D1264348

From Royal Township
to Industrial City
Cornwall
1784-1984

Town Crier — Guy Lalonde proclaims Bicentennial Year 1984, at the New Year's Eve Inaugural Ball.

Credit: *Le Bicentenaire de Cornwall Bicentennial Corporation.*

From Royal Township to Industrial City Cornwall 1784 - 1984

by
Elinor Kyte Senior

Mika Publishing Company
Belleville, Ontario
1983

Second Printing, 1984

From Royal Township to Industrial City
Copyright © Le Bicentenaire de Cornwall Bicentennial Corporation

ISBN 0-919303-74-9

Printed and bound in Canada

4

Contents

List of Illustrations

Introduction

In 1984, the City of Cornwall will be celebrating the 200th anniversary of its founding by United Empire Loyalists.

Settled June, 1784, by Lieutenant-Colonel Sir John Johnson and the First Battalion King's Royal Regiment of New York, and their families, Cornwall is one of Ontario's oldest permanent settlements.

In the early years, Cornwall originally named New Johnstown, became an administrative centre for Eastern Ontario. Over the last two centuries Cornwall has played an important part in the development of Ontario's history. One of the most notable contributions to the province's growth was made by the Reverend John Strachan and his Cornwall Grammar School, known as the breeding ground of the "Family Compact", the province's ruling class until the 1850s.

Up to the 1880s Cornwall remained a rural and political centre inhabited largely by the English, the Scots, and the Irish. With the coming of the textile and paper mills, the town was transformed into an industrial centre. As industrialization spread the town changed to include a large French-Canadian element. This steady growth was capped in the 1950s with the building of the St. Lawrence Seaway.

Now no longer a small outpost of Empire, Cornwall is a truly representative Canadian City where town and country, and Canadians of British and French descent work and live with people from many lands, for the future.

To mark its rich past, and reaffirm its commitment to the future, the City of Cornwall in 1977, on the advice of the Stormont, Dundas and Glengarry Historical Society created the Bicentennial Committee to investigage ways to mark 1984.

This first sub-committee comprised Alderman Angelo Lebano, Alderman Pat Armstrong, City C.A.O., Mr. R.J. Hamilton, Stormont, Dundas and Glengarry Historical Society Representatives Miss L. Jean Cameron, and Mr. R. Pearson.

The Committee immediately set to work and in 1979 contracted historian Dr. Elinor Kyte Senior to write this history. Not remaining content with this they studied similar celebrations in other centres and formulated plans to make this a year long event. In 1983 the Committee held a public competition to find a logo. This was won by local artist Bob Eadie.

In order to properly oversee the year's activities the Committee was incorporated in 1982, and became known as "Le Bicentenaire de Cornwall Bicentennial Corporation". At this time a co-ordinator was hired, and a temporary office opened.

On December 1 1982, the Corporation was registered as a non profit charitable organization under the laws of Ontario, and created "To promote, plan, co-ordinate and operate projects, functions, programmes, and celebrations for the general benefit of the City of Cornwall in the marking of the 200th anniversary of its settlement."

The new corporation made immediate plans to expand. One of its first activities was to initiate a series of historic publications. The City of Cornwall demonstrated its continued support by providing us with generous financial assistance.

During the summer of 1983 our task was made easier with the awarding of a grant from the federal government that permitted us to hire three permanent employees, and to open an office at 156 Pitt Street Cornwall.

Many special events are scheduled for 1984. As Chairman it is my privilege to invite you to share our rich heritage through the pages of Dr. Senior's excellent book, and to partake in the festivities for the upcoming year.

Robert Pearson
Chairman, Le Bicentenaire de Cornwall Bicentennial Corporation.

Le Bicentenaire de Cornwall Bicentennial Corporation

Chairman, Mr. Robert Pearson,
Vice-Chairman, Mr. Edward Armstrong,
Vice-Chairman, Leo J. Brisson,
Secretary-Treasurer, Mr. Richard Allaire,
Mr. Leo J. Brisson,
Mr. Dennis Carter-Edwards,
Mrs. Fernande DeSerres-Fobert,
Mr. Robert Kilger
Mrs. Terri Lalonde,
Mr. Bryan Lynch,
Mr. Gerald J. Parisien,
Mr. Maurice Roy
Brig. Gen. William Patterson,
Mr. J. Shea
Mr. Ron Sullivan.

Mr. Ian Bowering,
Mr. Claude Poirier.

9

Preface

The mandate I received four years ago from the Bicentennial Committee of the City of Cornwall was to write a scholarly narrative account of Cornwall in a style which could be read with ease and, hopefully, with satisfaction by the people of Cornwall and others interested in Cornwall's past. It was an awesome and moving experience to observe and study whole generations of families as they appeared on the stage of history over a period of two hundred years — solved problems, faced changed conditions and rubbed shoulders with newcomers in their midst.

As the research and writing progressed, I have had invaluable help and encouragement from many in Cornwall and elsewhere. Councillor Angelo Lebano, first chairman of the Bicentennial Committee, and his successor, Robert Pearson, have given un-stinting support. Brigadier-General William J. Patterson read with great care the first seven chapters in the early stages of the work and offered many useful observations and suggestions. Jules Renaud and L. Jean Cameron not only provided kind moral support, but frequently research materials and advice. In a special category is the aid given by Fernande DeSerres-Fobert whose enthusiasm, efficiency and thoroughness in research has been a constant source of strength during the writing. City Clerk Richard Allaire and his secretary, Yolande Fobert, have, at all times, provided assistance promptly and graciously.

I am grateful, too, to Laurier Courville, administrative assistant to the chief executive officer of Cornwall, and to Stephen D. Alexander of the City's Planning Department, for the advice and research materials they provided. Bicentennial Coordinator Ian Bowering has been helpful in solving several research problems, particularly in tracking down a copy of the 1926 Old Home Week souvenir booklet.

The writing was greatly facilitated by the work of two teams of students who carried out research throughout the summers of 1979 and 1980 under the federal government's Young Canada Works

Programme. The 1979 team, headed by Ron Parisien, was composed of Richard Irving, Christine Hart, Kathy Ray and Suzanne Yvette Poirier. The 1980 team, under John MacGillis, was made up of Richard Irving, Christine Hart and James McDonald. I wish to express my deepest appreciation to these students for the serious approach which they took towards their work. An author could not have had more pleasant, enthusiastic and efficient researchers.

I owe a special debt to my father, Fred L. Kyte, who undertook preliminary research for me right up until his death in early 1980. His wide circle of close friends, especially among Legion members, gave him access to memoir material and other documents that might otherwise have been lost. My sister, Jean Kyte, undertook, in her usual cheerful and competent way, to be literary critic, researcher, proof-reader and all-round assistant. Without my husband's faithful support, nothing would have been done.

To numerous other people in Cornwall, Ottawa, Montreal and elsewhere who so patiently and generously helped by answering queries by mail or telephone, by granting personal interviews, allowing me to peruse private documents or forwarding research materials to me, I offer my deepest thanks.

Elinor Kyte Senior
Cornwall, April 1983

Chapter I
Pointe Maligne — Royal Township No. 2

Disappointment, defeat and doubt wore heavily on the officers and men of the King's Royal Regiment of New York over the winter of 1783-84. For seven long years they had fought hard and ruthlessly, but never without hope that victory would perch on the Royal Standard. Then they would return to their homes on the Mohawk River in upper New York, to Vermont, Connecticut, Massachusetts, or, to whichever place they had been driven from or escaped from during the civil turmoil that had ended in revolution in America. Now the winter never seemed to end. These soldiers of the 1st Battalion were in their winter quarters at Montreal wondering what the new year would bring for them and their scattered families.[1] Many of them had spent five or six such winters in Montreal, Pointe Claire,[2] Ste. Anne or Lachine from where they had fanned out on campaigns and raids into northern New York and Vermont. At other times they had made furtive sorties into the rebellious territory to rescue families or friends or to persuade neighbours to come north to enlist in the Crown forces that were trying to bring the revolting colonies to heel. As volunteers in the northern army of the British command, they had taken up arms on the side of law and order, convinced not only that their choice was the right one, but that they would be on the winning side. The fortunes of war, however, turned against them and victory perched on the standard of revolt.

Impatiently the officers and men of the Royal Yorkers, as they were familiarly known, waited news of the peace negotiations between England and their homeland that acknowledged not only their defeat in arms but also their disinheritance. They knew that whatever concessions might be made by the victorious States to others who had remained loyal to the Crown, those who had borne arms in the Royal cause could expect no favours. Rumours and speculations abounded about the way the British government would redeem its enlistment promises of land grants. As the rumours spread, the men of the Royal Yorkers became more disgruntled, dismayed and edgy. When definite word was received at the beginning of December 1783 that the regiment would be disbanded on Christmas Eve of that year, one thing seemed certain. The government wanted the soldiers and their families out of the settled area of the French Catholic province of Quebec. This meant one more move for families that had been on the move, some of them, since 1776. If they must make new homes out of the forests of western Quebec, the Royal Yorkers were anxious to get on with the job as soon as navigation broke in the spring of 1784.

These men of Sir John Johnson's regiment had no fear of the western part of the province. Most of them had travelled back and forth along the St. Lawrence as far as Oswego or further many times in the campaigns and raids of the war. Some had even come along that route in 1760 with their colonel's father, Sir William Johnson, when he commanded some 1,000 Indians who formed part of the army converging on Montreal under General Jeffery Amherst. One of these soldiers was Samuel Anderson, a young lawyer from Boston, who had been with the Crown forces when they invested Ticonderoga and Crown Point in 1759. As Amherst's army sailed down the St. Lawrence from Oswego, Anderson was put in command of a scow with thirty men acting as marines. Their job was to help clear the French from Fort Levi on Isle Royale (Chimney Island), near Oswegatchie.[3] It took several days for Amherst's troops to reduce the strong French fort that commanded the upper St. Lawrence. Then the army proceeded towards Montreal where the young lawyer from Boston was among the British forces entering the city in September 1760. Eighteen years later Anderson and his family, along with thousands of other colonists and Indians, would again head for this northern city, this time seeking asylum.

Not only did men like Captain Samuel Anderson have no fear of the western part of the province; they had no fear of the Indians either. The men of Sir John Johnson's regiment had been close allies of the Mohawk Indians all during the war and some of the Royal Yorkers stationed at Lachine were now close neighbours of the refugee Indians who were temporarily settled there.[4] While officers of other provincial corps, especially those quartered along the Richelieu River, protested against being sent "to a very remote part of the Province (where) the transport is long, dangerous, and expensive, and what is worse in the Vicinity of the Savages,"[5] men of the 1st battalion of the Royal Yorkers were prepared to move as far west as Oswegatchie, but no further.[6]

Wives and children of the Royal Yorkers were scattered about in various refugee camps to which they had been sent as they escaped over the boundary into the province of Quebec. Some were as far away as Machiche near Three Rivers. Others were north of Montreal at Isle Jésus, Lachenaye, Rivière de Chêne, Terrebonne and L'Assomption.[7] Twenty-seven women and children were at Coteau-du-Lac. Others were with their soldier husbands at Lachine. Lieutenant Joseph Anderson, for instance, already had a farm in Lachine, located near the area of the King's stores.[8]

Still more enterprising was a corporal of the regiment, Adam Empy (Empey). By April of 1784 Empy petitioned the governor for permission to "trade Dry Goods and Liquor from this place (Montreal) to Cataraqui or to Niagara where opportunities will serve to dispose of it for the benefit of his large and distressed family."[9] Major-General Haldimand, the Swiss who had become governor of the province of Quebec in 1778, had more pressing matters on his mind. His most immediate concern was re-locating the thousands of distressed people and disbanded provincial soldiers who were daily increasing the numbers at the refugee camps along the Richelieu River and at other locations. The home government had decided that these Loyalists, soon to be known as the United Empire Loyalists, should be settled on Crown lands west of Rivière Beaudette beyond the western boundary of the last seigneury holding. French-Canadian settlement had halted at the Rivière Beaudette because beyond it was seven miles of uninviting cedar swamplands.

As soon as General Haldimand had told Sir John Johnson that his regiment was to be disbanded and disarmed on Christmas Eve of 1783, the blond, slightly-built commanding officer, whose steel grey eyes gave a hint of the iron will and nerves that lay beneath the rough hauteur, nodded. What he asked for his men was that the "lands to be granted to (the Royal Yorkers) might be laid out from the upper end of Mr. Longueuil's Seigniory."[10] A survey made that fall had shown that just beyond Pointe Mouille Bay from the Raisin River to Mille Roches the land was "excellent for three miles deep, and where creeks come into...the River, the land is good for six miles." The surveyor had reported that "in almost every place I examined, I found one foot and a half of black mould with a Crown loam." The forest was partly of "Maple, Hickory, Beech, White Oak, with a few trees of bitter Nutt."[11] Sixty years earlier Father Pierre-François-Xavier Charlevoix had made a similar observation. "I never saw a country more charming," he wrote, "and the lands appear good."[12] The one serious deficiency in the area was the lack of a waterfall for a mill. Only at the upper part of the Raisin River did the surveyor find a possible site for a mill near a waterfall some five feet eight inches high.

Just as Sir John Johnson had taken the lead among the Loyalist forces in upper New York at the beginning of the revolution, he now took the lead in re-settling those men who had fought under him with such determination. By the end of January 1784 he had made plans to "go up(the St. Lawrence)and chuse(sic)a place for myself and set some of my own servants to work which...will be an encouragement to some of my followers." Johnson feared that rumours being spread by some "evil-designing persons" would dissuade his "disbanded men and other Loyalists from taking up the lands offered them by Government."[13] More than rumours were circulating. Some of the disgruntled and disbanded officers, soldiers and refugee Loyalists were circulating petitions complaining about the conditions and locations of the proposed Loyalist settlements. And seigneurs, both French-Canadian as well as English-speaking, were offering attractive terms to "industrious Americans" to take up vacant lands on their seigneuries.[14] The rumour-mongers warned the soldiers that if they accepted Crown lands "they will be as much soldiers as ever and liable to be called upon at pleasure."[15] In a sense the rumour had an element of truth in it. The proposed new "Royal-Townships" that were to stretch out along the St. Lawrence from Rivière Beaudette to Cataraqui were not only to be settlements of military personnel, but were also to be military settlements in the sense that the disbanded soldiers would be kept together in contiguous settlements, ready if need be to form a protective cordon along the St. Lawrence should the new United States again become bellicose.[16] But the future military role of the disbanded men would be defensive, not offensive, as it had been in the past. In addition to the rumour that the provincial corps were to be settled in military array in order to be more readily available for a return to military duty, there was also the complaint among the men that the terms for the new settlements were not as favourable as those granted in the "neighbouring states where they are not prohibited from erecting mills." This was the beginning of the Loyalists' objections to the seigneurial system of land-holding already established in the province in which they had sought haven. Yet despite these objections to the seigneurial land-holding system, Sir John Johnson feared that many of his men might nevertheless agree that "it will be better for them to take up lands from the Segniors (sic) in the heart of the Province,...if timely steps are not taken to prevent it." Johnson pressed Haldimand to "hold out (to the disbanded soldiers) in the most public manner every encouragement...to prevent their dispersing in the spring."[17]

The slowness of government machinery in getting surveyors to lay out the proposed townships irked Johnson and his men. Johnson wrote repeatedly to Haldimand and his military secretary, Major Robert Mathews, urging that surveying parties be sent off. By 1 March 1784, Johnson took matters into his own hands. He ordered Patrick McNiff, a recently-arrived Loyalist who had been a substantial merchant on Staten Island, New York, and twenty-six of his own men to begin surveys.[18] Within a few days Johnson himself set off to "our cantonment," the site of the future town of Cornwall, which was then known by the foreboding name of Pointe Maligne.[19] Jutting out from the north bank of the St. Lawrence in jagged rifts, the point had received an even more ominous name from earlier French explorers. They referred to it as Pointe à la Maudie — the cursed point.[20] In 1760 when Crown forces camped overnight on the Point while en route to Montreal, Sir Jeffery Amherst called it Point de Maline,[21] while Captain John Knox in his *Journal* referred to it as Johnson's Point.[22] Throughout the 1770s there were still references to Maligne Grande Pointe, Maligne Petite Pointe and Johnson's Point.[23]

What was there about this "cursed" place that made it so attractive to Sir John Johnson and his soldiers that they were prepared to wrangle with the Indians of St. Regis over possession of it? For the Indians it was a source of revenue. French Canadians and others had paid them "considerable sums of money for the liberty to cut timber thereon,"[24] an indication that the land on the north side of the St. Lawrence opposite the Indian village of St. Regis had been regarded as part of the Indian seigneury. As soon as Sir John Johnson arrived at the camp site on Pointe Maligne he was visited by "a great number of the Chiefs and Warriors" who said that they "thought it would be unjust...to take away from them...the lands they had always looked upon as theirs." They claimed the land from the "River au Raisin Six Leagues in depth to a creek a little above the Long Saut (*sic*)." The Indians rested their claim on deeds or papers which they said had been burned when their church went up in flames. In addition, the chiefs informed Sir John that his father, Sir William Johnson, had promised to have the lands confirmed to them.[25]

On top of the other delays in getting the township lots surveyed, this new development was almost too much for Sir John. He told the Indian chiefs that he was sure that the governor would not "have sent us up to those lands" if they were not the property of the Crown; that if a grant had been made of them to the Indians of St. Regis, "it must have been recorded" and consequently known to the governor. Yet Sir John, bred to the ways of Indian diplomacy, manoeuvred adroitly. He asked whether the Chiefs would be willing to relinquish their claims "to two or three Leagues in Depth from the (Raisin) River to the Long Saut for a reasonable compensation." The Chiefs' reply was that "it was a matter of weight and merited serious consideration...(at an assembly) of the whole of their People."[26]

This disturbing Council with the Indians meant that Sir John and his surveying party could not get on with the job of selecting the most suitable site for the new town. What Johnson wanted was to choose a town plot and then to lay out townships for five companies of his regiment on each side of the town, rather than to run a line of townships along the river front from Rivière Beaudette to the Long Sault.[27] His plan, he thought, would make the land available for settlement more quickly. However, once the Indian objection was raised, Johnson had to abandon his plan and return to Montreal to consult with Governor Haldimand. Pointe Maligne had again lived up to its name. The first attempt at settlement had run into snags. Fearing that the Indians might stop the survey, Sir John told his surveyors, Louis Kotte and Patrick McNiff, to lay out as many townships as they could in the undisputed space between the Longueuil Seigneury and the Raisin River. Johnson was annoyed. "Should the (Indian) claim be found groundless, which I believe will be the case," he told Haldimand, "they merit a severe reprimand."[28]

Whether dealing with friend or foe, Indian relative or Indian ally, there was nothing maudlin or patronizing about Johnson's attitude. He had had to assume his father's mantle just before the outbreak of the American revolutionary war, for the elder Johnson died suddenly in 1774 in the midst of a great Indian Council at Johnson Hall. The younger Johnson, then 32 years old, boldly and unequivocally took his stand under the Royal standard. So, too, did his relatives and allies among the Mohawks as well as his numerous tenants. Many of these were Highlanders whom Sir William Johnson had invited to come from Glengarry in Scotland and who now had extensive farms on the 240,000 acres that comprised the Johnson holdings in upper New York.[29] Just hours before officers of the revolutionary army arrived at Johnson Hall in June of 1776 to arrest Sir John, Indian allies warned him of the impending arrest. Johnson hastily gathered up a few personal belongings, including the deputation authorizing him to direct Masonic affairs in New York.[30] With 200 of his tenants and Mohawk allies he made a gruelling nineteen-day trek through the forests and over the Adirondacks to St. Regis

Indian village just opposite the point bearing his father's name. To avoid detection, Sir John split his party into smaller groups. When his own party was down to the last loaf of bread, he sat down with his back to a tree and with his sword he divided the loaf. As he handed each man a slice on the point of his sword, he drily commented, "Here is the Staff of Life on the Point of Death." For the rest of the trek, Sir John and his men survived on "the flesh of a few horses, their dogs" and what roots and berries they could find. Left behind at Fort Johnson were his young pregnant wife and fifteen-month-old son, both soon imprisoned by the American revolutionaries.[31]

Johnson's safe arrival and welcome at St. Regis put him under obligation to his Indian hosts. Like his own family which had Indian blood relations through his father's liaison with Molly Brant, the sister of Chief Joseph Brant, many of the Indians of St. Regis, including the chiefs, were of mixed blood.[32] Thus when Sir John Johnson faced the Council of St. Regis Indian chiefs and warriors over the question of the land at Pointe Maligne, he met them on grounds of equality. If the Indian claim to the area was just, he would be the first to acknowledge it. On the other hand, if there was any deception about the claim, he would come down heavily on the Indians. He was a man hardened by strife, inured to victory and defeat, and wise in the ways of Indian and white. While his faithful Indian ally, Captain Joseph Brant, was known to have recognized the secret Masonic distress signal and spared American revolutionaires, Sir John reputedly neither recognized the signal nor spared the maker.[33]

The problem surrounding the site of the town plot that eventually became the city of Cornwall was tackled skilfully by Governor Frederick Haldimand. First he had the register of Crown Lands carefully checked to see if the disputed lands had been granted to the St. Regis Indians or to their Jesuit priest, Father Anthony Gourdan.[34] Finding no record of such a grant, Haldimand tactfully suggested a way around the difficulty. As the Indians had no "legal right to the Lands," Haldimand reasoned, but had been taught "to consider them as their property and have been in the custom of reaping advantages from them, together with the consideration of the Americans having encroached so much upon them with their Boundary Line," he urged that it would not be "political or right to contend the point with them provided they are to be satisfied with reasonable terms." In fact, Haldimand expected that "ere long (the Indians of St. Regis might) find it necessary or wish to cross the River" and that their "settling near the Loyalists might produce a good Effect."[35] Johnson was of a contrary opinion. When it was suggested that the Indians receive a tract of land to run northwards between the new townships so that the Indians would continue to have a direct access to their Algonquin allies of La Petite Nation to the north, Johnson commented dourly, "Their coming in between the settlements, let this Tract be ever so confined, will be disagreeable and injurious to the Settlers."[36]

Through the good offices of the Mohawk Indian Chief, Captain Joseph Brant, the difficulty with the St. Regis Indians was cleared up. Brant undertook the task of conferring with the Indians whom he found "reasonable enough about the lands." In fact, Brant told Johnson that "they mean to make you a present of the Island facing your lott (sic), (and) they mean to allow you the land you wish to have....But on your part," Brant wrote, "I hope you will please to get writings for the remainder of the Indian land." Brant assured the Indians that they would still have three miles or a little less river frontage on the north bank as a throughway to the Petite Nation River. The Mohawk Chief emphasized to Johnson the need "to use those Indians in easy manner...about land matters at this present unhappy times for us, for many reasons, in first place, it gives the dam Rebels larger mouths for many things against us and it is very good example for them, to get all our lands from us, if those Saint Rechis (sic) Indians was any ways forced about lands."[37]

By 6 May 1784 Johnson was able to assure the governor that Brant's mission had been successful. The Indians were satisfied to have the second settlement that became Cornwall Township begin near the Raisin River with the town plot in the centre of the township near the river frontage. This reduced the Indian holding on the north bank of the St. Lawrence to a tract of about two and three-quarter miles between the first and second townships. For giving up their claim to the rest of the area on which the new township was to be laid out, the Indians were granted valuable land south of the St. Lawrence from which they eventually received substantial rent.[38]

The amicable settlement with the Indians gave Sir John Johnson and his men the most prized of the Royal Townships. Sir John and his team of surveyors quickly laid out the mile-square town plot in the centre of the township, its front facing the commodious bay that lay between Maligne Grande Pointe and Maligne Petite Pointe, a bay that has long since been filled in. A few miles below the site of the township, the St. Lawrence widened into the stretch of water known as Lake St. Francis. A short distance above it were the swiftest and most frightening of the rapids of the entire St. Lawrence

River system — the Long Sault.[39] Though not particularly dangerous, the rapids were rough enough to force most travellers to take a land portage from above the Long Sault to beyond Pointe Maligne. Immediately in front of the township were two islands, Grande Isle of St. Regis, now called Cornwall Island, and Petite Isle of St. Regis. As the stretch of open water between Grande Isle of St. Regis and the township site was only about a quarter of a mile wide, the new town commanded the north channel of the St. Lawrence, the river system that was the major route of communication for fur traders and military personnel moving back and forth from Montreal to Oswegatchie, Cataraqui, or Niagara and beyond. Thus, it was of some strategic importance.[40]

Now that the Indian claim had been settled, Sir John was eager to get his men moving to the new townships. The original plan was to lay out areas six miles square, divided into 200 family lots of 120 acres each, with twenty-five lots along the river fronts and 175 lots to the rear.[41] In practice there were usually 37 lots laid out along the river fronts. Long before the townships were surveyed, Haldimand and Johnson had anticipated the tensions that would arise over who would secure the best locations and the better quality lands. In September of 1783 Haldimand remarked to Sir John, "To give satisfaction to all Parties, I need not tell you, will be impossible."[42] More than this, Haldimand warned Johnson, "I know there are many speculating for large Grants in order to turn Land-Jobbers, a System I shall entirely discourage as being subversive to the Plan of general relief and assistance intended for the distressed Loyalists."[43]

Several difficulties immediately arose when the surveyors attempted to put the general plan into effect. The first was that lots of 120 acres did not fit easily into the British government instructions that heads of families and common soldiers were to receive grants of 100 acres each.[44] The second difficulty was that the natural course of the river systems did not lend themselves to squares of 120 acres. Moreover, as the prized river frontage lots were very limited, officers and men eyed them enviously.

Haldimand's plan was to have the officers and men draw indiscriminately for both their townships and for their own lots, "an impartial plan," he thought, "that would give general satisfaction."[45] But both Sir John Johnson and Major Samuel Holland, the provincial surveyor-general, remonstrated with him that such an egalitarian system of distributing the land would create even more jealousy. Instead, Johnson and Holland pressed on the governor a system whereby the officers would receive a few of their lots on the river frontage and the rest immediately behind their front lots. Such an arrangement would be similar to the system of landholding in the settled part of the province where the seigneuries of the French Canadians were laid out in long narrow strips fronting the rivers, the natural means of transportation. Sir John assured Haldimand that "two thirds of the Gentlemen, late of my first Battalion, as well as many others, would rather relinquish their right to land than Accept it by Balloting for every hundred Acres," because this arrangement would result in their land-holdings being in detached blocks of 100 acres scattered here and there throughout the township.[46]

Haldimand disagreed. He scolded Sir John, expressing his "concern and disappointment on finding that your Officers have not entered cheerfully into the impartial Plan I have determined upon." Haldimand knew that the "advantages lye in having the front lotts" and that the disadvantages of the rear lots would then fall on the private soldiers and individuals, "who are the least able to contend with them, and who, without Cattle, and in every respect indigent, would be deprived of the Resources of Water Carriage, whilst the richer part of the Settlement would enjoy them." Haldimand argued with Johnson that if the officers not only had the waterfront lots but also the remainder of their lots immediately to the rear, this would "render the Situation of the Private (soldier) still more remote."[47]

Haldimand fully understood that the general appearance of the Townships would be more pleasing if the richer elements erected their houses in the front lots, but he insisted that the comforts and needs of the "Bulk of the People" must be attended to in order to ensure the "Success of those Settlements." Haldimand was looking to the future. If the "Royal Seigneuries" on the upper St. Lawrence became thriving communities, it would "not only draw many from the States, but will induce one half of the People who now prefer Chaleurs Bay, to apply for Land above."[48] Apart from all this, Haldimand gave another reason why the lots should be drawn for without distinction or advantage being given to officers. He noted to Sir John that many Loyalists considered themselves, because of their former situations, equal or superior in social rank to some of the officers.[49] And he again pointed out to Sir John that "it is a difficult matter to give general Content in the distribution of Benefits, each Individual considering His own Interest the point he is to gain, and rating His own merit at the highest Price."[50] Sir John fought for the honour of his men as well as for their due. He replied forcefully and with effect that "The distribution of benefits certainly most seldom gives general content unless very Impartially bestowed, Men in general, in every station of life, having an Eye to their own Interest, and Rating their own Merit according to what they conceive to be just." Indeed, Sir John argued, "the benefits to be received on this occasion in whatever Manner bestowed will be but trifling in Comparison to what many have sacrificed for them."[51] Haldimand took the rebuke in good part. Much as the grumbling and demands of the Loyalists added to his burdens in the re-settlement process, he knew that the officers and men of the provincial corps had fought steadfastly, believing that the Royal cause would triumph. What they were about to receive as the bounty of the Crown did not, in many cases, begin to compensate them for the losses and sacrifices they had suffered during the long war.

The one thing that both Haldimand and Sir John were in full agreement about was the need to get the Loyalists to their lands as quickly as possible. The delays over the surveying, the late opening of the rivers for navigation, and the difficulty over the Indian claim to the proposed township opposite St. Regis — all this had served to increase the anxiety and discontent of the distressed soldiers and refugees. When April and May of 1784 went by without embarkation for the upper St. Lawrence, it is not surprising that tempers were wearing thin and some of the Loyalist leaders were circulating petitions complaining about the terms of settlement.[52] Still others were actually thinking of returning to the States as it was reported that the persecution of Loyalists had diminished.

Captain Jacob Maurer, who had served in the 60th Regiment and then in the King's Royal Regiment of New York, was appointed inspector of batteaux. By 24 May 1784 he was at Lachine wrestling with the task of hiring skilled French-Canadian batteaux-men to transport the Loyalists and their baggage to the new settlements of the upper St. Lawrence. Within a week detachments of Loyalists began to crowd in on him at such a pace that Maurer embarked them onto the batteaux as fast as he could. Then, after consulting with Sir John and Major Samuel Holland, he sent them off with only a month's provisions. Clothing and additional supplies were to be sent later.[53] By June 3rd, Sir John reported to Haldimand that "the People are moving up as fast as they can but they have been delayed for want of Boats, Tents, etc."[54] Captain Maurer reported on June 7th, "Sir John Johnson setts off this day — His Boats are now receiving their Provisions — I am forwarding all the Tools, seeds and Grindstones...in Ten Batteaux."[55]

23

For tidy-minded officials of the quarter-master's department like Maurer, the confusion at Lachine on 7 June 1784 as the Royal Yorkers and their families moved off was "unaccountable." Maurer found that "Every Person pretends to a Superior Command." Some batteaux of the first battalion had been ready for several days, but the Royal Yorkers sent their French-Canadian pilots back to Maurer to ask for more provisions. Maurer adamantly refused the supplies, and he later explained to Haldimand's military secretary, Major Robert Mathews, that "those men in genl. move without any officers or even Sergt. to conduct them which creates very great delay and confusion."[56]

Yet all the disbanded soldiers and other Loyalist refugees who headed for the site that became Cornwall were on their way from Lachine by 17th June.[57] Thus the township which was officially called simply no. 2 of the Royal Seigneuries received its first complement of inhabitants during the first two weeks of June 1784, most of them likely arriving at the site by June 10th. Though Haldimand had at first given the townships only numerical names,[58] Sir John Johnson and his surveyors referred to the town plot of No. 2 seigneury as "New Town."[59] Almost as soon as the people reached the various township sites they began to call township no. 2 "Johnstown" and referred to the whole area of the five townships where the 1st battalion of the King's Royal Regiment of New York settled as "New Johnstown."[60] To complicate matters more, the town site at "New Oswegatchie" where Major Edward Jessup's Loyal Rangers settled was for a time also called "New Town" and then "New Johnstown."[61]

Probably the first letter to be written from what became Cornwall was sent on 18 June 1784 when Sir John Johnson wrote to Major Mathews urgently requesting whip and cross-cut saws, smiths' tools, broad axes, and hollow adzes. Dating his letter simply "New Town," Sir John told Mathews that the settlers also were in need of "a Bull or two...there being near Two Hundred Cows now on the ground."[62] One of the first visitors to the new township and perhaps the first to record its name as "Johnstown" was Baron de Reitzenstein, the commanding officer of the disbanded Hessian Troops who were then en route to their new settlement at the Bay of Quinte. When Baron de Reitzenstein arrived at the site of the new town on June 20th, he found Sir John and Major Holland "occupés pour regler les nouveaux établissements pour le régt. de Sir John."[63]

The waterfront was a mass of tents. Here the families were sheltered until huts could be built from the felled trees. Government stores and provisions were housed in a temporary hut located on the town plot. Haldimand had insisted that all the wives and children of the disbanded soldiers and refugees should proceed to the new settlements with the men, rather than remain in the temporary camps until the clearings had been made and huts built. Such an arrangement, Haldimand felt, would "enforce (on them) the necessity of settling rapidly." This meant, as he realized, that "means will (have to be) furnished for encamping the common People, whose wives and children will be useful in many respects from the moment a Tree is cut down." However, he agreed that "the Families of Officers and others of the more decent Order must, of course, have some preparations made for them previous to their going upon their ground."[64] Thus the town-planners of 1784 tried to reconcile the plans for a pioneer re-settlement with some regard for the social rank of the settlers, an unenviable and far from easy chore since the settlers themselves had, in many cases, suffered upheavals in their financial and social status during the long revolutionary war.

By June of 1784 Pointe Maligne had become Johnson's Point in reality.[65] Sir John Johnson was there with his cohorts, busily inspecting the various lots to see which were fit for settling on. Women and children were jostling together in tents, sorting out food supplies and setting up temporary quarters with makeshift cooking arrangements. There was some wailing, but little time for weeping. The spring planting season was long past; yet enough land had to be cleared for huts and fall seeding if the people were to have any sort of a harvest the next year. And it was at Johnstown that many of the women and children destined for other townships remained over the summer and early fall of 1784 while their men moved east and west to clear the land. Still other men asked permission to go to the States to bring out their families or to buy cattle. For the refugees, Pointe Maligne had become their point of hope.

NOTES

1. E.A. Cruikshank, *The Settlement of the United Empire Loyalists on the Upper St. Lawrence and the Bay of Quinte in 1784: A Documentary - Record*, 34.

2. William Faden's *Map of the Inhabited Parts of Canada from French Surveys; with the Frontiers of New York and New England from the large survey by Claude-Joseph Sauthier*, 25 Feb. 1777.

3. Benjamin Hough, *History of St. Lawrence and Franklin Counties*. 90-92; S. Rowe, "The Anderson Record from 1699 to 1896", in *OHSPR*, vol. vi, 1905, 113.

4. Return of Indians at Mohawk Refugee Camp, near Lachine, 21 Jan. 1784 (Haldimand Papers, MG21/B115/220).

5. Petition of Lt.-Col. John Peters, Queen's Loyal Rangers, on behalf of Loyalists, n.d. (*ibid.*, B215/206).

6. Sir John Johnson to Haldimand, 1 Dec. 1783 (*ibid.*, B158/338).

7. Recapitulation of Loyalists settled in the Province of Quebec, 24 Jan. 1784 (*ibid.*, B167/II/367; see also pp. 364-65).

8. Lt. J. Anderson to Haldimand, 8 Oct. 1783 (ibid., B215/II/65).

9. Petition of Adam Empy to Haldimand, 15 April 1784 (*ibid.*, B215/157-58).

10. Johnson to Haldimand, 1 Dec. 1783 (*ibid.*, B158/338).

11. Surveys relative to the Settlement of the Loyalists, c. 31 Oct. 1783 (*ibid.*, B169/46-50; see also, 15-26 and 31).

12. Hough, *St. Lawrence and Franklin Counties*, 43.

13. Johnson to Haldimand, 26 Jan. 1784 (Haldimand papers, MG21/B115/221).

14. Hereward Senior, "The Loyalists in Quebec: A Study in Diversity", paper presented to Canadian Historical Association at the Learned Societies, Halifax, June 1981, 3.

15. Johnson to Haldimand, 20 Jan. 1784 (Haldimand Papers, MG21/B115/221).

16. Elinor Senior, "Loyalist Regiments after the American Revolution", in *Canadian Genealogist*, ii, no. 1, 1980, 37.

17. Johnson to Major Robert Mathews, 2 Feb. 1784 (Haldimand Papers, MG21/B115/232-33.)

18. Johnson to Mathews, 1 Mar. 1784 (ibid., 232); for details on Patrick McNiff's background, see his Petition to Lord Dorchester, 21 Jan. 1787 (RG4/A1/31/10228.)

19. See D'Anville map 1755 (Facsimile at McGill University Rare Book Room.)

20. M. Pouchet, *Memoir upon the late war in North America between the French and English 1755-1760*, trans. Benjamin Hough, ii, 52.

21. Sir Jeffery Amherst, *Journal*, ed. J. Clarence Webster, 242.

22. Captain John Knox, *An Historical Journal of the Campaigns in North America for the years 1757, 1758, 1759 and 1760*, ii. 556.

23. See Thomas Jeffrey's *An Exact Chart of the River St. Lawrence from Fort Frontenac to Isle of Anticosti*, 25th May 1771; see also, William Faden, *A Map of the Inhabited Parts of Canada*, 25 Feb. 1777; *Map of the Province of New York*, 1 Jan. 1779, prepared by the order of Maj. General William Tryon; see also, *A Short Topographical Description of His Majesty's Province of Upper Canada in North America, to which is annexed a Provincial Gazetteer*, drawn up by David William Smyth, Surveyor-General of Upper Canada, at the desire of Major-General Simcoe, 1st October 1799, published by W. Faden, Geographer to His Majesty, London, 1799.

24. Johnson to Haldimand, 11 Mar. 1784 (Haldimand papers, MG21/B115/234-6.)

25. *Ibid.*

26. *Ibid.*

27. *Ibid.*

28. *Ibid.*

29. Sir John Johnson, *The North American Johnsons*, 45.

30. A.J.B. Milborne, *Freemasonry in the Province of Quebec, 1759-1959*, 37.

31. Johnson, *The North American Johnsons*, 57; see also, Memorial of Sir John Johnson to Commissioners...to enquire into the losses and services of the American Loyalists, *ibid.*, app. III, 89-92; Bishop A. Macdonell to J. Joseph, 7 March 1836, in Macdonell Letters, 1836-39, (MG24/J13); Rhodes Grant, "Settlement of the Counties traced by an Area Resident: a descendant of Angus Grant who was with Sir John Johnson on the trek," see *Standard-Freeholder*, Cornwall, 5 July 1976.

32. *Hough, St. Lawrence and Franklin Counties*, 112-15.

33. Milborne, *Freemasonry*, 37-39.

34. Haldimand to Johnson, 15 Mar. 1784 (Haldimand Papers, MG21/B63/128-31).

35. *Ibid.*

36. Johnson to Haldimand, 8 April 1784, (*ibid.*, B115/245).

37. Capt. Joseph Brant to Sir John Johnson, 4 May 1784 (*ibid.*, B115/254-55).

38. Johnson to Mathews, 6 May 1784 (*ibid.*, B115/256).

39. Amherst, *Journal*, 1 Sept. 1760, 242; see also, J.F. Pringle, *Lunenburgh, or the Old Eastern District*, 44; for Lt. Gov. J.G. Simcoe's appreciation of the site of Cornwall, see Simcoe to the Committee of the Privy Council for Trade and Plantations, 1 Sept. 1794 (*Simcoe Papers*, iii, 58).

40. For a discussion of the strategic importance of the new town, see, James R. Miller, "The Town of Cornwall, 1784-1867," unpublished M.A. thesis, University of Toronto, 1967, 2.

41. Haldimand to Johnson, 1 Sept. 1783 (Haldimand Papers, MG21/B115/142-43); see also Instructions to Surveyor John Collins, 11 Sept. 1783 (*ibid.*, B124/91-94).

42. Haldimand to Sir John Johnson, 1 Sept. 1783 (*ibid.*, B115/142-43).

43. *Ibid.*

44. See Instructions to Haldimand, 18 Nov. 1783, cited in Cruikshank, *Loyalist Settlements*, 35.

45. Haldimand to Johnson, 20 May 1784 (Haldimand Papers, MG21/B65/31-35); Haldimand to Johnson and Major Samuel Holland, 31 May 1784 (*ibid.*, B63/372-74).

46. Johnson to Haldimand, 27 May 1784 (*ibid.*, B115/264-65).

47. Haldimand to Johnson, 31 May 1784 (*ibid.*, B63/372-74).

48. *Ibid.*

49. Haldimand to Johnson, 10 June 1784 (*ibid.*, B63/398-99).

50. Same to same, 31 May 1784 (*ibid.*, B63/372-74).

51. Sir John Johnson to Haldimand, 3 June 1784 (*ibid.*, B115/267-68).

52. See Cruikshank, *Loyalist Settlements*, 72, 77, 87, 90, 94-96, 99.

53. Captain Jacob Maurer to Major Mathews, 27 May 1784 (Haldimand Papers, MG21/B188/262-63).

54. Johnson to Haldimand, 3 June 1784 (*ibid.*, B115/267-68).

55. Maurer to Major Mathews, 7 June 1784 (*ibid.*, B188/264-65).

56. *Ibid.*

57. Maurer to Mathews, 17 June 1784 (*ibid.*, B188/268-69).

58. Haldimand to Sir John Johnson, 20 May 1784 (*ibid.*, B65/31-35).

59. For early references to Cornwall as New Town, see Sir John Johnson to Major Mathews, 7 June 1784 (*ibid.*, B115/271); Mathews to Johnson, 10 June 1784 (*ibid.*, B62/393-94); Johnson to Capt. Maurer, 18 June 1784 (*ibid.*, B188/270).

60. See, for instance, John Crysler's claim, 8 Mar. 1788, *Second Report, Ontario Bureau of Archives*, 1904, 481; and William Cameron's claim, 15 Nov. 1787, (*ibid.*, 375); for township no. 2 as Johnstown, see Haldimand Papers, MG21/B168/61-62; 88-89, 92-93, 95.

61. Capt. J. Sherwood to Mathews, 23 July 1784 (*ibid.*, B162/339-41).

62. *Ibid.*, B188/270.

63. Baron de Reitzenstein to Haldimand, 26 June 1784 (*ibid.*, B152/157-58).

64. Mathews to Maurer, 15 April 1784 (*ibid.*, B63/210-211).

65. See Reminiscence of George Annable, son of Sergeant John Annable, in which he claims the first pioneers called the site Pointe Maligne, in *Freeholder*, 6 December 1889.

1792 Map No. 1 Credit: Public Archives of Canada, V3/440.

'Encampment of the Loyalists at New Johnstown (Cornwall), June 6, 1784. Watercolour by James Peachy.
Credit: Public Archives of Canada, Picture Division, neg. C-2001.

F.Bartolozzi.R.A.

John Johnson

Sir John Johnson, 1742-1830, (1813). Lieutenant-Colonel
Sir John Johnson led the First Battalion King's Royal Regiment
of New York, to Cornwall in 1784.
Credit: Public Archives of Canada, neg. C-2847.

Silhouette of 'Peggy' O'Sullivan Bruce,
one of Cornwall's first Loyalist settlers.
Credit: Marianne K. Davis, great, great, great,
great grand-daughter.

Chapter II
Growing Pains

During the summer of 1784 Royal Township no. 2 was a conglomerate of settlers. There were Roman Catholic Scots, Presbyterian Scots, American Episcopalians, German Lutherans, Dutch Calvinists, a few Irish, some Blacks, and even an Englishman or two. Before the end of the decade even stranger bedfellows would appear in the township. One was a captured soldier of the Continental Army that had tried to seize Quebec City on New Year's Eve of 1775. On his release from jail, the soldier had married a French-Canadian girl and brought her with him to the new township when he got a job as farm assistant to John Knave, one of the privates of Sir John Johnson's regiment. Thus as early as 1787 not only was there a French-Canadian presence in the new township, but also an American revolutionary soldier settled among the Loyalists. What was more surprising was that the American revolutionary and his French-Canadian wife lived together quite contentedly with his American Loyalist master and his young wife, sharing a single room hut that Knave had built on his river-front lot no. 25. Lord Dorchester's military secretary, Major Robert Mathews, stayed overnight with the two couples, when he was en route from Quebec City to Niagara in May of 1787. He found the pioneer hut "the neatest and most cleanly I ever saw."[1] Nor was the revolutionary soldier's wife the only French Canadian living in the township at this time. Louis Nadau was also there, able and willing to give evidence at the enquiry set up that year into the Loyalists' complaints.[2]

The six-mile square township no. 2 was the first choice of the senior officers of the 1st battalion of the King's Royal Regiment of New York. For one thing, it was the best up-river site nearest to Montreal and the heart of the province. For another, it was the township with the best soil. Patrick McNiff described it as "high, dry and rich and it is so with very little exception for six concessions back." The other townships all had serious drawbacks, according to McNiff. The first settlement that became known as the "Lake Township" was flat and very rich as far as lot no. 5, but then it became "high and stony." The third township site became Osnabruck and had land in front that was "very indifferent — stony or sandy."[3]

Thus township no. 2 seemed destined to become the chief town of the new settlements, perhaps even the capital of a new province. Sir John Johnson probably thought so that first summer as he set about distributing lots of land to his disbanded soldiers and dreamed of becoming lieutenant governor.[4] In spite of Governor Haldimand's injunction to have the men and officers draw indiscriminately for their lots,[5] Johnson stuck to his own proposal to allow his officers the first choice of the lots that ran along the river front for ten miles. When Johnson informed Haldimand that he had departed from the original instructions "at the earnest request of the Men of my own and those of Major Jessup's Corps" and yet had "given general satisfaction to the Bulk of the People,"[6] Haldimand was a little miffed but had to accept the accomplished fact. "If it turns out well," he told Johnson glumly, "I shall be satisfied."[7]

Eleven commissioned officers received waterfront lots.[8] Major James Gray chose a site three miles east of the town plot just beyond where the surveyors had laid out the first waterfront lots. Gray's land extended back from the river through the second and third concessions. So, too, did the lands of his neighbour, Captain Samuel Anderson, who received lots nos. 1 and 2 in the first, second and third concessions of the township. At the extreme western end of the township, Captain Patrick Daly of the 1st battalion received the two last waterfront lots nos. 36 and 37. Three of Captain's Anderson's sons got waterfront lots. Lieutenant Joseph Anderson secured no. 18 to the west of the town site.[9] Ensign Ebenezar Anderson shared lot no. 24 with Sergeant Samuel Moss. A third son, Elisha, shared lot no. 35 with Matthias Snetsinger. Sir John Johnson was content to take only two waterfront lots, nos. 33 and 34. He preferred to have a temporary cottage erected on what came to be known for a time as Johnson's Point and later as Fraser's Point, located in Township no. 1. In the fall he had a log hut built on the Raisin River and began construction of a mill on the site that he named Williamstown in honour of his father.[10]

By October of 1784 the official muster returns showed that there were at township no. 2 some 215 men, 87 women and 214 children.[11] In reality, the settlement was still very much in flux. Only ninety-nine settlers were reported "on their lands." Of these twenty-eight were Scots of whom twenty were Macdonells, all settled on the back concessions. A fair number of the ninety-nine settlers on the lands were either women or children, not men. Twenty-two other settlers were reported to be in Montreal; ten were "in Canada"; ten were "gone to the States," many of them "for their families"; eight were still at Lachine; six at Carleton Island; four at Coteau du Lac and one at Machiche getting his family.[12] Many of those who had drawn lots in township no. 2 may have come to the township only for the original drawing and then returned to Montreal or gone to some other location. On the other hand, there were some in the area of the township over the summer who had drawn lots in the adjacent township no. 3, but whose lots had not been surveyed yet. The one medical man of the regiment who elected to settle in New Johnstown, Surgeon James Stuart, formerly of the 42nd Regiment, was still in Johnstown over the summer. Although he drew a lot in no. 3 township, Stuart established himself just south of the town plot.[13]

Fairly satisfied with his new holdings in township no. 2 was Major James Gray, a former captain in the 42nd Black Watch.[14] Just twenty-one years earlier he had sold his commission and settled down comfortably in Pownal, Vermont, with his new bride, Elizabeth Low of Newark, New Jersey. Then political agitation took an ugly turn. Gray's comfort turned to exceeding discomfort and by 1776 he headed for Montreal bringing with him his wife, a nephew and two nieces, Jacob, Hannah and Catherine Farrand, and his black servant woman, Dorine.[15] As an experienced regular officer, Gray was soon commissioned as major in Sir John Johnson's first battalion. Now, the war over, the major strutted about in kilts, surveying his large riverfront grant of land, "a hoary-headed little man (with) a large fat Dutch American lady," as one traveller described him and his wife.[16] Not only had Gray received this choice waterfront lot that became known as Gray's Creek, he also received land in township no. 4 and laid claim to a large slice of Pointe Maligne which had been intended for a town common.[17]

Gray's nearest neighbour was his old Vermont friend, Captain Samuel Anderson, who had commanded the Light Company of the King's Royal Regiment of New York. Captain Anderson was a first generation American, the eldest son of Benjamin Anderson who had emigrated to the colonies from County Antrim, Ireland, in 1720. His mother was a native of County Down, Ireland. The family had settled on a farm near Boston where Samuel was born in 1739. After some time spent in the West Indies for the sake of his health, the tall and powerful Samuel returned home to study law. During the Seven Years' War he did his stint of duty in the army, returning home a hero from the capture of Montreal. In 1761 he married Prudentias

Deliverance Bates and settled at Pownal, Vermont. Here a steady stream of sons and two daughters were born to the young couple. Then, as affairs in the colonies assumed a nasty air, Samuel Anderson was soon spotted by the radicals as a "King's man."[18] In 1775 he tried to raise men to join the King's troops and to help succour those Loyalists who were being persecuted by the revolutionaries. One of his acts was to hide twenty-six barrels of beef in the vault of his neighbour, Major James Gray, for the use of Loyalists. But it was soon discovered and confiscated by the revolutionaries.[19]

In 1776 Samuel Anderson and his brother, Joseph, emphatically opposed the radical measures of the Congress party at Albany and refused proffered commissions in the revolutionary army. For his bluntness, Joseph Anderson was imprisoned but managed to escape. By May of 1776 Samuel and Joseph Anderson had raised a number of men whom they tried to get to Quebec. Both brothers were intercepted with their men and imprisoned in Connecticut, charged with "enlisting men in the British service."[20] At the end of 1776 the Andersons escaped again from prison, Samuel heading for Bennington, Vermont, where he joined General Burgoyne's army and was soon commissioned a captain in Sir John Johnson's Regiment.[21] Joseph made his way to New York City and eventually to Quebec where he was commissioned a lieutenant in the same regiment.

By 1779 Captain Samuel Anderson and his younger brothers headed the list of those banished forever from the State of Vermont. The Act "to Prevent the Return to this State of Certain Persons," left no doubt about its intention. "Whereas Samuel Anderson, Joseph Anderson, Benjamin Anderson of Pownal,... Jeremiah French of Manchester...Justus Sherwood of New Haven...have left this State... and joined the enemies thereof...(should) they voluntarily return to this State it shall be the Duty of the Sheriff...to apprehend...such persons...and order (them) to be whipped on the naked Back, not more than forty, nor less than twenty Stripes; which Punishment... inflicted, the Delinquent shall be ordered to quit the State immediately; if any person shall continue in this State one Month or shall presume to come again in this State...he shall be put to Death."[22]

When the Anderson brothers had first fled from their homes in Pownal, Vermont, they left behind 440 acres of land, most of it cleared, three dwelling houses, one of which was burned by the insurgents, five horses, four oxen, six cows, ten cattle, twelve swine, poultry, furniture and farming implements as well as a supply of hay and grain.[23] All was confiscated by the state and sold in 1778, "The money arrisening (sic) from such sales...to be put into the Public

Treasury."[24] Samuel Anderson's 36-year-old wife, like so many other wives and mothers of loyalist soldiers, had to manage on her own amongst hostile neighbours. Her decision in 1778 was to try to join her husband in the province to the north. She paid the Vermont government the price of a pass — two shillings and six pence — and with her family of six children ranging in ages from three to sixteen, she made her way to Sorel where Captain Anderson was then stationed.[25] By the time that the regiment was disbanded in 1783, the eldest son, Joseph, was serving as a lieutenant while a younger son, Ebenezar, was ensign.[26] As one of the senior captains of the regiment, Samuel Anderson received the grant of lots no. 1 and 2 in Royal Township no. 2 not by chance, but by choice. So, too, were the grants of riverfront lots to his sons. Few begrudged these grants of land to the Andersons. They not only had served long and faithfully; they were also related by marriage or blood ties to many of the settlers. Joseph Anderson's wife was Hannah Farrand, the sister of Lieutenant Jacob Farrand and niece of Major James Gray. Township no. 2 was, above all, a settlement of family groups, not only fathers and sons, brothers and sisters, but also of families related by marriage connections such as the Andersons, Grays and Farrands. Before long, other marriage ties would bind the disbanded officers and men of the King's Royal Regiment of New York more closely together and establish links with the other Loyalist families that trickled into the new township from Montreal, Oswego and from other towns at the mouths of rivers that flowed northward from the States along which refugees continued to move over the next few years.

The Andersons were typical of most of the families who were now clearing land at no. 2 township. Few had been able to save anything but their skins when they fled their homes to head for the Quebec border. George and John Barnhart of Ulster County, New York, were, like the Anderson brothers, American born and had had substantial farms on the Delaware River. But their family roots lay on the banks of the Rhine River in the Palatinate, Germany. Their grandparents had been part of the 30,000 refugees uprooted by warfare and religious persecution at the turn of the eighteenth century who eventually found a new home in America. Now their grandchildren faced a similar upheaval. Civil war rent their family's adopted country and political persecution took the place of religious persecution. George and John Barnhart remained firm in their allegiance to the Crown of England that had offered protection to their grandparents during their persecutions. In 1778 the two brothers joined the loyal Indian Chief, Captain Joseph Brant, and served under him as scouts.[27] When George was wounded and imprisoned at Poughkeepsie, his home and possessions were confiscated. The revolutionary party allowed his pregnant wife and four children to stay in one of the barns for a few days before they set off on the long trek towards Quebec by way of the Hudson River and Lake Champlain. As a souvenir of her home, Mrs. Barnhart was allowed to take one item from among her most cherished possessions: a pewter teapot, still in the possession of a Cornwall descendant.[28]

Just as the Andersons were considered by their Vermont neighbours as "wealthy people,"[29] so, too, were the Barnharts. According to Jacob Kairn who had lived near the Barnharts on the Delaware River, George Barnhart was considered to be "the richest man there about except Mr. Burch."[30] Barnhart's farm holdings of 430 acres, most of which was under lease, and his large stock of nine horses, twenty-eight cattle, forty-four sheep, fifty hogs, indicated a substantial farmer, though not a wealthy one compared with a man like Captain Richard Duncan of nearby township no. 4, who counted his confiscated lands in thousands of acres.[31] By the end of the war the Barnhart family had supplied four privates for Sir John's regiment and one sergeant, George, who secured a waterfront lot to the west of the town plot of no. 2 township.[32]

When Sir John Johnson informed Haldimand that the selection of lots had been made to the satisfaction of the "Bulk of the People," he was likely right for although officers secured waterfront lots west and east of the town plot, so, too, did non-commissioned officers and privates, an indication that the selection took into account the length and quality of services of families during the long revolutionary war. It is not surprising, then, that the Impey and Gallinger families, like the Andersons and Barnharts, found themselves on the banks of the St. Lawrence rather than on the concessions to the rear. Philip Impey had owned 1,800 acres on the Mohawk River in Tryon County, New York. There he had built a frame house and had three black servants.[33] Like the Barnharts and Gallingers, his family roots were in Germany, but with the migration of the family during the early part of the eighteenth century, family roots were also established in England and Ireland.[34] When political dissent turned to rebellion in the American colonies, Philip Impey was among those who openly and fearlessly declared loyalty to the British Crown. For his steadfastness, the elder Impey was disarmed by the revolutionaries and forced to flee from his home in 1777. It was not until 1780 that he had an opportunity to join the Crown forces. The sudden and devastating raid that Sir John Johnson and his men made into the Mohawk Valley in May of that year permitted many of the men of the valley, including Impey, to enlist in Sir John's Regiment and to come away with him to Canada.[35] Before the revolutionary war ended, the elder Impey and six of his sons served as privates. Now, while his sons cleared part of the family holdings on lots no. 4, 5 and 6 on the waterfront and lot no. 4 on the third concession of the township, the elder Impey waited in Montreal with his two younger children.[36]

The elder Impey's decision to stay in Montreal until the land at No. 2 Township had been partly cleared was an indication of the unsettled state of the new township. All through the summer and fall of 1784 settlers were constantly coming and going, either to Montreal, St. Johns, Machiche, or into the States. Some went to collect their families; others to harvest crops they had sowed in the spring; still others to buy provisions, implements or seed. Others, like Impey, simply preferred to remain in the city until the first clearings had been made. Then there were many who never came to the settlement at all though they had drawn lots there. Reverend John Stuart, the chaplain of the 2nd Battalion, King's Royal Regiment of New York, who had established a school at Montreal, preferred to settle at Cataraqui though he drew a choice riverfront lot no. 13 at township no. 2.[37] It is unlikely, too, that Lieutenant J.F. Holland, the son of the provincial surveyor-general, or Captain Patrick Daly and Ensign John Connolly settled even temporarily at township no. 2 though they all drew waterfront lots in the township.[38] On the other hand, at least one officer of the 2nd Battalion preferred to settle with the men of the 1st Battalion. This was the Vermonter, Lieutenant Jeremiah French. By October of 1784, French had ten acres cleared on his waterfront lot, the largest clearing of any of the settlers.[39]

Overflow Roman Catholic Scottish soldiers from township no. 1 followed the contour of the Middle Branch of the Raisin River to take up lots in the 4th concession of township no. 2. Most of their officers, however, settled to the east or west in townships no. 1 and 3. Although the Scots likely had cleared some land by the fall of 1784, the muster report of October gave no hint of what was going on in the rear concessions.[40] Perhaps this was because the muster-master, John Barnes, did not personally visit the rear concessions as he went through the various new settlements making his report for the governor.

For the new settlers their first task was to erect as quickly as possible some more substantial dwelling than the government-provided tents that lined the banks of the St. Lawrence. Men helped each other in building a type of log hut, usually about twenty by fifteen feet.[41]

From the trees hewn down to clear the land, the settlers piled round logs on top of each other to form solid walls, the ends notched in order to hold them together. Each wall of the hut stood some seven or eight feet high. The spaces between the logs were chinked with wood splinters and plastered inside and out with clay. Smooth straight poles were laid lengthways inside to serve as walls and to support the roof which was made of strips of elm bark overlapping each other. In most huts there was but one door and a single window. A floor was made of split logs flattened to make a level surface. The other essential was the hearth, usually made of flat stones with a backing of field stones or small boulders mortared up the wall to meet a crude chimney made of round poles plastered with mud. Though many of the settlers erected these shanty-type huts at first, other more affluent Loyalists set about at once to build frame houses that even boasted a type of shingle. Captain Samuel Anderson lost no time in erecting a frame house for his large family that had welcomed an addition in March of 1784 when the forty-one year-old mother bore her tenth child and eighth son.[42] But even before the Andersons had partitioned the house or built a door and windows, they and other Loyalists at New Johnstown were dismayed on Sunday, 16 October 1785 to see the sky turn fearsomely dark and remain in total darkness for two hours. Then torrential rain burst from the sky, flooding many of the newly-constructed huts and houses.[43] It was but one more instance in the long series of misfortunes that seemed to stalk the path of the Loyalists.

Although most settlers had had to leave all their possessions behind in the States when they fled to Canada or joined the King's forces, there were many who, by 1784, had begun to recoup their losses. Soldiers had been paid regularly over a number of years and, in some cases, had even re-established homes in the older part of the province where they had sown crops, had some livestock, and furniture. Officers, too, had been on the army payroll for a number of years and their families had been subsidized by government with quarters and rations. Though half-pay did not represent wealth, it represented a steady source of income for the rest of their lives. This income, which coupled with a growing income from cultivated lands, government jobs and other means of industry, including the timber trade, put men like Captain Samuel Anderson and other American Loyalists in a privileged financial position. Major Gray for instance could count on £133 9s. half pay a year; Captain Anderson on £88 19s. 4d., and Lieutenant Joseph Anderson £41 10s. 4d., part of the £1,707,655 that reached British North American from 1784 to 1813 in half-pay entitlements.[44] Moreover, the Loyalists of township no. 2 and the other four townships settled by the men of the King's Royal Regiment of New York showed a surprising tenacity about collecting compensation from the British government. These disbanded soldiers and Loyalists of New Johnstown accounted for more than half the claims presented to the commissioners sent out in 1786 from Britain to investigate Loyalist losses.[45] Though the Loyalists did not get anything near the amount they claimed — in most cases the compensation amounted to about two-fifths of their claim[46] — the settlers at New Johnstown shared abundantly in the close to half a million pounds that the British government gave as compensation to the Loyalists during the first decade that they were settled in the new townships.[47]

This input of capital was of considerable significance in the infant settlements. It meant that those receiving half pay could hire help to hew the trees, build their homes and cultivate their farms. When the compensation money arrived some five years after the initial settlement of the township, it provided a sudden and fresh inflow of capital into township no. 2 and its surrounding townships at a time when many of the settlers were growing excess crops and were in need of some means of transport to market.[48] A riverfront was an advantage for those with boats capable of carrying to market such crops as wheat. Many settlers now needed capital to buy boats. For those on the rear concessions, money was needed to purchase horses, wagons and carts.

The picture of Cornwall's beginnings is not entirely one of grinding poverty, back-breaking work and bitter hardship. On the contrary, its origin was a highly orchestrated move, organized and heavily subsidized by government. The land in township no. 2, like that in township no. 1, had been the most carefully and swiftly surveyed of all the townships. Government surveyors had been at the site since early February of 1784 running out the individual lots long before the batteaux of settlers began arriving in the first week of June.[49] Some officers and the more affluent Loyalists waited in Montreal and other centres in the settled part of the province while their land holdings were cleared and dwellings erected before they moved to the settlement. And even in the nebulous state of frontier society, Cornwall's first settlers already had a distinct sense of their own importance and place in society and, what was more pertinent, of their neighbour's. Thus minor social pretensions and conflicts were soon apparent. Within a month of the arrival of the first settlers, the governor was receiving reports that the most serious disputes arose between "the Master and Servant where Severe Correction Seems to take place."[50]

Those who had slaves expected them to help clear and cultivate the lands.[51] In township no. 2, Major James Gray brooked no dilatory behaviour from the young sons of his black servant woman, Dorine. One of them described the major as "strict and sharp. (He) made us wear deerskin shirts and deerskin jackets, and gave us many a flogging. At these times he would pull off my jacket, and the rawhide would fly around my shoulders very fast."[52]

Captain Samuel Anderson had at least one black women servant whom he had procured in a somewhat unorthodox fashion. He snatched her from her master, Adam Fonda of Caughnawaga, Tryon County, during one of the lightning raids that the Royal Yorkers made into the Mohawk territory during the revolutionary war. Now her rightful master concocted an ingenious scheme for securing his "negro wench, his actual property, born in his own family," as he put it. When Fonda was asked by Alexander Campbell, a Montreal-based Loyalist, to repay a debt, Fonda sent Campbell a power of attorney to "take his wench, (from Anderson) sell her and pay his debt." Campbell soon found that the deed was easier said than done. Anderson had no intention of parting with the servant; nor would any magistrate give an order for "taking this wench."[53] How many other settlers in township no. 2 had household servants is impossible to say, for the muster of October 1784 lists only one servant, that of Ensign John Conolly, who was at Cataraqui in 1784 and likely did not settle in township no. 2.[54]

Other Blacks had served in the various provincial corps. They now expected to be treated as discharged soldiers as far as land grants were concerned.[55] When Haldimand consulted Sir John Johnson on the matter, Sir John replied bluntly, "The negroes...alluded to must be the property of Loyalists, many of whom as well as those stiling themselves freemen, have served in some or other of the Corps, and Consequently, should (be) I suppose, intitled (sic) to the same proportion of land as the other Men are."[56] A number of these Blacks received land grants in the Lake Township, but there is no record of any Black soldiers receiving grants in township no. 2.[57]

By early October of 1784 Township no. 2 had a semblance of settlement. There was an elite of army officers of some independent means and a wider base of soldier-settlers who had cleared some 101-1/2 acres of land.[58] Many of the soldier-settlers counted themselves the social equals or even superiors of the local officers though few officers and fewer settlers could afford servants to help soften the workload of pioneer life. Five-year-old Thomas Gummersall Anderson, the second youngest son of Captain Anderson, claimed his parents "worked like slaves to render their children more fortunate."[59] Youngsters like young Tommy Anderson were glad enough that first year to share with the other settlers in the steady diet morning and evening of "sup-on," a dish of ground-up Indian corn that had been boiled several hours and was eaten with butter, sugar and milk.[60]

The Loyalists at Township no. 2 had been, like those in other settlements, irritated when they learned in early June 1784 that the British government had sent orders to reduce their daily government rations to two-thirds of the usual amount. Most of them had reached their various settlements far too late in the season to raise any crops for the coming winter. The most they accomplished was to clear some land to plant winter wheat and turnip. Luckily, most of them had had the foresight to supply themselves with turnip seed, for by early July seed was so scarce that Sir John Johnson was able to procure only enough to dole it out at the rate of "four drinking glasses to each company of my First Battalion."[61] What was even more difficult to procure in the early fall was wheat seed. By shopping around in Vermont and upper New York, Haldimand's agents were able to secure enough to supply each settler with about three bushels for fall planting. When the wheat appeared next spring, it was attacked by a grub that ate the stem through near the root and ruined the crop.[62] It was one more bitter pill for the settlers who had to depend again upon the bounty of the government to save them from hunger.

Haldimand kept his ear to the ground with regard to the complaints of the new settlers. Much as he himself might grumble about their "fickleness," he realized that these people represented the continuance of the British presence in North America. He was worried when he learned that "the Men are changeable in their opinion Since They have heard that the Americans persecute the Loyalists not so violently as formerly."[63] On top of that John Johnson reported that, "I have seen this day (July 16) two families who had been up to the lands, returning into the Colonies. Many others have come away, and are likely to continue daily so if not timely prevented by a continuance of their former allowance of Provisions, as none but those who had been fortunate enough to save a little money will be able to support themselves on the Land."[64] Fearing that discontent might reverse the flow of settlers coming in from the United States, Haldimand immediately increased the rations to the full quota, though he had no authority from Britain to do so. The daily ration was one pound of beef or twelve ounces of pork and a pound of flour.[65] Haldimand proposed to increase the ration by adding peas and butter, though Sir John reported that his men in New Johnstown had been most hurt by the reduction in the supply of flour. However the ration, when supplemented by peas and butter, was not all that meagre, especially when larger families like the Andersons were able to get their younger children on the adult ration list.[66] Moreover, the younger children of the settlement amused themselves with hunting squirrels, fishing or trapping pigeons to vary the diet of "sup-on." Pigeons were a special delicacy. Millions migrated at once, completely blackening the sky for hours on end.[67] Fish were plentiful, especially sturgeon and black bass and the settlers soon took to the Indian method of catching them by the dozen. This was to wait until nightfall and then to light a fire to attract the fish. The fish could then be speared without much effort.[68] Though the soldier-settlers had been disarmed when they were disbanded in 1783, the governor allowed one man in every five to retain a musket for hunting. Many others probably had their own firearms which they brought to the new settlements along with the axe, hoe, spade and portable corn grinder that the government supplied to each family.

Sir John Johnston was well aware of the immediate need for a saw mill and grist mill. In early August of 1784 he examined the mill site on the River au Raisin on one of his lots and was so pleased with the prospect that he wrote Haldimand that "it will admit of both Grist and Saw Mills on the same Dam." Though Johnson anticipated that the erection of mills at that location "will be very expensive," he determined to begin construction at once because the "numerous inhabitants now settling on that River will stand in great need of boards." All Johnson asked of the governor was that he would allow the very competent millwright employed at the Cedars Canal to super-intend the work.[69]

Apart from the essentials for their livelihood, the settlers asked Sir John Johnson to intercede for them in the matter of magistrates "to prevent the confusion and disorder that must otherwise ensue."[70] Rudimentary methods of law and order existed from the beginning in what was in reality a paramilitary settlement. The disbanded soldiers were accustomed to regulations and obeying superior officers; the latter were prone to exercise law and order in a somewhat arbitrary fashion. On the whole there were less "Complaints and Jealousies" reported from the new Johnstown area than from New Oswegatchie and Cataraqui that first summer.[71] It was the two latter areas that Sir John Johnson had to keep visiting to sort out difficulties and it was to these areas that the first magistrates were appointed.[72] It was not until 18 April 1785 that Captain Anderson was named a Justice of the Peace for the District of Montreal which then included the Royal

Townships in the western part of the province.[73] This was an indication that Captain Anderson, a lawyer by training who was also in charge of the commissary operation for the whole of the New Johnstown district, was considered by the government as the most suitable person for the job of justice of the peace. By 29 July 1786 Anderson was also named a Commissioner of Oaths. That township no. 2 was attracting most of the Loyalists who were being forwarded from Montreal to the western settlements was evident in the daily commissary transactions. For instance, in October of 1785, Captain Anderson distributed by far the largest number of plowshares in township no. 2, indicating that there were more heads of families in that township than in any of the other townships from Pointe Mouillée to township no. 8.[74]

Religion and education were not entirely neglected in township no. 2 in the first decade of its existence. The Church of England made gestures towards the settlers the very first summer that they arrived in their townships. In July 1784 Rev. John Stuart, the chaplain of the 2nd battalion of the King's Royal Regiment, visited "every encampment of the Loyalists (from) Niagara down to Coteau du Lac and baptised the children in each Place, the whole amounting to 150."[75] The settlers at township no. 2 did their best to encourage Stuart to settle among them as their clergyman, but he opted for Cataraqui, partly for financial reasons.[76] As the Society for the Propagation of the Gospel had reduced his salary from £70 to £50, Stuart hoped to recoup his loss by an army chaplaincy which was only possible if he were near a regular garrison,[77] and it was Cataraqui that had the garrison. Thus, although later Stuart spoke about his choice being mainly influenced by Cataraqui "being a large and widely-extended settlement (which) would probably afford a larger field for usefulness,"[78] he, like most Loyalists at this stage, took into account his personal needs and he headed for Cataraqui with his family in the summer of 1785.

Disappointed in not persuading Reverend John Stuart to settle among them, the Episcopalians of township no. 2 then began to raise a subscription for the support of a clergyman.[79] By September of 1786 they successfully persuaded the Episcopalian clergyman at New Oswegatchie, John Bryan, to come to them. Bryan, a Loyalist from Arlington, Connecticut, had been chosen by the people at New Oswegatchie to minister to them in 1784.[80] By 1786 Bryan had run into difficulties with Major Edward Jessup, the principal settler there,[81] and Bryan removed to New Johnstown by October 1787. Carpenters were hired to build him a parsonage of two floors with a "roof of Gable cords with two Dorman windows in a workmanlike manner," at a cost of eighteen pounds fifteen shillings, Halifax currency. Bryan was soon caught up in the local political turmoils for by 20 November 1787 he was among those signing a memorial from there to Deputy Surveyor John Collins.[82] As a recognized minister of the Church of England, even though his credentials were later questioned,[83] Bryan received £50 allowance from the government,[84] and took up his residence in the town site on a plot on the north side of Second Street west of Pitt Street where a parsonage house was erected by 1789.[85] This was the site that had originally been laid out for a public square,[86] but by 1790 Bryan had fenced in some three acres and made improvements.[87] That the people of township no. 2 were well organized and on the move with regard to establishing churches and getting land set aside for their clergymen was indicated in their petition of 15 April 1787 to Lord Dorchester in which they asked for "assistance in establishing the Church of England, and Scotland, in this Infant Settlement, and that a Glebe of Four Hundred Acres of Land in each Township, be set apart for a Clergyman."[88]

The Roman Catholics of the township received an increase in their numbers in September of 1786 when the first large influx of settlers directly from Glengarry and Knoydart in Scotland arrived, most of them settling in township no. 1, but a number settled to the rear of Cornwall Township and founded St.Andrews. They numbered 345 men, women and children and among them was their priest, Father Alexander Macdonell (Scotus) and Lieutenant Angus Mac-Donell, half-pay officer of the 71st Regiment.[89] Up until the arrival of Father Alexander Macdonell, the Roman Catholics of township no. 2 had probably been ministered to by Father Roderick Macdonell of St. Regis, brother of Captains Archibald and Allan Macdonell of the King's Royal Regiment of New York who had emigrated to the Loyalist settlements in 1785 at the solicitation of his brothers and others.[90]

With the coming of Reverend John Bethune to township no. 1 in 1787, the Presbyterians of township no. 2 began to have regular services of worship as often as Bethune could come to the town site. Imprisoned in North Carolina for his loyalist activities, Bethune, upon his release, had gone to Halifax where he helped organize the 84th Royal Highland Emigrants and became their chaplain. In Montreal at the close of the revolutionary war, he organized the first Presbyterian church in that city before he decided to move to Charlottenburg where many of the men of the 84th Royal Highland Emigrants chose to settle, to claim his land allotment as a Loyalist in township no. 1. He brought his growing family to a waterfront lot where he resided for some time before settling at Williamstown, which was then more often termed simply Johnson's Mills. From his location in township no. 1, Bethune travelled to township no. 2 to minister to the Presbyterians there as well as to those in the surrounding area.[91] By 1787 the Presbyterians had erected a small church of logs on the east side of what became known as Pitt Street, south of Second Street. This modest church was described as "neither large, nor very substantial...(but was) well adapted to the existing state of the Congregation."[92] Two years later their burial ground extended from First to Second Street along Pitt Street. Then in 1792 they erected a frame building on the southwest corner of lot 15 on or near the site of the log church.[93] Thus the Presbyterians in township no. 2 outdistanced other denominations in enthusiasm, organization and likely in numbers also. Part of their superior organization was undoubtedly due to the early arrival in the area of Bethune whose forceful personality was not surpassed until the arrival of the Reverend John Strachan some sixteen years later.

As for schooling, the young were not entirely free to amuse themselves by squirrel hunting and fishing. Though Thomas Gummersall Anderson claimed that "the first generation born in Upper Canada were without book learning because there were no means of education in the upper province in those days,"[94] a school was in existence by 1790. It was located at the north east corner of Second and Augustus Streets, likely established by Reverend John Bryan when he arrived in Johnstown in 1787.[95] The Loyalists had always been careful to get schools going as soon as their families were established in the refugee camps in the heart of the province; this had been as true of the Indian Loyalists as of the others.[96] One of their earliest requests on reaching the settlements was to ask the government for help in establishing schools in each township.[97] That rudimentary schooling at least was available for the youngsters at Johnstown was indicated by the fact that young Tommy Anderson had enough "book learning" by the age of sixteen to be apprenticed to one of the leading merchants of Kingston.[98] His comment that there was no means of education probably referred to a lack of means for securing a higher education or university training in those early years, rather than a lack of elementary schooling.

In the summer of 1784 it was far from clear which of the Loyalist settlements would pull ahead in terms of population and importance. Certainly neither the town-planners of 1784 nor the Loyalists ever dreamed that it would be the obscure little Indian village of Toronto that would out-distance all the carefully-planned and heavily-subsidized Loyalist settlements. Cataraqui township no. 1 where Rev. John Stuart chose to settle had but 220 settlers in October of 1784. Township no. 2 of the Royal Townships had 489 according to the muster lists of October 1784 which are not entirely accurate but are useful as a comparative guide to the pattern of settlement. The largest muster of all in October 1784 was Township no. 3, Cataraqui, that later became Fredericksburg.[99] This was settled by part of the second battalion of the King's Royal Regiment of New York under the popular senior captain, Thomas Gummersall, and by Major James Rogers' King's Rangers. For many settlers it was the presence of a regular garrison at township no. 1, Cataraqui that attracted them. Not only did the garrison provide an air of security; it also was a market for excess crops. The most that the town site of "Royal Township" no. 2 could offer was a small commissariat operation that distributed the government rations monthly to the Loyalists. Unlike the town site of township no. 1, Cataraqui, which was soon studded with substantial homes neatly fenced in,[100] the mile-square town site of township no. 2 of the Royal Townships failed to attract settlers.

NOTES

1. Maj. R. Mathews, Journal of his trip to Detroit, May 1787, in J.A. Macdonell, *Sketches, Glengarry in Canada*, 82.
2. Louis Nadau's testimony, 25 July 1787 (RG4/A1/33/10715).
3. Patrick McNiff map, 1 Nov. 1786 (H2/400).
4. Haldimand to Johnson, 17 May 1784 (MG21/B65/29-30); Same to same, 24 May 1784 (MG21/B115/262-63); Simcoe to Dundas, 7 Dec. 1791 (*State Papers, Upper Canada*, 1891, i, 6); see also, Hereward Senior, "Loyalists in Quebec: A Study in Diversity", paper presented to Learned Societies of Canada, Halifax, Nova Scotia, 5 June 1981, 14.
5. Haldimand to Johnson, 17 May 1784 (MG21/B65/22-29).
6. Johnson to Haldimand, 11 July 1784 (MG21/B115/272-73).
7. Haldimand to Johnson, 15 July 1784 (MG21/B64/53).
8. For the distribution of lots, see McNiff map, 1 Nov. 1786, H2/400.
9. On the McNiff map it is incorrectly recorded that James Anderson received this lot; see Mrs. S. Rowe, 'The Anderson Record from 1699 to 1896", in *OHSRP*, 1905, vi, 110.
10. Joseph Hadfield, *An Englishman in America, 1785, being the diary of*, 56-57; Johnson to Haldimand, 11 Aug. 1784 (MG21/B115/287-88).
11. MG21/B168/101-109.
12. *Ibid.*, see remarks made on each settler.

13. Return of disbanded troops and Loyalists settled at Township no. 3 mustered 25 Sept. 1784 (MG21/B168/62); Return of officers 1st Battalion King's Royal Regiment of New York, 6 Oct. 1784 (MG11/Q23/367); see also, William Chewett map, 1792 (V3/440).

14. Return of Officers of the late 1st Battalion, King's Royal Regiment of New York, encl. Haldimand to Lord Sydney, 6 Oct. 1784 (MG11/Q23/367).

15. J.F. Pringle, *Lunenburgh, or the Old Eastern District*, 318-19.

16. Patrick Campbell, *Travels in the interior parts of North America in the Years 1791 and 1792*, 144.

17. MG21/B168/92; see also, Minutes of the Land Board, Quebec City, 26 Feb. 1790 (RG1/L4/10/68).

18. Rowe, "The Anderson Record", *OHSPR*, 1905, vi, 113.

19. Samuel Anderson's testimony before the Claims Commission, Montreal, 21 Feb. 1788, *Second Report, Ontario Bureau of Archives*, 1904, 426.

20. Joseph Anderson's testimony, *ibid.*, 424.

21. Subsistence account of Loyal Volunteers commanded by the late Capt. Samuel MacKay on the campaign under Lt.-Gen. Burgoyne, 1777, (MG21/B167/I/109-112); see also, Capt. S. Anderson's Orderly Book 1779-80, King's Royal Regiment of New York (MG23/B23).

22. *State Papers of Vermont*, 1941, vi, 38-39.

23. Samuel and Joseph Anderson's testimony before Claims Commission, 21 Feb. 1788, *Second Report, Ontario Bureau of Archives*, 1904, 425.

24. List of Estates ordered confiscated by the Court of Confiscation, Arlington, Vermont, 23 Apr. 1778, *State Papers of Vermont*, 1941, vi, 15.

25. Rowe, "The Anderson Record", 115.

26. MG21/B168/104.

27. George Barnhart's testimony before Claims Commission, 29 Jan. 1788, *Second Report, Ontario Bureau of Archives*, 1904, 1101.

28. For details on the Barnhart family, see Dr. Barnhart's Genealogy, privately held by Mr. and Mrs. Benson Stidwill, Cornwall.

29. Alex Nicholson's testimony before the Claims Commission, *Second Report*, Ontario *Bureau of Archives*, 1904, 426.

30. *Ibid.*, 1102; John Burch, a Londoner who came to America in 1772, became a merchant at Albany and owned 5,000 acres on the Delaware River, confiscated by the revolutionaries. He settled at Niagara. (Hadfield, *Diary*, footnote 100; see also, A list of persons... to settle and cultivate Crown Lands opposite Niagara, 20 July 1784 (MG21/B168/38).

31. Captain Richard Duncan's testimony before the Claims Commissions, 5 Mar. 1788. *Second Report, Ontario Bureau of Archives*, 1904, 474.

32. McNiff map, 1 Nov. 1786, (H2/400).

33. Philip Impey's claim, heard before the Claims Commission, 6 Dec. 1787, *Second Report, Ontario Bureau of Archives*, 1904, 1069.

34. "Notes on the Empey (Impey) Family of Stormont", in *OHSPR*, 1931, xxvii, 392-93.

35. *Ibid.*, 392-99; *Second Report, Ontario Bureau of Archives*, 1904, 1069; for Sir John Johnson's own account of this raid, see Johnson to Haldimand, 3 June 1789, (MG21/B158/128), also printed in Pringle, Appendix A, 347-48.

36. Haldimand Papers, MG21/B168/107.

37. See McNiff map, 1 Nov. 1786 (H2/400); for Rev. John Stuart, see MG11/Q24/I/72; see also Petition of Rev. John Stuart to Haldimand, 31 Dec. 1783 (MG21/B215/2).

38. Return of Discharged Troops and Loyalists settled in Township no. 2, 9 October 1784 (MG21/B168/105); Daly is reported at Montreal and Conolly at Cataraqui.

39. *Ibid.*, 101.

40. *Ibid.*, 104-05.

41. For a description of the log huts, see James Croil, *Dundas, or a Sketch of Canadian History*, 131; Macdonell, *Sketches, Glengarry*, 62-63, gives an identical description.

42. Rowe, "The Anderson Record", 110.

43. Reminiscence of Thomas Gummersall Anderson, cited in "The Anderson Record," 117; McCord Museum: Thomas McCord Papers M8450; William Kingsford, *History of Canada*, VII, 240-41.

44. Howard Temperley, "Frontierism, Capital, and the American Loyalists in Canada", in *American Studies*, Cambridge University Press, 1979, 13, I, 20-22.

45. *Ibid.*, 16.

46. *Ibid.*, see 17, table 3.

47. *Ibid.*; other sources cite £3,000,000, see J.G. Harkness, *History of Stormont, Dundas, and Glengarry*, 55.

48. For testimony that most of the Loyalists' claims had been paid by 1789, see John Richardson to John Porteous, Montreal, 20 Oct. 1789, in E.A. Cruikshank, "The John Richardson Letters", in *OHSPR*, vi, 1905, 30; Campbell, *Travels to the Interior*, 156.

49. See Lt. Walter Sutherland's statement of his account as a surveyor employed from 20 Sept. to 12 Nov. 1783 and again from 15 Feb. to 23 May 1784, MG21/B120/163.

50. Major John Ross to Major R. Mathews, 7 July 1784 (MG21/B126/114-15).

51. Capt. John Barnes to Mathews, 5 Feb. 1784 (MG21/B138/336-7).

52. John Baker's memoir, 15 Dec. 1869, cited in Pringle, 321.

53. For details of Anderson's black servant, see Alexander Campbell to Major Mathews, 16 Aug. 1784 (MG21/B162/351).

54. MG21/B168/105.

55. Stephen de Lancey to Mathews, 17 May 1784 (MG21/B165/235-36); Mathews to de Lancey, 24 May 1784 (MG21/B63/342).

56. Johnson to Haldimand, 27 May 1784 (MG21/B115/264-65).

57. See Pringle, 403, for identification of Blacks.

58. Return of Disbanded Troops and Loyalists settled in Township no. 2 (MG21/B168/101-09), shows the amount of land cleared in 1784.

59. Rowe, "The Anderson Record", 117.

60. *Ibid.*

61. Johnson to Mathews, 22 July 1784 (MG21/B115/277-78).

62. Mathews to Sir John Johnson, 17 July 1784, and Mathews to French, 24 July 1784 (MG21/B64/66-67, 91); *Hadfield*, Diary, 57.

63. Maj. John Ross to Haldimand, 14 June 1784 (MG21/B126/104-07).

64. Johnson to Haldimand, 16 July 1784 (MG21/B169/55).

65. Haldimand to Sir John Johnson, 14 June 1784 (MG21/B63/401-02); Hadfield, *Diary*, says the daily rations were 10 oz. flour, 10 oz. oatmeal, 8 oz. pork fat and 1 oz. butter.

66. See the five-year-old Thomas Gummersall Anderson and the sons of Jeremiah French listed as men in the Muster List of October 1784 (MG21/B168/103 and 108).

67. Reminiscences of T.G. Anderson, in "The Anderson Record", 117.

68. Hadfield, *Diary*, 57.

69. Sir John Johnson to Haldimand, 11 Aug. 1784 (MG21/B115/287-8).

70. Same to same, 12 July 1784 (MG21/B115/274-75).

71. Mathews to Sir John Johnson, 19 July 1784 (MG21/B64/66-67); Johnson to Haldimand, 11 Aug. 1784 (MG21/B115/287-88).

72. Mathews to Ross, 20 July 1784 (MG21/B64/69-71); *Gazette de Québec*, 1 Jan. 1785.

73. For Anderson's appointment see, List of General Commission of the Peace of the District of Montreal, 18 Apr. 1785 (RG4/A1/28/9092); *Gazette de Québec*, 1 Jan. 1786.

74. For Anderson's appointment as Commissioner of Oaths, see Pringle, 47; for Anderson's distribution of plowshares see RG4/A1/29/9324-26.

75. Rev. John Stuart to Maj. R. Mathews, 14 July 1784 (MG21/B162/333-34).

76. *Ibid*.

77. Petition of Rev. John Stuart to Haldimand, 31 Dec. 1783 (MG21/B215/2).

78. Stuart to Bishop Inglis, 6 July 1788, cited in Richard Preston, *Kingston Before the War of 1812*, 134.

79. Rev. John Stuart to Secretary, Society for the Propagation of the Gospel, 26 Sept. 1786, cited in A.H. Young, "The Mission of Cornwall 1784-1812", in *OHSPR*, 1929, xxv, 487.

80. Byran is listed as a clergyman at Township no. 8, 18 Aug. 1784 (RG4/A1/29/9394); see also, James Miller, "The Town of Cornwall 1784-1867", unpublished M.A. thesis, University of Toronto, April 1967, 5-6.

81. Rev. John Stuart to Society for the Propagation of the Gospel, 26 Sept. 1786, in Young, "The Mission of Cornwall", 487; DAO: Trinity Church papers, 59-1, see account Voucher with carpenter Brackett, signed by John Smith and John Pescod, 4 Oct. 1787.

82. *Gazette de Québec*, no. 1176, Supplement, 28 Feb. 1788.

83. Rev. John Stuart to Society for the Propagation of the Gospel, 4 Oct. 1790, in Young, "The Mission of Cornwall", 488.

84. Lord Dorchester to Rev. John Stuart, 24 Oct. 1787, in Young, "The Mission of Cornwall," 487.

85. William Chewett Map, 1792 (V3/440).

86. *Ibid*.

87. Minutes of the Land Board, Quebec City, 26 Feb. 1790 (RG1/L4/x/68).

88. Petition of the Western Loyalists to Lord Dorchester, 15 Apr. 1787, New Johnstown, in Adam Shortt and A.G. Doughty, *Documents relating to the Constitutional History of Canada 1759-1791*, 648; Chewett map 1792 (V3/440).

89. John Craigie to Stephen de Lancey, Inspector of Loyalists, 4 Sept. 1786; Governor H. Hope to Lt. Angus McDonell, September 1786 (RG4/A1/31/9909-11).

90. J.A. Macdonell, *Sketches, Glengarry in Canada*, 125-26; see also, Nancy Cameron of Brodelbin, New York, to her cousin, Margaret MacPherson, in Scotland, 12 Nov. 1785 (PAO: MU2098).

91. "History of St. John's Church 1787-1975", 1-2; Macdonell, *Sketches, Glengarry*, 119-22; Robert Campbell, *A History of the Scotch Presbyterian Church, St. Gabriel Street, Montreal*, 28.

92. Minutes of Session, St. John's Church, Cornwall, 1 July 1827, cited in Miller, "The Town of Cornwall, 1784-1867", 15; Pringle, 84; see also, History of St. John's Church, prepared by a Committee of the Church headed by Frederick MacMillan, 2-3.

93. For burial ground, see William Chewett Map, 1792 (V3/440); Harkness, 52.

94. Reminiscences of T.G. Anderson in Rowe, "The Anderson Record", 117.

95. Chewett Map 1792 (V3/440).

96. See List of Schoolmasters and their pay, 8 April 1785 (MG11/Q24/I/66).

97. Petition of Western Loyalists to Lord Dorchester, New Johnstown, 15 April 1787, cited in Shortt and Doughty, *Documents*, 648.

98. Reminiscences of T.G. Anderson, in Rowe, "The Anderson Record", 120-21.

99. For these figures, see Musters of Disbanded Troops and Loyalists, Sept. and Oct. 1784, (MG21/B168/76, 83 and 109).

100. See James Peachey's map, dated 16 July 1784 (C1512).

Chapter III

The McNiff Controversy

The town site of no. 2 township, like its name, had a haphazard existence during its first ten years. At first the town site was called simply "New Town." Then, to distinguish it from the whole district of New Johnstown that included the five first townships settled by Sir John Johnson's regiment, the town site was called "Johnstown" in honour of Sir John Johnston. By the late 1780s the town itself was more frequently called "New Johnstown," or was beginning to be called "Cornwall", in honour of the Prince of Wales who was also Duke of Cornwall.[1] Thus within the first decade of its nebulous existence, the town was known by four different names, a fact that created confusion for future historians. If the town site boasted many names within the first few years of its existence, the same can not be said for the number of its inhabitants. One traveller who visited the town on 29 June 1785 found "a few huts here." As an afterthought, he added, "they have cleared a fine piece of ground around. The Commissary lives here."[2] The traveller, Joseph Hadfield, who was en route from Montreal to Niagara, secured from the Commissary an account of the actual number of inhabitants in the New Johnstown district. If Hadfield's figures are at all accurate, township no. 2 had, in 1785, only 64 men, 25 women and 77 children, making a total of about 166 in all.[3] This was a far cry from the 489 recorded in the muster of the previous fall, but the figure of 166 is more in accord with the estimate of inhabitants made according to the remarks on the muster list, that is, that there were about ninety-nine people actually on the land in the fall of 1784.[4] However, Hadfield noted that some 300 or 400 people were making their way towards the settlements that June. He himself met at least 100 on the way.[5]

Few of these settlers found the town site of no. 2 township attractive. There were several reasons for this. Foremost was the cumbersome way the town lots were laid out. The 640 acres of land within the mile square that formed the town site were divided into 81 lots of about six acres each.[6] Each of these lots was then subdivided into squares that contained 24 lots along the perimeter of a square. In the centre of each square was a reserve for back yards for each lot. On the paper plan for the town, nine major streets ran horizontally across the town site from east to west and were numbered from first to ninth. In reality the township road followed the road nearest the river which was called Water Street and wove its way up through the town site to Second Street.[7] Moreover, there was the customary grant of town lots to officers and soldiers: five to field officers, that is, fifteen acres; three to captains, two to subalterns, and one to non-commissioned officers or privates.[8] However, few officers laid claim to any of the town lots. The one condition for anyone who wanted a town lot was that the lot must be cleared within twelve months. When Major Samuel Holland, the surveyor-general, laid out the town, he had hoped that the town site would attract traders who would be given a preference if they applied for town lots.[9] But even with this preference, few traders appeared.

Although the town lots were distributed according to Holland's general plan, a town did not emerge. Very few people applied for the lots. Those who did fenced in more and more land as they improved it and "instead of forming a town," Deputy Surveyor William Chewett informed the Land Board Committee at Quebec City in 1789, "they have made farms of a town."[10] Complicating the matter of the town site further was the fact that no tickets or certificates were issued to those who were granted town lots.[11] The only record of the transactions was a plan of the town site prepared by Patrick McNiff, one of the deputy surveyors in Holland's department who listed the various proprietors on the master plan.[12] By 1790 the town was described as being a series of "large tracts...fenced around in the heart of the town and the streets are included in those enclosures."[13] These tracts of land included forty acres owned by Joel Stone who described his holdings in 1789 as "a small temporary purchase and my buildings equally temporary."[14] Identified by Chewett as the other holders of town lots by 1789 were Jacob Rambough, nine acres, Thomas Swan, twelve, Reverend John Bryan, three, Mrs. Margaret Bruce, a widow, twelve, Captain John (Spanish) Macdonell, Scotus, twelve, and John Robertson and the heirs of Daniel Robertson, five acres.[15] Major James Gray was reported to hold "part of Pointe Maligne originally intended as a common for the use of the Town."[16]

The lack of development in the town site proper came to the attention of government officials at Quebec City when three inhabitants of the township, William Impey, Jacob Ross and Matthias

Snetsinger applied successfully to Lord Dorchester, the governor, for permission to use what they described as a vacant town lot as a Lutheran burying ground.[17] When Impey and Ross buried two children in the town lot, they found themselves faced with a lawsuit brought by Major James Gray who charged them with trespassing. The case was tried before Captain Richard Duncan on 14 October 1789. The jury listened to the evidence, visited the burial ground, and concluded that Gray was in the right and awarded him £10. Though Gray won that round, he lost out eventually for the case led to an inquiry into the whole system of land-holding in Cornwall.[18] This resulted in the Land Board Committee at Quebec City ordering the town site to be re-surveyed and laid out under a new system that would, the Board hoped, "tend greatly to the speedy settlement of the town."[19] To eradicate the complaint that there was "a monopoly in some instances (of the town lots) and interference with the possession (of them) in others," the Land Board recommended that each town lot of six acres be subdivided into six lots of about one acre each, and that "all persons who have at present more or less land in their possession in Johnstown (Cornwall) than this quantity (one acre) shall be reduced or augmented according to that standard, with a reserve that the improvements shall be paid for before any possessions are relinquished."[20]

The Land Board at Quebec then threw the ticklish task of adjudicating "all disputed titles and other matters of controversy relative to Johnstown" back to the local Land Board that met under Captain Richard Duncan in Williamsburg Township.[21] No matter which decision the Land Board at Quebec made to untangle the thorny problem of the ownership of lots in Cornwall, the decision could not please all parties involved. And any decision that interfered with titles to land tended to cause general uneasiness in the whole district. The only record of the land grants were the tickets or certificates that had been issued hastily and often without even a date by the deputy surveyors in the area. Many such tickets and certificates had been granted by Patrick McNiff, but as he had been dismissed from his post as deputy surveyor, he refused to give up the only plan on which the names of owners were recorded.[22] To complicate matters more, many settlers who received grants of land had exchanged them for others and not all such exchanges had been officially recorded. Moreover, in some cases where tickets or certificates had been issued for grants of land, the deputy surveyor had neglected to enter the grant on the master plan for the town.[23] One final problem in the system of land-holding for the people of township no. 2 was that

McNiff and the other deputy surveyors had run some of the concession lines perpendicular to the sidelines of the township instead of parallel to the river.[24] This meant that some lots were too long in one place and too short in another.[25] These were problems that arose because of the feverish haste in which the hard-pressed deputy surveyors had worked prior to and after the arrival of the first contingents of Loyalists. With goodwill, patience and mutual trust, such overlapping of lots and discrepancies in the surveys were problems that could have been ironed out without too much difficulty.

The creation of a town with shops, post office, school, churches, streets, a common and parks was more difficult as long as the owners of the town lots treated their property as farm holdings. It was the local deputy surveyor, Patrick McNiff, the holder of one of the choice waterfront lots as well as lands in township no. 1, who spearheaded agitation that eventually provoked government intervention in the township. Though McNiff's calculated campaign was designed to undermine confidence in the leadership of the officers and was directed particularly against Captains Samuel Anderson and John MacDonell, it was the constant stream of petitions and complaints to Quebec City from New Johnstown that led to a public enquiry in the summer of 1787,[26] and eventually forced the Land Board at Quebec to grapple with the problem of the original ownership of town lots. Until the large holdings within the town site were legislated out of existence, Cornwall remained a town in name only.

Political agitation began in township no. 2 quite independently of Patrick McNiff and was first directed against the non-commissioned officers who were assisting Captain Samuel Anderson in distributing provisions, clothing and tools from the commissary stores. It took the form of a petition signed by thirty-three Loyalists who unanimously complained to Captain John Macdonell that Sergeants John Pescod, John Smith and John Annable "sold different Barills of provision and firkins of Butter to one Fox and different other Pedlars come here." The petitioners demanded to know by what right the sergeants disposed of such goods when they (the petitioners) "find it very hard to subsist upon what they receive from one month to another."[27] The appearance of this petition as early as February 1785 indicated that the less affluent settlers were beginning to imitate their officers who had been accustomed to dash off petitions almost without end to the government on various pretexts. What was particularly revealing about this petition was that it was signed by a number of those who held lots in the town itself and who henceforth would form the hard core of Patrick McNiff's followers. These included William

Impey, Jacob Rambough (Rombough) and Jacob Ross. But it also included a number of settlers who drew back from radical agitation almost immediately — men such as Sergeant George Barnhart, Christopher Seron, John Loney, Jacob Algier, (Alguire) Henry Merkley and Joseph Cryderman. This affair was soon hushed up for the sergeants readily admitted selling the goods, but assured government officials that what they had sold was their own rations or items they had purchased from others.[28]

A far more elaborate petition was prepared by all the senior officers from the various settlements for presentation to the King himself on 11 April 1785 by Sir John Johnson. Major James Gray signed for township no. 2. The very first clause of the petition was a protest against the system of "Tenure of Lands in Canada (which is) such as to subject them to the rigorous Rules, Homages and Reservations, and Restrictions of the French Laws and Customs, which are so different from the mild Tenures to which they had ever been accustomed." The suggested solution was to make the country west of Point Baudet into a District quite distinct from the Province of Quebec "where they might enjoy the Blessings of British Laws and of British Government." The establishment of "a liberal System of Tenure, Law and Government in this new Settlement," the officers declared, "would invite and encourage Emigration to it" from among those "now in the United States...whose Dislike of the Republican Government they now live under...would...strongly induce (them) to remove to this new Colony."[29]

Time and again the officers as a group were to petition against the seigneurial system of land-holding, and yet the Legislative Council in Quebec City somewhat rashly decided in the fall of 1786 that the cost of erecting grist and saw mills in the new settlements would be offset by allowing those who constructed them the seigneurial right of banalité for fifteen years.[30] By this right the owners of the mills would have a monopoly on the mills and could impose certain fees on anyone using them. This proposal suddenly drove home to the settlers that their lands were really under the seigneurial system. Four officers from New Johnstown were the first to compose a hurried petition to the governor protesting that the "late Resolution of His Majesty's Council of this Province relative to the right of erecting mills fills them with fear and jealousy." They added the oft-repeated theme that "they have always flattered themselves with the idea of getting their lands on the footing of British subjects on the same terms they held their Possessions in the Colonies and to have at least the same indulgence with their fellow soldiers in Nova Scotia."[31]

Hard on the heels of the officers' protest against the new regulations about the erection of the mills came Patrick McNiff's personal campaign against the mills. As a government employee, McNiff was taking a risk in opposing the Council's decision. It was not the first time he had taken risks. He had put his own life in jeopardy helping Captain Samuel Anderson escape from prison during the revolutionary war.[32] McNiff was an able, warm-hearted Irish Roman Catholic prone to nurse not only his own grievances but those of others. He had been chosen especially by Sir John Johnson to begin the surveys of the townships in the spring of 1783. Since then he had gained the confidence of many of the settlers in the rear concessions, surveying their lots as fast as he could and refusing any extra fees from them other than his surveyor's salary even though his own finances were in a precarious state.[33] As a wealthy merchant on Staten Island he had been bilked of some £6,000 worth of goods by the revolutionaries and then spent much of his surveyor's salary trying to recover the confiscated goods.[34] But he had a streak of stubbornness that led him to adopt extreme positions even when he knew that such persistence would bring him to grief. Thus, when he learned about the new edict from Quebec City concerning the erection of mills, he jumped to the conclusion that this was the first step towards a more pronounced policy of enforcing the seigneurial system on the new settlements. Moreover, by some undefined means he concluded that his old friend, Captain Samuel Anderson, endorsed such a policy.[35] Almost single-handedly he began to build up a political party within New Johnstown.

In the early spring of 1786 McNiff prepared a draft petition in a somewhat ranting style asserting that the new regulations about the mills were "measures to reduce us to a state of conquered people... that His Gracious Majesty never meant...in the least to entail Slavery on them (our Posterity) in which State we consider such of the Canadians as hold Lands of Seigniors to be." Instead of letting it go at that, he then held out a thinly-veiled threat that many of the settlers would return to the United States, that the "numerous and cordial invitations which many of our Friends and relations have lately received to return again to their places in the Different States from whence they fled, no doubt will be embraced sooner than holding lands in the manner lands are generally held by Canadians."[36] Having prepared copies of the petition, McNiff set out for the various settlements of New Johnstown along the St. Lawrence and distributed them to friends, directing them to get the petitions signed by the inhabitants. Though the language was strong, the petition was not dissimilar to those written by officers who at various times also suggested that unless their demands were met, the settlers might find it more convenient to return to the States.[37] One of the settlers whom McNiff approached was Sergeant Morgan of township no. 3 who turned the petition over to the magistrate.[38] The circulation of these petitions without the sanction or knowledge of the officers caused such a furore among the officers that McNiff's literary production was termed "factious and seditious."[39] By August 1786 McNiff learned that another deputy surveyor had been sent to the settlement to replace him.[40] Even his rations were cut off by the local officers, an act of meanness, as McNiff had both wife and family to feed. Though the rations were later restored by government order,[41] McNiff now had a personal grievance to add to the general grievances he had taken up as his own. Sharing McNiff's annoyance with the powers that be in New Johnstown and Quebec City was another resident of township no. 2, William Impey. Like McNiff whose waterfront holding was just west of the town site, Impey's choice waterfront grant was immediately east of the town site. Four other members of his family were located on lots 4, 5 and 6 beside him. Still, William Impey felt hard done by as far as the distribution of lots was concerned. "When we first came," he complained, "we expected to draw our lands agreeable to the Governor's proclamation, but when we drew our land, we found that the officers and some of the sergts. did not draw with the privates. The reason of their drawing their proportion of land in front diferent (sic) from the Privates we did not at the time Discover...but some time after...Ensign McCarty informed me...that the Officer of Each Company had given in a petition to Sir John and Major Holland that the...officers might have their full proportion of land in front and their families land in rear."[42] As Haldimand had feared, not all the settlers had been satisfied with the method of distributing lots. Yet, had Sir John Johnson and Major Samuel Holland not taken into account the expectations of the officers that they would receive waterfront lots, even more serious discontent might have existed. Impey is the only settler to harp on this grievance. He may have been, like McNiff, inclined to take upon himself and exploit what he considered the grievances of others. Certainly he himself had been as well treated in the distribution of lands as the officers and better than some, for the Impey family lots were closer to the town site than even Captain Anderson's and Major Gray's.

The straw that broke McNiff's and Impey's patience was the petition signed by all the officers of the New Johnstown district bidding Lord Dorchester welcome when he arrived for a second time in Canada as governor in the fall of 1786.[43] Most of the Loyalists, whether soldier or civilian in the Royal Townships, had had dealings with Sir Guy Carleton, now Lord Dorchester, when he had served in the New York Command during the dramatic times of the revolution and the evacuation of Loyalists from the coastal cities. Therefore, when the petition was sent off with only the military represented on it, the pride of the other Loyalists was hurt at being left out of the general expression of good will to the new governor, none more so than Patrick McNiff and William Impey. Impey admitted that "if the petition from the officers had been read to the people at large, they would have been perfectly satisfied and the present jealousy and uneasiness in the settlement would not have taken place."[44] Undoubtedly the officers had made a political blunder in ignoring the other more socially prominent Loyalists in the settlements, for the petition stirred up a tempest that almost upset the influence of the officer class in the settlements. Not only had the officers sent off the memorial welcoming Lord Dorchester, but they had also penned a second petition requesting among other things financial aid in establishing schools in each district, a post road from Montreal to Cataraqui with post offices at New Johnstown, New Oswegatchie and Cataraqui, and exemption from the French seigneurial tenure. Signing on behalf of the inhabitants of no. 2 township was Captain Samuel Anderson.[45]

Neither McNiff or Impey would have objected to anything in the petition. They just wanted to be part of the hierarchial machinery. If they could not share in that hierarchy, they wanted to replace it, not by more democratic elements but by themselves and their friends. The struggle for social recognition in New Johnstown was not a conflict between classes, but one within the same class. McNiff and Impey had been socially prominent and substantial people in their own communities in the old Colonies. Their reduced economic circumstances in the new settlements, they felt, did not warrant their exclusion from the top society composed of half-pay officers. What McNiff and his party failed to take into account was that the officers themselves were, for the most part, military men by circumstances, not by profession. Moreover, they had had plenty of experience with radical politics, having been among those in the rebellious states who stood up and were counted as King's Men under the Royal Standard.

During the long war years they had been politically organized as a group with regard to making ample use of the machinery of petitions to publicize their wants and expectations to government. Against such organized rivals, McNiff did not stand a chance, but he tried.

Lord Dorchester's reaction to the various petitions and the reports of latent discord in the settlements was to sweeten tempers by granting an additional 100 acres of land to all settlers in order to put them on an equal footing with the soldiers of the 84th Royal Highland Emigrants who had been promised 200 acres upon their discharge.[46] Then, what was more extraordinary, the new governor ordered that each township should hold town meetings to elect delegates who would act as representatives to the government with regards to requests and complaints from the settlers.[47] Thus, the first political meetings of the new townships were orchestrated at government initiative. McNiff's reaction to this news was to try to isolate the officers as a group, using whatever methods he could devise, so that the officers would be eliminated as candidates for election. He industriously spread rumours that not only Captain Anderson but other officers as well wanted the seigneurial tenure retained for the settlements[48] and he played upon the fears of the settlers that such tenure would entail on them and their children a form of servitude. As the township meetings were to be held in January of 1787, McNiff quickly prepared instructions for his friends in each township, advising them how to go about calling the meeting and even sent a draft copy of a vote of thanks to himself which ended with a request that he be "continued as King's Surveyor in this District."[49] Then McNiff and William Impey personally delivered the instructions to various friends in the different townships. At Williamsburg, township no. 4, for instance, they visited Sergeant Michael Haines (Haynes) and Sifrinis (Suffrenus) Casselman to sound them out about their choice of delegates and to implant fears of the officer class. McNiff asked Casselman whether he was for seigniories or not. Casselman replied, "I would rather be a free man and have no Seigniory as I used to...in the Colonies." Casselman asked McNiff "if there was any likelihood of our holding our lands on Seigniorial terms." McNiff replied, "Certainly, for some officers had sent a petition to Sir John Johnson and Major Holland signifying that the men would rather hold their lands on Seigniorial terms." McNiff then told Casselman that he (Casselman) was the proper person to be elected at the town meeting and that "if Captain Duncan (the senior officer in township no. 4) did not come up, the people might call a meeting themselves for the purpose of electing representatives."[50]

As the time drew near for the meetings of the various townships, the air was tense. The officers had not been napping while McNiff and his friends travelled about the townships handing out copies of petitions, together with a prepared vote of thanks to himself and instructions about how the meetings should be organized and run.

Captain Samuel Anderson consulted his officers about the coming confrontation with McNiff. The meeting at township no. 2 was scheduled for 12 January 1787. As magistrate of the district, Anderson was empowered to call the meeting and to assume the chairmanship. The meeting began innocuously enough. Anderson read the memorial that he and other officers had sent to Lord Dorchester upon his arrival in the colony showing that they had asked for a change in the "Tenure of our Lands, Laws, etc." He also read a letter from Stephen de Lancey, the Inspector of Loyalists, in which Anderson was asked to lead the inhabitants "to a choice of such person or persons as they should judge proper to transact the important business (of the township)." Anderson then paused to ask the inhabitants if there was anything "against their liberties contained in the Memorial."[51] Before anyone else had a chance to speak, McNiff grabbed the floor and shouted at Anderson that "certainly there would be nothing against their liberties in so public a paper as that."[52] McNiff then flourished the petition he had prepared the previous spring signed "by 136 principal inhabitants" and which had been labelled "a factious and rebellious libel." Anderson ordered McNiff to be silent. Instead, McNiff mounted a sled, exclaiming that he was for the liberty of the people and that "this township was composed of two denominations of men, vizt. Gentlemen officers enjoying half-pay from the Crown, and the Comonality (sic). That they should inform him which of those classes they would choose to Elect from." Some of the people called out, "No Officers, No Officers. They have rode long enough and now it's our turn."[53] Others shouted to "turn out all those half-pay Gentry" at which McNiff said it "was by their means that this Settlement would be held under Seigniors." At this, Peter Fitzpatrick shouted, "By the eternal God, they should all be murdered."[54] When McNiff called on the people to choose a clerk of the township, several called out, "Mr. McNiff, Mr. McNiff." McNiff then bowed and graciously replied, "Gentlemen, I thank you, follow me and I shall execute your orders."[55] The first round went to McNiff. There was no doubt that he had packed the meeting.

Captain Anderson and the other officers threw up their hands. "Mr. McNiff takes everything upon himself," Anderson muttered. Some of the people began to insult Anderson, particularly William Impey who snarled, "they would pay no regard to what he said or did, that he was no more Capt. Anderson but Sam Anderson and that he (Impey) was now in authority and that they had the power to punish him (Anderson) for his conduct towards them last spring respecting their petition."[56] At this stage in the lively meeting, Anderson and most of the officers left. As soon as they retired, McNiff told the people that the officers had taken his bread from him on account of his writing the petition for them last spring.[57] At this, one of McNiff's friends called out, "Damn the officers. They ought all to be slaughtered and it was a pitty (sic) that they went off so soon or they would have got their heads broack (sic).[58] When the meeting got down to voting, McNiff proposed William Impey as one of the delegates. Impey was unanimously elected. Then McNiff nominated Jonas Wood, but Sergeant Samuel Moss proposed another name. The vote went to McNiff's man. The final delegate chosen was Donald McDonnal.[59] Throughout the meeting McNiff acted as the clerk and from that time on assumed the role of delegate too.[60] As soon as the election was over, the meeting voted to thank McNiff for the "past attention that he has paid to settling the Inhabitants of this Township as well as for the Impartiallity (sic) with which he has distributed the Land to all Classes...and Praying Lord Dorchester to continue him (McNiff) as King's Surveyor in this District."[61] Thus ended the first and what was probably the liveliest town meeting ever held in Cornwall.

Immediately after the meeting ten of the men who disapproved of McNiff's proceedings made a joint deposition before Anderson describing what occurred both before and after the officers withdrew. Among the ten were Sergeant George Barnhart, Ranald McDonell, David Bruce, John Robertson and Richard Prosser.[62] Others came before Anderson individually to make depositions confirming what the other ten men said.[63] Then both McNiff and the officers sent off petitions to Quebec City. The one from Patrick McNiff took the form of a personal petition asking Lord Dorchester to re-instate him to the post of deputy surveyor. Included in McNiff's petition were the various recommendations from the town meetings which he himself had drawn up, praying that he be continued as King's surveyor.[64] The memorial from the officers was sent to Stephen De Lancey as Inspector of Loyalists. This memorial was signed by fifteen men, including six captains, six lieutenants and two who were listed as Gentlemen, though one of these was a retired major of the regular army who was in charge of Sir John Johnson's plantation at Johnson's Point. The fifteen men informed De Lancey that the "tranquillity which we lately enjoyed is banished from our Settlements." The officers reported that "There is a general outcry against the officers by reasons of a report, industriously circulated, that they have petitioned to hold their lands on a Seigniorial footing, in order to lord it over the inhabitants, two of whom are particularly pointed out, vizt, Capt. Sam Anderson and Capt. Richard Duncan." Moreover, the memorial stated, "The most ignorant and some of the most factious of the people are chosen for their representatives. The most poisonous and seductive arts have been practised to influence them in their choice, and to inspire them with contempt and hatred against their officers. We are publicly represented as the betrayers of their rights." What was more ominous was their report that "It is criminal as well as dangerous for anyone to speak in our behalf...our influence is lost and the authority of the magistrates wantonly set at naught. In short," the officers told De Lancey, "our situation in several respects is exactly similar to that of the suffering Loyalists previous to the commencement of the late Rebellion."[65] Here was a situation which De Lancey and government officials could scarcely credit. From the infant settlements peopled by men and women who had been driven out of their own country by persecution came this report of a new form of persecution brewing. The officers told De Lancey that "Mr. Patrick McNiff is the author and fomenter of all this disturbance." They asked De Lancey "as our inspector" to report McNiff to headquarters as "a seditious and dangerous incendiary as well as a common disturber of the peace" and they implored De Lancey to come to the settlement "as soon as possible to aid us in restoring public tranquillity and to quiet the Minds of the People." Finally the officers protested to De Lancey on behalf of themselves "as well as the Whole of the Gentlemen and Many of the Inhabitants" against the "proceedings of any of the late Elections that may be delivered to you through the channel of Mr. McNiff or any of his Associates on the principle of their being illegal, disorderly and inconsistent with your instructions."[66]

McNiff's men were quick to parry. His supporters in township no.3 included three members of the Impey family, each of whom spelled his name in a different way, and Jacob Rambough who owned several lots of the town site of township no. 2. They added a note to their report to government on the meeting in township no. 3, declaring, "We were not in any respect either directly or indirectly influenced by any Council or advice said to be given to us by Mr. McNiff respecting said Elections." In fact, they added, "nothing else but the bad treatment they had received from Numbers of the Officers while we were imbodied (sic) as well as since settling these lands was the only thing that caused us to put no more confidence in them."[67] Undoubtedly McNiff had managed to pack this meeting too. Only forty-six out of a possible ninety-six settlers in the township attended.[68]

The degree to which social unrest and even fear existed in township no. 2 and its neighbouring townships was indicated by the way Captain John Macdonell was treated after his election as a delegate for township no. 1. "Being treated," as he said, "with great abuse and scurrility by some persons (who) apprehended that his majority might have been obtained by the numbers of Highlanders present," Macdonell threw up his nomination to preserve peace. Nevertheless for a month after the meeting, he was subjected to such threats that he went about "armed with his fusil."[69] It had been more difficult for McNiff to pack the meeting in no. 1 township where the Gaelic-speaking Roman Catholic Highlanders had both a majority and an in-built immunity to external political overtures. McNiff had tried to get one of his friends in that township to "send him one of the Scotch people" as his friends "could not speak Erse."[70] McNiff's attempts to influence the election proved futile. Yet his men made it so uncomfortable for Captain Macdonell that he withdrew. Similarly, an officer of the 84th Royal Highland Emigrants, Lieutenant Neil McLean, fearing for his safety, sought and received a sort of passport[71] from Patrick McNiff. McNiff denied that he had alluded to McLean in a letter he had addressed on 16 January to "Inhabitants of township no. 2," warning the people settled in the rear concessions along the Raisin River that if they were planning to hold a meeting "for the purpose of transacting any business in which the Public may be concerned, it is itself Irregular and Improper." He cautioned them against signing "any paper whatever presented as a Public Affair by any person except your Delegates and not even then without the concurrence of three out of four of them."[72] This was the first whiff of discord or dissent within McNiff's hitherto closed ranks. If McNiff had to insist that three out of the four delegates from township no. 2 sign petitions, it meant that he had already run into resistance from one or more of his fellow delegates. It was obvious that he still feared officer influence, for he pointed out to the inhabitants that "it will perhaps be told to you that you, as formerly belonging to this Regiment or that Regiment, have a Right to sign as a Distinct body from the other inhabitants of the Township. In this you are not to be deceived...(do not suffer) such division to take place among you."[73]

Not only were people in township no. 1 going in fear of being assaulted. When Patrick McGuire of township no. 2 was beaten up about a week after the town meeting and said he would report the assault to Captain Samuel Anderson as the magistrate, he was told by Ranald and John McDonell that "Capt. Anderson and his constables both were broke, that they had no more to do, and that Mr. McNiff and the other three men who were elected for the Township were to take cognizance of all matters that might happen in the Township." As far as the two McDonells were concerned, both McGuire and Anderson could "both go to the Devil."[74] This was the first indication that Cornwall now possessed police constables. From the evidence it is not clear whether there were two or more, But one constable was identified as one of the Barnhart brothers.[75]

McNiff's final move that spring was to order all the elected delegates from Point au Baudet to the Bay of Quinte to a meeting at Philip Shaver's house in Matilda township, no. 5. The meeting took place on March 19th when perhaps as many as eleven delegates, including McNiff, assembled. A petition was prepared for Lord Dorchester in which they spoke of their "Distresses and Complaints... for want of clothing and other necessities which they say was sent by His Majesty but was withheld from them by such persons as were ordered to distribute the same." The delegates asked Lord Dorchester to appoint a Court of Enquiry to find out whether such "donations were justly distributed."[76] Of the eleven delegates purporting to sign this petition, two at least signed their names differently than they had on previous petitions. Jacob Rambough's name was spelled Ramback and Sifrinis Casselman's name was spelled Kasselman a hint that these names may have been signed by some other person.

The upshot of this steady run of complaints and petitions to Quebec City was the appointment of a Board of Enquiry to be held at Cornwall on 23 July 1787 "to give a fair and free hearing to all parties relative to their memorials and complaints."[77] Deputy surveyor John Collins and lawyer William Dummer Powell were to journey to Cornwall after attending a similar enquiry at Sorel where bickering and petty complaints of a different nature had broken out.[78]

The enquiry at Johnstown was taken up almost entirely with McNiff's charges against the officers. They ranged from accusing Captain John McDonnell of embezzling government property and disturbing the tranquillity of township no. 3 just prior to the town meeting there to accusing Captain Samuel Anderson of malad-ministration of justice and a partial distribution of donations.[79] A stream of witnesses appeared before the two commissioners, many of them recounting what occurred at the town meeting on 12 January, some supporting McNiff, others supporting the officers. Most of the principals involved such as McNiff, Anderson, Macdonell and Impey appeared more than once. Macdonell answered the charge of embezzlement. The government property that McNiff said he had embezzled were two company ammunition boxes containing small cartridges that Macdonell had retained after his company was reduced in 1783.[80] With this explanation from Macdonell, the charge was thrown out. The charge that Anderson had kept some pieces of iron out of the King's stores for his own use was similarly dismissed.[81] One by one the various accusations were whittled away or explained away until finally a distracted McNiff admitted to the Board that he had been "driven by the misconduct and abuse of power of the late officers to suggest to the people their independence (from them)" and claimed that it was he who had "prevented the people from rash resentment of the improper conduct of their late officers."[82] By July 29 McNiff collapsed and was reported too ill to continue his testimony. The next day the Board closed its hearings at Cornwall and moved on to New Oswegatchie and Cataraqui.[83] By 18 August 1787 the Board reported their findings to Lord Dorchester. Their first statement indicated that by 1787 township no. 2 was already being called Cornwall. Their second statement confirmed what McNiff and the officers were saying. "A few hours sufficed us," Collins and Powell reported to Lord Dorchester, "that a very dangerous Jealousy and want of Confidence mutually, subsisted in that Settlement, between the Majority of the settlers, and their late Officers." The report then went on to condemn not only the officers but also "heads of Townships," presumably some of the more prominent Loyalists. "We plainly perceive that the People have been uniformly, and as if by System, kept ignorant of the exact extent of the bounty of Government to them...Secrecy has been observed by the Officers and heads of Townships...we apprehend with a View only to sustain an appearance of Consequence and the Shadow of former power." Their analysis of the situation was that the "Jealousy has from various trifling Circumstances been gradually increasing untill the Certainty of some joint Communication with your Excellency and Ignorance of its purport inflamed their Suspicions into Rivalship and hatred." Just as William Impey had told them, the commissioners concluded that "We are thoroughly convinced that if the Petition from the Heads of Townships to your Excellency had been communicated to the Inhabitants, before it was forwarded, your Lordship would not have heard a Murmur from these People on the Subject of a general Charge or Complaint against their Officers."[84]

The Commissioners spent five days at Cornwall listening to about a dozen or more witnesses. Some complained about the commissary operation in township no. 2. These showed that complaints about the commissary were endemic as they usually were about any commissary operation. One witness swore that his neighbour had been a rebel in the United States.[85] The evidence showed that the fears about the seigneurial system increased from the time of the government's announcement as to the method of erecting mills. Jealousy of the officer class had become more pronounced after the government made known its intention to permit town meetings at which delegates were to be elected, and especially subsequent to McNiff's calculated campaign to undermine the officers' influence and thus eliminate them as possible rivals during the elections. As in any other frontier society, there existed a number of personal feuds. Some of these were directed against Captain Anderson and sprang largely from his role as magistrate and chief commissary officer. For instance, there had been some unpleasantness between William Impey and Anderson ever since Anderson had judged a case in which Impey had been involved.[86]

Similarly Anderson had had an altercation with Thomas Robertson over the distribution of plough shares and other farming implements. As Cornwall was the major distribution centre of the commissary, not only for the New Johnstown district but also for New Oswegatchie and Cataraqui, the job of handling the distribution of large consignments was considerable. Thus, when Anderson was called upon to distribute hundreds of pieces of iron and steel plough shares and other farming items to heads of families in the whole eight townships from the Lake Township to New Oswegatchie in 1785, he thought himself entitled to "selling a bar of steel to pay him his trouble in issuing the rest."[87] Thomas Robertson thought no such thing and accused Anderson of embezzling the King's stores. This was too much for Anderson's hot temper and he took a swing at Robertson.[88] Thus the enquiry at Cornwall produced a series of petty complaints and grievances. At New Oswegatchie and Cataraqui the enquiries hardly produced enough to warrant the commissioners making the long trip. As far as the commissioners were concerned they found that this first effort by the government to organize the settlements politically had led to rampant party spirit and they came down heavily on the officers as the culprits, so much so that McNiff and his followers publicly thanked Deputy Surveyor John Collins for "the patience and candour with which you have heard the various complaints on the late enquiry" and proffered him "their most sincere thanks." Their notice appeared in a supplement to the *Quebec Gazette* on 28 February 1788, along with similar votes of thanks from other townships, most of which were signed by officers and magistrates. The notice from "the inhabitants of Cornwall," however, had but one officer's name, that of Ensign Francis McCarty, who had risen from the ranks.[89] Heading the names of those thanking Collins was that of Patrick McNiff. It was followed by John Emerson, Reverend John Bryan, the newly-arrived Episcopalian clergyman who had had a squabble with Major Edward Jessup at New Oswegatchie, Joel Stone, Thomas Swan, Thomas Robertson and John Smith. Fifty-eight other inhabitants of the township signed McNiff's public notice, an indication that he still had considerable prestige and support in township no. 2.

In 1787 the infant township no. 2 that was now called Cornwall still lacked a proper town site and a sound economic base for survival. It had long lost out in importance to township no. 1, Cataraqui, (Kingston) which, by 1785, had already been picked out by the officers as the more suitable place for a metropolis.[90] But one thing Cornwall did not lack was political involvement. Township no. 2 was the heart of the turbulent political upheavals of 1787. The turbulence stemmed partly from its position as the major commissary operation west of Montreal and partly because it was the bailiwick of Patrick McNiff. Within a year from the time of the enquiry, the chief source of complaint had disappeared. Most of the commissary operations were phased out when the government rations of food, clothing and farm implements ceased. This threw the settlers entirely upon their own economically for the first time. Within a year they faced famine conditions when their crops failed and there was no Haldimand to take it upon himself to restore rations. By 1791 when the imperial government agreed to establish the loyalist settlements as a separate province — Upper Canada — with a lieutenant government and all the appurtenances of local government including a legislative assembly, the town and township of Cornwall had had enough of factionalism, and the officer class was once more firmly in the saddle. It was not Patrick McNiff or William Impey who were elected to the first parliament of Upper Canada in 1792 but Lieutenant Jeremiah French of Cornwall who was chosen to represent the newly-named county of Stormont that included townships no. 2 and 3. French was succeeded in the second parliament by Solicitor-General Robert Isaac Dey Gray, the only son of Major James Gray. A slave owner himself, Solicitor General Gray distinguished himself by voting against a law that would have permitted owners to bring their slaves with them into the province.[91] Gray held the Stormont seat until his accidental drowning in 1804. In the neighbouring township, of Charlottenburgh now part of the county of Glengarry, it was Captain John Macdonell and his brother, Lieutenant Hugh Macdonell, who were elected. Captain Samuel

Anderson remained the chief magistrate of Cornwall. Eventually he was appointed judge of the Eastern District, the name given in 1791 to the old Lunenburg District that included the New Johnstown and New Oswegatchie townships. Anderson also became judge of the Surrogate Court and finally postmaster of Cornwall.[92] If Patrick McNiff won the first round, clearly the officers won the second. They retained more than a shadow of their former power.

NOTES

1. By 18 August 1787 John Collins and W.D. Powell noted that the township was "now called Cornwall"; see their report to Lord Dorchester on Loyalists' Grievances, cited in Preston, *Kingston before the War of 1812*, 122; see Lord Dorchester's proclamation, 24 July 1788, cited in James Croil, *Dundas*, or *a Sketch of Canadian History*, 218.

2. Hadfield, *Diary*, 58.

3. *Ibid.*

4. Returns of Disbanded Soldiers and Loyalists settled in Township no. 2, October 1784 (MG21/B168/101-109).

5. Hadfield, *Diary*, 58-59.

6. Deputy Surveyor William Chewett to Capt. Richard Duncan, 26 Nov. 1789 (Land Board Minutes, RG1/L4/10/43-45).

7. For a discussion of the way the town site was laid out, see Report of the Land Board, Quebec City, c. November 1789, Minutes of the Land Board, RG1/L4/10/60.

8. RG1/L4/9/30; see also, William Chewett Map, 1792, though likely drawn in 1787 (V3/440).

9. Minutes of the Land Board, Quebec City, 2 Oct. 1789 (RG1/L4/10/64).

10. Chewett to R. Duncan, 26 Nov. 1787 (RG1/L4/9/27-28).

11. Minutes of Committee of the Land Board, Quebec City, 26 Feb. 1790 (RG1/L4/10/68).

12. Remarks and Suggestions by the Luneburg Land Board to Lord Dorchester, (*Ibid.*, 148); see also, RG1/L4/9/29-30).

13. *Ibid.*

14. Joel Stone to _____, 18 Feb. 1789 in Minutes of the Land Board (RG1/L4/11/008-010).

15. Chewett's testimony before the Land Board, Quebec City, 26 Feb. 1790 (RG1/L4/10/68); see also, Chewett Map, 1792 (V3/440).

16. *Ibid.*

17. John Collins's testimony before the Land Board Committee, Quebec City, 2 Oct. 1789 (RG1/L4/10/64).

18. For details see, RG1/L4/10/45, 60 and 66; see also, RG1/L4/9/29-30; and "Notes on the Empey (Impey) Family of Stormont" in *OHSPR*, 1931, xxvii, 397-98.

19. Remarks on New Johnstown (RG1/L4/10/60).

20. *Ibid.*, 61.

21. *Ibid.*

22. Land Board Minutes and Records, (RG1/L4/9/29-30); as late as 5 Mar. 1790, the Land Board was still trying to get the survey plans from McNiff; see Journal of the Land Committee, 5 Mar. 1790 (RG1/L4/10/80-82).

23. See List of persons who have produced Deputy Surveyor General Tickets or Certificates and who have never been entered on the Plans of their Respective Towns (RG1/L4/10/151B).

24. RG1/L4/10/212.

25. *Ibid.*, 218.

26. Papers respecting the complaints of the Inhabitants of Johnstown (RG4/A1/29/9464-65); Minutes of a Board of Enquiry held in the new Western Settlements, dated Cornwall, 25 July 1787 to 29 July 1787 (RG4/A1/33/10714-10742); for general discussions see, A.L. Burt, *The Old Province of Quebec*, 389-90; J.H. Harkness, *History of Stormont*, Dundas *and Glengarry*, 53-54; Preston, *Kingston before the War of 1812*, introduction, vi, and 122-24.

27. Petition to Captain John Macdonell, 8 Feb. 1785 (RG4/A1/28/8980).

28. See note no. 5, RG4/A1/28/8981.

29. Petition of Sir John Johnson, Bart, and others in behalf of the Loyalists settled in Canada, 11 Apr. 1785 (MG11/Q24/I/76-84), also cited in Adam Shortt and A.G. Doughty, *Documents relating to the Consitutional History of Canada 1759-1791*, 524-27.

30. Burt, *Old Province of Quebec*, 387; see also, Wilbur Seibert, "The Loyalists and Six Nations Indians", in *Transactions*, Royal Society of Canada, section II, 1915, 97.

31. Petition of the Inhabitants of the New Settlements to Governor Henry Hope, spring, 1786, signed by Captain Alex McDonell, no. 1. Township, Captain Richard Duncan, no. 4 Township, Captain Allan McDonell, no. 5 Township, and Captain William Fraser, no. 6 Township. (RG4/A1/27/8957-58).

32. Captain Samuel Anderson's testimony, Board of Enquiry, 25-30 July 1787, Cornwall, (RG4/A1/33/10722).

33. Board of Enquiry, 24-30 July 1787 (RG4/A1/33/10721).

34. Patrick McNiff's petition to Lord Dorchester, 21 Jan. 1787 (RG4/A1/31/10228); see also, Thomas Robertson's testimony, Board of Enquiry (RG4/A1/33/10736).

35. Moses Williams' testimony at Board of Enquiry, 25-30 July, 1787 (RG4/A1/33/10719).

36. See draft of McNiff's petition, March 1786 (RG4/A1/30/9564).

37. For instance, see Sir John Johnson's dissent from the report of the Legislative Council relative to granting Crown Lands, cited in Shortt and Doughty, *Documents*, 641-42.

38. See note at bottom of McNiff's draft petition, March 1786 (RG4/A1/30/9564); see also, Petition of Inhabitants of New Johns Town, 7 April 1786 (RG4/A1/30/9630).

39. Report of McNiff's speech at the meeting of Township no. 2, 12 Jan. 1787 (RG4/A1/31/10180).

40. McNiff's petition to Lord Dorchester, 21 Jan. 1787 (RG4/A1/31/10228).

41. Ranald McDonell's testimony, 12 Jan. 1787 (RG4/A1/31/10147).

42. William Impey to the Board of Enquiry, 24 July 1787, Johnstown, (RG4/A1/33/10703).

43. Address to Lord Dorchester, 2 Dec. 1786, New Johnstown, cited in J.A. Macdonell, *Sketches, Glengarry in Canada*, 70-71.

44. Impey's testimony at Enquiry, (RG4/A1/33/10725).

45. Petition to Lord Dorchester from the Settlement of New Johnstown, 19 Dec. 1786 (RG4/A1/31/9095-96); for a discussion of this petition, see A.C. Casselman, 'Pioneer Settlements" in Adam Shortt and A.G. Doughty, *Canada and its Provinces*, xvii, 35-37.

46. Instructions from Lord Dorchester, 26 Dec. 1786 (RG4/A1/31/10075).

47. Stephen de Lancey to Loyalists, giving instructions about the calling of town meetings and the election of town delegates, 24 Dec. 1786 (RG4/A1/31/10073-74).

48. See Moses Williams' testimony at Enquiry, (RG4/A1/33/10719); William Falkner's deposition, 11 Jan. 1787 (RG4/A1/31/10147); deposition of Lt. Jeremiah French, 24 Jan. 1787 (*ibid.*, 10244); Duncan Murcheson's deposition, 11 Jan. 1787 (*ibid.*, 10147); Ensign Francis McCarty's deposition, 12 Jan. 1787 (*ibid.*, 10174).

49. See copies of the vote of thanks to McNiff, all having identical wording and spellings, Townships nos. 1, 2, 3, and 5 (RG4/A1/31/10139-46, 10184 and 10187).

50. Sifrinis Casselman's deposition before Captain R. Duncan, 16 Jan. 1787 (RG4/A1/31/10215); see also, Sergeant Michael Haynes's deposition, 16 Jan. 1787 (*ibid.*, 10217), William Reid, *Loyalists of Ontario*, 138 and 222.

51. Report of ten inhabitants of Township no. 2 on the meeting of 12 Jan. 1787 (RG4/A1/31/10180-81 and 10185-86).

52. *Ibid.*

53. *Ibid.*

54. Ensign Francis McCarty's deposition, 12 Jan. 1787 (*ibid.*, 10174).

55. Report of ten inhabitants of Township no. 2 on the meeting of 12 Jan. 1787 (RG4/A1/31/10181).

56. *Ibid.*

57. Ranald McDonell's deposition, 12 Jan. 1787 (*ibid.*, 10187).

58. *Ibid.*, see also, 10178.

59. *Ibid.*, 10184 and RG4/A1/33/10734.

60. See McNiff's letter to the Inhabitants of Township no. 2, 16 Jan. 1787 (RG4/A1/31/10219); Petition of Representatives of the Loyalists settled from Point au Baudet to the Bay of Quinte, 17 Mar. 1787, in which McNiff signs as a township representative, (RG4/A1/32/10333).

61. RG4/A1/31/10184.

62. For signatures see, RG4/A1/31/10181.

63. See, for example, Ensign Francis McCarty's deposition (*ibid.*, 10174).

64. Petition of Patrick McNiff, 21 Jan. 1787 (RG4/A1/31/10228).

65. Memorial to Stephen de Lancey, 18 Jan. 1787 (RG4/A1/31/10221-23).

66. *Ibid.*

67. Memorial of Township no. 3, 9 Jan. 1787 (RG4/A1/31/10139-40).

68. *Ibid.*, see note at the foot of the memorial.

69. Captain John Macdonell's testimony, RG4/A1/33/10118-19.

70. Moses Williams' testimony at Enquiry (*ibid.*, 10719).

71. Patrick McNiff's note relative to Lt. Neil McLean and other officers of the late 84th Regiment, 30 Jan. 1787 (RG4/A1/31/10220).

72. Patrick McNiff's address to the Inhabitants of Township no. 2, particularly those on the River au Raisin, Johnstown, 16 Jan. 1787 (RG4/A1/31/10219).

73. *Ibid.*

74. Deposition of Patrick McGuire, 19 Jan. 1787 (RG4/A1/31/10326).

75. See cases tried by Magistrate Samuel Anderson in which it is noted "by the confession of Barnhart, his Constable", Minutes of the Board of Enquiry, 23 to 30 July 1787 (RG4/A1/33/10740).

76. Memorial to Lord Dorchester from Patrick McNiff and ten others, Township no. 5, 19 Mar. 1787 (RG4/A1/32/10333).

77. RG4/A1/31/10112.

78. For the Sorel enquiry, see RG4/A1/31/10034-35, RG4/A1/32/10525-30, 10569-82, and RG4/A1/33/10656-75.

79. Deposition of Patrick McNiff, 24 July 1787 (RG4/A1/33/10897, see also 10669).

80. See John Collins' note at the foot of McNiff's charges, 24 July 1787 (RG4/A1/33/10897).
81. See List of Papers respecting the complaints of the Inhabitants of Johnstown, (RG4/A1/29/9465).
82. McNiff's testimony at Enquiry, (RG4/A1/33/10738).
83. *Ibid.*, 10742.
84. Report of John Collins and William Dummer Powell to Lord Dorchester on the Loyalists' Grievances, 18 Aug. 1787, cited in Preston, *Kingston before the War of 1812*, 122.
85. R. Wilkinson's charge against John Burton, no. 1 Township, (RG4/A1/33/10715).
86. List of cases tried by Magistrate Samuel Anderson: Impey vs Carpenter (RG4/A1/33/10740).
87. Declaration of Thomas Robertson and Jacob Wagenar at Enquiry (RG4/A1/29/9465).
88. McNiff's Testimony at Enquiry (RG4/A1/33/10736 and 10699).
89. Roll of non-commissioned officers, drummers and privates of the 1st Battalion, King's Royal Regiment of New York, 17 May 1781 (MG21/B158/208).
90. Petition of Sir John Johnson and others on behalf of the Loyalists settled in Canada, 11 Apr. 1785, in Shortt and Doughty, *Documents*, 525.
91. Macdonell, *Sketches, Glengarry*, 90; see also, Fred Armstrong, *Handbook of Upper Canadian Chronology and Territorial Legislation*, 23 and 59.
92. Rowe, "The Anderson Story", 115; J.F. Pringle, *Lunenburgh, or the Old Eastern District*, 169.

Chapter IV

Strachan's Cornwall —
A Centre of Learning

In the first twenty-seven years of its existence, Cornwall's claim to fame was due more to three outstanding personalities than to any particular characteristic of the town itself. In their turn, Sir John Johnson, Patrick McNiff and John Strachan kept the tiny town on the north bank of the St. Lawrence from falling into obscurity. In fact, when John Strachan passed through the village for the first time on the night of 26 December 1799 en route to Kingston he scarcely noticed it.[1] Little did he dream that he would, within three years, return to spend almost a decade of his life there and, by the sheer force of his personality, transform Cornwall into a unique centre of learning, attracting the sons of the most prominent families of York, Kingston, Montreal and Quebec City to his academy.

Part of Cornwall's original importance lay in its good bay and its location at the east end of the Long Sault rapids. These rapids forced travellers on their way west from Montreal or moving towards the metropolis to leave their river transport and go by foot through the town to beyond the rapids while boatsmen dragged their batteaux past. Thus the town had a steady stream of travellers coming and going through it. For the first fifteen years most of these travellers found what overnight accommodations they could at various farmers' homes. Which of these homes first assumed the status of inn or tavern is not known; probably the first of Cornwall's public houses was the St. Andrew's and St. Patrick's on First Street just east of Pitt where a Scottish Loyalist sergeant, Alexander Bruce, and his Irish wife, Peggy O'Sullivan, set themselves up in a log cabin. They were one of the first families, along with Gilles McBean, to erect a dwelling place in the town. Across the front of the tavern, the Bruces hung a long board decorated with a likeness of St. Andrew at one end and St. Patrick at the other, the whole surrounded with a wreath of shamrocks and thistles. The couple welcomed strangers to their "log hotel," especially those of a military caste. When the young husband died prematurely, Peggy Bruce kept up the inn. By 1804 she had at least one rival — John Miller, who described himself as an inn-keeper when he applied for membership in the newly-formed Hiram Masonic Lodge at Cornwall.[2]

In the 1790s the more prominent travellers usually recorded their overnight resting places, giving credit to their hosts for the warmth of the hospitality that was supplied generously and gratuitously. Major Robert Mathews, Lord Dorchester's secretary who travelled to Niagara from Quebec City in 1787, stopped overnight at the modest home of the veteran soldier, John Knave.[3] Patrick Campbell in 1791 stopped overnight with Lieutenant Miles Macdonell, "at a place formerly called New Johnstown, but now Cornwallis (sic). Here the stance of a town is lined out," Campbell remarked, "and the place is very centrical for that purpose, being nearly midway between Kingston and Montreal."[4]

When the province of Quebec was divided into Upper and Lower Canada, in 1791, the new lieutenant governor of Upper Canada, Lieutenant Colonel John Graves Simcoe, and his wife, travelled through Cornwall heading for Kingston, the town at Cataraqui that had outdistanced Cornwall in size and importance. Some 120 houses lined Kingston's shore, providing homes for about 345 people. Before setting off to Kingston to call together his first Council in the new province, Simcoe enjoyed the gracious overnight hospitality of Major James Gray at his estate three miles east of Cornwall. One traveller described Gray's location as "strikingly beautiful, being situated upon an easy regular slope facing the south and defended from the raking east winds."[6] Mrs. Simcoe found Cornwall "a settlement...(of) about fifteen houses and some neat gardens in them."[7] Her estimate of fifteen houses probably referred only to those more substantial frame houses in the town.

William Chewett's map, which he dated 1792 and dedicated to Governor Simcoe though it was probably drawn in 1790, shows thirty-one names listed with various holdings on enclosed town lots and nine others located just south of Water Street.[8] Although Mrs. Simcoe did not mention it, the town in 1792 had a small Presbyterian log church, and an Episcopalian parsonage house of sorts, likely a log cabin, and a school that had been erected for and improved by Reverend John Bryan.[9] The town had, too, its own medical doctor for by this time Doctor James Stuart, the former surgeon's mate of the 1st battalion, King's Royal Regiment of New York, had permanently settled in a house south of Water Street and just east of what became Amelia Street.[10] It also had the King's stores, still one of the most important of the town's operations, located on Water Street at the foot of present-day Pitt Street. Among those listed as having a building on Water Street was J. Judah, likely a member of the prominent Montreal Jewish family and thus probably the first Jewish settler in the town.[11] Judah may have been one of the few traders attracted to the town site or he may have been a forwarding agent for one of the Montreal fur-trading operations further west. A second Montreal trader in the town site at this time was Rosseter Hoyle. Hoyle claimed three separate lots, two on Water Street and one on the north side of First Street. Buildings are shown on two of his lots, suggesting that one may have been a dwelling and the others some sort of trade or business establishment.[12] Hoyle evidently spent little time in Cornwall. In 1792 he was in Montreal acting as curator of the estate of Captain John Johnson, and was among those prominent Montreal citizens joining in a public testimonial to Sir John Johnson upon the latter's departure for England that year.[13]

By the turn of the century, Cornwall had sixty-six families totalling in all 397 who occupied thirty-two houses.[14] Among them were some professional men—district judge and postmaster Samuel Anderson, the former sheriff of Manchester, Vermont, Jeremiah French, solicitor general Robert I.D. Gray, doctors James Stuart and George Wood, lawyer Jacob Farrand and schoolmaster Elijah Leavens. Then there was the sprinkling of townsmen supplying special services — blacksmith Samuel Dow, clothiers Asabel Stevens and Matthew Gray, tinsmith Alexander Watson, master carpenter John Anderson, weaver James Watson, David Sheek, the first local man to be identified as a merchant, and innkeeper John Miller.[15]

In the township itself at the turn of the century the population numbered 1080 people living in some 91 houses scattered throughout the countryside. Thus the number of people in the town and township combined was but 1,477 by 1804. It was a slow-growing area, its settlement probably impeded by the vast areas of land that had been granted to the original Loyalist settlers, far more than they could cultivate though some of the land was eventually turned to profitable timber land. As all the good land in the first eight or nine concessions of townships 1 and 2 had been granted, it meant that there were no free grants of land left for latecomers who had to purchase from other settlers or seek free land further west or go into the interior. Joel Stone, for instance, who arrived at Cornwall 16 March 1787 with his family and enough heavy baggage to fill three batteaux, had to be content with a purchase of forty acres in the town site itself because he was "unable to find any ungranted lands."[16] Stone was one of those enterprising merchants from Connecticut who, with his father, had suffered at the hands of the revolutionaries. He made his way to England in 1783 with other Loyalist refugees, returning a few years later to seek a new fortune in British North America. A man of Stone's education and drive was just what Cornwall needed. He applied for a grant of land such "as usually given to captains in His Majesty's established Regiments," and immediately set about to build a "dwelling house and still house" in the town.[17] Within a month he learned to his disappointment that there was no free land available. What was more irritating he discovered that the land he held in the town was "under French tenure."[18] By 1789 he was completely disgruntled with his Cornwall holdings and worried about the scarcity of provisions. He wrote to his supplier in Montreal, that "the appearance of want in (this) quarter is every day more alarming."[19] To the Land Board at Quebec he declared that "all the settlement I have (here) is a small temporary purchase and my buildings equally as temporary and that I ever intended to settle myself and family at Cananuque (Gananoque) as soon as possible."[20] By 1793 Stone was one of the Cornwall settlers who opted for a free grant on a river further to the west.[21] He made his way to the Gananoque River to found that settlement and within a year or so owned one of the most prosperous inns on the Montreal-Kingston route.

If Stone's experience at Cornwall was typical of the more enterprising latecomers to the township, then it was the pattern of land distribution at the beginning of the Loyalist settlements that made the area unattractive to newcomers because all the land had been granted, though it was neither settled nor under cultivation. Thus Cornwall and the Eastern District grew slowly. According to the 1829 census returns there were but 812 in the town and 3,040 in the township of Cornwall and the newly-partitioned township to the rear called Roxborough.[22] What was significant about this census return was that it showed that fifty percent of the total population was under sixteen years of age. In addition, the census revealed the gradual movement of French Canadians into the town and township.[22]

Cornwall's first French Canadian resident was the wife of a revolutionary soldier who had fought at the siege of Quebec in 1775. The couple were living with John Knave and his wife as hired help in 1785. By 1787 another French Canadian, Louis Nadau, was listed as a resident of Cornwall. He gave evidence at the enquiry into

Loyalist grievances conducted by John Collins and William Dummer Powell. By 1793 the French Canadian presence in Upper Canada was sufficiently felt to warrant Assemblyman Hugh Macdonell of Charlottenburg to make a motion that all Acts passed by the Assembly should "be translated into the French language for the benefit of the inhabitants of the Western District of this Province and other French settlers who may come to reside within the Province." Hugh Macdonell, like his brother, the Speaker of the House, Captain John Macdonell, and A. Macdonell, the Clerk of the House, were all French-speaking, as were most of the Highland gentlemen living in the Lancaster-Charlottenburg area. By 1829 there were, perhaps, as many as ten French Canadian families in the town itself and some twenty-seven in the Townships of Cornwall and Roxborough.[23]

When Sir John Johnson's Regiment had first arrived that hot month of June in 1784, the official muster showed 302 adults and 214 children under sixteen. Even though the settlement had not kept up this birthrate of seven children to every adult, its rate of five children to one adult in 1829 was still impressive and suggests that the increase in population was due largely to natural increase of the original settlers rather than to emigration in the years before 1829. By the time the town of Cornwall was incorporated in 1834, its population had barely risen to 1,000.[24]

The picture that emerges of the town of Cornwall from 1790 through to the post 1812-14 war period is one of a small rural settlement of about 500 people by 1816.[25] As the eighteenth century drew to a close the town seemed, if anything, to be falling behind its nearest neighbours in terms of size and social organization. Charlottenburg, township no. 1, had several increases to its population from Scotland before the Napoleonic wars effectively cut off emigration. By 1815, Charlottenburg had some 494 people listed on its assessment rolls while Cornwall, including the town and Roxborough, had but 298.[26] The township of Matilda, twenty-five miles to the west had, at this time, only 111 on its assessment rolls, but it had pulled ahead of Cornwall in other respects. In the early 1790s settlers of Matilda had built two grist mills, two churches, several schools, a number of shops and taverns and one inn.[27] Yet Cornwall shared in the general prosperity of the Eastern District throughout the 1790s. This prosperity was so evident by 1799 that one American visitor exclaimed that in the townships "possessed by the late loyal corps and the adventurers from Europe and the States, People of every language and nation have come hither and formed prospering colonies. Heaven has blessed their labors, industry and enterprise. Few have experienced greater success."[28] This eulogy was all the more flattering as it came from an observant American anxious to see how the settlements of people, who had lately been his fellow countrymen, compared with those in his own country.

In the Cornwall of the early 1790s the inhabitants did not look at their town through the eyes of the town planners of 1784. They saw the town as visitors did[29] — a thinly-settled area fronting the river. No one at that time thought of the town site as a square mile of settlement bounded by Water Street on the south and Ninth Street on the north and to the east and west by Marlborough and Cumberland Streets. The east and west boundary streets were sketched in on the original paper plan of the town site, but were not named until some time in the early part of the next century. Flowing through the town's centre were two muddy creeks. One of these ran down part of what is now Pitt Street and emptied into the river a little to the east of Pitt Street which was then swampy on both sides and covered with small willows and alder bushes. The town itself in the early 1790s was characterized by the transitory state of many of the holders of the town lots. For instance, Joel Stone, who laid claim to the largest amount of land within the town, had left the town for Gananoque by 1793. Another holder of several town lots, Thomas Swan, who eventually settled permanently in Cornwall, listed his residence in 1788 as Montreal.[30] By the winter of 1789, the Episcopalian clergyman, Reverend John Bryan, left Cornwall abruptly for the United States from whence he had fled in 1780. His return flight to the United States in 1789 was precipitated by a visit from Reverend John Stuart of Kingston who was ordered by the Society for the Propagation of the Gospel to make enquiries into Bryan's standing as an ordained Episcopalian priest. Stuart had protected Bryan in 1785 when similar questions were raised in New Oswegatchie about Bryan's qualifications. At that time, Stuart had found Bryan a man "of good moral character, although of moderate talents and slender education." Yet Stuart assured the Society for the Propagation of the Gospel in 1785 that "from his great industry and the good opinion which the People have conceived of him, he (Bryan) may be very useful, especially in the present infant state of the Settlement."[31]

Since that time, however, Bryan had been on the fringes of the McNiff party[32] and perhaps because of this, he found himself again under suspicion of not being a properly-ordained priest. Thus, when Stuart arrived in Cornwall in the fall of 1789 to inspect Bryan's credentials, Stuart found that Bryan had gone "to the United States some time last Winter, and has not been heard of since."[33] Deputy Surveyor William Chewett lists Bryan's property on the 1792 map and even remarks that the parsonage house and school could be removed to their "proper situation," that is, above Third Street on the east side of Pitt Street, when the people were in a condition to rebuild them "otherwise it would be a great detriment to Mr. Brian who has improved (them)."[34] Like most buildings in the town, the Episcopalian parsonage and school had been erected by the people without regard to the original plan of the town set up by the provincial surveyor-general, Major Samuel Holland. When it was mooted about that the buildings might have to be removed from their present site, the Episcopalians dug their heels into the lots north of Second Street and there the parsonage and school stayed.

Who and how many people actually lived in Cornwall in 1792 still remains a puzzle as those listed on Chewett's map may only be those who claimed ownership of the town lots, but may not have resided in the town itself. An examination of the first patents granted for town lots from 1803 to 1810 does not clarify the picture either.[35] Only two names in those patents are identical to those on the Chewett map of 1792 — those of Mrs. Peggy Bruce and Thomas Swan. Four other family names are recorded — those of Empey, McLean, Kay and Emerson. Whether Jacob Rambough lived in Cornwall or Osnabruck Township is uncertain. On Chewett's map of the town Rambough is shown to have fenced in some nine acres above Second Street on what became York Street. However in 1787 Rambough was elected a delegate for township no. 3, an indication that he resided in that township.[36] Many of the original claimants to town lots obviously had not bothered to apply for patents for many years, probably because there was so little pressure for land in the townsite for the first quarter century of its existence. Then, as other settlers began to dribble in after the turn of the century, the owners of town lots decided to formalize their holdings.

Just as religious denominations and educational facilities were slowly beginning to be institutionalized in Cornwall by the 1790s, so, too, were local judicial and administrative bodies. The governor, Lord Dorchester, had reacted somewhat coolly to the first elections in the new townships and the subsequent Board of Enquiry into the various complaints. If he had had reservations about popular assemblies and democratic elements before, the results of the elections in 1787 and the enquiry confirmed them. Apart from McNiff's efforts to call a general assembly of the elected delegates in the Royal and Cataraqui Townships, these delegates were brushed aside as township representatives. Dorchester seemingly took into account the reports from the officers and magistrates that the elections had been rigged. Nor did the governor relish the accounts from magistrates that they were being abused and terrorized by McNiff supporters. The whole effort at democratic procedures in the townships smacked too much, he concluded, of what went on in the old colonies just prior to the outbreak of rebellion and revolution. What he proposed was to administer the townships from the top down once more, rather than to invite a wider representation from the townships to act as consultants in their own affairs.

Dorchester's first move at simplifying the administrative and judicial processes in the new settlements was to divide the western part of Quebec into four separate districts. Up until 1788, Cornwall and all the other western settlements had been included in the District of Montreal. Now Cornwall became part of the Lunenburg District and Captain Richard Duncan of township no. 4, Williamsburg, was made judge of the new district court. In June of 1789 Duncan called all the magistrates of the eight Royal Townships to Osnabruck for the first sitting of a Court of General Quarter Sessions of the Peace. This was the body that was to manage local affairs, appoint local officials and make regulations about roads, markets, harbours and a hundred other affairs. It was also the body that imposed tolls for ferries, bridges and roads, fees for marriage licences and other possible revenue-raising fees. Thus the new districts were to begin the unpopular task of providing some of the revenue for police, road construction and other improvements in the townships. Above all, this was the Court that heard the more important cases of those charged with civil or criminal offenses. As the first sitting of the Court was to be at Osnabruck township, this meant that the Cornwall magistrates, Major James Gray, Lieutenant Jeremiah French, and Thomas Swan, a McNiff supporter, had to journey to a neighbouring township to attend the Quarter Sessions. For some reason the senior magistrate of Cornwall, Captain Samuel Anderson, did not attend this first session.

By 1793 Cornwall was named as one of the six places in the new province for holding Quarter Sessions.[37] By that time, Captain Samuel Anderson's eldest son, Lieutenant Joseph Anderson, had been added to the magistrates of the town, making a total of five. Their job was suitably impressed upon them when they took the oath of office. They were to "enquire...(into) all manner of felonies, poisonings, enchantments, sorceries, arts magick, trespasses, forestallings, regratings, ingrossings, and extortions whatsoever."[38] If one can judge from the first few cases heard by the Court of General Quarter Sessions in Osnabruck, cases of assault and trespass were far more common than murders, enchantments or sorceries. Corporal punishment by flogging or the pillory and the imposition of fines were the usual sentences of the Court rather than confinement in prison, as Cornwall had neither court house nor jail.[39] Major Gray, in a letter to Lieutenant Governor J.G. Simcoe in 1792 complained about the burden put on inhabitants if prisoners had to be confined for any length of time in the town. The alternative was to send prisoners to the fort at New Oswegatchie or Kingston.[40]

When the Court of Quarter Sessions proposed to build a district court house and jail at New Johnstown in Edwardsburg, two Cornwall magistrates, Lieutenants Joseph Anderson and Jeremiah French, raised such a row that the magistrates then agreed to build court houses and jails at both New Johnstown and Cornwall,[41] a financial undertaking quite beyond the resources of the district at that time. Though steps were taken to begin construction of the jail and court house in Cornwall as early as 1794, neither was finished until 1808. Yet Anderson's and French's timely intervention on behalf of Cornwall assured that the town would become the administrative centre of the eastern district, rather than Osnabruck or Williamsburg to the west. The delay in getting a court house or jail under construction forced the Court of King's Bench to convene sometimes in the Presbyterian Church on Pitt Street or even in a tavern,[42] while Sheriff Cornelius Munro farmed out prisoners to people who posted bonds for their safe-keeping. Whatever the shortcomings of the jail and courthouse facilities in Cornwall, the magistrates did not neglect the police force. Two constables were appointed in 1789, David Wright and David Scheik.[43] Evidently the Court considered it unwise to re-appoint constable Barnhart who had served under Magistrate Samuel Anderson and had come under attack from McNiff's supporters.[44]

The other gesture towards law and order made at the first sitting of the Court of General Sessions in 1789 was to empanel Grand Jurors. Among the Cornwall men chosen to serve was Sergeant John Pescod.[45] He had been one of the non-commissioned officers accused in 1785 of fraudulently selling goods from the King's Stores.[46] His accusers were a group of thirty-three fellow townsmen including William Impey, Jacob Rambough and Jacob Ross who became the hard core of McNiff's supporters. Pescod had easily exonerated himself from the charge and he steadily rose in the rural society of Cornwall. He was likely among those men who founded the first Cornwall Masonic Lodge in 1790, Union Lodge no. 9, which was registered with the Grand Lodge of England as no. 521.[47] Nine years later he was master of the Cornwall Lodge.[48]

Although the influence of the Masonic Order on the new settlements can only be hinted at, Masonic links were legion. As the most powerfully organized fraternal society in the country at this time, the Order, which included Roman Catholics and Jews,[49] was far better represented in the western part of the province of Quebec than any religious denomination. Cornwall's founder, Sir John Johnson, had been Provincial Grand Master in New York before he fled to Canada. In 1788 he accepted the post of Provincial Grand Master of Canada when Deputy Surveyor John Collins relinquished the post after serving since 1767. So prominent were members of the surveying department in the Order that they had their own "Select Surveyors Lodge."[50] Members of the Order stood at the pinnacle of power in the province. They also stood at the doors of political opposition to the ministerial party. For instance, Adam Lymburner, one of the Montreal merchants most active in the opposition, was a member of Montreal's most exclusive lodge, St. Paul's.[51] Yet whether Masons were within the government party or in the opposition, all at the top, whether Masons or not, preferred orderly developments within the province. Thus it is not surprising that Sir John Johnson, who had remained quiet during the enquiry into Loyalist complaints, decided to accept the post of Provincial Grand Master and quickly began to bring the various Masonic Lodges in the western part of the province under his jurisdiction. In so doing he was to use the Masonic Order, if not as an agency of social control, at least as an agency of social direction in the infant settlements.

The past grand master, John Collins, had been one of the two commissioners sent by Lord Dorchester to enquire into the grievances. In their report, Collins and Powel had deplored the deterioration in manners and conduct in the Loyalist settlements. "The Licentiousness of Manners and Conversation appears," they wrote, "to be no longer the subject of shame or reproach."[52] They analyzed the root of the difficulties as due to the absence of churches and schools that usually had re-enforced or instilled recognized moral precepts and manners among settlers. Masonic leaders, perhaps unwittingly, tried to fill the vacuum by providing a fraternal organization within which the rough edges and ruffled feathers of pioneer society could be smoothed. Cornwall, New Oswegatchie and Niagara were part of that rough edge that came within the provincial Masonic orbit by 1790. Officers of the military Masonic lodges at New Oswegatchie and Niagara had applied for affiliation with the Provincial Grand Lodge of Quebec by

1787, the former being registered by the Grand Lodge of England as no. 520 and the latter as no. 521, the same number that was given to Union Lodge, Cornwall, when it applied for registration in 1790. Cornwall Lodge had been warranted on 30 November 1788 and given the local number of 21. It was renumbered 9 in 1792.[53] No evidence exists concerning the members of the first Cornwall lodge, but the fact that it applied for affiliation in 1790 suggests that it, too, like the lodges at New Oswegatchie and Niagara, had been a military lodge and was now simply regularizing its standing as part of the Canadian provincial organization. One of Cornwall's first land-owners, Rosseter Hoyle, was a Mason at this time.[54] Though it is not known whether he had anything to do with the provincial registration of Union Lodge no. 9 at Cornwall in 1790, he became master of a new Masonic lodge in Montreal, St. John's Lodge of Friendship, no. 11, in 1792.[55] This was the next lodge to be registered, after the Cornwall lodge, with the Grand Lodge of England.

Within a year Cornwall received its second Royal visit and a fillip to its Masonic connections when Prince Edward, the future Duke of Kent and father of Queen Victoria, arrived in town.[56] Whether the visit was purely in connection with military duties or had a Masonic connection is uncertain. Prince Edward had accepted the post of Grand Master of the Lower Province almost as soon as he arrived in the country in 1791 upon the retirement of Sir John Johnson. How popular the Royal nomination was is indicated by a letter of Surgeon Alex Wilson of the Royal Artillery who had acted as temporary Grand Master until the Prince's appointment. Wilson reported to the Grand Lodge of England, "We have already had applications from the Upper Province for warrants, people of all descriptions wishing to have their authority from the Prince; as they very justly observe it carried with it weight and gives dignity and consequence to the whole craft."[57] Prince Edward made several visits to the upper province, lingering long enough in Cornwall to enjoy the hospitality of Lieutenant Jeremiah French at his lovely home, west of the town site. A turkey hunt was organized for the Royal guest, but tragedy stalked the French family.[58] As French entertained his Royal guest, his young daughter ran out in front of the hunters and was shot by her father.[59]

Prince Edward's Masonic activities among the new settlements resulted in three lodges being warranted by him before he left Canada in 1794, one of them being in Cornwall.[60] The other two lodges were no. 1 Glengarry Lodge in the 2nd battalion of the Royal Canadian Regiment and no. 5 Royal Edward Lodge at New Johnstown in

Edwardsburg.[61] Whether these lodges were being re-registered under a new numbering system initiated by the new Grand Master is uncertain. By 1799 the Cornwall lodge was run by Sergeant John Pescod as Master, with Robert McGregor as Senior Warden, Robert McGloghlon as Junior Warden, Daniel Campbell, treasurer, and Thomas Johnson, secretary.[62] As Master, Pescod welcomed his old antagonist of 1785 — William Empey[63] — as a member, an indication that the Masonic Order could oil the wheels of social intercourse in the Loyalist settlements.

If the Masonic Order was pouring oil on troubled waters in the young settlement by the late 1790s, one other force was soon to be at work to give the town of Cornwall preeminence in an area that no town-planner could have foreseen. The young Presbyterian schoolmaster who travelled through the town on a cold wintry night at the end of 1799 en route to Kingston retraced his steps three years later and turned the small town into the top English-speaking centre of learning in the country. Schoolmaster John Strachan was no ordinary individual. Son of a Scottish stone quarry foreman who was killed accidentally, Strachan found himself at sixteen the main support of his family. At the insistence of his mother, he studied at Aberdeen Grammar School and then won a bursary to King's College, Aberdeen, where he was a scholar when the disaster of his father's death struck the family. From then until he received the invitation to take over a small school at Kingston, Strachan had worked as a private tutor and schoolmaster in various parishes in Scotland, winning the friendship and respect of several prominent intellectuals such as Thomas Chalmers, Thomas Duncan and Doctor James Brown of the University of Glasgow. It was to Doctor Brown that Richard Cartwright and Robert Hamilton of Kingston, Upper Canada, wrote enquiring for a schoolmaster and offering a contract for three years at eighty pounds a year and passage out. When Brown offered the post to Strachan, the twenty-one year old Scot did not hesitate too long before casting his lot on the other side of the Atlantic.[64]

Kingston's school had been closed for several years since its schoolmaster, George Okill Stuart, son of the Presbyterian convert to Anglicanism, Reverend John Stuart, had gone off to Princeton to finish his studies. Now Strachan settled comfortably in Richard Cartwright's large home and for three years went to the schoolroom in town to teach his wards, a dozen boys and one girl, Cartwright's daughter. Half his salary went home to his family. With one eye on prospects in New York and the other on a possible vacancy at St. Gabriel Street Presbyterian Church in Montreal, Strachan studied

French and kept abreast of the established church and its openings. During the three years he was in Kingston, his school work was done competently but not spectacularly. As the time for his contract renewal drew near, Strachan's needs and ambitions called for something more than a teaching job at eighty pounds a year. By embracing Anglicanism,[65] he secured the vacant parish of Cornwall in the spring of 1803.

Cornwall's Episcopalians had been without a resident clergyman from the time of John Bryan's disappearance in 1789. The new Bishop of Quebec, Jacob Mountain, deplored the absence of clergymen in the new province when he made his first visitation westward in 1794. He told authorities in England that "A Church should be immediately built at Cornwall and a Minister sent there for that township and neighbourhood,"[66] but it was not until 1801 that the town secured a Church of England clergyman in the person of a young missionary priest, James Sutherland Rudd, sent out by the Society for the Propagation of the Gospel. By the time he arrived, Rudd found the "Township of Cornwall consists of various Sects (and) those who belong to our Church bear a very small proportion to the whole."

Some sort of an Episcopalian parish organization had existed since 1788 when Sergeants John Pescod and John Smith were church wardens under Reverend John Bryan.[67] Since that time the families which had been associated with the Episcopalian parish had probably been in the habit of attending the Presbyterian services conducted by Reverend John Bethune. Rudd found no house on the glebe lands. The parsonage house noted on the Chewett map of 1792 may have been a rough frame house erected for Reverend John Bryan and too rude a habitation for the young missionary priest fresh out from England with an ailing wife. An appeal in Montreal for funds to build a parsonage resulted in £50 being raised there but local fundraising was less enthusiastic, and Rudd found himself living in a very modest house.[68] The new incumbent soon discovered that other denominations such as the Lutherans made use of the burial ground at the rear of the church grounds without the services of a clergyman. When Rudd insisted that it was his right to conduct all burial services, the Lutherans, finding themselves once more embroiled in a squabble over the burial of their dead, found another place for a graveyard.

Rudd stuck it out in Cornwall for less than two years. The house and salary promised by his parishioners did not materialize and by February of 1803 he readily accepted a vacancy at Sorel,[69] thus opening the way for John Strachan's entry into Cornwall life. Strachan's first reaction to Cornwall was not flattering. In a private letter to his Scottish mentor, Doctor James Brown, Strachan described his new situation. "My flock is not numerous. A great part of my parish belongs to the Lutheran persuasion, a greater has no religion at all. A number of the people are Catholics and plenty of Presbyterians with a few Methodists. You see, I am in a pickle."[70] Strachan soon unpickled them. By 1814, his successor reported that all dissenters had been cleared out of Cornwall with the exception of a "few Scotch Presbyterians."[71] Despite this report some Methodists and Lutherans remained, but undoubtedly Strachan's proselytizing efforts had succeeded beyond his expectations, partly because the Lutherans in the neighbouring county of Dundas had neglected to furnish their Pastor, John Gunter Weagandt, with his promised salary. By 1811, with Strachan's concurrence, Weagandt decided to opt for the Church of England and persuaded his congregation to follow suit.[72] For a brief period after the 1812-14 war the new congregation of Lutheran Anglicans was threatened with a secessionist movement led by a previous pastor, Reverend Friederich Myers, but he, too, eventually went over to the Church of England. Not only did Strachan's influence prevail among the Cornwall and County Dundas Lutherans; it also brought within the Church of England the talented sons of the Presbyterian minister, Reverend John Bethune, who were entrusted to Strachan's care as scholars.

John Strachan's success in the fields of religion and education in Cornwall was staggering. Both fields demanded and received his attention. On his arrival in town he found only a rough log cabin as a dwelling. With the help of one of his young students, the orphaned John Beverley Robinson, he made some temporary repairs to the cabin and moved in. The tone of society left something to be desired as far as Strachan was concerned. He privately described it as a "serious evil" and found the minds of the people "prone to low cunning."[73] What was more, he soon discovered that "An Honorary Degree...would be of great service to me here, for although there are no distinctions of rank in this country, no people are so fond of them."[74] These were problems he could deal with in his own time. Degrees of Licentiate of Divinity and Doctor of Divinity were bestowed on him, the first by St. Andrew's University in 1807 and the second by his Alma Mater, Aberdeen, in 1811. What he needed first of all was a proper parsonage, a church, a school and a wife. With his customary thoroughness and vigour, Strachan set about to secure all four.

The parsonage and stables went up first at a cost of £520, only £180 of which was provided by the parishioners. Later Strachan successfully applied to the Executive Council in 1815 for the balance of £340 to be paid from the rents of the Clergy Reserves. By 9 September 1805 Strachan was able to report to the Society for the Propagation of the Gospel that the parsonage "is now habitable and will be sufficiently commodious when completed."[75] Cornwall Episcopalians had begun a subscription fund in 1800 towards a church,[76] but it was not until 1805 that Strachan finally got a subscription raised and a committee appointed, composed of Captain Samuel Anderson, John Pescod and Joshua Young Cozens, to superintend the building of a church.[77] By January of 1806 the church was ready for use — a wooden building on a stone foundation, some fifty-two feet long. Strachan reported in November 1806 that "the people showed great alacrity in the business and deserve much praise...It is the poorest Parish in the Province," he remarked "and yet more has been done there than in any other. They not only have the handsomest Church, but the only Parsonage House in Upper Canada."[78]

When the bell tower and the tin-coated spire were added to the Cornwall church in 1810, it could be seen for miles up and down the St. Lawrence River.[79] Pews were sold to pay the cost of the building, though a number of free pews were reserved for the poor of the parish. The highest bidder was the first Sheriff of the District, Cornelius Munro, who paid £30 for pew no. 1.[80] The pew sales indicated how some of the disbanded soldiers of the Royal Yorkers had fared in the first twenty-two years of life in their new township. Though Strachan had described Cornwall as the poorest Parish in the province, he did not mean that the town was the poorest, nor his parishioners poor. Some of the non-commissioned officers of the Royal Yorkers had managed very well since settling at Cornwall. Whether their new-found affluence came from timber, potash or wheat or a combination of all three is uncertain, but by 1806 Sergeant John Pescod was able to put down £24.10 for a pew. His old captain, Samuel Anderson, now a District Judge, offered £16 10s. Sergeant George Barnhart paid £19 and Lieutenant Jeremiah French £20. Lieutenant Joseph Anderson managed £8 and Philip Empey £4.2.6. Sergeant John Smith's contribution was £10 and Andrew Milross paid £5 5s.[81] Altogether, forty-three Cornwall parishioners subscribed £457 14s towards the purchase of pews that first year. The Episcopalians now out-classed the Presbyterians as far as their church building went and even snubbed the Court of Quarter Sessions by refusing to allow the Court to hold a sitting in the church.[82]

Though the Episcopalian church was now the most imposing building in the small town,[83] it was Strachan's school that put

Cornwall in a class by itself. There were several distinctive features about this academy, as Strachan preferred to call it,[84] though subsequently it was more often referred to as a Grammar School, today's equivalent of a high school. To begin with, the physical plant can hardly be said to have existed. The school shown on the Chewett map of 1792 was likely a village elementary school, probably taught by Reverend John Bryan. At the time of Strachan's arrival in Cornwall, there was a local schoolmaster, Elijah Leavens, who was also secretary of the newly-founded Masonic Lodge, Hiram Lodge no. 20.[85] Whether Leavens used the school indicated on the Chewett map is uncertain. When Strachan's students arrived in Cornwall in the summer of 1803 hard on the heels of their master, they found Strachan ensconced in a snug log cabin in which he lived and taught for the time being.[86] John Beverley Robinson boarded with Strachan as did John and William Macaulay of Kingston. George Ridout of York (Toronto) boarded at one of the Vankoughnet's. Four other scholars lived at the Wilkinson home.[87] Thus, as the academy grew from twenty scholars in 1804 to about forty in 1808,[88] more and more Cornwall homes were benefiting in a modest pecuniary way by providing quarters for the lads. As the building of the church came first in Strachan's scheme of things, school classes were held in the church once it was completed. Then in 1807 he acquired both his wife and his school building, the latter perhaps owing something to the former. He took as his bride Anne Wood McGill, the twenty-two-year old daughter of a Cornwall doctor and recent widow of Andrew McGill of Montreal. Strachan's new wife had a settled yearly income of some £300. Strachan's own salary from his church and academy rose to £500 a year.[89] Thus money was no longer a worry. One of his students reported in 1807, "Mr. Strachan...lives in great style, keeps three servants...is a great friend to the poor, and spends his money as fast as he gets it."[90] Strachan agreed. In a letter to his friend, Dr. James Brown, in 1808, he admitted, 'I have saved very little...I shall assist some of my relations in Scotland — purchase books and live well."[91]

With his marriage and his relief from financial worries, Strachan's generous and boisterous character blossomed. Shorter in height than many of his scholars, he could crack a cane as well as the next over an errant student's back, but his strength lay not in the cane but in the force of his example and self discipline that brought him to the classroom by nine in the morning and kept him there until after four in the afternoon, intent on the moral and intellectual development of each of his scholars. Then, there was his zest for life. One of his students, young George Ridout, told his parents, "When Mr. Strachan laughs, he laughs heartily."[92] His influence and force of personality extended beyond his students. One father contrasted Strachan with his clerical rival, Reverend George Okill Stuart, "the one (Strachan) sociable and cheerful," the other "haughty, sullen and austere."[93] Within a year Strachan had another reason for sociable cheerfulness. His first son was born, named after his friend, James McGill, who frequently visited his sister-in-law and her husband. It was on one of these visits in February 1811 that Strachan put the idea into McGill's head of using part of his considerable fur-trade fortune to found a university in Montreal. Thus, from a Cornwall parsonage grew the seed of one of Canada's great universities.[94]

In Cornwall itself the long-desired school house was not under construction until June 1807 - a wooden structure forty by thirty feet, arched and with twelve windows so high above the floor that students could not look out or be distracted by the passing sights.[95] Thus school facilities were negligible for the first four years of the Cornwall Academy's existence. The quality of teaching came, then, from the character of the master. This was a constant factor in the lives of the scholars for, unlike modern high schools where the students move from class to class each year and from teacher to teacher every forty minutes, Strachan's school had but one master who could afford only one assistant.[96] The school's special features were not only the quality of Strachan's teaching, but the quality of his scholars — all sons of the principal inhabitants of the provinces. There was, too, the special curriculum that was a mixture of classical studies and practical courses adapted to the needs of the country where Strachan realized that the "parents are anxious to get them (the students) introduced to business and they can seldom appreciate the advantages of a liberal system of Education."[97] With the help of a tidy sum of £400 from the provincial Assembly, Strachan imported for his academy a variety of scientific apparatus that included a model steam engine, prisms, magnetic bars, air pumps, glass tubes, thermometers, hydrostatic balances, lenses, telescopes, microscopes, astronomical quadrants and even "an Electrical machine."[98] From the Society for the Propagation of the Gospel he secured a supply of Bibles, Testaments, Common Prayer Books and other theological books, the nucleus of a select Mission Library at Cornwall.[99] The lack of ready textbooks for the school presented problems. Strachan, practical man that he was, overcame some of these difficulties by writing his own textbooks. One such was *A Concise Introduction to Practical Arithmetic*, published in Montreal in 1809.

Above all, it was the way that Strachan managed the school that kept a keen spirit of emulation and competition alive among the scholars. This spirit was maintained by a system of monitors, "censors" as Strachan called them, from among the older students who helped teach and discipline the younger boys. It was maintained, too, by several of Strachan's educational innovations. These included a daily register in which each student's achievements were recorded and compared, and a monthly book of merit in which Strachan recorded special exercises of excellence that the students had done voluntarily. Then, too, there were the annual public examinations to which parents and the general public were invited. Elocution classes and debates helped to train the scholars for the annual examinations that highlighted the school's activities.

The school day began with prayers at nine in the morning; classes continued all day to four in the afternoon and then went on in the evening with studies that could extend well past midnight for the older lads. There was no holiday on Saturday either. This was the time when the scholars, whether Church of England, Presbyterian, Roman Catholic or other denomination, attended a short religious and moral lecture given by Strachan. The students were required to make copious notes of the lecture. These were collected the following Monday by the censors who then compiled a review from the reports and presented it again on the Thursday. Thus, as Strachan noted with some satisfaction, "it becomes impossible for any young man to leave...ignorant of religion." His "first and most anxious care," he avowed, "is to store the youthful mind with sound moral principles for it is a maxim with us that without knowing God, all knowledge is vain." Thus for Strachan moral training was paramount. "When once good principles are well fixed in the mind we conceive that the most valuable and essential part of education is finished," Strachan wrote in 1811.[100]

These were the principles under which Strachan taught, the methods he used, and the equipment and selection of scholars he had that made Cornwall the top centre of learning in the province. The result for Cornwall was that, for a generation afterwards, the men who dominated the administrative and, for much of the time, the political machinery of the province had spent four or five years in an intellectual environment in Cornwall that they appreciated and under a master whom all respected and many loved. Thus Cornwall and the Eastern District itself were well known at the centre of power. Moreover, as many of Cornwall's own sons and those from neighbouring areas attended Strachan's school, some of them found their ways to the corridors of power in the provincial capital. It was because of the school's location in Cornwall that these men of prominence, many of them within the orbit labelled the "Family Compact," looked to Cornwall with continued interest and affection. In 1833 several returned to the old school where they formed a committee to raise a subscription in order to present their schoolmaster, now the Archdeacon of York, with a piece of silver plate.[101] A tribute from another direction indicated that Strachan's firm belief in the "obligation of Charity among different denominations" was realized.[102] The Roman Catholic historian of Glengarry County, John A. Macdonell, in his *Sketches*, stated unequivocally, "Mr. Strachan's school in Cornwall was an unequalled seminary in its day. It was a school for Protestants and Catholics alike, where not only were their minds improved and an education given such as enabled those who were fortunate enough to partake of it to achieve in after life the highest positions in the gift of country, but where were also impressed upon them those sound and loyal principles which actuated the Bishop himself throughout his life, to the great advantage of the country."[103] Seldom has a man received greater tribute. When Strachan left Cornwall in 1812 to take up duties as rector of York, he left behind not only a greatly enlarged congregation of the Church of England and the only one in the province boasting its own parsonage and the best church, but he also left a Grammar School of exceptional quality, endowed by the government, which he turned over to the local trustees.

More than this, Strachan made it a point to keep in touch with his old students, writing to them, advising them, encouraging them, and in later years, as they approached death, he was at their bedside.[104] It was a relationship of intellect and affection, fostered by the unifying personality of the schoolmaster. With Strachan's departure from Cornwall and his absorption into the hierarchy of the church and assumption of political responsibilities in the capital, his academy at Cornwall continued under such able masters as the Presbyterian ministers, Harry Leith and Hugh Urquhart, who taught, among others, John Sandfield Macdonald,[105] the Roman Catholic from Glengary who would make Cornwall his permanent bailiwick and turn its political colours from those of moderate toryism to those of moderate liberalism. If, as some avowed, Strachan and his school, had been the nursery of the Family Compact,[106] and Cornwall a safe tory seat where as early as 1804 a political unknown from Brockville, D'Arcy Boulton, could be assured of a seat,[107] Cornwall over the first half of the nineteenth century did a complete political somersault, winding up in the liberal palm of John Sandfield Macdonald. But before that happened, Cornwall and the country underwent war and rebellion.

NOTES

1. T.A. Reed, "John Strachan's Journey from Montreal to Kingston in December 1799", in *Ontario History*, xlii, 1950, no. 4, 216.

2. For Alexander Bruce, see Return of Disbanded Troops and Loyalists settled in Township no. 2, October 1784 (Haldimand Papers, MG21/B168/101); G. Murray Logan, *Scottish Highlanders and the American Revolution*, 94; for a description of Mrs. Peggy Bruce, see Dr. William Dunlop.

   Recollections of the War of 1812, 36-42; for McBean, see J.F. Pringle, *Lunenburg, or the Old Eastern District*, 84; for John Miller, see A Return of the Membership of Hiram Lodge, no. 20, held at Cornwall, 11 Dec. 1804, in John Ross Robertson, *History of Freemasonry*, i, 875.

3. Maj. R. Mathew's Journal, cited in Macdonell, *Sketches, Glengarry in Canada*, 82.

4. Patrick Campbell, *Travels into the Interior*, 142.

5. Duc de la Rochefoucauld-Liancourt, *Travels through the United States of America, the Country of the Iroquois, and Upper Canada in the years 1795-1796, and 1797*, 69; William Canniff, *Settlement of Upper Canada*, 431.

6. Mathew's Journal, cited in Macdonell, *Sketches, Glengarry*, 82.

7. Mrs. Elizabeth Simcoe, *Diary*, 26 June 1792, 103.

8. William Chewett Map, Cornwall, 1792, (V3/440).

9. *Ibid.*

10. *Ibid.*

11. *Ibid.*; see also, Petition of Your Majesty's Ancient and New Subjects, Inhabitants of the Province of Quebec, 24 Nov. 1784 (MG11/Q24/I/1).

12. For Hoyle's holdings in the town, see Chewett map, Cornwall, 1792 (V3/440).

13. *Gazette*, Montreal, 3 May and 12 July 1792.

14. Population statistics provided by Rev. John Strachan to the Society for the Propagation of the Gospel, 22 May 1804, cited in Young, "The Mission of Cornwall, 1784-1812" in *OHSPR*, xxv, 1929, 494; Harkness's estimate of seventy houses in Cornwall at this time is too high, see his *History of Stormont, Dundas and Glengarry*, 61; Judge J.F. Pringle's estimate of the 1815 population as 296, based on the assessment rolls of that year, is too low, see his *Lunenburg*, 72.

15. For occupation identification see, A Return of Membership of Hiram Lodge, no. 20. held at Cornwall, 11 Dec. 1804, in Robertson, *History of Freemasonry*, i, 875; Pringle, 314-17.

16. Joel Stone to _____, 25 April 1787, cited in H.S. McDonald, "Memoir of Colonel Joel Stone, a United Empire Loyalist and the Founder of Gananoque", in *OHSPR*, 1920, xviii, 59-90.

17. *Ibid.*

18. *Ibid.*, 74.

19. Stone to John Wilson, 29 Mar. 1789, (*ibid.*, 75).

20. Stone to Land Board, Quebec, 18 Feb. 1789 (RG1/L4/11/008-010).

21. Stone to Governor John Graves Simcoe, 2 Feb. 1793 (McDonald, "Memoir of Col. Joel Stone", 78).

22. 1829 Census Returns for the Town of Cornwall and the Townships of Cornwall and Roxborough, prepared by Alexander McDonell, Assessor.

23. *Ibid.*; Motion by Hugh Macdonell, House of Assembly, 3 July 1793, cited in Macdonell, *Sketches, Glengarry*, 105; for earlier references to French Canadians in Cornwall, see Maj. R. Mathew's Journal, in *ibid.*, 81-82, and Deposition of Louis Nadau, Board of Enquiry, Cornwall, 25 July 1787 (RG4/A1/33/10715).

24. Pringle, 147.

25. *Ibid.*, 72.

26. *Ibid.*, 74.

27. James Croil, *Dundas, or a Sketch of Canadian History*, 144.

28. John Cosens Ogden, *A Tour Through Upper and Lower Canada by a Citizen of the United States*, 51.

29. George Heriot, *Travels Through Canada*, 124.

30. Swan's testimony before the Claims Commission, 22 June 1788, *Second Report, Ontario Bureau of Archives*, 1904, 838.

31. Rev. John Stuart to the Society for the Propagation of the Gospel, 1 Oct. 1785, cited in Young, "Mission of Cornwall 1784-1812," 486.

32. *Quebec Gazette*, Supplement, 22 Feb. 1788.

33. Stuart to the Society for the Propagation of the Gospel, 4 Oct. 1790, cited in Young, "Mission of Cornwall 1784-1812", 488.

34. Chewett Map, Cornwall, 1792 (V3/440).

35. For a list of the first patents issued, 1803-1810, see Pringle, 71-72.

36. Memorial of Township no. 3, 9 Jan. 1787 (RG4/A1/31/10139-40).

37. Canniff, *Settlement of Upper Canada*, 538.

38. Macdonell, *Sketches, Glengarry*, 75.

39. Pringle, 52-54.

40. Maj. James Gray to Governor J.G. Simcoe, 15 Jan. 1792 (*Simcoe Papers*, i, 104).

41. Pringle, 55-56.

42. *Ibid.*, 57-60.

43. *Ibid.*, 52, probably David Sheek.

44. Deposition of Patrick McGuire, 19 Jan. 1787 (RG4/A1/31/10326).

45. Macdonell, *Sketches, Glengarry*, 76.

46. Petition of Settlers at New Johnstown, 8 Feb. 1785 (RG4/A1/28/8980).

47. A.J.B. Milborne, *Freemasonry in the Province of Quebec 1759-1959*, 40, 43; Harkness, 90.

48. John Ross Robertson, *Freemasonry*, i, 820-82; Harkness, 90; Arthur Youngs, "Freemasonry in Cornwall and area first recorded in the late 1700s".

49. Milborne, *Freemasonry*, 49 and 56.

50. *Ibid.*, 53.

51. *Ibid.*, 36.

52. Report of John Collins and W.D. Powell to Lord Dorchester on Loyalist Grievances, 18 Aug. 1787, in Preston, *Kingston before the War of 1812*, 123.

53. Milborne, *Freemasonry*, 42-43 and 36; McCord Museum, Montreal: Miscellaneous Masonic papers, No. 12291, List of lodges for which warrants have been granted in Canada from the conquest to the year 1792.

54. Milborne, *Freemasonry*, 40.

55. *Ibid.*, and see 42.

56. *Gazette*, Montreal, 16 Aug. and 6 Sept. 1792; Prince William Henry had visited Cornwall in 1787, see "Address to Prince William Henry from the citizens of Cornwall, 1787", in archives of the Stormont, Dundas and Glengarry Historical Society, Simon Fraser Centennial Library, Cornwall.

57. Wilson to Grand Secretary of the Grand Lodge of England, 5 Nov. 1792 cited in John Ross Robertson, *History of Freemasonry*, i, 354.

58. Harkness, 187-88; Pringle, 160.

59. Harkness, 69; Hadfield, *Diary*, 59.

60. Robertson, *Freemasonry*, i. 869.

61. *Ibid.*, i, 182; Milborne, *Freemasonry*, 47.

62. Harkness, 90.

63. Milborne, *Freemasonry*, 40, gives the name as William Emery.

64. J.L.H. Henderson, *John Strachan*, 3-11; Gerald Craig, "John Strachan", in *DCB*, ix, 752-53.

65. Alison Smith, "John Strachan and Early Upper Canada 1799-1814", in *Ontario History*, lii, 1960, 164-66; see also Robert Campbell, *History of the Scotch Presbyterian Church, St. Gabriel St., Montreal*, 183-199.

66. Bishop J. Mountain to Henry Dundas, 15 Sept. 1794 (*Simcoe Papers*, iii, 92).

67. Joel Stone to Church Wardens John Smith and John Prescod (Pescod) 23 Feb. 1788, DAO: Trinity Church papers, 59-1; Young, "The Mission of Cornwall 1784-1812", 482.

68. Rev. J.S. Rudd to the Society for the Propagation of the Gospel, 19 Nov. 1802, (*ibid.*, 490-91).

69. *Ibid.*

70. Strachan to Brown, 27 Oct. 1803, cited in Henderson, *John Strachan*, 11.

71. Smith, "John Strachan and Early Upper Canada," 167.

72. James R. McCartney, "Sectarian Strife in Dundas County: A Lutheran-Episcopalian Land Endowment Controversy", in *Ontario History*, liv, June 1962, 74.

73. Smith, "John Strachan and Early Upper Canada 1799-1814", *Ontario History*, lii, 1960, 164.

74. *Ibid.*, 171.

75. Strachan to Society for the Propagation of the Gospel, 9 Sept. 1805, cited in Young, "The Mission of Cornwall 1784-1812", 494; for details of the financing of the parsonage see, Petition of John Strachan to Executive Council, 3 May 1814; and statements of S. Anderson, Neil McLean and David Sheek, 20 Aug. 1813; and statement of Church Wardens, Joseph Anderson and Benjamin Eastman, 20 Aug. 1813 (State Papers, Upper Canada, RG1/E3/79/42-44).

76. John Cosens Ogden, *A Tour Through Upper and Lower Canada by a Citizen of the United States*, 53.

77. Pringle, 227.

78. Strachan to Society for the Propagation of the Gospel, 4 Nov. 1806, cited in Young, "The Mission of Cornwall 1784-1812", 494.

79. Henderson, *John Strachan*, 12.

80. George Ridout to his parents, Cornwall, 24 Feb. 1806, cited in Matilda Edgar, *Ten Years of Upper Canada in Peace and War: being the Ridout Letters with Annotation*, 19.

81. For prices paid for pews, see Pringle, 227-28.

82. *Ibid.*

83. When Strachan's brother, James, made a tour of the province in 1819, Strachan had published under his brother's name, *A Visit to the Province of Upper Canada in 1819*, 26, in which he described Cornwall - "though not large, is neat and clean, and is ornamented with an excellent church", see Gerald Craig, "John Strachan", in *DCB*, ix, 755.

84. Smith, "John Strachan and Early Upper Canada," 162.

85. A Return of the Membership of Hiram Lodge, no. 20, Cornwall, 11 Dec. 1804, cited in Robertson, *Freemasonry*, i, 875.

86. Henderson, *John Strachan*, 11.

87. George Ridout to his parents, 17 Sept. 1805, in Edgar, *Ridout Letters*, 16; same to same, 27 Jan. 1806, (*ibid.*, 18-19).

88. George W. Spragge, "The Cornwall Grammar School Under John Strachan 1803-1812", in *OHSPR*, 1942, xxxiv, 64-65, 77; Craig, "John Strachan", in *DCB*, ix, 753.

89. Strachan to Brown, 9 Oct. 1808, in Spragge, "Cornwall Grammar School", 79.

90. Thomas Ridout to his father, 16 June, 1807, Edgar, *Ridout Letters*, 25.

91. Strachan to Brown, 9 Oct. 1808, in Spragge, "Cornwall Grammar School", 79.

92. George Ridout to parents, 27 Jan. 1806 (Edgar, *Ridout Letters*, 18-19).

93. George Ridout to his brother in England, 19 Oct. 1811 (*ibid.*, 64).

94. Strachan to the United Society for the Propagation of the Gospel, London, 17 Apr. 1824, cited in Henderson, *John Strachan*, 15.

95. Thomas Ridout to his father, 16 June 1807 (Edgar, *Ridout Letters*, 25); Pringle, 242.

96. Spragge, "Cornwall Grammar School", 66.

97. Strachan to Brown, 13 July 1806, in Spragge, "Cornwall Grammar School", 67.

98. Strachan to Brown, encl. 9 Oct. 1808 (*ibid.*, 79).

99. Young, "The Mission of Cornwall 1784-1812", 494-95.

100. *Kingston Gazette*, 3 Sept. 1811, cited in Spragge, "Cornwall Grammar School," 70-71.

101. *The Cornwall Tribute*, 3, 13-14.

102. Smith, "John Strachan and Early Upper Canada", 166.

103. Macdonell, *Sketches, Glengarry*, 123.

104. When Hon. Archibald McLean died in Toronto, Strachan was at his bedside, see Harkness, 149.

105. For a list of students, though it is not complete, see Pringle, 243-46.

106. H.E. Belden, *Historical Atlas*, see his Historical Sketch, Counties of Stormont, Dundas and Glengarry, i; Harkness, 143, for his comment; see also, *Histoire de Cornwall, Experience '78*, 26-28.

107. Harkness, 86; Pringle, 228.

Bishop John Strachan, 1778-1867. Rector of Cornwall Parish from 1803 to 1812. Later first Anglican Bishop of Upper Canada.

Credit: the United Counties of Stormont, Dundas and Glengarry, Harkness, J.G. *Stormont, Dundas and Glengarry: A History 1784-1945.*

Rev. Hugh Urquhart, (1793-1871).
Minister at Cornwall 1827-1871. Head
Master Cornwall Grammar School
1827-1840.
Credit: United Counties of Stormont, Dundas
and Glengarry, *Stormont, Dundas and Glengarry: A History 1784-1945.*

South view of the District School House Cornwall. This school
was used from 1807 to 1855. The Reverend John Strachan
first taught here.

Chapter V
Cornwall — A Garrison Town

War was never far from the thoughts of the first settlers of Cornwall. Their city owed its origin to war. When its soldier-founders laid aside their arms in favour of the axe and the plough, they did so half expecting that they would have to take up arms once more should their former neighbours and foes in the United States again sound the war tocsin. Throughout the early 1790s there was an uneasy peace until the British vacated the western fur posts that lay within the boundary of the United States. From then on, as long as the new republic kept its revolutionary army dismantled, fear of invasion from the south was not as worrisome as the situation in Europe where Napoleonic France was flexing its muscles over the continent. The Loyalist settlements had been deliberately located side by side to form a protective cordon along the north bank of the St. Lawrence. Quasi-military in their infancy, the new settlements had a loosely-structured military organization. Their old commanding officer, Sir John Johnson, was brigadier-general at the head of some 1,525 men who were liable for service under the 1787 Militia Act.[1] However, the Loyalist settlements along the St. Lawrence were to enjoy a generation of peaceful development, for the long revolutionary war had exhausted warlike appetites to the south.

Politically, the constitutional arrangements of 1791 had answered the most pressing demands of the Loyalists. The new province of Upper Canada was to have its own representative body — an elected House of Assembly. Its laws were to be the familiar British civil and criminal law with trial by jury. Above all, land would now be held in free and common soccage, not under the seigneurial system. McNiff's party and the Loyalists had what they wanted. And if Sir John Johnson was not to be their lieutenant governor, as he and they had fully expected, they welcomed as governor, John Graves Simcoe, a former soldier under whom some of them had served and whom all respected. In other words, the provincial political and judicial establishment was their own creation and they supported it. It is not surprising, then, that when Robert Issac Dey Gray, the only son of Major James Gray of Cornwall, went to a premature and watery grave while en route to a trial at Presqu'Ile in 1804, his post as solicitor general and his Stormont seat were accorded to the government's choice, D'Arcy Boulton, though Boulton had no Cornwall connections. And as for continuing reform within the governmental machinery, John Graves Simcoe's imaginative mind kept producing so many changes that people in Cornwall and elsewhere scarcely had time to formulate petitions or make suggestions.

One of the areas that Simcoe immediately set about improving was the military establishment of the new province. His plan was to imitate the English system where the county was the military unit and a lieutenant of the county — some distinguished citizen — would be in charge of the militia, appoint officers, and act as the King's military deputy. Thus the county lieutenant represented the direct link between the military and the Crown.[2] In 1792 the township of Cornwall became part of the County of Stormont, named in honour of the Chief Justice of England, Viscount Stormont, a native of Perth, Scotland.[3] As the administrative and judicial arrangements of the province were already organized within the framework of district divisions, the new county divisions were partly for electoral purposes and partly military in nature. The military importance of the county divisions was spelled out by the Duc de la Rochefoucauld-Liancourt who travelled through Upper Canada in the mid-1790s. "The division of Upper Canada into Counties is purely military," he wrote, "and relates merely to the enlisting, completing and assembling of the militia...(which) is commanded by a lieutenant and a second lieutenant."[4] All males between the ages of sixteen and sixty were required to enrol themselves under their militia officer or pay a fine of four dollars. Every militia company was inspected by a captain twice a year and each militiaman provided his own musket.

The County of Stormont's first military establishment drew its strength from two old Loyalist regiments. Major James Gray and Captain Archibald Macdonell of the Royal Yorkers became the colonel and lieutenant-colonel of the sole regiment of Stormont militia. In addition, Archibald Macdonell was named lieutenant of the county. Lieutenant Neil McLean of the 84th Regiment became major of the Stormont Regiment. Most of the new captains were former lieutenants of the two old regiments — Jeremiah French, Jacob Ferrand, Joseph Anderson, Ranald Macdonell and Miles Macdonell. Three sergeants of the Royal Yorkers now found themselves lieutenants of the county militia — John Smith, John Pescod and John Annable. Other lieutenants were John Beikie, John Gallinger, Alexander Macdonell, John Cones, George Stewart, Angus Fraser, Elisha Anderson and Alexander Morgan. Thus, it was the military families of the county re-asserting themselves in the new militia arrangements, most of the individual officers moving up a peg in the military hierarchy. Like other counties, Stormont and its town of Cornwall, found it difficult to keep the county regiment at full strength, though by 1796 a volunteer Troop of Horse, commanded by John Beikie, was attached to the Stormont militia. In 1800 Stormont had 398 enrolled militiamen with thirty-four commissioned officers and thirty-one sergeants. Though its militia record was not quite as good as Glengarry County's, it was better than Dundas's.[5] By 1806 there was no appreciable change in the number of militiamen enrolled.[6]

Cornwall also supplied officers and men to the Second Battalion of the Royal Canadian Volunteer Regiment of Foot. This was one of two provincial regiments raised in 1794 to take over garrison duty at strategic points in the country, thus allowing some of the regular line regiments to be withdrawn for service overseas.[7] The second battalion of the Royal Canadian Volunteers, commanded by Lieutenant-Colonel John Macdonell (Aberchalder) of Glengarry, drew to its ranks several Cornwall militia officers including Neil McLean, Miles Macdonell, Ranald Macdonell, Angus Macdonell, and two Cornwall civilians, Richard Wilkinson and Cyrus Anderson. Thus, for six years from 1796 until 1802, when a temporary European peace resulted in the disbandment of Royal Canadian Volunteers, a number of Cornwall men were once more under full-time military discipline and employment. When war struck in 1812, these trained officers and men were quickly absorbed into the wartime military establishment, for Cornwall was a communications pivot between Upper and Lower Canada as far as supplies and reinforcements were concerned.

The people of Cornwall experienced the rattle of the sabre even before the United States declared war on Great Britain in June of 1812. The original quarrel that led to the outbreak of war was the impressing of American seamen into the Royal Navy. Then, too, there were fears, principally among American frontiers-men and southerners, that the British military were encouraging Indian attacks on frontier American settlements. Flank companies of the Stormont Regiment began training six days a month shortly after the Upper Canadian Assembly passed a special Act on 6 March 1812, providing for the raising of two flank companies from the county regiment. Each company was to be composed of 100 picked men, unmarried and under forty years of age, ready for service at a moment's notice. As soon as it was learned in Cornwall that war had been declared, not only the flank companies hastened to the town. Men of the sedentary militia arrived, eager for the fray. Their most important immediate duty was to escort stores being forwarded to the west from Montreal. As the St. Lawrence water route was subject to attack from American gunboats and where the river narrowed, to gunfire from the American side, the land route from Cornwall westward to Kingston was the only alternative until a bateaux convoy system was worked out. One military traveller who examined the land route was impressed. "The streets of Cornwall," he wrote, "(are) wide and straight...The roads are good enough, particularly so from Cornwall westward." This was true as far as Elizabethtown (Brockville), but thereafter the roads were poor.[8] Colonel Richard Cartwright, the leading merchant of Kingston, wrote to the military commander in Montreal, Sir George Prevost, in early June 1812 that, "the Roads would soon be made tolerably good along the whole line from Lake St. Francis to this place (Kingston if) Detachments of the Militia...work on them."[9] Cartwright feared that government stores, destined for Kingston and points farther west, were not secure at Cornwall and he urged that they be forwarded by land to Elizabethtown.

The British military command was just as concerned about Cornwall's security. The Adjutant-General, Colonel Edward Baynes, ordered Colonel Robert Lethbridge to take command at Kingston and, while en route, to inspect the militia units and general defence and security of the communications between Cornwall and Kingston. Lethbridge was impressed with the zeal of the Stormont militia. He decided to keep the flank companies on continuous duty in Cornwall, allowing the rest of the militiamen to return home for the harvest. The flank companies were to post guards at all points where the river channel was narrow or where there were rapids, and they were to provide relay escorts for the convoys of bateaux that were bringing up supplies. As for arms, Lieutenant-Colonel Neil McLean of the Stormont militia reported to the adjutant-general, "we are greatly deficient in serviceable arms and a large proportion of those we have are unfit for service." McLean explained that "a considerable part of them (the arms) have been in possession of the Militia of Glengarry and Stormont for nearly thirty years," that is, since the townships were first settled.[10] The remaining part of the arms, McLean noted, "were used by different corps serving in these Provinces for probably fifty years." He did not have to add the obvious that such arms, left to the care of militiamen, would soon become defective. By July 1812, 100 stand of arms with fifty rounds of ball cartridges for each musket were sent to Cornwall from Montreal military stores and "the twelve cases containing 114 stand of old arms" stored at the Court House in Cornwall were returned to Montreal for repair.[11] As quarters for the flank companies that were Cornwall's sole defence force at the start of the war, a store was hired for £20 and wooden berths fitted up. Additional flank companies from the Glengarry militia were posted to Cornwall by the autumn,[12] forcing military authorities to look for more barrack space. The Court House and jail and, eventually, even St. John's Presbyterian Church were pressed into service.[13] By winter the troops in the temporary barracks in the Court House were reported to be "miserably accommodated which occasions discontent and some have deserted in consequence." The inspecting officer ordered berths to be fitted up "to make the place as comfortable as the seasons require."[14]

To increase the town's security, officers of the Stormont militia asked permission to raise a Troop of Horse for patrolling and dispatch purposes.[15] By 10 February 1813 permission was granted. Gradually the town was strengthened militarily in order that its role as a relay post for supplies and reinforcements to the west would not be interfered with. But it was hard to overcome its inherent weakness as a defensive position. Lt. Col. Ralph Bruyeres, who had been sent along the route from Montreal to Prescott to inspect all important points, complained that Cornwall was "not a good position for Troops in point of defence as it does not possess any strong or commanding ground."[16] Another officer put it more bluntly. "This (Cornwall) is an open town and presents formidable features for defence."[17]

The strong defensive position was above Cornwall at Osnabruck township where Lt.-Col. Neil McLean of Cornwall had the Stormont militia build a crude blockhouse in which he stationed a company of men in the fall of 1812.[18] The Raisin River to the east of Cornwall was guarded by a company of 100 men of the Glengarry militia who were as poorly accommodated in a "very slight and miserable barracks" and the river guarded by only one gunboat. Lt.-Col. Ralph Bruyeres complained that this was not sufficient, that "there should be two (gunboats) stationed here and two at Cornwall."[19] He reported to military headquarters in Montreal that "good boats for the purpose may be purchased on the spot," and by 1814 regular officers were commenting on "the fine Boats being constructed in Cornwall."[20] Boat building was but one of the fillips given to the town's economy by the war.

102

However, in the fall of 1812, with only one gunboat on the Raisin River, navigation was particularly exposed in the area from Lake St. Francis to Cornwall. Therefore an outpost was established across the river at St. Regis Indian Village by detachment of the Corps des Voyageurs Canadiens, a unit raised in Montreal largely from among the officers and men of the North-West Company.[21] As soon as the Americans at French Mills learned of the outpost at St. Regis, they made a devastating suprise attack on it, killing Ensign Pierre Rototte and seven other Voyageurs and taking the remaining twenty-three men captive. In addition, the raiders helped themselves to the supply of blankets, muskets and other items meant as presents for the Indians at St. Regis.[22]

News of this raid electrified the people of Cornwall. For a month they bided their time, awaiting a favourable opportunity to retaliate. They were well aware that the officer commanding the whole area from Cornwall to Kingston, Lieutenant Colonel Robert Lethbridge, had received positive orders from military headquarters in Montreal not to provoke hostility or to engage the enemy. Indeed, he was "to use every precaution to preserve the tranquillity of that part of the Province which does not in itself afford an eligible position for offensive operations."[23] This policy notwithstanding, the Cornwall military men were determined on a punitive expedition against the American force at French Mills on the Salmon River that had pulled off the raid. Their opportunity came with the arrival in town of Captain Andrew Gray, the Acting Deputy Quartermaster General. Gray brought with him seventy regulars, including a detachment of Royal Artillery, as part of an escort convoy for bateaux on their way up river. Lt.-Col. Neil McLean and Lt.-Col. Alexander McMillan lent their weight to the persuasive overtures made to the regulars to help the Cornwall militiamen carry off a raid across the river at the American position near French Mills. McMillan had some seventy to eighty militiamen ready to join the regulars and McLean was prepared to see to the safe embarkation of the raiders. Early in the morning of 23 November 1812 they set off and were joined by Indians from St. Regis.[24] According to Captain Gray who accompanied them, the whole manoeuvre was carried out with "great judgment, alertness and spirits (and) the enemy fled to a Block House for protection."[25] The Block House was soon surrounded by the combined regular-militia party from Cornwall and the American force surrendered. One captain, two subalterns and forty-seven men along with four bateaux and fifty-seven muskets were captured.[26] Some of the Cornwall soldiers were so encumbered on the return trip with captured arms and accoutrements that McMillan and Gray ordered them to break up the muskets and throw them into the river. The booty was not confined to war loot, however. Several houses and stores in the nearby towns of French Mills and Constable, New York, were pillaged.

The news of the successful raid, followed as it was by the arrival in Montreal of the American prisoners brought warm praise from the Commander of the Forces, Sir George Prevost, though he soon had to face the less agreeable task of adjudicating the various claims made by the plundered inhabitants of French Mills and Constable, New York.[27] The Cornwall men had only one regret. The Americans they captured were not the identical men who had raided St. Regis the previous month.[28]

What the British military command feared was that the Americans would retaliate by a direct attack on Cornwall.[29] One commissary agent in Cornwall had intelligence that the state of Vermont was "far more anxious to invade Canada than any other (state), though he admitted to Lt.-Col. McNeil that the Americans had been suitably impressed when the militiamen had broken up the captured muskets and thrown them in the river. "Destroying the arms had the desired effect," he gloated, "of conveying an idea of our being amply supplied."[30] Psychological warfare was useful over that winter in Cornwall. By February of 1813 the local commanding officer, Lt.-Col. Neil McLean wrote to the new military commander at Kingston, Major-General Baron Francis de Rottenburg, "I presume that your knowledge of the defenceless situation of this place (Cornwall) supersedes the necessity of saying much upon that subject." Nevertheless McNeil spelled it out. "We are entirely destitute of artillery, we have no place of defence, and are deficient in small arms."[31] What was more, McNeil had intelligence that a large proportion of the 6,000 troops raised in Vermont "are to be sent to the Salmon River station to make a descent on or about Cornwall before the ice breaks up on the St. Lawrence...to cut off the communications between Upper and Lower Canada."[32] In the face of this build-up of American troops opposite Cornwall, the military command at Montreal ordered McNeil "to assemble all his Militia at Cornwall in case the enemy should make any attack there."[33]

Worrisome, too, were the 200 Indians at St. Regis. Some had already entered the American service, but it was reported, "several would be very faithful to us if a proper officer of the Indian Department was stationed with them."[34] In fact, Lt.-Col. Bruyeres told Sir George Prevost that "Indians are much required (as scouts)...at River Raisin, Glengarry House, and at this post (Prescott)." He urged that "they should be immediately sent, if possible," but warned against sending "the few encamped in the vicinity of Cornwall (as) they are from St. Regis and not much to be depended upon." To what extent the St. Regis Indians were influenced by American overtures was not known by British intelligence, but British agents in the Salmon River area kept the military alert to American plans. Bruyeres knew that "the enemy is engaged in cutting...a road through the wood from Salmon River to St. Regis...with a view to taking possession of that post." Moreover, the Americans were known to be building "gunboats above the Mills (French Mills) ready to be launched with the spring floods" opposite Cornwall.[35]

All this enemy action just across the river from Cornwall kept the inhabitants on their toes. Guards were posted at Captain Joseph Anderson's farm to the west of the town where they exchanged occasional shots across the river with a guard of American militia stationed at Massena Point.[36] Regimental hospitals were set up in rented houses for the 1st Stormont militia.[37] Master Carpenter John Anderson was busy with his workmen, David Mason and Jacob Waggoner, in repairing barracks, erecting cook houses and guard houses, and converting Lt.-Col. Neil McLean's blacksmith shop into a carpenter's shop and armoury repair centre.[38] Other Cornwall men were reaping some of the harvest from the military chest. Evan Roys received pay for two days' work carting cannon. Walter Buchanan was happy to supply boards for the barrack department at Cornwall for a price.[39]

The Governor and Commander of the Forces, Sir George Prevost, decided the situation was serious enough to warrant his making a tour of inspection to the upper province. He travelled by quick sleigh most of the way, reaching Prescott by 21 February 1813. Here he placed Major "Red George" Macdonell of the 8th King's Regiment and Glengarry Light Infantry in command of the fort. Immediately Macdonell pressed on the Commander of the Forces a proposal to relieve the pressure at Cornwall. What Macdonell had in mind was a surprise attack on Ogdensburg, the American town across from Prescott that had been the source of numerous raids on Canadian towns and shipping.[40] Prevost gave conditional permission to Macdonell to make a demonstration on the ice to divert attention at Ogdensburg while the Commander of the Forces and his party sped away towards Brockville. Macdonell followed up his demonstration by such a sudden and devastating attack on the fort itself that Ogdensburg was eliminated as a source of future trouble.[41] The raid on Ogdensburg freed Cornwall from the threat of imminent attack, for the American militiamen assembling at Salmon River made no attempt at counterattack against Cornwall that spring. For some

Cornwall soldiers the action at Ogdensburg had more permanent effects. Ensign Philip Empey of the flank company of the 1st Stormont Regiment came home without a leg.[42] Thirty-one others suffered various wounds. But the town of Cornwall returned to its normal war-time establishment by May of 1813 when the garrison was reduced to a strength of 132 men.[43]

So secure was the Eastern District, it was thought, that John Strachan decided it was safer to send his wife, who was six months pregnant, to Cornwall for her confinement rather than to have her remain in York over that winter. He sent her off in a batteau with the other children and servants under the care of her brother. They reached Cornwall safely only to find that the town was experiencing fresh war alarums. The activity of Major-General Wade Hampton and his American troops near Chateauguay, New York, made the British military command at Kingston apprehensive for Cornwall's security.[44] But the town saw nothing of Hampton's troops for they moved down the Chateauguay River to do battle with the forces under Lieutenant-Colonel Charles de Salaberry. Instead, Cornwall received a visit from the American army that was assembling at Grenadier Island opposite Kingston under Major-General James Wilkinson.[45] By the 6 November, Wilkinson made up his mind for a descent on Montreal by way of Cornwall, "if not prevented," as he said, "by some act of God."[46] And indeed, so impressive was Wilkinson's flotilla of 8,000 men in "180 immense boats, besides schooners with provisions," that one commissary agent at Kingston, the former Cornwall schoolboy, Thomas Ridout, exclaimed, "Unless this armament is destroyed, Montreal will go."[47]

By 8 November 1813 the American force reached Iroquois. Here Wilkinson called a war council at which it was decided that Brigadier-General Jacob Brown should advance on the Canadian side by land to Cornwall in order to clear the way and secure the government stores at that town. Brown's brigade of 1,200 men, including detachments of artillery and cavalry, pushed on in advance of the main American army under Wilkinson.

At the same time a large convoy of supplies from Montreal had got as far as Rapide Plat beyond the Long Sault under escort of a small number of regulars and a unit of the Glengarry militia. In the face of the American invading force, the commanding officer at Prescott sent word to the convoy escort to land part of the goods and transport it to Prescott by wagon, the remainder of the cargo to be returned by boat to Cornwall to avoid capture by the American force. The convoy of supplies got back to Cornwall just a hair's breadth before the American troops under Brown arrived. All the wagons that could be secured from the country-side, some 150 of them, were pressed into use to convey the stores from Cornwall out by the rear road to St. Andrews and from thence to Coteau du Lac.[48]

While the men of Cornwall and its surrounding country were quickly removing the King's stores so that they would not fall into enemy hands, militia intelligence officers were keeping keen eyes on the approaching American army. Overhead, leaden skies threatened icy sleet on that cold morning of 11 November 1813 as one British officer at Cornwall reported, "Enemy cavalry are entering the town, but in what force I am unable to tell."[49] Donald McKay began a report to Captain William Cochrane of the Royal Marines that same morning. "Mr. Koughnettes (sic) and myself have arrived at Cornwall... and have been...some distance above Cornwall and by all our endeavours cannot ascertain the strength of the enemy. At this moment they have made their appearance at Cornwall with their advance guard of horse... their boats have not yet passed Cornwall, but most probably will...tonight." Later that same day, McKay continued his report. "The enemy's force (is) near Cornwall, some say two thousand infantry and cavalry...many of their boats are two miles from Cornwall near the Widow Bernard's (Barnhart's) house... The enemy did not enter Cornwall until towards the morning; only a few of their cavalry patrolling within a quarter of a mile of it."[50]

Brown's army took possession of Barnhart's Island and spread out in Lots 17, 18 and 19 where the officers occupied the houses, including that of Captain Joseph Anderson. Their men bivouacked in the surrounding fields, awaiting news of the battle at Crysler's Farm from where the booming of cannon could be heard. The American soldiers helped themselves to whatever provisions they found in the farmhouses and barns. They then tore down all the fences to use as wood for their campfires and burned the bridge near Anderson's home. Most of the men huddled close to the campfires, hoping that the sleet and rain of the previous night would hold off. Others went into town to confiscate the King's stores only to discover that the cupboard was bare. That night the whole of Wilkinson's flotilla arrived off Barnhart's Island, bringing news of their defeat at Crysler's Farm. Anxious eyes watched the arrival of the American force. The Stormont and part of the Glengarry militia were posted in the rear concessions keeping a sharp lookout. Early next morning, 12 November, they saw the American troops re-embark and head for Salmon River, taking with them all the goods they had plundered from Cornwall merchants.[51] When Wilkinson learned that he would get no support from Major-General Wade Hampton, he gave up all idea of an advance on Montreal.[52]

Once more the people of Cornwall breathed more easily as they watched the enormous American flotilla pass by their town and head for home waters. Those who scurried away from their homes at the approach of the enemy troops now hurried back to inspect their losses. Captain Anderson's wife discovered that her device of burying her stock of winter preserves in one of the garden beds had been of no use. A sentry had prodded the ground with his iron ramrod and discovered it. Her small stock of plate and jewellery had been more successfully concealed.[53]

Authorities in England were glad to hear of the success at Crysler's Farm over the American force. From Downing Street came praise for the action, tinged with a barb for Sir George Prevost, the Commander of the Forces. "The result has been such as the uniform good Conduct of the Troops under your Command would have led me to anticipate," wrote Lord Bathurst, the Secretary of State for War. "I will, however, be very prejudiced to your future operations if Gen. Wilkinson has been allowed to establish himself at Cornwall."[54] Wilkinson did not make a descent on Cornwall, but by moving into winter quarters just across the river at French Mills on the Salmon River, he was still too close for comfort. Cornwall's first reinforcements arrived within a week of the battle of Crysler's Farm — four companies of the Canadian Fencibles whose job was "to protect communications between River Raisin and Long Sault."[55] Early in January of 1814 Major General de Rottenburg received intelligence that 1,000 men were being sent to reinforce the American army at Salmon River.[56] The British military command feared that this movement of American troops nearer Cornwall meant a renewed attempt to break communications between the upper and lower provinces. Lieutenant General Gordon Drummond ordered "the utmost vigilance to be preserved at Cornwall... against an attack by the enemy."[57] Cornwall thus became a hub of military activity with regular troops moving in to take up garrison duty there. By 1 February 1814 barracks were hastily fitted up for 481 Royal Marines, thirty-one Royal Artillerymen and six Provincial Dragoons.[58] This was in addition to the 181 Canadian Fencibles already stationed there along with the flank companies of the 1st Stormont Militia. A few days later Drummond reported to Prevost that the American plan to have troops "cross over at or above Cornwall to intercept some of the convoys of Stores and render the guns useless...it would appear, has been given up for the present."[59] With this news, the regulars and militiamen garrisoning Cornwall relaxed a bit. Then, when word reached them that General Wilkinson had divided his army, part of it moving off towards Niagara early in

February and the remainder withdrawing to Plattsburg,[60] the Cornwall garrison levelled off to about 500 men and remained about that strength throughout 1814.[61]

This enlarged garrison at Cornwall and the continual movement of troops through the town to posts in the upper province meant that a much larger commissariat and barrack establishment had to be located in the town. Assistant Commissary-General Thomas Ridout was moved there from Kingston in January of 1814. In early February he exclaimed to his father, "Only think of 1700 rations a day and no one but myself and a storekeeper (to issue them)." Since 24 January his disbursements had reached £4,000, much of it going to American beef and flour contractors and to secret service agents.[62] The Commissariat at Cornwall had given up trying to pry grain out of the local farmers. So exorbitant had prices become in the Eastern and Johnstown Districts — $17.50 a barrel for flour,[63] for instance — that the Commander of the Forces put the two districts under martial law in November of 1813.[64] This permitted commissary agents to set their own prices and make their own demands. One commissary agent, Edward Doyle, lost no time in sending parties out to various farms to take the grain for threshing. One of the farmers thus divested of his grain supply was Jacob Empey who brought charges against the commissary and won a substantial settlement.[65] The unpleasantness of this arbitrary method of seizing grain eventually forced the commissariat into clandestine deals with American beef and flour suppliers. Though prices continued high, the supply was fairly certain.

Indeed, the question of supplies was foremost on many minds. Cornwall merchants were still incensed over the seizure of their merchandise by the American troops the previous fall. One of the top Canadian secret agents who acted as an officer of the Quarter Master General's Department in Cornwall, Captain Reuben Sherwood, discovered that this stolen merchandise was to be auctioned off at a public sale in the small American town of Hamilton near the Salmon River. Sherwood, whose own store had been despoiled of some £500 worth of merchandise, suggested the idea of "plundering (the merchandise) back again."[66] No sooner was the proposal made than it was acted upon. On the night of 6 February 1814 some twenty Royal Marines joined ten Stormont Militiamen under Captain Sherwood for a swift trip over the ice on the St. Lawrence River to the Salmon River. Bundled up in warm sleighs drawn by horses, they reached Hamilton safely, seized the goods, packed them up in the sleighs and made off back across the ice. According to Deputy-Commissary Thomas Ridout at Cornwall, "The inhabitants (of Hamilton) made no opposition; indeed, they rather enjoyed the joke at the expense of the Yankee officers who were charged with the sale of the stolen goods."[67] This was the last expedition of a warlike nature into enemy territory from Cornwall. For the rest of 1814 what expeditions there were to the Salmon River were all in the interests of commissariat. Thomas Ridout frankly and boastfully admitted, "We drive a pretty good trade with the Yankees from Salmon River,"[68] he being "well supplied with specie" from the military chest for that purpose.[69] Indeed, with large contingents of soldiers from the 70th, 81st, 89th, 90th 103rd and 104th Regiments stationed in the town at various times during 1814, all requiring a plenteous supply of food, forage and drink, Deputy Commissary Ridout was often hard put to find the wherewithal to cope with all of them. One of his smuggling deals he described to his father. "I have contracted with a Yankee magistrate to furnish this post (Cornwall) with fresh beef," he wrote. "A Major came with him to make the agreement but as he was foreman of the Grand Jury at the Court in which the Government prosecute (those engaged in) Smuggling, he turned his back and would not see the paper signed."[70] By September of 1814 Cornwall found itself temporarily the headquarters for General James Kempt who arrived with 4,000 British troops.[71] These included the 70th Regiment which marched into town with a brigade of flying Artillery consisting of "brass six-pounders, 180 horses, 120 Artillerymen and eighty drivers." Ridout had to find two tons of hay and fifty bushels of oats daily for this brigade. He was able to purchase "sixty tons of hay from the Yankees in batteaux but am afraid of great difficulty in December."[72]

This movement of troops in and out of Cornwall not only affected the commercial activity in the town. When the 81st Regiment arrived September of 1814 en route to a post in the upper province, a young officer of the regiment, James Pringle,[73] was invited by Captain Joseph Anderson to breakfast and then for a fishing trip. On meeting Anne Anderson, the eldest daughter of Captain Anderson, Pringle was beguiled at once when the young lady "kindly asked me to take an apple."[74] Before the month was out they were married "at Cornwall Church by Mr. Baldwin"[75] and the young bride went off with her soldier husband to Kingston. In the spring of 1815, when the treaty of peace was signed, the newly-weds were on their way to Spain with the regiment.

Officers like James Pringle and Dr. William 'Tiger' Dunlop of the 89th Regiment found Cornwall an agreeable if "insignificant" village in which to be quartered.[76] Indeed, Pringle found it far preferable to Kingston which "lies in a swamp," he exclaimed, and "is a very shabby-looking (town whose) people are a race of extortioners."[77] The town of York did not receive unqualified praise either. George Ridout referred to York as "this miserable hole"[78] while most travellers passing through Cornwall spoke of the town's neatness and its "very agreeable society, composed principally of old officers of the revolutionary war."[79] Dr. William Dunlop found that he was soon at home "with the highest circles (in Cornwall), "asserting with tongue in cheek that even in a town as small as Cornwall where he had counted but twenty houses in 1814 there was a highest circle, "for these exist in all societies, and the smaller the society, the more distinctly is the circle defined." Thus the officers of the garrison "walked into (Cornwall) houses as if they had been our own and no apology was offered...The old gentlemen when in town came to Our Mess (and) regaled us with toughish yarns of their military doings during the revolutionary war."[80] It is not surprising, then, that some of the officers and men returned to the little town when the war ended, their discharges or half-pay status allowing them to take up civilian life. By 1838 some twenty-one privates and non-commissioned officers of regular regiments were living in the town.[81] Young Lieutenant James Pringle sold his commission as soon as the Napoleonic Wars ended and retraced his steps back to the banks of the St. Lawrence with his Cornwall bride, eventually becoming Clerk of the Eastern District Court and Town Treasurer.[82]

The war had kept the small town from falling into complete insignificance, just as Strachan's School had kept Cornwall on the map for the previous eight years. During the war years it was Cornwall's location as a relay post for stores, provisions and reinforcements that had made it a possible target for American attack. In spite of several threats of invasion, the town was briefly occupied only once by American troops. Thereafter, Cornwall remained a garrison town with local and regular troops in barracks and many others passing through, all consuming far more than the town and its surrounding countryside could provide. Farmers and merchants profited from the military chest though some farmers had to be coerced into providing grain at a reasonable price. The war brought its anxious moments to the people of Cornwall. It also brought a wartime excitement and social conviviality that most Cornwall people found agreeable. Thus when the announcement of the peace treaty was received, it was almost with an air of regret that Assistant Commissary General Thomas Ridout closed out his accounts and wrote to his father at York, "All stores are stopped at Montreal and nothing but provisions will now be sent up."[83]

NOTES

1. E.A. Cruikshank, "A Memoir of Lt.-Col. John Macdonell, of Glengarry House", in *OHSPR*, 1925, xxii, 41; William Boss, *The Stormont, Dundas and Glengarry Highlanders*, 2.

2. Boss, *Stormont, Dundas and Glengarry Highlanders*, 3-4.

3. C. Hume Wilkins, "Stormont, Dundas, Glengarry", a paper presented to the Stormont, Dundas and Glengarry Historical Society, 17 Jan. 1972, 3-4.

4. Duc de la Rochefoucauld-Liancourt, *Travels in Canada*, 41.

5. Boss, *Stormont, Dundas and Glengarry Highlanders*, 7.

6. Stormont Militia Returns, 24 July 1806 (RG4/B29/I).

7. Cruikshank, "Memoir of Lt.-Col. John Macdonell," 43-44; for a list of officers, see J.F. Pringle, Lunenburgh, or the old Eastern District, appendix E, 412-413; Pringle gives 1796 as the date of the unit's formation; William Boss, *Stormont, Dundas and Glengarry Highlanders*, 5-6, gives 1794.

8. See Mackey Hitsman, *The Incredible War of 1812*, 52.

9. Cartwright to Prevost, 5 July 1812 (RG8/C676/124).

10. McLean to Maj.-Gen. Shaw, 5 June 1813, in Pringle, 419.

11. Lt.-Col. Edward Baynes to Lt.-Col. R. Lethbridge, 7 July 1812 (RG8/0688A/103).

12. Prevost to Brock, 19 Oct. 1812 (RG8/C681/323 and RG8/C1707/110); Lethbridge to Brock, 10 Aug. 1812 (RG8/C688A/171).

13. See John Young Cozens' deposition relative to barracks in the Court House and jail, 20 Mar. 1815 (RG8/C88/24-25); Jospeh Anderson's statement, 11 Aug. 1815 (RG8/C89/187); for St. John's Church, see RG8/C556/102.

14. Lt.-Col. Ralph Bruyeres to Prevost, 14 Jan. 1813 (RG8/C387/6); see also, Paul Fortier, "Accommodation for Militiamen in the Eastern and Johnstown Districts of Upper Canada during the War of 1812", Upper Canada Village, 1977, 2.

15. Lethbridge to Brock, 10 Aug. 1812 (RG8/C688A/169).

16. Bruyeres to Prevost, 14 Jan. 1813 (RG8/C387/6).

17. Report on the preparations for defence and reinforcements on the St. Lawrence and the River Raisin, 31 Dec. 1814 (RG8/C388/252).

18. Bruyeres to Prevost, 14 Jan. 1813 (RG8/C387/6).

19. *Ibid.*

20. Maj.-Gen. Sir Thomas Beckwith to Maj. F.L. Coore, 21 Oct. 1814 (RG8/C686/82).

21. See list of officers of this unit in the *Quebec Almanac*, 1813, cited in J.A. Macdonell, *Sketches, Glengarry in Canada*, 185.

22. General Orders, 27 Nov. 1812 (RG8/C1169/82-83); see also, Hitsman, *The Incredible War of 1812*, 99.

23. Hitsman, *The Incredible War of 1812*, 54.

24. Deposition of Joseph Spencer of French Mills, New York, 17 Dec. 1812 (RG8/C677/272); Major W. Tanner of Constable, New York, to McLean, 17 Dec. 1812 (*ibid.*, 271-72).

25. General Orders, 27 Nov. 1812 (RG8/C1169/82-83).

26. *Ibid.*

27. See deposition of Joseph Spencer, 17 Dec. 1812, in which he asked $661.55 compensation for pillaged goods (RG8/C677/272); see also Lt.-Col. Neil McLean to Lt.-Col. Thomas Pearson, (RG8/C677/268); Major W. Tanner to McLean, 17 Dec. 1812 (RG8/C677/271-72).

28. Edward Doyle to Lt.-Col. Neil McLean, 29 Nov. 1812 (RG8/C677/224).

29. Lt.-Col. T. Pearson to Col. Edward Baynes, 2 Dec. 1812 (RG8/C677/226-28).

30. Edward Doyle to McLean, 29 Nov. 1812 (RG8/C677/224).

31. McNeil to De Rottenburg, 7 Feb. 1813 (RG8/C678/75-76).

32. *Ibid.*

33. Maj.-Gen. de Rottenburg to Col. Edward Baynes, 9 Feb. 1813 (RG8/C678/84).

34. Bruyeres to Prevost, 14 Jan. 1813 (RG8/C387/6).

35. *Ibid.*

36. Pringle, 75.

37. C.R. Redmond, Inspector of Hospitals, to Noah Freer, 22 Jan. 1813 (RG8/C290/5 and RG8/C1220/175); for Lt.-Col. Neil McLean's premises used as a hospital, see John Empey and Philip P. Empey's statement, 8 June 1815 (RG8/C89/25).

38. RG8/C554/148 and RG8/C701/90, 99; for the blacksmith shop, see, John Anderson's letter, 14 Sept. 1815 (RG8/C90/30); see also, RG8/C89/25.

39. See RG8/C701/104 and RG8/C557/25.

40. Hitsman, *The Incredible War of 1812*, 117-18; Boss, *The Stormont, Dundas and Glengarry Highlanders*, 14.

41. For Maj. George Macdonell's role in raising the Glengarry Fencibles and in the Ogdensburg raid see, Macdonell, *Sketches, Glengarry*, 178-180, 215-16.

42. Ensign P. Empey's petition, 8 Mar. 1813 (RG8/C515/24 and RG8/C1220/249); Boss, *The Stormont, Dundas and Glengarry Highlanders*, 17.

43. Monthly returns of Troops...under the command of Col. Thomas Pearson, 26 May 1813 (RG8/C688E/77).

44. Pearson to Baynes, 7 Oct. 1813 (RG8/C680/227).

45. Thomas Ridout to his father, 1 Nov. 1813 (Edgar, *Ridout Letters*, 243).

46. Wilkinson to Maj.-Gen. Wade Hampton, 6 Nov. 1813 (*ibid.*, 249).

47. Thomas Ridout to his father, 9 Nov. 1813 (*ibid.*, 250); Hitsman, *The Incredible War of 1812*, 167, gives the figure of the American army as 8,000.

48. James Croil, *Dundas, or a Sketch of Canadian History*, 79-81; James Smart, "St. Lawrence Projects: Events in Military History 1760 to 1814", Upper Canada Village, 19-20; Elizabeth Hoople, *The Hooples of Hoople's Creek*, 54-55.

49. Pearson to Bussel, 11 Nov. 1813 (RG8/C681/31); Pringle, 77, incorrectly gives 12 November as date of Brown's occupation of Cornwall.

50. Donald McKay to Capt. William Cochrane, 11 Nov. 1813, cited in E.A. Cruikshank, *Record of the Services of the Canadian Regiments in the War of 1812*, 93-94.

51. Thomas Ridout to his father, 20 Nov. 1813 and 9 Feb. 1814 (Edgar, *Ridout Letters*, 255-256 and 274-75); see also, Dr. William Dunlop, *Recollections of the American War*, 41-42.

52. Hampton to Wilkinson, 8 Nov. 1813 (Edgar, Ridout Letters, 250).

53. RG8/C681/51-53; and see, Pringle, 77.

54. Bathurst to Prevost, 27 Dec. 1813 (RG8/C681/83).

55. General Orders, 17 Nov. 1813 (RG8/C1171/102).

56. De Rottenburg to _____, 7 Jan. 1814 (RG8/C682/14).

57. Drummond to Prevost, 27 Jan. 1814 (RG8/C682/57).

58. Weekly distribution of British troops in Upper Canada, 1 Feb. 1814 (RG8/C1709/35-36).

59. Drummond to Prevost, 5 Feb. 1814 (RG8/C682/93).

60. Thomas Ridout to his father, 9 Feb. 1814 (Edgar, *Ridout Letters*, 274); Hitsman, *The Incredible War of 1812*, 181.

61. General Orders, Aug. 1814 (RG8/C1707/109).

62. Ridout to his father, 9 Feb. 1814 (Edgar, *Ridout Letters*, 274).

63. Same to same, 15 May 1814 (*ibid.* 281).

64. Archibald McDonell to Lt.-Col. Foster, 1 Aug. 1815 (RG8/C621/57); J.G. Harkness, *History of Stormont, Dundas and Glengarry*, 136; Hitsman, *The Incredible War of 1812*, 180.

65. Empey vs. Doyle, 30 June 1814 (RG8/C688D/55); Doyle to Drummond, 30 June 1814 (*ibid.*, 54).

66. Edgar, *Ridout Letters*, 274; for instances of stolen merchandise see Capt. R. Sherwood to Lt.-Col. Thomas Pearson, 16 Nov. 1813 (RG8/C681/51); M. Gillison to Pearson, 17 Nov. 1813, (*ibid.*, 52-53).

67. Ridout to his father, 9 Feb. 1814 (*ibid.*, 275). This is likely the same exploit described by Pringle, 78, and repeated by Boss in his *The Stormont, Dundas and Glengarry Highlanders*, 23, though the details are somewhat different. Ridout's account is likely the more accurate, being written a few days after the incident occurred. See also Barrack Master Benj. Comins to Noah Freer, 10 June 1814 (RG8/C553/129) and Noah Freer to Maj.-Gen. de Rottenburg, 24 Mar. 1814 (RG8/C1224/64).

68. Ridout to his father, 11 April 1814 (Edgar, *Ridout Letters*, 279).

69. Same to same, 15 May 1814 (*ibid.*, 281).

70. Same to same, 19 June 1814 (*ibid.*, 282); for a description of a similar transaction see, Dunlop, *Recollections of the American War of 1812*, 32-35.

71. Ridout to his father, 25 Aug. and 1 Sept. 1814 (Edgar, *Ridout Letters*, 318).

72. Same to same, 1 Sept. 1814 (*ibid.*, 318).

73. For identification of Pringle, see his application for the post of Clerk of the Eastern District Court, 1819 (State Papers, Upper Canada, 1791-1841, RG1/E3/70/43-66).

74. Pringle Diary, 22 Sept. 1814 (MG24/I29/44).

75. *Ibid.*, 45.

76. Dunlop, *Recollections*, 30.

77. Pringle Diary, MG24/I29/48.

78. George Ridout to Thomas Ridout, York, 19 Oct. 1811 (Edgar, *Ridout Letters*, 108).

79. Dunlop, *Recollections*, 30-31.

80. *Ibid.*

81. Returns of commuted Pensioners in the Eastern District, 16 Oct. 1838, in Pringle Papers, (MG24/I29/191-93).

82. See Pringle's application for office, 1819 (State Papers, Upper Canada, 1791-1841, RG1/E3/70/43-66, Harkness, 161, 415.

83. Thomas Ridout to his father, 27 Feb. 1815 (Edgar, *Ridout Papers*, 336).

Chapter VI
Cornwall Politics and Canal Conflicts

The end of the war and the removal of the garrison threw Cornwall back on its own economic and social resources, meagre as these were. A few external sources of revenue remained. Old officers of the American revolutionary war still received half-pay from the British Crown. Discharged regular soldiers got their Chelsea pensions. A few townsmen had access to local government jobs, and clergymen and schoolmasters could count on some financial aid from the government or the Society for the Propagation of the Gospel. Apart from these sources, however, the people of the town had to rely on themselves. Yet, whatever economic dislocations arose at the end of the war, Cornwall men and women did not, like their neighbours in Glengarry, succumb to the lures of the newly-arrived Scot, Robert Gourlay, who urged them to list their grievances and formulate their thoughts about the factors that might be holding their town back in terms of economic progress.

Glengarry spokesmen were candid in their report to Gourlay. What the township lacked, they said, was capitalists — men with money and willing to put it to use improving the area.[1] Cornwall people and, on the whole, those of Stormont and Dundas would have nothing to do with Gourlay's questionnaires. They accepted their former townsman's judgment on him. John Strachan at York thundered that Gourlay was a troublemaker whose questionnaires were based on "principles inimical to the peace and quiet which the inhabitants of this province so happily enjoy."[2]

Undaunted by Strachan's blast, Gourlay set out for the Eastern District in the spring of 1818. In Glengarry he was received with some interest and held meetings there for four days. Then, as he neared Cornwall, he learned that his pamphlets had been publicly burned and threats against him were being bandied about. Thus his stay in the town was brief. By the time he reached Johnstown near Prescott, he was arrested and eventually brought before the same man who had listened to somewhat similar charges against Patrick McNiff almost thirty-two years before in Cornwall. William Dummer Powell, now

Chief Justice of Upper Canada, banished Gourlay and his question-naires from the country. Thus Cornwall and Stormont were not included in Gourlay's useful statistical analysis of 1818. The best Gourlay could do was to give an estimate of the town and county's population as 2,500.[3]

Gourlay had his own way of hitting back. "The parson of York," he wrote scathingly, "had for a series of years kept a school in the village of Cornwall; and here he whipped a very considerable portion of youths into due submission...before he was installed in the pulpit and Executive Council... Magistrates, members of parliament, and militia officers, besides the attorney-general and the solicitor-general, had sprung up in the school of Cornwall and were all zealots in the cause of their master."[4] That the master could evoke such loyalty in his students says something for the master and his school. Later critics of the ruling government party adopted Gourlay's pin-pointing of Strachan's school at Cornwall as the cradle of the "Family Compact."[5] Whatever claims Strachan's school had with regard to peopling the province with staunch tories, Cornwall and Stormont for two decades after the war of 1812-14 remained almost solidly tory.

Two Loyalist families held sway politically — the Vankoughnets and the McLeans. The Vankoughnets were not original settlers, but they had impeccable Loyalist credentials as the family of a soldier of the King's Royal Regiment of New York. The McLeans straddled the other Loyalist regiment — the 84th Royal Highland Emigrants. By 1832 Michael Vankoughnet was the single largest landowner in Corn-wall. His son, Philip, took the Stormont seat in the provincial election of 1816 and held it, except for two years, until 1834. When Stormont became a two-member riding in 1820, Vankoughnet's colleague at the provincial Assembly was the tory Presbyterian from Cornwall, Archibald McLean. McLean was a son of Lt.-Col. Neil McLean, the former lieutenant of the 84th Royal Highland Emigrants who had headed the local militia effort during the 1812-14 war and was now sheriff. Reformers did not begin to make a dent in the tory armour until 1828 with the election of Dr. Ambrose Blacklock of St. Andrew's, a retired naval surgeon.[6]

The changes in the town of Cornwall in these post-war years from 1816 to 1840 were not so much in terms of size of population or economic expansion, but a gradual growth of municipal institutions and improvement in transportation and communications. The only significant immediate post-war immigration to the town was in the fall of 1815 when some 300 emigrants from Scotland arrived suddenly and unexpectedly. Unprepared to handle such a number of newcomers, the immigration agent reported that at Cornwall "the conditions are...

poor...there were no adequate accommodations as the Barracks and hired Buildings had been given up and were in a bad condition."[7] This lack of ready accommodations, together with the lack of free or cheap land in the Cornwall area, may explain why Cornwall and other areas in the Eastern District did not fall heir to more of the emigrants who swept into Canada at the close of the Napoleonic wars, as many as 12,000 a year by 1819 and 1820.[8]

In the immediate post-war years the townsmen applied to government for funds to repair their court house and jail so that these buildings could be once more used for their intended purposes.[9] Within ten years the renovated court house burned down and makeshift accommodations had to be found for the court sittings and jail in various town buildings. It was not until 1831 that the Court of General Quarter Sessions authorized £4,500 towards the construction of a new court house and jail on the north side of Water Street which was completed in 1833.

Cornwall had its "Gallows Hill" on the north side of Fifth Street where public hangings drew their crowds. The quadruple hanging in August of 1821 of four young men convicted of killing a storekeeper brought a multitude of onlookers who were not disappointed. One of the convicted men named McGarry, before he mounted to the scaffold, kicked off his boots declaring he was making a liar of his mother who had told him he would die with his boots on.[10] Public floggings continued as late as 1832 when two young thieves were sentenced to receive thirty-nine lashes each and to be imprisoned for fourteen days. The flogging took place at the corner of Pitt and Fourth Streets, its public nature designed both as an additional punishment to the convicted men and as a deterrent to would-be wrongdoers.

Attempts to establish a market, to hold semi-annual fairs,[11] and to regulate the weekly markets met with indifferent success. Weekly markets had been held in Cornwall as early as 1794, but they had tended to be loosely-structured affairs.[12] Then, in 1818, the town received a grant of £50 from the provincial government to establish a permanent market house. It was two years before the market house was opened for business on the north side of Water Street. The magistrates at Quarter Sessions drew up elaborate regulations for this market. Fresh meat, vegetables, hay, and grain had to be exhibited for sale at the market for three hours on Tuesdays and Saturdays. Fines were imposed for trying to sell these products elsewhere without first trying to sell them at the market. Whether it was the location of the market, the amount of rent demanded for market space, or the harassing regulations, the market house was used only once for displaying goods. In 1838 efforts were made to repair the unused market house and to re-establish a market on Water Street, but it was not until 1843 that another market house was built, this one located on the south side of Fourth Street. Within two years, market rents were wiped out in an effort to attract more business to the market place.[13]

Cornwall had had postal arrangements of a sort since its founding. At first as batteaux plied back and forth to the various Loyalist settlements, letters were sent by private hands. The first official post-carrier was Jacques Morriseau. He was paid by government to carry the mail three times during the winter from Montreal to Kingston. Travelling on snowshoes, he munched sea biscuit and fat pork while sitting on a snow bank and afterwards "would puff away dull care in clouds of smoke curling from his old clay pipe, the stem of which was just long enough to keep the burning punk with which he lit it about two inches from his nose." From Lachine to Cornwall the settlers were so scattered that he was obliged to sleep out of doors three nights, resting on green boughs with a blanket to cover him. By the time he reached Postmaster Samuel Anderson's home, he was glad enough to spend the fourth night under a warm roof.[14]

In May 1789 a public postal service was established, and Captain Samuel Anderson, as Postmaster, operated out of the King's Stores located below Water Street just to the west of Pitt Street. Every four weeks letters and parcels were conveyed to Cornwall and other settlements along the St. Lawrence from Montreal to Kingston.[15] Captain Anderson, who was also chief magistrate of the town, continued as Postmaster until 1803 when a young barrister, Walter Butler Wilkinson, took over the post briefly. Wilkinson was the eldest son of a former officer of the King's Royal Regiment of New York and a namesake of the son of the founder of Butler's Rangers. Married to a daughter of the Reverend John Bethune and called to the Bar in 1801, young Wilkinson probably operated the post office out of the family store on the south side of Second Street at the corner of Sydney Street. Just four years after taking over from Anderson, young Wilkinson died suddenly.[16] His work as postmaster was carried on by the man who would remain on the job for the next half century — Guy Carleton Wood. Named in honour of Lord Dorchester and son of a retired surgeon of the 1st Dragoon Guards, the new Postmaster set up an office in his store at the corner of First and Sydney Streets.[17]

The duties of postmaster were not too onerous, especially in the winter when the courier passed through Cornwall only once every fortnight, enroute to Kingston and back to Montreal. A more systematic method of conveying mail was started in 1812 when an enterprising American, Barnabas Dickinson of Massachusetts, secured a government contract to deliver mail westward from Montreal to Kingston by boat and stage. This system became so regularized by 1819 that Upper Canadian mail from Kingston passed through Cornwall and reached the metropolis of Montreal twice a week on Wednesdays and Saturdays and left Montreal for the west on Mondays and Thursdays. Thus stage coach inns came into their own. Over the years the busiest spot in Cornwall was the stage coach stop at Chesley's Inn on the north side of Second Street near the Church of England rectory. Built in 1814, this inn soon out-distanced the old St. Patrick's and St. Andrew's "log hotel" kept by Mrs. Peggy Bruce.[18] But Chesley's Inn lost some of its importance when the Cornwall Canal was completed, allowing mail and passengers to sail past the town without a nod. Winter mail still came by stage, but by the mid-1850s when rail service was inaugurated, the familiar stage post gave way to railway stations.

Means of transportation grew with the city. From the time when the first township road wound through the various Royal Townships in the late 1780s,[19] roads, ferries, bridges and a canal eventually smoothed out travelling to and from Cornwall. As early as July 1799 David McCuen was authorized by government to keep a boat or batteau as a ferry between Cornwall and St. Regis. Then in 1806 Richard McBean took over the ferry from the town to St. Regis. The small creek on Captain Jeremiah French's property to the west of the town was bridged in 1810 only to be burnt by American troops in 1813, and restored in 1814 by the government.

After the war of 1812-1814 some attention was given to the streets of Cornwall. In 1816, £20 was voted by the Court of General Sessions for road repairs, but it was not until 1835 that the first sidewalks, four feet wide, were laid along Second Street from Pitt to Augustus Street. These were probably built with flagstones in imitation of the sidewalk which Guy Carleton Wood had had constructed in front of his home on First Street. Plank sidewalks were put down in 1838 on Pitt Street north of Second Street and on the south side of Second Street from York to the west of the town. Efforts to raise a loan for a macadamized road from Cornwall to Roxborough partly succeeded in 1853 when a sum of £3000 was authorized for a stretch from Pitt Street to Eamer's Corners. Then in 1858 a gravel sidewalk was made on the east side of Pitt Street as far as the Grand Trunk Railway station. The town came into its own with regard to local transportation when Thomas Murphy began the first cab service in town in 1873.

Important as these means of land transportation were, they were dwarfed by the developments in river transport until it gave way to the age of steel. By the 1820s Cornwall, with its produce of potash, timber, and some excess wheat and flour, was looking for an easy outlet to its natural market — Montreal. Thus, when the merchants of Montreal began to organize meetings in the early 1820s to promote the idea of a political and economic union of Upper and Lower Canada, Cornwall was one of their stomping grounds. Its role as a distribution centre of goods had changed over the years. As the forest was felled to make way for crops and homes, Cornwall had turned to the timber trade and potash manufacture. Thus, it was not only a distribution centre of goods coming into the district, but also of staples leaving the district for the larger market at Montreal. By the time of the war of 1812-14, wheat and flour were beginning to surpass timber as the major produce of the area, and the people of Cornwall opted for union in the early 1820s, expecting that a political merger of the two provinces would give them a greater voice in such matters as transportation improvements. They sought the pages of the Montreal *Herald* in 1822 to publicize their views. "The greatest difficulties now exist," Cornwall businessmen declared on 22 December 1822 "regarding the transportation of produce from the interior parts of this district to market, there being no direct land communication with Montreal, this being the consequence of the interested conduct of those persons holding seigniories near the line, and of the inattention of the Legislature of the Lower Province to the internal improvement of this portion of Canada, notwithstanding repeated applications have been made to the House of Assembly of Lower Canada, to open the different communications."[20]

With the defeat of the union proposal in 1822 and the construction of the Erie Canal, Montreal merchants again sought support from the towns along the river from Quebec to Cornwall to pressure the government at Quebec City to improve the St. Lawrence route. These efforts were formalized in the St. Lawrence Association of 1824-25, which had a branch at Cornwall. Out of these joint manoeuvres with a parent organization at Montreal, the Cornwall men of the future secured their first regular river communication in the early 1820s when a horseboat plied between Cornwall and Coteau-du-Lac, the horses steadily treading the wooden paddle wheels that propelled the boat back and forth. Within a few years a steamboat, the *Neptune*, took over this route, with mail, freight and passenger connections between Cornwall and a steamboat on Lake St. Louis that ran from the Cascades to Beauharnois and then to Lachine for a final connection by stagecoach for Montreal. Thus, by the 1820s, Cornwall and the surrounding Loyalist townships were coming out of their relative isolation and within the orbit of regular stagecoach and steamer connections with the metropolis of Montreal.

The great leap forward in river transportation came in the 1830s when work began on the Cornwall Canal that was to give shipping a way around the treacherous Long Sault Rapids. Convinced that any improvement in the mode of water transportation would be good for the town, Cornwall merchants like Philip Vankoughnet pressed the project of a canal on the government. Surveys began in the late 1820s after the Lachine Canal was finished and the Welland Canal was well underway. Chief Justice John Beverley Robinson, the orphan boy who had helped John Strachan repair his log hut for a school house in Cornwall, returned to the town in August of 1834 to do the honours at the turning of the first sod. Even more impressive was the appearance of the lieutenant governor of the province, Sir John Colborne, who journeyed to Cornwall to participate in the ceremonies which ended at Chesley's Inn where speeches, toasts, and conviviality reigned. Outside, the town was brilliantly illuminated and burning faggots added to the festivities. Watching these developments with interest and pride was one of the town's founders, Captain Samuel Anderson, who died in 1836 at the age of 101.[21]

The start of work on the Cornwall Canal went hand in hand with the incorporation of the town in 1834. As soon as the number of people living within the town boundaries reached 1,000, application was made to the provincial government to incorporate the town and thus bring taxation and other municipal matters directly under the control of elected townsmen. Unlike the modern city administration, Cornwall's first corporate existence was managed by a Board of Police, formed from the four men who were elected for the two wards into which the town was divided. A fifth member of the Police Board was chosen as chairman from among the town's population at large by these four elected members.

The first municipal elections in the spring of 1834 brought few surprises. Philip Vankoughnet was returned for the first ward that comprised all the town east of Pitt Street. His running mate was Martin Carman. Two members of the popular Chesley family, Peter and John, easily swept the second ward that included all the town west of Pitt Street. Their choice for president of the Board of Police was Archibald McLean, the township's tory member of the provincial Assembly since 1820 and Speaker of the House since 1831.[22] These initial municipal elections gave the people of the town of Cornwall for the first time, a sense of their identity as a distinct body quite separate from the township of Cornwall. Only those living within the square mile bounded on the north and south by Ninth and Water Streets and on the east and west by Marlborough and Cumberland Streets could vote in the elections for town officials. Moreover, these elections showed that, strong as the tory leaven was within the town, a leaven of reform still smouldered since the days of the McNiff controversy. There was no doubt about McLean's and Vankoughnet's politics — they were tory supporters of the ministry in power. But the Chesleys represented all political shades. As one of the few post-revolutionary American immigrant families that opted for Cornwall, rather than pushing on further west to cheaper lands, the Chesleys had arrived in 1800 from Rensselaer County, New York, with sons who soon married into prominent Cornwall families, including the Vankoughnets.[23] Captain Peter Chesley, who won the West Ward in company with his brother, John, was an acknowledged reformer.[24] His brother, Solomon, was a moderate conservative.[25] Whether the third brother, John, was reformer, tory, or moderate conservative, is unknown, but this first local election indicated that from the beginning of Cornwall's municipal history, there was political diversity.

The newly-elected ward representatives met every week to get down to the job of appointing essential officers such as bailiffs, a treasurer, and a poundkeeper and drawing up a code of local laws. They published this code in the *Observer*, Cornwall's first newspaper which was started in 1833 by Christopher Fulton who was both owner and editor. One of the first decisions of the new Board of Police was to set the price of bread in town, a task that had previously fallen to the Court of General Sessions. They fixed the price at nine pence for four pounds, thus keeping the staff of life independent of the market place so that its price could not get beyond the means of the less fortunate in the town. The finances of the town were simple. Real estate in the town was taxed one penny to the pound.[26] Other revenue would come from the sale of licenses for taverns, inns and stores — set at £2/10 a year, and from the fines for non-payment of these fees. Salaries to the street surveyor of £10 a year and to the town clerk of £12/10 came out of these sources. The town treasurer received payment by deducting 2-1/2 percent of all the money that passed through his hands. Horace Spencer, who was appointed High Constable of the Town, could keep 25 percent of all the fines he collected for infractions of the law prosecuted on his complaint.[27] To help with executing warrants for arrests and other police duties, eight bailiffs were appointed. Because of rowdiness among canal workers, bailiffs soon found their jobs far more onerous than they had expected.

The introduction of municipal politics gave more than a boost to the small town. No sooner had politically-ambitious townsmen a taste than they cast their eyes about for new lands to conquer or, at least, to annex. In the early spring of 1835 lawyer George Stephen Jarvis gathered together a number of like-minded cronies, including the hard-drinking barrister, George McDonell, and, amidst the hospitality of Thomas Marshall's inn, they decided to annex the Island of Montreal to Upper Canada. Resolutions to that purpose were proposed by the two McGillis brothers, Hugh and John, who included in their demands all the peninsula east of the Eastern District as well. Fully in accord with these territorial ambitions were such Cornwall stalwarts as Philip Vankoughnet, William Cline and John McGillivray who were commissioned to draw up a petition to the lieutenant-governor, Sir John Colborne. The Cornwall *Observer* of 13 February 1835 printed details of the meeting which soon produced repercussions in Montreal where the Constitutional Association of that city expressed its decided approval of the "annexation of the County of Vaudreuil and the Island of Montreal of Upper Canada."[28] Whether this was a case of the Cornwall tail wagging the Montreal dog or vice versa is unknown, but the brashness of the Cornwall Constitutionalists in proposing to annex Montreal showed that they were not reluctant to dabble in big-time politics or even to fish in the troubled waters between the two provinces.

However, Cornwall politicians were able to exercise their aspirations a little nearer home. Within a few months of this meeting, George Jarvis was elected President of the Board of Police, George McDonell was elected councillor of the West Ward and Thomas Marshall, at whose inn the meeting took place, was one of the new councillors for the East Ward. Nor was this all as far as aspiring politicians were concerned. They could also compete for a third seat in the provincial Assembly, for Cornwall was set aside as a separate riding, even though the number of residents eligible to vote was likely under 300 out of a total population of 1,000. Only men could vote and to qualify as a voter they had to own property valued at forty shillings at least or, if they were tenants, pay a minimum rent of £6 yearly. In 1834 Cornwall had but 192 assessed lots. Even by 1850 there were but 221 houses and shops in the town. Thus, the number of local men eligible to vote was extremely limited, and it was not until 1884 that women were given the right to vote.[29]

A contemporary, J.D. Dent, in his history of the rebellion in Upper Canada, claimed that Cornwall was one of "the notoriously rotten boroughs...(in the province which) always returned Tory members prepared to do the bidding of the executive."[30] With ample hyperbole, he added, "By such means was the Assembly corrupted." It is true that conservatives swept the town for the first twenty years, but by 1853 when the township was annexed to the town for electoral purposes, moderate liberals took the seat consistently, first Dr. Roderick Macdonald and then John Sandfield Macdonald. Thus, although future election results did not justify Dent's description of Cornwall as a consistent Tory stronghold, the label stuck. As late as 1879 H.E. Belden in his *Historical Atlas of Stormont, Dundas and Glengarry* still declared that Cornwall had been made a constituency in order to "create a little pocket borough whence the "Compact" could always be sure of a supporter."

In the fall of 1834 when elections to the Assembly were called, reform overtures were more pronounced in the county of Stormont than in the town riding, but the political action was in the town itself. The contestants, two tories and two reformers, were all Cornwall men, all four were former pupils of Strachan's Academy, all were second or third generation Loyalists, and all were officers of the 1st Stormont Regiment. For the tories were Archibald McLean, the Speaker of the last Assembly, and Philip Vankoughnet;[31] for the reformers there were Lieutenant-Colonel Donald Aeneas Macdonell[32] and Dr. William Bruce,[33] grandson of the innkeeper, Mrs. Peggy Bruce.

The hustings were set up on Second Street opposite the Grammar School and within a stone's throw of the homes of the two keenest rivals — McLean and Macdonell. As polling began in early October 1834 both contestants had their banners ready — a Union Jack waving in the breeze — a piper to pipe each voter to the hustings and back to the home of the candidate of his choice where the voter would be refreshed with cold beef or ham, bread and cheese, and more than a whiff of rum, whiskey or beer. For those voters who had come into town from as far away as Osnabruck or the rear concessions, the refreshments proved welcome.

Philip Vankoughnet had represented the county since 1816 with the exception of two years, but in the face of the reform onslaught, he withdrew early from the contest, leaving his old sidekick, Archibald McLean, to uphold the tory interests. Dr. Bruce's popularity gave him an overwhelming lead for one of the Stormont seats. Thus it was two Scots who fought over the second seat: McLean, the tory chief pillar of St. John's Presbyterian Church,[34] and Roman Catholic reformer Donald Aeneas Macdonell, son of Lieutenant Miles Macdonell and grandson of Captain John (Spanish) Macdonell of the King's Royal Regiment of New York.[35] Nomination preliminaries

124

were carried out for McLean by Lieutenant-Colonel George Singleton Anderson, the youngest son of Captain Samuel Anderson and brother-in-law of Philip Vankoughnet. McLean's seconder was George Stephen Jarvis, the New Brunswick Loyalist who had opened a law practice in Cornwall in 1820 and had been named Judge of the Ottawa District in 1825, though he continued to reside in Cornwall.[37] Proposers for the reformers were almost as impressive — Captain Peter Chesley and Michael Link, a second generation Loyalist, for Macdonell. Captain George Morgan and Robert Grant for Dr. Bruce.

When the counting was over, the two reformers of Cornwall, Dr. William Bruce and Lt.-Col. Donald Aeneas Macdonell, captured the county seats, Bruce leading with 408 votes and Macdonell winning some 342.[38] Archibald McLean the tory candidate, trailed thirteen votes behind Macdonell, thus losing the county seat, but he had the consolation of taking the new seat for the town of Cornwall uncontested. From then on, the Cornwall seat was far from a safe or pocket borough for either tory or reform interests. Each succeeding election saw the seat challenged, sometimes by members of the same political persuasion. Therefore, although tories tended to win the seat, they did so only after a struggle, occasionally between former presidents of the Board of Police who found that occupancy of this important town post often proved a stepping stone to provincial politics.

Politics and canal construction difficulties occupied the centre of the stage in Cornwall for the next few years as the town and its township coped with the influx of boisterous canal workers and then found itself caught up in the waves of reform politics that engulfed tory strongholds like Cornwall in the early 1830s. At first canal construction brought a wave of expansion in the town centre. Optimistic merchants and businessmen leased lots on Water Street and along First and Second Streets where they began putting up substantial buildings.

It was the canal workers who first brought the town into an unwelcome limelight on 13 December 1834. Trouble began at the Mille Roches quarry early that morning when one of the workers was arrested for debt. A party of his fellow Irish workers soon forcibly rescued him from the bailiff. Immediately Deputy Sheriff Ewen Stuart, together with Cornwall lawyer George McDonell and bailiff Henry Thain set out for Mille Roches to arrest the rescued man and the party that affected his rescue. At the quarry the bailiff pointed out Robert Quinn as one of the men involved in the rescue. While Deputy Sheriff Stuart was questioning Quinn, the man's brother, Richard, ran up, shouting violently and instantly aimed an iron crowbar at the head of the bailiff. Thain jumped back to avoid the blow and tripped backwards over some rubble. Quinn was about to attack Thain again when Deputy Sheriff Stuart cocked his pistol at him and ordered Quinn "to stand back and be careful what he was about." Immediately Robert Quinn struck the deputy sheriff from behind with a six-foot crowbar and as Stuart fell, Quinn struck him again across the temple. Lawyer George McDonell stood aghast at the bloody scene, "muffled up" as he later reported "in his cloak and greatcoat, unable to render the least assistance," for Quinn threatened to do the same to him. Indeed, one of the workmen snapped his pistol at McDonell, but it was not properly loaded and failed to discharge.[39]

The deputy sheriff survived but a few days. On his death, the Quinn brothers were imprisoned in Cornwall where the town people nervously awaited the trial and petitioned the lieutenant governor, Sir John Colborne, for troops. "After this sacrifice of one of our most respectable and most respected townsmen," wrote the editor of the Cornwall *Observer*, "Sir John Colborne cannot refuse two companies at least to guard our jail and maintain our laws."[40] Barracks were built in September of 1835 on the court-house lot, but it was not until the shock of a second murder reverberated from Cornwall to Toronto that the government sent a company of the 15th Regiment to restore tranquillity and ordered the Irish-speaking troubleshooter, James Fitzgibbon, to Cornwall to investigate.[41]

This second murder occurred on 5 February 1836, just a day or two after the dismissed lieutenant-governor, Sir John Colborne, had stopped at Cornwall for a three-day visit before proceeding to Montreal. The town was agog with festivities as Sir John and Lady Colborne, together with their suite and servants, attended service at Trinity Episcopal church and finally on Monday were seen off with an impressive procession headed by Sheriff Donald Macdonell, Philip Vankoughnet, Lt.-Col. George Anderson, and Indians from St. Regis. In the rear George Stephen Jarvis carried aloft a banner inscribed with Sir John's parting words "The Constitution will be firmly upheld."[42] Five days later Lt.-Col. Albert French drove along the same route in his horse and sleigh heading for his elegant country home, Maple Grove, just to the west of the town. He was accosted by two canal workers and a woman who asked for a ride. When French refused, the trio dragged him out of the sleigh, struck him over the head with a rake and left him dying on the road as they rode off in his cutter.[43]

Contemporary newspapers and accounts show how bitter Cornwall people were over these murders. The records of Trinity Church, for instance, minced no words. "Wantonly and barbarously murdered on the evening of 5th of February in broad daylight by a band of Irish Papists, who dragged him out of his sleigh opposite William Wood's barn, was Albert French, Esq., buried on 9th February 1836." The editor of the Cornwall *Observer* burst out in a torrent of abuse against the canallers. "Good God! How long will such a state of things be tolerated — an inoffensive gentleman to be waylaid within a musket shot of our very door? Poor Stuart fell at the hands of the sanguinary and heartless ruffians while in the discharge of his duty, and now Mr. French has become their second victim because he would not permit three savages to sit in his own cutter!"[44]

Reprehensible and unprecedented as these two murders were, the circumstances surrounding them pointed out a new development in Cornwall's history. The Irish labourers who arrived in such large numbers to work on the canal were not only poor. They were, unlike the earlier successive waves of Scots immigrants, without friends or relatives in the Loyalist-Scots settlements along the eastern shores of the St. Lawrence. Huddled in makeshift shanties outside the town in conditions somewhat similar to those faced by the original United Empire Loyalists half a century earlier, the Irish immigrants were conscious of class distinctions and a certain amount of nativist hostility, even though Cornwall had always had a number of Irish among its inhabitants. Its founding father, Sir John Johnson, came from an ancient Irish family. So, too, did the senior captain of the first battalion of the Royal Yorkers — Samuel Anderson. But these men of Irish-American background had been protestant, the Johnsons from Meath and the Andersons from Antrim.[45] Irish in origin, too, was the Presbyterian Pringle family that gained such prominence in nineteenth century Cornwall.

For the descendants of the original Irish-American settlers and the people of Cornwall generally, their worst fears seemed confirmed when not one but two murders were perpetrated by the Irish canallers in an area where most of the judges' time had usually been taken up with litigation involving money rather than acts of violence. Yet the murders involved two elements not unknown to the Loyalist-Scots founders of the town: family loyalty and racial pride. In the first murder, the initial difficulty had involved the arrest of a canaller for debt. The murder occurred when one labourer tried to prevent the arrest of his brother. The second murder occurred when three Irish canallers asked for a ride on a late afternoon in December as they were returning somewhat the worse for liquor, to their shanty near the Mille Roches quarry after attending a funeral in Cornwall.

Lt.-Col. Albert French may have had good reasons for refusing them a lift, just as many a modern driver would hesitate to pick up a solitary hitchhiker, let alone a group of three. Yet there was a fierceness about the attack on French that suggests that, in the verbal exchange, the pride of the Irish labourers had been hurt at the curtness of French's refusal and the conveyed slight that they were not good enough to ride beside one of Cornwall's native sons.

Only one of the men involved in the murder, Michael Connell, was apprehended. As the time of Connell's trial drew near, Sheriff Donald Macdonell of Cornwall wrote to the civil secretary at Toronto urging "a detachment of troops for this town...especially as a man who was employed on the canal is to be tried for murder at the Assizes. If condemned, an execution would be difficult to enforce without troops."[46]

In the midst of this excitement over the murder of French and the reverberations over Sir John Colborne's dismissal as lieutenant-governor and his subsequent visit to Cornwall in January of 1836, political tensions ran high in the little town. To bolster tory morale in Cornwall, the Constitutionalists called a meeting on 12 February, presided over by Archibald McLean's brother-in-law, John MacGillivray, the retired Montreal fur-baron who had settled in Glengarry and was now doing a lucrative business in land speculation.[47] Conservative newspapers snorted that "Radicals of the District attempted to disturb the meeting and to negativize the resolutions proposed by the Constitutionalists...but the division showed their numbers were too weak and...they contented themselves with yelling."[48]

There is no mention that Irish labourers were present at this Cornwall political rally of the Constitutionalists, but as the time neared for the provincial elections of July 1836, their presence was expected and feared. James Fitzgibbon, who had been sent to Cornwall to help maintain order among the canal workers, hurriedly wrote to the civil secretary at Toronto on 6 July 1836. "A man named Brown, son of a neighbouring farmer, and Terrence Curran, who had been discharged from the works for misconduct, came with a piper and persuaded a number of men to quit work and go to the election in Cornwall." Fitzgibbon got out warrants for their arrest, but the contractor succeeded in convincing the workers that "it had been Brown's intention to bring the labourers into contact with the country people under such circumstances as would make it appear that the labourers had left work and went to town to beat the country people." So alarmed was Fitzgibbon that he urged government to form a Rifle Corps or armed company to keep the peace at Cornwall and suggested that a regiment of regulars be sent to the town from Kingston or Montreal.[49] A company of the 15th Regiment marched from Kingston and occupied the barracks that had been built the previous year. On the day that Michael Connell was executed on Gallows Hill for the murder of Albert French, the regulars were kept under arms in barracks, but no disturbance occurred, nor was there any further serious trouble among the canal workers. Soon after the execution the regulars returned to Kingston and the townsmen and canallers, having taken stock of each other, relaxed to a more easy relationship.

From another direction the people of Cornwall, both protestant and catholic, were singled out with the voters of Counties Stormont and Glengarry for a special address from the Roman Catholic Bishop of the upper province, Alexander Macdonell, who two years earlier had moved his seat from St. Raphael, just northeast of Cornwall, to Kingston. Bishop Macdonell had persuaded the Presbyterian, Archibald McLean, not to stand for re-election in the town of Cornwall, but to seek the county seat that he had held during several other sessions of the Assembly, a seat that was now held by the popular reformer, Dr. William Bruce of Cornwall.[50] It was not the first time that the aging but still vigorous bishop had raised the political battle-axe. Taking a direct swing at the reformers, Bishop Macdonell told the people of the two counties, "If you believe that I have your interest at heart, and that I know better than yourselves the most effective means of promoting it, you will elect men to represent you...of sound and loyal principles...who will not allow themselves to be duped or misled by wicked hypocritical radicals, who are endeavouring to drive the Province into rebellion...and to subject you to the domination of Yankee rulers and Lynch Law."[51]

Observing these developments from the sidelines was a lanky lad from Glengarry who had just quit his job in a Cornwall dry-goods store in order to study law in Archibald McLean's office. Young John Sandfield Macdonald's first taste of Cornwall politics and legal training was thoroughly tory as he watched his patron, Archibald McLean, toss his hat into the county elections of July 1836 and come out ahead of the two incumbent reformers, Lt.-Col. Donald Aeneas Macdonell and Dr. William Bruce.[52] McLean led Macdonell by only one point, but that was enough to restore a tory voice to one of the county seats. Dr. Bruce was out of the running entirely, capturing only 283 votes to McLean's 334.[53] Election ructions had been partly avoided by the quick work of Colonel James Fitzgibbon, the Toronto man sent to investigate labour unrest in Cornwall. Learning that there was trouble at the western end of the canal on election day, Fitzgibbon rode out to find that an agent of Dr. Bruce, the genial Irishman, William Browne, was enlisting Irish canallers to go into Cornwall to support Dr. Bruce, Fitzgibbon's ploy was to collect affidavits against Browne and his cohorts and prepare warrants for their arrests, a manoeuvre sufficient to cool Browne's ardour and keep most of the canallers away from the polls.[54]

The town election was just as lively that year as the Stormont County elections. Two avowed Constitutionalists rivalled each other for the Cornwall seat. Solomon Yeomans Chesley of the politically-diverse Chesley family crossed swords with George Stephen Jarvis, McLean's choice as president of the Cornwall Board of Police. When the counting was over, Jarvis was chaired through the town as Cornwall's second representative to the provincial Assembly. That the rival candidates belonged to the same brand of politics did not prevent "some rioting...between the rival parties parading the streets in procession after the close of the polls."[55]

Just as the Eastern District of the province and Cornwall in particular had remained unmoved by Robert Gourlay's agitation for reform in 1818, so, too, did the area of Stormont, Dundas and Glengarry repudiate overtures from the radical wing of the reformers led by William Lyon Mackenzie. Once the 1836 elections were over, Cornwall settled down to a more mundane routine, glad enough to be listed among those towns anxious to attract incoming immigrants. James Pringle, the young officer who had wooed and wed the daughter of Captain Joseph Anderson during the war of 1812-14, and was now Clerk of the Session of St. John's Presbyterian Church, took on the job as government agent in Cornwall to whom immigrants could apply for information for maps and about lands for sale in his neighbourhood.[56] Among those who applied were large numbers of Irish immigrants who soon merged with the more conservative elements of the population, both politically and religiously. When rebellion struck in Upper Canada in the late fall of 1837, the Irish remained solidly loyal to the established government.[57]

NOTES

1. Robert Gourlay, *Statistical Account of Upper Canada*, i, 564.
2. *Ibid.*, i, 567.
3. *Ibid.*, i, 565; *Upper Canada Gazette*, 23 July, 1818.
4. Gourlay, *Statistical Account*, i, 565.
5. H. Belden, *Historical Sketch of Stormont, Dundas and Glengarry*, i, ii.
6. For Stormont and Cornwall elections from 1792-1840 see F.H. Armstrong, *Handbook of Upper Canadian Chronology and Territorial Legislation*, 99-100.
7. Sir Sidney Beckwith to Lt.-Gen. Sir Gordon Drummond, 21 Nov. 1815 (RG8/C621/103-06).
8. See figures cited in *Report of a Missionary Journey made by the Hon. and Rev. Charles James Stewart through Upper Canada in 1820*, ed. J.J. Talman, 16.
9. Petition from magistrates of the Eastern District to Government for remuneration for occupation of the Gaol and Court House at Cornwall by H.M. Troops, 20 Mar. 1815, £250 allotted for repairs (RG8/C88/24); for remuneration for the use of St. John's Presbyterian Church by troops, see payment of £65 to John Anderson and John Kay, 14 Nov. 1815 (RG8/C556/102-03).
10. J.F. Pringle, *Lunenburgh or the old Eastern District*, 65-68; see also, J.G. Harkness, *History of Stormont, Dundas and Glengarry*, 151, 162.
11. State Papers Upper Canada, 1791-1841 (RG1/E3/26/18-22).
12. E.A. Cruikshank, ed. *The Correspondence of Lieut-Governor John Graves Simcoe*, v, 193.
13. Pringle, 63 and 136.
14. S. Rowe, "The Anderson Record from 1699 to 1896," in *OHSPR*, 1905, vi, 115, 118.
15. *Almanack de Québec*, 1801, 81 and 131; E.A. Cruikshank, "Memoir of Lt.-Col. John Macdonell," in *OHSPR*, 1925, xxii, 42.
16. Harkness, 86 and 89.
17. *York Almanac*, 1803, cited in Pringle, 169-70.
18. *Gazette*, Montreal, 24 December 1810; Thomas Doige, *Montreal Directory*, 1819, 43-44; William Dunlop, *Recollections of the War of 1812*, 37.
19. See William Chewett map of Cornwall, 1792, V3-440.
20. *Montreal Herald*, 14 December 1822, cited in Donald Creighton, *Empire of the St. Lawrence*, 221.
21. *Cornwall Observer*, 15 Aug. 1834; William Reid, *Death Notices of Ontario*, 147; at the time of his death, Captain S. Anderson was drawing half-pay of five shillings a day and his son, Joseph, was getting two shillings four pence daily, see RG8/C634a/108.
22. Minutes of the Board of Police, Cornwall, 21 and 26 April, 1 May 1834, cited in H. Belden, *Historical Sketch*, v.
23. George Mainer, "Solomon Yeomans Chesley," in *DCB*, x, 163-64.
24. Peter Chesley nominated reformer Lt.-Col. Donald Aeneas Macdonell for the county election in the fall of 1834, see, *Gazette*, Montreal, 16 October 1834; see also, *Cornwall Observer*, 30 November 1837, in which Peter Chesley is identified as a reformer.
25. *DCB*, x, 163-64; Harkness, 183.
26. Pringle, 144.
27. Minutes of the Board of Police, 6 May 1834, in Belden, *Historical Sketch*, v.
28. *Morning Courier*, Montreal, 1 March 1836.

29. Pringle, 73; A. Shortt and A.G. Doughty, *Canada and its Provinces*, xviii, 466-67.
30. Cited in Harkness, 144.
31. *Gazette*, Montreal, 16 October 1834; Harkness, 146; *Chronicle and Gazette*, Kingston, 27 September 1834.
32. *Vindicator*, Montreal, 17 and 21 Oct. 1834; J.K. Johnson "Donald Aeneas Macdonell", *DCB*, x, 470.
33. *Vindicator*, Montreal, 17 and 21 Oct. 1834; Mrs. Charlotte Bruce Carey, "Sketch of the Bruce Family" in *Annual Transactions, United Empire Loyalists Association*, (Toronto, 1900) iii, 51; Harkness, 165-66.
34. History of St. John's Church, typed manuscript, Simon Fraser Centennial Library, Cornwall, 7, 12; Harkness, 146, 149-50.
35. W.D. Reid, *The Loyalists of Ontario*, 196.
36. For details of the nomination of candidates, see, *Gazette*, Montreal, 16 Oct. 1834.
37. J.K. Johnson, "George Stephen Jarvis", in *DCB*, x, 379-80; James Croil, *Dundas, or a Sketch of Canadian History*, 227.
38. *Gazette*, Montreal, 16 Oct. 1834; *Vindicator*, Montreal, 17 Oct. 1834.
39. For details of the affair see, *Gazette*, Montreal, 23 Dec. 1834, reprinted from the *Cornwall Observer*.
40. Pringle, 158, says the Quinns escaped; Harkness, 187, repeats this. However, the contemporary *Cornwall Observer*, states that the Quinns were arrested, see *Gazette*, Montreal, 23 Dec. 1834.
41. James Fitzgibbon to Joseph, Cornwall, 6 July 1836, Upper Canada Sundries, RG5/A1; *Cornwall Observer*, 15 August 1836.
42. *Cornwall Observer*, 5 Feb. 1836.
43. For contemporary accounts of the murder see, *Chronicle and Gazette*, Kingston, 10 Feb. 1836, re-printed from the *Cornwall Observer*; see also Trinity Church Records, Cornwall, 5 Feb. 1836; *Morning Courier*, Montreal, 11 Feb. 1836; for general discussions, see Pringle, 160; Harkness, 187-88.
44. Re-printed in *Chronicle and Gazette*, Kingston, 10 Feb. 1836.
45. For the Johnson family genealogy, see Sir John Johnson, *The North American Johnsons*, 19; for the Andersons, see Rowe, "The Anderson Record from 1699 to 1896", in OHSPR, 1905, vi, 109.
46. Macdonell to Joseph, 26 July 1836 (Upper Canada Sundries RG5/A1). For another instance of acts of violence on the part of Irish canallers whose pride had been hurt see, Elinor Senior, *British Regulars in Montreal: An Imperial Garrison 1832-1854*, 63.
47. Bruce Hodgins, *John Sandfield Macdonald*, 11-12.
48. *Morning Chronicle*, Quebec, 1 Mar. 1836.
49. Fitzibbon to Joseph, 6 July 1836 (Upper Canada Sundries RG5/A1).
50. J.E. Rea, *Bishop Alexander Macdonell and the Politics of Upper Canada*, 171.
51. Address of Bishop Alexander Macdonell to the Catholic and Protestant Free Holders of the Counties of Stormont and Glengarry, in Toronto *Patriot*, 17 June 1836, cited in Rea, *Bishop Alexander Macdonell*, 171-72.
52. See Bruce Hodgins, *John Sandfield Macdonald*, 5-6.
53. *Gazette*, Montreal, 5, 7, 9 July 1836.
54. J.K. Johnson, "Colonel James Fitzgibbon and the Suppression of Irish Riots in Upper Canada", in *Ontario History*, lvii, 1966, 153.
55. Fitzgibbon to Joseph, 6 July 1836 (Upper Canada Sundries, RG5/Al).
56. *Gazette*, Montreal, 20 Aug. 1836.
57. For an appraisal of the loyalty of the Irish community during the rebellion see Sir John Colborne to Lord Hill, confidential, 23 June 1838 (RG8/C1278/76-77).

District Court House and Gaol, the central portion of this building was completed in the summer of 1833.
Credit: Ian Bowering.

Chapter VII
Loyalist Reformers and Tories Face Rebellion

Political tension had been increasing in both Upper and Lower Canada since the early 1830s. In the upper province it did not come to a head until December of 1837 with William Lyon Mackenzie's attempted *coup d'état* in the small capital city of Toronto. For the people in Cornwall the uprising in the Toronto and London area in December was felt far less than the repercussions of the earlier outbreak in Lower Canada in late November when Sir John Colborne, by now Commander of the Forces in both provinces, called hurriedly on the men of Glengarry and Stormont for help. Once more external factors showed how closely Cornwall was allied to military and economic interests in Montreal, rather than to those of the more distant capital of Upper Canada. The reality of this fact is driven home by a glance at contemporary newspapers. News of Cornwall's politics, personalities and developments can more readily be found in contemporary Montreal daily newspapers than in Toronto newspapers or even those published in Kingston or Brockville.

For Sir John Colborne, the man who faced the task of suppressing rebellion in Lower Canada, his chief contact in Cornwall was his close personal friend, Captain George Phillpotts of the Royal Engineers. Phillpotts, a brother of the Anglican Bishop of Exeter, had taken over the superintendency of the work on the Cornwall Canal in March 1836 after Civil Engineer J.B. Mills resigned in a huff after a dispute with the canal commissioners appointed by government, one of whom was a local man, Philip Vankoughnet,[1] and Peter Shaver. But the Commander of the Forces was no stranger to Cornwall and its people. When he had left the upper province a year earlier, Sir John Colborne had received from the people of Cornwall and from the Indians at St. Regis one of the warmest receptions of any along the route as he made his departure from the province he had governed for close to eight years.

Just as Cornwall was a mobilization centre in 1812-14, so, too, when internal security was threatened, the town was a hub of military action for the regiments of Stormont and Glengarry. However, on 17

November 1837, Colborne received disturbing news from this focal point. Captain George Phillpotts wrote a long intelligence report on the St. Regis Indians and the Roman Catholics of Glengarry, warning Colborne that neither community could be taken for granted in the event of an uprising. In fact, it may well have been Phillpotts' initial alarmist reports from Cornwall that spurred Colborne into immediate counter-rebellion measures against St. Denis and St. Charles on 23 November. The doleful report from Phillpotts on 17 November, the day after the first overt attack on Crown forces occurred near Longueuil opposite Montreal, informed Colborne that "The Highlanders in Glengarry are not, I fear, to be depended upon, or at least they have not as yet come forward to offer their services."

With regard to the Indians of St. Regis, Phillpotts told Colborne it had been unwise of the government to dismiss Solomon Yeomans Chesley, the Indian agent at St. Regis, just at the very time when his presence there was most required to prevent "many other Indians... (being) drawn over to the Rebels." Already one deposed chief, Joseph Teorakaran, whom Phillpotts described as a "shrewd, clever man... well informed (who) had visited France and other parts of Europe," had interrupted an Indian Council called for the purpose of drawing up a loyal address to Lord Gosford, the Governor of the two provinces. Teorakaran made an impassioned speech on behalf of Louis-Joseph Papineau, the leader of the Patriotes in Lower Canada, declaring that "Papineau is fighting for the liberty of the Roman Catholics and the King is fighting against it — that he w^d. join Papineau, and the first use he w^d. make of his protection w^d. be to shoot the old fool, his head Chief." Another Indian at the Council agreed with Teorakaran, saying he felt "strong in the cause of Papineau, as did all the other Warriors except the Chiefs, who were sworn slaves to the King." Phillpotts warned that there were rumours that Teorakaran had threatened to blow up the government stores at St. Regis where the gunpowder was stored, and he urged that Chesley be retained at his post.[2]

Chesley's post as Indian agent at St. Regis had become suspect because of his support of Major William Plenderleath Christie's measure to provide a stipend for a protestant schoolmaster at the Roman Catholic Indian village. This was Reverend Eleazar Williams who arrived at St. Regis in 1835.[3] Thus at the time that Patriote political agitation was making itself felt among the Indians as well as among the French-and English-speaking inhabitants of both provinces, there was also a minor tempest about the attempts to draw the Indians of St. Regis back within the hegemony of Cornwall and the Eastern

District of Upper Canada and away from the pull of French Catholic Lower Canada. The controversy embarrassed Lord Gosford's government at Quebec City and this, together with Chesley's attempt to challenge the government's choice for the Cornwall seat in the 1836 elections, probably resulted in the government decision to abolish his post in 1837.

Phillpotts at Cornwall saw Chesley's presence at St. Regis as imperative, both as a source of intelligence on the Indians and as a means of stemming the pro-Papineau propaganda among the people of the village. On November 20th, he sent off another alarmist report to Colborne, elaborating on the attitude of the Glengarry Roman Catholics, his views likely reflecting those of some of the military men of Cornwall. "The Protestants in Glengarry," he wrote, "are, I believe, all loyal, but I have heard that the R. Catholics are determined not to act agst. the R. Catholics in Lower Canada. — They say, or at least some of them say, that they look upon it not in a Political point of view, but that their Religion is in danger. To this it was replied that the Bishop's letter,[4] lately published, ought to satisfy them...when it was ans^d. that the Bp. rec^d. a salary and was in some measure dependnt. on the Govt., but that they did not (receive a salary), and they knew well that if the Govt. succeeds in putting down Papineau, the next step will be to put down the R. Catholic Religion."[5] Phillpotts was not one to look on the bright side of things and he tended to repeat too willingly the various rumours circulating in Cornwall. As such, he was a barometer of Cornwall's perturbed state as news arrived each day of fresh disturbances in the lower province.

While Colborne was receiving these intelligence reports from Phillpotts at Cornwall, local militiamen were taking matters into their own hands as rumours spread that insurgents in the Vaudreuil and Rigaud area were planning to cut communications between the two provinces. Col. Philip Vankoughnet of the 2nd Stormont Regiment called a meeting of his officers at battalion headquarters in Osnabruck Township on 23 November. Twenty-seven officers were on hand to take into account "the present alarming state of Lower Canada." Six of them were avowed reformers. All declared their willingness to "march to Lower Canada whenever the Commander of the Forces (Sir John Colborne) shall think that the emergency...may require their aid in checking the rebellion which has already so unhappily commenced." Spokesmen for the reformers among the officers was Captain Peter Chesley of Cornwall. Declaring himself "still a reformer, but not a revolutionist," he pledged that he and his fellow officers and men "whether Tory or Reformer...would follow where their Colonel chose to lead them." The entire corps of officers then unanimously resolved to lend "their assistance in effecting every reasonable measure of reform, and in redressing every real grievance; yet when a party, under the garb of reform, should attempt to thwart the due administration of justice, to alienate the people from the Government, subvert the Constitution, and encourage Treason and Rebellion, they would use their utmost endeavours to put down such traitorous designs and bring the offenders to justice."[6] Their colonel, delighted with the response of his officers, rose to the occasion. "Let the Second Regiment of Stormont," Vankoughnet exclaimed, "be one of the first to march to the assistance of our friends in Lower Canada and prove to them that although a greater portion of it is composed of those who stand out in favour of reform, yet they will be among the first to stand forward and protect the Constitution and maintain their connection with Great Britain."[7]

At the same time that the 2nd Stormont Regiment was meeting at battalion headquarters under Col. Philip Vankoughnet and pledging themselves to put down rebellion, so, too, the officers of the four Glengarry regiments met at Lancaster on 23 November to declare their loyalty. "Accounts have reached us, shewing that the leaders of the revolution in Lower Canada have so far succeeded as to have persuaded their deluded countrymen to take up arms, and although we are convinced," they stated, "that these infatuated and misguided men can never effect more than harassing and attacking the loyalists... still we feel that our fellow subjects in Lower Canada have not only a right to our sympathies but a claim upon our services in support of our common cause, the maintaining and upholding the British Constitution and our connexion with the British Empire." The officers went a step further. They published their declaration in the Montreal *Transcript* of 2 December 1837. Another writer from Glengarry wrote to the editor of the *Morning Courier* in Montreal stating that in Glengarry alone "they can raise at least 2,000 effective men at very short notice." This writer assured the editor that both the catholic and protestant Highlanders "are all ready to turn out, even those we used to call Radicals....They say that although they were and are radical for reform, they never will fight against Britain."[8]

Thus, at the very moment that British regulars and a handful of Montreal Volunteers were being beaten back from an unsuccessful attack on the insurgent camp at St. Denis on 23 November 1837, the officers of the 2nd Stormont and Glengarry Regiments were pledging their services to succour the loyalists in Lower Canada whenever Sir John Colborne called upon them. All that was needed was the permission of the new lieutenant-governor, Sir Francis Bond Head, to allow them to cross the provincial boundary into the lower province.

The only officers who remained strangely silent were those of the 1st Stormont Regiment which comprised the town and township of Cornwall and that of Roxborough.[9] This Regiment had been commanded continuously by United Empire Loyalists, their sons and grandsons. When the Honourable Neil McLean retired as colonel in 1825, Colonel Joseph Anderson took his place and in 1830 Lieutenant-Colonel Albert French took the command. When French was murdered in early 1836, the command of the Regiment devolved on Neil McLean's second son, Archibald. He resigned early in 1837 when he was appointed to a judgeship and Donald Aeneas Macdonell became lieutenant-colonel. Thus as reform gave way to radical agitation and turned into rebellion, the command of Cornwall's own regiment, the 1st Stormont, devolved on Donald Aeneas Macdonell, the reform member for the county. At this point Macdonell evidently hesitated to call a meeting of his officers for fear that the more radical reformers in the regiment would hang back.[10]

Matters came to a crisis on Saturday, 2 December. On that day Colonel Philip Vankoughnet received urgent messages from the Commander of the Forces at Montreal, Sir John Colborne, and from John Simpson, the Collector of Customs at Coteau-du-Lac, pressing for assistance from the people of Cornwall.[11] Simpson had been a close friend of Louis-Joseph Papineau and an avowed reformer. Yet his reform leanings had nothing to do with rebellion. When he discovered that insurgents planned to seize the fort at Coteau-du-Lac, he hastily conveyed the cannon from the fort to boats on the St. Lawrence where, to avoid their capture by the insurgents, he had them sunk in fourteen fathoms of water.[12]

Then, after removing the bridge near the fort in order to intercept the march of the insurgents, Simpson, together with Captain W. Cox and Lieutenant Henry Roebuck of the Coteau-du-Lac Loyal Volunteers, went through the surrounding country to collect as many loyalists as they could muster to undertake the defence of the fort. Some forty to fifty volunteered their services. These men took up their position in the fort where they remained day and night. When it was learned that a party of insurgents were on their way from Vaudreuil, Simpson sent a hurried appeal to Cornwall. As soon as Philip Vankoughnet received this note on November 30, 1837, he enlisted fifty Cornwall volunteers, "fine, young men of this town," as the *Cornwall Observer* reported, who marched to Coteau-du-Lac the next day "to join the gallant little band who had collected there."[13] Led by Colonel Philip Vankoughnet of the 2nd Stormont Regiment, the Cornwall volunteers included Captains B.G. French, Martin McMartin and Ensign S.I.B. Anderson, all of the 1st Stormont Regiment. Among the private volunteers was Jacob F. Pringle, the future country judge and historian.[14] Each man carried a musket, "all the arms we have here," according to Vankoughnet, and they took some powder from one of the local merchants. The Indians of St. Regis lent them a ceremonial field piece and provided them with some barrels of pork.[15] Captain George Phillpotts marched with the Cornwall militiamen and stayed long enough at the fort to instruct Simpson that he was to inform the leading French Canadians in the area that "this was merely an earnest of what Upper Canada will do and that we will not allow communication with Montreal to be interfered with."[16] Colonel Vankoughnet agreed. He found that the arrival of the contingent from Upper Canada had "struck consternation and amazement into the hearts of the French rebels who had been led, by false representations of their leaders, to suppose that the inhabitants of this province are as ripe for rebellion as themselves."[17]

This movement of Cornwall volunteers to the lower province together with the news of two battles between Crown forces and insurgents at St. Denis and St. Charles south of the St. Lawrence soon produced a change of attitude on the part of those men of the 1st Stormont Regiment who had shown hesitation. Phillpotts reported to Colborne on 4 December that "Mr. Alex McLean (a brother of Judge Archibald McLean) has just informed me that the 1st Militia (Stormont Regiment) from St. Andrew's will all turn out. There are some Radicals among them who w^d. rather remain behind, but he says the spirit shown by the Loyalists has had a good effect on them and they will be ashamed to hang back." The Indians of St. Regis showed their colours, too. Phillpotts remarked that "Solomon Chesley has been told you do not like to employ the Indians of St. Regis. He says you may depend upon them and they are quite under control."[18] Moreover, Phillpotts told Colborne that the Glengarries were "all ready to turn out and march in a body to assist you in putting down the rebellion. The Radicals are as forward as any others now in showing their loyalty. The great fear now expressed by many is that you will quiet them all without their assistance."[19] Part of this martial enthusiasm stemmed from the threats that the Glengarries were now receiving from the radicals on their border. The radicals told the Glengarrians that if they should march to Lower

Canada, the Canadians of Rigaud will come in and destroy their farms." Phillpotts warned Colborne, however, that the Highlanders "will not go without arms" and he urged that they be immediately armed and sent down. "The fifty Volunteers at Coteau have been of the greatest service," he pointed out, "in encouraging the Loyalists and dampening the rebellious spirit of the Canadians in that neighbourhood."[20]

Thus Phillpotts' initial fears that the Indians of St. Regis, the Roman Catholics of Glengarry, and even the reformers of the district generally could not be depended upon in a conflict with co-religionists and political colleagues in the lower province proved groundless. Undoubtedly there was hesitation as long as the agitation in the lower province remained within the bonds of legal opposition, but once the threshold of rebellion had been passed, Indians, reformers and catholics were as eager as any tory in Cornwall to discountenance revolt.[21]

The defeat of the insurgents at St. Charles on the Richelieu River on Saturday, 25 November 1837, by British regulars and a few Montreal volunteers gave Sir John Colborne a breathing space. This victory of the Crown forces eliminated the major insurgent camp south of the St. Lawrence and meant that the Commander of the Forces could concentrate his disposable force north of Montreal in the Lake of the Two Mountains where the other major insurgent thrust was expected. To confine the insurgent force north of the St. Lawrence, Colborne was anxious to have the Stormont and Glengarry militia regiments mobilized and ready to reinforce his troops at St. Benoit.[22] He sent repeated appeals to Sir Francis Bond Head to allow the volunteers from the eastern district of Upper Canada to cross the provincial boundary, but Head held back. The lieutenant-governor of the upper province had already sent all the regulars from Upper Canada to Colborne's aid and he was reluctant to start any movement of militiamen out of the province for fear that such moves would upset the somewhat precarious tranquillity of his own province.[23]

Head did not give permission for the Stormont and Glengarry militia to cross the boundary into Lower Canada until after he had coped successfully with Mackenzie's abortive efforts at revolt from December 4th until the 7th. In the final attack on Mackenzie's stronghold at Montgomery's Tavern on Yonge Street north of Toronto on December 7th, Cornwall's pride, Judge Neil McLean, the former commanding officer of the 1st Stormont Regiment, was at the head of the left wing of 250 men with Colonel William Chisholm of the Gore Militia.[24] As soon as Mackenzie's forces were routed, Head sent permission for the border militia units to cross into Lower Canada. By this time Colborne's army had already moved north to St. Eustache and had fought the last battle of the 1837 rebellion. Thus the two Stormont Regiments and the four Glengarry Regiments, though anxious to serve and fully dependable,[25] remained at their battalion headquarters during all the military engagements in the lower province. Only at Coteau-du-Lac in the lower province did Cornwall volunteers serve. Here Colonel Vankoughnet urged the military secretary at Montreal headquarters to keep a strong garrison of 200 or 300 men. "If the Rebels know that this fort is strongly garrisoned, they will not think of an attack upon it or taking up positions at the Cedars, Cascades or Pointe Claire."[26] The first contingent of Cornwall volunteers who had so promptly crossed the provincial boundary to hasten to Coteau-du-Lac were relieved within ten days by another contingent of Cornwall Volunteers. When they were dismissed on 20 December, the commandant of the fort paid special tribute to "the officers, non-commissioned officers and gentlemen composing the second detachment of Cornwall Volunteers for the very soldierly and gentlemanly conduct and behaviour whilst under his command...that (there was) not a single complaint (against them) by the inhabitants of the country."[27]

Although the hand of revolt had been stayed in both provinces by the second week of December 1837, Sir John Colborne could not rest easy for Mackenzie set up an armed camp on Navy Island opposite the Niagara frontier. In addition, rumours circulated that the insurgents who had fled over the American border were planning border raids. Colborne therefore mobilized various corps of Volunteers along the St. Lawrence. At Cornwall on 8 January 1838 Colonel Philip Vankoughnet raised a local unit which was almost completed by 29 January, 1838.[28] In addition, George Stephen Jarvis, now a captain, was given permission to raise a Troop of Dragoons. The Cornwall Dragoons, whom the local inhabitants usually referred to as Lancers, were composed of sixty armed men. Together with a newly-raised troop at Brockville, their job was to provide for express despatch service between Montreal and Kingston, to keep open communications along the frontier, furnish escorts, and to act as intelligence agents by reporting to military headquarters in Montreal any hostile movement on the opposite side of the St. Lawrence.[29]

With the arrival of regular reinforcements from Great Britain in the spring of 1838, Sir John Colborne ordered the volunteer corps disbanded, including the Cornwall Troop of Dragoons.[30] Colborne now posted a number of regular officers at key positions along the

St. Lawrence and the land frontiers to act as liaison officers with local militia officers, to keep military headquarters at Montreal informed of any suspicious activity in their immediate neighbourhood and to report any insurgent moves from the American side.[31] A veteran of the Peninsula War, Colonel C.B. Turner, was stationed at Cornwall from the spring of 1838 on and, together with Captain George Phillpotts, the Royal Engineer officer overseeing canal construction, kept Colborne informed of local developments. By June of 1838 the people of Cornwall were not the only ones greatly alarmed by rumours that a secret society called the Hunters had emerged in the United States. The Hunters were responsible for the burning of the new Canadian steamer, *Sir Robert Peel*, and for the renewal of border raids along the Niagara River. Once more Colborne ordered volunteer companies formed for frontier duty at various towns, including Cornwall.[32] One of the contractors on the canal, George Crawford, who had been a captain in Colonel Vankoughnet's volunteer unit earlier in the year, raised an infantry company that took up quarters in the vacant barracks adjoining the jail in Cornwall.[33]

Cornwall experienced no more war alarums until the first few days of November 1838 when a courier galloped into town with a terse message from Sir John Colborne for Colonel Turner. Dated Quebec City, 1 November 1838, the note ordered Turner to "explain to the officers of Militia in the District...that Canada, being threatened with an attack from the American frontier by a horde of rapacious brigands, every man that can bear arms, I am persuaded will not hesitate to join his regiment and prepare to repel the wicked and unprovoked invasion."[34] Scarcely had this courier arrived than another despatch rider rode into town carrying orders from the Deputy Quarter-Master General at Montreal, Colonel Charles Gore, to call out two regiments of the Glengarries.[35] For three Cornwall men — Lieutenant Martin Carman of the Cornwall Troop of Dragoons, John S. McDougall and Duncan McDonell, the rebellion struck sooner than for most. They were among the passengers on the mail steamer, *Henry Brougham*, that plied back and forth between the Cedars, Beauharnois and Lachine. As the steamer docked at Beauharnois about seven o'clock on Sunday morning, 4 November, the crew and passengers were astounded to find themselves suddenly imprisoned by a party of insurgents commanded by François-Xavier Prieur of St. Timothée.[36]

When Colborne's appeal for reinforcements arrived at Cornwall, it took Captain George Phillpotts three days to convey by the steamer, *Neptune*, all the Highlanders who crowded into Cornwall or Lancaster anxious to be part of the brigade converging on Beauharnois. The only men from Cornwall permitted to embark were a small detachment of Captain George S. Jarvis's Troop of Volunteer Cavalry under Lieut. John Chesley.[37] While the Glengarries and the Cornwall Cavalry were embarking on the *Neptune* for Coteau-du-Lac from where they would make a direct descent on Beauharnois, the military authorities in Cornwall received another urgent plea for reinforcements from another direction. This despatch came from Major John Campbell, the regular officer in charge of the Huntingdon Loyal Volunteers. These Huntingdon men had travelled down the Chateauguay River as far as the insurgent camp at Baker's Farm near Ste. Martine. Fearing that the insurgents far out-numbered this force, Major Campbell sent an express to Colonel Turner at Cornwall asking for reinforcements. Immediately Lt.-Col. Donald Aeneas Macdonell of the 1st Stormont Regiment offered the services of his regiment and just as quickly his offer was accepted.[38] This was the Cornwall regiment that had given some cause for concern at the beginning of the outbreaks in Lower Canada a year earlier. At that time the more ardent reformers in the regiment had not been convinced that the political agitation would turn to rebellion. Now the officers and men of the 1st Stormont were the first to stand forward. Some 237 under the command of their lieutenant colonel immediately boarded the *Neptune* on 7 November 1838 and crossed to the Salmon River where fifty Indian Warriors from St. Regis joined them, under the command of the Indian agent, Captain Solomon Chesley.[39] Marching with them was Rev. John MacKenzie, the Presbyterian minister of Williamstown.[40]

It took the Cornwall contingent three days to make their way from the Salmon River to Huntingdon and thence down the Chateauguay River to the camp of the Huntingdon Volunteers. Enroute they encountered a party of loyalist volunteers carrying the body of one of their men who had been killed in a brief skirmish with the insurgents at Baker's Farm camp the previous day. At the sight of the dead volunteer soldier, the Indians raised a warwhoop that echoed through the forest, striking fear into the hearts of insurgent and loyalist alike along the Chateauguay. Then on Saturday, 10 November 1838, as the Stormont Highlanders and the St. Regis Indian Warriors neared the camp of the Huntingdon Volunteers, their pipers struck up "The Campbells are coming" and strutted into camp, a welcome sight to Major John Campbell and his men. In the nearby insurgent camp, news of the arrival of the Cornwall contingent together with the news that Colborne's army was converging on Napierville prompted the insurgent leaders at Baker's

Farm to make a quick decision to disperse. Thus, when the Huntingdon Volunteers with their reinforcements from Cornwall and St. Regis advanced on the insurgent camp, they found it deserted.

After putting the torch to the insurgent camp at Baker's Farm, the combined volunteer troops under Major John Campbell and Lieutenant-Colonel Donald Aeneas Macdonell moved off down the Chateauguay towards Ste. Martine. The cavalry under Captain Solomon Chesley made contact with Captain Edmund Thomas Campbell of the 7th Hussars who headed the brigade that attacked the insurgent camp at the small village of Chateauguay on Saturday night, 10 November.[41]

Meanwhile, the main force moving from Cornwall and Lancaster directly on Beauharnois under Colonel Lewis Carmichael and Major George Phillpotts, marched seventeen miles from Hungry Bay where they had disembarked after crossing from Coteau-du-Lac and reached Beauharnois at about eight o'clock on Saturday evening, 10 November. How many Cornwall men were with the brigade is uncertain, but a member of one of the town's most prominent families managed to join the brigade for he was mentioned in despatches. This was Neil McLean's brother, Alexander, who would soon succeed his older brother as the member of the provincial Assembly for Cornwall.[42] As 1,200 troops from Upper Canada invested Beauharnois, insurgents fired one volley before they dispersed or were captured. The next day Colonel Carmichael ordered the two Glengarry Regiments to march towards St. Martine to effect a juncture with the troops of the 1st Stormont Regiment.

This movement of the militia units from the Upper Canadian border counties of Glengarry and Stormont, together with the Cornwall Cavalry and the St. Regis Indian Warriors to the lower province in 1838 gave a new dimension to relations between the peoples near the provincial boundary and indeed, between the people of Cornwall and those of Montreal. Hitherto there had been a growing rapport between Roman Catholic Scots and their French Canadian co-religionists. As well there had been a certain amount of political sympathy between reformers in both areas. But the rebellions of 1837-38 put a temporary damper on this merging of the varied communities. By the time of the second rebellion in November of 1838 residents of Cornwall as well as those of the county were firmly within the "loyalist" orbit of Montrealers who had rallied to the government. They assumed something of the anti-French attitude of that section of the Anglophone community of Montreal that tended to regard all French Canadians as disaffected. Indeed, Bishop

Alexander Macdonell minced no words when he came to Cornwall in December of 1839 and preached at St. Columban's Church what proved to be his last sermon in Canada. Taking as his text "Render unto Caesar the things that are Caesar's and unto God the things that are God's", the warrior bishop summed up his analysis of the rebellion in the neighbouring province.[43] "The Canadians had no real grievances to complain of," he told his Cornwall congregation. "They paid no tythes but to their own clergy; no taxes or other burthen but what was imposed upon them by laws of their own making; their religion was not only free and uncontrolled, but encouraged and protected by the Government when threatened to be shackled by their own Catholic Assembly; parishes were multiplied by the consent of the Government, and subscriptions were raised by Protestants and even by the representatives of His Brittanic Majesty to build their churches". The Catholic Bishop warmed to his topic. "In a word," he exclaimed, "the French-Canadians lived freer, more comfortably and more independently than any other class of subjects perhaps on the whole surface of the globe and they were perfectly contented and seemed quite sensible of the blessings they enjoyed under the British Government until the folly and madness of Irreligious Papineau, Atheistical Giraud (Girod) and Camelion O'Callaghan (whose religion is as changeable as the colours of that animal), of the Protestant Nelsons, Browns, Scotts and others of that kidney, who, taking advantage of the ignorance and simplicity of the unfortunate habitants, made them believe that they were groaning under a galling yoke". Macdonell spoke of the "unfledged gang of briefless lawyers, notaries and...a numberless horde of doctors and apothecaries, like the locusts of Egypt, (who) spread themselves through the land, and...flattering their vanity with the hopes of the distinguished situations which they would occupy in the new republic, they unfortunately succeeded in seducing but too many of the credulous Canadians".

For Macdonell, "the most inexcusable part of the conduct of the Canadians was not to listen to the advice of their clergy, who knew well the intention of Papineau and his associates was to destroy their influence and extinguish the Catholic religion". His parting exhortation to the Cornwall Catholics whom he knew well was to remind them that "your loyalty is based upon the sacred obligation of your holy religion. The Apostle commands us to obey and be submissive to the powers that be...and give unto Caesar the things that are Caesar's.[44] His powerful political sermon, preached to men who just a year earlier had marched to Lower Canada to help suppress the insurgents, left no doubt that the church hierarchy continued to regard with misgivings those who had trod the road to rebellion. Bishop Macdonell castigated both the French and English leaders, whom he identified as lapsed or non-Catholics, and deplored those French Canadians who had refused to listen to the Catholic clergy when they advised against rebellion. Thus the Catholics of Cornwall regarded with some suspicion those few intrepid French Canadians who continued to move towards their boundaries in the post-rebellion era.

This rupture in cordial relations, caused by the rebellions, may partly explain the small number of French Canadians who moved into the Cornwall area prior to 1850. In the twenty-two years from 1829 to 1851 their numbers had risen only from ten to 132.[45] The town did not attract French Canadians from the lower province in large numbers until the 1870s with the advent of manufacturing. Then, in the decade from 1871 to 1881, the French-speaking community in the town increased from 313 to 1,223.[46]

If the rebellion period tended to disrupt cordial relations between the French-, Gaelic- and English-speaking communities on both sides of the Upper and Lower Canadian border and discouraged movement of French Canadians into the town of Cornwall, the continued disturbed state of the American-Canadian frontier after the rebellions forced military authorities in both provinces to mobilize the first standing Canadian army in peace time. Part of this local peace-time force was stationed at Cornwall from 1838 until 1843, thus turning the small town once more into a garrison town and keeping its military men on the alert with regards to its defences. After Hunters occupied the old windmill near Prescott for five days and were dislodged only after a fierce battle on 16 November 1838, the new lieutenant-governor of the upper province, Major General Sir George Arthur, warned local military commanders to occupy "any Mills or strong Buildings within our command, so that the Vagabonds may not make a footing anywhere."[47] Colonel C.B. Turner, the regular officer on particular duty in Cornwall, lost no time in turning the large deserted windmill to the east of Cornwall into a powder magazine. To strengthen the defenses of the windmill, a breastwork was thrown up round the southern portion of the tower that faced the river. Here a twelve-pounder was mounted.[48]

In the town itself the garrison over the winter of 1838-39 included Captain George Crawford's Independent Infantry Company, an Artillery Company commanded by Captain James Pringle, the 1st Provisional Battalion under Colonel Philip Vankoughnet and the 3rd Regiment of Glengarry Militia under Colonel Alexander Chisholm, one of the most ardent reformers and ardent loyalists. Then in 1839 new military arrangements were inaugurated with the raising of battalions of incorporated militia. Colonel Philip Vankoughnet was authorized to raise the 5th Battalion and did so within a few days, the men enlisting for a two-year engagement. This battalion garrisoned Cornwall until the spring of 1842 when it exchanged quarters with the 4th Battalion of Incorporated Militia at Prescott.[49]

Just as the last stretch of work was being completed on the Cornwall Canal after a long disruption due to lack of money and the unsettled rebellion period, Cornwall residents awoke one night to the rattle of drums — as the 4th "played ourselves in our new quarters...shortly after midnight." The Cornwall commandant, Colonel Turner, and his wife, tumbled out of bed thinking the Hunters were at their door, and the colonel gave the men of the incoming battalion "a jobation for disturbing his rest." Before the year was out the colonel would have more than one restless night as this jolly battalion made themselves at home in Cornwall which they found to be "an extremely pleasant place to be stationed in, having a very nice society, pleasant and hospitable."[50]

Officers of the 4th Battalion took up quarters in the commodious house at the southeast corner of Water and York Streets. They immediately proclaimed their arrival by placing the Roman numerals IV above the door. From then on the house was known as Ivy Hall and eventually became the elegant home of Cornwall's rising young politician, John Sandfield Macdonald.[51] The rank and file found quarters in the large brick building on lot 15 on the north side of Second Street,[52] owned by Dr. Noah Dickinson. The men of the 4th Provisional Battalion soon were favourites in town. They were invited to all the festivities including the all-day and all-night picnic at Lancaster in celebration of the completion of the cairn that Colonel Lewis Carmichael and the people of Glengarry had erected on the small island near the shore of the River aux Raisins to commemorate the district's loyalty during the rebellion and to honour Sir John Colborne.

With the disbandment of the battalions of incorporated militia in the spring of 1843, Cornwall lost its garrison and the excitement that went with the movement of troops in and out of the little town. The completion of the Cornwall Canal in November of 1843 meant that many of the migrant canal workers moved on to the work at the Beauharnois Canal that began almost immediately. Thus Cornwall was bereft of two large groups of outsiders who had formed part of its consumer ranks for local produce and who had added zest to the social life of the town. For the next decade Cornwall seemed to slip back to its pre-rebellion status of a remote county seat. As the town reached the half century mark, one writer somewhat condescendingly wrote, "Cornwall remains rather stationary...the actual number of its inhabitants being but 1,506." Describing the town as a "neat, quiet, pleasant, old-fashioned place (with) several good houses scattered through (it)," he concluded, "Cornwall is not a place of any great business."[53] Modern historians tend to agree. Cornwall did not even rate a dot on the map of Upper Canada prepared for Gerald Craig's scholarly work, *Upper Canada: The Formative Years 1784-1841.*[54]

NOTES

1. Alan Wilson, "John Colborne", in *DCB*, ix, 138; J.F. Pringle, *Lunenburgh, or the Old Eastern District*, 156-9.

2. Phillpotts to Colborne, Cornwall, 17 Nov. 1837 (Colborne Papers, MG24/A40/2952-55).

3. For details on Rev. Eléazar Williams see, George Mainer, "Solomon Yeomans Chesley", in *DCB*, x, 163; Rev. S.B. Lindsay, "The Romance of Louis XVII", in *Gazette*, Montreal, 6 June 1922; John H. Hanson, *The Lost Prince*.

4. See pastoral of Bishop Ignace Bourget, Roman Catholic Bishop of Montreal, admonishing against agitation and insurrection, see *Missiskoui Standard*, Frelighsburg, 21 Nov. 1837, re-printed from *Montreal Weekly Herald*.

5. Phillpotts to Colborne, 20 Nov. 1837 (MG24/A40/2969-71).

6. For details of this meeting see *Gazette*, Montreal, 5 Dec. 1837, re-printed from *Cornwall Observer*.

7. *Cornwall Observer*, 30 Nov. 1837.

8. *Transcript*, Montreal, 2 Dec. 1837.

9. William Boss, *The Stormont, Dundas, and Glengarry Highlanders*, 43.

10. Phillpotts to Colborne, 4 Dec. 1837, (MG24/A40/3072).

11. *Ibid.*

12. *Gazette*, Montreal, 9 Dec. 1837, see also, Gowan, Memoirs of the Rebellions, Ferguson papers, MG27/IE30/v/19.

13. *Gazette*, Montreal, 9 Dec. 1837.

14. Pringle, 260, 275.

15. Phillpotts to Colborne, 4 Dec. 1837 (MG24/A40/3072).

16. *Ibid.*, see also, Robert L. Seguin, *Le Mouvement insurrectionnel dans la Presqu'ile de Vaudreuil 1837-38*.

17. *Gazette*, Montreal, 9 Dec. 1837, re-printed from *Cornwall Observer*.

18. Phillpotts to Colborne, 4 Dec. 1837 (MG24/A40/3072).

19. Same to same, 4 Dec. 1837 (MG24/A40/3111).

20. *Ibid.*

21. *Gazette*, Montreal, 9 Dec. 1837.

22. See for instance, Captain T.L. Goldie to Col. Donald Macdonell, 2nd Regiment Glengarry Militia, 8 Dec. 1837 (RG8/C1271/74).

23. Elinor Senior, "The Glengarry Highlanders and the Suppression of the Rebellions in Lower Canada 1837-38", in *Journal of the Society for Army Historical Research*, LVI, no. 227 (London, 1978), 147-49.

24. Gowan, Memoirs of the Rebellions, in Ferguson Papers MG27/IE30/v/23.

25. Phillpotts to Colborne, 12 Dec. 1837 (MG24/A40/3161).

26. Vankoughnet to Capt. T.L. Goldie, 9 Dec. 1837 (MG24/A40/3128).

27. Garrison Orders, Coteau-du-Lac, 20 Dec. 1837 (RG4/A1/S392/91).

28. General Orders, 8 Jan. 1838 (RG8/C1192/88-89).

29. Phillpotts to Colborne, 29 Jan. 1838 (MG24/A40/3820-21); James Croil, *Dundas, or a Sketch of Canadian History*, 230; Pringle, 265-66, 275, 279.

30. General Orders, 21 April 1838 (RG8/C1192/154).

31. *Transcript*, Montreal, 29 Mar. 1838.

32. Colborne to the Commander-in-Chief, Lord Hill, at Horse Guards, Confidential, 23 June 1838 (RG8/C1278/73-77).

33. Pringle, 157, 161, 260.

34. Cited in Gowan, Memoirs of the Rebellions, (MG27/IE30/v/51).

35. *Ibid.*, 51-52.

36. *Ibid.*, see also, Pringle, 265.

37. Gowan, Memoirs of the Rebellions, MG27/IE30/v/57; Pringle, 265.

38. Gowan, Memoirs of the Rebellions, MG27/IE30/v/58.

39. Major John Campbell to Capt. T.L. Goldie, 11 Nov. 1838 (MG24/A40/5578-79).

40. Robert Sellar, *History of Huntingdon*, 603.

41. Lt. Thomas Colville to Maj.-Gen. Sir James Macdonell, 13 Nov. 1838 (MG24/A40/5596).

42. Gowan, Memoirs of the Rebellions, MG27/IE30/v/58.

43. *An Historical Sketch of St. Columban's Parish, Cornwall, commemorative of the opening of the new church*, June 1896, 4.

44. Extracts from Bishop Macdonell's sermon are found in J.A. Macdonell, *Sketches: Glengarry in Canada*, 276-77.

45. Population List, Cornwall and Roxborough, 1829; *Census*, 1851, 26-27.

46. *Census*, 1871, 274-75; *Census*, 1881, 262-63.

47. Cited in *Heritage Cornwall*, i, 2.

48. *Ibid.*, 3.

49. See Pringle, 266-67 and 281.

50. For details of the 4th Provisional Battalion of Incorporated Militia see, Wily Memoirs, MG29/E1/81-86; for a list of officers see, Pringle, 283.

51. Wily Memoirs, MG29/E1/84; Pringle, 267.

52. Pringle, 85.

53. W.H. Smith, *Canada, Past, Present and Future*, ii, 387.

54. Gerald Craig, *Upper Canada: The Formative Years 1784-1841*, 127.

Windmill Fort, built prior to 1837, converted for military purposes in 1838. Demolished in the late 1940's.

Chapter VIII

Cornwall at the Half-Century Mark

To the passing observer, Cornwall in 1850 did, indeed, appear backward in comparison to the booming towns to the west. "Muddy York" of 1812 had become by 1850 a city of 25,166 souls with a municipal revenue of £17,323 and yearly exports of £77,829.[1] Kingston's population had risen to 10,097 and it exported £47,414 worth of goods.[2] Even nearby Brockville, a town that was only laid out in 1802, had nearly 3,000 inhabitants and exports of £18,099 by 1850.[3] By comparison, Cornwall, the first of the Royal Townships settled in 1784, had but 1,646 souls[4] and its exports at mid-century amounted to only £1,067.[5] What increase in population there was in the years from 1834 to 1850 had resulted largely from natural increase or immigration from the United States and Ireland. Out of the 1,646 inhabitants of the town in 1850, 1,173 were born in Canada,[6] and of these, 132 were of French-Canadian origin.[7] The largest number of immigrants came from the United States, 376, among whom were many Irish. These immigrants, casualties of the commercial slump in the United States in the late 1830s, crossed the border seeking work in the lumber trade and at the canal construction sites.[8] When to the Irish coming in from the United States were added 269 arriving directly from Ireland, most of them Catholics,[9] the population of Cornwall in the 1850s continued to be an ethnic and religious mosaic.

Cornwall Township still dominated the town with respect to population and productivity. A total of 3,897 people lived in the township where 13,711 acres had been brought under cultivation by 1850. In terms of production these farmers in the township accounted for 17,900 bushels of wheat, 42,000 bushels of oats, 9,500 bushels of peas, 11,000 bushels of Indian corn, 13,000 bushels of potatoes, 43,900 pounds of maple sugar, 13,000 pounds of wool and 24,900 pounds of butter. Moreover they had built, by 1850, three grist mills and four saw mills.

The rear of Cornwall Township had been partitioned in 1791

into a new township called Roxborough. By 1850 Roxborough had 1,704 people and 8,472 acres under cultivation. Apart from the rather small amount of this agricultural produce that was exported through Cornwall — only 3,224 bushels of oats and 1,410 bushels of wheat, for instance — most of the produce of the township was consumed locally or sent to the Montreal and Quebec City markets.[10]

If the township of Cornwall still dominated the town in terms of population and productivity, it was the reverse with regard to politics. The town of Cornwall was the political centre, not only of the township, but of the whole county of Stormont that included the townships of Roxborough, Osnabruck and Finch, and, until 1830, the county of Russell. On long winter evenings the men of Cornwall and their cohorts from the countryside warmed themselves around the over-heated stove at the county court house on Water Street or gathered at one of the numerous taverns that dotted the centre of the town, a glass of whiskey in their hands, deciding who would represent the town and county in the provincial Assembly. Not only did the men of the town discuss local political personalities, and note carefully their strengths and shortcomings in terms of success at the hustings, the politically-keen also watched with interest the shifts in electoral districts over the first fifty years of the century. In 1820, for example, when the county of Stormont claimed more than 4,000 souls, it could at last send two members off to the provincial Assembly at York instead of only one. It was at this time that the county of Russell was detached from Stormont. Then, in 1834, as Cornwall's population reached 1,000, the town was entitled to elect a member to the Assembly. Proudly Cornwall took its place as one of the province's towns large enough to attain local representation at the capital, now called Toronto. Thus, for a brief period from 1834 to 1841, Cornwall was at the peak of its political prestige, having three of its townsmen as representatives at the provincial Assembly.

The new constitutional arrangements, worked out in 1841 after the rebellion period, saw the upper province once more re-united to Lower Canada as it had been prior to 1791. Instead of a re-united province of Quebec, however, the two provinces now formed the province of Canada. For Cornwall, this meant diminished political prestige because the county was reduced to a one-member riding. However, these changes did not necessarily mean diminished political clout. As far as the people of Cornwall were concerned, they had seldom lacked a direct line to the corridors of power at Toronto. In the earliest days of the settlement, one of their townsmen, Robert I.D. Gray, had been solicitor-general. By 1815 the former Episcopal rector and school master of Cornwall, John Strachan, had become a member of both the Executive and Legislative Councils at York. Moreover, many of his former pupils, who knew Cornwall intimately, were moving into positions of power in the provincial bureaucracy or Assembly.

Another former merchant of the town, John Beikie, who represented the county in the Assembly from 1812 to 1816, became Clerk of the Executive Council from 1820 to 1825. Then, when the tory combination of Philip Vankoughnet and Archibald McLean became virtual tenants of the Stormont county seats for about eighteen years after 1816, the town and county exhibited for the first time what was to be a characteristic of the Cornwall and Stormont voters — political stability or, perhaps more accurately, political fidelity to local sons whose metal they had tested and found to their liking. And this metal tended to be moderate and measured, whether labelled tory, liberal or reformer. Nor did Cornwall Assemblymen warrant the description of "yes-men". When Philip Vankoughnet left the political arena to accept a seat on the Legislative Council in 1836 at the recommendation of the departing lieutenant-governor, Sir John Colborne, he by no means proved a docile supporter of the powers that be. This was particularly true over the issue of settling the claims of militiamen who had served during the rebellion. In fact, Vankoughnet, as Cornwall's chief protagonist, was exhibiting such irascible behaviour by 1840 at meetings of the Legislative Council that the new lieutenant-governor, Sir Gordon Arthur, exclaimed, "Politically, we owe Coll. Van Koughnet nothing. — On the contrary his conduct last session was factious and very hostile."[11] Needless to say, Vankoughnet was not among those re-appointed to the Legislative Council in 1841.[12]

Another Cornwall Assemblyman, the reformer Dr. William Bruce, publicly and privately snorted his vehement disapproval of any Executive Council that was appointed by the lieutenant-governor and consulted by him only if he wished such consultation. When the Executive Council dramatically defied the new lieutenant-governor, Sir Francis Bond Head, in 1836 by resigning rather than continue to sit simply as a part-time consultative body, the young Cornwall medical doctor wrote gloatingly to his good friend in Cornwall, Irishman William Browne. Browne was a graduate of Trinity College, Dublin, whose home in Cornwall was a haven for any Irishman coming to Canada without friends or money. It was also a rendezvous for Cornwall reformers, as Bruce's letter indicated. "We are determined," Bruce reported to Browne on St. Patrick's Day, 1836, "to ask for...and insist on what you say we must have, that is, a responsible

Executive Council. This House must have the above, or we must be dissolved, or we will dissolve ourselves."[13] Thus tory Vankoughnet and reformer Bruce both kicked up their heels at the central political establishment. It was otherwise with Vankoughnet's political colleague, Archibald McLean. Rather than falling from grace, McLean continued to rise, favoured with a judgeship in Toronto in 1837, and thus providing his stay-at-home constituents in Cornwall with yet another direct line to authorities in the provincial capital.

For half a century the people of Cornwall had looked increasingly westward to Toronto as the focal point of political power — the only real drawing card the west held for them. Their commercial, business and cultural links were still eastward towards Montreal. Now as the century neared its half-way mark, the political direction was shifting from the west to a more central position, first Kingston, then Montreal as the location of the Provincial Assembly. After 1849, the Assembly ambulated between Toronto and Quebec City until the politicians and their entourages, tired of the constant shifts, welcomed Queen Victoria's decision to make nearby Ottawa the provincial capital, once more drawing the attention of Cornwallites away from the western part of the province.

The shift in Cornwall's political allegiance from tory right to left-centre reform became more apparent in the 1850s when the long McLean ascendancy ended with Alexander McLean's retirement from politics in 1851. The first serious break in the solidly pro-government ranks in Cornwall had come in 1834 with the victory of reformers Donald Aeneas Macdonell and Dr. William Bruce at the county elections. Macdonell won two subsequent elections in 1836 and again in 1844, thus keeping the county divided between reformers and tories. The town of Cornwall, however, remained within the tory or, as it was more frequently labelled, "Constitutionalist" orbit, until 1851. It even provided a safe seat in 1846 for the future Grand Master of the Orange Lodges, John Hillyard Cameron, when he was named solicitor-general in the Draper ministry. Obligingly, Cornwall lawyer Rolland McDonald stepped down from the seat in order to make room for Cameron. It was the second time Cornwall had given a safe seat to tory interests.[14] The man who obliged was the son of a retired fur-trader living at the palatial "Inverarden" — John McDonald of Garth. Just two years earlier the young McDonald had wrested the Cornwall seat from another moderate conservative, Solomon Y. Chesley.[15] Although John Hillyard Cameron won the seat again in 1848 at the general elections that saw a great Liberal sweep of the two provinces under Robert

Baldwin and Louis-Hippolyte La Fontaine, it was the last time that Cornwall people would give their votes to someone from outside the town and county.

Though Cameron was an outsider from Toronto, Cornwallites in 1848 probably thought they were voting for the future leader of the conservative forces in the province, perhaps even a future premier. Only the previous year the retiring conservative leader, William Draper, had invited Cameron to assume the mantle of attorney-general, a post that was tantamount to leadership of the government.[16] With such a rising star in their midst, the conservative elements in Cornwall gave Cameron their support. However, by 1851, Cameron decided not to contest the Cornwall seat again and it fell to a local doctor, Roderick Macdonald. He held it for two sessions until Cornwall lawyer John Sandfield Macdonald decided to shift his bailiwick from Glengarry to Cornwall. For the next fourteen years it was John Sandfield Macdonald who occupied the centre of the political stage in Cornwall, another example of the town's stability in politics.

Not only did the town turn consistently liberal at a time when the country as a whole was experiencing severe political instability: so, too, did the county hoist liberal colours. Cornwall's mayor, William Mattice, tossed his hat into the county electoral proceedings in 1851. As the son of a United Empire Loyalist and one of the town's leading merchants, Mattice had impeccable credentials. He was an elder and trustee of St. John's Presbyterian Church, a pioneer in Masonry in the Eastern District, town reeve, and lieutenant colonel of the 5th battalion Stormont militia.[17] The popular mayor swept the county and continued to do so for the next decade.

Thus Cornwall seemed to have made a complete political somersault in the first half of the century. From a pro-government tory complexion at the beginning of the century, it surfaced at mid-century as a centre of moderate liberalism. A closer look at this apparent political metamorphosis reveals that the shift may not have been that pronounced. For one thing, their current lodestar, John Sandfield Macdonald, was a product of tory Archibald McLean's law office. His entry into politics had been fostered by tory elements in Glengarry and he at first enjoyed the support of Cornwall's only newspaper, the moderate conservative *Observer*.[18] Had John Sandfield Macdonald remained solidly tory, it is likely that Cornwall voters would have continued to back him just as they did when he eased himself out from close association with the old-line tories and moved closer to the liberal reformers, eventually assuming a centrist position in liberal politics. This was a position that harmonized with the moderate position of most of his constituents in Cornwall.

The extremism of George Brown in religious matters, the regional pulls of Toronto and the area to its west, and the nationalist overtones in the French-speaking section of the province — all these John Sandfield Macdonald regarded as political anathema that would divide the country. His home in Cornwall was a living example of how the pluralism of the country could be harmonized. At his lavish entertainments at Ivy Hall, Cornwallites and provincial notables rubbed shoulders as bagpipes filled the air and vast quantities of strong drink loosened tongues. Gaelic, English and frequently French flowed, as the charming hostess, the soft-spoken Marie Christine Waggaman Macdonald, greeted her guests. This was the Louisiana belle whom John Sandfield Macdonald had persuaded to elope with him from a French finishing school in Baltimore.[19] Christine now graced the drawing room at Ivy Hall and, unlike her husband, she rarely missed Mass at the Roman Catholic St. Columban's Church, a modest wooden building erected in 1829-30 on lot 17 on the north side of Fourth Street.[20] Thus while John Sandfield Macdonald's devotion was more to politics than to religion, his wife's influence as a devout Catholic balanced her husband's lack of religious ardour.[21] Nor was John Sandfield Macdonald alone in his lack of a hard sectarian line. Many of his Cornwall and Glengarry cohorts shared his easy attitude towards religion, especially those whose families had marriage ties that bridged the various religious communities in the town and county.[22] Inattentive as he was to religious observances, Macdonald and his family were generous financial supporters of the new St. Columban's and helped finance the purchase of the parish bell.[23]

Though essentially a liberal Catholic whose lack of enthusiasm for separate sectarian schools in Cornwall and Glengarry brought clerical wrath on his head, John Sandfield Macdonald found little comfort in the demands of George Brown and the Toronto *Globe* that churches be funded entirely by voluntary subscriptions of their members. Nor did John Sandfield Macdonald relish the disruptive influences of the Free Kirk movement that were already being felt in Cornwall in the early 1840s. Presbyterians had been the first religious group to erect a church in the small village, their log church going up in 1787. By 1820 they were well enough organized to play host to ministers and elders of the four presbyteries of Upper and Lower Canada which met that year in Cornwall to form the United Synod of Canada.[24] When their first minister, John Bethune of Williamstown, died in 1815, the small congregation was served from 1817 until 1823 by the master of the District Grammar School, Reverend Joseph Johnston. Being of Irish background and a licentiate of the Synod of Ulster, Johnston did not suit the more ardent Scots Presbyterians of Cornwall.[25] When Johnston resigned as master of the District School in 1822, his post was assumed by a minister of the Church of Scotland, Reverend Harry Leith. Leith began to hold services in the District School, attracting a number of the families away from the original congregation. This created the first, though temporary, split in Presbyterian ranks in Cornwall. It was not until Johnston left Cornwall for Osnabruck in 1823 that the division was healed and the congregation, numbering something under 200 at this time, reunited in the old church under Leith.[26] They soon put their energies to work to build a new and bigger church on lot 15 on the east side of Pitt Street between First and Second Streets.[27] Substantial financial aid came from many leading men in Montreal, Quebec City and Kingston, some of whom were not Presbyterians. By 1827 the new white frame church, St. John's, was finished, topped by a turret instead of a steeple. Through the generosity of the Cline family, St. John's acquired a bell which not only summoned worshippers to service, but soon became part of the life of all Cornwallites, calling them from their beds at six in the morning, reminding them at noon that it was time for lunch, and sounding a nine o'clock curfew at night. Until 1889 it also served as the fire alarm for the town.[28]

No sooner was St. John's church ready for worship in 1827 than its minister decided to return to Scotland. This left a vacancy into which stepped a young schoolmaster and minister who quickly became one of the town's most forceful personalities. Reverend Hugh Urquhart would have shone anywhere he set foot. Like two of his eminent predecessors in Cornwall — John Bethune and John Strachan — Urquhart was a Scot and a graduate of King's College, Aberdeen. Ordained into the Church of Scotland in 1822, he set sail later that year for Canada. Here a post awaited the young minister at the Montreal Academic Institution, a private high school founded and run by a fellow Scot and graduate of Marischal College, Aberdeen, Reverend Harry Esson. Urquhart, like his employer, was but twenty-nine years old when he began his five-year stint at Esson's Academy which soon attracted many of the sons of leading Montreal families, boys who would otherwise have attended the government-subsidized Grammar School of Alexander Skakel. The new academy, according to historian-minister Robert Campbell of the Montreal Scotch Presbyterian Church, "owed not a little of its popularity to Mr. Urquhart."[29]

It was to Hugh Urquhart that the trustees of the new St. John's Presbyterian Church in Cornwall turned in 1827. The call to Urquhart, signed by Neil and Archibald McLean, John McDonald and Dr. Ambrose Blacklock, fell on receptive ears.[30] Both Urquhart's letter of acceptance and the manner of his induction showed that he was an ardent adherent to the idea that a minister could be installed only with the consent of the congregation. This was to be one of the moot issues that led within a decade to serious disruption within Presbyterian ranks, both in Scotland and Canada, including Cornwall. Urquhart's early stance indicated that he would influence his Cornwall flock towards what came to be known as the "non-intrusion" position. This meant that patrons of a church could not install or "intrude" a minister into a church against the wishes of the congregation. It also meant that should disputes arise about the appointment of a minister, such disputes were not to be settled by a civil court.[31] In his letter to the Trustees of St. John's Church, Urquhart carefully noted that he accepted "the Call...which you...present to me, with consent of said Congregation". Moreover, as soon as he was inducted as minister, "the Heads of families and Members of the Congregation immediately thereafter took Mr. Urquhart by the hand in testimony of their receiving him to be their Minister".[32] There could be no doubt that Urquhart was installed by the congregation.

The new minister stepped not only into the pulpit of St. John's but also into the master's seat at the District Grammar School, bringing it back almost to the stature it had enjoyed under John Strachan. He was also the third Presbyterian minister to hold the post of master at what had started out as an Episcopalian high school but which, by 1817, had come under successive Presbyterian ministers and continued to do so almost without exception until the 1850s.[33] Urquhart's students included the not-so-young John Sandfield Macdonald, who would become premier of Canada, Archibald McLean, the future associate judge of the King's Bench, Donald McAuley, a future lumber merchant, Roderick Macdonald, who would become one of Cornwall's leading medical men and county treasurer, Jacob Farrand Pringle, the future historian and county judge, Philip Vankoughnet, one of the future leading merchants of the town and a legislative councillor, and George C. Wood, the future postmaster of the town.[34] Drawn to Cornwall, too, by the high quality of Urquhart's teaching were a number of Montreal lads — John and William Molson, sons of the brewer, and Joseph Shuter and William Arnoldi.

For thirteen years Urquhart combined preaching and teaching, winning from his students the affectionate nickname of "Polycarp", an acknowledgement of his great scholarship and simplicity of character. Friends and clerical colleagues spoke of Urquhart's "unparalleled grace and kindness". His home in Cornwall was a "model in which, with dignity and a liberal hand, hospitality was extended alike to strangers and acquaintances".[35] A new honour came to Urquhart in 1840 when he was named Moderator of the Synod of the Presbyterian Church in Canada, an appointment that lent considerable prestige to the town. His added duties as Moderator, together with his work as pastor of St. John's prompted Urquhart to give up his work as master of the District Grammar School in order to devote full time to his ministry.

Urquhart made no secret of his sympathies with the party in Scotland that was protesting against what he considered "the spiritual thraldom of the Church". According to those of his flock who were coming increasingly under the influence of the Free Kirk movement in the early 1840s, Urquhart went so far as to raise a fund to help finance Free Kirk people in erecting churches.[36] Thus, when deputies arrived in Cornwall from the Scottish Free Kirk, they were welcomed by some members of St. John's church who fully expected that, in the event of a split in the church, Reverend Hugh Urquhart would, like his good friend in Montreal, Reverend Henry Esson, withdraw to join the Free Kirk.[37] However, Urquhart, as outspoken as he was on the issue, rejected the idea of separation. He thus kept most of Cornwall's Presbyterians within the parent church. These included such prominent families as the Clines, Kays, Colquhouns, McLeans, Mattices and Pringles.

It was, then, but a small group that severed their ties with St. John's church in 1844. Their views were reinforced by articles in the newly-established Toronto journal, the *Banner*, published by Peter Brown and his son, George, in the interests of the Free Kirk.[38] At the head of the Cornwall dissenting group was Doctor William Johnston, a native of Scotland and a graduate of the University of Edinburgh, and James Craig, a contractor and farmer, both of whom had been among the first elders of St. John's church. Associated with Johnston and Craig in the leadership of the separation movement were John Sandfield Macdonald's legal assistant, A.M. Mackenzie, Austin Edson Cadwell, head of Cornwall's only iron foundry, school teacher John McKerras, tinsmith John Hunter, the future town councillor James Smart, and jeweller Robert Atchison.[39] At first the Free Kirk adherents held services in the home of John Hunter on lot 10 at the corner of First and Amelia Streets.[40] They were soon joined by Reverend John Fraser, a Free Kirk minister from the Presbytery of Montreal. Under his leadership, the seceding group formed a committee in 1846 to raise funds for a church.[41] By 1851 they numbered 109 in Cornwall itself and 103 in the township. Another Free Kirk minister, Rev. Charles Quinn, took charge of the small congregation, and it was under his charge that the foundation for a new church was laid in July 1851 on lot 11 on the south side of Second Street. Until 1876 the new church was known simply as the Free Kirk.[43]

The parent church retained the vast majority of the town's Presbyterians, though there must have been a fair number in Cornwall not associated with either parish. The 1851 census showed 362 Church of Scotland adherents in Cornwall and another 742 in the township.[44] The official history of St. John's Church, compiled from church records, states that there was not "any great increase in the number of church members in Dr. Urquhart's time" and that at his death there were about 190 members of the congregation, perhaps the starkest evidence of the effect of disruption in 1844.[45] Still, St. John's weathered the split, setting up a committee to help raise funds for the new Church of Scotland university being founded at Kingston in the 1840s.[46] It even looked somewhat askance at its offspring when the Free Kirk came out for total abstinence.[47] In fact, the stance of the Free Kirkers provoked one of the few remaining Methodists in Cornwall to tease one of them by remarking that he understood that Presbyterians liked a drink at times. The Free Kirker promptly and soberly replied, "That is not true of (the Free Kirk), though I have heard they do at St. John's."[48]

The effects of the disruption within Presbyterian ranks were watched carefully by the politically-minded men of the town, especially by John Sandfield Macdonald who had been moving up in the Cornwall bureaucracy. In 1840 the young barrister took his place as first lieutenant in the newly organized fire company under fellow barrister, Captain George McDonell.[49] A year later Macdonald was elected president of the Cornwall Board of Police, a post that was tantamount to being mayor and which served many ambitious men as a training ground and a stepping stone to higher politics. While Presbyterians were debating the Free Kirk issue with gusto, Macdonald was acquiring land and building up a solid financial base through a lucrative legal business in Cornwall. The only cloud on his horizon was recurring attacks of tuberculosis. What began to interest him even more than the Presbyterian squabbles were developments within his own religious milieu in the town.

From the time of the founding of Cornwall in 1784, Roman Catholics had remained a small segment of its population. There had been Catholic soldiers among the Irish and Scottish disbanded troops, and a few of these settled in Cornwall township, among them Ensign Francis McCarty,[50] Patrick and Daniel McGuire,[51] and John Loney.[52] Probably the most influential of the Scottish Catholics to settle in the town of Cornwall itself was Captain John McDonell (Scotus), known as Spanish John because of his service in Spain.[53] McDonell settled on lot 19 on the north side of Water Street and his family laid claim to all the property bounded by Water and Second Streets between Augustus and Bedford Streets.[54] In addition, Spanish John had property on the River aux Raisin where he spent most of his declining years. Calling it "Scothouse" after the family estate in Scotland, the elder McDonell caused his sons some concern. Captain Miles McDonell informed his brother, "My father still keeps possession of his favourite seat at the River aux Raisin (where) he lives very uncomfortably, tho' at great expense", pursued by and pursuing the widow of Donald McAlistir, much to the delight of the gossips of the village and the chagrin of his sons. They spoke of "that cursed artful widow (who) pilfers him of everything, of which she is not ashamed to boast publicly".[55] The elder McDonell was not that aging or lonely that he rushed into matrimony, however. He assured his sons that he went to the widow's house "to pass an idle hour (thinking) it no harm to shew some little attention to her more than to the rest of the vulgar of the place. But...as to matrimony with her or any other, I shall change my mind before I can think of it".[56]

An even more colourful personage in the early years of the town was Peggy Bruce, daughter of a substantial Roman Catholic Irish farmer of New York, Cornelius O'Sullivan.[57] After the death of her soldier-husband, Alexander Bruce, Peggy kept up the log tavern that served as a public house and inn. With a sharp tongue and an Irish wit, she shattered whatever pretensions her neighbours assumed. One such was a corporal turned militia captain by 1812 whom she always addressed as "Captain Corporal John". Hearing Captain Corporal John explode one day into profanity when he discovered that his whole company had disappeared overnight as soon as they saw the American troops set sail for the southern bank of the St. Lawrence, Peggy Bruce stuck her head out of the window to chide the newly-promoted captain. "Oh, John," she scolded. "Don't let the devil get so great a hould of ye as to be blaspheming like a heathen in that fearful way; things are not bad with you yet; sure you have twice as many men under your command as you had when I knew you first."[58] Feared because of her waspish tongue, Peggy was also greatly beloved in Cornwall because of her care of the sick. No matter what time of the day or night, those who needed medical care sent for Peggy Bruce. Her usual method of dealing with sickness was to stuff as much food into the patient as possible and then to plunge the sick one into a warm bath of her favourite herbs. When these specifics were over, her parting gesture was to dig into her deep pockets and fish out a bottle or two of wine as a recuperative for the patient.[59]

These were some of the identifiable Roman Catholics of Cornwall in the late eighteenth century. Together with Catholics of Glengarry they probably had as their first priest Father John McKenna, an Irishman who had come to Glengarry prior to 1785 with a group of Scottish Catholics from New York.[60] However, as soon as the Highland Catholics settled, they took steps to procure a priest acquainted with Gaelic, preferably a Highland Scot.[61] Their eye fell on Roderick Macdonell, whose father and two brothers had been captains in the King's Royal Regiment of New York. Not only was Father Roderick Macdonell closely allied to officers of this loyalist regiment, he also had served for some time as priest in Glengarry, Scotland, after being educated, as were most Highland gentlemen of the time, at the Scots College at Valladolid, Spain, and at Douay, France.

With impressive credentials from Secretary of State Lord Sydney, Father Roderick Macdonell arrived in Canada in 1785, highly recommended to receive a government bounty in the form of an annual subsistence allowance.[62] Father Macdonell soon found himself pressed into duty in several parishes, for the resources of the church in the Quebec Diocese were being taxed severely to find sufficient priests to supply the new western settlements. Moreover, the small Indian village of St. Regis across the river from Cornwall had been without a resident priest since 1783.[63] Thus Father Macdonell had to cover three parishes at first — Glengarry, St. Regis and Cornwall. Travelling by canoe and horse, he visited the rear of Cornwall township where the Catholic population was more numerous along the River aux Raisins,[64] and there he organized the parish of St. Andrews.[65] This was the parish that the Catholics of Cornwall belonged to for the first fifty years of the town's existence. A rude log chapel was built as soon as the settlers first arrived. Then by 1788 they began a more substantial stone church that was finished at the turn of the century, its construction partly paid for by men of the North-West Company then wintering in the far west.[66]

The difficulty of serving several widely-separated parishes was only too evident to the thirty-year-old priest. On one occasion when he was asked to officiate at a marriage in the Cornwall parish,

Father Roderick Macdonell awaited the bride's father who came to fetch him at St. Regis early one cold spring morning. As they neared the northern bank of the St. Lawrence to make their way through Cornwall to the church at St. Andrews, the accumulation of ice and snow on the bank suddenly gave way, swamping the canoe and throwing its occupants into the icy swift current. The priest and the bride's father struggled to the shore where they dried themselves off as best they could at the cabin of a settler. Then the pair started off through Cornwall, the priest seated on the solitary horse. Hour after hour they toiled on through deeper and deeper mud. Finally they reached the clearing that was St. Andrews. Shouts of delight greeted them and hot collations were served by the jubilant Highlanders who were anxious to begin the three days of festivities that accompanied the wedding.[67]

The priest's heavy parish load was somewhat lightened in 1786 with the arrival of a second Highland priest, Father Alexander Macdonell, who accompanied 345 members of his parish from Knoydart, Glengarry, to the new Glengarry in the western part of Quebec.[68] The newly-arrived priest, who was fluent in Gaelic, French and English, took over the duties in Glengarry where he soon organized St. Raphael's Parish.[69] His arrival cleared the way for Father Roderick Macdonell to be appointed resident priest at St. Regis in 1789, though he continued to serve the Catholics in Cornwall and its township as well.

The death of Father Alexander Macdonell in 1803 threw the burden of the whole district back on Father Roderick Macdonell until a successor was found. The manoeuvres surrounding a new appointment revealed the problems of supplying a priest for places like Cornwall where ethnic tensions could surface on such vital matters as the language or nationality of a local priest, militia officer, sheriff or other official.[70] At the time of the death of Father Alexander Macdonell, it was already expected that another Father Alexander Macdonell would be arriving from Scotland with a body of immigrants. In the meantime, there was but one itinerant Recollect priest, Father Luke Fitzsimmons, the former chaplain of the North-West Company, available for the vacancy. As an Irish priest, Father Fitzsimmons was not as readily acceptable to the Highlanders as a Highland priest and no one knew this better than Father Fitzsimmons and Father Roderick Macdonell. Indeed Father Macdonell found "the people of the New Lands...very troublesome" and feared that he might "have to pass the remaining part of my life among them and those of St. Andrews parish".[71]

To smoothe the way for Father Fitzsimmons at the parish of St. Raphael's, Father Roderick wrote a half-chiding, half-coaxing letter to the Highlanders there. He informed them that "Reverend Mr. Fitzsimmons has come to this country to serve you as a Pastor, and that he is appointed by the Lord Bishop of Quebec for your Parish at St. Raphaels." Macdonell assured them that "If Mr. Macdonell (Father Alexander Macdonell, the future bishop) arrives this year, it will rest with the Bishop to appoint him or not". But, the St. Regis priest went on, "You know that no priest can be a pastor in any parish unless he is appointed by the Bishop and that it entirely depends on the Bishop to appoint anyone he pleases." Coming from one of their own priests, this recommendation had something of a rebuke about it. Father Macdonell went on to tell the parishioners that they were "bound and obliged to receive him (Father Fitzsimmons) with every mark of esteem and attention in your power".[72]

The Irish priest lasted only six months at St. Raphaels. By 24 March 1805, after the arrival of Father Alexander Macdonell and his immigrants, Fitzsimmons moved to St. Andrews.[73] He thus became the first resident priest for Cornwall and its township, taking over the duties previously carried out with such difficulty by Father Roderick Macdonell of St. Regis. This long rapport between the parishes of St. Regis and St. Andrews survived well into the nineteenth century. In 1839, the Indians looked to the priest at St. Andrews to succour them when their own priest, Curé François-Xavier Marcoux, fell ill. Just as Father Roderick Macdonell was transported by canoe and horse to St. Andrews at the turn of the century to perform marriages and baptisms and to officiate at the grave for Cornwall Catholics, so, too, the St. Andrews priest of 1839, the aging Father Aeneas McDonell, was carried through Cornwall by horse and canoe across the St. Lawrence River to the Indian village on Christmas eve, 1839, escorted all the way there and back by a party of Indians.[74] Again, as late as 1878 when the St. Regis Indians raised a storm against their old priest, Father Marcoux, because the "church took possession of a certain road and the Indians claim that no white man can take Indian land", the priest fled to Cornwall until tempers cooled.[75]

Father Fitzsimmons remained at St. Andrews for three years, from 1805 to 1808. There is little doubt that his departure from the parish was hastened by the arrival of the Catholic priest who, above all others, was to stamp the Highland image on the Catholics of Upper Canada during the first forty years of the nineteenth century. This was the warrior priest, Father Alexander Macdonell, a powerful man some six feet four inches tall, who towered over even those giants of Highlanders to whom he ministered. Many of the men he brought with him in October of 1804 were soldiers of the Glengarry Fencible Regiment, the first Catholic corps raised in Great Britain since the Reformation and formed at the suggestion of Father Alexander Macdonell who became chaplain.[76] On his arrival in Canada, Father Macdonell carried in his pocket a letter from the Secretary of State, Lord Hobart, authorizing the lieutenant-governor of Upper Canada, Peter Hunter, to grant 1,200 acres of unappropriated Crown Lands to the priest and 200 acres to every "family he may introduce into the Colony".[77]

In Upper Canada Macdonell found "but two clergymen and two Catholic churches in the whole province. One of these," Macdonell bluntly remarked, "soon after deserted his post".[78] The priest referred to was Father Fitzsimmons who left Cornwall in 1808 to do missionary work on the Gaspé coast and eventually returned to Ireland in 1811.[79] If feathers were ruffled at times between the Irish and Scots Catholic clergy, the task of providing the "comforts of religion to the Catholic inhabitants", as Macdonell described his work, left the newly-arrived priest little time for in-fighting. With the departure of Father Fitzsimmons, Father Macdonell had to take over the duties of the parish of St. Andrews and the care of the Cornwall Catholics as well. These amounted to twenty-three families in 1806, an indication that there had been little Catholic immigration into the area since the original founding of the township.[80]

By the late 1820s there was a trickle of Irish Roman Catholic immigrants to Cornwall, some of them from a group of 200 who had settled temporarily and discontentedly at Lancaster prior to 1821.[81] A number of these Irish moved westward to the Indian tract that lay between Cornwall and Charlottenburg townships.[82] It was on this Indian Reserve, commonly called Bois Sauvage, that the Irish and French-Canadian newcomers to Cornwall first brushed shoulders with each other in the 1820s. That French Canadians were settling at Bois Sauvage in the early 1820s is indicated in the correspondence between the Bishop of Montreal, Jean-Jacques Lartigue, and Alexander Macdonell who, by 1819, had become the first Catholic bishop in Upper Canada. Lartigue assured Macdonell that in future the priest at St. Regis would no longer minister "d'aucune des habitants du Haut Canada qu'avoisant sa Mission, Canadiens comme autres, excepté dans les cas de nécessité, et que tout ce qui appartient au Bois Sauvage dépendrait à l'avenir de la jurisdiction de vos Prêtes."[83] Thus jurisdictional disputes in the developing Catholic dioceses were being ironed out as the area of Cornwall was being gradually filled up by increasing numbers of Catholics, some of them French-Canadians.

The St. Regis Indians were annoyed at the steady intrusion of settlers into their tract, so much so that their superintendent, Solomon Y. Chesley, warned settlers on 22 October, 1835, that "arrangements were made with the Attorney-General, during the last Assizes in Cornwall, for prosecuting and ejecting all defaulters and intruders settled on the Indian Reservation between the Counties of Stormont and Glengarry".[84] Within the next fifteen years so many had intruded on the Indian Tract or had leased land from the Indians on which they had farms that the Indian tenants eventually petitioned the government for freehold titles to their farms. The government allowed them to commute their rents for a fair amount of money and to obtain patents for their farms. When this was done, the money paid into government was invested for the benefit of the Indians who received an annual interest from the investment.[85]

By 1829 ten of the westward-moving French Canadian families had reached Cornwall itself, numbering in all seventy-four souls. As Cornwall's population at this time was only 812, this meant that these French Canadian families may well have represented the largest single Catholic group in the town.[86] Culturally, the French-Canadian presence in Cornwall was announced on 18 December 1835 in the Cornwall *Observer*. On that date, an advertisement appeared notifying the public that Clet. Raizenne "has commenced a day and night (French) school in Mr. Chesley's brick house near Mr. Lane's tavern, where he intends, by unremitting assiduity, to advance his pupils". For their spiritual guidance, these newly-arriving Catholics of Cornwall still had to look outside the town. From the time of Father Fitzsimmons' departure in 1808 until 1821, the Catholics were ministered to by the priest from St. Raphaels, Father Alexander Macdonell. When he was appointed Bishop in 1819, Macdonell's additional duties made it imperative that a resident priest be appointed once more to St. Andrews. The choice fell upon another Irish priest, Father John O'Meara, even though the bishops in Kingston, Montreal and Quebec City had reservations about employing Irish priests whom they found difficult to discipline.[87]

It was with the departure of Father O'Meara from St. Andrews in 1827 that the Catholics of Cornwall began to think seriously of building a church and securing a resident priest of their own. Small as their numbers were in 1829, these local Catholics turned the first sod on Fourth Street, west of Pitt Street, to begin work on St. Columban's Church, named in honour of the Irish saint who converted the Highlanders of Scotland to Christianity.[88] Work halted several times over the next few years for lack of funds, but always families like the Macdonells, Macdonalds, Rodriques, Loneys and Flanigans (Flanagans) sustained the work by their financial support.[89] By the time St. Columban's was finished, the Macdonells were by far the most important of the Cornwall Catholic families. Head of the family was Donald Macdonell (Greenfield), sheriff of the Eastern District from 1819 to 1837. As early as 1827 he had been named the Catholic representative to the Board of Education for the Eastern District, together with Archibald McLean for the Presbyterians and Joseph Anderson for the Anglicans.[90] With his wife, a daughter of Ranald Macdonell (Leek), Macdonell was foremost in forwarding the interests of the Catholics of Cornwall.

Just as faithful were members of the Loney family whose head was John Loney (Looney), a private in the 1st Battalion of the King's Royal Regiment of New York.[91] Loney was one of the first of the disbanded soldiers to arrive at Township No. 2 in 1784 with his wife and five children.[92] The Flanigans were among those Irish settlers who moved as far as the Indian Tract in the 1820s and established themselves on the Point at Glen Walter which bore their name.[93]

The most dramatic change in the growth of the struggling Catholic parish in Cornwall occurred suddenly in the fall of 1834 and started the denominational somersault in town from a pre-dominantly Protestant population in the early nineteenth century to a predominantly Catholic one by the end of the century.[94] With the start of construction of the Cornwall Canal, Irish labourers swarmed to the site seeking work. It had been five years since the Welland Canal had been finished and many workers were glad enough to see another huge construction project begin. The local labour market could not supply the initial demand for workers needed to undertake the tough job of building an embankment on the south side of the canal from Dickinson's Landing along the great rapid of the Long Sault.[95] Many, perhaps most of the incoming labourers, were Irish Catholics who brought their wives and families with them. Rough shanties and huts were thrown up along the canal line to house the transient workers and their families. It was this sudden flooding of the town and its immediate environment with Catholics that at last precipitated the appointment of a resident priest at Cornwall, Father James P. Bennett, likely of Irish background.

Father Bennett moved quickly to Cornwall, taking up residence on Second Street, and began his formal ministry on 24 November 1834 with the baptism of the infant son of John Kelly and his wife,

Margaret Caroll, "now living on the Canale line".[96] Between November 24th and December 9th, Father Bennett baptised fifteen children, all from families living on the Canal line. The fact that the children brought to him for baptism were newly-born infants indicated that these Irish Catholic families had been associated with a parish prior to their arrival at Cornwall. Otherwise, Father Bennett would have been swamped with a large number of older children requiring baptism. As it was, he officiated at baptisms for newly-born children only, an increasing number of whom were born of Irish-French parents.[97]

While the local Catholics were eminently law-abiding, the newcomers arrived in such force that they competed for the available jobs, and on occasion engaged in feuding and fighting. Considering the number of transient workers who were employed on the canal from 1834 to 1838 and again from 1842 to 1843 — amounting at peak seasons to 2,500[98] — it is not surprising that social adjustments within the town did not always go smoothly. Though many of the workers were single men, there is evidence of extended families whose presence on the canal line brought the number well above 3,000.[99] These families looked to Cornwall for their social and religious amenities, particularly to the Catholic parish of St. Columban's though there were Protestants among the migrant workers as well.[100] The town experienced some tensions when occasional fisticuffs between drunken canallers ended in vicious biting contests in which the combatants bit off each other's ears or noses.[101] There was an attack on the Episcopal church by canallers who threatened its rector, George Archbold, an old officer of the 68th Regiment.[102] And when the peace of the town was disturbed by "some two or three women of ill-fame" and their customers, the inhabitants of the town and the shanties combined to warn the women to leave. When they refused, the inhabitants burned down the brothel.[103] These were some of the more bizarre incidents which, taken together with the two murders that were associated with the canallers, gave the Irish a bad press. Yet eventually the press began to modify its tone about the Irish. On 4 September 1835, for instance, the Observer pointed out that a woman, arrested for stealing a jack-knife from a store, "was not Irish, as it happened, but French".[104]

Over the decade from 1834 to 1843 the miracle was not that there were so many incidents, but that there were so few. During these years while the Cornwall Canal was being built, the majority of those who helped to build it merged into the community as consumers, parishioners and townsmen, amenable to the social controls exerted in some cases by the able hand of Father James Bennett. The intrepid priest did not hesitate to charge his horse into the midst of unruly and drunken canallers with whip in hand. "He dispersed them instantly," an admiring colleague reported. "Then he dismounted and entered the tavern where many others were drinking. (These) he expelled...through the windows and door and, on coming out, he called from a distance a number of sober men and made them convey the drunken men to their several huts".[105]

With the close of work on the Cornwall Canal in 1843, most of the Irish workers and their families moved on to find similar work at the Beauharnois Canal or other construction sites. Left behind in the town of Cornwall was a sprinkling of their numbers, sufficient to make Catholics the largest single denominational group by 1850. Though the town was still predominantly Protestant, Catholics now numbered 562.[105] That St. Columban's parish reflected the ethnic composition of its flock is indicated by the continued service of priests of Irish background. Father Bennett, the priest who had seen the town through the worst of the canal troubles, moved from Cornwall in 1841. Then, from 1843 on, the parish was served by Fathers John Francis Cannon, Gallagher, Walsh, J.S. O'Connor, Lynch, Charles Murray, D.C. McCrae and George Corbet.[106]

If St. Columban's boasted the largest congregation by the 1850s, Trinity Anglican Church ran a close second in numbers. The town's Anglicans in 1850 numbered 557.[107] Not only were Anglicans increasing in size, they were increasing in militancy over the 1830s and 1840s. Since Strachan's departure in 1812, Cornwall's Anglicans had been served for a year by John Bethune, a son of the first Presbyterian minister of Cornwall. Bethune had been educated at Strachan's Academy and converted to the Church of England. From June 1813 until 1817 the Cornwall parish was ministered to by Reverend W.D. Baldwin. Both Bethune and Baldwin assumed Strachan's dual mantle as rector and master of the District Grammar School, thus keeping the school under Anglican tutelage.

The clergyman who took over the Cornwall parish in 1817 was Salter Jehoshaphat Mountain, the forty-seven year old son of Doctor Jehoshaphat Mountain, Rector of Christ Church, Montreal. What was perhaps more important, the new rector of Trinity was a nephew of Jacob Mountain, Bishop of Quebec. Ordained in 1796, Salter Mountain travelled extensively in Upper Canada with his uncle and father, helping to organize the Church of England in the pioneer loyalist settlements. Before coming to Cornwall, he was rector of what was probably the most influential parish in the country — that of Quebec City.[108] Thus he came to the small town on the northern bank of the St. Lawrence well-connected, experienced as a clergyman and knowledgeable of the locality. His arrival in 1817 coincided with that of the new Presbyterian minister, Reverend Joseph Johnston, but, whether by mutual agreement or otherwise, it was Johnston who became master of the District Grammar School rather than Mountain. The new Anglican rector, therefore, concentrated largely on his parish duties, though he acted for a time as one of the school trustees for the Eastern District. Aided by his wife, the Irish-born Anna Maria Scott, Mountain quietly built up the parish until his death in 1830 at the age of sixty.

The vacancy in the Cornwall parish was filled by an Irish clergyman, Reverend George Archbold, a retired officer of the 68th Regiment who entered the ministry after serving in the Peninsular war. Archbold kept in touch with affairs in Ireland and was aware of the proselytizing efforts of the Irish Readers Society, a protestant group that financed teachers who taught Roman Catholics to read in Irish, particularly the Bible, with a view to conversion.[109] Among Archbold's Cornwall parishioners was the Indian agent at St. Regis, Captain Solomon Chesley, who had long nursed an ambition to open a school in the village, largely as an agency for converting the Roman Catholic Indians to the Church of England.[110] His hopes were sparked into action in 1835 with the visit to St. Regis of an Episcopalian half-Indian minister, Reverend Eleazar Williams. Williams was the son of an aged Indian couple then living at St. Regis his mother being descended from an English family named Williams. At the age of ten, young Williams was taken by his father to Connecticut where he attended a common school and then went to a higher seminary where he converted to the Episcopalian church. Ordained in 1815, he was sent as a missionary to the Oneidas and other Indians at Green Bay in the far west.[111]

Tall and majestic in appearance and bearing such a remarkable likeness to the Bourbons that some credited rumours that he was the son of the last King of France, Williams returned to St. Regis, fired with evangelical zeal to convert "my Brethren" whom he found "in a most deplorable condition...their minds unable to discern the nature and design of Christianity".[112] With such a willing instrument at hand, Captain Chesley and Reverend George Archbold immediately formed a plan "for instructing the Indian children at St. Regis...who may be brought to a knowledge of their Redeemer and his Salvation through the means of School instruction".[113] Well aware that any attempt to open a school by a protestant clergyman in a Roman

Catholic village would provoke opposition, Chesley and Archbold proceeded cautiously. The two men pooled expenses in hiring a house at St. Regis for Williams who opened a modest school on 9 July 1835. It was to be on a trial basis to see "how far it might be practicable to obtain the Indian children's attendance and how far it might meet the concurrence or opposition of the Indians themselves as well as their pastor, the resident Roman Catholic missionary".[114] At first seventeen boys attended, despite what Williams described as the "violent opposition of the Romish missionary against teacher and school". Several girls began to attend and eventually Williams counted forty pupils in his school.[115]

Chesley managed to persuade the governor, Lord Aylmer, at Quebec City to provide Williams with a stipend as schoolmaster, but as soon as Williams realized how deep the hostility to him and his school was, he quickly resigned the government appointment, fearing that it might interfere with his teaching that was being carried on with English language textbooks.[116] However, the school did not survive against the combined opposition of the Roman Catholic priest, many of the chiefs and Indians. Chesley's own post as resident Indian agent was saved only by the outbreak of rebellion in Lower Canada which made the government hesitate to remove from St. Regis an employee whose residence extended back twenty-nine years. Yet the manoeuvres surrounding the school experiment by the Cornwall Anglican rector and one of his foremost parishioners indicated a missionary militancy originating from the small town opposite the Indian village of St. Regis which, with 700 souls, was almost as big as Cornwall itself.[117] The fact that the first prize at the new school was awarded to a thirteen-year old Indian boy for having "learnt the whole English alphabet in the short space of two days" showed that the school was meant to be, as the Roman Catholic hierarchy insisted, an agency of assimilation to the English community as well as an agency of conversion.[118]

Not only were Cornwall Anglicans embarking on the seas of educational missionary work at St. Regis, they also provoked several teapot tempests in the 1840s. The most serious was a denominational uproar in 1842 when another Anglican clergyman set the town agog briefly. The occasion was a meeting on 5 November to form a Parochial Association of various parishes in the Eastern District in association with the Diocese of Toronto. The new Anglican rector, Reverend Alexander Williams, recently-arrived from England, presided at the meeting in such a fashion, according to the elders of St. John's Presbyterian Church, "as calculated to sow religious dissention in this community".[119] Williams announced at the meeting that he did not recognize Presbyterian ordination as valid and he went on to rank St. John's Church and its members "with all kinds of dissenters". As soon as a report of the meeting appeared in Cornwall's *Observer*, Reverend Hugh Urquhart, who was now Moderator of the Presbyterian Church of Canada, hastily called a Session of Elders where the matter was heatedly debated. Three resolutions were shot off to Williams testily accusing him of disturbing "that harmony and good feeling which have hitherto happily existed between the members of the Church of England and Scotland in this town".[120] Moreover, the Presbyterians informed the Anglican rector that their church was just as good as the Anglican one inasmuch as the "Church of Scotland was an Established Church of the Empire". Their final bolt was to protest "against such sentiments (as William's) that tend to tear asunder the bonds which ought to unite Christian communities".[121]

Thoroughly reproved by the Presbyterians, Williams turned his attention to another area — social control of the town's morals — by disparaging the attempts of the resident soldiery to initiate live theatre in town. By his appeals to the local commandant, Williams forced the officers of the 4th Battalion of Incorporated Militia to seek private quarters for their theatricals, though he was unsuccessful in getting the plays stopped altogether.[122] On a more positive level, he promoted the growth of the separate boys' and girls' parochial schools during the brief two and a half years that he lasted in Cornwall. Begun partly in rivalry to the Grammar School that had been preempted by Presbyterian ministers since 1817, the boys' school suffered an eclipse in the fall of 1841 because of lack of funds. It re-opened under P.G. Mulhern at the end of November when subscribers agreed to pay the master's salary for two months.[123] Under a new master, Thomas Pitts, appointed in 1842, the school expanded to some sixty-one boys by 1847, including thirty-nine Anglicans, fifteen Roman Catholics, six Presbyterians and one Baptist.[124] Funds for the school came from the government in the form of a grant for the master, and additional income came from the Church Society and private subscribers such as Judge George S. Jarvis and Captain George Crawford, as well as fees from the pupils.[125]

While the Anglicans of Cornwall were expanding and generating a certain amount of heat by their religious, moral and educational zeal in the 1840s, the town's third largest denomination, the Church of Scotland, was still suffering from the split of 1841. It reported 362 adherents in 1850, while its sister Presbyterian church, Knox

Free Church, had 109. Holding out against both congregations was a single Presbyterian who labelled himself in the 1850 census simply as "Other".[126] Cornwall Methodists remained small in numbers. Though they welcomed an American bishop, Francis Ashbury, in 1811, they did not increase in numbers significantly until the second half of the nineteenth century.[127] In 1850 there were but twenty-five Methodists in town. Even these were divided, eighteen being Wesleyans and seven Episcopal Methodists. Lutherans were reduced to four and Baptists to three in 1850.[128] This, then, was the religious complexion of Cornwall at the middle of the nineteenth century when its political complexion was transformed by John Sandfield Macdonald from one of moderate conservatism to one of moderate liberalism.

NOTES

1. W.H. Smith, *Canada, Past and Present and Future*, ii, 4, 13, 10.
2. *Ibid.*, ii, 279, 283.
3. *Ibid.*, 304-5.
4. *Census*, 1851, 26-27; Smith, *Canada*, ii, 387, incorrectly gives figure of 1506 for 1850.
5. Smith, *Canada*, ii, 387.
6. *Census*, 1851, 26-27.
7. *Ibid.*, in the township of Cornwall there were 274 of French-Canadian origin in 1850 while in County Stormont as a whole there were 758 French Canadians and 10,548 others.
8. Ruth Bleasdale, "Irish Labourers on the Cornwall, Welland and Williamsburg Canals in the 1840's" (unpublished M.A. thesis, University of Western Ontario, Sept., 1975, 8); Ruth Bleasdale, "Class Conflict on the Canals of Upper Canada in the 1840's", in *Labour/Le Travailleur*, Spring, 1981, 9.
9. *Census*, 1851, 26-27.
10. Figures for townships are from Smith, *Canada*, ii, 388.
11. Arthur to Governor Charles Poulett Thomson, 8 April 1840, private; (Charles R. Sanderson, *Arthur Papers*, iii, 16.)
12. Bruce Hodgins, "Philip Vankoughnet", *DCB*, x, 693.
13. Bruce to Browne, Toronto 17 March 1836, see Mrs. Charlotte Bruce Carey's "Sketch of the Bruce Family", in *Annual Transactions, United Empire Loyalists' Association*, 1899-1900, iii, 51; for Browne's role in trying to persuade canallers to come to Cornwall during the elections in early July in support of Dr. Bruce, see J.K. Johnson, "Colonel James Fitzgibbon and the Suppression of Irish Riots in Upper Canada", in *Ontario History*, lviii, 1966, 153.
14. The first time was to Darcy Boulton in 1804.
15. H. Senior, "John Hillyard Cameron; Canadian Scot and Orange Grand Master," in *Journal of Scottish Studies*, 1983.
16. *Ibid.*

17. *Canada Directory*, 1851, 69; William Boss, *Stormont, Dundas and Glengarry Highlanders*, 66; J.G. Harkness, *History of Stormont, Dundas and Glengarry*, 203.

18. Bruce Hodgins, *John Sandfield Macdonald*, 10-13, 20, 24.

19. *Ibid.*, 19.

20. *An Historical Sketch, St. Columban's Parish*, 1896, 3-4, 25; Pringle, 233.

21. Hodgins, *John Sandfield Macdonald*, 16.

22. *Ibid.*, see 24 especially.

23. *150th Anniversary, St. Columban's Parish, 1829-1979*, Cornwall, 7; Father Charles Murray, "Reminiscences", 7.

24. Robert Campbell, *History of the Scotch Presbyterian Church, St. Gabriel Street, Montreal*, 289; Fred Armstrong, *Handbook of Upper Canadian Chronology*, 229.

25. Fred MacMillan, Dr. Simon Fraser, Philip Robertson, "History of St. John's Church." 3.

26. *Ibid.*, 6.

27. *Ibid.*; J.F. Pringle, *Lunenburgh, or the Old Eastern District*, 214-215.

28. "History of St. John's Church", 3-4.

29. Campbell, *Scotch Presbyterian Church*, 310.

30. "History of St. John's Church," 4.

31. *History of Knox United Church 1846-1975*, 1-3.

32. H. Urquhart to Trustees, 20 Jan. 1827, cited in "History of St. John's Church," 5.

33. Alexander Caldwell and Mary H. Stewart, *Cornwall Collegiate and Vocational School: An Historical Sketch*, 4-8.

34. Pringle, 245-6.

35. Campbell, *Scotch Presbyterian Church*, 312.

36. Knox Church Session Minute book, 1851, cited in *History of Knox United Church, 1846-1975*, 2-3.

37. Esson accepted a post at Knox College, Toronto, in 1844, (Campbell, *History of Scotch Presbyterian Church*, 290-91).

38. J.S.M. Careless, *Brown of the Globe 1818-1859: The Voice of Upper Canada*, i, 2-22; 33-34.

39. *History of Knox United Church*, 3.

40. Pringle, 222.

41. *History of Knox United Church*, 3.

42. *Census*, 1851, 62-63.

43. *History of Knox United Church*, 5 and 8; Harkness, 353. The church is now an apartment house at 116 Second Street East.

44. *Census*, 1851, 62-63.

45. "History of St. John's Church," 11.

46. *Ibid.*, 8.

47. *History of Knox United Church*, 31.

48. Harkness, 353.

49. Pringle, 134.

50. J.A. Macdonell, *Sketches: Glengarry in Canada*, 48.

51. McNiff map. 1 Nov. 1786 (H2/400).

52. Haldimand Papers: MG21/B168/106.

53. G.A. Morice, "A Canadian Pioneer: Spanish John", in *CHR*, 1929, x, 215.

54. Chewett map, 1792 (V3/440). William Reid, *Loyalists of Ontario*, 196.

55. Miles MacDonell to his brother, John, 6 April 1804, in Morice, "A Candian Pioneer: Spanish John," *CHR*, x, 232.

56. Captain John McDonell to his son, John, 27 February 1802, *ibid.*, 232.

57. Mrs. Charlotte Bruce Carey, "Sketch of the Bruce family," *Annual Transactions, United Empire Loyalists' Association*, 1899-1900, iii, 60; Interview with Miss M. Davis, Montreal, Bruce descendant, who says that the family tradition is that Peggy Bruce was Roman Catholic.

58. William Dunlop, *Recollections of the American War*, 42.

59. *Ibid.*, 40.

60. *Canada and Its Provinces*, iii, 26; Brother Alfred, *Catholic Pioneers in Upper Canada*, 4, see also, Joseph Cossette, Father Pierre René Floquet, *DCB*, iv, 271.

61. Macdonell, *Sketches*, 125.

62. Lord Sydney to Lieutenant Governor Henry Hamilton, 24 June 1785, cited in Macdonell, *Sketches*, 125-26.

63. L.J.A. Derome, *Le Canada écclesiastique*, 223.

64. Rev. James S. Rudd to Society for the Propagation of the Gospel, 24 July 1801, in A.H. Young, "The Mission of Cornwall 1784-1812," in *OHSPR*, xxv, 1929, 490.

65. H. Belden, *Historical Atlas of Stormont, Dundas and Glengarry*, see p. V for brief description of Roman Catholics at St. Andrew's.

66. Morice, "A Canadian Pioneer: Spanish John", in *CHR*, 1929, X, 230; Harkness, 116, 119, 124; Pringle, 234.

67. Pringle, 234-35.

68. John Craigie to Stephen De Lancy, 4 September 1786, in RG4/A1/31/9909-11); see also, Macdonell, *Sketches*, 127, quoting the Quebec *Gazette*, 7 September 1786, which lists 520 steerage passengers. This figure is frequently quoted as the number which came to Glengarry. However, some of these passengers settled elsewhere.

69. Father Alexander Macdonell was educated in France, see Macdonell, *Sketches*, 128.

70. See, for instance, Macdonell, "*Sketches*," 215, re George Macdonell being replaced by an Irish Protestant in the regiment. See also letters concerning Vankoughnet being in command of the Highlanders. In a letter of Governor General Charles Poulett Thomson to Sir Gordon Arthur, 8 April 1840, he remarked, "As the Highland blood seems amazingly excited at the prospect of being commanded again by a Dutch man, it may be worth your while to consider if any change can be made when the new arrangements take effect." (Sanderson, *Arthur Papers*, iii, 16); see also Arthur to Thomson, 14 April 1840, "You will, also, perceive, by the accompanying letter from Colonel Fraser, who is a very worthy man and fine old soldier - that his blood would have been up in no time if a preference had been given to the McDonell! The Dutchman was quite beneath his notice." (*Ibid.*, 30-31.)

71. Father Roderick Macdonell to John McDonell, 25 April 1804, cited in Morice: "A Canadian Pioneer, Spanish John," *CHR*, 1929, X, 232-33.

72. Father Roderick Macdonell to the Church Wardens of St. Raphael's, 12 September 1804, cited in Macdonell, *Sketches*, 128-29.

73. See original parish register, St. Andrews, March 1807, cited in Harkness, 120.

74. Father Aeneas McDonell to Bishop of Montreal, 6 January 1840, in Archdiocese Archives, Montreal, file 255, 102/840/1, Kingston diocese letters 1836-42.

75. *Reporter*, Cornwall, 8 June 1878; "Reminiscences of Father Charles Murray", 10.

76. An account of Catholics who emigrated from the Highlands of Scotland to the British Colonies of North America and of the 1st Glengarry Fencible Regt, 9 November 1837; see also, Macdonell to Head 7 March 1836 in Macdonell Letters, 1836-39; see also *Canadian Literary Magazine*, April 1833, i, 3.

77. Lord Hobart to Lieutenant Governor Hunter, 1 March 1803, cited in Macdonell, *Sketches*, 148.

78. Bishop Macdonell to J. Joseph, Civil Secretary, 7 March 1836, Macdonell Letters, 1836-39, MG24/J13.

79. Boss, *Stormont, Dundas and Glengarry Highlanders*, 3, 391; Cyprien Tanguay, *Répertoire Général du Clergé Canadien*, i, 147.

80. Father Alexander Macdonell to Bishop J.O. Plessis, 10 May 1806, cited in Brother Alfred, *Catholic Pioneers in Upper Canada*, 103, see footnote.

81. Bishop J.J. Lartigue to Bishop A. Macdonell, 12 May 1821, in Archdiocese Archives, Montreal, Lartigue papers, 63. Bishop Lartigue to Father Dufresne, 12 May 1821, *ibid.*, 62.

82. An Historical Sketch of St. Columban's Parish, June 1896, 4; see also, Births, Marriages and Deaths Register, St. Columban's Parish, for the marriage of John Flanigan, son of John and Margaret Flanigan, of the Indian Reserve, lot no. 8, 1st Concession, and Elizabeth Colquhoun, daughter of Robert and Elizabeth Colquhoun, of the Indian Reserve, B.D.M., 1834-38, 6, dated 7 January 1835.

83. Bishop J.J. Lartigue to Bishop Macdonell, St. Raphael's, 3 April 1821, (Archdiocese Archives, Montreal, J.J. Lartigue Papers, i, 34-35.)

84. *Cornwall Observer*, 23 October 1835.

85. Pringle, 194.

86. Cornwall Census, 1829.

87. Bishop J.J. Lartigue to Bishop Plessis, 21 April 1821, and Bishop Lartigue to Bishop Macdonell, 12 May 1821, Archdiocese Archives, Montreal, Lartigue papers, i, 39 and 63; see also Kingston Diocese papers, Bishop Prince to Bishop Bourget, 13 August 1840; No. 255.102/840/7; Bishop Macdonell to Bourget, 1 February 1839, Kingston Diocese, No. 255.102/839/3; see also, F.A. Walker, *Catholic Education in Upper Canada*, 21.

88. *150th Anniversary of St. Columban's Parish, 1829-1979*, 1-3.

89. *An Historical Sketch, St. Columban's Parish, 1896*, 3-4; Father Charles Murray, "Reminiscences", 2.

90. Harkness, 107.

91. Roll of Non-Commissioned Officers, drummers and Privates, enlisted for the 1st Battalion, K.R.R.N.Y., Pointe Claire, 17 May 1781, in Haldimand Papers, MG21/B158/209.

92. Haldimand Papers, MG21/B168/106.

93. St. Columban's Parish Register of Births, Marriages and Deaths, 1834-38, see 6; see also Register for 1886-1931, death notice of Dr. Darby Bergin, 4 October 1896, interred at Flanigan's Point.

94. *Census* 1851, i, 62-63; *Census* 1891, i, 258-59.

95. Pringle, 157.

96. St. Columban's Parish Register of Births, Marriages and Deaths, 1834-38, 1; see also, *150th Anniversary*, 6; Father Charles Murray, "Reminiscences," 2.

97. St. Columban's Parish Register of Births, Marriages and Deaths, 1834-38, 1-39.

98. J.K. Johnson, "Colonel James Fitzgibbon and the Suppression of Irish Riots," in *Ontario History*, lviii, 1966, 147; see footnote; see also Ralph Ellis, "The Economic, Social and Demographic Impact of the Cornwall Canal: 1834-43", unpublished paper prepared for History Dept., McGill University, April 1982, see appendix, table 6 - estimates of number of men employed on Cornwall Canal, 30.

99. See the list of births and some marriages among families of canal workers, in St. Columban's Parish Register of Births, Marriages and Deaths, 1834-38.

100. See Trinity Church records of Births, Marriages and Deaths 1835 for burial of workers killed on canal site.

101. *Cornwall Observer*, 17 July 1835, cited in Ellis, 21.

102. *Ibid.*, 20-21.

103. *Cornwall Observer*, 27 November 1837, cited in Ellis, 21.

104. James Miller, "The Town of Cornwall, 1784-1867," unpublished M.A. thesis, University of Toronto, April 1967, 40. Colonel James Fitzgibbon to Civil Secretary Joseph, 26 June 1836 in Civil Secretary's Letter Book, RG7/G16C/36, cited in Johnson, "Colonel James

Fitzgibbon," in *Ontario History*, lviii, 1966, 152.

105. *Census*, 1851, i, 62-63.

106. *150th Anniversary of St. Columban's Parish, 1829-1979*, 7-10; Rudolph Villeneuve, *Catholic Education in Cornwall*, 6.

107. *Census*, 1851, 62-63.

108. For details on Mountain, see G.B. Stidwill, "The Mountains and Trinity Church," 4.

109. See extract from letter regarding the Irish Readers Society, January 1835, in Trinity Church Papers, Diocesan Archives, Ottawa, 59-1/3b.

110. Chesley to Archbold, 27 August 1835, in *ibid.*, 59-1/2b.

111. *Ibid.*; see also Archbold to Major William Plenderleath, 18 June 1835, in *ibid.* 59-1/2a; see above 135.

112. Reverend E. Williams to Reverend Archbold, 21 March 1836, *ibid.*, 59-1/2c.

113. Archbold to Plenderleath, 18 June 1835, *ibid.*, 59-1/2a.

114. Chesley to Archbold, 27 August 1835, *ibid.*, 59-1/2b.

115. Williams to Archbold, 21 March 1836, *ibid.*, 59-1/2d.

116. Williams to Archbold, 18 November 1835, *ibid.*, 59-1/2c; see also George Mainer, "Solomon Chesley", *DCB*, X, 163-4.

117. For population figures, see Archbold to Plenderleath, 18 June 1835, Trinity Church Papers, Diocesan Archives Ottawa, 59-1/2a. Chesley to Archbold, 27 August 1835, *ibid.*, 59-1/2b.

118. Archbold's appeal for financial support for St. Regis School, *ibid.*, 59-1/2a.

119. Reverend Hugh Urquhart to Reverend Alexander Williams, 5 December 1842, *ibid.*, 59-1.

120. *Ibid.*

121. *Ibid.*

122. Trinity Church Papers, Diocesan Archives Ottawa, 59-1/34a.

123. *Ibid.*, Boys' Parochial School, 59-1/19.

124. *Ibid.*, see list of students in 1847.

125. *Ibid.*, see Receipts for 1842.

126. *Census*, 1851, i, 62-63.

127. Richard Preston, *Kingston Before the War of 1812*, xcvii.

128. *Census*, 1851, i, 62-63.

St. Regis Indian Village, (St. Lawrence), around 1840.
Print by W.H. Bartlett.

Cornwall Grammar and High School, 1856. Moved to the north-west corner of Fourth and Sydney Streets in 1877. This school is the ancestor of the present Cornwall Collegiate and Vocational School, which can trace its history to 1803 when the Reverend John Strachan opened the Cornwall Grammar School.

Credit: Ian Bowering.

Inverarden Regency Cottage Museum, built in 1816 for John McDonald of Garth.

Credit: Ian Bowering.

Mrs. John Sandfield Macdonald, 1850. (nee Marie Christine Waggaman). Oil painting by T. Hamell.
Credit: Public Archives of Canada, neg. C-4807.

John Sandfield Macdonald, 1812-1872. M.L.A. for Cornwall, 1858-1872; M.P. for Cornwall 1867-1872. First Premier of Ontario.
Credit: Public Archives of Canada, neg. C-7543.

Chapter IX

Cornwall's Institutions Develop

The town's municipal complexion underwent changes since the time when townsmen received their first charter. In the intervening years from 1834 to 1850, there had been a gradual growth of municipal institutions and local services. For one thing, the arrangements of 1834 soon proved inadequate for administering the town. A new municipal act came into effect in 1847. Under this legislation, seven councillors were elected, two each from the East and West wards, and three from the more populous Centre ward. The Board of Police gave way to a council of seven who chose one of their numbers to be Cornwall's first mayor. This honour went to a barrister, George McDonell, who had had ample experience at running the town, having been President of the Police Board in 1843 and again in 1845. In fact, with the exception of Roderick Macdonald, a medical doctor, all Cornwall's chief municipal officers were drawn from members of the bar up to 1848. And this was in spite of the fact that Cornwall legal men were such notorious drinkers that John Sandfield Macdonald's abstemious legal assistant, A.M. MacKenzie, reported to his boss that it was not unusual to see "barristers stretched out upon the street in a helpless state of intoxication".[1]

These were the days in Upper Canada when a man was considered a moderate drinker if his daily intake did not exceed four glasses of whiskey.[2] Town fathers took measures to try to curb excessive drinking of canallers and Indians, but they drew the line at too close a scrutiny of their fellow barristers. In 1836, for instance, the Cornwall *Observer* noted that the provincial Assembly had recently passed a statute prohibiting "all persons (from) selling, bartering, exchanging or giving to any Indian man, woman or child, any kind of spirituous liquors in any shape, manner or way, under a penalty of £5."[3] When the number of taverns increased from eleven in 1838 to twenty-three in 1842, town fathers finally attempted to initiate some social control of the canallers' drinking habits by limiting the number of licensed taverns. Yet even though a Cornwall Total Abstinence Society was reported "fully organized and in a flourishing condition" by May of 1841, unlicensed grog shops continued to flourish along the canal line until the construction work ended in 1843.[4]

Whatever the drinking habits of his townsmen, Cornwall's first full-blown mayor, George McDonell, had sown his wild oats during a stint of legal work and carrousing in the Ottawa District before he settled down to a more staid life in Cornwall in the 1830s.[5] By the mid-1849s townsmen found him sober and sound enough for three terms as their chief magistrate. Then in 1850 when all three wards were able to elect three councillors each, the popular merchant, William Mattice, a descendant of one of the original United Empire Loyalists, was chosen mayor for three successive terms from 1849 to 1851. It was not until 1859 that a new act came into force by which the town's mayor was elected directly by the people, rather than chosen by the councillors. The popular reform doctor, Charles Rattray, who had arrived from Perthshire, Scotland, in 1835, and married into the Chesley family, was the first mayor elected by the people, though he had already served a term in 1848 as the choice of the councillors.

Along with the maturing by mid-century of the town's central administrative body there were improvements in the police establishment, fire protection, health and sanitary measures and educational facilities. The importance of local police arrangements in assuring that Cornwallites obeyed the laws and maintained public order was evident in the fact that the first elected municipal body in 1834 was a Board of Police. And one of its first acts was to appoint innkeeper Horace Spencer as high constable and surveyor of streets. Assisting him in executing warrants for arrests were a number of bailiffs including Alexander McDonald, Aaron Walsh, Peter and Lewis Carpenter, James Clemmens, Andrew Duesler and William Hessel.[6] During the construction of the Cornwall canal there were, at various times, five to seven constables in the town.[7] With the departure of most of the canallers in 1843, the town's police force returned to its normal establishment of a high constable and bailiffs. Instead of canal riots, fights and murders, the law officers now found themselves occupied with the more mundane jobs of arresting careless horse-drivers on Pitt Street, or gamblers at the travelling circuses that came occasionally to Cornwall, and warning bathers against choosing "unreasonable hours" for their swimming activities.[8] Petty offences, whether theft, assault, drunkenness or disturbing the peace, were often settled out of court at the urging of the barristers, thus saving the offenders from a jail sentence or fine which would interfere with his ability to support himself or his family.[9]

This liberal treatment of offenders was a far cry from that meted out to wrong-doers earlier in the century. A woman convicted in 1800 of petit larceny was sentenced to be tied to a post and "whipped with small cords until your body be bloody."[10] A man found guilty of theft was sentenced to stand in the pillory for an hour.[11] This was a rack with holes for the prisoner's head and hands to be stuck through. It was a form of public humiliation during which passers-by could and sometimes did throw objects at the culprit. For a man found guilty of manslaughter in this early era, the punishment was to be burned on the hand.[12] The lash, pillory and branding gave way to jail sentences and fines once the town had its own jail. By the 1850s trespassers against the law were so infrequent that the High Constable, Daniel Daly, spent most of his time at his saddle and harnessmaking shop.[13] In the next decade the High Constable, William Skeith, was given the extra job of street surveyor.[14] His successor, Samuel Pollock, hired in 1868, assumed more and more duties including market clerk, fire warden, pound keeper and, to top it off, he was given an extra $10 a year "to take care of the hearse and keep it properly cleaned and ready for use at all times".[15]

Volunteer firemen remained Cornwall's chief protectors against fires for the first 160 years of the town's existence. Until 1832 the men of the village used hand-to-hand bucket methods to quell flames. In that year the magistrates, meeting in Quarter Sessions, allotted £10 to Guy Carlton Wood for the purchase of a fire engine.[16] Three years later, in 1835, the first volunteer fire company, composed of twenty-eight men, was organized. Among the volunteers were some of the most influential citizens of the town including Walter Colquhoun, James Loney, D.W.B. McAuley, Jacob F. Pringle, William M. Park, George S. Jarvis, Thomas Marshall, Donald McDonell, George McDonell and two French Canadians, Vincent Masson and G.A. Masson.[17]

A serious fire on the north side of First Street in the early winter of 1841 prompted the Cornwall Board of Police to re-organize the fire company that had suffered a disruption during the rebellion era.[18] George McDonell, one of the first volunteer firemen, was named captain, together with John Sandfield Macdonald and Jacob F. Pringle as lieutenants. Hiram Pitts was branchman and Ranald McDonell and Richard Allen sergeants. Two fire engineers were appointed — Thomas Palin and James Gilley. Fifteen firemen were named to the company. Another eight formed a hook and ladder company and two others were bucketmen.[19] From the time of this serious fire in 1841 and the re-organization of the town's firemen, houses and shops in the heart of the town began to be built of brick or stone. In keeping with this general trend towards more fire-proof buildings in the centre of the town, the trustees of St. John's Presbyterian Church began to make it a condition of their leases that any buildings constructed on their property would be of brick or stone with metallic or other fireproof roofs.

Cholera struck Cornwall suddenly and severely in 1832 and again in 1834. The appearance of this dreaded Asiatic plague prompted the Board of Police to create a Board of Health whose job it was to see to the town's sanitary arrangements. A number of the town's most prominent citizens were named to undertake the task of examining premises where "nuisances" existed, that is, where garbage was thrown, and to order the rat-infested material to be removed. Taking on the unpleasant job were Postmaster Guy Carlton Wood, barristers Alexander McLean, Robert Cline and George S. Jarvis, Sheriff Donald McDonell, Doctor John Goodall, town treasurer James Pringle, and shopkeeper William Mattice. The efficiency of the Board of Health in 1847 prevented the spread of typhus, then raging that summer among the newly-arriving Irish immigrants. A quarantine hospital was erected on Petite Pointe Maligne to the east of the town below the canal. Here Doctors Darby Bergin and Roderick Macdonald worked each day, caring for 234 patients. They cured 182 who were discharged; another fifty-two died of the disease.[21] In 1849 and 1854 Asiatic cholera again swept the town, but not so severely as in 1832.

Educational facilities developed slowly in Cornwall. The earliest record of any school was the one built sometime prior to 1792 by the first Episcopalian clergyman, Reverend John Bryan. This school, probably a log hut, was located at the north-west corner of Second and Augustus Streets.[22] The town had at least one schoolmaster in 1803, Elijah Leavens, who was also secretary of the local Masonic lodge.[23] Reverend John Strachan's Academy, which opened in 1803, is the second school for which any records exist. This became the District Grammar School in 1807 under new provincial legislation establishing public schools in each district. After Strachan's departure for York in 1812, the school had a succession of five different masters until 1827. In the frequent changes of masters, the quality of teaching suffered. Moreover, the government grant to the district school did not pay the master's whole salary. Thus the students had to pay a tuition fee which, though not high, was enough to put secondary education beyond the reach of most village children. This was evident in the low numbers attending the Academy. In

1829, two years after Reverend Hugh Urquhart took over the school, there were only thirty-four students. Nine years later it had but thirty.[24]

There was no doubt that the academy was for those who could afford it, and thus arose the criticism from some quarters that the grammar schools of the province were looked upon as "seminaries exclusively instituted for the education of the children of the more wealthy classes of society, and to which the poor man's child is considered unfit to be admitted."[25] The criticism was justified generally but in Cornwall a "poor Glengarry boy", as John Sandfield Macdonald described himself, could and did pass through the grammar school portals to gain a "liberal education," the key to entry into the "learned professions".[26] Two years before his death, John Sandfield Macdonald paid tribute to the Cornwall Grammar School where, he admitted, he had "to strive with those who were able to be maintained by their parents. I worked with them at a great disadvantage, and would have succumbed but that I was cheered on by my Preceptor, the Rev. Dr. Urquhart."[27]

The Grammar School's curriculum in the 1830s contained large doses of the Latin classics such as Ovid, Sallust, Caesar and Virgil, and mathematics including algebra and the first book of Euclid. What was astonishing was that female students had somehow slipped through its portals. Strachan, the former master and now President of the General Board of Education, among other duties, returned to Cornwall to inspect his former academy in 1827. Though he found his old school worthy of favourable mention in his report, he found the presence of "female children interferes with the government which is required in classical seminaries". This "inconvenience", he was sure, "would pass away as the population increases in wealth and numbers".[28]

Elementary schooling did not receive government attention until 1816 when the Assembly passed an act to establish what were called "common schools." These were a type of school in which the tenets of Christianity common to Roman Catholics and protestants alike would be taught. Objections to these schools were soon voiced by Catholic parents who wished their children to be educated only by those who shared their faith.[29] What was less apparent at first to non-English speaking parents was that the common schools would act as an agency of assimilation. Thus first generation Gaelic-speaking immigrants found that while their clergymen were obliged to give their sermons in Gaelic in order to be understood, the second generation no longer understood Gaelic because, as one Macdonell remarked, "The common school has brought the new generation to use the English tongue."[30]

According to the School Act of 1816, parents could obtain a government grant of £25 yearly providing there were at least twenty pupils to be taught and that parents were prepared to provide a school house and to pay part of the teacher's wages. The 1816 legislation also provided for three trustees to be appointed for each school and that Boards of Education be appointed for each district. Shortly after 1816 a common school was established in Cornwall on lot no. 10 on the north side of Second Street at the corner of Amelia Street and this spot remained the site of a public school down to the present day. By 1827 a Board of Education was in operation, composed of one Catholic, one Episcopalian and one Presbyterian.[31] That more than Catholics were uneasy about the common school system is evident by the fact that members of Trinity Episcopalian Church were the first to opt out of the common school. By 1834 they applied for a government grant to open their own school on lot no. 19 on the south side of Third Street.[32] A private school for young ladies already existed, for the *Cornwall Observer* of 30 October 1835 announced that "the young ladies of Cornwall" were being solicited to attend "Miss Sherman's Seminary in the house then occupied by Miss Malvo". The *Observer* assured the public that Miss Sherman's "acknowledged acquirements will secure for her school the high character so justly earned by her predecessor", an indication that a young ladies' seminary existed prior to 1835 in town. This school catered to the more affluent families who could afford to pay fees for their daughters' education.

A free school for girls was organized in 1842, largely through the efforts of the widow of Reverend Salter Mountain, the indefatigable Anna Maria Mountain. This native of Carrick-on-Seur, Ireland, who had organized the first Cornwall bazaar and had devoted much of her time to the Sunday school of Trinity Episcopal Church, had set her mind on a free school for the girls of the parish. By 1843 the school, situated on York Street, had fifty-five students and drew £18.6.3-1/2 from the provincial government. Its teacher was Eliza Brown. Not only was the free girls' school in operation by the early 1840s, largely for the benefit of Episcopalian children, a boys' parochial school was underway by 1841 with a graduate of Trinity College, Patrick Gildes Mulhern, as its first master. Fees came in somewhat irregularly at first and Mulhern moved to the Cornwall Common School where he soon became principal.[33]

The first Catholic school began in 1842 when Julia Cozens began teaching children privately, her fee being but twenty-five cents per month for each child. Her pupils may have been girls only to whom she taught needlework, singing, and catechism as well as elementary academic subjects. By 1849 she was receiving a modest government allowance of £2.10.5, but the school closed when the teacher's mental health broke down and she was placed in an insane asylum. Educational facilities in Cornwall in the 1840s, then, consisted of the Grammar School and six elementary schools, two of which were associated with the Episcopalian parish and one with St. Columban's Roman Catholic Parish, all receiving some government financial support. The largest of the elementary schools was the Church of England school run by Eliza Brown with fifty-five pupils. The other five elementary schools accounted for another 136 pupils.[34]

In the early years of the town, young girls of more affluent families were sent to Montreal to be educated, though John Strachan found this expedient not conducive to great intellectual progress. His own wife, the daughter of Dr. Charles Wood, a 1st Dragoon Guards officer who settled in Cornwall, had, according to Strachan, "as good an education as this country can afford, which by the way is not very great".[35] The twice-widowed Captain Miles McDonell sent his daughters to be educated at a nunnery in Montreal where "they were happy" enough, though the father soon found, "they have ruined me in expenses...having been noticed by Gen. Drummond's Lady, Mrs. McGillivray and others, (which) led them to considerable expenses in dress to attend Balls, Bouts and evening Parties given by those Ladies".[36] However, the father was reconciled to the expense, as "we have the satisfaction of their (the McDonell girls) having received more advantages than any of the family ever got".[37] This practice among affluent Cornwall families of sending their daughters to finishing schools or nunneries in Montreal continued into the early twentieth century, even though high schools were well established in Cornwall and girls were admitted.[38]

As the mid-century drew near, Cornwall, like other centres in Canada West, was experiencing mounting pressure for denominational, or, separate schools, rather than common schools. Episcopalians had been the first to open a school in Cornwall, though children of other denominations attended. Then, after the first common school was established, it was again Episcopalians who opted for a largely denominational school in 1834. Within the next decade, Catholics organized their first private school and, as the Catholic population increased so, too, did pressure for government aid to subsidize a separate school where Catholic teachers would teach Catholic children. For Bishop Alexander Macdonell, the advancement of "Catholic religion and Catholic education" went hand in hand. "What tends to that," he wrote the year before his death, "will afford me not only the greatest but the only satisfaction I can enjoy in this life".[39] There were few Catholics who did not whole-heartedly concur in the papal pronouncement that "he who in education neglects the will, directing all his efforts to the training of the understanding, succeeds in making instruction a dangerous weapon in the hands of the wicked".[40] Indeed, most Presbyterians and Episcopalians agreed.[41] Yet Cornwall at this time was coming under the spell of the secular-minded John Sandfield Macdonald whose views on separate schools, like his attitude towards denominationalism, tended to be hostile.[42] Still, Sandfield Macdonald did not press hostility too far and, by 1863, he secured a Separate School Act under which Cornwall's first separate school, Centre Ward Separate School, was organized in 1871 in connection with St. Columban's parish.[43]

Culturally, Cornwall in the first half of the century had developed a few amenities. Both Trinity Episcopal and St. John's Presbyterian churches had small lending libraries, devoted largely to religious reading material. Reverend John Strachan had established a "Mission library" by 1806.[44] In 1831 a library was organized for Presbyterians in the manse by Reverend Hugh Urquhart.[45] Books valued at £21.17.9 were ordered in Glasgow and a set of rules drawn up governing the use of the Presbyterian library. Strachan's contributions to the cultural life of the small village in the first decade of the nineteenth century included annual "popular lectures in Natural Philosophy" which he began each January.[46] Strachan was responsible, too, for one of the gala balls each year. At the close of the yearly public examinations at his academy, he and his wife entertained at dinner and a ball where as many as forty or more would relax after the day's activities.[47]

For most of the fashionable parties in the 1830s the music was supplied by a one-legged fiddler, known as "Black Jim", who knew several popular tunes. These he played indifferently until liquor got the better of him. Then some less accomplished amateur took over. The fiddle sometimes gave way to the bagpipes when reels and strathspeys were danced, and a contemporary noted that, "young folks gathered, flirted and made love just as satisfactorily (then) as in the present enlightened age".[48] One of the favourite places for balls and concerts in the first half of the century was the large building on the north side of Second Street, lot no. 15, that became the American Hotel. This building, owned by Dr. Noah Dickinson, had been used as a court house in the 1820s and as a barracks for the incorporated militia units stationed in Cornwall up to 1843.

Thereafter one of the large rooms served as a ballroom and concert hall for many years.[49]

Live theatre came to Cornwall in the early 1840s with the arrival of the 4th Battalion of Incorporated Militia from Prescott. Like most large groups of soldiers, the men of the 4th Battalion amused themselves during the long winter nights with amateur theatricals. As soon as they arrived in Cornwall, they rented a vacant building and went ahead with plans for opening a small theatre. One of the most enthusiastic of the actor-soldiers was Lieutenant Joseph Lee who later became Montreal's leading Shakespearean actor. No sooner had Lee got his theatre well advanced, with staging and seating arrangements completed, than a minor uproar ensued. According to the battalion's adjutant, Captain Thomas Wily, it all started when the "parson, a pleasant English gentleman (Reverend Alexander Williams) allowed himself to be influenced by some goody, goody old women of the place to...prevent our...small theatre..the said 'goodies' being apprehensive that the morals of the place would be contaminated, if the project was not staid."[50]

Williams called on the commandant, Colonel Turner, to interfere and succeeded so well that the commandant vetoed the project. As the officers considered the theatre proceedings a private matter, they resented the interference of the garrison commandant and the Anglican rector. Their dander aroused, they determined to turn their messhouse, Ivy Hall, into a theatre. It was ideally suited for the purpose, as the room used for the mess was divided by an open arch. The smaller portion was converted into a stage. The larger area of the room was turned into an auditorium large enough to seat about a hundred. Only the orchestra had to be in an anteroom. The adjutant, Thomas Wily, got into the act by painting all the scenic backdrops, several of which later found their way onto stages in Montreal. Thus the theatricals were to be strictly private in the officers' mess. Invitations were by cards, distributed by the officers amongst their friends. These were eagerly sought by all, even by some of those who had initiated the prohibition, while the "goodies", as Wily put it, "could only look on idly and blaspheme."[51]

By 1843 the provincial regiments were disbanded and Cornwallites bade farewell to the itinerant soldiers and their theatricals. It was not until 1882 that the town secured its own theatre on the second storey of the enlarged town hall on the south side of Fourth Street. A stage with scenery was fitted up with dressing rooms below and a large room in front capable of seating 700 or 800. As in the 1840s there was still a slight taint of disapproval about live theatre. A contemporary remarked that many "thought it would have been better...to have left the work of providing a theatre... to a joint stock company that would have done it much more satisfactorily."[52]

Cornwall's first venture into journalism came in the early 1830s when a discarded hand press was brought to Cornwall from Montreal. Merchant-innkeeper William W. Wyman used it to begin publication of a weekly four-page newspaper, the Cornwall *Observer*.[53] Claiming to be politically independent, the new journal was moderately conservative in tone, its masthead bearing the legend, "King and Constitution". By 1836 the *Observer* was bought out by John Carter, Wyman's partner. The new owner announced on 25 July 1836 that the newspaper would be devoted to "Commerce, Politics and Literature". Like other growing towns in the province, Cornwall boasted not only a local newspaper but even a reading room, located next door to the Post Office on the north side of First Street.[54] Here townsmen could gather to read the latest news or back issues of the *Observer*.

A second newspaper appeared in 1836, the Cornwall *Argus*, but it seems to have had an ephemeral existence.[55] By 1844 Carter lost control of the *Observer*, perhaps because of financial difficulties, but by 1845 he was back into Cornwall journalism, establishing a new paper, the *Cornwall Chronicle* whose first issue came out on 8 February. Carter declared that "by an undeviating and unflinching perseverance in those principles which characterized the *Cornwall Observer*, whilst under our management, we hope to show that the Eastern District can and will support two constitutional Conservative Newspapers". All this was to be done, Carter hoped, "without any injury to our contemporary (the *Observer*)".[56] Like the *Argus*, the *Chronicle* was short-lived. Its publisher shortly returned to the *Observer* fold and faced a far more serious challenge the next year when John Sandfield Macdonald embarked in journalism in the interests of the reform party. With Henry Patterson as editor, he founded the *Freeholder* in 1846. At first issues came out sporadically and then it became a regular weekly.[57]

The *Freeholder* and the *Observer* engaged in mutual vituperation of a type common among rival newspapers at that time, the *Observer* adopting a patronizing air towards the upstart *Freeholder*. Describing Cornwall as "our Conservative Town", the *Observer* gloated, "will our Radical friends now believe that the Town of Cornwall is Conservative, or will they...have the impertinence to make another attempt (to secure the Cornwall seat in the Assembly)?"[58] John Sandfield Macdonald took up the challenge. Within two years the *Freeholder* had pushed the *Observer* into its grave, although another conservative journal sprang up to take its place.[59] This was the

Constitution which survived throughout the decade of the 1850s. The appearance of these rival newspapers may not have raised the cultural level of the small town, but they raised political consciousness to a fine point. Whether the *Freeholder* spurred John Sandfield Macdonald to pre-eminence or vice-versa, both Macdonald and his newspaper came out ahead of their respective local rivals.

In their own way, the women of the town were beginning to organize by the 1830s, not that they felt any need to assert themselves. The pioneer women of the early settlement had often been forced to take the initiative in fleeing to the province of Quebec with their children during the revolutionary war when their men were either serving in loyalist regiments or imprisoned. The wife of the senior captain of the settlement, for instance, Mrs. Samuel Anderson, was one of the many wives who had to survive in a hostile neighbourhood in Vermont for several years until she found a way to head north through the dense forests to Sorel in 1778, bringing seven children with her. Peggy Bruce had no illusions that life was easy. Having eloped with a handsome soldier of the Royal Highland Emigrants, she knew the rigours of camp life. When, at war's end, and the couple settled in Cornwall and death fell suddenly on the discharged soldier, the mother did as a number of other widowed women did in those days. She turned the family inn into a profitable business, sufficient to provide for herself and her four children and still find time to tend to the village sick.

By the 1830s many of the first generation of pioneer women had gone to their graves. Now their daughters and the wives and daughters of more recent immigrants to the town began to think of group efforts, usually centred around their churches. Thus, in the autumn of 1834 the ladies of the town ran their first bazaar. Judging from those in charge, the bazaar was largely the work of members of the Episcopal church. Mrs. John Goodall, wife of Dr. Goodall, was president. Mrs. Mountain, widow of Reverend Salter Jehosophat Mountain, was treasurer and Miss Sherman was secretary. The committee included Mrs. Solomon Chesley, Mrs. Philip Vankoughnet, Mrs. George S. Jarvis, Mrs. Robertson, Mrs. Campbell, Mrs. Hart, Miss Malvo and Miss McDonell.[60] The first record of a bazaar organized by Catholic women was in the summer of 1856. Heading the group was the wife of John Sandfield Macdonald. She was assisted by Mrs. D. Macdonald, Mrs. Angus Macdonald, identified as "Deputy", and another Mrs. Angus Macdonald, distinguished as "Mrs. Col.", Mrs. Donald McMillan, Mrs. Lachlan McDonald, and Mrs. John S. McDougald.[61] These ladies netted $600, no mean accomplishment even by today's standards.

Cornwall never lacked for sports, though it was not until the second half of the nineteenth century that organized sports took hold. Pupils at John Strachan's academy bragged about the "excellent sleighing here and very fine skating for the boys who have skates". The favoured children at school also enjoyed impromptu games on New Year's Day, 1807, when Judge Samuel Anderson invited sixteen of them to his farm on the eastern side of the town. The aging judge threw a barrel of apples and hickory nuts into the snow for the boys to scramble for.[62]

One of the favourite summer sports for young people was lacrosse, a game learned from the St. Regis Indians who were playing it as early as 1795.[63] Informal matches were held between Indians and townsmen in the 1840s, but it was not until 1863 that the first Lacrosse Club was organized in Cornwall.[64] From then on Cornwall lads challenged the Indians to matches that went on from noon until darkness put an end to the game. Out of these matches developed some of the finest lacrosse players in the country who went on to win world championships in the latter part of the century.[65]

For the horse-lovers of Cornwall, the old race course had its delights. This course wound its way through the heart of the town along Second Street to Adolphus and Fourth Streets and thence down Sydney Street, about a mile in all.[66] The annual races brought horsemen and breeders from near and far. By the half century the game of curling had taken on among Cornwall buffs who enjoyed sunny days on the frozen bay between Farlinger's and Flanigan's Points, chasing stones around with brooms. In the 1850s the stones were made of blue beachwood with a handle on top for throwing. Among early curling enthusiasts were innkeeper John Gibson, John Greenfield Macdonald, William Colquhoun, James Young and John Ben McLennan.[67]

If Cornwall lacked organized sports in the early part of the nineteenth century, it did not lack young men and not-so-young men with larking propensities. Opportunities for larks often presented themselves with the annual arrival of circuses in town. On one occasion, A.P. Macdonald, who in later life was the very respectable partner in the firm of Worthington and Macdonald, decided that the then visiting circus had not provided sufficient entertainment in the ring for him and his cohorts. The young men-about-town met to discuss the matter. Their decision was to raise a fund of $100 which they offered to the manager of the circus if he would allow the circus elephant to show his abilities as a swimmer. The offer was accepted. Following the afternoon performance, the elephant was taken to the river bank where most of Cornwall's stalwarts had gathered. After much prodding and persuasion, the elephant was coaxed into the water but, once in the water, he made straight for the south shore. This was more than the circus proprietor or the youths had bargained for. They hastily put off in boats "to turn the huge beast back," but as Macdonald admitted, "they might as well have attempted to stop an ice-berg. Mr. Elephant was bound for the south shore and he pushed the obstructing boats away as though they were so many straws." When he landed, the elephant showed no disposition to return. It took the combined efforts of the circus people and townsmen to shove the beast back into the water, but by that time, the circus itinerary was so disrupted that it missed its performance at Prescott.[68]

Cornwall's reputation may have prompted the circus manager another year to strike the town completely off its tour. When A.P. Macdonald and the other young bucks of Cornwall learned of this, they hit upon a scheme to see the elephant. Learning that the circus people had arranged to travel through Cornwall before daylight, the young men scattered several bushels of small potatoes, which elephants love, along the road. Then they hid and watched. About two o'clock in the morning the sound of wheels was heard as the cavalcade approached the sleeping town. There was the elephant, striding along majestically between several strings of wagons. Suddenly he stopped, and began feeling about the road with his trunk. He struck a potato. The keeper did everything he could to get the beast moving, but the elephant began a slow zig-zag course along the road, fearful of missing one of his gastronomical treats. A rosy tint eventually began to appear in the sky and still the cavalcade moved along at a snailspace while the star attraction made sure he did not miss a single potato. The upshot was that the circus entered Cornwall, elephant and all, long after daybreak and Cornwall people not only saw the circus but saw it without charge.[69]

Fraternal societies did not flourish in Cornwall in the first half of the nineteenth century. The Masonic lodge that had blossomed shortly after the settlement was founded — Union Lodge no. 9 — warranted under the Provincial Grand Lodge of Upper Canada, seemed to have disappeared sometime after 1799. When two new Cornwall lodges were warranted in 1804, members of the new lodges were not identical to any known members of the older lodge. One of the new lodges was a "gentlemen's" lodge, Athol no. 3, which took over the name and number of the prestigious lodge that had existed in the Queen's Rangers before they disbanded in 1804. The other lodge was a more plebeian one, made up largely of farmers and artisans in the village, though among the fourteen members was one innkeeper, a merchant and a schoolmaster. It was named Hiram lodge and warranted as lodge no. 20.[70]

The emergence of two small lodges and the subsequent negative reports by the master of the gentlemen's lodge, Joshua Y. Cozens, about the master of no. 20, Asabel Stevens, a clothier, and his lodge, indicated considerable acrimony rather than harmony between the local Masonic brethren. By 1806 the gentlemen's lodge had diminished to three members and was about to break up, especially as there was unpleasantness about the purchase of a set of Masonic jewels by the first Master, Walter Butler Wilkinson. Failing to receive payment for the jewels, the Provincial Grand Secretary sent two agents to Cornwall to investigate the lodges in 1807. The agents were told that the members had paid Wilkinson for the jewels, had received his receipt and "that was enough for them". The stymied agents testily reported to the Grand Secretary, "There, Right Worshipful Sir, you hear the Last Dying Speech and Confession of the Gentlemen's Mason Lodge at Cornwall, and from such Masons, I say, Good Lord Deliver Us".[71] Payment for the jewels eventually got sorted out after the sudden death of Walter Butler Wilkinson in 1807, and the gentlemen's lodge, Athol no. 3, gained in membership and importance under Joshua Y. Cozens as master. Its officers were delegated by the Provincial Grand Lodge in 1810 to officiate at the installation of other lodges in the area, but by 1812 both Athol no. 3 and Hiram no. 20 disappeared from the records, presumably casualties of the war of 1812-14. It was not until the 1860s that another Cornwall lodge, no. 125, was instituted with John McLellan as master.[73]

Although one scholar asserts that there were Orange clashes in Cornwall in the 1820s, no evidence has been found to show that an Orange Lodge existed in the town prior to 1857.[74] Yet there may have been some interest in Orangeism in the 1820s. The former Cornwall clergyman, John Strachan, who had rapidly risen in the government machinery at York, did not think it beneath his dignity to preach to members of the York Orange Lodge on the Glorious Twelfth in 1822. Nor did Cornwall's leading merchant, Philip Vankoughnet, support Doctor William W. Baldwin's bill in the Assembly to ban Orange processions in 1823. Vankoughnet may simply have voted with the government which had decided that existing legislation was sufficient to deal with disorders arising out of Orange processions.[75] In any event, Cornwall's Orangemen did not become organized until Robert Gordon formed a lodge in 1857. Orange initiative was far from vigorous, for it was not until 1895 that the local lodge was incorporated under the name of Monroe Loyal Orange Lodge, no. 880. By choosing this name the lodge honoured its master,

Cornwall's "Insurance King", Duncan Monroe, the conservative Presbyterian who continued to stand during prayers at St. John's long after the rest of the congregation had adopted the habit of kneeling. At first the Orangemen met in a building on the north side of Second Street between Augustus and Pitt Streets. Then they built their own hall on the west side of Pitt Street below First Street, chiselling the name "Monroe Orange Hall" across its front so deeply that it remains in full view today even though the hall has passed to other hands. Township Orangemen had their own hall by 1878, located in the fifth concession on lot no. 19, an indication that rural Orangemen were sufficiently numerous and affluent to erect a hall.[76]

There is no evidence that Irish canallers at Cornwall were organized into secret societies such as Ribbonmen, Shamrocks or Hibernians.[77] Nor is there any record that a Friends of Ireland Society was formed in the town in the late 1820s as occurred in a number of other towns. Yet there was contact with larger Irish movements overseas. The Catholic Association of Ireland which won Catholic emancipation for the Irish in 1829 had an agent in the Cornwall area as early as 1824 — Aeneas Macdonell — through whom financial aid could be funnelled to Ireland.[78]

Closer to home was the Highland Society of Canada, organized by Bishop Alexander Macdonell in St. Raphaels in 1818. Among Cornwall men who were original members were Colonel Neil McLean and his sons, Archibald and Alexander, and John McDonald of Garth. Largely devoted to helping distressed Highlanders, the Society also assisted those engaged in publishing works in Gaelic and gave awards to Gaelic scholars, pipers and to the best-dressed Highlanders.[79] By the 1830s the Highland Society of Canada gave way to the St. Andrew's Society which in 1837 was presided over by John McGillivray.[80] Vice presidents were Hugh McGillis and Alex Fraser; managers James McDonald, Archibald Stewart, John Hay and Fennan McDonald. In charge of accounts were Donald Fraser and Alexander McBean. Like the earlier Highland Society of Canada, the St. Andrew's Society drew on both the town and township of Cornwall and the neighbouring area of Glengarry for its membership. Apart from these societies, Cornwall people did not feel the need for more elaborate fraternal, charitable or sport organizations during the first half of the nineteenth century. The loose fraternal and social ties within their church structures and at the local taverns and inns provided for their more immediate needs.

As far as the town's institutions were concerned, one of the oldest was the court house with its adjoining jail. This was the provincial government's reminder to townspeople and their adjacent township neighbours that they were linked to the larger entity of Upper Canada. The first court house was a two-storey wooden building begun in 1802 and finished in 1808. It lasted until 1826 when fire destroyed it.[81] The second court house was built of a more substantial sombre grey stone and was ready for use in 1833. It survives today as one of Cornwall's oldest buildings. In the first part of the century the justices of the peace, as members of the Court of Quarter Sessions, operated out of the old court house. They handled most of the judicial, financial and administrative work for the eastern part of the district. With the union of Upper and Lower Canada in 1841, a major change took place. The Court of Quarter Sessions was relieved of its administrative and financial duties and limited to serve as a court of criminal jurisdiction. Duties such as the management of finances, property, and the building and repair of roads and bridges were turned over to the newly-created district councils.[82] These councils were composed of wardens and clerks, appointed by the government directly, and of a body of councillors elected by the townships. With this change from government by the justices of the peace in Quarter Sessions to government by district councils, the old local wielders of patronage and political power — the justices of the peace — were jostled out of their saddles. Cornwall's rising political star, John Sandfield Macdonald, fought vigorously against the new arrangement that tended to centralize appointments and patronage in the hands of the provincial administration, but lost.[83]

The local objections to the centralizing tendencies within the district councils made themselves felt by 1846 when the councils were given the right to elect their own wardens from among council members. Then, in 1849, new legislation abolished the district councils and established the county as the administrative unit. The "poor Glengarry boy", John Sandfield Macdonald, had been assiduous throughout the forties in securing jobs for minor postal clerks, lock masters and land officers, thus tying their fortunes to his. When the new act abolished the old districts, John Sandfield Macdonald prevented the disruption of the Eastern District by keeping the county of Stormont united with Glengarry and Dundas for administrative, judicial and financial purposes. The county continued to serve mainly as an electoral and military unit.[84]

These refinements in the district and county arrangements had their repercussions for the town of Cornwall. For one thing, the wardens, clerks, judges, sheriffs and other provincial officials operated out of the county court house that was located in the heart of Cornwall. For another, councillors had to come to Cornwall for the quarterly meetings of the different councils each year. Thus Cornwall retained its importance as the administrative and judicial centre of the united counties. It secured additional influence in 1850 when the town was permitted to elect a reeve to the county council. By 1869 it could elect a deputy reeve as well. Thus Cornwall now had two voices in the council. It was not surprising, then, that Cornwall men monopolized county offices. In 1851 the council for the united counties elected as warden Cornwall's own mayor, William Mattice. From 1850 until 1884, Dr. Roderick McDonald was treasurer. From 1842 until 1850, James Dunbar Pringle was clerk and then his older brother, Jacob Farrand Pringle, held the post from 1858 until 1866 when he was appointed junior county judge.[85]

The judicial arm of the united counties was well represented by Cornwall men. George S. Jarvis was county judge from 1841 until 1878 when he was succeeded by Jacob Farrand Pringle. Judges of the surrogate court from the time of Samuel Anderson in 1793 until J.F. Pringle's term began in 1878 were all Cornwall men with one exception, John McDonald of Garth, whose beautiful home, Inverarden, was then outside the town's limit.[86] Most of the sheriffs of the district were Cornwall men, including the first sheriff, Cornelius Munro, and Neil McLean and Donald Aeneas McDonell.

By 1850 there were twenty civil servants connected with the county courts and provincial administration working out of the court house and jail in Cornwall, or holding jobs as post master, land agent, high constable, judges, clerks and registrars of the various courts, canal superintendent, and jailor, all drawing their pay from the provincial government. Thus, although the business and politics of the county court house encompassed an area far beyond the immediate town of Cornwall, the personalities immediately concerned in the everyday business of the county court, jail and council were centred in Cornwall and added a dimension of prestige and importance to the small town that would have been lacking had the county seat been elsewhere.

This proliferation of provincial civil servants put such a strain on the facilities of the court house that by 1852 the county council erected a small brick building containing four rooms to house the clerk of the county council, the clerk of the peace, the county treasurer and registrar. A second storey was added for use as a lecture and assembly room. This building soon proved too small and, by 1885, another county building was put up to provide offices for the increasing number of bureaucrats working out of Cornwall.[87]

In addition to the provincial civil servants whose work was centred in and around Cornwall, mid-century Cornwall had some small-scale manufacturing, a business milieu of eleven shopkeepers, and a discernible professional circle. Cornwall's first saleable product was ready for market almost as soon as the first settlers cut down trees to make room for their homes and crops. The innumerable felled trees, far more than the settlers could use to build homes or for warmth, were burned, simply to get rid of them. Their pearl white ashes, known as potash, could be sold by the bushel to the Cornwall firm of Wilkinson and Beikie in 1795 in exchange for credit or goods, a form of bartering in the early life of Cornwall that proved as convenient as a straight sale for cash. Thus, for instance, loyalist settler Adam Johnston bought a scarlet milled cap and a pound of Bohea tea, valued at seven shillings, but paid no cash for the items. Instead, he bartered 51 bushels of ashes, priced at four pence a bushel, for his purchases and received a credit for the extra 43 bushels from Wilkinson and Beikie.[88]

If the settlers preferred, they could sell their potash, not to the local storekeepers, but to a potash factory. Cornwall, like other early loyalist settlements, boasted its own potash establishment located on Pointe Maligne, which became known as Potash Point. The promoter of the factory was likely loyalist Michael Vankoughnet, who was fast becoming Cornwall's largest land-owner.[89] Vankoughnet and other Cornwall businessmen understood well the profits that could accrue from turning potash into lye as a disinfectant or for use in making soap. Crude buildings were put up on Pointe Maligne near a creek. Here leach tubs made of basswood or cedar slabs were constructed to hold the mixture of potash and water from which the lye was extracted. Near the tubs, large iron kettles stood on stone or brick arches under which a brisk fire was kept going day and night until the lye boiled down sufficiently to be poured into moulds for cooling and hardening.[90] This primitive method of turning potash into lye continued well into the nineteenth century until newer methods replaced the old leach tubs and arched fireplaces, and Potash Point no longer welcomed the ash-ladened wagon and its ash-covered driver.

Potash manufacturing and small hand carding and weaving production at home were the beginnings of industrial life in Cornwall. The town also benefitted financially from the lumbering operations that were carried on to the rear of the town. Most of the men who spent their winters hewing and cutting up trees for rafting to the Montreal market in the spring were paid off in or near Cornwall. Then, to the delight of Cornwall merchants, innkeepers, and tavern owners, the lumbermen, "having earned their money like horses, spent it like asses", as one Cornwall contemporary remarked.[91]

More prosaic products came from the first Cornwall flour and saw mills. At the mid-century the two local flour mills were operated by Andrew Elliott and Myron Hitchcock. A man named Hawkins ran the single sawmill in town in 1850. Free Kirker Austin Edson Cadwell owned the more impressive iron foundry. Here ploughs, brass castings and threshing mills were turned out.[92] The town in 1850 also boasted two firms of saddlers and harness makers: McDougall and Robertson and that of Daniel Daly. Local carriage-makers were Vincent Annable, James Irving and Ranald McDonell. John Carr was the boot and shoe-maker. The town's three tanneries were run by Robert Craig, Henry Perkins and a man named Farlinger.

The number of general stores and grocery stores rose and fell with the ebb and flow of the town's prosperity in the first half of the nineteenth century. At the height of canal construction in 1836, there were seventeen licensed shopkeepers in town: Philip Vankoughnet, William Cline, Howard Thompson, Lachlin McDonell, Felix McLaughlin, Peter Chesley, William Lindsay, Keezar and Dix Company, James Groves, George Robertson, William Mattice, Martin Carman, Guy Carlton Wood, Caleb Knight, James Forsyth, George Sutherland and John Bell. Anyone else trying to sell goods in Cornwall was warned by town fathers that "they would be liable to a penalty of £20".[93] This alerted canal contractors not to scab on local merchants by operating a "truck" system which would oblige canallers to buy their provisions from the shops of contractors.

The influence of shopkeepers as a class was clearly discernible in early municipal politics. Three of the five members of the first town council were shopkeepers: Philip Vankoughnet, Martin Carman and John Chesley. In spite of a drop in their numbers from seventeen in 1836 to eleven in 1850, merchants at the mid-century edged barristers out of their entrenched position as top men in the town council. With two exceptions, all the presidents of the Police Boards and mayor from 1834 until 1850 had been barristers. Then, in 1850 merchant William Mattice, a leading man at St. John's Presbyterian Church, was chosen mayor by a council of nine that included grocers P.E. Adams and D.W. McDonell, jeweller Robert Atchison, carriage-maker Vincent Annable, and iron manufacturer Austin E. Cadwell. From then until the end of the century merchants and doctors, almost without exception, held the mayoralty seat. Mattice's victory in 1850 also marked the eighth time in the sixteen years since the town was incorporated that a member of St. John's Presbyterian Church headed the town's administration.

The drop in the number of merchants in Cornwall resulted from the decline that set in after canal construction ended. Yet the decline may not have been as severe as statistics would indicate. Five of these eleven shopkeepers survived from the 1830s: Philip Vankoughnet,

John Bell, William Park, William Cline and William Mattice. Except for Thomas O'Callaghan who confined himself to groceries, all the others carried on extensive trade in a great variety of goods including groceries, bakery products, hardware, crockery, drugs and medicines, dry goods and china. One, Donald McMillan, also sold liquors, competing with the only other local liquor merchant and brewer in town, John Bell.[94] Thus, although there was a drop in the number of local merchants between 1836 and 1850, it may be that the surviving merchants had considerably expanded establishments over those that had existed in the mid-1830s.

Some specialized shops began to appear in the first part of the century, one of the earliest being that of William M. Park who established himself as the town's undisputed watchmaker and jeweller. Located on lot 14 on the north side of Water Street by the 1820s, Park assured his customers that "particular attention (would be paid) to work from a distance".[95] A rival jeweller appeared in the next decade when Robert Atchison established a store on Pitt Street.[96] One of the longest continuing businesses in Cornwall in the nineteenth century was that of John Hunter who had a tinsmith and coopersmith shop on Water Street in 1834.[97] It was at Hunter's home that the Free Kirk secessionist group from St. John's Presbyterian Church first held services in 1844. Another merchant of the 1830s, John Bell, blossomed out in the next decade as Cornwall's first brewer. At his shop, farmers could barter their wheat, oats and barley for "Jamaica rum, cogniac brandy, Holland gin, port and other wines".[98] The following chart indicates the breakdown of trades, professions and civil bureaucracy operating in Cornwall in the mid-century:[99]

Bank Agents
1. William Mattice: Bank of Montreal
2. Jacob F. Pringle: Bank of Upper Canada
3. Guy C. Wood: Commercial Bank

Blacksmiths
1. Robert Campbell
2. Wellington Lonney
3. George Cook
4. Joseph Johnson

Boots & Shoemakers
1. John Carr
2. McDougall & Robertson

Brewer
1. John Bell

Bricklayers
1. Francis Campbell
2. David Perkins
3. Charles Stafford
4. Archibald Mason

Cabinet & Chairmaker
1. John Shirkey

Carpenter & Builder
1. John Clough

Carriagemakers
1. Vincent Annable
2. James Irving
3. Ranald McDonell

Grocers & General Stores
1. P.E. Adams
2. A. Fulton
3. Alex McDougall
4. Donald McMillan
5. William Mattice
6. Thomas O'Callaghan
7. Samuel Cline
8. William Cline
9. D.W. McDonell & Co.
10. Angus McPhaul
11. Philip Vankoughnet

Tailors & Clothier
1. James Hunter
2. Joseph Tanner
3. Michael J. Smart

Tanners
1. Robert Craig
2. Henry Perkins
3. _____ Farlinger

Telegraph Agent
1. G.S. Hickey

Tin & Coppersmiths
1. John Hunter
2. William Percy

Watchmakers & Jewellers
1. William M. Park
2. Robert Atchison

Insurance Agents
1. William M. Park: Canada Life
2. Jacob F. Pringle: Colonial Life
3. A.S. McDonald: National Loan Fund Life

Millers
1. Myron Hitchcock (flour)
2. Andrew Elliott (flour)
3. _____ Hawkins (saw)

Printers
1. Henry Patterson
2. Little & Mitchell

Saddlers & Harnessmakers
1. Daniel Daly
2. McDougall & Robertson Co.

Hotel & Innkeepers
1. William Wagner
2. Benjamin Wagner
3. W.J. Pitts
4. Benjamin Burton (St. Lawrence House)
5. Coombs & Hickey (Steamboat Hotel)
6. A.W. McDonell

Cornwall — 1850 — Professions

Attorneys & Barristers
1. John (Greenfield) McDonell
2. William Ross
3. John Sandfield Macdonald
4. George McDonell
5. Peter U. McDonell
6. Jacob F. Pringle
7. John Walker

Bookkeeper & Accountant
1. Robert Stuart

Clergymen
1. Father J.F. Cannon (Roman Catholic)
2. Rev. J. Quin (Free Kirk)
3. Rev. Hugh Urquhart (Presbyterian)
4. Rev. Henry Patton (Anglican)

Doctors & Chemists
1. Darby Bergin
2. William Cox Allen
3. Roderick Macdonald
4. Daniel E. McIntyre
5. Charles Rattray
6. James J. Dickinson

Teachers
1. William Kay (Grammar School)

Civil Servants

Canal
1. Duncan McDonell (Superintendent)
2. D. Phelan

Clerks
1. Angus S. Macdonald (of county court)
2. Charles Poole (division court & town)
3. Guy C. Wood (deputy clerk of the crown)
4. James Pringle (clerk of the peace)
5. Peter J. McDonell (county council)

Crown Land Agent
1. Samuel Hart

High Constable
1. Daniel Daly

Jailor
1. Duncan McLennan

Judges
1. George S. Jarvis (county)
2. George McDonell (surrogate)

Landing Waiter
1. Angus McDonell

Postmaster & Customs Collector
1. Guy C. Wood

Registrars
1. A. McLean (surrogate court)
2. John McLean (county Stormont)

Sheriff
1. Daniel E. McIntyre
2. Angus Bethune (deputy)

Treasurer
1. Roderick Macdonald

Warden
1. Daniel E. McIntyre (county)

Social welfare had yet to appear in Cornwall, but there were gestures towards the needy, particularly in the winters when labouring jobs were scarce. Provincial government aid and private charity were provided to canal workers in the winter of 1837. At that time Colonel George Phillpotts, one of the Royal Engineer officers connected with canal construction, reported that sixty families in the Cornwall area were close to starvation. He asked that their winter wages of one shilling three pence be raised to two shillings six pence in order to keep the people alive and available for work in the spring. The provincial Assembly voted relief on 16 February 1837 and arranged to advance provisions to the needy families. Cornwall contractors also took up a subscription for thirty sick men and their families.[100] Clergymen undertook some welfare work, especially Father James Bennett of St. Columban's Church, but his financial resources were extremely meagre.[101]

Cornwall at the half-century did, indeed, appear to observant travellers as "not a place of any great business".[102] Yet by 1850 some small industries had appeared. There was the well-established potash factory, an iron foundry, three mills and three tanneries. The town supported two weekly newspapers and enjoyed a modest prestige as the county seat. Yet neither the visitors to Cornwall nor the inhabitants of the little town on the north bank of the St. Lawrence suspected in 1850 that within a generation water power from the new canal would turn the sleepy town into an industrial giant.

NOTES

1. Mackenzie to John Sandfield Macdonald, 25 September 1855, cited in Bruce Hodgins, *John Sandfield Macdonald*, 33.

2. William Hutton to editor, the *British Farmers' Magazine*, April, 1835, cited in Edwin C. Guillet, *Early Life in Canada*, 298.

3. *Cornwall Observer*, 8 January 1836.

4. For Total Abstinence Society see *Cornwall Observer*, 6 May 1841; for social controls by town fathers see, Ralph Ellis, "The Economic, Social and Demographic Impact of the Cornwall Canal, unpublished paper submitted to History Department, McGill University, April 1982, 11.

5. J.G. Harkness, *History of Stormont, Dundas and Glengarry*, 190.

6. H. Belden, *Historical Atlas of Stormont, Dundas and Glengarry*, v.

7. RG22/7, Minutes of General Quarter Sessions of the Peace for the Eastern District, 25 April 1834, 24 January 1838, 24 April 1839, 29 April 1840, 30 April, 1841, 27 April 1842, cited in Ralph Ellis, 32.

8. Minutes, Town Council, 18 May 1868, cited in *Standard-Freeholder*, 24 June 1967.

9. George S. Jarvis, "Reminiscences," in *Canadian Illustrated News*, 26 January 1878.

10. J.F. Pringle, *Lunenburgh, or the Old Eastern District*, 59.

11. *Ibid.*, 54.

12. Harkness, 71.

13. *Canada Directory*, 1851, 68.

14. Minutes, Town Council, 18 May 1868, 12.

15. For the various appointments see, Minutes, Town Council 18 May, 26 October, 1868, 18 January, 8 February, 23 August, 1869.

16. Pringle, 67.

17. *Ibid.*, 69; *Old Boys' Reunion*, 1906.

18. *Cornwall Observer*, 7 January 1841; Pringle, 135, says the reorganization was in 1840.

19. *Cornwall Observer*, 7 January 1841.

20. Pringle, 285.

21. *Ibid.*, 133 and 138.

22. Chewett map, 1792, V3/440.

23. Return of Membership, Hiram Lodge no. 20, Cornwall, cited in Robertson, *History of Freemasonry*, 875.

24. Alexander Caldwell and Mary Stewart, *Cornwall Collegiate and Vocational School: An Historical Sketch*, 5.

25. *Ibid.*

26. Hodgins, *John Sandfield Macdonald*, 18; for contemporary view of a liberal education, see Dr.Charles Duncombe, *Report on the subject of Education*, cited in Caldwell and Stewart, 5.

27. *Ibid.*, 6.

28. *Ibid.*, 4-5.

29. Walker, *Catholic Education and Politics in Upper Canada*, 13; Pringle, 247-48.

30. J.A. Macdonell, *Sketches: Glengarry in Canada*, 150.

31. Pringle, 85 and 248; Harkness, 107.

32. Pringle, 249; Harkness, 338.

33. Until well into the mid-1840s, Trinity was usually referred to as the Episcopal Church, an indication that its pioneer founders were of American origin. For details on the parochial school see, Diocesan Archives Ottawa: Trinity Church records 59/1/19; Mary Mack, "History of Bishop Strachan Memorial Trinity Church" in *Souvenir of the Dedication of the Restored and Modernized Memorial Pipe Organ*, 1968, 2; G.B. Stidwill, *The Mountains and Trinity Church*, 7; Pringle, 249.

34. For the Catholic School, see, Father Charles Murray, "Reminiscences," 6; for the number of pupils see Appendix, *Journal of the Legislative Assembly*, 1843, no. 2, iii, app. Z, Statistical Schedule for 1842; Pringle, 249.

35. Strachan to Reverend Dr. James Brown, Professor of Natural Philosophy at University of Glasgow, 20 October 1807, cited in Allison Smith, "John Strachan and Early Upper Canada, 1799-1814"; in *Ontario History*, lii, 1960, 170.

36. Miles MacDonell to his brother, John, 21 May 1809, cited in A.C. Morice, "A Canadian Pioneer: Spanish John," in *CHR*, x, 1929, 232-35.

37. *Ibid.*, 235.

38. For instance, Cornwall's first woman councillor, Mary Mack, attended Miss Edgar's and Miss Cramp's School, Montreal; see, Emily MacInnes, Tribute to Mary Agnes Mack, 28 May 1978.

39. Macdonell to Francis Baby, 10 March 1839, cited in Walker, *Catholic Education and Politics*, 22.

40. *An Historical Sketch, St. Columban's Parish*, 1896, 8.

41. See Walker, *Catholic Education and Politics*, 37-39.

42. Hodgins, *John Sandfield Macdonald*, 24.

43. Minutes, Town Council, 1893-1896, 13 February 1895, 277; Father Charles Murray, "Reminiscences," 9; Rudolph Villeneuve, *Catholic Education in Cornwall, Ontario, Yesterday, Today and Tomorrow*, 4-5.

44. A.H. Young, "The Mission of Cornwall 1784-1812," in *OHSPR*, xxv, 1929, 494.

45. History of St. John's Church, 1787-1975, 8.

46. *Gazette*, York, 5 December 1810, cited in Richard Preston, *Kingston Before the War of 1812*, cv-cvi.

47. Joseph Frobisher's diary entry dated 30 July 1809, cited in George W. Spragge,"The Cornwall Grammar School under John Strachan, 1803-1812," in *OHSPR*, xxxiv, 1942, 72.

48. Pringle, 93.

49. MG9/D8/6, Eastern District Quarter Sessions, 1826-35, entry dated 12 July 1827, 40; Pringle, 85; Harkness, 446.

50. Thomas Wily Memoirs, MG29/E1/83-85.

51. *Ibid.*

52. Pringle, 142-43.
53. For early accounts of the development of the press in Cornwall see *Cornwall Observer*, 8 January 1836; *Standard-Freeholder*, 30 December 1944; Belden, *Historical Atlas*, 1878, vi; *Saturday Globe*, Toronto, 18 November 1893; Pringle, 69, 99; Harkness, 371.
54. *Cornwall Observer*, 25 July 1836; Pringle, 83.
55. Thomas Rolph, *A Brief Account...with a Statistical Account of Upper Canada*, see appendix.
56. *Cornwall Chronicle*, 8 February 1845.
57. Belden, *Historical Atlas*, vi; *Old Boys' Reunion*, 1906.
58. *Cornwall Observer*, 8 January 1848.
59. W.H. Smith, *Canada, Past, Present and Future*, ii, 387-8.
60. Pringle, 342; Harkness, 449.
61. *An Historical Sketch, St. Columban's Parish*, 1896, 26.
62. Thomas Ridout to his parents, 10 January 1807, in Edgar, *The Ridout Letters*, 21.
63. Duc de la Rochefoucauld-Liancourt, *Travels in Canada 1795*, 120.
64. *Saturday Globe*, Toronto, 18 November 1893; *Standard-Freeholder*, 3 August 1946.
65. *Canadian Illustrated News*, 26 January 1878.
66. Pringle, 86.
67. *Canadian Illustrated News*, 26 January 1878; *Saturday Globe*, Toronto, 10 November 1893; Harry H. Moffat, Early History of Curling in the Cornwall area, 1.
68. *Canadian Illustrated News*, 26 January 1878.
69. *Ibid.*
70. Robertson, *History of Freemasonry*, i, 872, 875.
71. John Darley to Grand Secretary Jermyn Patrick, 2 October 1807, cited in *Ibid.*, i, 872.
72. *Ibid.*, 873-74.
73. *Standard-Freeholder*, 29 June 1934.
74. Ruth Bleasdale, "Irish Labourers on the Cornwall, Welland and Williamsburg Canals in the 1840s", unpublished M.A. thesis, University of Western Ontario, September 1975, 83; *Standard-Freeholder*, 29 June 1934.
75. For Strachan, see *Weekly Register*, York, 18 July 1822; for Vankoughnet, see *Parliamentary Register*, 7 March 1823, bound with *Upper Canada Gazette*, 1 May 1823; for a discussion of Baldwin's bill to ban Orange processions, see H. Senior, *Orangeism: The Canadian Phase*, 9-10.
76. For Monroe Lodge, see *Saturday Globe*, Toronto, 18 November 1893; *Standard*, Cornwall, 7 February 1918; *Standard-Freeholder*, 29 June 1934; for township Orange Hall, see Belden, *Historical Atlas*, 6-7.
77. Bleasdale, "Irish Labourers on the Cornwall, Welland and Williamsburg Canals in the 1840s," unpublished M.A. thesis, University of Western Ontario, 1975, 76.
78. For Friends of Ireland Societies, see H. Senior, *The Fenians and Canada*, 13; for Catholic Association Agent, see Bishop A. Macdonell to Lord Bathurst, 18 December 1824, MG11 Q337/1-2.
79. Macdonell, *Sketches*, 326-7; J.E. Rea, *Bishop Alexander Macdonell and the Politics of Upper Canada*, 55-56; Harkness, 128.
80. *Cornwall Observer*, 30 November 1837.
81. Pringle, 55-56.
82. F.H. Armstrong, *Handbook of Canadian Chronology and Territorial Legislation*, 150; Pringle, 70, 210-211.
83. Hodgins, *John Sandfield Macdonald*, 13.
84. *Ibid.*, 17; James Croil, *Dundas, or a Sketch of Canadian History*, 219.

85. Belden, *Historical Atlas*, v; for listing of county officers, see Pringle, 211-12.
86. *Ibid.*, 314.
87. *Ibid.*, 138.
88. Account voucher, 2 August 1795, Cornwall, in *Freeholder*, 15 February 1889.
89. Harkness, 137.
90. Pringle, 93-94.
91. *Ibid.*, 95.
92. *Canada Directory*, 1851, 68.
93. *Cornwall Observer*, 8 January 1836.
94. Canada *Directory*, 1851, 69.
95. *Ibid.*; Pringle, 82.
96. *Standard-Freeholder*, 29 June 1934; Pringle, 137-8.
97. *Old Boys' Reunion*, 1906; *Canada Directory*, 1851, 69.
98. *Cornwall Observer*, 4 September 1845; Pringle, 73; *Standard-Freeholder*, 13 March 1943.
99. *Canada Directory*, 1851, 68-69.
100. *Appendix, Journal Legislative Assembly*, 1836-37, 135-136, cited in Ralph Ellis, "Economic, Social and Demographic Impact of the Cornwall Canal: 1834-43," unpublished paper submitted to History Department, McGill University, April 1982, 27.
101. Father Charles Murray, "Reminiscences", 2.
102. W.H. Smith, *Canada, Past, Present and Future*, ii, 387.

Chapter X

Fenians, Confederation and Cornwall

Cornwall did not escape the political turmoil and invasion threats that faced Canada as a whole during the 1860s. As far as defense went, Cornwall remained within the Montreal orbit whenever tensions with the United States arose, but for military administrative purposes, it was within the orbit of the upper province. In 1846, as the Oregon crisis loomed in Canadian-American relations, a new militia act produced a reorganization of the sedentary militia battalions. The three Stormont battalions were grouped with the Glengarry and Dundas battalions to form a single unit called the Regiment of the Eastern District. Cornwall men commanded three of these battalions: John Sandfield Macdonald remained lieutenant-colonel of the 4th Glengarry, Donald Aeneas Macdonell commanded the 1st Stormont and George Anderson the 2nd Stormont. By 1851 two additional battalions had been raised. Again it was Cornwall men who were appointed to the command — George McDonell to the 4th Stormont and Mayor William Mattice to the 5th.[1]

Cornwall's Troop of Dragoons, raised in 1838 by George Stephen Jarvis, evolved over the 1840s into the Stormont Independent Troop of Cavalry with Dr. James J. Dickinson as captain.[2] The Cornwall Independent Artillery Company survived the militia reorganization of 1846, commanded by Captains R.K. Bullock and Jacob Farrand Pringle, the latter a son of half-pay British officer, James Pringle, who had founded the company in 1838.[3] The Stormont battalions underwent a further reshuffling in 1852 when the Regiment of the Eastern District was discarded in favour of the county as the unit of militia organization as it had been prior to 1846. These various paper reorganizations of local militia battalions did not hide the fact that since the rebellion era of 1837-38, Cornwall militiamen had done little soldiering apart from the annual muster day.

Although no serious external threats to Cornwall or the rest of Canada arose in the 1850s, the withdrawal of most of the British troops from Canada for duty in the Crimea in 1854-55 made Canadian military authorities more aware of militia inadequacies. A new militia act came into force in 1855. Under this, Cornwall became headquarters for military district no. 2 that embraced the counties of Stormont, Dundas, Glengarry, Grenville, Leeds and the town of Prescott. Appointed to command the new military district was Alexander McLean, the sixty-two-year-old son of Neil McLean who had served in the 84th Royal Highland Emigrants during the American revolutionary war and had seen Cornwall through the war of 1812-14. Under this new legislation, Cornwall once more raised a troop of cavalry, this one designated the Cornwall Troop of Volunteer Militia Cavalry. Dr. James J. Dickinson was appointed captain and remained in command until 1862 when Captain William D. Wood assumed command. Thus, as Cornwall's military organization adjusted to the new militia laws, it was the military families of the town, many of them descended from the early loyalist and military pioneers, who still commanded and filled the ranks.[4] For instance, one of the first men to apply, in 1858, for a commission in the 100th Royal Canadian Regiment — the first Canadian unit to be raised for service overseas — was Captain M.J. Anderson of Cornwall. Anderson was a third generation member of Captain Samuel Anderson's family of loyalist days. The young Anderson had served during the rebellion period and had been for six years in the incorporated militia under Colonel Philip Vankoughnet.[5] As such, he represented yet another link of the old loyalist military families with the military might of the succeeding generations. In the years from 1843 until 1861, Cornwall men saw little military activity except the two weeks' annual drill undertaken by the Troop of Cavalry and its splendid appearance at Cornwall and at Dickinson's Landing in 1860 when the youthful Prince of Wales arrived during his Canadian tour.[6]

With the outbreak of the American Civil War in the spring of 1861, two companies of the Royal Canadian Rifles were moved to Cornwall and remained encamped west of the town over the summer months. Then, as the American Civil War intensified in the late fall and relations between the United States and England became increasingly strained over the *Trent* incident, Cornwall military leaders were ordered by the government to call out seventy-five volunteers from the sedentary Stormont Battalion.[7] Although tension between the two countries subsided by the end of 1861, Canadian military authorities encouraged the formation of Rifle Companies. Cornwall immediately responded. In January of 1862, Captain Darby Bergin, one of Cornwall's most popular doctors, raised No. 1 Volunteer Rifle Company. His officers included Lieutenants James Alexander McDonell and John E. Cline. A second Volunteer Rifle Company was raised by Captain Edward Oliver. Among Oliver's officers were Cornwall's mayor, Dr. William Cox Allen, and George Sherwood Jarvis, as lieutenants, and Donald Alexander Macdonald as ensign.[8]

A third Cornwall volunteer unit was raised by Captain Jacob Farrand Pringle in November of 1862. Like the other two recently-organized volunteer rifle corps, the new unit was officered by politically-active men. Pringle had served as mayor of Cornwall in 1855-56; his lieutenant was lawyer Donald Ban MacLennan, legal partner of John Sandfield Macdonald.[9] Hugh McDonell was ensign. These Cornwall volunteer riflemen and infantrymen drilled once or twice a week, at first under non-commissioned officers sent from the regular garrison in Montreal and afterwards by their own officers, a system that Pringle considered more efficient for giving the men a knowledge of squad and company drill than the later system by which volunteers trained for a period of twelve days annually.[10]

Military enthusiasm waned among the volunteers in Cornwall and elsewhere as the Americans turned more fiercely on themselves. It was not until the Civil War ended and countless Irish-American war veterans were released from military service, that a new threat appeared on the Canadian border in the form of Fenian raids. These Fenians hoped to secure Irish independence from Great Britain by the round-about method of attacking a conveniently nearby neighbour, Canada, which was a colony of Great Britain. By establishing a military presence in Canada, no matter how brief, the Fenians hoped to gain belligerent status and thus press home their demands for Irish independence. Cornwall held two important features in the Fenian scheme of things — its canal was an essential part of the St. Lawrence communication route, and secondly, its railroad linked Montreal and Toronto. "The possession of Cornwall is a prize worth striving for," the editor of the Quebec City Mercury noted. "Whoever holds the canal and railway holds the key to communication between the two parts of the country." Fenian leaders had also noted the obvious. Indeed, their leading military expert, General Thomas W. Sweeny, had already written his appreciation of Cornwall. "Canada is shaped somewhat like an hour-glass," he wrote. "The occupation of the line dividing its centre, near Montreal, will cut the provinces in two, and by isolating the Western District give us entire command of the enemy's line of communication and supplies".[11]

Anxiously watching these developments in Canada and in Cornwall was John Sandfield Macdonald, who had decided in 1857 to switch his political bailiwick from Glengarry to the smaller and more manageable constituency of Cornwall. The switch meant that he had to cope with something less than 700 voters to secure a seat, even if the Cornwall seat had proved somewhat uncertain in the past. In his first Cornwall election in 1857, Macdonald faced Philip Vankoughnet, in every sense a worthy and formidable opponent. The town's tories were sure that Vankoughnet's long political, military and business career in the small town would be sufficient to overcome Macdonald's obvious polling attractions. However, the boy from Glengarry likely heeded the Catholic delegation from St. Andrews which marched into Cornwall to warn him to desist opposing separate schools or lose their votes. He walked away from the hustings with 428 votes against 246 cast for Vankoughnet.[12]

By the time of the next elections in the spring of 1861, Macdonald had won his spurs as spokesman for central Canada. He firmly upheld the duality of the country and insisted on a majority vote from each section of the country for all major bills. The cry from the more western part of Canada West for representation according to population held no attraction for him. As the elections drew near, he made one of his most aggressive speeches in Cornwall on 3 July 1861. ''To Montreal we send our grain, our timber, our ashes. From Montreal we obtain our money'', he told his Cornwall constituents, reminding them once more that their natural business and financial orientation was still towards Montreal, not Toronto. They agreed and gave him their votes, some 374 against 260 to his opponent.[13] Thus Cornwall had the right man in the right place at the right time in the spring of 1862 when John A. Macdonald's shaky government went down to defeat on the issue of a new militia bill. The governor-general, Lord Monck, gave the nod to the member for Cornwall and catapulted John Sandfield Macdonald into the leadership of the government, the first and only time that a Cornwall man headed the Canadian government. Not only was he Canadian premier, Macdonald was also minister of militia affairs as well, assuming the new post that John A. Macdonald had created and taken on the previous year in the face of the international crisis.

John Sandfield Macdonald was no stranger to military matters. His first taste of military duty had been during the rebellion era when he served as lieutenant in the Queen's Light Infantry, a Toronto militia unit.[14] Then, in 1857, when he shifted his political base from Glengarry to Cornwall, he also switched from command of the 4th Glengarry Regiment to the 3rd Stormont Battalion.[15] Moreover, the new Canadian premier from Cornwall had close personal ties with the contending sides in the American Civil War. His wife's family was of the Southern gentry, and her younger brother, Eugene, soon became a Confederate colonel. When Colonel Waggaman was imprisoned in Boston by federal troops, it was the Canadian Premier who personally intervened to try to secure his release and confinement in Canada for the duration of the war.[16]

Macdonald coped with the emergency militia situation by bringing in two bills, one for the sedentary militia and the other relating to the volunteers. He managed to keep his defence budget at $163,500, slightly below that projected by the defeated John A. Macdonald. Nevertheless, John Sandfield Macdonald's administration survived precariously only until 24th May 1864. Then he went somewhat sadly back to his usual opposition role. "It has been my misfortune," he remarked, "to have spent nearly nineteen years of my political life in the cold shades of opposition." Yet he did so by adhering, he said, to the wishes of his constituency, Cornwall, on all major issues. "I have always believed," he asserted, "that I was here for the purpose of representing the constituency which sent me, and not for the purpose of misrepresenting them...on any leading question coming before this House."

John Sandfield Macdonald's opposition to Confederation was consistent and in accordance with the wishes of his Cornwall constituents. "I was never an advocate of any changes in our Constitution," he announced in 1865, insisting that any proposed constitution must have the approval of the majority of Canadians and not be imposed by imperial decree as it had been in 1841. On economic questions, he also pursued policies that reflected local interests, that is, he rejected George Brown's plea for free trade, claiming it would endanger the family homestead. "Our wealth is in our lands," he pointed out, "we own but little money." He feared that free trade would mean an increase in interest rates on debts of farmers who were already heavily mortgaged.[17] With views as strong as these on Confederation, it is not surprising that John Sandfield Macdonald was not among the fathers of Confederation, though once Confederation was accomplished, he accepted the new scheme of things and became Ontario's first premier.

His reconciliation to Confederation came, as it did for many other central Canadians, partly because of the Fenian threat that jolted many out of any feelings of complacency they might have harboured with respect to defence. Cornwall's involvement in the Fenian threat came sooner than any of its townspeople had expected. Local militia volunteers, like others across Canada, were suddenly called out by the government on 7 March 1866 when rumours persisted that the Fenians would invade Canada on St. Patrick's day.[18] A week later Cornwall experienced its own kind of rumours that set the town in an uproar. The story was that no less than 500 Fenians from Malone in New York were crossing the ice at Summerstown ten miles to the east, prepared to pounce on the town and its canal. Fire bells rang out an alarm and "within a few minutes the streets were filled with citizens all asking to have arms placed in their hands."[19] Men from the surrounding countryside hastened to town to offer their services. Within a few minutes of the alarm, the volunteers were under arms with "alacrity and good spirit", their commanding officer, Major Darby Bergin, reported to Lieutenant Colonel F.T. Atcherley, the regular officer in command at Prescott. When no Fenians appeared, Bergin began a careful inquiry into the origin of the rumour. He discovered that some of his idle volunteers had indulged in "a bit of chaff...towards a silly French lad whom they were endeavouring to persuade would be eaten up by the Fenians." This was overheard by a servant who reported it to her mistress with the result that by eleven o'clock in the evening what had begun as a bit of teasing was magnified into a rumour that put the town on its head. Bergin assured the commanding officer at Prescott that positive orders had now been given that the "Bells shall not again be rung or alarm made (except) by order of the Commanding Officer of the Force". Yet he believed that the scare had done some good in that it showed that the volunteer force could be roused and got together within a short period "except for those billeted in their own houses in scattered and distant parts of the town", and he planned to remedy this. Atcherley found Bergin's letter "so truly ridiculous" that he decided not to forward it to Major-General James Lindsay at Montreal.[20]

Within a month Cornwall got its second Fenian jolt. On 11 April 1866 St. John's church bell clanged a sudden alarm once more and volunteers poured from their billets and homes, clutching their Enfield rifles. The mayor, Doctor William Cox Allen, himself an officer of no. 2 Rifle Company, ordered the men to the Grand Trunk Railway station to await the inbound train from Toronto. He had just received a telegram from two cabinet ministers, George-Etienne Cartier and Alexander Galt, in Montreal, ordering him to arrest the Fenian Head Centre of Toronto, Michael Murphy, and other Fenians who were en route from Toronto to Montreal, heading for Portland, Maine, to join the Fenian raiders gathering there for an attack on New Brunswick. Escorted by a party of volunteers, Allen lost no time in boarding the train and apprehending the startled Fenians who were quickly handcuffed and marched off to the town jail. Murphy and his seven companions were heavily armed and carrying train tickets billeted for Portland.[21] No sooner had Cornwall's mayor and volunteers arrested Murphy and his followers, than they found themselves under fire from the Crown prosecuting attorney, Jacob Farrand Pringle, who had the task of making out a legal case against the arrested Fenians. It was no easy job, even though Grand Trunk manager, C.J. Brydges, had been on the train to swear out affidavits as the basis for the arrests. It seems that Cartier and Galt had acted independently of the government leader John A. Macdonald, in ordering the arrests. Macdonald had given instructions that Murphy was to be followed to Portland by a confidential agent, not arrested. Thus, when Mayor Allen was reprimanded by Pringle, a fellow officer of the Cornwall volunteer force, for precipitous action in arresting Murphy and his cohorts, Allen testily sent off a letter to John A. Macdonald. In it he protested that he had taken on the "serious reponsibility of arresting Michael Murphy and his associates in crime...by direction of *two members of your government.*"[22] John A. Macdonald reprimanded Pringle for repeating to the mayor what had been told to him in confidence. He advised Pringle that as the arrests were ordered by Cartier, he should seek further instructions from Cartier about the Fenian prisoners.

Excitement in Cornwall knew no bounds as telegrams flew back and forth to Ottawa, Toronto and Montreal, trying to straighten out the messy affair and to secure witnesses for the preliminary hearing. To provide greater security for the town, the commander of the British forces at Montreal, Lieutenant General Sir John Michel, ordered two Montreal volunteer companies, one from the Victoria Rifles and the other from the Royal Light Infantry, to entrain immediately for Cornwall.[23] It was only after local magistrates finished their examinations and the Fenians, charged with treason, were remanded for trial at the autumn assizes, that the tense situation eased. The two Montreal companies were relieved on May 2nd by three companies of the Hochelaga Light Infantry, another of Montreal's volunteer units.[24] Thus Montreal amateur soldiers moved by train to help defend the town that guarded the right flank of Canada's metropolis.

Cornwall citizens had made some gestures in the early sixties towards military preparedness. With funds raised by private subscription, a drill shed large enough to accommodate two companies was built on lot no. 11, north side of Water Street, in 1863. It was subsequently removed to lot 16 on the south side of Fourth Street.[25] The strength of the local volunteer units in 1865 had declined somewhat in the three years since their formation. Only the Rifle

Company of Major Darby Bergin remained at full strength of 55 men. Captain Edward Oliver's Rifle Company had 48 men present at the annual inspection in 1865, while Captain Jacob Farrand Pringle's Infantry Company had only 39 present out of a total strength of 55.[26] Not only had enthusiasm for volunteering slackened off between 1862 and 1866, the Cornwall Troop of Cavalry suffered an entire disruption in 1865 and was disbanded in March.[27] Despite this decline in numbers in volunteers or perhaps because of it, the two commanding officers of the Rifle Companies, Captains D. Bergin and Edward Oliver, undertook training at the Military School in Montreal in the summer of 1865, receiving their first class certificates.[28] This, then, was the state of Cornwall's military might when it was confronted with the possibility of invasion in 1866.

At the time when Fenianism was posing a threat to Cornwall and other areas along the Canadian border, the town's Irish population had been increasing slowly but steadily, largely through natural increase, rather than immigration. In the decade from 1861 to 1871 the population increased slightly from 1,915 to 2,033. Of this total, those claiming Irish descent almost equalled the largest ethnic group in town — the Scots. The Irish in 1871 numbered 616, only four less than the Scots. Beyond the immediate perimeters of the mile-square town there was a gradual filling up of the more fertile areas, so that by 1871 the Irish in the township numbered 867, French Canadians accounted for 644 of the township's total population, and the Scots maintained their predominance with 2,038.[29] These figures were in contrast to the sluggish growth of the town in the previous decade when Cornwall had experienced a slight drop in the number of Irish immigrants settling in the town — 269 in 1851 and 206 in 1861. This decline paralleled a similar decline in the number of French Canadians living in Cornwall in the same decade — 132 in 1851 and only sixty-nine in 1861, though by 1871 the number of French Canadians had increased to 313. The other novel development in Cornwall's population at the start of the decade that experienced Fenian alarms was that for the first time the town attracted a few continental European immigrants — its first three Italians.[30]

If any of the Cornwall Irish harboured sympathy for the Fenian cause, no trace of it was evident during the hectic days of the Fenian scares. Cornwall's foremost Roman Catholic Irishman, Dr. Darby Bergin, was commanding officer of the local volunteers, a staunch conservative who would, in the next three decades, keep the Cornwall seat almost as his private domain in the interests of the party headed by John A. Macdonald. Bergin was a second-generation

Irishman, his father having emigrated in the early part of the century to York, where he engaged in moderate reform politics but actively opposed the radical stand taken by William Lyon Mackenzie and the Irish priest, Father William O'Grady.[31] A more recently-arrived leading Irishman in town was Patrick Gildea Mulhern. Prior to emigrating, he had taught for many years in Ireland and resumed his teaching career in Cornwall, eventually becoming principal of the Cornwall Public School.[32] Marrying into the liberal family of the Snetsingers, Mulhern and his family hoisted liberal colours too. The parish priest of St. Columban's church was Father John S. O'Connor who, like his Irish predecessors, steered the Irish members of his flock away from radical politics into local ventures such as building a bigger church in 1864.

Probably the most important Irishman in Cornwall in the decade of the 1860s was its mayor, Dr. William Cox Allen, ten times elected to head the town's administration. A powerful, strikingly handsome man who stood over six feet tall and carried himself erect, Allen came to Cornwall from Ireland where he had been born in 1820 at Killaloe. He was one of the Cornwall medical men who threw himself into the work of succouring cholera patients in 1854. He married into the powerful Vankoughnet family, but the marriage proved unstable and there was unpleasant litigation over the custody of the children.[33] Yet Allen's popularity was unbounded during the time when Fenian troubles arose. Not only was he mayor of the town and lieutenant of No. 2 Rifle Company, he was a prominent member of the newly-formed Loyal Orange Lodge, no. 880 "Prentice Boys of Cornwall". By 1870 he was Master of the Lodge with Gregor Mattice, an officer of No. 2 Rifle Company, as his deputy master.[34] The extent of influence exercised by the new Orange Lodge in Cornwall can only be hinted at, but its presence in the town during this decade of Fenian fever undoubtedly added to the intensity of local defence efforts against the invaders.

In early June of 1866 as the pressure of Fenians and their sympathizers increased at border points, including Malone, New York, just eighteen miles south-east of Cornwall, townspeople, including the Irish, called a public meeting on June 2nd to appoint a committee to work in concert with the military commandant to put the town in a state of defence. Patrols were established by the three local volunteer companies to mount guard up and down the river front for a distance of ten miles. The next day, as Fenians invaded the Niagara area at Ridgeway, regular and volunteer troops from Kingston, Montreal and rural areas crowded into Cornwall. The first to arrive were regular British soldiers — the 30th Regiment from Montreal. They were accompanied by fifty sailors of the *Pylades* who brought with them two cannons to man a tug, the *Royal*, stationed below the town.[35] They were followed on June 4th by part of the 25th King's Own Borderers and part of the 47th Regiment from Montreal, as well as a battery of Royal Artillery, all British regular troops.[36] The units of volunteers from neighbouring areas ordered to Cornwall were the 14th Rifles from Kingston, the 11th Argenteuil Rangers, a half battery of volunteer Artillery and two companies of Rifles from Ottawa. The regulars and volunteers, including the three Cornwall companies, numbering about 2,000 men, were formed into two brigades under Lieutenant-Colonel T.H. Pakenham of the 30th Regiment.[37] The sudden arrival of these large contingents of regular and volunteer troops meant vastly-increased duties for the local clergymen, including Father O'Connor of St. Columban's church, as many of the soldiers were Irish Roman Catholics. The Irish priest's devotion during this trying time was acknowledged by the soldiers who presented him with a "modest purse" and a letter of thanks composed by one of the sergeants.[38]

With such a formidable and patriotic array of regulars and volunteers at Cornwall and an armed tug nearby, the Fenians at Malone hesitated to attack the town. Then, with the defeat and retreat of other bodies of Fenians from the Quebec border and the Niagara area, the Fenian scare subsided. Cornwall people were treated to a grand military display at William Mattice's farm east of the town on June 9th. By June 21st all the British regulars returned to Montreal. The Cornwall Administrative Battalion, consisting of three Cornwall companies, three companies of the Hochelaga Light Infantry and two Rifle Companies from Ottawa, remained in camp at Cornwall. With no Fenians to fight as the summer grew hotter, the amateur soldiers grated on one another's nerves. Tempers flared on the night of July 3 and a full-fledged fight broke out during which shots were fired by both the Hochelagas of Montreal and the volunteers from Ottawa. It was one thing for volunteers to quarrel, but another thing to fire their rifles. This called for a Court of Enquiry which resulted in a reprimand from the Commander of the Forces at Montreal who deplored the lack of discipline in the Cornwall Administrative Battalion. Non-commissioned officers were reported drinking "in the canteen with two of the officers," a situation certain to destroy discipline, he warned. As for the lieutenant-colonel neglecting to have his men clean their rifles after firing and before they returned them to the rack, "this was most discreditable."[39] The upshot was that the three companies of the Hochelaga Light Infantry were sent back to Montreal; the Ottawa Rifles headed for home, and the three Cornwall companies of Rifles and Infantry were relieved from duty. From then until November, Cornwall was garrisoned by two volunteer companies from Brockville and two from Belleville.

The Fenian invasion threat of 1866 served to demonstrate anew the importance of Cornwall as a central point of Canadian defense against any attack originating in the United States. It also gave local volunteer troops their first taste in over a generation of acting in concert not only with regular troops of the line, but also with fellow Canadians from the Montreal and Ottawa areas.

As for the eight Fenians lodged in the Cornwall jail over the summer awaiting their trial in September, they spent their time concocting escape plans. Indeed, Cornwall jail was notorious for its escapes, especially of Irish prisoners.[40] But during the detention of the Fenians, military sentries had been posted around the building to prevent an escape. Nevertheless, the Fenians succeeded in raising a plank in one of the passages of the jail. Then, for about a month they dug their way under the stone wall of the prison. On September 2nd, a severe thunderstorm facilitated their plan. One of the sentry boxes stood close to the point where their tunnel emerged, but the storm had driven the sentry inside the box where he remained while five of the eight men crawled through the tunnel, scaled the primitive wooden fence and found a boat conveniently awaiting them on the river. The prisoners made it safely across the St. Lawrence to the American side, much to the relief of all concerned including the head of the Canadian government, John A. Macdonald, and the governor-general, Lord Monck, not to mention Cornwall's Mayor William Cox Allen, Judge Jacob Farrand Pringle, and Major Darby Bergin. Michael Murphy so appreciated the waiting boat that he arranged for its safe return to its Cornwall owner.[41] Few doubted but that the escape had been contrived or, at least, winked at by the authorities.[42] The three remaining prisoners were brought before the fall Assizes in Cornwall but were ordered to stand trial in Toronto where they were speedily admitted to bail and the government did not proceed against them.[43]

As the last of the Fenian prisoners were disposed of, the Brockville and Belleville volunteers, who had formed the town's garrison since July, were dismissed to their homes in November. War's alarums faded into the background even if the Fenian issue did not as Cornwall's citizens settled back to observe the constitutional changes brought about by the Confederation scheme that their political leader, John Sandfield Macdonald, had so frequently denounced. On the eve of Confederation, Cornwallites were treated to one of the most important addresses of the era when Canada's foremost Irishman, Thomas D'Arcy McGee, delivered an address entitled, "The New Dominion", a prophetic vision of Canada's future. McGee had been relentless against Fenianism, regarding it as the greatest enemy of the Canadian Irish because it brought the Irish community into disrepute. Though his address to the people of Cornwall on 2 June 1864 was mainly directed towards the future, he repeated his warnings against Fenianism and the need to be on guard.[44]

As soon as the first federal administration under Confederation was underway, it brought in legislation to reorganize the various volunteer cavalry, artillery, rifle and infantry companies into regiments. The three Cornwall companies were amalgamated in 1868 with the rifle and infantry companies from Lancaster, Williamstown and Dickinson's Landing to form a new battalion styled the 59th Stormont and Glengarry Battalion of Infantry, with headquarters at Cornwall. Major Darby Bergin who had commanded the local troops during the 1866 Fenian scare became lieutenant-colonel of the regiment in 1869 and piloted it through its first seventeen years. The newly-formed battalion, at first 439 strong and boasting "a fair brass band with twelve performers", went to brigade camp at Prescott for six days under canvas in 1869, some twenty-one officers and 248 men undergoing summer training.[45]

When an alarm sounded again on 24 May 1870 with the reappearance of Fenians at the border, the 59th Battalion turned out eagerly along with a mounted corps of sixty men under Captain Corydon J. Mattice, son of the former mayor of the town. Volunteer troops from Ottawa, Iroquois, Gananoque, Aultsville, Hawkesbury and Brockville, converged quickly on Cornwall to help the 59th Stormont and Glengarry Regiment with the town's defence. Within twenty-four hours some 1,440 officers and men were posted at various points to guard the canal, its locks and bridges. William Cox Allen still headed the town's administration and he, with members of the town council, procured billets for the troops, placing the town hall at their disposal. Townsmen vied with each other in their efforts to make the troops comfortable.[46] However, the volunteers imposed on townsmen only a few days for the Fenians gathering at Malone, New York, struck down the Trout River towards Huntingdon in the Lower Province rather than moving down the Salmon River towards Cornwall. They were repulsed on May 27th by the Huntingdon Borderers and soldiers of the 69th Regiment in what proved to be the last Fenian raid against Canada. Their defeat marked the last occasion on which the town of Cornwall was threatened with invasion.

NOTES

1. *Report on the State of the Militia,* 1857, 51, for list of officers and numbers of men; William Boss, *History of Stormont, Dundas and Glengarry Highlanders,* 66.

2. Boss, 71.

3. *Ibid.,* 55.

4. For cavalry of 1856, see General Orders, 15 February 1856 (RG9/1C6/19); and *Report on the State of the Militia, 1857,* 25.

5. Anderson to Captain Retallack, Military Secretary, Montreal, 25 February 1858 (RG7/G19/5).

6. J.F. Pringle, *Lunenburgh, or the Old Eastern District,* 140 and 268; Boss, 74.

7. Elinor Kyte Senior, *Roots of the Canadian Army: Montreal District 1846-1870,* 44; Boss, 74.

8. See General Orders, 22 and 31 January 1862 (RG9/1C6/19, 161 and 223); see also, Boss, 436-37.

9. Bruce Hodgins, *John Sandfield Macdonald,* 120; Boss, 79 and 437.

10. Pringle, 269.

11. *Mercury,* Quebec, 5 June 1866; for an appreciation of Cornwall's military importance, see Brigadier-General T. W. Sweeney's report to Pittsburg Fenian Convention, February 1866, in Joseph Denieffe, *A Personal Narrative of the Irish Revolutionary Brotherhood,* 270; see also, J. A. Macdonald, *Troublous Times in Canada,* 107.

12. Hodgins, *John Sandfield Macdonald,* 36.

13. *Ibid.,* 51.

14. Boss, 64.

15. *Report on the State of the Militia,* 1857, 51.

16. Hodgins, *John Sandfield Macdonald,* 62.

17. *Ibid.,* 80-82.

18. Hereward Senior, *The Fenians and Canada,* 88; Elinor Kyte Senior, *Roots of the Canadian Army,* 79; Pringle, 269.

19. Major D. Bergin to Lieutenant Colonel F. T. Atcherley, 14 March, 1866 (RG9/1C8/8).

20. *Ibid.*

21. For details of the arrests, see C. P. Stacey, "Michael Murphy: A Fenian Interlude," in *CHR,* June 1934, xv, no. 2, 146-48; Francis W. Campbell, Fenian Raids of 1866 and 1870, 13; for names of Fenians arrested at Cornwall, see *Le Pays,* Montreal, 12 April 1866.

22. Allen to Macdonald, April 1866, cited in Stacey, "A Fenian Interlude," 149.

23. Colonel Patrick L. MacDougall to Lieutenant-Colonel William Earle, 11 April 1866 (RG7/C185/44); see also, Campbell, *Fenian Raids,* 13.

24. Pringle, 269; Campbell, *Fenian Raids,* 26.

25. *Report on the State of the Militia, 1870,* 180-81; Pringle, 141.

26. *Report on the State of the Militia for 1865-66,* 56; for 1862 figures, see Boss, 77.

27. Boss, 83.

28. *Report on the State of the Militia for 1865-66,* 100.

29. For population figures see, *Census,* 1871, i, 274-75.

30. *Ibid.,* 1851, i, 61-63; 1861, i, 152-153; 1871, i, 274-5.

31. J.G. Harkness, *History of Stormont, Dundas and Glengarry,* 299; Pringle, 251.

32. *150th Anniversary, St. Columban's Parish, 1829-1979,* 8-9.

33. For biography of Allen, see Harkness, 450-51.

34. See Hugh MacCallum's warrant, L.O.L. no. 880, signed by William Cox Allen, 14 Mar. 1870; Boss, 89.
35. *La Minerve*, Montreal, 4 June 1866.
36. Macdonald, *Troublous Times*, 107-8; Pringle, 270.
37. Macdonald, *Troublous Times*, 108.
38. Father Charles Murray, "Reminiscences", 8.
39. For details of this incident, see Report of Court of Enquiry, 3 July 1866, cited in Boss, 85.
40. J. K. Johnson, "Colonel James Fitzgibbon and the Suppression of Irish Riots in Upper Canada," in *Ontario History*, lviii, 1966, 149; Harkness, 230.
41. Stacey, "A Fenian Interlude," 151-152.
42. *Freeholder*, Cornwall, 7 September 1866; *Leader*, Toronto, 3, 7 September 1866.
43. Stacey, "A Fenian Interlude," 153.
44. *Standard-Freeholder*, 26 June 1946.
45. *Report on the State of the Militia*, 1870, 180-1; Boss, 89-90.
46. Boss, 91-92; Macdonald, *Troublous Times*, 170-171.

Dr. Darby Bergin, April 1879. (1826-1896) M.P. for Cornwall, Town
and Township 1872-1874 and 1878-1882. M.P. for Stormont 1882-1896.
Credit: Public Archives of Canada neg. PA-33903.

Chapter XI

The Mill Town Emerges

Although Fenian scares and constitutional issues occupied the centre of the stage during the 1860s in Cornwall as elsewhere in Canada, there were other developments in the town, scarcely noticeable at first but which, as the decade wore on, became more pronounced. These developments indicated that Cornwall was taking a new economic direction. With the building of the canal, the town gained what it had lacked from its birth — a source of water power. In 1845 town fathers led other local entrepreneurs in urging the Board of Works to grant water privileges on the canal.[1] Within a year, several water privileges were surveyed and sold by public auction, the first three going to John Harvey, Andrew Elliott and Austin Edson Cadwell.

Harvey shortly afterwards constructed the first grist mill on the south bank of the canal nearly opposite lot no. 21 on Water Street. Elliott erected a rival grist mill just to the east of Harvey's mill, while Cadwell located his mill to the west of Harvey's mill and nearer the river. Although these three mills were in operation by 1850, along with a sawmill operated by a man named Hawkins,[2] they were not booming successes. Harvey soon sold his to Myron Hitchcock. Anxious to improve the mill's production, Hitchcock looked around the country for a capable manager and found what he was looking for in the small border town of Huntingdon in the neighbouring province. William Mack at twenty-one was already known as a young man who really knew the milling business, having learned the trade after his family emigrated to Huntingdon from their native Lanarkshire, Scotland, in the 1820s.[3] Mack came to Cornwall in 1849 where he worked first for Hitchcock and then for Andrew Elliott. When Hitchcock died, his flour mill was bought by merchant William Mattice. Elliott sold his mill and water rights to Andrew Hodge who, with his son, William, expanded the operations to include a sawmill and carding and fulling works that developed into a small woollen factory. Hodge ran the factory on what was known as "custom work", that is, local farmers brought in the results of their shearing and had it made up into wools or exchanged it for some manufactured products, a method of trade that was, as a contemporary noted, "bothersome, but certainly safe." By 1878 Hodge employed twenty men.[4] Austin Cadwell sold his sawmill to hardware merchant P.E. Adams, who operated it until fire struck in 1874.

These first flour, saw and woollen mills were all located on the south bank of the canal to the west of Pitt Street. They represented Cornwall's first thrust into manufacturing in the 1850s apart from the potash factory at Potash Point that was operated by Joseph Dennison, and smaller boot, shoe, and carriagemaker operations underway by 1850.[5] The only expansion in the mill business in the 1860s was William Mack's venture into express milling on his own. He was the first to locate in the eastern area of the town. It was here at the head of the Cornwall Canal that Philip Vankoughnet had invested in the water rights and had laid out a somewhat primitive industrial park site. Attracting no prospective mill owners, Vankoughnet sold the water rights and his farm to William Mattice who was speculating in industrial sites. Mattice realized the importance of a channel being constructed from the north side of the canal eastward along the site to which he hoped to attract industrialists. He set out determinedly and successfully to persuade the Board of Works to undertake its construction.[6] As soon at this was done, William Mack bought one of the water privileges and in 1861-62 erected at the foot of Marlborough Street what proved to be one of Cornwall's thriving flour mills, producing 100 barrels of flour daily by 1893, all consumed locally.[7] Another firm, that of David A. Flack and Isaac Van Arsdale, became Mack's neighbour in 1868, buying up the pottery works to the east that had been begun by an American, A.L. Ballard, in the early 1860s.[8] Today the Flack and Van Arsdale pottery pieces are valued collectors' items.

Montreal industrialists did not begin to look closely at Cornwall as a possible location until the end of the 1860s. The man who paved the road to Cornwall was George Stephen. This carpenter's son and firm Presbyterian from Banffshire, Scotland, arrived in Montreal in 1850 to work in a drygoods store established by his cousin.[9] As the Stephen Company specialized in imported British and foreign drygoods, the twenty-one-year-old newcomer soon found himself making regular buying trips to Great Britain for his employer. Then, as trade suffered dislocation, first because of the Crimean War in 1854-55, and then because of the American Civil War and the cancellation in 1866 of the Reciprocity Treaty between Canada and the United States, Montreal businessmen began to explore the possibilities of home manufacturing, especially as rail communication expanded across Quebec to Ontario. Cornwall had been linked by rail to Montreal as early as September 1855 and to Toronto by November of the following year. George Stephen followed these advances in transportation with great interest. As Canadian tweeds were becoming increasingly popular, his firm began to specialize in them and Stephen soon took an interest not only in their sales, but in their production as well.

One of the small woollen mills that attracted Stephen's attention was in Almonte, Lanark County, where Bennett Rosamond and his brother, William, were running their father's mill on the Mississippi River.[10] In 1866 when the brothers had doubled the capacity of their mill, they admitted Stephen as a partner. Then Stephen's eye hit upon Cornwall. He immediately perceived that Cornwall had several salient features as far as a location for manufacturing was concerned. Unlimited waterpower awaited exploitation. It was close to a major market — Montreal. And a labour force was at hand.[11] With characteristic vigour, Stephen organized a joint-stock company, the Cornwall Manufacturing Company, to put the town to the test as a manufacturing location. He managed to get one of Montreal's top businessmen, Hugh Allan, to become president of the new company. Stephen took the vice-presidency, John Warwick was manager and Alex G. Watson, secretary. The firm secured water rights on the canal and erected a woollen factory in 1868 between Mack's Express Flour Mill and the Flack and Van Arsdale pottery works.[12] The popularity of their high quality blankets soon provoked imitations from abroad and by October of 1870 the Cornwall Manufacturing Company had to insert advertisements in the Toronto *Globe* warning the public against imitations of their blankets imported from England and tagged with the label, "Canada Manufacturing Company."[13]

Another group of Montreal financial men watched, with considerable interest, the nascent mill operations at Cornwall, especially those being undertaken by their drygoods competitor, George Stephen. The Gault brothers knew a good thing when they saw it. Their father, a substantial shipowner and merchant from Strabane, County Tyrone, Northern Ireland, had shifted his operations to Montreal in the 1840s, anticipating more advantageous business opportunities. By 1857 two of his sons, Andrew Frederick and Robert Leslie, began a highly successful partnership in drygoods.[14] They, too, hoped to produce as well as sell goods and their eyes hit upon Cornwall. They bought out John Harvey's mill and water rights on the canal west of Pitt Street and in 1870 replaced the old mill with a stone one. Incorporating themselves as the Stormont Cotton Manufacturing Company, these Irish Church of England brothers began producing a variety of cotton materials.

Cornwall town fathers were delighted with this increasing industrial activity in their midst. They had long urged the sale of water rights on the canal to encourage industry. Now they promoted the idea of granting cash bonuses and tax exemptions to outside capitalists willing to locate in Cornwall.[15] The question of granting bonuses was first raised in 1867 at the time that Stephen began plans for his first woollen mill.[16] Public meetings were held to discuss the pros and cons. The result was an informal vote indicating that the majority of ratepayers favoured financial assistance to any companies locating in Cornwall. However, it was not until fire levelled the Stephen's woollen mill in a spectacular Christmas night conflagration in 1870 that town fathers and citizens responded more actively to a request from the Cornwall Manufacturing Company asking for tax exemptions and a cash bonus. Mayor Angus Bethune, who had had ample mill experience as manager of the Hitchcock flour operation, called a special meeting of Town Council on 9 February 1871 to consider the request. Another former mill owner, Councillor Andrew Hodge, was quick to move that "this Municipal Council, duly recognizing the importance of manufactories in this country and that such add considerably to the welfare of the community where (they are) established, pledge themselves to aid and assist all cotton, woollen and other similar factories which may be...established within this municipality." This done, the town fathers announced that they would seek approval from the electors for a by-law to give $6000 to the Cornwall Manufacturing Company at a rate of $600 per year for ten years if the company erected another woollen factory "on the site of the one lately destroyed by fire." Then councillors dealt with the problem of taxation of the new factories. As the industrial site to the east was outside town boundaries, they decided to ask permission from the provincial government to annex all the land "on the south side of the main road leading to Montreal," bounded by the eastern boundary of the Mattice farm, and to exempt this industrial land from municipal taxes for twenty-one years.[17]

Nothing was hurried as far as the Town Council was concerned. Before taking action on the motion, the town fathers called a public meeting of Cornwall inhabitants to sound them out on the feasibility of granting such bonuses and tax exemptions to manufacturers. Ratepayers approved the grants on condition that the Cornwall Manufacturing Company's new factory would give employment "to an equal or nearly equal number of operatives as were employed in the same, previous to its destruction." Ratepayers were cagey enough to reduce the amount of the total bonus to $4000 and added a proviso that, should the new factory burn down, the town would discontinue the yearly grants of $400 to the company. They were also astute enough to suggest offering cash bonuses of $4000 to any other company that opted to erect a factory in Cornwall.[18]

Stephen and his associates were delighted with this general approval from the citizens of the proposals by Town Council to grant special privileges to factory promoters. They lost no time in getting the charred ruins of their woollen factory cleared away to make room for another mill. By November of 1871 they petitioned Town Council for a larger grant than $4,000 on the grounds that the new factory would be bigger than the one destroyed by fire.[19] Speaking for the company, Donald McInnes assured the Council that his company was particularly interested in expanding in Cornwall because the local "Labour (force was) of a superior class."[20] Council agreed to grant extra bonuses "if the benefits derived from the factory are adequately great." At first the rebuilt woollen mill employed 100 workers who produced tweeds and blankets.[21] Within six years the number of its employees had doubled and its monthly payroll averaged between $3000 and $4000. By 1878, 350,000 yards of woollen material were being produced in the expanded factory that now included a dye-house, store-houses for wool, and a number of tenant cottages for its workers.[22]

Montreal industrialists not only rebuilt the woollen factory to the east of the town; they also persuaded a number of other Montrealers such as Edward Mackay and Donald A. Smith, along with Bennett Rosamond, Stephen's partner in the Almonte woollen mill, John Harvey, the first Cornwall mill owner, and Donald McInnes of Hamilton, to promote a second cotton mill in Cornwall.[23] These men announced the formation of the Canada Cotton Manufacturing Company in the Montreal *Gazette* on 30 January 1872, declaring that they hoped to achieve for the manufacture of cotton goods the same success that had attended their production of Canadian woollens. They lost no time in applying to the Town Council for a cash bonus and tax exemption on the large parcel of land that lay east of the industrial property already annexed by the town for taxation purposes. This was the site on which they planned to build the new cotton factory.[24] Their rival, the Gault brothers of the Stormont Cotton mill, also petitioned for similar privileges. Ratepayers voted favourably and the system of paying debentures of $400 per year to each of the three new factories began.[25]

Even before the bonuses and the tax exemptions were finalized, the promoters of the new Cornwall cotton mill began construction of what became the pride of the Canadian textile industry. The red brick building, four storeys high, sprawled along the canal front for 310 feet and ran back for ninety. As soon as construction ended, 20,000 spindles and 500 looms were installed for the 400 workers that were taken on, almost all of them "principally of Scotch descent, natives of the locality, who were trained at the new factory", an indication that the great wave of French-Canadians into Cornwall — from 323 in 1871 to 1,323 in 1881 — did not get underway until late in the 1870s.[26] The Scottish-Canadian workers brought home a monthly payroll of $10,000 for producing a great variety of cotton goods — sheeting, shirting, ducks, ticking, denims, cottonades, seamless bags for flour and grain, hosiery, and yarns and warps. Plant machinery, imported from the Platt Company of Oldham, England, was driven by two turbine water wheels of 250 horse power. Should the canal water supply fail, there was a Corliss engine of 500 horse power as an emergency unit. Besides the main factory, large warehouses were constructed, as well as a dye-house, gas works, and cottages for the overseers and mill operatives. The company also constructed a large boarding house, "leased by a skilled caterer", where workers could get "good, honest board at the rate of $8 per month for females, and $10 for males."[27] If any male worker was brash enough to complain about the unequal price structure, he would probably be quickly told that females earned less and perhaps ate less. By 1879 the new mill, together with the nearby woollen mill of the Canada Manufacturing Company, employed a total of 500 workers who began work each day at 6:30 a.m. and worked until 6:30 in the evening with an hour off for lunch. On Saturdays they worked from 6:30 a.m. to noon. Their wages ranged from $1.75 to $3.00 a day for skilled male labour, sixty cents to a dollar a day for unskilled male labour; sixty to eighty cents a day for what was called "inferior classes of labour," evidently females, and children earned from twenty-five cents to sixty cents a day. To keep these workers busy, the company imported nearly two million pounds of raw cotton a year, costing about $208,000.[28]

This expansion of industry in Cornwall from 1870 to 1880, at a time when the rest of the country was experiencing severe recession or depression, resulted in a doubling of the town's population, from 2,033 in 1871 to 4,468 in 1881.[29] Accompanying this expansion in industry in Cornwall was the increase in the number of Roman Catholics to predominance by 1881. By then, the town's Catholics numbered 2,290 as compared to 2,183 Protestants. Not only was there a shift in the religious balance, there was also a shift in ethnic composition. The great increase in French-Canadians, some 1,323 by 1881, meant that this group was the largest single ethnic group in town. Townsmen of Scottish origin now numbered 1,109. The next largest ethnic group was the Irish with 1,070. What was also apparent in 1881 was the gradual increase in the number of continental Europeans who were making Cornwall their home — six Dutch, 357 Germans, fifteen Jews, seventeen Italians and fourteen Poles.[30] In addition, the census for 1881 showed that there were fourteen Blacks living in Cornwall. Another indication of Cornwall's capacity to attract settlers from other parts of Canada was the Patrons' Directory of H.E. Belden's *Historical Atlas of Stormont, Dundas and Glengarry*, published in 1879. None of the forty-three Cornwall partrons of the Atlas was a native of the town, though thirty-one of them were natives of Canada.[31]

It is not surprising then that the local Member of Parliament, Dr. Darby Bergin, having regained his seat in the 1878 federal elections, rose in the House to brag somewhat about his constituency. "Cornwall was no longer a pretty little village," he declared in May 1879, "but a prosperous and flourishing town, that had withstood the depression of the past few years and had rode through the storm which had almost swept away towns of greater size." Bergin praised his fellow townsmen, claiming that it was "by their energy, their industry, their frugality, and their practical common sense for manufacturing everything for themselves, not handing over the produce of their labour to be sent out of the country to support foreign industries and laborers, (that) they had improved their positions so as to have a rich heritage (for) their children."[32]

A somewhat less flattering appraisal came from the pen of the editor of the liberal opposition newspaper, the *Freeholder*. Its editor, Alexander McLean, in an article entitled "What Cornwall Has", listed the following: "An 8-cent store, a dollar paper, a debating society, first-class hotels, any quantity of old bachelors, a junior judge, the most peculiar Council that ever graced the Chamber, a lockgate contractor, more trotting horses to the acre than any town in Canada, several financially-embarrassed merchants, the meanest man in Canada, the laziest man in America, and the biggest sneak in the universe."[33] Cornwall's press never lacked spunk when it came to calling names, but in this instance the editor left it up to his readers to fit the name to the personality. In any event his darts were not pointed directly at the town's manufacturers. They basked in the sun of the town fathers' liberal treatment, reciprocating by vastly expanding their Cornwall operations in the 1880s. In 1882 Canada Cottons constructed the largest weave shed in the world, some 500 by 120 feet in size, employing 231 additional hands. To safeguard the factory and its new extension from fire, water hydrants were placed throughout the various buildings and male employees were drilled periodically in the use of the apparatus.[34]

To add still another feather to its own and to Cornwall's cap, Canada Cottons decided to illuminate the new weave shed by the latest in lighting equipment — the incandescent electric lights recently invented by Thomas Edison. Throughout the fall of 1883 workmen toiled for weeks building two houses to hold six boilers each capable of producing 100 horse power. These boilers produced steam for the six generators that were installed to operate the new electric system, a system crude by today's standards but representing unprecedented efficiency for that time. Edison himself supervised the wiring of 100 carbon filament electric lights that were suspended from the ceiling of the weave shed. Early in 1884 when everything was ready, Cornwall prepared for a gala occasion when, for the first time in Canada, electric lighting would be used for industry. Canadian and United States officials headed for the small town, together with industrial leaders and scientists from Toronto, Montreal and Ottawa. They joined with hundreds of Cornwall people in the official opening of the new lighting. Oil lamps were extinguished in the weave shed. Edison pressed the switch. A feeble glow appeared. Then, as the generators gained speed, the light strengthened and the familiar yellow glare of the early incandescent lights shone out, throwing a glow across the canal and over the St. Lawrence which could be seen for miles.[35] Just as the white spire of old Trinity Church had been a familiar landmark in the first half of the nineteenth century, so, too, the huge factories with their yellow glow at night became beacons for new generations of Cornwall people and their neighbours.

With such unrivalled modern equipment and facilities, the directors of Canada Cottons were determined that their product would be unrivalled as well and they succeeded. At the Centennial Exhibition, their cloth carried off the highest honours. Their label, a portrait of old Baptiste, the famous Indian pilot of the St. Lawrence rapids, became as familiar in Canadian homes as the novel device attached to the bolt of family cotton — a yard measure printed on the material surrounded by the words "Honest width" — assuring customers that they would get full value for their money.[36]

Canada Cottons weathered the severe depression of the late 1870s, though it was unable to provide "its shareholders (with) a fair profit upon their investment," a situation that the *Canadian Illustrated News* of 26 January 1878 claimed would not be rectified "until Canadian manufacturers are placed upon a better footing as regards foreign competition." This widely-read journal devoted four pages to Cornwall's development, an indication that the town had achieved country-wide notice because of its textile factories. Describing Cornwall as "lacking, in some degree, the spirit of enterprise characteristic of your thorough-going Western town", the reporter of the *Canadian Illustrated News* added, "It is only fair to state that Cornwall is in a transitory state. In the old days, it was quite an aristocratic place, the Belgravia of Canada, so to speak (but)...the town, as a whole, has changed in character, and is developing into a commercial centre."

While George Stephen and his business associates were expanding their two mills in Cornwall, their nearest competitor, the Stormont Cotton mill, fell victim in 1874 to the same destructive force that had carried away Stephen's first woollen mill. Fire broke out in a small paper plant, run by the Martin and Crilly Company, located just to the east of the Stormont mill. The fire spread to the cotton mill warehouses and then to the mill itself, the intensity of the heat cracking the stone walls and causing them to fall. Flames leaped from the cotton mill to a small saw-mill owned by P.E. Adams and before the night was over, all three mills had been wiped out in one fell swoop.[37] The only mill to escape the general conflagration was that of Andrew and William Hodge which continued to turn out tweeds, flannels, blankets and yarn, in addition to flour and saw mill operations adjoining their woollen mill. Moreover, R.A. Hodge, who ran the planing and saw mill, manufactured the portable Fanning Mill and Seed Separator known as "The King of the West."

It was five years before the Gault brothers had the heart or perhaps even the capital to begin again in Cornwall. But begin they did, notwithstanding the depressed state of the economy. Their determination might even have been spurred by the large spread on Cornwall in the January 1878 issue of the *Canadian Illustrated News* in which two terse lines appeared at the end of the glowing accounts of Cornwall mills. The lines read, "Close by are the charred ruins of a paper mill and Gault Bros. & Co.'s cotton mills."[39] By April of 1878 the Gaults asked Town Council for a grant of $10,000 towards the construction of a new cotton mill, some $6,000 more than the town had been accustomed to give.[40] Townspeople showed their interest by holding informal meetings of leading property owners in April and early May to consider the request. The local press put in its two cents' worth, too. The Cornwall *Reporter* reminded its readers that the "main cause which has lifted the ancient settlement of Cornwall from the condition of a mildewed village to a position of a flourishing and populous town is the establishment of magnificent manufacturing facilities or plants."[41] The same journal was delighted to report that another mill was about to be erected by Flack Brothers, local manufacturers of cotton batting. The new mill to be located to the east of the pottery works of Flack and Van Arsdale.[42]

By October of 1878 Canadian manufacturers breathed more easily, for the new government of Sir John A. Macdonald returned to power pledged to provide high tariffs to protect budding industries from foreign competition. Within a month, "negotiations were underway between the Town of Cornwall and the Gault Bros. Ltd. from Montreal with a view to having the latter re-build the mill."[43] The enthusiasm of local people knew no bounds. Led by George McDonell, Postmaster and merchant who, among other things, had been a millowner, 200 townsmen got up a petition urging Town Council to grant the Gault Brothers $10,000.[44] Council responded by submitting a by-law to ratepayers asking their approval of the grant. The vote was overwhelmingly in favour, 222 voting for it and 23 against.[45]

With such local support, the Gaults went ahead with plans to buy the adjoining land from P.E. Adams. Within a year construction began on the new six-storey Stormont mill which commenced operations in 1880 with 250 looms and 300 workers.[46] So successful was the new plant that an extension was built in 1881 to increase the number of looms to 500 and the operatives to 500. By the early 1890s a third extension had been made, bringing the mill's capacity to 632 looms and 620 hands. Thus the Stormont mill ran a very close second to the huge mill of Canada Cottons which, by 1893, had 864 looms.[47] By this time, however, the two cotton plants were no longer rivals but part of the same company. The Stephen and Gault interests combined in 1892 to form a company called the Canadian Colored Cottons Mills Limited with Archibald F. Gault as president and Samuel Greenwood as manager. The woollen mill of the Canadian Manufacturing Company joined the new company in 1903.[48] The three mills combined had a work force of 1,453 in 1891, producing $1,647,397 worth of goods and providing $446,588 in wages each year.[49]

Not only was the Stormont Cotton mill rebuilt in the early 1880s and Canada Cottons expanded to include a huge weave shed in 1882, but a third major industry was born in the town when, for the first time, capitalists from the western part of the province found Cornwall attractive as a location for a paper mill. Cornwall officials had been anxious to secure a paper plant ever since 1874 when fire had destroyed the small mill operated by Patrick Martin and Crilly. This mill had been in operation at least since 1870, employing fifteen men and women, two boys and seven girls, whose annual production amounted to $11,000 worth of felt and coarse paper.[50] Former Mayor William Cox Allen thought he had Montreal financiers lined up in 1879 to promote a new paper plant in town, but this fell through.[51] Then, in 1881, John Roaf Barber, a paper mill owner of Georgetown, Ontario, decided to locate in Cornwall. Barber's father, James, with his brothers, had emigrated from Ireland in the early part of the century and established paper mills at Georgetown where John Roaf Barber was born and educated. When his father died in 1880, John Roaf Barber became sole proprietor of the Georgetown mills and president of the Toronto Paper Manufacturing Company. In an expansive mood, he decided that Cornwall offered exceptional advantages for paper manufacturing. He bought the property owned by G.C. Smith on the western outskirts of Cornwall near the canal and, unlike the cotton and woollen manufacturers, Barber and his associates asked no favours or privileges from the town.[52]

Associated with Barber's company, the Toronto Paper Company, were Charles Riordan of Merritton and Edward Trout of Toronto. With James D. Finlay as first superintendent and W.J. Wallace as secretary-treasurer, these men set out to produce, exclusively from rags, the finest type of paper for writing and books, and for tinted, lithograph and chromo work.[53] The brick factory built on stone foundations was finished by the spring of 1882 at a cost of $141,674. Machinery worth $126,397 was then installed, driven by five water wheels of 100 horse power each, the water supplied from the canal.[54] On 27 April 1883 the first sheet of paper rolled off the paper machine.[55] Barber and his associates made use of the most modern paper-making techniques, being able to produce fine paper in a continuous roll at the rate of 120 feet a minute, while newsprint came off at a rate of 240 feet a minute. This was a far cry from the cruder methods employed in his father's mill where the paper was made by hand and hung up, sheet after sheet, to dry. The more efficient and speedier method meant a great reduction in manufacturing costs and a subsequent reduction in the price of paper. So voluminous were the company's sales that the machinery was kept going day and night, except on Sunday.[56]

At first the Toronto Paper Company secured pulp from the province of Quebec, but this pulp was not of high enough quality and the company decided in 1887 to erect their own sulphite mill. By using the process developed by a Viennese chemist, Kellner, the

Toronto Paper Company was able to supply not only their own paper plant with what was acknowledged to be the finest pulp in the country, but also supplied a number of other paper plants.[57] By 1891, the paper plant, with a work force of fifty men and forty women, was producing $122,322 worth of paper and paying annual wages of $28,147.[58] Within two more years, its work force expanded to 130 hands.[59]

The Toronto Paper Company mill was the only one of the four major mills in Cornwall in 1891 that employed more men than women. The two cotton mills employed 522 men and 524 women.[60] The woollen mill had 89 men and 124 women. As for child labourers, the cotton mills had 104 boys and 41 girls under sixteen years. The woollen mill employed 27 boys and 22 girls. These 1,191 workers in the cotton mills produced goods valued at $1,310,892 yearly and received wages totalling $372,172 for the year. The woollen mill produced $336,505 worth of goods annually and paid its 262 workers $74,416 in yearly wages.[61] This meant that the average yearly wages of $312.50 at the cotton mills was somewhat higher than that of workers at the woollen mill whose pay averaged $284 a year. By comparison, a police constable's yearly pay in the 1870s was $220 and by 1883 it was $1.25 daily or about $400 a year.[62]

That Cornwall had attained the distinction of being Canada's pre-eminent "Factory Town" was evident in the recognition that the Toronto *Globe* afforded the town in its issue of 18 November 1893. Devoting its first page and four subsequent pages to the town, and amply illustrating the material with pictures of the various Cornwall mills, town personalities, residences and hotels, the *Globe* eulogized its citizens for "the spirit of fairness, liberality, and the honorable manner in which the people of Cornwall have carried out their pledges, many of them verbal, with those (factories) already established here." The editor pointed out that property value in 1874 had been $667,300. In 1893 it was $2,760,635. What was more, the revenue of the town increased proportionally so that "it might be said that every dollar invested in bonuses or exemptions has been returned four-fold."[63]

The road to this pre-eminence had not been entirely without its thorns. In 1884, for instance, the Canadian market suffered from a glut of cotton goods, forcing the Stormont mill to shut down temporarily and lay off its 400 operatives, and Canada Cottons cut back from 648 to 490. However, work interruptions because of over-production were rare. What gradually became part of the industrial picture in Cornwall over the 1880s were strikes and threats of strikes. Labour discontent was not unknown in Cornwall. Work stoppages had occasionally complicated canal construction in the 1830s and

1840s. When work got underway to enlarge the Cornwall canal in the mid-1870s and eliminate a curve in the original lock, stone cutters threw down their tools in early February 1877.[64] They were protesting with their foreman against a change in the texture of the stone they were cutting. These workers were part of some 200 men housed in a large shanty or boarding house erected south of the canal by the contractors, Gordon and Woodward Company. They refused to return to work until the contractors guaranteed them that they would continue to be paid at a rate which would enable them to earn the same amount they had been making when working on softer stones. In addition, they insisted that the foreman be fired.[65]

Labour trouble at the mills arose in May of 1882, four years before any of the mills were organized into Assemblies of the Knights of Labor.[66] This was the year that the huge weaving shed was being erected at Canada Cottons and it was here that a strike was first threatened. The workers protested against a company order to work all day Saturday instead of breaking off at 12:30 o'clock. Millhands worked sixty and a half hours a week, eleven hours from Monday to Friday and six and a half hours on Saturday. That the workers as a group were worth courting was evident in the reaction of the editor of the *Freeholder* to the labour conflict. Its editor berated the company for its policy. "The workers are paid starvation wages," he declared, "and are being forced to work themselves to death for an ungrateful company."[68] The threatened strike was averted by a mishap at the plant. The main belt broke, throwing the entire mill into idleness for some time. When work resumed, the company backed down on its demand for work on Saturday afternoons.

The *Freeholder* continued to champion the workers, especially as the federal election campaign warmed up on the issue of continued protection for home industries. The leading Cornwall candidate was Dr. Darby Bergin, the conservative Irish Roman Catholic bachelor doctor who had been elected by acclamation in 1872. Bergin was re-elected in 1878, and although unseated on a charge of alleged bribery, he still went on to win the by-election.[69] Bergin's opponent in 1882 was the popular lawyer, James Bethune, who had taken the Stormont seat in the provincial elections of 1873.[70] After a successful career as John Sandfield Macdonald's partner and county attorney from 1866 to 1871, Bethune moved to bigger fields in Toronto in 1871, fast becoming one of Ontario's foremost lawyers.[71] With impeccable credentials as a United Empire Loyalist descendant and a long residence in Cornwall, James Bethune entered the lists under the liberal banner against the formidable Bergin.

The *Freeholder* did its best for Bethune, informing its readers, "We are credibly informed that those in authority in the Cotton Mill here are already beginning to hint to the voters in the mill that they can leave as soon as they like if they do not support the Government candidate (Dr. Darby Bergin)." The editor scornfully asked, "Are they to be vassals of the monopolists?"[72] Whether this alleged attempt by the cotton company officials to coerce their workers' votes had any effect or not, the outcome of the election was unanimous support for Bergin. Bergin was the popular choice of both workers and manufacturers. Not only did he promote legislation aimed at securing safer working conditions for the millhands, but he also endorsed heartily the policy of high tariffs to protect native industries from foreign competition. He won every one of the 244 votes cast in Cornwall, as well as those in the Township, in Osnabruck and Finch. Only in Roxborough did Bethune have support. In all, he secured 95 votes to Bergin's 545.[73] The *Freeholder*'s wooing of the workers was thus without effect, partly because the conservative press, the *Reporter*, had shown considerable aptitude at wooing the workers as well, reporting factually and without harshness on the stone-cutters' strike of 1877.[74] But the deciding factor in the 1882 election was that millhands and manufacturers agreed with Sir John A. Macdonald's policy of high tariffs to protect their jobs and industries from foreign competition. Cornwall voters continued to support the conservative government, even though federal liberals sent some of the top French-Canadian speakers such as Laurent-Olivier David, former editor of Montreal's *L'Opinion Publique*, to Cornwall to try to win French-Canadian votes away from Dr. Bergin in 1887. Councillor James Plamondon of Cornwall East proclaimed French solidarity with English voters. "We have done our duty in the East end at any rate," he announced with satisfaction when the East end votes were cast almost entirely for Dr. Bergin.[75] It was a case, the *Standard* declared, of the "National Policy asserting itself in Cornwall" once more.[76] Politically, workers and manufacturers were of one voice.

There was less agreement between management and millhands during the 1880s with regard to wages and conditions of work. In 1883 thirteen weavers of the Canada Cotton mill went on strike to protest a cut-back in their wages.[77] But the more serious strikes occurred in 1887, 1888 and 1889 after both the Stormont and Canada Cotton mills were organized into Assemblies of the Knights of Labor in 1886.[78] The man responsible for organizing the textile workers in Cornwall was undoubtedly John James Bickley, an overseer in the Cornwall Spinning mills.[79] This was a small company owned by Joseph Moyes, who employed eighteen men and women.[80] Bickley was a dedicated member of the Knights of Labor, whose first Assembly in Canada was founded in Hamilton in 1881.[81] Like many of the early adherents of the Knights of Labor, Bickley was captivated by the chivalric ideals of the Order which gave workers, whether skilled or unskilled, a sense of the worthiness of their labour and, at the same time, combined them in a fraternal bond to secure better working conditions and fair wages. "If the teachings of the Order were lived up to, nothing but good could come to the workingman." Bickley declared. More than this, he was certain that "if labor is properly and thoroughly organized, strikes will seldom occur (because) if grievances exist, the Knights state the case to the executive board of the local Assembly. They investigate and if the grievances are real, they try to effect a remedy with management. If no settlement is reached, then the executive would call the help out (on strike)...If a place is organized, they cannot jump up at the spur of the moment and leave (their work.)"[82]

The first strike organized by the Knights of Labor in Cornwall occurred in 1887 when dyers demanded that their hours be reduced from ten to nine per day. The Order provided $400 to striking members but the strike was unsuccessful.[83] More impressive was the strike of spinners and weavers at both the Canada Cottons and Stormont mills that began 26 January 1888. Perhaps because of their lack of success the previous year, the dyers did not go out on strike, nor did the carders at the Stormont mill.[84] The workers at both mills were protesting an intended cut in their wages which the companies maintained was not so much a reduction in wages as a scheme to equalize wages, that is, the company claimed that while some workers would receive less, others would receive more.[85] The Knights of Labor did not accept this company rationale, but expected that the new scheme would reduce real wages by 30%.[86] At Canada Cottons there had been a slight increase in average yearly wages from $282 in 1883 to $298 in 1887 and, meagre as this increase was, the workers were determined to keep it. The following shows the increases at the Canada Cottons mill:[87]

Year	No. hands	Annual Payroll	Average Wage Paid
1883	648	$183,000	$282
1884	490	129,000	263
1885	537	149,000	277
1886	655	190,000	290
1887	696	208,000	298

Apart from their concern about the possible wage cutback, the striking workers were also protesting a boycott imposed by the Cornwall mill officials against a number of "men who were fired or left their jobs", presumably organizers of the Knights of Labor.[88]

Strikers gathered at the Canada Cottons mill about one o'clock on Thursday afternoon, 26 January 1888, just as the non-striking workers were beginning to return from their lunch period. The strikers jostled a few of the non-strikers and nearly tumbled a company man, Fred Rowe, into the nearby raceway. No one was injured and the strikers moved off when the company called in policemen Allan Cameron and Michael Reardon.[89] At the Stormont mill all was quiet. On the very day that the millhands decided to strike, the canal water sank to a low level due to an ice jam and the Gault brothers decided to close the mill rather than operate at a decreased speed.[90]

Because of the scuffles between strikers and non-strikers the previous day, Canada Cottons officials asked Police Magistrate Angus Bethune to send "a sufficient number of constables to protect such of the employees as wished to enter the mill to work." On January 27 the three regular policemen, Allan Cameron, Michael Reardon and Robert Smythe were sent, together with Special Constables George Crites, John Graham, and three others named Shaver, McGarity and Kippen. When the police arrived at the mill about 5:30 in the morning, they found small groups of strikers already near the entrance. More arrived as the time of opening neared. No disturbances whatever occurred. Operatives of the dye room, the finishing room, the bleachery and the machine shop all passed in without a word said to them by the striking weavers and spinners. The crowd then dispersed until lunchtime. The police and special constables returned to find a larger crowd of strikers and sympathizers outside the mill entrance but there was no trouble, except for a single arrest of a young man named Peter Bilodeau. Another worker, Charles O'Brien, had sworn out a warrant against Bilodeau, complaining that the previous day Bilodeau had pulled him back as he was entering the gate of the millyard and thrown him down and torn off his coat. When police arrested Bilodeau he was carrying a "heavy stick (which) he gave up immediately." He was taken to the Police Station where he was identified as a bartender at Albert Beaucage's tavern, not a millhand.[91]

By Monday morning, February 1st, the strikers were in a more truculent mood. They gathered at both Stormont mill, which had re-opened, and at Canada Cottons' mill, making noises at those workers who were going inside. At the Stormont mill, the strikers obeyed a police order to "go about their business", but at the Canada

Cottons mill police arrested four men, identified by the *Standard* reporter as "Richard Sennet, a man with one eye, seemingly inoffensive, Maurice Bellanger, Louis Pard, a youth not out of his teens, and Issac Blum."[92] The arrests created a sensation. Strikers followed the police to the station, while women strikers paraded Pitt Street, "taking a great interest in the Court proceedings."[93]

By February 2nd the strike had gone on for a week. "No event since last year's flood has caused so much excitement in Cornwall", exclaimed the editor of the *Standard*. "Some very hard language is used by the operatives and others at the mill authorities because of the cutdown (in wages). Supers of both mills claim that the reduction of the mills is really an equalization of wages and will not reach more than 5% or 10% reduction." The superintendent of Canada Cottons, Albert T. Knight, assured the *Standard* that "if the operatives went to work at the prices we offer, they would be better paid than any mill in the Dominion."[94]

The degree of tension is indicated by the efforts made by the Knights of Labor to exert social control during the strike, and the executive took credit for keeping the strike from becoming violent. When strikers threatened to go to the house of an overseer "for the purpose of molesting him", it was the Knights of Labor that met and prevented it. John James Bickley asserted that "had it not been for the Order of the Knights of Labor,...certain persons in authority at the mills would have been severely dealt with."[95]

Townsmen became alarmed at the interruption of work at the mill and the increasing tension. Some tried to mediate between the strikers and company officials. One of these was the minister of Knox Presbyterian Church, Reverend James Hastie. He approached the mill superintendents, Albert Knight of Canada Cottons mill and W.S. Turner of the Stormont mill, to try to persuade them to remove the company boycott against some of the millhands who had been fired, presumably the Knights of Labor organizers.[96] Alex McDonald and his partner, J.M. McDonald, who owned the largest furniture store in Cornwall and managed the Victoria Skating Rink and auditorium, offered the rink to the striking millhands for a meeting on February 2nd.[97] Here several hundred met at ten o'clock in the morning to discuss the strike and the company offers. Among those in attendance was Cornwall's mayor, Angus R. Maclennan, the priest from the newly-formed parish of the Nativity in the East end, Father J.J. Kelly, two ministers, Reverend James Hastie of Knox Presbyterian Church and Reverend George S. Reynolds of the St. Paul's Methodist Church, indicating considerable public interest in, if not support for, the strikers. The chair was taken by Hugh Rambo. After the workers urged Reverend James Hastie to speak, he gave the gist of his interviews with the two mill superintendents and recommended that the workers appoint a committee to negotiate.

Indicative that this first mass meeting of strikers in Cornwall was orchestrated by the executive of the Knights of Labor is the fact that the chief speaker was from Montreal, a man named Shehyn, who spoke at length. Declaring that the boycotting of discharged millhands "was infamous," Shehyn insisted that "there was safety only in organized labor". He assured the Cornwall strikers that "men were getting less pay in Cornwall than anywhere else" and that the cutback in wages would be as much as 12 percent. The meeting appointed Mayor Maclennan, Father Kelly, Reverend George Reynolds, and two English and two French laymen to act as a committee to convey the views of the committee of the strikers to the superintendents of the mills "to come to some agreement whereby work shall be resumed on a basis suitable to both." This meant that the Knights of Labor executive agreed to using a committee of townsmen to mediate for them with the company officials."[98]

Townsmen were worried at the impasse that had been reached at the mills, with both of the major ones closed down completely. More ominous was the procedure on the previous day at the Canada Cottons mill when the millhands were paid off and told that their backpay would be paid the following Wednesday.[99] Noticed, too, was the departure from Cornwall of mill operatives. The *Standard* reported on 2 February 1888 that two families had gone to Fall River, Massachusetts, another to Manchester, New Hampshire, and two had left for Montreal. Other families had moved to Lowell, Massachusetts, and some to Rimouski. The one bright spot that cold and fearful week in Cornwall was that the Canada Cotton Company decided not to press charges against the four men arrested at the mill. Huge crowds of strikers surrounded the magistrate's court on the morning that the arrested strikers appeared, but the managing director of Canada Cottons, the Honorable Donald McInnes, announced that "as matters have reached a more pacific aspect, the company did not wish to prosecute."[100]

John James Bickley was the most active member of the Knights of Labor on the arbitration committee appointed by the operatives. This committee set as its objective to equalize wages paid to Cornwall operatives with those of the best-paid mills in Canada. The citizens' arbitration committee carried out the negotiations with company officials who invited the operatives to meet with them to compare their scale of wages with those paid by other mills in the province.[101]

However, when the Knights of Labor secured the wage list of the mills at Merritton, Ontario, and presented it to Canada Cottons superintendent Albert Turner, he refused to believe it was a correct wage scale.[102] In addition, Bickley was fired from his job at the Cornwall Spinning Mill and black-listed from getting another job though his former boss, Joseph Moyes, denied that Bickley was fired because of his labour organizing activities.[103]

Resentment over Bickley's dismissal and in particular over the failure of the Canada Cotton Company to live up to the agreement led to a second strike in the spring of 1889. After a month-long walkout, this was settled by two arbitrators, one appointed by the millhands and one by the company, who were able to agree on the wage scale, but Bickley was not reinstated.[104]

Stormont mill also went on strike in February of 1889, not over wages, but over the lengthening of the cuts, that is, the number of yards each worker had to weave in order to earn a certain amount of money. Weavers wanted the cuts kept at fifty yards.[105] This strike continued from 15 February until 8 March when some weavers began to return to work. In fact, the *Freeholder*, which more often than not took the side of the workers, insisted that the weavers were under a misapprehension and that they received better pay with the longer cuts.[106] These strikes resulted in wages at the Cornwall mills being raised to a par with the best of those paid in other Canadian factories. Cornwall millhands not only were among the best paid in the country by 1893, but their skilled workers received higher wages than their counterparts in the United States. According to the Toronto *Globe*, Cornwall manufacturers had to pay such wages "in order to retain their workers as they want to go away as soon as they become at all familiar with the business".[107] This drain of skilled laborers to the United States caused the Cornwall mills great expense and meant, as the *Globe* remarked, "That the Cornwall mills are really the training schools for the other mills across the line".[108]

By the late 1880s Cornwall's textile mills had been organized by the Knights of Labor, though it is not clear whether all workers joined the Order or not. At the time of the strikes in 1888, the chief organizer, John James Bickley, stated that the millhands were only partly organized and that accounted for some going on strike and others not.[109] Work conditions were as good if not better than in most factory towns across the country inasmuch as the Cornwall factories were relatively new and used the most modern equipment. In the investigation carried out by a Royal Commission in 1889, commissioners heard of only one severe accident at a Cornwall mill and only one case of what could be considered harsh treatment towards women employees. The accident occurred when a man fell from staging he had erected at the Stormont mill and he plunged into a vat. When the man died from injuries some days later, the company gave the widow a month's extra pay, looked after the medical and funeral expenses and paid the family grocery bill.[110] The one complaint of harshness resulted from the practice of the Stormont mill bosses to allow female employees to remain in the mill in winter to eat their lunches. The boss of the carders, Edward King, said the trouble arose because he would not let the women "run the room as they liked". At first King paid a man to look after the room during the lunch hour "to see that order was kept and that (the workers) did not damage company property". However, the forty or so women workers, as soon as work stopped, chatted like magpies and enjoyed themselves so heartily, laughing and making noise, that the attendant told them they would have to take their lunches outside. In the uproar that followed, the boss, Edward King, lost his temper and called the women workers "bitches", though he later apologized for his language when they returned to work.[111]

At the Canada Cottons plant the employees by 1889 were almost equally divided between English-speaking and French-speaking workers, whereas in 1878 they had been entirely Scottish operatives.[112] This trend towards more and more French-speaking hands being hired meant also that the company cottages and boarding houses were beginning to be occupied by French as well as English millhands. What was true at the Canada Cottons mill in the East end was just as true at the Stormont mill in the West end of town. Here Archibald Gault, secretary of the company, posted French and English signs outlining the work rules for each department, and all pay envelopes had the chief rules printed on them in English and French so that operatives of both language groups knew what was expected of them.[113] Working conditions were still far from ideal at the turn of the century. Air conditioning was unheard of. One factory inspector reported that a "person passing through from one end of the weaving room to the other (at Canada Cottons mill) would be as wet with perspiration as if dipped in water."[114] Social relations at the Stormont plant seemed to have been better than at the Canada Cottons mill. Some attempts were made by the company to promote good public relations. There was, for instance, the annual excursion of employees and their families to Port Lewis on the steamer *Bohemian*. In 1882 some 750 boarded the steamer at 9:30 on a Saturday morning in late August for the three hour sail across the St. Lawrence, returning at 8:30 in the evening. Adding to the day's enjoyment was the band of the 59th Battalion. The fact that the mill secretary, Archibald Gault, and manager, A. Tweed, went along indicates that top management did not hesitate to mingle with their employees on the day's outing.[115]

Once wages were brought up to par with those of other mills in the country, Cornwall mill workers settled down to a decade of strike-free operations over the 1890s. It was not until late August of 1898 that the Stormont mill ran into difficulties once more. Spool-room hands walked out in protest over an improvement in machinery which they thought would reduce their earnings. After a week of strike action, they returned to work, assured by the company that "if, after a fair trial, the company finds that...the spoolies' earnings (were reduced) they will make it up to them."[116]

To what degree the Cornwall Knights of Labor suffered from the disruptions that faced the Order at the national level is uncertain. In the municipal elections in Cornwall in 1890, the successful mayoralty candidate, M.M. Mulhern, made it a point to deny specifically that he was a candidate of the Knights of Labor. However, he carefully and publicly acknowledged that he agreed with much of the "platform of the Knights of Labor...that he was opposed to all exemptions from taxation except for churches and schools... (yet) while approving of the combination of labor to protect their interests, as was done by capitalists, he considered strikes totally unnecessary in this enlightened age."[117] Another contestant for municipal council, Angus J. Lalonde, who had been first elected to Council in 1885 for the East Ward and who was the second French-Canadian to contest successfully a seat on Council, also denied that he was a Knights of Labor candidate, but noted that he "would accept votes from all." Although both Mulhern and Lalonde repudiated direct candidacy as Knights of Labor men, they did so in such a manner as not to alienate the Knights' support. A third candidate for Council, Fred Rowe, who had been jostled by strikers at Canada Cottons, announced his strong support for day labour in preference to contract work and reminded voters about the "important recent legislation that had been secured by working people." Still another Canada Cotton Company man, James P. Watson, who had been councillor in 1889 for the East Ward, discussed the question of factory exemption from taxation in his nomination speech.[118]

These speeches showed that the issues during the 1890 municipal election were closely linked to those of the Knights of Labor and to labour and industrial problems in Cornwall. This 1890 election represented the height of the Knights of Labor influence in Cornwall. They still had an Assembly in the town in 1895, but by the turn of the century the demise of the Knights left Cornwall's textile labour force of 1,300 in a disorganized state and so it continued for the next thirty years.[119] There was a fraternal society in 1893 called the "Ancient Order of United Workmen", with John Ridley as secretary, but whether this was a type of union or simply a workmen's fraternity is unknown.[120]

While labour over the 1880s became organized and then disintegrated, the textile industry itself consolidated. The merger of the two rival cotton companies with the woollen factory in the early 1890s under a new name, the Canadian Colored Cotton Mills Company, lent substance to the generally-accepted Cornwall dictum that "prosperity depends wholly upon the continuance and prosperity of the factories, and the location of more industries in our midst."[121] In a handsomely-prepared souvenir booklet that accompanied the Cornwall Old Boys' Reunion of 1906, the editors emphasized that the factories "are the life of the town...and everything that would act in a prejudicial way against them is looked upon with justifiable indignation." This was particularly so by 1906 when the giant textile company, now headed by D. Morrice and Sons of Montreal, began to update the factory machinery, rather than replace worn-out machines by the same type. The renewal of machinery involved enormous expenditure by the new company, but it allowed the mills to lessen the cost production and thus to compete more favourably with rivals in the United States and Europe.[122]

The operation of the four major mills in Cornwall stimulated the growth of secondary industries, as well as created numerous jobs for those employed in the construction and expansion of the mills. One of the most important secondary works established to service the mills was that of the Cornwall Foundry and Machine Works, now Bingley Steel Works on William Street. Built in 1889 by Walter J. Derochie and his brother Joseph, and conveniently located just to the rear of the Canada Cottons and the woollen mills, the foundry soon earned a reputation for skill in repairing machinery for cotton and woollen mills and its workmen were sent to serve the Gault Brothers cotton mills at Hochelaga near Montreal, and elsewhere.[123] In addition, Derochie's foundry made all kinds of iron and brass castings, shafting, pulleys, beaming machines and school and church seats. A specialty of the shop was an invention of Walter Derochie — a water motor that could be used to drive a variety of office and household machinery such as sewing machines. One of the publishing firms to make use of Derochie's invention was the *Freeholder* which installed a water motor in the basement and used it to drive all the press equipment.[124]

A firm that grew from a small sash and door operation in 1857 to the first Cornwall planing mill by 1880 was that of William Atchison on Gloucester Street between Second and Third Streets East.[125] Atchison enlarged his plant in 1884 to two storeys and operated his mill machinery by steam. His construction accomplishments included the new Cornwall Public School, the impressive Kirkpatrick block and the Turner block. A second sash and door mill was operated in 1882 by L.A. Ross who bought out the business founded by P.E. Adams. By 1891 these two mills employed forty-six men who earned $20,000 a year in wages.[126] Other firms to open their doors in 1889 were C.Y. Kyte's stationery and fancy goods store; a new bottling works run by G.R. McLennan; Cornwall's first greenhouse operated by two brothers, Henry E. and John J. Whittaker; and a slaughter and butcher business, opened by H.T. Donihee.[127] An electroplating firm, the largest of its kind in Canada, was established on Fourth Street by the Shields Brothers with Wilbur R. Hitchcock as supervisor.[128]

One of the most famous and long-lived secondary businesses to spring up in 1887 was Duffy's Candy Store, operated by Patrick Duffy and his wife. For many years they made most of their own candy, their biggest seller being home-made taffy made in vanilla, strawberry or chocolate flavour, "in chunks or jaw-breaker form". It was a treat sufficient to draw Cornwall children by the dozens to their store at 243 Pitt Street.[129] For different reasons, Frank and P.J. Lally attracted hundreds of sports enthusiasts to their factory on Cumberland Street. This was the plant which, in 1881, began making lacrosse sticks using only hickory. The factory became known the world over as the finest supplier of lacrosse sticks, England being the largest purchaser, but the United States running a close second.[130]

Other firms already established in the 1870s reaped the harvest of the industrial expansion of the 1880s. One of these was the large merchant tailoring business of James McDonell who opened the Cornwall Cloth Hall on Pitt Street in 1878. Here some forty hands were employed.[131] Another was the Glasgow Warehouse, a firm handling ladies' clothing and furs, that opened on Pitt Street in 1879 by Cornwall's Member of Parliament, John G. Snetsinger.[132] The Cornwall Marble and Granite Works, established in 1879 by Harry Williams, secured contracts with the Canada Cottons Company and for work on the canal expansion and repairs. Henry Weber was the town photographer as early as 1871. His pictures provided the *Canadian Illustrated News* with Cornwall's first nation-wide coverage in 1878. Besides photography, Weber dealt in jewellery, toys, fancy goods and picture frames.[133]

By 1891 the town's population had reached 6,805 of whom 2,319 were French-Canadians.[134] By this time, too, the suburbs were expanding rapidly, bringing the total population of the town and its immediate environs closer to 10,000.[135] "The dull, stodgy, old town" that John S. Grant first visited in the early 1870s, with its streets lighted by a few coal-oil lamps and covered here and there with planks twelve feet wide, was transformed by the 1890s.[136] Handsome modern factories lined the waterfront, surrounded by more and more cottages for millhands and their families. Churches, schools, hospitals, secondary services and institutions all mushroomed and the people of Cornwall felt the pulse of that expansion, usually with pride, sometimes with anxiety and occasionally with resentment.

NOTES

1. J.F. Pringle, *Lunenburgh, or the Old Eastern District*, 136.
2. *Canada Directory*, 1851, 69.
3. J.G. Harkness, *History of Stormont, Dundas and Glengarry*, 256.
4. *Canadian Illustrated News*, 26 January 1878, 55.
5. *Lovell's Ontario Directory*, 1871, 28; *Canada Directory*, 1851, 69.
6. Pringle, 292.
7. Mary Mack to Editor, *Standard-Freeholder*, 13 March 1943; *Cornwall Freeholder Souvenir* issue, 1900; *Old Boys' Reunion*, 1906; *Saturday Globe*, Toronto, 18 November 1893.
8. *Cornwall Freeholder Souvenir* issue, 1900.
9. Heather Gilbert, *Awakening Continent, The Life of Lord Mount Stephen*, i, 7 and 15; William Wood, *The Storied Province of Quebec*, iii, 178.
10. Gilbert, *Awakening Continent*, 15.
11. *Ibid.*, 7, 14-16; for a modern explanation of Cornwall's good location, see, *Fifty Years of Progress, Yesterday, Today and Tomorrow...Courtaulds (Canada) Limited*, 1975, 2.
12. In a petition of the Cornwall Town Council to the Lieutenant Governor of Ontario, 19 February 1872, 164, the date of the factory's construction is given as 1867, Minutes, Town Council, 19 February 1872, 164; *Canadian Illustrated News*, 26 January 1878, gives the date as 1868; Pringle, 293.
13. *Globe*, Toronto, 17 October 1870; see also *Standard-Freeholder*, 12 May 1978.
14. William Wood, *The Storied Province of Quebec*, iv, 471.
15. H. E. Belden, *Historical Atlas of Stormont, Dundas and Glengarry*, vi; *Globe*, Toronto, 18 November 1893.
16. Pringle, 141.
17. Minutes, Town Council, 9 February 1871, 92.
18. *Ibid.*, 18 April 1871, 98.

19. *Ibid.*, 7 December 1871, 132.

20. *Ibid.*, 22 January 1872, 149.

21. Petition of Town Council to Lieutenant Governor, 19 February 1872, in Minutes, Town Council, 164.

22. *Canadian Illustrated News*, 26 January 1878, 55.

23. Gilbert, *Awakening Continent*, 15.

24. Minutes, Town Council, 19 February 1872, 164.

25. *Ibid.*, 10 March and 4 November, 1874, 211, 261; Pringle, 142.

26. *Canadian Illustrated News*, 26 January 1878, 55; Canada *Census*, 1871, 275, 1881, 262-63.

27. *Canadian Illustrated News*, 26 January 1878, 55.

28. Details from *Reporter*, 10 May 1879.

29. *Census*, 1871, 134, 1891, ii, 398.

30. All population figures from *Census*, 1881, 262-63.

31. Belden, *Historical Atlas*, 55.

32. *Reporter*, 10 May 1879.

33. *Freeholder*, 30 March 1883.

34. *Canadian Illustrated News*, 26 January 1878, 55.

35. D. Ross-Ross and A. L. Farnsworth, *History of Engineering in Cornwall*, 18; *Standard-Freeholder*, 29 September 1971; John S. Grant, "Reminiscences" in *Standard-Freeholder*, 28 September 1946.

36. *Canadian Illustrated News*, 26 January 1878, 55.

37. *Ibid.*, Pringle, 142, 293; Harkness, 236.

38. *Canadian Illustrated News*, 26 January 1878, 55.

39. *Ibid.*

40. *Reporter*, 20 April 1878.

41. *Ibid.*, 4 May and 15 June, 1878.

42. *Ibid.*, 23 May 1878.

43. *Ibid.*, 2 November 1878.

44. Minutes, Town Council, 11 November 1878, 412-13.

45. *Ibid.*, 8 January 1879.

46. *Reporter*, 26 April, 10 May, 1879; Pringle, 294.

47. *Saturday Globe*, Toronto, 18 November 1893, 7.

48. *Standard-Freeholder*, 29 June 1934.

49. *Census*, 1891, iii, 120 and 377.

50. For details of this early paper plant see, *Census*, 1871, iii, 427; *Lovell's Canadian Directory*, 1871, 28-29; Pringle, 293.

51. *Reporter*, 10 May 1879.

52. For details of J. P. Barber, see Henry Morgan, *Canadian Men and Women of the Time*, 48; *Saturday Globe*, Toronto, 18 November 1893; *Cornwall Freeholder Souvenir* issue, 1900; Pringle, 295, Harkness, 236.

53. *Saturday Globe*, Toronto, 18 November 1893.

54. *Census*, 1891, iii, 238; Pringle, 295.

55. *Standard-Freeholder*, 18 March 1972.

56. *Saturday Globe*, Toronto, 18 November 1893.

57. *Ibid.*, for a description of this process.

58. *Census*, 1891, iii, 238.

59. *Saturday Globe*, Toronto, 18 November 1893.

60. *Census*, 1891, iii, 120.

61. *Ibid.*, 377.

62. Minutes, Town Council, 17 January 1870, and 3 July 1883, 99.

63. *Freeholder*, 18 April 1884; Alex G. Watson's evidence before the Royal Commission on the relations of Labor and Capital, 1889, cited in Gregory Kealey, *Canada Investigates Industrialism*, 184.

64. *Canadian Illustrated News*, 26 January 1878, 55.

65. *Reporter*, 1 September 1876 and 10 February 1877; see also *Standard-Freeholder*, 28 June 1958.

66. Gregory Kealey and Bryan Palmer, "The Bonds of Unity: The Knights of Labor in Ontario 1880-1900", in *Histoire Sociale/Social History*, xiv, no. 28, November 1981, 408; Charles Lipton, *The Trade Union Movement of Canada*, 68-69.

67. *Freeholder*, 12 May 1882.

68. *Ibid.*

69. Harkness, 247-48, 259, 263.

70. Pringle, 256.

71. Harkness, 240.

72. *Freeholder*, 9 June 1882.

73. *Reporter*, 24 June 1882.

74. *Ibid.*, 10 February 1877.

75. *Standard*, 24 February 1887.

76. *Ibid.*

77. *Freeholder*, 2 November 1883.

78. Kealey and Palmer, "The Bonds of Unity: The Knights of Labor in Ontario, 1880-1900", in *Histoire Sociale/Social History* xiv, no. 28, November 1981, 408; Lipton, *Trade Union Movement*, 68-69.

79. J. J. Bickley's testimony before Royal Commission on the relations of Labor and Capital, 1889 in Kealey, *Canada Investigates Industrialism*, 188-191.

80. *Ibid.*, see Joseph Moyes's testimony, 186.

81. Lipton, *Trade Union Movement*, 68-70.

82. Bickley's testimony before Royal Commission, 1889, in Kealey, *Canada Investigates Industrialism*, 188-191.

83. *Ibid.*, 191; see also Kealey and Palmer, "*The Bonds of Unity*" in Histoire Sociale/Social History, 408.

84. *Standard*, 26 January 1888.

85. Archibald Gault's testimony before Royal Commission, 1889, in Kealey, *Canada Investigates Industrialism*, 179.

86. *Standard*, 2 February 1888.

87. Testimony of mill secretary, Alex Watson, before Royal Commission, 1889, in Kealey, *Canada Investigates Industrialism*, 184.

88. See Reverend James Hastie's address and Shehyn's address to Knights of Labor meeting in Cornwall, 2 February 1888, in *Standard*, 2 February 1888.

89. *Standard*, 26 January 1888.

90. *Ibid.*

91. For details see *Standard*, 2 February 1888.

92. *Ibid.*

93. *Ibid.*

94. *Ibid.*

95. Bickley's testimony before Royal Commission 1889, in Kealey, *Canada Investigates Industrialism*, 191.

96. See Hastie's address to Knights of Labor, in *Standard*, 2 February 1888.

97. *Standard*, 2 February 1888; *Old Boys' Reunion*, 1906, 73.

98. See *Standard*, 2 February 1888 for details of this meeting.

99. *Ibid.*

100. *Ibid.*

101. Alex Watson's testimony before Royal Commission, 1889, in Kealey, *Canada Investigates Industrialism*, 182.

102. Bickley's testimony, *ibid.*, 190.

103. *Ibid.*, 188-190; see also Joseph Moyes's testimony, 186.

104. Alex Watson's testimony, *ibid.*, 182; Albert Knight's testimony, 184; and Bickley's testimony, *ibid.*, 188.

105. *Freeholder*, 22 February 1889.

106. *Ibid.*, 8 March 1889.

107. *Saturday Globe*, Toronto, 18 November 1893.

108. *Ibid.*

109. Bickley's testimony before Royal Commission 1889, in Kealey, *Canada Investigates Industrialism*, 188.

110. Gault's testimony, *ibid.*, 181-82.

111. Edward King's testimony, *ibid.*, 186.

112. Alex Watson's testimony, *ibid.*, 184; *Canadian Illustrated News*, 26 January 1878.

113. Gault's testimony before Royal Commission, 1889, in Kealey, *Canada Investigates Industrialism*, 187-188.

114. *Heritage Cornwall*, 44.

115. *Freeholder*, 25 August 1882.

116. *Ibid.*, 2 September 1898.

117. M. M. Mulhern's nomination speech cited in *Freeholder*, 3 January 1890.

118. All the nomination speeches are reported in *Freeholder*, 3 January 1890.

119. Lipton, *Trade Union Movement*, 80; *Old Boys' Reunion*, 1906, 47.

120. *Saturday Globe*, Toronto, 18 November 1893.

121. *Old Boys' Reunion*, 1906, 45.

122. *Ibid.*

123. *Globe*, Toronto, 18 November 1893.

124. *Standard-Freeholder*, 29 September 1972.

125. *Lovell's Ontario Directory*, 1871, 27; *Old Boys' Reunion*, 1906; *Freeholder Souvenir* issue, 1900; Harkness, 358-59.

126. *Census*, 1891, iii, 286.

127. For Kyte, see *Freeholder*, 19 April 1889; *Old Boys' Reunion*, 1906; for McLennan, see *Freeholder*, 31 May 1889; for Donihee and Whittaker, see *Standard-Freeholder*, industrial edition, 1955, 8 and 13.

128. *Standard*, 15 February 1889.

129. *Standard-Freeholder*, 26 April 1946.

130. *Standard-Freeholder*, 29 June 1934.

131. *Canadian Illustrated News*, 26 January 1878, 55.
132. *Freeholder Souvenir* issue, 1900; *Old Boys' Reunion*, 1906.
133. *Lovell's Ontario Directory*, 1871, 29; *Canadian Illustrated News*, 26 January 1878.
134. Canada *Census*, 1891, iii, 42 and 151.
135. *Globe*, Toronto, 18 November 1893.
136. Grant, "Reminiscences," in *Standard-Freeholder*, 28 September 1946.

A woman worker in what is believed to be the Weave Shed of
Canada Cottons around 1900.
Credit: Heritage Cornwall.

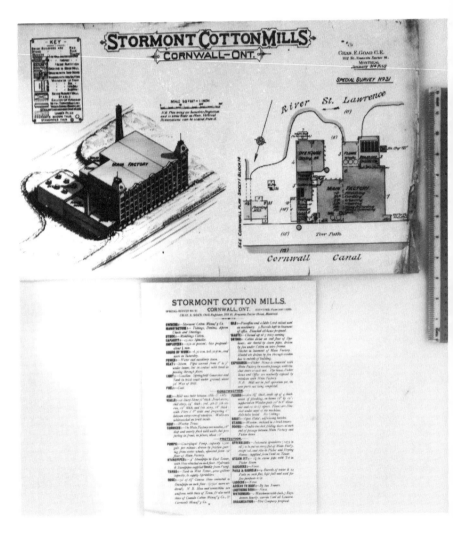

Stormont Cotton Mills, 1882.

Toronto Paper and Manufacturing Company, rear view of mills.
Credit: Cornwall: Old Boys' Re-Union, 1906.

Canada Cottons 1906. Built in 1872, the mill was 90 feet by 300 feet. In 1882 a weave shed was added and outfitted with electrical lighting designed by Thomas Edison. Edison was assisted by a local electrical contractor John MacMillan.
Credit: Heritage Cornwall.

Chapter XII
Cornwall Copes With Expansion

The emergence of a mill town with major cotton, woollen and paper mills put a strain on the somewhat primitive secondary institutions and services provided by the town. Police and fire protection, gas works, electricity, telephones, the press, waterworks, street railways and sanitation, all these and more were affected by the sudden influx of industries and people. None more so than the local police. A policeman's lot was not a particularly unhappy one in late nineteenth century Cornwall. He might suffer an occasional bite from a drunken prisoner or the less lethal but still annoying bite from local journalists who seldom hesitated to point out the shortcomings of police protection in town. From the 1860s when one constable was thought sufficient to cope with the evils of the day and night, the police establishment grew slowly. For one thing the seamier side of Cornwall's corporate existence, that is, the activities of its law-breakers, continued so innocuously that in a single year only 123 minor cases were recorded on the police blotter.

With the enactment of the provincial Municipal Act of 1873, Cornwall, with other municipalities, was obliged to hire a police magistrate to adjudicate minor offences. Former Mayor William Cox Allen stepped into the job on 4 September 1874 and back into his old spot at Town Hall, for Police Court sessions were held in the Council Chambers until 1877 when another room was fitted up as a Police Court Room.[1] A clerk of the police court was named in 1876 — George S. Jarvis, at a salary of $200. Job pluralism was neither unknown nor frowned upon in town. Jarvis, a son of Judge George S. Jarvis, already held the job of town clerk and continued to do so for the next thirty years.[2] Allen remained police magistrate until 1880 when Angus Bethune took over and served until his death in 1898. Then the job was taken for the first time by a French Canadian, thirty-year-old Daniel Danis, a native of St. Justine de Newton, Quebec. After studying at Laval University and at Osgoode

Hall, Toronto, Danis set up the first French law firm in Cornwall in 1894.[3]

Along with these elaborations in the police hierarchy and improvements in the police court and station, there was a slight expansion over the seventies and eighties of the force itself, stimulated by a number of complaints about minor fights, burglaries, smuggling, brothels and other crimes. At the time that Samuel Pollock assumed the sole policeman's uniform in October 1868, ratepayers insisted that there was not enough work to pay him a salary of $220 a year. He was therefore given the extra job of lighting the street lamps at night and shutting them off at daybreak. Before two years were up he found duty upon duty heaped upon him. Not only was he high constable, street surveyor, market clerk, inspector of weights and measures, town property and town hall guardian, hearse attendant, and poundkeeper, he was also expected to sit in on all meetings of the common school trustees, and to top it off, he was to make sure that "all weeds and thistles are cut down and no fences erected on public roads."[4] Occasionally Pollock was assisted by special constables, hired at a dollar a day, for such special occasions as the annual arrival of the circus in Cornwall or other festivals. By January of 1871, weighed down by the multiplicity of his duties, Pollock died suddenly.

Henry Silmser replaced Pollock as high constable, but he, too, found the job too onerous and quit by 3 April 1871.[5] At this time there was a second police constable in town, Adam Eligh, who was also the steamship agent. It is likely that Eligh was a private policeman hired by the steamship company, just as other constables were hired privately by the Grand Trunk Railway to guard its station and warehouses.[6] John Dewar took on the job as high constable in 1872 at a salary of $250 a year, but by April of 1873 he, too, resigned.[7] With one policeman dying on the job and two resigning, all within three years, town fathers realized that the combination of a meagre salary and heavy duties led to disenchantment. When they next advertised in Cornwall and Montreal newspapers for a police constable, they offered almost double the salary previously paid. The new constable could expect $420 yearly, providing he took no fees except in his role as poundkeeper.[8] The man who stepped into uniform and remained a constable for the next thirteen years was William Lawrence, familiarly dubbed "Sweet William."[9]

Like his predecessors, Sweet William found his duties piled higher and higher as each session of Town Council brought new by-laws that had to be enforced by the town's solitary limb of the law. By 1876 when Lawrence was promoted to high constable he was expected to "go to the scene of a fire as soon as the alarm is given and, under the direction of the Mayor or Chief of the Fire Brigade, in regard to the preservation of the public peace, (see to) the removal of idle and suspected persons and others not actually and usefully, employed in extinguishing the fire."[10] This chore was not removed from his list of duties until 1884 when the fire engineer took over the job of acting as a guard at fires.[11] From then on fire engineers were part-time constables as well. John Quig, for example, earned a yearly salary of $660 in 1885 for his dual roles.[12]

As sanitary inspector, the new high constable had to "inspect meat...offered for sale at the Market and all other places in Town at such hours daily (Sundays excepted) as he may deem fit...and to lay information against any lessees or persons...who expose for sale any tainted or unwholesome meat...and to seize and destroy the (same)." Moreover, if the lessees of market stalls did not pay their weekly rents, Sweet William had the unpopular task of seizing their goods and holding them until such time as the stall-lessees paid up. The cleanliness of market stalls and slaughter houses was also part of his responsibility,[14] though the town hired an assistant constable, Robert Lightbody, in 1876, who took over part of the sanitary inspection duties and was paid a dollar a day.[15]

Town fathers also tackled the sticky task of public morality by passing a series of by-laws in 1876 for the "prevention of vice and immorality." The list of prohibited activities in the new by-laws gives an idea of the type of behaviour found unacceptable. From now on no one was to serve intoxicating drinks to children, apprentices or servants, without the consent of parents or masters, an indication that drinking was not confined to the elders of the town. As for adults, it was "illegal to be drunk, to swear, to use obscene, blasphemous, or insulting language in public."[16] The framers of the new law went a step further in curtailing what they considered habitual drunks. The relatives of "any unfortunate who is addicted to excessive drinking" could notify the Inspector "who is bound to warn all vendors of the ardent, that the inebriate in question is not to be served with any intoxicant, unless the dealer is prepared to pay a heavy penalty for disobeying the injunction."[17] According to the Cornwall *Reporter*, these "unhappy ones" were now greeted derisively as they entered a bar with "No drinks for you, you're on the Indian List," that is, they were, like the Indians of St. Regis and elsewhere, prohibited by law from buying any kind of spirituous liquors.[18]

Another activity no longer to be tolerated by the upholders of law in Cornwall was that of posting "indecent placards or pictures in public places." Henceforth trespassers would be hauled into police court by Sweet William. Gambling establishments and the playing of "rouge et noir, roulette and other gambling games" were prohibited within the municipality, as was "bathing in water lying on the road, (or) public highway,...indecently exposing his person between six a.m. and 8 p.m." In a final cleanup, town councillors took exception to "charivaris or such gatherings...within the municipality." Violations of the new by-laws could mean a fine as high as $50.00 or thirty days in jail.[19]

In 1878 a night watch was set up when R. McCutcheon was hired at a dollar a night and occasionally served during the day as a special constable.[20] This meant, in effect, that the Cornwall police force had expanded by 1878 to three members, McCutcheon on night patrol, High Constable William Lawrence on regular patrol during the day, and Assistant Constable Robert Lightbody who carried out some of the overflow duties of the high constable. The Town Council also became more specialized by the early 1880s when councillors were put on specific committees such as Finance, Health, Building, Roads, and Fire, Light and Police.

In 1883 the Fire, Light and Police Committee, one of the most important, was composed of Chairman Albert W. Flack, and Councillors John E. Loney, M.O. O'Callaghan, Henry Adams, and Fire Chief John G. Hunter.[21] They had to deal with a complaint against Constable Lawrence brought in, curiously enough, by twenty-six citizens including a brother of Cariboo Cameron, Allan Cameron, the man who would dominate the police force until the close of the century. Cameron and his co-signers protested that High Constable Lawrence "can never be found at his post when his services are required and when present refuses to take any action in quelling any riot or disturbances." They went on to claim that Lawrence "on a recent occasion stood a looker-on and allowed an individual to carry on all sorts of rowdyism and when asked to interfere refused to do so." The petitioners asked the Council to "make a change and appoint someone that will fill the said office of policeman to the satisfaction of the Public."[22] Lawrence had his defenders. At the enquiry held by the Fire, Light and Police Committee, he presented a petition signed by James Watson, Hugh Adams and sixty-five other citizens who testified to his good and efficient behaviour as high constable.[23]

Discretion may have been the better part of valour for Lawrence. A single policeman or even a number of police have seldom been effective in quelling disturbances unless they have undergone special riot-control training. In any event, the upshot of the petitions was that Allan Cameron was taken on as a policeman and given Sweet William's old beat in the East End of town. Lawrence was to patrol on Pitt Street and just east of it, while a third town policeman, Constable Duffy, who had been hired sometime prior to 1883, was to patrol on Pitt Street and around the Town Hall.[24] Armed with their batons and handcuffs, the police trio were so resplendent in their new uniforms that the *Reporter's* lead writer was almost speechless. "Sweet William, Daisy Duffy and Canny Cameron", he exclaimed, "are now perfect dudes of policemen (in) skin-tight blue pants, tasty jackets, and swell overcoats of the same hue set off with two rows of refulgent brass buttons bearing the device of the Imperial Crown, the whole surmounted by ponderous otter-skin caps. Joking aside," he admitted, "the appearance of the police force is a credit to Cornwall."

Yet the difficulty of keeping up morale and discipline among the three policemen was soon evident. Duffy resigned in April of 1884, necessitating a new arrangement of duties in which Lawrence and Cameron were to handle all the outside work, Cameron's beat to extend eastward from Amelia Street, and Lawrence to handle the rest of the town.[26] The engineer of the Fire Brigade, John Quig, was detailed off by Town Councillors to act "as a Constable in and about the Town Hall and on Pitt Street between Third and Fourth Streets, and to reside within one hundred yards of the Town Hall." In other words, the highly-paid fire engineer was commandeered to the police force. By this time, a number of men had had some experience in police duties as special constables, and a few had been hired, either privately or by the Town Council, to act as detectives. Among the special constables who were on and off the force throughout the seventies and eighties was George Crites, likely a relative of one of the longest-serving policemen of the early twentieth century, George "Manny" C. Crites. The senior Crites served as a special constable as early as 8 August 1877 when he and three other men were hired as guards during the circus.[27]

John W. Graham and a man named Flaherty were what the editor of the *Freeholder* called the "Invincible Detective Force of Cornwall." They worked evidently on what was essentially an "awards system," that is, they would get part of whatever fine was meted out to people they arrested. They may also have been retained by the Grand Trunk Railway as private police. Like the police force, the detective force was not a favourite with the press. On 30 November 1883, for instance, the *Freeholder* informed its readers that "Last evening Det. J.W. Graham was lurking around the G.T.R. station looking for innocent victims to devour. A man from Brockville named Fox, who was the worse of liquor, happened to be at the station. When Graham saw Fox, his face lit up with brilliancy. Visions of a dollar floated before his eyes. Graham waltzed up to Fox and attempted his arrest. Fox resisted and Graham beat him brutally on the head with his baton. Several parties interfered and rescued Fox from Graham's grasp, after which it was necessary to telephone for a doctor to dress his wounds. He received three ugly gashes upon his cranium which bled profusely. The Proper authorities should investigate the matter and mete out the law with a vengeance to this "duffer" who should, if he had his deserts, be serving a sentence in the Kingston Pen. A term in the above institution would do this stool pigeon good. It would make him walk erect and fit him for something useful after being liberated."

Castigation of the police for doing their duty, no matter how unpleasant or unpopular, was not confined to the twentieth century. In this case, Cornwall journalists were aware that earlier that spring the Grand Trunk station agent, M. Wagner, had been brutally stabbed about the head by a tramp who was prowling around the station about three o'clock in the morning. Wagner's life was probably saved only by the fortuitous arrival of the night watchman who was able to secure medical help for him and, though a search was made for the attacker, he was not found.[28] The police were thus not the only ones meting out blows. In July 1884 Constable William Lawrence received such a deep bite on his arm from Joseph Seguin whom he was trying to arrest, that the constable had to take a week off to recover.[29] Fire Engineer and pro-tem Police Constable John Quig had no intention of suffering a like fate. Thus, when William Tyo, a young man from "Slab Town", as the *Freeholder* reporter put it, "got chuck full of Bajus' lager on Saturday, and acted like a Texan steer on a Stampede...he entered Policeman Quig's territory and kicked up a racket...That slim and supple limb of the law terminated the fandango by a double-footed kick, which stretched Billy prone and breathless upon the walk. He then dragged him over to the Hall and laid him out in the refrigerator. On Monday morning the P.M. (Police Magistrate) interviewed Billy and made him "anti" four dollars and 75¢. If he had not "antied" he would have sent down for ten days."[30]

The media's coverage of the police beat left little to be desired in terms of colourful description. The *Freeholder* informed its readers on 11 April 1884 that it took two policemen and a cab to convey Mrs. Cook to the cells. Quipped the reporter, "Now if it takes two policemen and a cab to take Mrs. Cook to the Police Station, how many cooks would it take to clean out the whole Police Force?" This constant put-down of the police by the press and, in particular, by the *Freeholder*, had its effect. By the fall of 1884 Constable Cameron was accused of being negligent in his duties and of spending too much time "lounging about hotels." Town fathers were being peppered from other quarters about the performance of the police, especially after a daring robbery at William J. Wagoner's jewellery store on Pitt Street. Shopkeepers and merchants were so alarmed that they discussed security measures and sent a deputation to Town Council offering to hire a night watchman at $35 a month, asking the town to pay $10 if they raised the extra $20.[32] Council offered $500 reward for the apprehension and conviction of the jewellery shop thief.

After this flurry of activity on the part of citizens and Council and the subsequent inquiry and reprimand to Constable Cameron to mend his ways, the town police force resumed its normal routine, the constables more or less making their own arrangements about their patrols and hours on and off duty.[33] Then in the spring of 1887 the Town Council was besieged with requests for better police protection in the East end where numerous assaults were reported.[34] At this time there were two regular constables, Allan Cameron and Michael Reardon, the latter replacing William Lawrence in June of 1886.[35] The town's two detectives were George Crites and John W. Graham.[36] In response to the complaints about inadequate police protection, Town Council decided to re-vamp the police system. Instead of a policeman patrolling all night along Pitt Street, the two constables were ordered to report to their respective beats at the sensible hour of nine o'clock each morning and to remain on duty until midnight.[37]

The hours may have been different but the duties remained the same. Constables went about impounding cows that still roamed at large over the town's streets or strayed into Gallagher's Pond. They confiscated fire crackers from boys in obedience to a new by-law. Fortune-tellers were chased out of town and two Frenchmen from "Old France" were arrested for giving an exhibition of their performing bear to an immense crowd of people at Brennan's Corners.[38] One constable was intrepid enough to corner "the terror of the north end", one Fred Chenney, whom the policeman noticed walking along trying to conceal something under his Prince Albert coat. As the constable neared, Chenney dropped the bundle and fled, leaving a newly-killed hen on the ground.[39]

Other constables enjoyed the occasional time that they outwitted Cornwall's smugglers. Special Constable George Crites was especially adept in this line of police work. One cold night in February of 1886, he took it upon himself to spy out two Cornwall men crossing the ice from the American side and heading for Gillespie's lock on the canal. The men had an abundant supply of Bourbon and were chuckling over the fun they were going to have with it. Up bobbed Crites from behind the lock and confiscated the whole cache.[40] Another night he waylaid Michael Beauvais of Cornwall Island whom he caught red-handed selling twelve bags of American onions to a Cornwall vegetable dealer. According to the *Freeholder*, Detective Crites "scared the fellow half to death by telling him he would have him arrested unless he planked down the customs duties", which he did and "walked out into the cold air a free and independent man."[41]

Another favourite item for smugglers was American coal-oil. Detective Crites kept a sharp lookout and managed to seize 236 gallons early one May morning in 1891.[42] There was a certain amount of cloak and dagger about thwarting the law-breakers who tried to sneak past Customs Officer John Cline in order to get their goods to the counters of Cornwall merchants, but the team of Cline and Crites soon became obnoxious to would-be smugglers. Nonetheless, smugglers continued to ply their trade, for Crites and Cline were still seizing teams of horses loaded with coal-oil as late as February 1897.[43]

Not quite so enjoyable from the point of view of the constables were the late night police chases. One such took place on Sunday night, 23 April 1886. Policeman Allan Cameron was making his rounds on William Street in the rapidly-growing East End when a ruction broke out. Cameron made a bolt for Henri Lanctôt who, according to the *Freeholder*, was calling the policeman "naughty names." In the colourful language of the press of the day, the chase was described. "No sooner did the "peeler" make the bolt than the offender made a break and the race that took place down William St. was much enjoyed by the hundreds who witnessed it and cheered all along the course." Lanctôt was the winner and got away, but Cameron charged him with using grossly insulting language and summoned him to Police Court. Like a number charged with minor offences, Lanctôt "quietly took his departure for Uncle Sam's domain leaving behind...only Policeman Cameron to mourn his loss."[44]

Another police chase that gave the media food for fun occurred late one hot Wednesday afternoon in 1890. Word came to police headquarters from the Grand Trunk Railway agent, R.P. Horsman, that the notorious burglar and jailbreaker, Archibald McDonald, and two or three of his pals were hiding in a culvert below the station. Boldly Constables Cameron, Crites, and their new partner in fighting crime, Robert Smyth, headed for the station culvert. As they neared the tracks, "The McDonald" and his friends took to their heels down the track. As Cameron weighed some 200 pounds, he was good for only a 100 yard dash. He therefore commandeered one of Cornwall's top lacrosse players, Alex Rivier, to join the posse. But even with Rivier's help, the posse could not catch up with the escaping trio, who had too good a head start. The police quickly put the way freight engine to use in pursuing the desperadoes. Down the engine bore on the fleeing men who took to the road. Off hopped the police to give chase. As Rivier closed in on the three fugitives, they threw up their arms and awaited the police. Instead of the notorious burglar, McDonald and his friends turned out to be tramps waiting a chance to jump the next freight train. Disgruntled, the posse returned to police headquarters and threw the tramps into cells for an overnight stay before ordering them to move on out of town the next day. The tramps lost no time. Their experience in Cornwall, like that of many another tramp, gave Cornwall a bad name among what the *Freeholder* termed the "Gentlemen of the Pike", so much so that by 1904 most of the "Weary Willies" had cut the town out of their time-table entirely.

A chase of another kind revived memories of the attack on Colonel Albert French in the winter of 1834. This time the chase again involved descendants of the town's founders. Colonel George Anderson and his wife were driving into town in a sleigh from the family estate on the East Front. Dusk had just fallen as they neared the eastern boundary of the town on a cold February evening. Here they encountered a party of four men who may have asked for a lift into town and were, like the Irish canallers in the earlier case of Colonel Albert French, refused. Two of the men jumped on the sleigh and tried to shove Anderson off. Anderson managed to topple the man off the sleigh, but they raced after it and struck Anderson on the back of his head. Only by pressing the horse forward did Anderson and his wife outdistance the quartet. Anderson recognized one of his assailants, Antoine Lefesse, against whom he lodged a complaint and police arrested the man immediately.[45] Unlike the earlier incident in 1834, the 1883 affair was a scuffle and chase, but it added to the growing demands for more police protection in the East End.

Two cases involving women of ill fame set the town on its ears. One led to the firing of Constable Michael Reardon and probably to his premature death. Reardon's downfall resulted from his leniency towards a woman prisoner while he was making his hourly rounds of the prison cells one night. The usual routine for the police, whenever there were prisoners in the cells, was for the constable on duty to visit the jail every hour of the night to make sure that all was well. In addition, the caretaker-constable was, according to the regulations set down by Town Council, supposed to remain overnight in the building whenever the cells were occupied. However, the police made their own arrangements whereby the caretaker did not stay overnight but prison security depended on the hourly visits of the night constable.[46] On the night in question, Constable Michael Reardon arrived at the station about one o'clock. In the cell was a solitary prisoner, a mulatto named Margaret Farran. No sooner had Reardon taken off his coat and cap and settled himself down comfortably to have a quiet smoke in the Magistrate's room than the prisoner asked him for a drink. Instead of fetching it for her, Reardon let her out of the cell to get it for herself and then chatted with her for some time. On hearing a noise, the girl hopped back into the cell and Reardon put out the light and left the building.[47]

Charges of immoral conduct towards the woman prisoner and dereliction of duty in not returning to the police station each hour throughout the rest of the night were brought against Reardon by the Town Council in October 1895 after one of his fellow constables, Robert Smyth, informed the Council of the incident.[48] The bizarre case became more bizarre when the accused constable, the mayor and town councillors all trotted off to the court house to hold the inquiry in the jail "as one of the parties to be examined is a prisoner in the gaol and cannot be removed from the building." Although both Margaret Farran and Constable Smyth gave evidence against Reardon, the charges were not sustained, but Mayor A.F. Mulhern and several other councillors voted against reinstating Reardon. They argued that although the immorality charge had not been proved, "Reardon's admissions, considering the reputation of the girl, told very much against him. The public would not condone the officer... that Reardon's conduct showed he was not attending to his duty as he should on the night in question...he let her (the prisoner) out of the cell..and then chatted with her...visited the cells a little after one o'clock in the morning...and says he did not intend coming back again." Mayor Mulhern demanded, "Who can tell what might have transpired in the interval?"[49]

That some townsmen did not approve of Reardon's dismissal from the force was evident in a petition presented to Council on 4 November 1895 and signed by merchant G.W. Runnions and 242 others.[50] However, the Council held firm in its decision not to reinstate the constable. Instead, it hired, for the first time, a French-

Canadian policeman, Joseph Lalonde, to replace him.[51] By 14 November 1895 Lalonde donned his new uniform and went on duty, the *Freeholder* describing him as a "fine soldierly looking officer."[52] Four years later the constable who had been dismissed under a cloud after ten years service with the Cornwall force died at the age of sixty-three.[53]

The second bizarre case revived far-off and fearful memories of the days when Cornwall's pioneers were fleeing from tar and feathers, riding the rails or other indignities inflicted upon them for their loyalty to the Crown in the colonies to the south. A century later the women of Mulberry Bend in the north end of Cornwall took to these extra-legal methods for dealing with Susan Blondin whom the *Freeholder* described as "past reforming...(as) for years she has been leading a dissolute life and has given the police quite a lot of trouble." According to the *Freeholder*, the women of Mulberry Bend "after riding her on a rail and improving her beauty with tar and feathers drove her off from that quarter." Blondin then set up in a house in the North End which was burned down, either accidentally or perhaps deliberately as had been done in 1834 in the case of a brothel.[54] The climax came a few days later when people complained to the police that "Susan and several tramps were having a drunken orgy in the barn adjoining the burnt house." Chief Constable Cameron and Officer Robert Smyth set off to arrest the disturbers of the peace. Susan received a sentence of six months in the Mercer Reformatory for women while the one man arrested was let off with a fine of two dollars and costs.[55] It was the only recorded instance of the methods of the American revolutionaries imported to Cornwall.

Haphazard attempts by Council to improve the discipline and organization of the Cornwall police were made throughout the 1890s. In March of 1891 Allan Cameron was promoted to Chief, though it was in name only.[56] Then in December of 1893 a deputy chief was appointed, hardware merchant Hiram Pitts, who strutted up Pitt Street in a "uniform gorgeous to behold," taking his cue from Chief Allan Cameron as to his new duties.[57] In spite of the appointment of a chief and deputy chief, the Fire, Light and Police Committee of Town Council kept a tight grip on the force. This led to increased bickering, resentment and confusion amongst the constables as to whom they were to take orders from or even what their duties were. For instance, Smyth was, among other things, in charge of the new fire alarm bell that had been installed in the fire station in 1893 to take the place of the alarm bell in Knox Church. In addition to his duties as a fire constable and caretaker of Town Hall, Smyth was ordered by Councillor Matthew J. Fraid, Chairman of the Fire, Light and Police Committee, to patrol Pitt Street each night from five to eleven because complaints had been received by Council that Pitt Street was unprotected until eleven o'clock when the night watch came on duty.[58] Fraid was backed up by other councillors with regard to Smyth taking regular police duties, and they ordered Chief Cameron to report to them any constable who refused to obey their instructions.[59] Somewhat plaintively, Smyth asked whether he would be allowed to rest until two o'clock in the afternoon if he was expected to take his share of night work as "he could not work night and day."[60]

The new policeman, Joseph Lalonde, also found himself at odds with the Police Committee when it ordered him to take turns at patrolling Pitt Street. Lalonde argued that he had been hired to do duty in the East end. Councillor Fraid said he found no such provision as was mentioned by Policeman Lalonde and told him he must patrol Pitt Street.[61] Lalonde retorted that he would not, upon which Fraid threw up his hands declaring that the "police were not required in the East end of town any more than in other parts, as the residents of that quarter were as law-abiding as those in other parts of town." Indeed, Fraid wished to know from Council "whom the Police were to take their orders from."[62] This discipline problem was not resolved until 1900 when Council finally handed control of the force over to Chief Cameron, relieving him of night duty and making him responsible for the supervision of the other constables who would henceforth take their orders directly from him.[63]

Thus, at the turn of the century, the police force came into its own with Cameron as Chief, Robert Smyth as second in command, George Crites and Joseph Lalonde as constables and Ed Larose, James Cowley and Fred Seymour assistant policemen.[64] The police force that in the 1860s had consisted of one constable had increased to a force of seven in 1900, paralleling the expansion of the town itself from a population in 1861 of 1,915 to that of 6,704 in 1900, the latter representing a slight decline from the population of 1891.

As far as improvements in town services were concerned, the fire department was at the top of the priority list. In the 1870s it was still manned by volunteers and its equipment consisted of a hand pump supplied with water from the canal. This was supplemented by water cisterns sunk below the streets in the central and northern areas of the town.[65] The disastrous fire of 26 July 1876 that destroyed the Commercial block on Pitt Street put an end to this old fire system. A steam fire engine, made by John D. Ronald's company at Chatham, Ontario, happened to be sitting on the wharf at the end of Pitt Street, awaiting inspection by city fathers who the manufacturer hoped would buy it. As flames jumped into the air from the Commercial block and threatened to spread across to stores on the other side of Pitt Street, the engineer of the steamer, *Bohemian*, took it upon himself to put the new fire engine to the test. With water pumped from the canal, the steam engine was able to keep the flames from spreading. So impressed were town councillors that they lost no time in finalizing the negotiations with Ronald, agreeing to a price of $3,450.[66] The new horse-drawn engine, with its three hose reels carrying 1,000 feet of hose, could operate even when the temperature dropped to twenty degrees below zero.[67] However, the new engine could not operate effectively beyond a thousand feet of the canal which was the source of its water.

One townsman suggested installing portable tanks of water "so as to be able to reach fires north of Second Street."[68] Town councillors did discuss the price of installing waterworks for fire and domestic purposes, but decided "nothing should be done at present...owing to the enlargement of the canal."[69] They appointed John Tobin as engineer of the Fire Department and passed an additional by-law giving the Fire Company power to appoint its own chief, deputy-chief, secretary and treasurer, subject to approval by the Council. Since 1874 Dr. William Cox Allen had headed the volunteer Fire Brigade. When he retired in 1879, Neil McLean became chief for a few years in the early 1880s until he moved to Brockville. The post then went to C.J. Mattice until 1886. In that year the man who would mould the Fire Brigade into a fine fire-fighting machine for the next thirty-nine years, John G. Hunter, became Chief. The fire station was located in one wing of the Town Hall which was enlarged in 1882 so that two fire engines could be housed there.[70]

Two small fires in 1883, one at the Canada Cottons mill and another at Annabelle's wheelwright and blacksmith shop on Amelia Street, were brought under control by the volunteer firemen with the aid of the new steam engine. But a devastating fire broke out in January 1884 in the kitchen of the Commercial Hotel at the corner of Pitt and First Streets. Not only was the hotel levelled; so, too, were three important retail shops — Duncan McRae's large grocery, Turner's hardware shop, and the impressive drygoods store of the Kirkpatrick brothers. This fire, together with one in 1888 that threatened the town hall and fire station itself and burnt to death two prisoners in the police cells, sparked town fathers to action in securing waterworks and fire hydrants.[71] A public meeting of ratepayers was called in the spring of 1886 to authorize the mayor to begin negotiations with an American firm of Watertown, New

York, to build the works. Within a year, eight miles of water mains were laid and fifty-two hydrants installed in the more populous part of town.[72] From then on, firemen could function with reels of hoses which would be attached to the hydrants. Thus the threat and dread of fire lessened as each additional water main was laid.

The waterworks remained in the hands of a private company, that of David and Albert Flack, Amercians who settled in Cornwall to operate the pottery works and expanded into other areas including the waterworks. When the Toronto *Globe* expressed surprise in 1893 that such an important public utility should be in private hands and suggested that public ownership would provide citizens with cheaper water and give the town a valuable source of revenue, Town Council began plans to expropriate the waterworks.[73] It offered the Flack brothers $87,059 but the sale became involved in lengthy litigation that was not resolved until 1900 when the works were bought for $104,000.[74]

Lighting of the town's main streets was by coal-oil lamps until 1882. Then the Cornwall Gas Company set up a small plant at the corner of Amelia and Water Streets. Here gas was extracted from coal that was heated in ovens and treated with oil and steam to improve the yield of gas. Town Council authorized the new company to lay pipes to carry the fuel to various streets and premises and, by the fall of 1882 the first gas lights appeared on the streets, making a considerable improvement over the oil-lamps, though these continued to be used on the streets not serviced by the gas pipe lines. Many other streets were without lights at all. Gradually some houses on the streets with mains began to install gas lighting to replace the coal-oil lamps.[75]

Gas lighting gave way to the more impressive electric lighting on the night of 24 August 1887. This achievement was the result of a single individual, Wilbur R. Hitchcock, and a group of men inspired by Hitchcock's faith in electricity. Hitchcock had helped with the installation of incandescent lighting at the Canada Cottons mill under Edison. He was so convinced of its potential that he leased a small water power plant at the Hodge woollen mill on the south bank of the canal near the Stormont Cotton mill. He then strung several power lines along Cornwall streets. Residents were skeptical and few were induced to receive electricity for home lighting purposes, even though Hitchcock offered to wire some homes free of charge. Frequent interruptions in the crude system kept most residents from experimenting with it. However, a group of Cornwall men watched Hitchcock's efforts with interest. One of them was the King of

Insurance, Duncan Monroe, whose tongue slid easily from English to French to Gaelic.[76] On the night of 27 April 1887 he met with other enthusiasts for electricity at his office to form the Stormont Electric Light & Power Company. Among the men were former mayors William Colquhoun and James Leitch, mill-owner William Hodge, John McIntyre, Peter E. Campbell and Edwin Kewin, partners in one of Cornwall's largest drygoods store, and Archibald Denny, manager of the Ontario Bank that opened in Cornwall in 1882. They pooled financial resources of $25,000 to buy the Hodge woollen mill power site which had two water wheels on the canal. Here they installed two 500 light generators and later added two 100 horse power boilers. In less than four months, these men pushed their project through and the main streets of Cornwall were illuminated with electricity.[77]

This company soon interested itself in supplying another much-needed service in Cornwall — that of a street electric railway system for both passengers and freight. In 1885 Town Council passed a by-law granting the Cornwall Street Railway Company "to build, operate and maintain a Street Railway...to be run at least thirteen hours in the summer and as many as practicable in the winter..at a speed of seven miles per hour...running power to be animals, steam or electricity but subject to safety regulations as set by the municipal government.'[78] By 1887 this company was incorporated but evidently used only horse-drawn cabs.[79] By 1893 the Toronto *Globe* was loud in its assertion that Cornwall needed above all an electric street railway service from the Grand Trunk Railway station to the various factories in town. "The enormous quantities of freight handled at this station, and which has to be hauled to and from the factories, would insure its success," the reporter remarked.[80] Within a few months of the appearance of the issue of the Toronto *Globe* containing the large-scale report on Cornwall, Wilbur Hitchcock was again on the move. After securing from Town Council authority to construct and operate an electric street railway, he persuaded local and outside financial interests to underwrite the project.[81] The first tracks were laid in May 1896 and soon three trolley cars were running from the Grand Trunk station along Pitt to Second Street, replacing "Old Dobbin" as the major means of transportation in town. Passengers paid five cents a ride. Workmen could buy six tickets for a quarter and children's tickets were ten for a quarter.[82]

Financed by a bond issue of the Sun Life Assurance Company of Montreal, the Cornwall Street Railway Company soon found itself in financial difficulties and by 27 January 1899 the Sun Life Assurance Company became the owner of the Street Railway

Company,[83] after receiving vigorous appeals from prominent citizens not to abandon the street railway. William Hodge was put in charge of the company and it merged with the Stormont Electric Light and Power Company. Thus Cornwall's public transportation and power system was owned by the Sun Life Assurance Company of Montreal until 1977 when the city of Cornwall purchased its shares.[84] By 1906 there were four miles of railway track connecting the paper and cotton mills and other manufacturing plants with the Grand Trunk station and with the station of the New York and Ottawa Railway line that opened just west of the town in 1900.[85]

Communications by post and telegraph improved over the latter part of the century. Cornwall's first pioneers were lucky to receive mail once a month in summer and three times over the winter. A traveller in 1878 found the local post office "a most dingy little hole" on the west side of Pitt Street south of First Street.[86] By 1882 construction of a new Post Office and Custom House got underway at the corner of Pitt and Second Streets but it was not opened to the public until June 1885.[87] Inhabitants complained bitterly in 1883 about the early closing hour of the post office — 5:30 p.m. each evening. Word that the Post Office Department would order the local office to remain open from 7:30 a.m. until 8:30 p.m. each day was received with satisfaction by the editor of the *Freeholder*. He remarked on 2 March 1883, "Not only will this prove a great benefit to the working classes, but it will be a great boon to the manufacturing establishments that now find the closing of the mail for the east at 5:30 very inconvenient and are obliged...to send special messengers to the station to post their mail on the train." The editor snorted, "In no other town of the size and importance of Cornwall would the system inaugurated here be tolerated by the people or approved of by the Department." Post Master George McDonell, who held the job from 1870 until 1902, was not so pleased. The new hours prolonged his working day considerably.

Postal communications had been supplemented by telegraph as early as 1847 when the first telegraph wire was installed by the Montreal Telegraph Company. By 1878 a rival telegraph company was in town, the Dominion Telegraph Company.[88] The larger mills maintained direct communications with other cities and towns by means of their own telegraph instruments and operators.[89]

Cornwall's first experiment with a telephone was in 1878 when George S. Jarvis arranged a call with Reverend Thomas Henderson, a friend of the inventor, Alexander Graham Bell.[90] Two years later the Montreal Telegraph Company agent, L.H. Stiles, established the first telephone service in town, with lines to the Grand Trunk station, the American House and all the factories.[91] Another milestone was reached in 1882 when R.W. MacFarlane, editor of the *Reporter*, chatted by telephone with L.B. MacFarlane, general manager of the Bell Telephone Company in Montreal, the first long distance call.[92] At first Stiles printed cards with the names and numbers of the few town telephone owners. Then, as more and more businesses and some homes installed telephones, Cornwall had its first directory in August 1887 prepared by the local agent, A.T. Porteous, who kept the switchboard in his bookstore on Pitt Street.[93] Among the thirty-four telephone subscribers was the *Standard* Publishing Company where for many years the telephone rated a special soundproof office of its own. News staff approached this office with considerable trepidation for the task of receiving news over the telephone, while reporters often preferred to bring their stories to the office rather than trust them to the "wire".[94]

The development of the press in Cornwall during the latter part of the nineteenth century tended to be an up and down affair with several weeklies having ephemeral existences. John Sandfield Macdonald's *Freeholder* was the exception. It weathered libel suits brought against it by Mayor William Cox Allen who did not like being called a thief of public money by the editor of the *Freeholder*.[95] Unrepentant, the *Freeholder*, in the free-swinging journalistic style of the era, returned to the attack with vigour. "For five years past the administration...of the Town of Cornwall has been directed solely by Dr. Allen...in our opinion, it has been a swindle.[96] The *Freeholder* sailed along smoothly during the 1870s under John Sandfield Macdonald's son, Henry, as proprietor, and Alexander McLean as editor, coming out regularly each Friday morning and collecting a modest annual subscription of $1.50 from its readers. It continued to lash out at political foes, especially those it considered turncoats. Cornwall's rising star, Dr. Darby Bergin, came in for his share of abuse. Accusing Bergin of being "a turncoat in the truest sense" who had deserted to the Conservatives after he had "failed to persuade Mr. Mackenzie (Prime Minister Alexander MacKenzie) that he was the man for the Irish Roman Catholic representation in the Liberal Cabinet of '73," the *Freeholder* called Bergin a "snapdragon, a degenerate and mongrel politician...who deserted to the enemy with the expectation that he would get from them what he had been refused by those whom he had deserted."[97] Bombast and abuse were part and parcel of journalism's lively production at this time and Cornwall's most stable weekly indulged with gusto and with impunity in the trade. By 1885 Charles W. Young bought out the *Freeholder* and within twenty years had nearly doubled its circulation, keeping it under moderate liberal colours and maintaining its format as a strictly local newspaper, leaving national and international news to the metropolitan dailies.[98]

While the *Freeholder* continued to appear regularly from its first printing in 1846, opposition papers came and went. The successor to the *Observer* was the *Constitutional*, founded by Watson Little in the late 1840s. It survived until 1863 when John McDonell resuscitated it in January 1865 under a new name, the *Advertiser*. This lasted only three years. A second Reform journal, the *Cornwall Economist*, was established in 1861 by William S. Johnston, but it continued only about a year.[99] Its owner-editor removed to Port Hope and eventually took a job with George Brown on the Toronto *Globe*. A third Reform newspaper appeared in 1867, the *Cornwall Gazette*, with George Burden as proprietor. Initially it was what was known in Cornwall as "an Anti-Sandfield" journal, that is, it opposed John S. Macdonald who by the late 1860s was arrayed against the majority of the Reform party. However, this newspaper fell by the wayside in the early 1870s. A new and decidedly conservative newspaper, *The Reporter*, started up on 1 August 1876 under R.W. MacFarlane as proprietor and editor. According to H.E. Belden's report in his *Historical Atlas* of 1878, this paper, "by utterly ignoring the factions into which the people of Cornwall were then divided... succeeded in organizing the Conservative party in that constituency from the demoralized condition into which the long prevalence of personal rancour had transformed it into a united and substantial political compact."[100] The founding of another weekly, *The News*, in 1883 meant that for a number of years in the mid-1880s Cornwall had three weeklies at the same time — the *Freeholder*, the *Reporter* and the *News*, another indication of the expansion of the town's population.[101]

The man who set up the first and most enduring of the conservative newspapers was another lad from Glengarry, Roderick R. McLennan, the world champion for hammer-throwing and heavy weight throwing whose records seldom, if ever, have been equalled.[102] After making his fortune in railway construction, McLennan returned to Eastern Ontario, spending his time between Cornwall and Alexandria. Along with erecting some of Cornwall's most imposing business buildings — the Glengarry block, the Ontario Bank and the Iron Block — he branched out into the publishing business, buying up the *Reporter* upon the death of its editor, Robert W. MacFarlane, and merging it with the *News*, which he bought from the Porteous brothers. Like many another ambitious man whose aspirations turned to the political field, McLennan realized that the ownership of a local newspaper, devoted to the party which he hoped to serve in Parliament, could have its advantages. McLennan's new paper, the *Standard*, made its first appearance in Cornwall on 13 May 1886,[103] and soon had a new home in the *Standard* block which McLennan constructed. Within two years he found the right editor for the *Standard*, thirty-six-year-old William Gibbens of the Ottawa *Citizen*. That religious affiliation no longer took first place over political affiliation was evident in that the fiercely Presbyterian McLennan chose the firm Church of England Gibbens to defend conservative interests in Cornwall, particularly those of Colonel Roderick R. McLennan. For almost fifty years, the *Standard*, under Gibbens, and the *Freeholder*, under Charles Young, continued in friendly and courteous rivalry until the deaths of both, Young in 1927 and Gibbens in 1932. It was then that the *Standard* and *Freeholder* buried their political axes and merged as the *Standard-Freeholder*.[104] It was published twice weekly, not becoming a daily until 1 April 1941.

Water communication had been Cornwall's first means of transportation. The building of the canal reinforced the east-west direction of trade past Cornwall, though it eventually led to the establishment of large factories dependent on water power from the canal. The north-south direction of trade and travel became more pronounced in the latter part of the nineteenth century when trade between Cornwall and Fort Covington, New York, was carried out by a daily line of small steamers operated by Captain Smallman of Dundee, Quebec.[105] Trade between Cornwall and Montreal was maintained by a large side-wheeler, the *St. Francis*, which made semi-weekly trips in the 1870s. When a rival company began operating a larger steamer, the *Bohemian*, in the late 1870s, competition became so fierce that Cornwall people could get cabin passage to Montreal for twenty-five cents. Deck passengers paid what they pleased, and those who simply wanted a trip through the Beauharnois Canal could enjoy it free.[106]

In 1896 the Montreal and Cornwall Navigation Company was incorporated with its head office in Cornwall and Arnold Neilson Smith as general manager. Established to carry freight and passengers between Kingston, Cornwall and Montreal, the company's steamers stopped at Cornwall chiefly to carry to Montreal cheese produced by the Cornwall Cheese Board that was organized in May 1898.[107] The *Brittanic*, a side-wheeler with steel hulls, was this company's best known steamship. Passage to Massena, New York was by the steamer, the *Triton*, which had "ample accommodation for horses and waggons". In 1889 the *Triton* plied between Cornwall, Barnhart's

Island and Massena Point.[108] Water communication along the St. Lawrence was also provided by the boats of the Royal Mail Line. Some of the favourite outings for Cornwallites were Saturday afternoon trips up the canal and down the Long Sault Rapids or moonlight excursions to Stanley Island and Lake St. Francis.

Sidewalks, sewers and sanitation all received attention from town fathers in the years of the town's expansion at the end of the century. Planked sidewalks and a few stretches of flagstone sidewalks were, for many years, the only improvement made to mother earth on the town's sidewalks. In 1891 Archibald Denny, manager of the Ontario Bank, urged that streets be numbered and their names placed at intersections "for the very great convenience of everybody."[109] Cornwall's Streets running east and west had been numbered First to Ninth Streets when the town was first laid out by Sir John Johnson's surveyors.[110] The adoption of names of royalty and of major political personages for the streets running north and south occurred some time after 1792 for they do not appear on the Chewett map of 1792. Cumberland, York, Augustus, and Amelia Streets were all named for children of George III. Gloucester Street honoured the King's brother, William Henry, Duke of Gloucester. Pitt was named for Prime Minister William Pitt, Sydney Street took its name from Thomas Townsend, Lord Sydney, one of George III's ministers. Bedford Street is named for Lord John Russell, the 4th Duke of Bedford, while Marlborough commemorates the famous Duke of Marlborough.[111] Although the town's streets may have been graced with signs bearing their names by 1891, it was not until 1893 that new road beds were laid and Mayor Roderick R. McLennan and ex-Mayor William Colquhoun set an example by having granolithic sidewalks constructed in front of their properties.[112] Other businessmen along Pitt Street promised to follow their example the next spring, but progress was slow. The *Freeholder* bitterly lamented as late as 1898 that "the Streets of the town are in a disgraceful condition and a standing hint to people of leisure and means to settle elsewhere than in Cornwall."[113] It was not until 1904 that the first concrete sidewalks appeared.

The sanitary condition of the town came in for scrupulous attention whenever epidemics threatened. Without such outbreaks, other needs took priority. A sewage system of sorts existed as early as 1871, for on April 14 of that year town councillors authorized the high constable to call upon the "different owners (of properties) on Pitt Street south of Second Street to the Wharf...to fill up with stones or earth the holes caused by the breaking of the Main Sewer."[114] The sewer system must still have been in a very primitive state by 1885, the year that Justice Robert Smith of the Supreme Court of Canada arrived in town as a young lawyer. "When I came here," he recalled, "there (was) no sewerage system. There were two sewers on Water Street along the canal and that was the whole sewerage system in those days."[115]

The outbreak of several cases of smallpox and diphtheria in the fall of 1878 led to a higher number of deaths that year than was usual in town — some 55.[116] It was not until the outbreak of scarlet fever in the spring of 1883 and the fear of cholera spreading in July of the same year that the Health Committee of Town Council ordered the town's two policemen, Allan Cameron and William Lawrence, to make a "thorough survey to ascertain the premises that were not in a proper state of cleanliness and to report such to the Health Commissioner."[117] The next year a Board of Health was appointed in conformity with a new provincial law regulating municipal Health Boards. The new Board consisted of Mayor James T. Kirkpatrick, Reeve James Leitch, Councillors Merritt Darby, Robert Brown, Homer Stiles, John Snetsinger, together with Doctors Edward A. Graveley and Charles J. Hamilton, and R.P. Eastman. The duties of the new Board were far more extensive than those of the old Health Committee. Its members were to keep the town free from "nuisances likely to affect the health of its inhabitants", inspect wells to make sure they were clean, and they could make regulations to "prevent the spread of any infectious disease that makes its appearance within the limits of the town."[118] Dr. Charles Hamilton was appointed Medical Officer of the town, a post he held, without pay, until his death in 1937.[119] To assist Dr. Hamilton, Police Constable Allan Cameron was named sanitary inspector for the area east of Amelia Street. Police Constable William Lawrence was to act in the same role west of Amelia Street.[120]

The Board of Health had its hands full in early January of 1887. Snow fell so heavily on 17 January that the cotton mills closed down at four o'clock that afternoon to allow the workers to get home before dark. Ice blocked the flow of water at Windmill Point and the water level of the river was high as the temperature level dropped to twenty-two degrees below zero. Few ventured out on such a night. As daylight dawned, some hardy souls made their way to work only to discover that the water was over the canal bank and forcing itself up the streets from the river. Quickly one man dashed to St. John's Presbyterian Church to ring the alarm bell. By six o'clock, water had reached up Pitt Street north of First Street, overflowing Fly Creek and circling to the north as far as the Grand Trunk station which could only be reached by Marlborough Street. Along the river front, the mills were flooded to the second storey. At the Canada Cottons mill, François Bergeron got to safety, but then returned to get his tools and, trapped by the waters, lost his life.[121] Two other workers, Joseph Miron and Frank Robidoux, fearful that the former's mother was trapped in her home near the river bank on Prince Arthur Street, took a rowboat and axe to reach the house. Water was already two feet from the second floor where the mother and her baby were stranded. Miron and Robidoux got through a top window and, by cutting a hole in the ceiling, were able to pull the mother and the child to safety and they reached Prince Albert Street by boat.[122] Though the city suffered fearfully from the water, no serious illness followed in the wake of the icy flooding. The main job of the town's medical officer and the members of the Board of Health was to ensure that the dirt swept up by the flooding was removed from the cellars and first storeys of homes and businesses. So thoroughly was the town cleansed and kept in good sanitary condition that, by 1893, it was described by the Toronto *Globe* as ranking "among the best in the Province" as regards its sanitary condition.[123] Only in 1899 did the town suffer a smallpox scare. As soon as the Board of Health learned that a case had occurred in town, it arranged for the "poor to be vaccinated free of charge" and ordered that all who had not been vaccinated within seven years were to be re-vaccinated.[124]

Although the Toronto *Globe* in 1893 acclaimed Cornwall generously, declaring that "The general appearance of the town, the manifestations of prosperity and progress, are not to be surpassed by any other place of the same size in the Dominion, and everything indicated that the people of Cornwall have faith in its future," more astute local businessmen such as Donald Ban Maclennan, who headed the law firm of Maclennan, Liddell and Cline, warned the Town Council in 1896 that the "town had been receding, instead of growing, for some years past; and unless we obtained some new industries, or more railway accommodation, it would collapse.[125] Maclennan may have overstated the case a little in his plea before Council for financial support of the New York and Ottawa Railway line. He argued that a railway running north and south would cut into the monopoly then held by the east-west Grand Trunk Railway, thus facilitating the export to the United States of the products of Eastern Ontario, including cereals, horses and horned cattle, and bring American trade to Canada.[126] Mayor A.F. Mulhern, himself a businessman, together with Reeve Angus Lalonde, Deputy Reeves Peter E. Campbell and Dr. Edward Graveley, and Councillors L.A. Ross and John A. Chisholm, favoured granting the proposed railway a bonus in the area of $15,000 to $20,000. Ratepayers approved a bonus of $35,000, providing the railway company built a passenger station in town.[127]

This municipal support for a second railway line and station in Cornwall was part of the town's forward-looking policy designed not only to hold the factories already established, but to attract new ones. So, too, was the establishment of the Cornwall Board of Trade in March of 1890.[128] Fifty-five businessmen, headed by John McIntyre as president, James T. Kirkpatrick vice-president, C.W. Brownell, secretary and Archibald Denny as treasurer formed the executive of the first Board whose members had to be resident within the district and who were in the category of merchant, broker, trader, mechanic, manufacturer, agent of a bank or insurance company. Among the charter members were Duncan Monroe, Edward O'Callaghan, Peter E. Campbell, A.W. Flack, William Hodge, A.T. Porteous, N.J. Fraid, J.J. Phillips, J.E. Snetsinger and F.C. Myers.[129] Indicative of the slight decline Cornwall was experiencing was the fact that the new Board after some initial successes in persuading the Canadian Express Company to set up an office in Cornwall and in helping to settle a strike of millhands, decided to dissolve in 1894 and it remained dormant until 1905.[130] More apparent as the decade neared the century mark was the lack of population growth as compared to the expansion in the 1880s. The town's population in 1901 was scarcely a hundred more than it had been in 1891 when it numbered 6,805. What was more distressing to business and municipal leaders was that within the next decade of the new century, the town's population fell to 6,074 and did not begin to climb until the decade of 1911 to 1921 when it reached 7,419.[131]

However, these ominous signs were not so apparent to the ordinary citizen of the 1890s who enjoyed the fanfare and excitement of the town's celebrations of Queen Victoria's Diamond Jubilee on 22 June 1897[132] and rejoiced in 1898 when the Stormont millhands ended their week-long strike after the company agreed to make up to them any loss of earnings the spoolroom hands might experience because of improved machinery.[133] In another direction, Cornwallites held to liquor prohibition by a slight majority even though the rest of the province voted to reject it.[134] Thus the town ushered in the new century dry, though its citizens had the consolation of being able to drink cold pure-running water from any of the four handsome drinking fountains recently put up by the Women's Christian Temperance Union.[135] One of these fountains was erected in front of the County House in memory of Judge Jacob Pringle, the town's historian. It also served as a silent reminder to members of the Bar and others that there were alternatives to the numerous splendid bars located in the Rossmore and other equally elegant hotels in late nineteenth century Cornwall. Not to be outdone by the women and their cold water drinking fountains, the military-minded of the town applied for and received four cannons on a permanent loan from the federal government in 1898.[136] Two of them flanked the water fountain at the Court House and the others were placed in the new Central Park at the foot of Amelia Street facing the canal, a park that had been the pet project of Councillor William Dingwall.[137]

NOTES

1. Minutes, Town Council, 4 September 1874; *Reporter*, 10 March 1877.
2. Minutes, Town Council, 18 January 1878; J.G. Harkness, *History of Stormont, Dundas and Glengarry*, 175; J.F. Pringle, *Lunenburgh, or the Old Eastern District*, 148.
3. Harkness, 432.
4. Minutes, Town Council, 18 January, 23 August, 1869; 17 January 1870.
5. *Ibid.*, 3 April 1871.
6. *Lovell's Ontario Directory*, 1871, 28; according to the *Reporter*, 19 May 1883, one of the Grand Trunk detectives in 1883 was Constable Madden.
7. Minutes, Town Council, 9 and 21 April 1873, 218-19.
8. *Ibid.*, 2 June 1873, 250.
9. *Ibid.*; see also *Standard-Freeholder*, 29 June 1934.
10. Minutes, Town Council, 21 February 1876, 6 November 1878, 152.
11. *Ibid.*, 3 April 1884.
12. *Ibid.*, 6 February 1885.
13. *Ibid.*, 20 March 1876.
14. *Ibid.*
15. *Ibid.*, 5 June 1876.
16. *Ibid.*, 1 May 1876.
17. *Reporter*, 15 September 1877.
18. *Cornwall Observer*, 8 January 1836.
19. For the by-laws, see Minutes, Town Council, 1 May 1876.
20. *Ibid.*, 8 June and 31 August 1878.
21. *Ibid.*, 15 January 1883, 7; *Reporter*, 19 May 1883.
22. Petition of Alick Lashamb, William Payment, James Tobin, Allan Cameron, Isaac Blondin and 22 others, in Minutes, Town Council, 1883-86, 48.
23. Minutes, Town Council, 5 April 1883, 56.
24. *Ibid.*, 24 April 1884, 52.
25. *Ibid.*, 16 November 1883, 196; 3 March 1884, 255; *Reporter*, 22 December 1883.

26. Minutes, Town Council, 3 April 1884.
27. *Ibid.*, 3 September 1877; *Freeholder*, 4 September 1883.
28. *Reporter*, 19 May 1883.
29. *Freeholder*, 11 July 1884; see also Minutes, Town Council, 7 July 1884.
30. *Freeholder*, 18 July 1884.
31. *Ibid.*, 7 November 1884.
32. Minutes, Town Council, 22 July 1884, 319.
33. *Ibid.*, 8 September 1884, 337; *Freeholder*, 7 November 1884.
34. Minutes, Town Council, 7 March 1887, 80.
35. *Ibid.*, 7 June 1886, 604.
36. *Ibid.*, 2 May 1887, 106.
37. *Ibid.*, 7 March 1887.
38. *Freeholder*, 7 May 1886, 3 July 1891, 11 and 17 May 1887; 20 June 1890.
39. *Ibid.*, 5 September 1884.
40. *Ibid.*, 19 February 1886.
41. *Ibid.*, 11 March 1887.
42. *Ibid.*, 15 May 1891.
43. *Ibid.*, 5 February 1897.
44. *Ibid.*, 23 April 1886.
45. For railway tramps, see *Freeholder*, 30 September 1904; for attack on the Andersons, see *Standard*, 2 February 1888.
46. Enquiry into charges against Constable Michael Reardon, Minutes, Town Council, 14, 17, 21 October 1895, 473-85.
47. Mayor A. F. Mulhern's summary, *ibid.*, 481-85.
48. *Ibid.*, 473-75.
49. *Ibid.*, 481-485.
50. *Ibid.*, 487.
51. Minutes, Town Council, 8 November 1895, 494-95.
52. *Freeholder*, 15 November 1895.
53. *Ibid.*, 8 December 1899.
54. *Cornwall Observer*, 27 November 1835.
55. *Freeholder*, 15 October 1897.
56. *Ibid.*, 4 March 1891.
57. *Ibid.*, 29 December 1893.
58. Minutes, Town Council, 20 October 1898, 3.
59. *Ibid.*
60. *Ibid.*, 14 November 1898, 12.
61. *Ibid.*, 20 October 1898, 3.
62. *Ibid.*
63. *Ibid.*, 14 May 1900; *Freeholder*, 18 May 1900.
64. *Standard-Freeholder*, 29 June 1934.
65. Grant, "Reminiscences," in *Standard-Freeholder*, 28 September 1946.
66. Minutes, Town Council, 17 August 1876, 104-05; Pringle, 142.
67. *Canadian Illustrated News*, 26 January 1878.
68. *Reporter*, 23 September 1876.
69. Minutes, Town Council, 1 May 1876 and 9 June 1876.

70. For various fire chiefs, see *Cornwall Observer*, 7 January 1841; Minutes, Town Council, 9 June 1876, 82, 13 October 1876, 137, and 2 June 1884, 294; *Canadian Illustrated News*, 26 January 1878; *Standard-Freeholder*, 30 December 1944; Pringle, 69, 135, 142.

71. *Freeholder*, 19 and 26 January 1883; Pringle, 144 and 287.

72. *Standard-Freeholder*, 6 August 1946.

73. *Globe*, Toronto, 18 November 1893; Harkness, 369.

74. Minutes, Town Council, 11 June 1897, 318; 12 July 1897, 329; 14 May 1900, 267-68.

75. Justice Robert Smith's paper to the Stormont, Dundas and Glengarry Historical Society, 15 January 1932, 7; *Standard-Freeholder*, 29 June 1934, 7 October 1946 and 24 June 1967; Pringle, 143.

76. *Old Boys' Reunion*, 1906.

77. Ross-Ross and Farnsworth, *History of Engineering in Cornwall*, 18; *Standard-Freeholder*, 29 June 1934 and 30 April 1937.

78. Minutes, Town Council, 11 December 1886, 513.

79. *Standard-Freeholder*, 3 August 1946.

80. *Globe*, Toronto, 18 November 1893.

81. Minutes, Town Council, 9 February 1894, 58.

82. *Glengarry News*, 1 May 1896; *Standard-Freeholder*, Centennial issue, 29 June 1934, 80; *Standard-Freeholder*, 7 October 1946; Harkness, 365.

83. *Standard-Freeholder*, 3 August 1946.

84. *Standard-Freeholder*, 25 March 1979; Ross-Ross, et al, *History of Engineering in Cornwall*, 16; Harkness, 366.

85. Ross-Ross and Farnsworth, *History of Engineering in Cornwall*, 26; *Old Boys' Reunion*, 1906.

86. *Canadian Illustrated News*, 26 January 1878, 55.

87. *Freeholder*, 9 June 1882, 26 May 1882; Pringle, 287-288.

88. *Canadian Illustrated News*, 26 January 1878, 55; Pringle, 137.

89. Grant, "Reminiscences", in *Standard-Freeholder*, 28 September 1946.

90. Harkness, 366.

91. *Reporter*, 27 February 1880.

92. *Standard-Freeholder*, 29 June 1934; Harkness, 367.

93. Grant, "Reminiscences", in *Standard-Freeholder*, 28 September 1946.

94. *Standard-Freeholder*, 29 June 1934, 29 September 1972.

95. *Freeholder*, 13 September 1867.

96. *Ibid.*, 8 December 1871.

97. *Ibid.*, 12, 19 and 26 May, 25 August, 1882.

98. *Old Boys' Reunion*, 1906.

99. *Cornwall Economist*, 14 March 1861.

100. H. Belden, *Historical Atlas of Stormont, Dundas and Glengarry*, vi.

101. For general discussion on newspapers, see *ibid.*, and Harkness, 371-376; Upper Canada Village: Cornwall Press Reel No. 1.

102. *Globe*, Toronto, 18 November 1893; *Old Boys' Reunion*, 1906.

103. *Standard-Freeholder*, 13 May 1936.

104. *Old Boys' Reunion*, 1906; *Globe*, Toronto, 18 November 1893; Belden, *Historical Atlas*, vi; *Standard-Freeholder*, 28 April 1932 and 13 May 1936; Harkness, 375.

105. Grant, "Reminiscences", in *Standard-Freeholder*, 28 September 1946.

106. *Canadian Illustrated News*, 26 January 1878, 55.

107. *Freeholder*, 3 June 1898; H.M. Stiles, *Official History of the Cornwall Cheese and Butter Board*, 196.

108. *Freeholder*, 7 June 1889.

109. *Ibid.*, 4 September 1891.

110. See the Chewett map, 1792, V3/440.

111. For a discussion of naming of streets, see *Standard-Freeholder*, 1 August 1942.

112. *Globe*, Toronto, 18 November 1893.

113. *Freeholder*, 3 June 1898.

114. Minutes, Town Council, 14 April 1871.

115. Robert Smith's Reminiscences, paper delivered to Stormont, Dundas and Glengarry Historical Society, 15 January 1932.

116. *Reporter*, 12 and 19 January 1878.

117. Minutes, Town Council, 3 July 1883, 96.

118. *Freeholder*, 13 June 1884.

119. Harkness, 322.

120. Minutes, Town Council, 11 June 1884, 310.

121. *Standard-Freeholder*, 18 January 1933.

122. A.D. Miron to editor of *Standard-Freeholder*, March 1977.

123. *Globe*, 18 November 1893.

124. Minutes, Town Council, 4 February 1899, 60-61.

125. *Globe*, Toronto, 18 November 1893; Minutes, Town Council, 19 October 1896, 160-64; Harkness, 424.

126. Minutes, Town Council, 19 October 1896; see also, Minutes, 11 June 1900, 279-280.

127. *Ibid.*, 29 November 1897, 413.

128. Minutes, Board of Trade, see first entry on 30 April 1890; *Standard-Freeholder*, 29 June 1934.

129. *Standard-Freeholder*, 29 June 1932.

130. *Ibid.*

131. *Census*, 1931, ii, 79.

132. *Freeholder*, 12 May 1897.

133. *Ibid.*, 2 September 1898.

134. *Ibid.*, 30 September 1898.

135. *Old Boys' Reunion*, 1906.

136. Minutes, Town Council, 14 March and 13 June 1898, 459 and 509.

137. Minutes, Town Council, 30 September 1895, 457.

TOWN o. CORNWALL

10   20   40   60   80 rods

10 chains or 40 rods to one inch

e-Industrial Cornwall — 1862

·e location of several tanneries on north Pitt Street, an ashery on
xth Street and one south of the Canal, a door and sash
anufactury on Fifth Street, and grist, saw and flour mills south of
·e canal to the west of Pitt Street.

AC: V1/420, Stormont, Dundas, Glengarry, Prescott and Russell,
·44923).

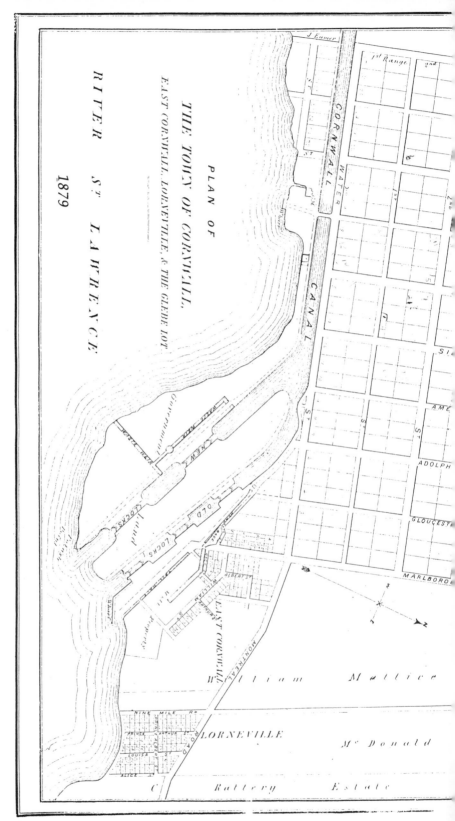

PLAN OF

THE TOWN OF CORNWALL,

EAST CORNWALL, LORNEVILLE, & THE GLEBE LOT

RIVER S.T LAWRENCE

1879

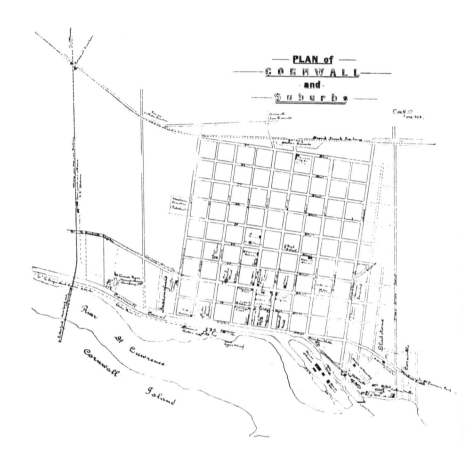

Cornwall in 1906

'Some of Cornwall's Notables', May 24, 1865. From left to right (standing) John (Cariboo) Cameron, John R. Woods, James Craig, Alex McLennan, John B. McKenzie, Sheriff D.E. McIntyre. (sitting) Dr. Wm. Cox Allan, Edward Allan, Arthur McLean, Duncan McLennan.

Credit: Public Archives of Canada: neg. PA 51609.

287

Cornwall, Pitt and First Street, 1906.
Credit: *Cornwall, Old Boys' Re-Union, 1906.*

Interior of J.E. Chevrier's store, 1906.
Credit: *Cornwall: Old Boys' Re-Union, 1906.*

Rossmore House, 1906.
Credit: *Cornwall: Old Boys' Re-Union, 1906.*

Old Cornwall Town Hall, Fire Station, and Fire Brigade, 1906.   Building 1863-1968.
Credit: *Cornwall: Old Boys' Re-Union - 1906.*

Chapter XIII

Victorian Cornwallites at Church and at Play

Cornwall had come a long way since the turbulent times of 1787 when John Collins and William Dummer Powell had visited the small pioneer loyalist settlement and concluded that the widespread social unrest and decline in public morals and manners were due to the absence of churches and schools. Within a hundred years the town had acquired eight churches, seven schools, a seven-man police force, and a county jail for those who defied the law.

This increase in the number of schools and churches in the 1870s and 1880s paralleled the growth in the population of the town and in the areas immediately surrounding it. Centre Ward remained the most populous in the 1870s when the first factories were being rebuilt. The area to the East where the Canada Cottons mill and the Canadian Woollen Manufacturing Company were located remained largely English-speaking during the 1870s. The census of 1881 showed that an ethnic melange existed in the East Ward — 497 French, 300 Irish, 238 Scotch, 175 English, 75 Germans and eight Italians.[1] Thus, although the French-speaking were the largest single language group in the East Ward by 1881, they were out-numbered by 796 residents of other backgrounds. At the Canada Cottons mill the millhands in 1878 were almost entirely Scottish in origin, and their families occupied the cottages and the boarding houses erected near the mill by the company.[2] Among the 200 operatives at the nearby woollen mill there were likely many French workers, but there was no concentration at that time of French in the East End. They were fairly evenly distributed in the three wards — 421 in the West Ward, 405 in the Centre Ward and 497 in the East Ward.[3]

It was the building of the huge weave shed at Canada Cottons in 1882 that probably accounted for the shift in the balance of population in the East End from a preponderance of English-speaking workers to one of predominantly French-speaking workers. Yet, in

292

this decade of factory expansion, the greatest population growth was felt in the West Ward. This had 2,397 people in 1891 while the East Ward numbered 2,292.[4] The most populous ward in preceding decades, Centre Ward, thus lost out to its flanks. The rebuilding of the Stormont mill at the end of the 1870s and the construction of the Toronto Paper mill, both in the western area of the town, accounted for this population expansion in the West Ward.

This expansion put pressure on schools and churches, so much so that the four churches of the 1850s had to be replaced by larger ones in the 1880s and 1890s and, before the century was out, three other churches were erected. The tiny congregation of Methodists, in all fourteen counting both Wesleyan and Episcopalian, had a small chapel in 1846. With the help of the much larger number of township Methodists, they erected a small brick church in 1861 on the south side of Fourth Street.[5] By 1878 when local Methodists had increased to just over 100 and township Methodists numbered 585, the congregation built a bigger church at the corner of First and Sydney Streets, capable of seating 500.[6] Cornwall's Methodists did not number 500 until 1891, but they undertook by 1893 to establish a mission on Cornwall Island under Reverend E. Tennant, the second time within the century that a Cornwall protestant congregation attempted to proselytize among the St. Regis Indians.[7]

Cornwall Episcopalians, or as they were now more commonly called, Church of England members, experienced little increase in their numbers from 1851 to 1871. At the mid-century they numbered 557. Twenty years later they had increased by only forty-five members.[8] Yet even this slight increase in numbers put pressure on the facilities of the small wooden church that Strachan had erected in 1806. By 1867 parishioners began plans for a new church. Then, when they received news in the fall of that year of the death of Bishop John Strachan, it was decided that a new church, rising up in the place of the old one, would be a fitting memorial to the man who had done so much for Cornwall and the province. The Rector, Archdeacon Henry Patton, appointed an imposing committee of twenty churchmen to manage the undertaking. Among them were Mayor William Cox Allen, Postmaster and County Registrar George Carleton Wood, Honourable Philip Vankoughnet, the Chancellor of Ontario, Dr. George Pringle, P.E. Adams, one of Cornwall's master builders, Judge George Stephen Jarvis, who had been president of the old Board of Police in the 1830s, and his son, Town Clerk George Sherwood Jarvis. Also on the committee were a number whose names bore testimony to their direct descent from the original Loyalists — Jacob Gallinger, A.J. Barnhart and W.G. Barnhart,

Philip Vankoughnet, Thomas G. Anderson, John G. Snetsinger and R.P. Eastman.[9] Four members of the committee, Gallinger, Anderson, Eastman and Vankoughnet also boasted forbears who had been on the committee set up in 1805 by Strachan to make plans for the first Trinity Church.[10]

With impressive ceremony the cornerstone was laid in July 1869, but from then on quarrels with the contractor, Albert Gordon French, arose. Settling of the foundation of the belfry, which was built on the site of the old church, caused difficulty, and the contractor was accused of substituting materials, all of which led Dr. William Cox Allen to take over the contract. Allen was promptly sued by French with the result of long-drawn out litigation.[11] The church, finally completed in 1875, was built in Gothic style with dark limestone from Cornwall quarries, relieved by Ohio sandstone.[12] Officially named the Bishop Strachan Memorial Church, its old name of Trinity seemed to stick. Though the architect's plans called for a lofty spire and many published illustrations of Trinity Memorial Church show the church with a steeple, the spire was never erected because it was feared that the tower would not support one.[13] The seating capacity of 580 and choir stalls for twenty barely accommodated the total number of Church of England people in town, an indication that the church builders anticipated backsliders.

A reporter of the *Canadian Illustrated News* described the new Trinity as a "beautiful stone church...erected to the memory of Bishop Strachan. It takes the place of the venerable Trinity Church,...which has been moved back bodily and serves for Sunday school purposes during the summer. The new church cost $37,000, of which $30,000 has been paid....In the graveyard...there is a quaint old relic in the shape of an enclosure some twelve feet square and six feet high. At one corner is a padlocked door almost off its hinges. Outside, leaning against the stones, stands an oaken slab or tablet which sets forth that the enclosure contains, with others, the remains of Colonel James Gray who died in 1795."[14]

As the factories attracted more and more people to town, the congregation at Trinity Memorial, like that of other local churches, began to increase rapidly and by 1884 had some 180 families, probably accounting for most of the 912 Church of England members reported in the 1881 census. In this year the parish built a hall with funds supplied by Canon Jacob Mountain. Known as Mountain Memorial Hall, it was a one-storey building on Augustus Street, capable of providing much-needed Sunday school facilities and a rendezvous for the ever-increasing social and service organizations of the church. The benefactor, Canon Mountain, was the son of Reverend Salter Mountain who had served the parish as rector from 1817 until his death in 1830, and whose wife, Anna Maria Mountain, died forty-three years after "a life in the parish that has never been surpassed," as her son dutifully recorded.[15] Indeed, the children of the parish acknowledged her dedication. A window was placed in the south wall of the nave in her memory "by the pupils of the Sunday and Parish Schools of Cornwall of which she was the founder."[16] Canon Jacob Mountain's beneficence did not end with the donation of the parish hall. In 1885 he gave a set of nine chimes as a memorial to various members of his family who had served the church. The chimes rang out over Cornwall for the first time on Christmas Eve, and ever since have been part of Cornwall's musical heritage. For forty-seven years, from 1888 to 1935, John Sugden was chimer. Then Burton Heward and his son, William, became the carilloneurs.[17]

With the crowding of Church of England workers and others into the East End to get jobs in the cotton and woollen mills, a second church was needed. Trinity parish undertook this mission, becoming the first of the established Cornwall parishes to provide a place of worship for workers in the East End. Through the continued generosity of Canon Jacob Mountain, a small wooden church, known as Mountain Memorial Church, was built on Marlborough Street in 1886.[18] Two years later, Canon Mountain, then sixty-four, took on the work of the mission church. Within five years the parish had out-grown the small church. Once more Canon Mountain dipped into his pocket to supply funds for a new brick church. Financial help came also from the ladies of the parish who held bazaars to aid the church fund.[19] Built in Gothic style with a fine spire, the Church of the Good Shepherd was ready for service in 1893. The Toronto *Globe* observed that it was well named. "While it is to be dedicated to Him who is the shepherd of His people, yet we think that Dr. Mountain has shown the true spirit of a careful under-shepherd in providing such a beautiful place of worship for those in his charge."[20]

In the same decade that saw the erection of the second Church of England in Cornwall, both Presbyterian congregations expanded into larger and more impressive churches. The divisions of the 1840s between Free Kirk and established Church of Scotland were healed in 1875 with a reunion of all Presbyterian congregations in Canada. There were even some talk in Cornwall of the Free Kirk and St. John's re-uniting as a single congregation, but this did not happen. Instead, the Free Kirk, to distinguish itself from St. John's and yet indicate its reconciliation with the parent church, voted itself a new name in 1876 - Knox Presbyterian Church. That the issue of a name did not command great attention is evident from the small number who voted, twenty-eight for Knox and eight for an alternative name - Arnott.[21]

Knox congregation began plans for a larger church in 1882, but they did not mature until 1884 when the old church on Second Street was sold for $2,175 and a new one built for $16,600. Dedicated on 14 June 1885, the new Knox Church was built of brick with stone foundation and facings, and described by the *Freeholder* as "one of the handsomest structures in the province."[22] Having provided a place for the spiritual needs of the congregation, the building committee did not forget other essentials. A drive-shed was built on the south-east corner of the church property where horses were blanketted down during the service and families exchanged greetings and gossip after worship. Knox gave into the innovation of musical instruments to lead the singing, voting 167 to 33 in 1888 to buy an organ. A number of the holdouts felt strongly enough about the "kist o'whustles" or "the instrument of the devil", as they called the organ, that they quit Knox Church for St. John's where the congregation still sang unaccompanied. Yet even conservative St. John's soon fell in line with the swing towards musical instruments, and by 1889 voted for an organ.[23]

St. John's had been enjoying steady expansion and vigorous spiritual leadership under Doctor Neil MacNish, acknowledged as the most distinguished Gaelic scholar on the American continent.[24] When MacNish first came to Cornwall in 1868 to act as assistant to the aging Dr. Hugh Urquhart, there were 100 communicants. At the time of his retirement thirty-five years later, there were 300.[25] This growth paralleled the increase in the town's Presbyterians from 583 in 1871 to 1,125 in 1901.[26] Among the latter at the turn of the century were members of the small French Presbyterian congregation, followers of the great Roman Catholic temperance leader, Father Charles Chiniquy, who had converted to Presbyterianism. Wishing to hold services in their own language, the French Presbyterians built a small church on Sydney Street nearly opposite Knox Church.[27]

The protestant church that emerged almost overnight was the First Baptist. Only two Baptists were recorded in Cornwall in the census of 1861, three in 1871. Whether these were a few of the Baptists converted in 1845 by a young student from Montreal, Allen McLean, and baptised by the outstanding Baptist minister and historian, Newton Bosworth of Montreal, is unknown. Some evangelical work was done in 1874 and 1875 by students and others sent out by the Baptist Home Mission Board so that by 1881 there were forty-five Baptists in town.[28]

The real beginning of the Baptist Church in Cornwall was due to two women, Jane MacArthur and Jennie Hamilton. They came to live in the town in 1880 but, finding no Baptist meeting of any kind, they decided to organize a Mission Circle. The first one, held Sunday 7 October 1880, was attended by ten members.[29] In addition to the monthly Mission Circle, to which men were invited and soon given the leadership, weekly prayer meetings were held on Sunday afternoons. Out of these small beginnings grew the desire for a church. Plans were matured by sixteen men and women who met at the home of Mr. and Mrs. William Andrews on 15 June 1882 and determined to secure both a regular place of worship and a minister. Kirkpatrick Hall was hired and Reverend P.H. McEwen of Thurso accepted the invitation to become pastor. Within a year a Sunday School was organized, and by 1884 a small stately church was erected for $5,000, capable of seating 260. It survives today as the House of Labour at 130 Sydney Street.[30]

The Baptists were not the only new protestant group to make their presence felt in Cornwall in the 1880s. The *Freeholder* facetiously announced in 1883, "It is said that several members of the Salvation Army are coming this way. Our Police force should be increased at once."[31] This was the body of Christian militants organized on the model of an army by William Booth in London, England, in 1865, to evangelize the masses in large cities. He sought out especially those who had become alienated from rural parishes through mobility to the factory towns seeking work. Cornwall at the end of the nineteenth century reproduced on a smaller scale the conditions that Booth had found in the factory cities of England, except in one important way. There was no wide-spread alienation of the mobile Cornwall population from church affiliations. As far as can be estimated from census figures and church membership figures in Cornwall at the end of the nineteenth century, there does not seem to have been an appreciable segment of Cornwall's industrial population which had no connection with any of the established churches.

It was the rural areas surrounding the factory town of Cornwall that first embraced the Salvation Army, probably because of the scarcity of rural churches. From Maxville, members of the Salvation Army corps marched to Cornwall on 10 March 1888, together with some Salvationists from Montreal, to hold their first street meeting in the mill town. With their band and hymn singing, they attracted a large crowd at the corner of Pitt and Second Streets, but the Cornwall Corps grew slowly.[32] By 1891 there were eighteeen converts meeting in the market house on Water Street.[33] Then, in the mid-

1890s the founder, General William Booth, decided to make Cornwall one of the centres of his Canadian tour. He arrived with his son, Herbert Booth, the commandant at Toronto, together with Mrs. Herbert Booth and the general's private secretary. His headquarters were in the large drawing-room of the elegant home of a member of the Methodist Church, Mrs. G.W. Armstrong.[34] The bustle and excitement created by the arrival of the Salvation Army entourage fascinated the small daughter of the household, Evelyn Armstrong (Stidwill.) For her, the old general with his flowing white beard created more of a sensation by his eating habits at breakfast than by his novel methods of "assaulting the ranks of sin in Cornwall", as the editor of the *Old Boys' Reunion* put it. Each morning when the maid brought General Booth some hot buttered toast, he carefully stood each piece upright against a dish to cool and dry out. Little Evelyn regarded him as "very odd" for many years until she discovered that "the English liked their toast" that way. Despite the visit from the founder, Cornwall's Corps remained small in numbers, only twelve in 1901 and forty-three in 1911. Like the early Methodists, however, the Salvation Army attracted adherents in the township where by 1891 there were 56. Members of the town and township Salvation Army Corps combined in 1904 to erect an imposing barracks on West First Street to serve as a place of worship and meeting house and, in army fashion, it was called "The Citadel", a fortress to protect the town against moral corruption.[35]

Education for the children of these protestant families was provided, for the most part, by means of the public schools which were, in essence, protestant schools since Roman Catholic children were enrolled within the separate school system by the 1870s. By modern standards, the elementary and high school facilities of Cornwall from 1850 until 1877 were woefully inadequate; yet they represented a workable arrangement whereby boys and girls coming out of elementary school at twelve or thirteen years could read, write and do simple arithmetic. What was more important, these children could and did find jobs in the ever-increasing number of factories. Going on to high school was only for more affluent children who would not be competing for jobs in the mills, shops and tailoring establishments of towns.

Pressure of numbers was thus felt sooner at the elementary level than at the high school level. The six schools operating in the 1840s could not handle the increasing number of small children. School trustees therefore obtained from Town Council a grant of £740 in 1853 to erect a two-storey four-room school on the site of present-day

Central Public School at the corner of Second and Amelia Streets. This site was already the location of two small schools, one facing Second Street, the other facing Third Street. By building a larger school, the trustees hoped to combine in one school all the children other than those attending the Church of England parochial schools run by Eliza Brown and H. Bartley.[36]

However, by the early 1880s the number of children crowding into the school was far beyond what the school built in 1854 could cope with. After some hesitation, Town Council passed a by-law, ratified by the rate-payers, to spend $25,000 on a handsome new public school which was erected in 1884 in the centre of the school property bounded by Second and Third Streets.[37] Cornwall contractor William Atchison was the builder.

The new school, soon termed the Model School, was under the direction of George Milden. To take care of the younger children, two "primary" or "ward" schools, as they were called, were also organized.[38] On the periphery of the town a number of small wooden schools were operating by the end of the century. One was on the Tollgate Road to the north of the town where Patrick Mulhern taught for a time.[39] Children in the East End attended classes in the Temperance Hall on First Street from January 1879 until a small school-house was erected on lot no. 2, south side of First Street. Then, in 1897, the first Gladstone Public School was built on Baldwin Avenue to accommodate children who had been attending school at Anderson's Ferry and those in the northeast area of town. A third school was located on the western outskirts. This was school section No. 2 on Second Street West where as many as seventy-three barefoot boys and girls tramped in from various farms and mill homes to learn from two teachers.[40] Heating and sanitary arrangements were not the most efficient, but they served. In the cold weather an older pupil started the wood stove at eight in the morning to get the heat circulating from one room to the other through a large opening cut in the wall. Even so, pupils like Elizabeth Good (Tilton) found it "bitterly cold and even when we were sitting on benches around the stove, we were burning in the front and freezing in the back. The ink would be frozen in the ink-wells, and it would be nearly noon before it thawed out." An old water bucket and a single tin cup sat on a box in the lobby of the school "and every kid in the school would wait his turn to get a cupful of that beautiful cold well water."[41] Less agreeable were the trips in the cold to the outside privies that were part of the school's and Cornwall's landscape until well into the twentieth century. Primitive as they were, these schools produced outstanding people such as Dorothy Tilton (Donihee) who became national president of the Catholic Women's League of Canada and has since written poignant and powerful memoirs of the area surrounding the paper mill known as Smithville.[42]

Secondary education in Cornwall was confined for fifty years to the old district grammar school on Second Street West long after it had passed its prime. In 1855-56 school trustees prevailed on Town Council to erect a new two-storey brick school on lot no. 12 on the north side of Fourth Street.[43] The building of the new grammar school probably owed much to the efforts of Headmaster William Kay who had had enough of the draughty old grammar school. He had been a student there under Strachan. Then he served as a teacher in it under Dr. Hugh Urquhart and spent fourteen years as headmaster. Although dismal and utilitarian in appearance, the new school was a slight improvement over the old grammar school. The latter went downhill rapidly, used for a time as a tenement house and then as a carriage house and stable in 1888, its blackened clapboards unrelieved by paint or whitewash.[44]

Neither teachers nor students found the new grammer school attractive. James H. Coyne who took over the headmastership in 1871 soon turned to the study of law in preference. Describing his one-year term at the high school, Coyne related, "I was headmaster-and the entire teaching staff...there were 40 or more pupils, 25 classes a week and 25 hours a week to teach them". High school students in those days attended school for five hours a day, Monday through Friday, their classes ranging from elementary English to Latin, Greek, French, Euclid and bookkeeping. Coyne recalled that, "As I taught them all, the effort broke down my health so that I was twice laid up with rather serious illness, and I made up my mind at the end of the year to take up something easier - so I went back to law."[45]

While Coyne taught all forty pupils in the grammar school in 1871, other children scattered throughout the city were taught by seven other teachers: Eliza Brown, Margaret Cozens, Elizabeth Kennedy, Colin MacKercher, Helen McDonald, Patrick G. Mulhern and Rachel Snetsinger.[46] These teachers got together in October 1877 with two other public school teachers of County Stormont to form a Teachers' Association, the first attempt at organizing what was essentially a teachers' professional association which could also be used as a pressure group for better wages and working conditions.[47]

Coyne's place was taken by James Smith, a Master of Arts, who had had ample teaching experience elsewhere in the province. Under his directorship from 1872 until 1885, the grammar school acquired once more "a reputation second to none in the Province."[48] More-over, Smith managed to persuade trustees that a new building was essential to replace the one built in 1855-56, though there were some philistines in town who regarded the project as a "useless and uncalled for extravagence." Nonetheless, a third high school, as it was now called, was erected in 1877 by Cornwall contractor William Atchison at a cost of $8,000. It could accommodate at least 200 students who were to be drawn from the school district that embraced Osnabruck, Finch and Roxborough, as well as Cornwall and its township.[49] How-ever, when the High School opened in the fall of 1877, only eighty pupils were enrolled. A number of them were females who, for the first time, were officially permitted to attend.[50] In 1828 a few females had slipped past the portals of Strachan's old school, but their stay had been short-lived. Now, under the School Act of 1871, females as well as males were eligible for entry to High School providing they passed entrance examinations. Another sign of the times was the hiring of a female teacher. When the school received its first formal visit from School Inspector Robert Johnston, in the spring of 1878, he congratulated the people of Cornwall on being "alive about the education of the rising generation." All three teachers received a nod of approval from Inspector Johnston who noted, "the teachers appear to me to be the right men in the right places. This, of course, refers to the lady also."[51]

With both a new high school, a new public school and several primary schools scattered throughout the town, there was sufficient space now for all the children of the town. Thus school trustees and teachers began to take a sterner view of the wide-spread truancy prevalent in town. The *Freeholder* of 4 September 1891, for instance, reported that there were only twenty-three pupils attending the Model School under Principal John Ritchie. Cornwall policemen were press-ed into the duty of acting as truant officers to make sure that all children fourteen years and under attended school.[52] But the problem of older children not making the jump from elementary to high school remained a perennial one until well into the twentieth century, partly due to economic stringencies within the family unit, partly because of educational difficulties within the elementary system that left some children unprepared for the entrance examinations to high school, and partly because of problems within the separate system that could not finance buildings at the high school level.

It was not until 1904 that the high school enrolment exceeded its 200 pupil capacity, an indication that probably less than one-third of the town's children went on to high school. Indeed, the town's future mayor, William A. Parisien, at the age of thirteen, was working at the Canadian Colored Cotton mill. Similarly, the man who became mechanical superintendent of the Howard Smith Paper Company, Stan Tilton, went to work at the age of ten in the Canada Cottons mill, his first job being to fill the lanterns with oil, trim their wicks and clean the shades.[54] Tilton's future wife, Elizabeth Good, passed the entrance examinations into high school but she, too, like most children in the town, did not go on to high school. Instead, she attended Kate Perkins' dressmaking establishment over James Tallon's drygoods store on east Pitt Street. Not liking that trade, she shortly afterwards gave it up for a job at twenty-five cents a day at the west end's best known grocery store, run by the crippled Teddy Fawthrop. Here Liz Good dispensed the best "butter and freshest eggs and cheese" that Fawthrop could find on buying trips through the countryside. She was content enough with her wages of $1.50 a week, but her Scotch pride drew the line against scrubbing up the store floor when asked to do so by Mrs. Fawthrop.[55] For young people who wished to secure more lucrative jobs, high school was a must. Therefore, when school trustees found some 217 pupils crowded into the space for 200, they pressed Town Council for the money to expand school facilities. By 1905 a by-law granted the high school building committee $8,000 to build a four-room addition.[56] Then, by 1907, the high school board began to ask Council for the right to designate the school a Collegiate Institute, a status which would enable the board to apply for a larger government grant. This status did not materialize until 1925 under the able principal who guided the high school from 1918 until 1939 - Alexander Caldwell, an honours graduate of an Irish university.[57]

A second institution of higher learning appeared in Cornwall in 1896 with the opening of the Cornwall Commercial College in the Snetsinger block under the direction of George F. Smith. Included among its staff was Oscar D. Skelton who became Secretary of State for External Affairs.[58] According to the Montreal *Standard* of 28 October 1905, the College was one of the "best equipped, most influential and widely-patronized business colleges in Canada." Its staff of seven in 1905 coped with 109 students, sixty-two of them men, who were taught shorthand, typing, and given a technical knowledge of commercial affairs.[59]

The need for expansion of Roman Catholic schools and churches became pronounced in the 1870s because of the inflow of French Canadian and Irish Roman Catholics. The 1850s had been a decade of decline in numbers of both Irish and French Canadians, but the 1860s saw the beginning of what became a continual flow of both into Cornwall, turning it into a predominantly Roman Catholic town by

1881.[60] This great increase in the number of Roman Catholics, from 562 in 1851 to 3,741 by 1891, was, to a large extent, owing to the influx of French Canadians who numbered 2,319 by 1891.[61] Yet the Irish newcomers were impressive in numbers also. They increased from 269 in 1851 to 1,070 in 1881.[62]

Even the moderate expansion of Roman Catholics over the 1850s, from 562 to 669, put pressure on the small wooden church of St. Columban's that had been built in 1829-30 for a much smaller parish. Under Father John S. O'Connor, a new Roman Catholic church was begun in 1864 east of the old church. Its walls were up and the roof about to be laid when a terrific windstorm smashed the walls down. Undaunted, the parishioners began anew. Giant bazaars helped finance the finishing of the interior, and by 1871 the debt of the church had been reduced to $2,000.[63] The church was no sooner built than the tide of newcomers swept in, the Irish, like the French, straddling the three wards of the town. By 1881 there were 323 Irish in the West Ward, 447 in Centre, and 300 in the East Ward.[64]

The Bishop of Kingston, James Vincent Cleary, made several visits to Cornwall in the early 1880s, confirming as many as 312 candidates at one time.[65] He was thus well aware of the growing Catholic population in town. Only too aware, also, of the expansion was the indomitable parish priest of St. Columban's, Father Charles Murray. He pushed ahead with school expansion, opening Centre Ward Separate School for boys at the corner of Fourth and Adolphus Streets in 1871. The next year a girls' school was opened, West Ward Separate School, at the corner of Fourth and Augustus Streets. Then Father Murray set about building a convent at Augustus and Fourth Streets so that he could persuade the teaching Sisters of the Congregation of Notre Dame of Montreal to come to Cornwall. When all was ready, he took a bold step. He dismissed all the lay teachers of the girls' school and set out early in January 1885 for Montreal. The Sisters of the Congregation were astonished at Father Murray's sudden appearance and request that they begin teaching on Monday, 7 January 1885. When the Mother Superior demurred, telling him that it was quite impossible for the Sisters to be in Cornwall that Monday, Father Murray replied, "Very well then! I shall expect them Tuesday." Sure enough, on Tuesday, January 8th, Father Murray was at the Grand Trunk Station with his carriage to conduct the three Sisters to their future abode on Fourth Street.

The influence of the Sisters soon spread far beyond the convent school on Fourth Street. Almost immediately they were pressed into additional teaching duties in the East End of town, organizing adult education classes for teenagers working in the mills. When the first group of millhands assembled one Sunday morning in February of 1885 for their class, the Sisters found thirty-five English and twenty French students ready to learn. Once these classes were established, French-speaking families asked the Sisters to provide classes for their children too. Thus, in September of 1886, the Sisters of the Congregation of Notre Dame opened l'Ecole de Bois, the first school in Cornwall where French children would be taught in French. The small frame school stood at the corner of Edward Street and Montreal Road, just across the street from the spot where the Church of the Nativity would be built in a few years' time. There were two classes, one for boys taught by a lay teacher, and one for girls, taught by the Sisters who had to travel to the East End each day from the St. Columban Convent. By the time that Father Charles Murray came to bless l'Ecole de Bois in November of 1886, there were 125 children, both French and English enrolled. Then, in 1888, another Sister of the Congregation arrived from Montreal, Sister Antoine du Desert. She took over the French classes, while a lay teacher, Doctor Emma McDonald, taught the English pupils.[66]

The French presence in Cornwall was making itself felt in directions other than education and religion. In July of 1882 the powerful St. Jean Baptiste Society established a branch in town. Designed to advance and protect French-Canadian interests and traditions, this society had local links for it was first organized in Montreal at the home of John Macdonell, the son of Lieutenant Angus Macdonell of the 71st Regiment who had been among the founders of the original parish at St. Andrews in 1786.[67] The parent Montreal body of the St. Jean Baptiste Society, organized in 1834, was composed of English, Irish, American and Scottish, as well as French adherents of the radical Patriote party of Louis-Joseph Papineau, most of them anticlerical in attitude. Yet over the years since 1834 the society had become increasingly Catholic and nationalist in character. The newest branch in Cornwall soon boasted its own banner, imported from Montreal in time for a parade in 1884 and its members fraternized with the Montreal society that year participating "in the grand celebrations in honor of their patron saint."[68]

To what extent members of the Cornwall St. Jean Baptiste Society put pressure on ecclesiastical authorities to establish a second Roman Catholic parish in the East End of Cornwall is unknown, but by 1884 Bishop James Vincent Cleary named a twenty-eight-year old priest, Father J.J. Kelly, to organize a parish which was put under the protection of the Nativity of the Blessed Virgin.[69] It is possible that at first the new parish was expected to be territorial in composition, and thus would include the large number of Irish Catholics as well as French Catholics in the East end. Father Kelly, being fluently bilingual was thus an obvious choice as the mission priest for the mixed congregation. A site on Montreal Road just east of Marlborough Street was chosen for the new church. Bishop James Vincent Cleary travelled from Kingston on 7 September 1887 to do the honours at the laying of the cornerstone. He noted with satisfaction that the cornerstone bore testimony to the fact that the church "was about to be erected by the voluntary contributions of the faithful, the Irish and the Scotch cooperating with the French", all part of his growing Cornwall flock.[70] Four days later Father Kelly made the first entry in the parish register, that of the baptism of "Cordélia Préscillie, fille légitime de Joseph Adélard Breault, et de Marie Anne Masson, de cette paroisse, neé le quatre Septembre."[71]

Father Kelly lost no time in putting up a small wooden chapel to serve until a church was constructed.[72] Then, in January of 1888, he organized a spectacular concert in the Music Hall of the Town Hall to aid the building fund. Local newspapers, including the *Standard*, advertised the event, informing readers that 'It is Father Kelly's special effort to make his church a success. Cornwall will certainly help him.'[73] And it did. The town's professional musicians such as Professor C.H. Fleck, the organist of St. Columban's and Professor Robert, contributed their talents, Fleck conducting the orchestra and Robert playing a cornet solo. Bella Finlay, one of the outstanding dancers in the Eastern District, performed along with a host of other singers and comic artists. Father Kelly was overwhelmed by the response. In his vote of thanks at the concert's end, he acknowledged that the majority of the concert's promoters and performers "were of a different denomination to the one under which the entertainment was sponsored," an indication of the existing goodwill among Cornwall's various denominations and language groups.[74]

Later in 1888 Father Kelly was moved to a mission parish near Brockville and an older priest, well experienced in building up new parishes, Father Paul-Antoine de Saunhac, was sent to Cornwall. Father de Saunhac was a native of Toulouse, France. Ordained at Ottawa in 1858, he served for fourteen years as pastor at Brewer's Mills, Ontario, where he had succeeded in building up that mission parish.[75] His arrival in Cornwall coincided with an upsurge of French-Canadian nationalism in Quebec, under Honoré Mercier, and rampant anti-Catholicism that was being fanned in Ontario by people like Dalton McCarthy.[76] This anti-Catholicism, which was soon tinged with anti-French overtones, became institutionalized in the ephemeral Equal Rights Association of 1889. Promoted by McCarthy, this Association's main objective was to secure the removal of public financial support from denominational schools. It thus represented a threat to the survival of Cornwall's separate schools and a threat to the emerging French-language schools in Cornwall. In fact, the editor of the *Freeholder* regarded the latter threat as the more serious. "To prohibit the imparting of French instruction to French children would be tyrannical," he declared. "They must be instructed in French before they can receive instruction in English."[77] Others in Cornwall agreed. Shopkeepers such as Messrs. MacHaffie and Elvidge of the East End Drug Store returned to their school desks to study French in order to "keep up with the growing demands on their business."[78] And, indeed, exchanging language skills became the thing to do. The incoming French soon took to learning English to get ahead, especially as more and more of the French-speaking entrepreneurs moved into the hotel business, into tailoring, grocery and meat retailing, photography, and into positions on the Town Council and police force.

The grocer who was to become Cornwall's pre-eminent French Canadian in the early years of the twentieth century was a young native of Vaudreuil, Quebec, Joseph E. Chevrier. Upon finishing his education at the College des Clercs St-Viateur in Vaudreuil, Chevrier wooed and won Malvina de Repentigny of Ste. Anne de Bellevue and, as soon as they were married in 1890, he persuaded his young bride to move west to Cornwall where he established a thriving grocery business. By 1906 Chevrier not only dealt in groceries and fruits, carefully selected in Montreal markets, but had expanded into coal and wood, and his Cornwall home was among the finest in town. Active in the St. Jean Baptiste Society, he got his first taste of local politics in 1906 when he was elected councillor for Centre Ward. By 1914 he became mayor by acclamation.[79]

Among the more prominent hotelmen at the turn of the century were J.E. Plamondon, proprietor by 1881 of the St. Lawrence Hall on Marlborough Street, and Louis P. Charlebois who owned the Windsor Hotel on Water Street near the swing gate.[80] This comfortable old hotel was built in the early 1870s and came into Charlebois's possession about 1884. He subsequently sold it to another enterprising young French Canadian, Alexandre Laplante, at the turn of the century. Still another young French Canadian, Joseph R. Duquette, bought out the Clifton Hotel opposite the Court House and transformed it into the Hotel Duquette. Not content with this, Duquette also managed the elegant summer hotel on Stanley Island, the Algonquin.[81] The Crosbie House, at the corner of Pitt and Third

Streets, was taken over by an ambitious French Canadian, Robert Lalonde, who had first worked as a millhand at the Canadian Colored Cotton Mill. Retiring early as yard master, he decided to go into the hotel business. For some years he ran the Gladstone House in Cornwall East and then opted for the Crosbie House which he completely overhauled and re-named the Empire House.[82]

Probably one of the best known hotelmen in town was Angus Lalonde, a popular master builder who converted the Brennan block at the corner of Water and Marlborough Streets into a modern hotel, the Stormont House, at the turn of the century. Lalonde was the second French Canadian elected to Town Council, the first being a grocer located on Pitt Street, Joseph Primeau, who for many years held the contract for supplying food to the county jail prisoners. Primeau was elected for 1879.[83] Angus Lalonde was elected for the East Ward in 1885 and continued to be elected as councillor or reeve for the next thirteen years, becoming mayor in 1904, the first French Canadian to hold that office.[84]

Photographer Thomas Lafleur established a studio on First Street next door to the *Freeholder* office in 1891, inheriting much of the photography trade of the late H.W. Weber.[85] Yet another French Canadian, J.T.A. Gauthier, opted for a flour, hay and seed business on Pitt Street, buying out R.M. Arthur's interests in the late 1880s.[86] Cornwall tailoring got a shot in the arm with the arrival of the French Canadians. Two men in particular moved into top positions as Cornwall tailors. One was a native of Rivière-Beaudette, Oscar Leblanc, who soon changed his location from Marlborough and Water Streets to more commodious quarters in the Snetsinger block on Pitt Street.[87] Another tailor who helped turn Cornwall men from their habit of patronizing only Toronto and Montreal tailors was J.A. Sauriol who set up business in Cornwall in the early 1890s.[88]

These were some of the men of the French community in Cornwall who, together with their families, were among the parishioners of Father de Saunhac when he undertook the task of designing and building the Church of the Nativity of the Blessed Virgin Mary. Having decided against giving a contract for the building of the new church, Father de Saunhac threw himself into the job of hiring stone masons and laborers in April of 1891 and ordering "280 cords of stone with lime and all necessary timber."[89] Chief mason S. Blair laid the first stone on 25 May 1891 and the work was pushed on with such speed and skill that Mass was said within the church walls on Christmas Day of that same year.[90]

Major ecclesiastical changes had taken place in the church hierarchy while the parish of the Nativity was building its first church. A new diocese was created in eastern Ontario in 1890 with the episcopal seat at Alexandria. Henceforth Cornwall Catholics came under the jurisdiction of the newly-created Bishop, Alexander Macdonell, instead of the Bishop of Kingston. One of the earliest and toughest decisions of the new bishop was to confirm the parish of the Nativity on linguistic lines, rather than territorial limits. This decision had already been made by the Bishop of Kingston, but Bishop Macdonell reiterated it on 18 March 1892 to enable, as he said, "Pastors...to know each one belonging to their congregation...to make sure that every Catholic family and each single individual shall belong to one congregation or the other." Macdonell therefore spelt out his instructions. "I hereby renew and confirm the basis adopted by His Grace, the Archbishop of Kingston, on the separation of the French congregation from that of St. Columban's, namely that it was not made by territorial limits, but on the lines of language, and that the French language was to be the one used in all public instruction and prayers within the French Church."[91]

To avoid as much as possible tensions over the separation of the two parishes, the new bishop stipulated that "it is now left to the choice of each French family and single French individual to select to which congregation he should belong and accordingly be responsible for the obligation of membership in regard to the requirements of Divine Worship, the sustentation of the Pastor and the maintenance of the sacred edifice." Finally, Bishop Macdonell decreed that "no one after having made his selection of church or congregation shall enjoy the freedom to join another."[92] These carefully thought out and precise instructions to the Cornwall Catholics indicated that there were thorny problems to be resolved. Many French, Irish and Scottish families were intertwined through marriage relations and many had looked to St. Columban's as their parish for years. Yet all realized that parish ties had to be broken, as St. Columban's was not big enough to cope with the great flood of Catholics coming into town. Indeed, the building of a bigger St. Columban's began the next year even after the withdrawal of many of the French parishioners.[93] Yet some of the French remained at St. Columban's. In 1892, for instance, thirty-one out of 104 baptisms were of French children.[94] As for the Church of the Nativity, it did indeed become the French-language church, but, like St. Columban's, it, too, continued to have a sprinkling of Irish and Scottish parishioners and its pastors, including Father de Saunhac, were bilingual. In fact, after the death of Father de Saunhac in 1904, one Irish and two Scottish priests were appointed pastors. It was not until 1942 that a French Canadian became pastor. This was the forty-nine-year old Father Joseph-Azellus Brunelle, one of five brothers of Joliette, Quebec, all of whom were priests.[95]

NOTES

1. *Census*, 1881, i, 262-63.
2. *Canadian Illustrated News*, 26 January 1878.
3. *Census*, 1881, i, 262-63.
4. *Census*, 1891, i, 42.
5. *Census*, 1851, i, 62-63 and 1861, i, 152-53; *Smiths' Gazetteer*, 1846, 38-39; Arthur Youngs' "History of St. Paul's United Church."
6. *Census*, 1871, i, 24 and 132-33; *Standard*, 2 Sept. 1886, refers to the church as the Canada Methodist Church.
7. *Saturday Globe*, Toronto, 18 November 1893; Mrs. Evelyn Stidwill, "Early Recollections of St. Paul's United Church."
8. *Census*, 1851, i, 62-63; 1871, i, 132-33.
9. Diocesan Archives Ottawa: Holy Trinity box 8/6S/C2; Mary Mack, "The Church of England in Cornwall", in *Souvenir of the Dedication of the Restored and Modernized Memorial Pipe Organ, Bishop Strachan Memorial Trinity Church*, 15.
10. J.F. Pringle, *Lunenburgh, or the Old Eastern District*, 227.
11. Mary Mack, "The Church of England in Cornwall", 15; Bishop R. Jefferson, *Faith of our Fathers: Story of the Diocese of Ottawa*.
12. *Saturday Globe*, Toronto, 18 November 1893.
13. Mary Mack, "The Church of England in Cornwall," 151; G.B. Stidwill, *The Mountains of Trinity Church*, 8.
14. *Canadian Illustrated News*, 26 January 1878.
15. Will of Canon Jacob J.S. Mountain, Cornwall, 25 June 1902.
16. Mary Mack, "The Church of England in Cornwall", 16.
17. *Ibid., Standard-Freeholder*, 25 September 1965.
18. *Saturday Globe*, Toronto, 18 November 1893; Jefferson, *Faith of Our Fathers' Story of the Diocese of Ottawa*, 182; Pringle, 288-89; *Old Boys' Reunion*, 1906, 172.
19. *Freeholder*, 6 December 1889.
20. *Saturday Globe*, Toronto, 18 November 1893.
21. *A Brief History of Knox United Church, Cornwall, 1846-1975*, 7.
22. *Freeholder*, 19 June 1885, cited in *ibid.*, 9.
23. Cameron, *History of Knox United Church*, 10; Pringle, 223.
24. Fred MacMillan, Dr. Simon Fraser, Philip Robertson, History of St. John's Church, Cornwall, 1787-1975, 14.
25. *Ibid.*

26. *Census*, 1871, i, 130; 1901, i, 190-91.
27. *Old Boys' Reunion*, 1906, 172; History of St. John's Church, 5; LACAC, *Exploring Cornwall's Heritage*, May 1978, 6.
28. L. Jean Cameron, *First Baptist Church*, Cornwall, 1882-1967, 6; *Census*, 1881, i, 160-61.
29. L. Jean Cameron, *First Baptist Church*, 6-7.
30. *Ibid.*, 11-12; LACAC; *Heritage Cornwall*, i, 32-36.
31. *Freeholder*, 26 January 1883.
32. *Standard-Freeholder*, 1 March 1923 and 15 March 1973.
33. *Census*, 1891, i, 258-59; Minutes, Town Council, 1896-1898, 16 April 1896, 65.
34. Mrs. Evelyn Stidwill, Early Recollections of St. Paul's United Church.
35. *Old Boys' Reunion*, 1906, 55; *Census*, 1901, i, 190-191; ii, 76-77, 1891, i, 258-59.
36. Diocesan Archives Ottawa: Trinity Church Schools, Cornwall, 59/1/19; Pringle, 249-250.
37. Minutes, Town Council, 17 May 1883, 66; Pringle, 250, for school figures; David Hickey, Principal, Central Public School, to E. Senior, 13 January 1982, re inscription on cornerstone; see also *Standard-Freeholder*, 3 August 1946, "Schools", Cornwall.
38. Belden, *Historical Atlas*, iv; *Standard-Freeholder*, 4 February 1932, see under Cornwall Public School.
39. Mary Mack, The Church of England in Cornwall, 14, in *Souvenir of the dedication of the restored and modernized memorial pipe organ*, 1968.
40. Dorothy Donihee, "In My Mother's Footsteps", see picture, 36; for Gladstone Public School, see Pringle, 251, and Rudolph Villeneuve, *Catholic Education in Cornwall, Ontario, Yesterday, Today and Tomorrow*, 3-4.
41. Donihee, "In My Mother's Footsteps," 33.
42. *Ibid.*
43. Alexander Caldwell and Mary H. Stewart, *Cornwall Collegiate and Vocational School: An Historical Sketch*, 8; LACAC, *Heritage Cornwall*, i, 27-31; Pringle, 242.
44. Pringle, 242.
45. Caldwell and Stewart, *Cornwall Collegiate and Vocational School: An Historical Sketch*, 8.
46. *Lovell's Ontario Directory*, 1871, 288-290.
47. *Reporter*, 27 October 1877.
48. Belden, *Historical Atlas*, iv.
49. *Canadian Illustrated News*, 26 January 1878; *Reporter*, 11 August 1877.
50. *Ibid.*
51. Cited in Caldwell and Stewart, *Cornwall Collegiate and Vocational School: An Historical Sketch*, 9.
52. *Standard*, 21 August 1891.
53. *Standard-Freeholder*, 28 July 1944, see obit.
54. Dorothy Donihee, "In My Mother's Footsteps," 36.
55. *Ibid.*, 37, 56-57.
56. Minutes, Town Council, 1902-07, 305-6, and, 30 October 1905, 439.
57. Minutes, Town Council, 1907-1914, 12 August 1907, 57; *Standard-Freeholder*, 21 September 1938; Caldwell and Stewart, *Cornwall Collegiate and Vocational School: An Historical Sketch*, 11.
58. *Freeholder*, 14 May 1897; *Standard-Freeholder*, 29 June 1934.
59. *Old Boys' Reunion*, 1906, 40-41.
60. *Census*, 1881, i, 160-161.
61. *Ibid.*, 1851, i, 62-63; *Census*, 1891, i, 258-59.
62. *Ibid.*, 1881, i, 262-63.

63. Father Charles Murray, "Reminiscences", 8-9.

64. *Census*, 1881, i, 262-63.

65. Murray, "Reminiscences", 11.

66. Details on Father Murray's part in the growth of separate schools are taken from Father Rudolph Villeneuve, *Catholic Education in Cornwall, Ontario, Yesterday, Today and Tomorrow*, 5-16.

67. Michele Guay, "Jean-(John)-François-Marie-Joseph Macdonell", in *DCB*, ix, 485.

68. *Reporter*, 20 June 1884; *Standard-Freeholder*, 29 June 1934.

69. Villeneuve, 14.

70. For various accounts of the founding of Nativity Church, see Villeneuve, 14-15; *Paroisse de la Nativité de la B.V.M.*, 1887-1962, 13; *Album Souvenir: Hommages à Mgr. J.A. Brunelle, P.P., Curé de la Nativité de Cornwall*, 1942-1960, 7; Fernande DeSerres-Fobert, Historique de la Paroisse de la Nativité depuis sa fondation, 1982, 13-14; *150th Anniversary of St. Columban's Parish*, 1896-1979, 12.

71. Registres des Baptîmes, Mariages et Sepultures de la Congrégation Canadienne Française de l'Eglise de la Nativité de la Sainte Vierge, cited in *Paroisse de la Nativité de la B.V.M.*, Cornwall, 1887-1962, 46-47.

72. *Album Souvenir: Hommages à Mgr. J.A. Brunelle, P.P., Curé de la Nativité de Cornwall*, 1942-1960, 7.

73. *Standard*, 19 January 1888.

74. *Ibid.*, 2 February 1888.

75. J.B. Allaire, *Dictionnaire biographique du Clergé Canadien français*, 493; Louis Flynn, *Built on a Rock: The Story of the Roman Catholic Church in Kingston, 1826-1976*, 296.

76. Hereward Senior, *Orangeism: The Canadian Phase*, 79-86; James T. Watt, "Anti-Catholicism in Ontario Politics 1894", in *Ontario History*, lix, no. 2, June 1967, 57-67.

77. *Freeholder*, 20 December 1889.

78. *Standard*, 3 February 1887; *Old Boys' Reunion*, 1906, 99.

79. For details on Chevrier, see, *Le Droit*, Ottawa, 30 Novembre 1937; *Old Boys' Reunion*, 1906, 106 and 136; DAC, St. Jean Baptiste Society, 8.

80. For Plamondon, see *Reporter*, 11 June 1881; for Charlebois, see *Freeholder*, 15 February 1889; and *Old Boys' Reunion*, 1906, 92.

81. *Old Boys' Reunion*, 1906, 90; see also, Donihee, In My Mother's Footsteps, 26.

82. *Old Boys' Reunion*, 1906, 93.

83. *Reporter*, 11 January 1879; Belden, *Historical Atlas*, vi; Smith, Reminiscences, paper presented to Stormont, Dundas and Glengarry Historical Society, 1932, 6.

84. *Old Boys' Reunion*, 1906, 95.

85. *Ibid.*, 108; *Canadian Illustrated News*, 26 January 1878.

86. *Old Boys' Reunion*, 1906, 134.

87. *Ibid.*, 60.

88. *Ibid.*, 66.

89. *Standard*, 17 April and 25 May 1891.

90. Album Souvenir: Hommages à Mgr. J.A. Brunelle, 7.

91. Bishop Alexander McDonell (sic) to Rev. George Corbet, 18 Mar. 1892, in Baptism Register, 1834-1921, St. Columban's Church, 8.

92. *Ibid.*

93. *Ibid.*, 14.

94. *Ibid.*, 429.

95. *Paroisse de la Nativité de la B.V.M.*, Cornwall, *1887-1962*, 12-13; *Album Souvenir: Hommages à Mgr. J.-A. Brunelle*, 4-6.

Cornwall Lacrosse Team, champions 1887-1888

Cornwall High School, 1877.
Credit: Heritage Cornwall.

Cornwall Public School, 1884.
Credit: Heritage Cornwall.

Trinity Bishop Strachan Memorial Church 1870's (Anglican). The steeple was never complete.
Credit: Heritage Cornwall.

St. John's Church, (Presbyterian) 1906.
Credit: Heritage Cornwall.

Chapter XIV

In Sickness and in Health

Catholics and protestants required medical care in addition to spiritual and educational care, but hospitals did not appear in Cornwall until 1897. Then, not one, but two suddenly emerged. Temporary army hospitals had been set up in town during the 1812-14 war and at the time of the 1837-38 civil conflict. Again in 1847 three temporary hospital sheds were erected at Petite Pointe Maligne east of the town to care for Irish immigrants stricken with typhus fever. But a permanent hospital did not get under way until 1897, even though Town Council as early as September of 1868 appointed a committee to "see about buying land for a hospital."[1]

The town's medical fraternity worked out of their own homes, while midwives tended the women who bore their children at home, the usual fee for a delivery being one dollar.[2] The doctor's lot was not a particularly lucrative one, judging from the number of medical men who took up other jobs in combination with doctoring. What was more surprising about nineteenth century doctors was the number who took to politics. The town's mayor for most of the 1860s, Dr. William Cox Allen, for example, combined municipal politics, doctoring and the post of police magistrate for many years. Then, at the age of sixty-eight, he decided to seek greener pastures, leaving Cornwall to begin a new life at Fort McLeod in the North West Territories.[3] Dr. Roderick Macdonald was County Treasurer from 1850 until 1884. Cornwall's leading federal politician from 1872 until his death in 1896 was Dr. Darby Bergin. Dr. Duncan Orestes Alguire was twice mayor of Cornwall, in 1899 and again in 1903. His contemporary, Dr. Charles J. Hamilton, also captured the mayoralty seat twice, the first time in 1889 and the second time in 1894. This was despite the fact that he was one of the busiest of the Cornwall doctors, beloved for his deeds of charity as well as his acts of healing, and honoured by his colleagues in 1929 with a cup and address in recognition of fifty years of service.[4]

In spite of this propensity of Cornwall doctors to dabble in politics and other jobs, medical men had been anxious to provide the town with a hospital where surgery could be performed under sanitary conditions and modern medical equipment would be available for the sick and accident victims. Not only were medical men concerned. Town fathers, clergymen and citizens generally were worried at the lack of hospital facilities in the expanding factory town. One of the wealthy families to express their concern in a practical way was the Purcells. This Roman Catholic family of three brothers, Patrick, Michael and John, born of mixed Irish-Scottish parents, were natives of Charlottenburg township. With little formal education, the brothers became prominent contractors, John settling in Cornwall in 1887 and occupying the house on First Street East that later became the rectory of the Church of the Good Shepherd.

Both John and his more prominent brother, Patrick, Member of Parliament for Glengarry from 1887 to 1891, died in 1891. John Purcell left a legacy of $15,000 to found a county hospital open to all and he named two protestants, former Mayor James T. Kirkpatrick and John McIntyre as executors of his will. Both executors understood that Purcell had endowed a non-denominational hospital. This was promptly disputed and lengthy litigation ensued.[5] When the dispute was finally settled in 1896, the judge deciding in favour of the "general" or non-sectarian hospital, Roman Catholics began negotiations to open their own hospital. Just as devout Catholics wished their children educated under Catholic teachers, so, too, they wished their sick and dying to be within the orbit of a wholly Catholic institution. Indeed, the Catholic hierarchy believed firmly that its institutions, whether they were religious, teaching or sick and welfare agencies, must be guarded against secular ideas that contradicted Catholic doctrines. There were less contradictions at the end of the nineteenth century than there were as the twentieth century lengthened into its second half. Nevertheless, Bishop Alexander Macdonell of Alexandria and Vicar-General George Corbet of St. Columban's Parish, borrowed $5,000 from the Ontario Bank to buy Ivy Hall from the widow of Henry Sandfield Macdonald for use as a hospital. Thus the large house at the corner of York and Water Streets in the western part of the town evolved from an officers' mess to the residence of Canada's premier and finally into a Roman Catholic hospital.

Bishop Macdonell and Father Corbet lost no time in securing a staff. They sought the services of the Sisters of the Religious Hospitallers of St. Joseph, five of whom arrived from Kingston one cold February morning in 1897. Mrs. Katherine Purcell offered them lodging while the Sandfield Macdonald home was being converted into a seventeen-bed hospital, the Hotel Dieu, with a small operating room.

The Sisters tended their first patient on 14 June 1897, almost at the same time that the cornerstone was being laid for the Cornwall General Hospital.[6]

Like its sister institution, the Cornwall General Hospital arose almost overnight. Its cornerstone was laid in June 1897 and the formal opening took place the following December. Located outside the town limits at the corner of Marlborough and Second Streets, it was near the eastern factory area where the new Church of the Nativity and Church of the Good Shepherd had recently been built. And, like the Hotel Dieu, the new general hospital received gifts and legacies from many hands. Former Mayor William Colquhoun donated $1,000. Furnishings for the public wards were supplied by the Golden Rule Circle of the King's Daughters, an organization of women dedicated to helping others, particularly the sick. This society, a branch of which was formed in Cornwall in 1894, continued well into the twentieth century, contributing liberally to the hospital.[7] Private wards were furnished by the ladies of St. John's Presbyterian Church, the ladies of Knox Church, the King's Daughters of Farran's Point, the Cornwall Public School, the Cornwall Masonic Lodge, and Mrs. S. Gower Poole, wife of the Church of England curate of East Cornwall. The congregation of Trinity Church gave $100 and a chair in lieu of furnishing a ward.[8]

The by-laws of the hospital decreed that the management of the hospital "shall be strictly non-sectarian, and the Institution will be open to all citizens of the Town of Cornwall and United Counties of Stormont, Dundas and Glengarry, irrespective of creed or nationality, in accordance with the terms of the Will of the late John Purcell, Esq., Founder of the Hospital."[9] Yet, the patrons and governors were almost entirely protestant, the exception in the first Board of Governors being the wealthy Roman Catholic merchant and postmaster, George McDonell, whose beautiful home at the north corner of Second and Sydney Streets eventually became Nazareth Roman Catholic Orphanage.[10] For the next two decades, protestant churches continued to have annual collections in aid of the general hospital that at first could handle thirty-six patients.

The Cornwall General and the Hotel Dieu were staffed by the same doctors. It was a Church of England doctor, Charles J. Hamilton, who admitted the first patient to Hotel Dieu, for instance. Other town doctors were Edward A. Graveley, Duncan Orestes Alguire, Adam Wagner and J.W. Wheeler,[11] all protestants, and Henry Joseph Harrisson, a Roman Catholic.[12] A second Roman Catholic doctor, Paul J. Maloney, was attracted to the town in 1897 from Perth.[13]

The Cornwall General had the advantage of great stability at the helm during the first twenty-five years of its existence when James T. Kirkpatrick remained chairman of the Board of Governors and Doctor Duncan Orestes Alguire president of the medical staff. These men, together with John McIntyre as first vice-president, Dr. C.J. Hamilton, the town's medical officer, and benefactors like the Colquhouns, Macphersons and Clines kept a tight rein and a keen eye on the hospital's management, finances and services. From the earliest days of the hospital, townspeople tried to establish a close working relationship between the Board of Governors and the medical staff by having monthly visits to the hospital by two of the Governors who were deputed to examine and hear complaints from the staff and patients. As the hospital expanded in 1902 to fifty beds and, by 1946, to seventy-five, the difficulties of keeping a balance between the policies of the Board of Governors and the needs and practices of the medical staff became more apparent.[14] Thus, in recent times, the Board confined its activities more to the financial and building requirements of the hospital, rather than a direct investigative role in the management and medical policies of the hospital.

The small Hotel Dieu had been operating a year when tragedy struck suddenly. About three minutes before noon on 6 September 1898 as men were busily completing the last section on the new New York Central and Ottawa bridge that spanned the St. Lawrence, they were horrified to see pier no. 2 suddenly give way and crumple into the river, dragging fourteen men to their deaths and wounding seventeen. Forty men on the south span leaped to shore. Others jumped or were carried down with the bridge. The men on shore at once put out in boats or swam out to rescue those who were hurt or wounded as they rose to the surface of the water. A nearby tug swung into action, gathering up the wounded and quickly conveying them to the nearest hospital, Hotel Dieu. As the alarm sounded in Cornwall, every medical man in town hastened to the new west-end hospital. The Sisters quickly moved patients upstairs from the public ward or out onto the balcony to make room for the wounded men who were carried in on stretchers.

It was partly due to this disaster that the Sisters began plans for a larger hospital. Once more it was a member of the Purcell family, the widow of Patrick Purcell, who spurred the project by a donation of $10,000.[15] Begun in May 1899, the second Hotel Dieu was finished in July 1901 after Vicar-General George Corbet visited different parishes in the diocese to solicit funds to aid with the construction.

The need for a home for old people and for orphans had been felt for some time in Cornwall. As these people were not sick, they could not be kept in the small hospitals. The Religious Hospitallers of St. Joseph found a temporary solution. They turned the spacious stable and carriage house on their property into St. Paul's Home for the aged. Father Paul de Saunhac of the Church of the Nativity and Vicar-General George Corbet of St. Columban's helped finance the renovations. A society called the "Children's Aid" had been formed sometime prior to 1897, its main object to house destitute children until they could be placed in permanent homes. As it became increasingly difficult to find shelter for ophans, the Society asked the Sisters to help. They responded by taking several of the children into two modest frame homes near the hospital in 1909. But so many children needed shelter that another house was fitted up on York Street where the orphans remained until 1919 when Mrs. John McMartin donated her beautiful home, "Highland Manor," at the corner of Second and Sydney Streets, to the Sisters. This orphanage, known as Nazareth Home, was used until fire destroyed it in 1950. A new one was not built, as provincial government policy now decreed the use of foster homes for destitute children.[16]

When not at work, church, school, or in hospital, the people of Cornwall found a surprising number of ways to enjoy their leisure hours. In 1893 the Toronto *Globe* listed twenty-one Cornwall societies and sports clubs. There were many others. In fact, as the first half of the twentieth century wore on, such a plethora of clubs, societies and associations emerged in Cornwall that it was scarcely possible for a citizen to survive in town in isolation from the friendly network of beckoning organizations. In 1893 the list was headed by the exclusive men's fraternal society known simply as "The Club", which was formed 20 December 1886 by a number of young men whose object was "to elevate and amuse" themselves. The Club's first president was Archibald Gault of the Stormont Cotton mill. Duncan Monroe, the affable Presbyterian insurance magnate, was vice-president, while hardware merchant Henry Turner was secretary. In 1893 members of The Club put their guests at ease" in a very quiet way" at their centrally-located club rooms which were, according to the Toronto *Globe*, "comfortably furnished and supplied with every amusement and means of recreation". A club house was built at 42 Second Street East in 1910 when the club was incorporated as "The Cornwall Club" and there it stands to this day. The original membership qualifications still hold - one must be male and a gentleman, and membership is limited to 125. Members meet together once a week for a buffet dinner and otherwise enjoy the club's library, pool room, card room and other amenities under the present executive headed by Lionel Grant and William Mack.[17]

Probably still the most powerful organization in town was Masonic Lodge no. 125, organized in 1860 with John McLellan, master, Thomas Bacon, senior warden, and E.F. Beaufort, junior warden. By 1890 Dr. Edward A. Graveley was master, W.J. Wallace senior warden, William Gibbens of the *Standard*, junior warden, W. Norris, secretary, W.H. Weber, treasurer, and Francis Bisset, tyler. Until 1897 Cornwall's Royal Arch Masons had to travel to Farran's Point to attend meetings of Covenant Chapter no. 113. These journeys caused local Royal Arch Masons some inconvenience, even though the monthly meetings took place always "on the Wednesdays after the full moon" so that country members could take advantage of the moonlight on their return drive home by horse and carriage. Those Cornwall members who went to Farran's Point by the evening train for the meeting had to wait until morning for a return train journey, a delay that caused Companion Nathan J. Fraid to petition the Grand Chapter for a charter to open a chapter at Cornwall. Instead, the Grand Chapter decided to move Covenant Chapter, which had been meeting at Farran's Point since 1894, to Cornwall. Thus Cornwall by 1897 had two Masonic bodies, Covenant Chapter of Royal Arch Masons and Lodge no. 125, both meeting on the top floor of the Kirkpatrick Block on Pitt Street.[18]

Closely trailing the Masonic Lodges in importance were the Odd Fellows. St. Francis Lodge, no. 18, was the first Cornwall Odd Fellows Lodge, organized in 1846 under the inspiration of the Montreal Odd Fellows. Its Noble Grand was J.D. Pringle and Vice Grand was Jacob Farrand Pringle. Secretary was L.F. Putnam and treasurer A. McDougald. Although the lodge boasted eighty-two members in June 1847, it collapsed in 1851.[19] A second Odd Fellows Lodge, Oriental, no. 163, was not instituted until April of 1875 with charter members Merrill Derby, Corydon J. Mattice, Lewis A. Ross, J.A. Simpson and Thomas B. Blyth.[20] Like the Masons, the Odd Fellows were a fraternal society pledged to assist each other, especially in times of distress such as bereavement and sickness, and to aid widows and orphans. Installations of officers usually took place in the parish hall of the Church of the Good Shepherd whose curate, S. Gower Poole, was chaplain.[21] Other early members were Doctors C.J. Hamilton and Edward A. Graveley. This society, which in 1884 was open to all "free, white males, of not less than 21 years of age, and of good moral character" tended to draw members from all classes of society and of different religious backgrounds. Thus members in the 1880s included two Jews, Samuel L. Goldstein and Abraham L. Fraid, both described as "travellers;" John M. Crites, a millhand; Max Wilhelm Nafe, a weaver; Francis Bisset, a teacher; George A. Grant, a carpenter;

M. Myers, a jeweller; and W.C. Kanier, a musician.[22] By the early 1890s laborers of French-Canadian origin were initiated. These included John Langevin and Zotique Brunett.[23]

Other clubs in existence by the end of the nineteenth century tended to be mutual-help fraternal societies, providing sick and death benefits, insurance protection, aid to immigrants, and cultural activities. Such a society was the Canadian Order of Foresters, which enjoyed great popularity for over sixty years. Its first Cornwall branch, Court Sydney, was formed in 1879. By 1893 two other courts were organized - Stormont, no. 3, and St. Columban's, no. 227. Nativity Court no. 576 was founded in 1896 under James E. Tallon. In 1900 a fifth court was formed in the East end, conducting its business entirely in French.[24]

Cornwall men of English extraction organized a Sons of England Benevolent Society in 1880. Among its charter members were R.H. Horsman, W. Ivens, A.G. Cuddsford, William Lawrence, A.T. Porteous, H. Williams, J. Gill, A. Baggallery, I. Eldridge, A. Hessel, A. Millson, and C.A. Graveley.[25] The Sons of Scotland, Aberdeen Camp, had as their chief in 1893 Duncan Monroe who also headed the St. Andrew's Society and the local Orange Lodge.[26] Such national societies straddled the various denominations. While the leading Orangeman might be chief of the Sons of Scotland one year, Roman Catholic grocer D.J. Gillies, Chief Ranger of the St. Columban's Court of Foresters, was Chief of the Sons of Scotland the next.[27] Like the Sons of England and the Sons of Scotland, the St. Jean Baptiste Society was a fraternal organization of nationalist character dedicated to preserving the traditions, language and culture of a particular community within the town and assisting the needy in the Parish of the Nativity and other French-Canadians in distress.[28]

St. Columban's Benevolent Society existed as early as 1884 when G.R. Davey was president and its members took to debating current events such as the Scott Liquor Act. The anti-Scott team of M.F. Harrington and J.F. O'Neil won the debate, proving statistically that liquor consumption had increased in the province since the Scott Act came into force and that there had been no diminution of crime.[29] Temperance lodges were also very much in evidence in Cornwall in the 1890s. St. Lawrence Council and Stormont Council of the Royal Templars of Temperance were buttressed by the Women's Christian Temperance Union which was in fighting trim as early as 1892. The Total Abstinence Society was still going strong in 1898.[30] So enthusiastic were the advocates of temperance that they were able to build a temperance hall on lot no. 2, south side of First Street, in 1894.[31]

The Young Men's Christian Association made its debut in Cornwall in 1876, promoted by undertaker James Kilgour who donated chairs to the new group. Announcing that its "rooms are available free", the Y.M.C.A. held its activities in the Ross Block on Pitt Street in the 1880s and later in the basement of St. John's Presbyterian Church.[32] Another group of militant Christians were united in the Lord's Day Alliance to combat what they considered desecration of Sunday. Drawing its main strength from Knox Presbyterian Church, with Elders William Mack and William Dingwall as president and secretary, the Alliance asked Town Council in 1897 to forbid streetcars to run on Sunday, May 23. Indeed, the vice-president of the Cornwall Electric Street Railway Company, D.A. Starr, assured the Council that even if granted the right, the company "had no intention of running the streetcars on the 23rd."[33]

From the cultural point of view, one of the most important developments in Cornwall in 1890 was the growth of the Mechanics' Institute under president James Hall and his board of directors J.P. Watson, Richard Tanner, A. Bates, Francis Bissett, William Gibbens, E. Oliver, J. Ritchie, J.F. Smith and J.A. Alguire.[34] This group laid the foundation for the Cornwall Public Library by starting a collection of books that could be borrowed by townspeople. At first those wishing to use the library paid an annual fee of a dollar which entitled them to borrow books or to use the reading room which was open from 1 p.m. to 10 p.m. every day. When the Institute library was inspected by a reporter of the Toronto *Globe* in 1893, the only criticism he had was the lack of Canadian literature of any sort among its holdings. "Why this should be is beyond comprehension," the reporter scolded, "with so many good books bearing on the history of our own country which have been recently published."[35] By 1895 the Institute had 1,500 volumes, undoubtedly some of them with Canadian content, and all housed in the Turner Block on Pitt Street.[36] Here the first volunteer librarian, insurance agent J.R. Adamson, lent books out to some 200 members of the Institute. In addition, the Mechanics' Institute organized adult night courses for the benefit of mill-workers who wished to better their education.[37]

Enthusiasm for the new library was keen. Thirty-five different donors gave grants of over $100 each for the purchase of books and, by 1895, some 327 townspeople petitioned the Town Council to make the library free. Dr. Duncan Orestes Alguire, president of the Institute and for forty years teacher of the Adult Bible Class at Knox Church, informed the Council that should the petition be granted, the Institute's assets of books, furniture and other equipment, valued at $1,400 would be made available free for the use of the public. While the finance committee mulled over the petition and eventually granted it, the library becoming a public one by 1900, its location was moved from the Turner Block to the Glengarry Block where the library remained until 1903, with Nellie Hollenbeck as librarian. She was succeeded by Linda Clark who was in charge of the library until the 1940s.[38]

Not only was the town becoming more culturally sophisticated in its library facilities, musically the town had graduated from a solitary fiddler in the 1840s to a Philharmonic Society in 1884 and concerts by the "Ladies Orchestra" in 1887.[39] In the late 1870s the Fire Brigade organized a band which practised in a small room off the Council chambers in the Town Hall, much to the annoyance of councillors and the town clerk.[40] Their efforts were more appreciated each Saturday night when the fifteen-member band provided music for a weekly dance at the popular Victoria roller skating rink on the west side of Pitt Street between Second and Third.[41] While townmen and women tripped the light fantastic on the roller skating rink, other dancers climbed to the second storey of the building to learn more sedate modes of dancing from Professor Macdonald of Montreal. His dancers formed a Quadrille Club whose members preferred the elegant ballroom of the Rossmore Hotel for their Friday night balls.

The Fire Brigade Band ran into stormy waters and disbanded in 1885 when it was unable to find a competent director. Within a year another town band was organized, known as the Citizens' Band. Contributions for instruments poured in and the new band was soon performing on street corners, and encouraging the efforts of a cadet brass band.[43] By the late 1890s the town built a large bandstand at Central Park where concerts were performed on sunny afternoons and sultry evenings to the delight of townspeople.

Most musical and dramatic performances as well as church bazaars, temperance conferences, strawberry festivals and large balls were held in the Music Hall of the Town Hall which, until well into the twentieth century, was by far and large the hub of community activities. Even the Cornwall Poultry Association held its annual exhibition there, rent-free in 1896 although councillors later complained that it cost the town $350 to pay for mop-up exercises after the champions of the barnyard departed.[44] Town Council took pains to keep the Music Hall equipment and furnishings in repair and its rental prices within reason, though many organizations found ten to fifteen dollars a day a bit steep.[45] In 1885, for instance, Roland Snetsinger was appointed to look after the

324

scenery backdrops.[46] And when the Tavernier Dramatic Club performed to small audiences for two weeks that year, its members received a rebate of four dollars from Council.[47] Not so lucky was the May Fisk Company "which could not pay their rent because of lack of patronage." Town authorities confiscated three new sets of scenery from the company in lieu of rent, these being "of greater value than their personal property and more preferable."[48] The King's Daughters prevailed on Town Council for the use of the Music Hall free of charge for their entertainment given in December of 1896 "for the benefit of the sick poor of the Town."[49] But the more professional Dramatic Club had to fork over rent when it performed "Robert Emmett" in aid of the sufferers of the New York and Ottawa Railway Bridge disaster in 1898.[50]

As the women of Cornwall began to organize, their first societies tended to be church-oriented, with women of the various congregations running tremendously successful bazaars to help finance the building and furnishing of their respective churches. Once the church buildings were erected and furnished, women moved into more sophisticated church work, especially fund-raising in aid of foreign missionary work. Thus, for instance, at St. John's Presbyterian church, while the general management of the church was solely in the hands of the all-male Kirk Session and Board of Trustees until well into the twentieth century, women organized themselves into the "Ladies Association" as early as 1863. President Mrs. Robert Cline kept a steady hand on the tiller of the Ladies Association for the next thirty-three years, providing consistent and discreet leadership to the women of the congregation. Once their major effort of raising $4,000 for the purchase of an organ was accomplished, the women of St. John's built up funds for direct aid to home and foreign missionaries. This was the work that captured the imagination of women in various churches for almost a hundred years.[51]

At Knox Church the women of the congregation organized initially as the "Mite Society", raising money to help furnish the church and the manse, but soon directing their efforts to missionary work that expanded to include no less than six different missionary groups by 1926.[52] Similarly, the women of the Methodist Church emphasized the importance of missionary work so much that young members of the congregation, as well as adults, tithed themselves for this work. Youngsters' tithing took the form of cultivating small plots of land on which they grew vegetables. Upon selling the vegetables, the children put the money aside as their contribution to the Women's Missionary Society.[53] It was women who began the

Baptist Mission Circle that led to the founding of the first Baptist Church in Cornwall. Their impetus in mission work continued. Not only did they raise money to provide for home and foreign missionaries. They also organized reading courses designed to acquaint church members with work in the mission field.

Trinity Church women did not organize as a distinct body within the parish until 1892, though they functioned effectively as a parish group from the early 1830s when they organized the first bazaar in town. Although they were barred from participation in the governing bodies of the church such as the corporation and vestry until well into the twentieth century, women tended to work with their male counterparts in promoting parish schools and Sunday schools. Later in the nineteenth century when Trinity emerged from the status of a "mission" parish partially subsidized by the Society for the Propagation of the Gospel, its women parishioners began to look outward towards the broader mission field.[54] Spurred by Mrs. Mary Bruce, they followed the lead of an Ottawa churchwoman, Mrs. Roberta E. Tilton, a convert to Anglicanism, in forming a local branch of the "Women's Auxiliary" to the Domestic and Foreign Board of Missions of the Church of England. Mrs. Tilton had, in 1885, solicited the Bishop of Ontario and members of the Domestic and Foreign Board of Missions to permit church women to organize themselves as an "Auxiliary" to the Board.[55] Thus was born the most powerful of all women's organizations within the Church of England in Canada, so powerful that by 1911 they became the Women's Auxiliary of the Church of England and by 1934 had paved the way to General Synod for women, hitherto an all-male preserve.

Throughout the nineteenth century Roman Catholic women vied with the men at St. Columban's in efforts to build up the parish and to provide schools and hospitals for their co-religionists. Just as Anna Scott Mountain, Mrs. Robert Cline, and Jane MacArthur and Jennie Hamilton occupied the centre of the stage in their various protestant congregations, so, too, did the generous American-born wife of John Sandfield Macdonald dominate women's activities at St. Columban's at a time when that parish was welcoming more and more French-speaking men and women. The fact that Marie Christine Waggaman Macdonald was not only the wife of Canada's prime minister, but spoke French as her mother tongue, lent prestige and cemented links within the dual-language parish. Her able seconders in works of charity and fund-raising projects were the wives of Dr. Roderick Macdonald, Colonel Angus Macdonell,

Lachlin Macdonald, J.S. Macdougall and Duncan Allan Macdonald.[56]

It was thus through church organizations that the women of Cornwall began to develop skills in public relations, organization and fund-raising, as well as to experience a sense of power through united efforts. When they branched out into more secular-oriented societies, their choice usually fell upon fraternal organizations closely allied to those already formed by their husbands, brothers or sweethearts, or they organized societies designed to promote some particular interest such as temperance. One of the first societies paralleling a man's organization in Cornwall was formed 27 February 1896, when members of Oriental Lodge of Odd Fellows helped institute a women's lodge, the Daughters of Rebekah. Like their male counterparts, the women undertook to visit sick members, provide relief for distressed members and to help maintain homes for aged and infirm Oddfellows, their wives and widows and for their own sisters of the Rebekah degree. Elected Noble Grand was the wife of the editor of the Cornwall *Standard*, William Gibbens who was a member of Oriental Odd Fellows Lodge and a Mason. Vice-Grand was Mrs. H. Hermiston whose family had been connected with the local Oddfellows since 1884.[57]

The two other prominent women's groups in town at the turn of the century were the King's Daughters and the Women's Christian Temperance Union, the first active by 1894, and the second formed in 1892. First president of the Women's Christian Temperance Union was the wife of Judge Jacob Farrand Pringle. Other stalwarts were Mrs. J.C. Alguire, Mrs. John H. Cline, Mrs. Robert Binnie, Mrs. John D. McLennan, and Mrs. R.S. Relyea, all determined to impress on the youth of the town and the not-so-young the evils of consuming liquors and narcotics.[58] The King's Daughters were primarily concerned with care of the sick and needy, but they sometimes combined their efforts with the W.C.T.U. In April 1900, for instance, the two women's groups jointly donated a fountain to the town in honour of Jennie MacArthur, one of the prime movers in procuring the town's other drinking fountains.[59] The more militant women who sought to exercise social control over the drinking habits of Cornwallites had ample cooperation from the still active Total Abstinence Society.

Though the rest of Canada may not always have agreed that Cornwall was the breeding ground of Canada's top athletes, Cornwallites were adamant on the subject as far back as 1865 and continued adamant for the next hundred years, pressing a claim to have the Canadian sports Hall of Fame located in the factory town in recognition of the many top lacrosse, hockey and other sportsmen that the town produced.[61] The town's first outstanding athlete and probably Canada's greatest athlete of the nineteenth century was Roderick R. McLennan, a native of Charlottenburg who began his astonishing career of hammer-throwing in Cornwall in 1865 almost by a fluke.[62] For years McLennan had topped various local youths in all feats of running, jumping and hammer throwing. Then he left Cornwall to work on railroad construction in the United States. This is where the twenty-three-year old McLennan was when Canada's champion hammer-thrower, Thomas Jermy, returned from Scotland after defeating the champion there. Full of justifiable pride, Jermy challenged any man in Canada to a match. Cornwall men took up the challenge, naming McLennan as their champion. Cornwall's mayor, George C. Wood, took off to locate McLennan across the line and a match was set for 24 May 1865 with a stake of $1,000 and a gold medal, emblematic of the world championship. Cornwall's pride won easily, swinging a twelve-pound hammer 216 feet. Jermy's supporters then challenged McLennan to the fifty-six pound weight with a stake of $2,000. Up until then McLennan had never attempted the heavier throws, so he and his supporters prudently declined the challenge. But it took McLennan only a few days to train for the heavier weight. Two weeks later he met Jermy in Toronto and threw the fifty-six weight five feet farther than his rival.

With mutual appreciation and goodwill, the two men toured Canada and the northern United States that summer, McLennan taking every honor in the running, jumping and throwing contests he entered. He threw out challenges all along the way, offering prizes to anyone who could beat him throwing the ordinary nail hammer weighing one and a quarter pounds against his twelve-pound hammer. In every case, McLennan won. At the end of the season, he returned to his work on railroad construction and did not enter any athletic competitions for five years. Then, in 1870, his Cornwall admirers persuaded him once more to compete at Toronto for the world Championship. With but a few days' preliminary practice, he won the heavy hammer throwing championship medal which was presented by the Honorable George Brown, editor of the Toronto *Globe*. In addition, he carried off the medals for light hammer and fifty-six pound weight throwing, and went on to Montreal where he took another champion gold medal. By 1872, when the young lad of twenty-three had changed to a sturdy man of thirty who disdained the lighter feats of running and jumping, McLennan again competed in Toronto for the world championship for the hammers and the fifty-six pound weight throw and won all. Unlike modern athletes who specialize in one weight or style, McLennan used all weights and all styles, entitling him to rank among the most remarkable Canadian athletes of all time. The editor of the 1906 *Old Boys' Reunion* did not mince words when describing McLennan. "He won great distinction as an amateur athlete, having made records in feats of strength and skill which have never been equalled by professionals or amateurs."

If McLennan took the spotlight in Cornwall and Canada with regard to individual sports, it was the Cornwall Lacrosse team that put Cornwall on the world sport map by bringing the world championship title home on three occasions. Cornwall men and boys had learned the game early in the century from the St. Regis Indians who taught them a form of lacrosse called hurls. One of the earliest recorded hurl matches between Cornwall and St. Regis took place on 28 August 1840. In spite of lowering clouds, the Indians began to gather in town about ten o'clock in the morning. By eleven o'clock, they lined up behind the band of the 5th Battalion of Incorporated Militia and marched with their hurls and banners to Colonel Philip Vankoughnet's meadows east of the town where the matches were to be held. Captain Solomon Y. Chesley and a number of Indian chiefs selected sixteen of the top young Indians for the first match and, as the *Observer* reporter noted, "at a signal, the beautiful and manly game of Hurl commenced, and was kept up with great spirit through four games, three of which were gained by the Married Men against the young Men."[63]

Since that time until the first world war thinned the ranks of lacrosse players in the area, Cornwall remained the greatest centre of lacrosse in the Dominion.[64] The first formally-organized lacrosse club came into being in 1863 and hosted a team against the St. Regis Indians in 1868.[65] Two new clubs emerged in the late 1870s — the Young Victorias, active by 1876, and the Independents, organized in the spring of 1878.[66] Members of the Young Victorias, many of whom went on to bring lacrosse fame to Cornwall, were Frank Lally, goal, J. McAteer, point, J. Hunter, cover point, William Martin, J. Broderick and J.Plamondon, defence field, A.E. McDonald, Alex McDonald and George Pringle, centre field, G. Hunter and C. Liddle, home field, S. Page, home, J.F. Smart, field captain, J.G. Hunter and M. Callaghan, umpires.[67]

With two teams in the field in the 1870s, Cornwall lacrosse enthusiasts organized a Lacrosse Club in 1879, determined to produce a Championship team. Its president was Mayor C.J. Mattice, an indication that town fathers fully supported efforts to nurture a top team. Among other officers were some of the top lacrosse players — Frank Lally, J.G. and G.A. Hunter, R. Tanner, J. Broderick, J. Plamondon, J. McAteer, and S. Page.[68] By 1881 Cornwall players emerged under a new name, the Young Canadians. This was the aggregation that brought to Cornwall that same year its first lacrosse championship, the Eastern District trophy.[69] Two years later the Cornwall lacrosse team swept through Montreal, Kingston, Iroquois, Aultsville, Brockville and Brantford, to win the junior title. By 1885 they brought home the title of intermediate champions of Canada.

The steady climb upwards of the Cornwall Lacrosse Club was evident two years later in 1887 when they formed a tough senior team of players, averaging about twenty-three years of age. Younger players re-organized in a junior team called the "Young Emeralds."[70] In 1887 the lacrosse teams in Western Ontario pulled out of the National Amateur Lacrosse Association, forming a circuit of their own. The new senior Cornwall lacrosse team played the eastern circuit, winning seven out of eight games against the Montreal Shamrocks, and the Ottawa and Brockville teams. The local boys then prepared for the crucial playoff game against the winning Toronto team of the western circuit to mark the world championship, still very much a purely Canadian affair. The playoffs were held in Montreal with an exciting well-played match that ended in a draw. Cornwall wanted to decide the issue by a second game the next day, but the Toronto team returned without another game and the title went to Cornwall.[71] Charges that the playoffs had been rigged dampened the glory of this first world championship title for Cornwallites, but the Cornwall team showed that it was of champion stuff by winning the world title for the next three years.[72]

This team, which went down in Cornwall sports history as "The Immortals", was Cornwall-bred except for three players, defence men Billie Hughes of Lindsay, George Tudhope of Orillia and Gerry Sullivan of Williamstown.[73] The home boys included Norm Carpenter, acknowledged as a "marvellous goalkeeper," Hugh Adams, a "superb athlete who could throw a pass 148 yards"; Dr. A.A. Smith, the fastest man on the team; Alex Black, a brilliant shot;John J. Broderick who could always be counted on to be "sure and effective;" Frank Lally, the manufacturer of lacrosse sticks who was looked upon as a "tower of strength and one of the finest all-round athletes in the country," and the part-time policeman, George "Manny" Crites, termed, "one of the all-time greats."[74] This senior team's honorary president was none other than Cornwall's greatest athlete, Major Roderick R. McLennan who, by now, had become a wealthy railway magnate and builder of some of Cornwall's finest building blocks, including the McLennan Block on Pitt Street that housed the Victoria roller skating rink.[75] With such players and such support, Cornwall expected and got outstanding results. The senior team's last world championship was in 1891. Thereafter, for a number of years, Cornwall teams became seriously handicapped by the migration of some of its best players to the west, drawn by large salaries offered by clubs in the Canadian Lacrosse Association. Wryly, the *Freeholder* commented on 8 May 1903, "Cornwall has again been raided, which is an excellent tribute to the quality of its players, if not to their loyalty."[76]

New lacrosse teams emerged, promoted by the Cornwall Junior Lacrosse Club and the Aberdeen Lacrosse Club.[77] One of these was formed in 1897 by the newly-established Cornwall Commercial College. The team's honorary president was Member of Parliament for Stormont, John G. Snetsinger, and the chairman was C.E. Duquette.[78] Snetsinger's business partner, William Fitzgibbon, shared Snetsinger's enthusiasm for lacrosse and by the end of the century he served not only as president of the Cornwall Lacrosse Club but also as president of the National Lacrosse Union. It was this constant support and enthusiasm amongst all levels of Cornwall society that created the backdrop for the emergence of a second generation of lacrosse greats in the twentieth century when Edouard "Newsie" Lalonde and Dalton Phelan blazed a trail across Canada as Cornwall's contribution to the sport.[79]

In its heyday, lacrosse was vastly different than its later development. For one thing, there were twenty-eight men on a much larger field, twelve players on each team, a field captain on each side and two other officials. Games were usually played at the Cornwall Agricultural Society's grounds on St. Andrew's Road north of the railway station.[80] Early lacrosse players donned only jersey sweaters, pants and running shoes. Padding from head to foot and helmets were unheard of in the late nineteenth century and would have been frowned upon, not only as slowing up the player, but also as an unnecessary barbarism among gentlemen players who would not use the gutted stick to slash an opponent's kidneys, shoulders or shins.[81] For the younger lads who could not afford proper lacrosse sticks, they made their own and played a more primitive type of lacrosse called "Clinkers",[82] a game that continued in vogue until the early 1930s.

Although lacrosse was Cornwall's showpiece sport at the turn of the century, other individual and team sports drew fans as well, particularly curling, boxing, cricket, horse-racing, golf and baseball.

Curling was the winter counterpart of lacrosse. Curling buffs trekked out to the ice on the St. Lawrence between Farlinger's and Flanagan's Points every winter for some thirty years until they finally got around to building a club house in 1882 at the corner of First and Augustus Streets.[83] Then in 1886 they successfully petitioned for a portion of the Town Hall lot facing Fourth Street for a term of ten years on which to build a curling rink.[84] Major Roderick R. McLennan turned his attention to curling as well as lacrosse, donating a trophy to be competed for annually by the two rinks of the Cornwall Curling Club. In 1888 these were composed of Frank Lally, Hugh M. Watson, A.A. Smith and skip Robert Ferris, rink no. 1, and G.C. Smith, Henry Turner, William Pollock, and skip J.D. Finlay, rink no. 2.[85] The next year the Curling Club had fifty-three members headed by Judge Jacob Pringle as patron, Mrs. Archibald Gault, patroness, and Archibald Denny as president.[86] These Cornwall curlers competed with the Burns Curling Club from Ogdensburg, New York, as well as with rinks from Montreal, Ottawa, and Brockville. In 1891 they got as far as the playoffs for the Governor General's Trophy. Friendly matches with the Montreal Royal Caledonia Curling Club and other outside rinks continued until 1908 when the local club disintegrated and the property was sold, marking the end of organized curling in Cornwall until 1946.[87]

Hockey took a great leap forward in 1897-98 when John Snetsinger built a huge rambling frame structure on lot 16 south side of Third Street which came to be known as Victoria Rink. For thirty-five years it provided citizens with some of their happiest moments. With an entrance on Pitt Street, the rink, one of the largest covered rinks in Canada at the turn of the century, gave protection from the elements for players and fans on stormy nights. Prior to this, hockey enthusiasts played on an open air rink that adjoined the curling rink on the north side of First Street west. Eight inch high boards surrounded the ice surface, their job supposed to be to prevent the puck from hopping into the snow banks that lined the rink area. Near one end of the rink two large trees jutted out of the ice surface but players paid little heed to these unusual adornments, skating around and between them.[88]

Once the covered rink was built, Cornwall hockey pundits lost no time in entering its team in the senior series of the Ontario Hockey Association in 1899. Cornwall was in the section that included Iroquois and the Ottawa Capitals. In their first year of play in the senior league, the Cornwall team drew blood by beating the Ottawa Capitals, then the star team of the section.[89] By 1902 and 1903 the Cornwall senior hockey team was strong enough to capture the colours in the championship playoffs against Iroquois and the Ottawa Capitals, but went down to defeat in the provincial playoffs in a match with the Toronto Wellingtons.[90] Among the top players were Billy Peacock, Jack Hunter, James Milden, Billy Turner, Fred MacLennan, Stuart Layside, Randy McLennan, Harlow Stiles and Fred Degan. Cornwall then entered the Federal League with Ottawa, the Montagnards and the Montreal Wanderers. Subsequently they played in the Ottawa Valley Hockey League.

To keep strong senior teams on the ice, young hockey blades needed encouragement in improving their skills, getting uniforms, and organizing their matches. Cornwall youngsters secured such able and enthusiastic management in 1903 when George Eastwood, N. Contant, H. Flanagan, H. Stewart and George Leponcier undertook to organize them in a Junior Hockey League composed of the Rovers, Buffaloes and Red Stars.[91] From these early teams emerged such twentieth century hockey greats as Edouard "Newsie" Lalonde, Carson Cooper, Cyril and Corbet Denneny, Joseph, Tilly and Garth Donihee, Ralph Gault, Cyril Dextras, Elzéar, Arthur and Joseph Contant and Clarence Gallinger.[92]

Cricket and baseball were flourishing in Cornwall by the mid-1870s. Mayor Corydon J. Mattice headed the men who gathered on 21 August 1877 to consolidate the town's cricket talent into one general organization, the Cornwall Cricket Association.[93] A baseball team, the Cornwall Key Stones, was in existence by 8 June 1878.[94] And in 1886 a new cricket club was formed at a meeting of some thirty men at the Sons of England Hall.[95] Billiards had long been a favourite sport, so much so that town fathers found it profitable to impose licences on the keepers of billiard saloons. Thus in March of 1868 Mrs. Littlefield secured a licence "for keeping a billiard room for the current year."[96] By 1881 the *Freeholder* took umbrage at a proposal to open two billiard saloons that year. "Such places of resort will not by any means add to the morality of the town," it scoffed. "These billiard saloons will result in the downfall of many a man."[97] More to the liking of the editor was the promotion of the Cornwall Snowshoe Club which was in full swing in the winter of 1878. This was the year the club was immortalized by Montreal's famous artist, Henri Julien, when he produced an engraving of club members for the *Canadian Illustrated News* from a photograph by Cornwall photographer, H.W. Weber. Nine years later the club was still active, its members journeying to Montreal to attend the winter carnival there.[98]

Military men in their role as citizens were conspicuous in most of the town's sporting events, especially lacrosse, horse racing, and curling. Men like Corydon J. Mattice who had organized a company of infantry in Cornwall during the Fenian raid of 1870, Doctor Darby Bergin, lieutenant colonel commanding the 59th battalion, Major Roderick R. McLennan, and Lieutenant A.A. Smith, one of Cornwall's top dentists, were renowned for their participation in and promotion of local sports endeavours. As soldiers and sportsmen, one of their particular interests was in good marksmanship and, as in lacrosse, Cornwall men excelled. As youths they began their apprenticeship with sling shots, "Whether to shoot at a target or at some poor bird," as Dorothy Donihee recollected, "the accuracy of the shot was unbelievable and after just a little practice the "bull's eye" could be hit every time." Simplicity and ingenuity were all that were needed for equipment. Practice took care of the skill. Limbs of trees were carefully searched for the straight "Y" shaped branch to make the best slings. A piece of rubber about three-quarters of an inch wide was fastened tightly with string to form the sling, while the tongue of an old shoe formed the centre from which the pellet was expelled. The apprentice marksman then looked for hundreds of little round smooth stones as ammunition.[99]

Graduating from slingshots to rifles, the young men of Cornwall could practice their markmanship in any of the shooting galleries in town, which by 1875 were coming under stricter surveillance and licensing by the Town Councillors.[100] To encourage good rifle shooting, military men, with a sprinkling of civilians, formed a strong Rifle Association in 1886. At its head as honorary presidents were Lieutenant-Colonel James Henry Bredin, who took over the command of the 59th battalion in 1885 from Lieutenant-Colonel Darby Bergin, Major Roderick R. McLennan, now Member of Parliament for Glengarry, and Samuel Greenwood, manager of the Canadian Colored Cottons Company mills. The active president was a curling buff, J.F. Smart, under whose leadership the Rifle Association produced such crack shots that when they competed in the Canadian Military Rifle League matches in 1896, firing in Cornwall, several leading Canadian newspapers insinuated that the results had been dishonestly recorded. The adjutant of the 59th, Captain John L. Weller, who, among other things was a graduate of the Royal Military College and Chief Engineer of the Welland Canal, sent a blistering note off to the Canadian Rifle League demanding that two officials of the League be present at the second, third and fourth matches still to be shot. "We are satisfied," he snorted, "that we can come close enough to the previous score to clear us of the stigma which now rests upon us."[101]

Two officers of the 5th Scots arrived in Cornwall to represent the Canadian Military Rifle League when the second matches were fired. One of them, Major Ibbotson, officially reported that he had been at the butts only a short time when he realized there could be no doubt about the reliability of the figures of the first match. Captain Weller put on a score of 94 in spite of a wind of gale proportions blowing across the range. Six other Cornwall men scored over 90. A strong team from the Regiment attended the Quebec Rifle Association matches in 1896, winning the Active Militia and Battalion matches and the Merchants Match. Even more impressive was the choice of two Cornwall military men, Captains John L. Weller and G.W. Runions as members of the Canadian Bisley team that year. Runions, a popular Cornwall grocer and Town Councillor, represented Canada a second time two years later at Bisley. Cornwall continued to draw top honours in rifle shooting for the next four years, with Sergeant R. Corrigan on the Bisley team in 1897 and 1990, and Lieutenant A.A. Smith on the team for three years, in 1896, 1897 and 1900.[102]

Horse lovers abounded in Cornwall from the earliest days of its settlement. At first, a race track was located just north east of the mile-square town. By 1825 it was located in the heart of the town, the track circling the block where Central Public School now stands.[103] For many years winter horse racing took place along the canal on the straight stretches of ice, when large crowds lined both banks of the canal for the events.[104] This may have been the course referred to in 1858 as the St. Lawrence Race Course for which the Town Council authorized "persons to take out a special licence to sell wine, brandy and other spirituous liquors, also Ale and Beer, and to furnish refreshments generally to the public."[105] By 1879 the race track was located at the Agricultural Society's grounds north of the railway station and east of Pitt Street.[106]

Top men in the horse racing field were Dr. Darby Bergin and his lawyer brother, John Bergin, and Veterinary Surgeon W.H. Craig, a graduate of McGill University, whose stables, infirmary and farm "Belleview", were renowned across the country for the fine horses he bred, bought, sold and cared for.[107] In 1893 Craig owned ten brood mares and fifteen Jersey cows. Among his four stud horses, the most famous was Saltpetre, winner of the gold medal at the Montreal fair in 1888. Saltpetre was a half-brother of Salvatore, the holder of the world's record as a running horse. His first cousin was Foxhall, the winner of the Grand Prize of Paris. Dr. Craig's French coach horse, Heristal, took all the prizes at the Quebec Provincial Exhibition in 1893. His pony, "Black Cloud, Junior," won the special for roadster stallions at the Ottawa Central Fair in 1893. His fourth prize horse, Hector, was the only pure bred French-Canadian stallion in Ontario at that time. This horse won every prize wherever he was shown, including Montreal and Ottawa.[108] With breeders such as Craig and the Bergin brothers, it is not surprising that the Cornwall Driving Park Association should mount well-patronized "Derby Days" in the 1890s.[109]

Less glamorous were the exhibitions of boxing by members of the Cornwall Athletic Club and the efforts of the Bicycle Club.[110] The latter was "growing in numbers" in 1899, and making plans to plot our "wheelways" through the town where enthusiasts such as George F. Smith, founder of the Cornwall Commercial College, could enjoy cycling uninterrupted by passing carts, street railways or other vehicles.[111] For those who liked an outdoor sport in summer that was less rigorous than lacrosse, golf answered their needs. A group of five men got together in 1896 to finance a golf course, located at first in the Dingwall pastures east of the present Athletic grounds. The location of the club shifted four times, first to the Agricultural Society grounds north of the railway station, then to the Woods property in west Cornwall, Gulf Street taking its name from the Club. In 1914 the club moved eastward once more to the river front just west of where St. Lawrence College now stands. Here a nine-hole course was laid out and the club affiliated with a boating club that had been formed by Dr. Ross Alguire in 1909; hence the sailboat on the early crest of the Club that was then the Cornwall Golf and Boat Club. The final move was in 1934 when the club purchased the Colquhoun Farm east of the town boundary. Members such as J.G. Harkness, the historian, his law partner, George A. Stiles, M.V. Boyd, manager at Canadian Cottons who had worked his way up from waterboy at the Stormont mill, Dr. W.D. Knight, J.H. Bonar, and H.F.C. Poste, took the lead in the club expansion which became the Cornwall Golf and Country Club. Over the twentieth century, it increased to some 800 members who, by 1958, purchased the adjoining land to expand into an eighteen-hole course, becoming one of Cornwall's most prestigious and popular clubs for golf and social events.

These were the sports undertaken by adults, mostly men, in the second half of the nineteenth century at a time when there seemed to be a wind sweeping across the town and the continent whipping up enthusiasm for sports, particularly organized sports. It had not hit the women of the town to the same degree, for there is little evidence of women taking to bicycles, golf courses, lacrosse fields and hockey rinks before 1900. It was not until the first world war disrupted male teams that Cornwall sported an all-girls' hockey team, the Victoria Ladies' Hockey Club, led by Albertine Lapensée whose prowess on the ice was so outstanding that a reporter of the Montreal *Star* commented, "Miss Lapensée is such a wonderful player and shot that for a long time her opponents thought she was a boy."[113] He was not far off for the hockey star underwent a sex change, altered her name to Albert, and resided in Cornwall with his wife.[114]

Although women did not participate to any great degree in organized sports until 1915, younger girls were far from reluctant to engage in the unorganized sports that took the fancy of the young boys of the town. Thus it was just as likely to be a couple of girls that would "catch a bob", that is, jump on the back runner of a sleigh being pulled up Wood's hill by a horse. Dorothy Tilton Donihee recalled the delight of "smoothly gliding over the fresh-packed snow, the cold wind hitting you in the face, and your heart leaping with the speed and exhilaration, and the beautiful sound of the bells on the horse's harness ringing loud and clear. On those really cold days, she recounted, "the horse's bodies were covered with frost and as they drew their heads high in the air and snorted, great gusts of hot breath would immediately turn to white frozen crystals shining like great diamonds."[115] Slingshots and rolling hoops remained the monopoly of town boys, but girls took to bows and arrows, home made from the long pliable limbs of the willow trees, the arrows carefully sanded down and a murderous nail sticking out the end so that the bull's eye could be pierced.[116]

As the twentieth century approached, Cornwall and its denizens were optimistic, but not buoyantly so. The cotton industry had levelled off and the paper industry had yet to show any great leap forward. Men who had gone off to the gold fields in the Yukon came back carrying huge potatoes from the prairies rather than gold nuggets and settled back into more mundane but steady jobs at the mills.[117] Though the population of the town had taken a slight dip, its figure of 6,704 in 1901 was misleading when compared with the other Loyalist towns of Kingston, with 19,264, Brockville, 8,793 and Belleville, 9,914. The Cornwall figure represented only those living within the square mile of the town, whereas the suburbs of Cornwall accounted for about an additional 4,000, making Cornwall's real population nearer 10,000 by the turn of the century. Its maturing municipal institutions, places of worship, educational facilities and social and sports activities all indicated a lively leadership and a deepening community spirit, unmarred by blatant class conflict or ethnic divisions.

NOTES

1. Minutes, Town Council, 4 September 1868, 15.

2. Dorothy Donihee, "In My Mother's Footsteps," 25.

3. *Standard*, 19 January 1888.

4. Donihee, 2; Jean Gogo, *A History of the Cornwall General Hospital*, 8.

5. For details, see, *Historical Sketch of Hospital, and By-laws of Cornwall General Hospital*, 1898, 3; Gogo, 3, 5, Glengarry News, 1 May 1896 and 24 December 1897; J.F. Pringle, *Lunenburgh, or the Old Eastern District*, 290; J.F. Harkness, *History of Stormont, Dundas and Glengarry*, 263, 478.

6. See, DAC: *Hotel Dieu Jubilee*, History of Macdonell Memorial Hospital, *Freeholder*, 14 June 1897; *Standard-Freeholder*, 22 May 1936; Gogo, 2.

7. Minutes, Town Council, 15 December 1896, 20; *Standard-Freeholder*, 3 August 1946.

8. *By-laws of the Cornwall General Hospital*, 1898, 4.

9. *Ibid.*, 5.

10. Pringle, 211; Harkness, 217; for list of governors, see Gogo, 4; *Standard-Freeholder*, 27 June 1972.

11. DAC: *Hotel Dieu Jubilee*; *Standard*, 2 February 1888.

12. *Freeholder*, 6 December 1889, identifies Harrisson as a Roman Catholic.

13. Harkness, 462-3.

14. Gogo, 5; *Standard-Freeholder*, 29 June 1934.

15. *Standard-Freeholder*, 29 June 1934.

16. *Hotel Dieu Jubilee*; *Standard-Freeholder*, 27 June 1972; *150th Anniversary of St. Columban's Parish*, 1896-1979, 18.

17. *Globe*, Toronto, 18 November 1893.

18. For details on Masons, see *Freeholder*, 6 December 1889; Benson Stidwill, *Covenant Chapter Royal Arch Masons, Jubilee Year 1894-1944, Fiftieth Anniversary*, 4-5; *Standard-Freeholder*, 29 June 1934.

19. Return of Lodges for the year ending 30 June 1847, enclosure; Gerald Revill to E. Senior, 2 July 1892.

20. Members Register, Oriental Lodge, 163, Cornwall, 1883-1948 gives 15 April 1875 as founding date; see also *Standard-Freeholder*, 29 June 1934.

21. *Ibid.*, see notice of open installation; *Reporter*, 20 January 1876.

22. Members Register, 1883-1948, see constitution of subordinate lodges, 1; for these members see lists for 1885-1889.

23. *Ibid.*, see initiations 15 December 1894 and 18 February 1895.

24. *Freeholder*, 19 January 1900; for others Courts, see *Globe*, Toronto, 18 November 1893; *Freeholder*, 4 September, 1891; *Standard-Freeholder*, 29 June 1934; and *150th Anniversary of St. Columban's Parish*, 50.

25. *Standard-Freeholder*, 29 June 1934.

26. *Globe*, Toronto, 18 November 1893.

27. *Old Boys' Reunion*, 1906, 77.

28. *Standard-Freeholder*, 29 June 1934.

29. *Freeholder*, 13 August 1884 and 6 December 1889; *Globe*, Toronto, 18 November 1893.

30. Minutes, Town Council, 14 March, 1898, 460; 9 April, 1900, 253; 1 May, 1901; *Old Boys' Reunion*, 1906, 161; *Standard-Freeholder*, 29 June 1934.

31. Minutes, Town Council, 23 October 1894, 191.

32. *Reporter*, 12 August 1876, 9 September 1876; L. Jean Cameron, First Baptist Church, Cornwall, 1882-1967, 7; History of St. John's Church, 24.

33. Minutes, Town Council, 17 May 1897.

34. *Standard*, 8 May 1891.

35. *Globe*, Toronto, 18 November 1893.

36. Minutes, Town Council, 4 March 1895, 293.

37. *Standard-Freeholder*, 29 June 1934.

38. *Ibid.*, see also *Freeholder*, 23 February 1900; Anne Nyland, History of the Cornwall Public Library, 1982.

39. *Standard*, 3 February 1887; *Reporter*, 20 June 1884.

40. *Reporter*, 19 May 1883.

41. *Standard-Freeholder*, 7 October 1946.

42. *Ibid.*

43. *Freeholder*, 3 January 1890; *Globe*, Toronto, 18 November 1893; *Standard-Freeholder*, 24 August 1948.

44. Minutes, Town Council, 10 February 1896, 2; for Poultry Association, see also *Freeholder*, 21 January 1915 and *Standard-Freeholder*, 29 June 1934.

45. Minutes, Town Council, 10 February 1896, and 22 April 1886.

46. *Ibid.*, 19 January 1885, 398.

47. *Ibid.*, 23 April 1885, 431-32.

48. *Ibid.*, 5 November 1899, 199.

49. *Ibid.*, 15 December 1896, 206.

50. *Ibid.*, 28 September 1898, 589-591.

51. History of St. John's Church, 30.

52. *History of Knox Church*, 40.

53. Evelyn Stidwill, History of St. Paul's United Church, 1966.

54. Cameron, History of First Baptist Church, 6 and 7.

55. Bishop Philip Carrington, *The Anglican Church in Canada*, 181-2; Winifred Jerrom, Our Story, the W.A. and A.C.W., Angelion, Cornwall, Spring, 1980.

56. Father Charles Murray, "Reminiscences," 8.

57. *Standard-Freeholder*, 29 June 1934; see also Members Register, Oriental Lodge 163, 1884-1951.

58. *Standard-Freeholder*, 29 June 1934.

59. Minutes, Town Council, 9 April 1900, 253.

60. *Ibid.*, 23 October 1894, 191; 14 March 1898, 460.

61. See Edouard "Newsie" Lalonde's claim in M2811/273; see also Dr. George Beers' claim, *Standard-Freeholder*, 3 August 1946; *City of Cornwall and the United Counties of Stormont, Dundas and Glengarry Old Home Week*, 1946, 61; *Old Boys' Reunion*, 1906, 163.

62. For details of McLennan's sporting career, see, Harry Moffatt, Early History of Curling in the Cornwall Area, 1980, 2-7; *Old Boys' Reunion*, 1906, 86; Harkness, 282, *Globe*, Toronto, 18 November 1893, 7.

63. *Cornwall Observer*, 3 September 1840; "hurls" or "shinny" was a cross between lacrosse and hockey and was played in summer and winter, for description see *Standard-Freeholder* 13 November 1936.

64. *Globe*, Toronto, 18 November 1893; *Old Boys' Reunion*, 1906, see pages 22-24 and 163.

65. *Standard-Freeholder*, 3 August 1946, see Dr. George Beers, compiler of the first rule book of lacrosse.

66. *Reporter*, 5 August 1876 and 23 March 1878.

67. *Ibid.*, 5 August 1876.
68. *Ibid.*, 10 March 1879.
69. *Standard-Freeholder*, 13 November 1936; for list of team members of this date see *Freeholder*, 25 August 1882.
70. *Freeholder*, 28 March 1884.
71. *Standard-Freeholder*, 3 August 1946; *Old Boys' Reunion*, 1906, 163.
72. *Standard*, 2 February 1888; see also *Standard-Freeholder*, 3 August 1946; *Globe*, Toronto, 18 November 1893.
73. *Old Boys' Reunion*, 1906, 22; *Standard-Freeholder*, 13 November 1936 and 3 August 1946.
74. For description, see *Standard-Freeholder*, 3 August 1946.
75. Minutes, Town Council, 7 June 1886, 604; *Standard-Freeholder*, 7 October 1946 and 27 December 1941; Pringle, 289; for mention of an earlier rink, Snetsinger's Albert Rink, see *Reporter*, 30 December 1876.
76. *Old Boys' Reunion*, 1906, 164.
77. Minutes, Town Council, 2 April 1894, 83, and 30 April 1900, 261.
78. *Old Boys' Reunion*, 1906, 72.
79. See account of Cornwall reception for these two men in 1911, PAC: reel no. M2811.
80. *Freeholder*, 25 August 1882.
81. *Standard-Freeholder*, 13 November 1936.
82. *Ibid.*, 29 September 1972.
83. Harry Moffatt, Early History of Curling in the Cornwall Area and the Cornwall Curling Club, 1884-1909, 1946-1978, 1.
84. Minutes, Town Council, 5 April 1886, 572, 589.
85. *Freeholder*, 23 March 1888.
86. *Annual Report*, Royal Caledonia Curling Club, Montreal, 1889-90, cited in Moffatt, Curling in Cornwall, 7.
87. Moffatt, Curling in Cornwall, 10-11; *Globe*, Toronto, 18 November 1893.
88. *See Old Boys' Reunion*, 1906, 165; *Standard-Freeholder*, 13 November 1936; 3 August 1946.
89. *Standard-Freeholder*, 13 November 1936.
90. *Ibid.*
91. *Freeholder*, 8 February 1923.
92. For extensive list of prominent hockey players, see *Standard-Freeholder*, 13 November 1936.
93. *Reporter*, 25 August 1877.
94. *Ibid.*, 8 June 1878.
95. *Standard*, 16 September 1886.
96. Minutes, Town Council, 9 March 1868, 8.
97. *Freeholder*, 2 December 1881.
98. *Canadian Illustrated News*, 26 January 1878; *Standard*, 3 February 1887.
99. Dorothy Donihee, "In My Mother's Footsteps," 38.
100. Minutes, Town Council, 6 April 1885, 430.
101. William Boss, *The Stormont, Dundas and Glengarry Highlanders*, 100-101.
102. *Ibid.*, *Old Boys' Reunion*, 1906, 102.
103. Pringle, 86; *Standard-Freeholder*, 13 November 1936; 28 June 1958.
104. *Standard-Freeholder*, 13 November 1936.
105. Minutes, Town Council, 13 September 1858, 27.
106. H.E. Belden, *Historical Atlas of Stormont, Dundas and Glengarry*, 6.

107. *Globe*, 18 November 1893.
108. *Ibid.*
109. *Ibid.*, for Bergin's farm, see J.K. Johnson, *The Canadian Directory of Parliament*, 39-40.
110. Minutes, Town Council, 10 April 1899, 93-94.
111. *Freeholder*, 26 May 1899.
112. For details on golf, see Winifred Mavor, History of the Cornwall Golf and Country Club, 1982; *Standard-Freeholder*, 3 August 1946, 31 May 1947 and 10 January 1958.
113. *Star*, Montreal, 14 February 1916.
114. M2811, 29.
115. Donihee, "In My Mother's Footsteps," 34.
116. *Ibid.*, 38.
117. *Ibid.*, 2, 4; Harkness, 236.

Cornwall General Hospital, around 1900.

Credit: Ontario Archives.

The Hotel Dieu, 1906.
Credit: *Cornwall: Old Boys' Re-Union, 1906.*

Cornwall Public Library, 1906.
Credit: *Cornwall: Old Boys' Re-Union, 1906.*

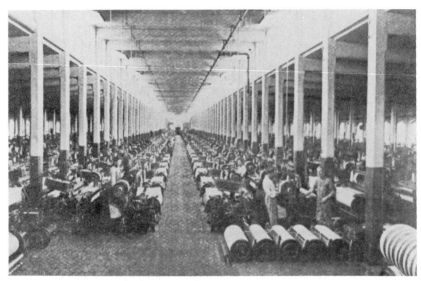

Canada Mill-Weave Room interior, 1906.
Credit: *Cornwall: Old Boys' Re-Union, 1906.*

Women's Christian Temperance Union Fountain, 1906.
Credit: *Cornwall: Old Boys' Re-Union - 1906.*

Chapter XV

Early Twentieth Century Cornwall

Trends in twentieth century Cornwall went in a number of directions. Industrially, the town's climb was moderate and fairly steady until the mid-century, weathering the 1930s with a mild boom in population and expansion in industry while the rest of Canada suffered severe depression. Thereafter, the collapse of Canadian Cottons and the completion of the St. Lawrence Seaway cast a shadow over what had been a climate of optimism, looking forward to the Seaway as an El Dorado. In religion, Roman Catholics continued far ahead of other denominations in terms of numbers, churches and schools, particularly in the 1940s when war-time industrial expansion and military bases attracted workers and service personnel to the town, many of them Roman Catholics. Municipal developments reflected these trends, Cornwall becoming a full-fledged city in 1945 and annexing 18,000 acres of suburbs in 1957 to jump its population overnight from 17,160 to 39,764 expressing for the first time the true demographic picture of the city.[1] Physical expansion could only be northwards as the east, west and south flanks of the city were hemmed in by natural barriers - Glengarry County boundary to the east, reserved Hydro land on the west and the St. Lawrence River to the south. Even development to the north encountered man-made obstacles - east-west highways, used and abandoned railway lines, and transmission lines.

Annexation of the surrounding suburbs and township area had been on the minds of Town Councillors since the beginning of the century, but it took fifty-seven years for them to do it.[2] Other ideas were in the minds of townsmen as they ushered in the new century. One was a drill hall and armoury fit for such a splendid regiment as the 59th, which thrilled with pride as it welcomed home its solitary hero from the South African war - Private Walter Lawrence of "D" Company, Royal Canadian Infantry Regiment.[3] That other Cornwall lads were missing on the South African front was no fault of theirs. "Volunteers were so numerous," a contemporary claimed, "that only a small percentage was accepted."[4] Indeed, the government at first limited the Canadian contingent to 1,000. Eventually 7,368 served.[5] In a wave of imperial enthusiasm, Town Council voted $200 to the Canadian Patriotic Fund, set up for wives and children of men serving in South Africa, while a writer to the *Freeholder* urged Cornwallites to drink only tea imported from Ceylon and India as a good-will gesture towards those countries whose "British tea planters are also fighting for the cause," an indication that the war aroused sentiments of solidarity with other parts of the distant empire.[6]

Pleas for an armoury and drill shed had been raised as early as 1884 when military men complained that the wooden drill hall at the rear of the Town Hall was inadequate.[7] Although Council granted a site for a new armoury in 1884, none was erected by the Department of Militia. In 1900 battalion officers Colonel Gordon Baker, Majors H.A. Morgan and Henry Turner, and Captains Archibald Denny, Dr. A.A. Smith and A.G.F. Macdonald made a strong representation for an armoury to the Minister of Militia, Dr. Frederick Borden. They stressed the efficiency of the 59th Regiment and Cornwall's strategic importance, especially noting that the canal might need protection by local troops at a moment's notice, an indication that there were lingering fears of the United States as a potential enemy. Indeed, the Yukon-Alaska boundary dispute was fresh in everyone's mind.[8] The Cornwall deputation's path to the corridors of power in Ottawa was smoothed by the local Liberal member, John G. Snetsinger, who met the officers as soon as they arrived in the capital. He then escorted them to the Minister of Militia and, after briefly setting forth the purpose of their visit, he allowed the officers to plead their own case. The persuasive arguments of the Cornwall officers convinced Borden that "from the size and importance of Cornwall, it had good claims to...(a drill hall as well as an armoury.)"[9]

Borden immediately sent the departmental architect to examine the sites offered by the town and to prepare plans for an armoury. Tenders were called and the ratepayers asked to ratify the amount needed to buy property. Officers and men of the 59th encouraged the formation of a cadet corps, especially when it was learned that the government was prepared to issue new Ross rifles to such corps.[10] However, with the end of the Boer War, the impetus towards military expansion lessened and plans for the armoury were shelved. Cornwall did get its first cadet corps, though. In March 1907 students of Cornwall High School were organized as a corps and, through the beneficence of Mrs. John McMartin and Duncan Monroe, they became one of the few kilted units in the province. By 1942, the cadet corps was increased by two companies of girls who dressed in white blouses, navy blue skirts, red berets and socks. Their performance at annual inspections established an unrivalled tradition of excellence. Moreover, Cornwall Collegiate Institute, as the high school was later called, provided the officers of the parent regiment with two small rooms in the basement for use as regimental headquarters for many years.[11]

Demands for an armoury were revived in 1913 when the town again offered a site to the Dominion government, but the magnificent armoury and drill hall on Fourth Street East did not materialize until 1939 when the threat of a second world war loomed large.[12] Its erection, some fifty-five years after the first overtures had been made by town military men for an armoury, was largely the work of Lionel Chevrier, Member of Parliament for Stormont. Chevrier worked quietly behind the scenes, so quietly in fact that when news that $100,000 had been set aside in the 1937 federal budget estimates for an armoury in Cornwall, its citizens were taken completely by surprise.[13] Chevrier's success in securing the wherewithal to begin the armoury and drill hall marked the first time since 1882 that Cornwall had secured a federally-financed public building, its last being the Post Office.

Businessmen fretted about the slight economic recession that set in at the turn of the twentieth century. They revived the defunct Board of Trade, using it as a pressure group to promote the enlargement of the drydock and to get the Canadian Pacific Railway to run a spur line to Cornwall.[14] It was largely through the efforts of the Board of Trade that a committee of thirty business and professional men - among them five French Canadians - promoted the very successful Old Boys' Reunion of 1906, enticing back to Cornwall for four days in mid-August many who had left the town to seek greener fields.[15] Their return prompted the Board of Trade to prepare an impressive 163-page souvenir booklet describing in prose and picture the growth of Cornwall and the three counties of Stormont, Dundas and Glengarry. Drawing on the excellent history of the three counties published in 1890 by County Judge Jacob Farrand Pringle, the writers cast aside the prophets of gloom and doom and the town's chronic whiners and complainers, telling them they needed to study the past more vigorously to see what had been accomplished. "What a marvellous contrast," the editors exclaimed, "from the time of the landing of the Loyalists to the Cornwall of today. Where once were dense and forbidding forests, are now paved streets and granolithic sidewalks, bordered with green boulevards and brilliantly illumined with electric light - all but the grand old St. Lawrence is changed."[16]

There were some hopeful signs of renewed industrial activity in town. Mack's express roller flour mill that had been inoperative for some time was bought up by G.D. Atkinson who renovated and refitted the mill in 1906.[17] Three foundries were in operation at this time - Jacob Miller's, located west of Hotel Dieu on the north side of Water Street, Gillies' on Pitt Street West above Fourth Street, and the older established foundry run by the Derochie brothers in the east near the cotton mills. By 1912 the Miller foundry was bought out by James E. Quig who, at twenty-nine, had blitzed his way up from mechanic with the Toronto Paper Company to master mechanic with the Canadian Pacific Railway Angus Shops in Montreal. In 1911 he returned to Cornwall to establish his own foundry, where he did a thriving business in acetylene welding, and cast iron and pipe fitting.[18]

The revival of the express flour mills and the expansion of the foundries opened up additional jobs in town, but the more practical and pragmatic members of Cornwall's business community and Town Council, much as they glowed with pride over the results of the Old Boys' Reunion, felt that the future must be safeguarded. Thus Councillors and townsmen continued to vote substantial bonuses to a number of companies which decided to build factories in Cornwall. Two of the earlier ones of the new century were the Cornwall Furniture Manufacturing Company and the Cornwall Paper Manufacturing Company. The furniture company was located in impressive new brick buildings at the head of Sydney Street in 1902. It was organized by Thomas S. Aspinall of Toronto and Andrew Edwards of Gananoque, who acquired some local investors such as hardware merchant R.J. Pitts. As soon as Council voted a bonus of $16,200 to the company, Aspinall and Edwards moved to Cornwall and were soon producing high quality bedroom and dining room furniture. A railway siding to the factory enabled them to ship goods directly to the main line for distribution across Canada. By 1906 the factory employed eighty hands and was described as "a success from the start and now one of the leading industries in town." Yet within two years its financial base collapsed and the company went into bankruptcy, local men as well as outside capitalists losing most of their investments. The large factory was then bought by a furniture-maker of Winchester, Charles A. Beach, who took a chance on the Cornwall location because of its rail facilities. Where others failed, he succeeded, building a modest fortune and producing prize furniture.[19]

The Cornwall Paper Company was located at Mille Roches where the mill could take advantage of the power plant owned by company president M.P. Davis of Ottawa. Financed largely by Cornwallites - Colonel Roderick R. McLennan, Samuel Greenwood, manager of the Canadian Colored Cottons Mills Company, R.J. Pitts, who had invested heavily in the Cornwall Furniture Company, and Curtis P.

Derochie, the new plant went up in record time. Ground was broken in April 1904 and by November 8 of the same year the first sheet of paper rolled off the press. A spur joined the paper plant to the main line of the railway so that ten to twelve tons of high grade paper could move easily each day to markets across Canada. Yet, like the Cornwall Furniture Manufacturing Company, the paper plant soon fell into financial troubles and was bought by Americans from Kalamazoo in 1909.

Like Beach from Winchester, they managed to operate the company successfully, and it evolved into the Provincial Paper Company which continued operations until the early 1950s.[20]

Another plant that was nurtured by the Town Council and the Board of Trade's industrial committee was a bedstead factory. This opened in 1907 as a branch factory of the Modern Bedstead Company of Sherbrooke, Quebec. Council voted the company a bonus of $20,000 and exemption from taxes other than school for ten years in order to entice the company, with its fully paid-up stock of $80,000, to locate in Cornwall.[21] Despite these advantages the iron and brass bed factory encountered financial difficulties and was bought out by the Ives Bedding Company of Montreal in 1908. Under the capable management of Major S. Morgan Gray and his brother, Fred, of Toronto, the new bed company met with a moderate success, employing fifty hands as late as 1946.[22] The new company brought to Cornwall a man who not only got the company out of the red, but in a quiet way proved a boom to the town's social and fraternal life. Transferring from the Queen's Own Rifles to the 59th Stormont, Dundas and Glengarry Highlanders, Major Morgan Gray served with the 59th overseas and helped found the Great War Veterans' Society that eventually became the Canadian Legion. This Toronto import was also instrumental in establishing the Stormont, Dundas and Glengarry Historical Society in 1920 and the Cornwall Kennel Club. As a dedicated Mason, he reached the highest degree, receiving his fifty-year Jewel and becoming a member of the Karnac Temple of the Mystic Shrine, Montreal.

Attempts to establish a viable brewery in town proved ephemeral. It was another group of businessmen from Sherbrooke, Quebec, who chose Cornwall as a likely locale, probably spurred on by one of the promoters of the Modern Bedstead Company, C.H. Nutter, whose brother, Seth C. Nutter, was the key man in the brewery's promotion.[23] What Seth Nutter and the other men from Sherbrooke asked of Council was ten years' exemption from municipal taxes and, what was more important, a change in the town's by-laws which limited the supply of water to 800,000 gallons a year. The brewery promoters expected to operate day and night and wanted Council to guarantee them an increasing supply of water to allow for plant expansion.[24] The $125,000 plant was erected on Water Street at the corner of Augustus in 1907, its kettle capable of brewing 8,000 gallons of beer daily.[25] Incorporated as the St. Lawrence Breweries Limited, the company's financial basis soon proved inadequate, and by 1909 Montrealer J. Frederick Schneider bought the plant.

For a short time Schneider succeeded in making "Cornwall ale" known from coast to coast.[26] However, before the decade was out, his business failed, either through poor marketing or financial difficulties, and he closed up the brewery in 1920, marking the first complete failure of an industry that had been encouraged by the Town Council in terms of tax exemptions. The vacant brewery stood for twenty years as a gaunt reminder to the town that industries could come and go. Then suddenly in 1939 it was turned overnight into "one of the busiest spots in Cornwall," as a storage place for cheese coming in from twenty-two district factories. Unlike the other items stored in the deserted brewery - machinery for a mattress factory, a sausage-making plant and a brick manufacturing concern - the cheese was stored in the curing room for a time and then moved to market.[27]

The McGill Chair Company enjoyed a longer success than the brewery. Started by Thomas McGill who received a loan of $20,000 from Town Council in 1905, the chair factory was erected, with the help of some local investment, at the corner of York and Third Streets. Unlike other companies which received cash bonuses, McGill's was required to repay the loan by yearly installments of $1,000. The business became insolvent in 1910, but McGill was able to re-construct a new company which continued in operation until 1931, when it was bought by a group of Cornwallites. Even so, the company tottered along only for a few years before collapsing completely and the factory was demolished in 1942.[28]

Probably one of the most successful of the smaller factories to locate in Cornwall in the early part of the twentieth century was the pants plant founded by Aaron and Louis Horovitz. These brothers had left their native Roumania in 1910 to seek their fortunes in the new world and succeeded. After looking over the Montreal clothing manufacturing field, they decided to make Cornwall their bailiwick starting out modestly in 1911 in part of the Brennan block at the corner of Water and Marlborough Streets, with twenty-five employees operating sewing machines. By 1920 their business had expanded enough to buy out the Plamondon Hotel on Marlborough Street.

350

Here they set up the Prince Clothing Company, soon acquiring the Collins dance hall to which they added a second floor. By 1934 they had 300 workers bringing home $250,000 in wages each year, and this in spite of a devastating fire that swept through their pants factory after a boiler exploded on 18 February 1933.[29] Materials were imported from the United Kingdom, France, Holland, Germany and Czechoslovakia, arriving at Cornwall station in huge bales. When the second world war cut off some of their suppliers, the Horovitz brothers moved into war-time production, more than half of their clothing going to the Royal Canadian Navy in the form of greatcoats and battledress slacks for the infantry and airforce.[30]

One of the most active Cornwallites in promoting the town as a location for industry was Doctor W.B. Cavanagh, mayor in 1906 and again in 1926 when the town celebrated Old Home Week. Cavanagh had been foremost in promoting an advertising scheme in 1905 and 1906 to put Cornwall on the map across the country. Moreover, to increase its industrial potential, he pushed for additional water power from the different by-washes on the canal. By 1910, as chairman of the industrial committee of the Board of Trade, Cavanagh met with agents of the J.C. McLaren Belting Company of Montreal to try to persuade them to locate in Cornwall, rather than move to the outskirts of Montreal. Though the town was prepared to meet the firm's demands in providing a town lot, exemption from municipal taxes, water at a nominal rate of twenty-five cents per 1000 gallons and a small cash bonus of $500 towards the cost of moving their plant from Montreal to Cornwall, the negotiations were not successful. This was just one of several such projects carried out by Cavanagh and the Industrial Committee and Town Council to try to diversify the town's industrial base at the beginning of the century.[31]

The last time Council tried to attract an industry to town by means of bonuses or loans and tax exemptions was in 1920 when $40,000 was loaned to the Canadian Linoleum and Oilcloth Company to purchase a large brick building on Fourth Street. The factory operated only five years, just long enough to repay the entire loan.[32] Thus, out of seven industries attracted to Cornwall in the years from 1902 to 1920, five received substantial help from the town in terms of money or tax exemptions and yet only one survived without suffering early bankruptcy. The furniture, bed and paper companies all went under financially within a few years of starting operations. The brewery collapsed completely by 1920. The chair company failed in the 1930s and the oilcloth company folded within five years. Only the pants factory sailed on smoothly, weathering the depression years and labour difficulties right up until 1975 when fire struck a disastrous blow, forcing the new owners to close the plant that had been operating since 1911.

At the turn of the twentieth century, Cornwall's major industries felt the need to consolidate and to initiate aggressive marketing policies. The three cotton and wollen mills had been absorbed and amalgamated under an umbrella company — the Canadian Colored Cotton Mills Company, which secured tax exemptions for a further ten years on one of its mills.[33] By 1904 the newly-organized company had 1300 operatives on its payroll. The Toronto Paper Company was not in a league with the local textile firm. Only 130 hands took home a weekly pay envelope, though their envelopes usually contained more than those of their counterparts at the textile mills. And scarcely anyone in Cornwall noticed when the Toronto Paper Company appointed Charles Howard Futvoye Smith of Montreal as its selling agent in 1905. Yet Smith was no ordinary salesman. At thirty-two, he had gone through various stages of the paper industry, beginning with his father's publishing and printing firm at St. John's, Quebec, then taking a year's stint with the Canada Paper Company and three years as manager of the Kinleith Paper mills. By 1900 he opened his own business as a paper jobber in Montreal, representing a number of firms that, by 1905, included the Cornwall plant, an indication that the small Cornwall plant was hoping to capture some of the Montreal market.[34]

Many of Cornwall's businessmen and professional men wore two hats. When they were not tending their shops, their dentistry or medical offices, or their legal and insurance trades, they were, more than likely, donning military uniforms as part of the town's defence force. Most of these militia officers took time out from their busy schedules to attend special courses to qualify for promotion, while the rank and file of the 59th Battalion undertook annual training at summer camps at Rockcliffe in Ottawa, Barriefield, near Kingston, or at the new central training camp at Petawawa. Despite the lack of suitable accommodation in Cornwall for company training, the battalion managed to keep fit and disciplined, winning high praise in 1913 from its inspecting officer, Lieutenant-Colonel John Hughes, a brother of the Minister of Militia, Sam Hughes. Hughes reported, "The Regiment is made up of a most superb body of young men of splendid physique, active and most willing to perfect themselves in military knowledge. Both officers and men work together...to do all in their power to make the 59th the best or one of the best Regiments in Canada."[35]

The test of any military unit comes in time of war. For Cornwall, war touched the town the moment Germany invaded Belgium on 4 August 1914. That same night military guards from the regiment were placed at vulnerable points along the canals, bridges and public buildings to guard against possible sabotage. For families living near the Toronto Paper Company mill, in the area known as Smithville, the movement of troops to patrol the New York and Ottawa Railway bridge, or, as it was familiarly dubbed, the "Nyando", brought the war very near. One mother, Elizabeth Good Tilton, gathered her children around her as they watched the soldiers set up camp right behind their house. "Never go near the bridge," she warned, for it was over this bridge that the dreaded German saboteurs were expected to come. Yet as the summer wore on, the dread turned to normalcy. Children ran to the soldiers' cook house, an old boxcar drawn up on an unused track, from where the jovial and rotund cook, Alex Eamer of Hazel Street, turned out meal after meal for the soldiers as they patrolled the nearby bridge, shouting out at night, "Halt! Who goes there?" Usually a muffled voice of some Indian from Cornwall Island answered. But one night there was a terrifying silence. Then shots rang out and all Smithville jumped out of bed to learn that an elderly Indian had been killed when he failed to respond to the sentry's challenge.[36] During all the war, there was only one case of a German being caught on the bridge. Night watchman Alex McCourt cornered the man as he was trying to get back to the American side after having crossed to Canada from Detroit a week earlier. The captured man admitted being a German chemist, but insisted that he was a naturalized American. Cornwall authorities took no chances. They shipped him off to Montreal for questioning.[37]

Along with this military activity on the home front in Cornwall and its immediate neighbourhood in the fall of 1914, townsmen also responded to the call for overseas volunteers. At this time these townsmen were a mixed lot ethnically. By far the largest single group were the French Canadians, now numbering 2,537, and almost entirely Roman Catholic. Those of Scottish origin were next in numbers — 1,184 — followed by the Irish, some 1,155, and the English — 1,067. There were smaller groupings of whom the Dutch were the largest and continued to increase in numbers from 241 in 1901 to 303 in 1911 to 348 in 1921. The decline in the numbers of Germans, Jews and Italians from 1901 to 1911 reflected the slowing down of Cornwall's industrial life. Italians had numbered seventy-seven in 1901, fifty-four in 1911 and ninety-six in 1921. Those of German background dropped from 206 in 1901 to 127 in 1911.

Similarly Cornwall's Jewish community had an unsteady demographic picture with seventy in 1901, 104 in 1911 and eighty-six in 1921. There was a smattering of Blacks, nineteen in 1911, seven Orientals and a small number of other Continental Europeans.

Out of this ethnic melange an estimated 500 men served overseas from 1914 to 1918, eighty-seven of them dying in battle.[38] Their names bore testimony not only to Cornwall's Loyalist founders, but to those who came later — Lieutenant George Henry Gallinger, Privates R.J. and S.P. Gallinger, A. Runions, Gunner O.H. Loney, Captain C.D. Hamilton, M.D., Clifford J. Eastman, Henry Atchison, Ralph Freeman, Clarence Murch, Stuart H. Hermiston, Joseph Albert Benoit, Alex Lalonde, and the brothers, Murdock John and Donald Malcolm Munroe, to mention only a few. At first the Cornwall volunteers fed a variety of battalions heading overseas — the 1st, 2nd 21st, 38th, 39th, 73rd and 77th. Then in December 1915 the United Counties own unit — the 154th Battalion — was authorized. Cornwall became the major recruiting centre with Major J.G. MacLaren, Captain G.A. McNaughton, Lieutenant J.R. Macdonald and Lieutenant B.L. Irwin operating out of Ross's mill on Water Street and drumming up recruits by huge advertisements in the local newspapers: "Young Man! Your Country Calls you! It is your Duty to yourself as a true Canadian, your Duty to your Home and Family, to Enlist." Another read, "If Germany Wins, Nothing else in the World Matters. Eligible Young Men who don't want Germany to Win Should Go to the Front!"[39]

Despite the prohibition against enlisting such categories of men as mechanics, machinists or any men employed in munitions factories, 1,150 men were recruited into the new local battalion by May 1916.[40] They went into training at Barriefield where, along with digging drains, building cookhouses, practising with the new Ross rifles and bayonets, they had an overnight bivouac at Collins Bay. Each recruit rolled up in blankets and groundsheets which proved so cosy that most of them awoke to find they had acquired overnight companions — cold, clammy watersnakes had coiled themselves comfortably inside the blankets.

That Cornwall looked upon the 154th as its own special battalion was apparent from the first day recruiting began. For one thing, members of the newly-organized St. Lawrence Chapter of the Imperial Order Daughters of the Empire, many of them still high school girls, undertook to provide colours for the new battalion.[41] This national patriotic women's organization had grown out of the South African War but it was not until August of 1914 that a number of women in

Cornwall banded together to form the St. Lawrence branch. Helping them in their organizational meeting were members from the I.O.D.E. Brockville Chapter and the Wolfe and Montcalm Chapter of Montreal. Una Stewart was named Regent with Lillian Phillips as secretary and Daphne Duquette treasurer. The chapter's membership included two sisters who were still members in 1982 — Marcia Hermiston Boyd and Ruth Hermiston Wood.[42]

In presenting the 154th with its colours, these women helped put on what was Cornwall's most impressive military display since the days of the Fenian invasion scares. The day chosen was 23 August 1916 when the 154th Battalion returned to Cornwall from its year's training at Barriefield. Through streets of cheering crowds, the troops marched to St. Lawrence Park to bivouac. As evening fell the Park was brilliantly illuminated through the generosity of the Stormont Electric Railway Company, thus allowing soldiers to mingle with friends and relatives from town and other parts of the United Counties. The next day was one that remained imprinted on the minds of every volunteer and townsman who shared in the moving ceremonies as three I.O.D.E. members presented the beautiful colours. These flags were consecrated by Reverend Hugh Sutherland, Moderator of the Presbytery of Glengarry, whose son had been killed in action. Receiving them was another man who would give his life for his country — Lieutenant Frank Pendergast. Then Mrs. John McMartin presented a large silk flag to the Pipe Band, a gift of the Long Sault Chapter of the Imperial Order Daughters of the Empire. The Pipe Band had been equipped and uniformed through the generosity of John McMartin, a native of Charlottenburg who, with his brother, Duncan, had made a fortune in railroad construction and gold mines. Returning in 1903 to make his home in Cornwall where he bought the beautiful R.R. McLennan property at the corner of Second and Sydney Streets, McMartin became Member of Parliament for Glengarry-Stormont in 1917-18. He and his brother typified the pluralism that existed in the Cornwall of that period. He died a Roman Catholic and Liberal, his magnificent home bequeathed to the Roman Catholic Church which subsequently transformed it into Nazareth Orphanage. Duncan went to his grave a Presbyterian and Conservative.[43]

On hand for the colour presentation ceremony at the Lacrosse Grounds were all three Members of Parliament for the United Counties. None was more enthusiastically applauded than Cornwall's own Dr. Duncan Orestes Alguire, Member for Stormont, who had served as medical officer of the 59th Regiment and whose son, Captain A. Ross Alguire, was to serve in France and Belgium with the Canadian Army Medical Corps. At nine o'clock that night after the colourful ceremonies had ended, the troops entrained for Kingston and within two months were embarking on the *Mauretania* for England.

Cornwall had proved so good a recruiting ground for the 154th Battalion that the 5th Pioneers of Montreal opened a recruiting office in town at the Ottawa Hotel. The officer in charge, Captain C.A. Palmer, lost no time in making use of the local press to announce that the Pioneers hoped to leave Montreal for England by July 1916 with a full strength of 1,034.[44] In 1917 and 1918 the war touched Cornwallites indirectly through the local press which printed news of the front and casualty lists. More direct were the letters and telegrams from overseas with news of loved ones. Mr. and Mrs. Nathan Copeland of the East Front, for instance, learned by telegram that their son, Corporal John G. Copeland, arrived in Quebec from the front in France, having lost his left leg in the Somme engagement.[45] Paul Besse, son of a town tailor, went off to Toronto to join the 216th Bantam Battalion, he being "well within the limit of the Bantams, standing about four feet eleven inches."[46] Mrs. Alex Cross, whose husband was wounded in France received a letter from her brother-in-law on his way back to the front. "I suppose there are a lot of slackers over there who would rather walk around than fight," he commented somewhat bitterly. "There will be a day when they will have to come over."[47] Indeed, as the fighting grew more tense, the letters took on a more sombre tone. Private Bryan wrote his parents: "If some of the fathers and mothers were to stand a few days by the Lens Road and watch the boys going back into the trenches from the hospitals, limping along, some of them with their bandages not yet off, to fill up the ranks, they would not hesitate a moment in sending them help. We have so much of the line to hold," he declared, "and we have to hold it."[48]

There were brighter moments to wartime duty as well. One Cornwall man who was gassed at Passchendale, Private Mack Kittle, was delighted by a visit while in hospital from Prime Minister Lloyd George and Sir Robert Borden, the latter quite surprised "when I told him I was from Cornwall." The invalided soldier exclaimed, "I tell you, Mums, this is the life! A bunch of us were up to Windsor Castle the other day and we were received by the King and Queen and Princess Mary. The King and Queen shook hands with us all."[49] Still another Cornwall soldier, Gunner Delmar T. Bowes, took time off to write to one of his old teachers at Cornwall High School, telling him, "Since I came to France, I have (met) many old Cornwall boys who, in previous years, were members of the Cornwall High School Cadets, and we have all agreed that our early training as Cadets has been of the greatest value to us in our present military work,"[50] a vindication of the faith that the Chief of the Canadian General Staff, Major-General Sir Percy Lake, had placed in cadet training.

By 1917 the drain of young men into the services was sufficient to produce a minor labour shortage in town and prompted the Board of Trade to establish a special labour-supplying bureau.[51] On the whole, though, Cornwall passed through the war years without serious dislocations in labour or life-style. Organized sports suffered some loss of players. Indeed, lacrosse never fully recovered from wartime attrition. Letters to the press may have aggravated its decline. One writer, for instance, urged that the game be suspended until the end of the war and the money usually spent on the teams be "turned over to buying comforts for the boys over in the trenches."[52] In another direction, Trinity Church ladies gave up their candy table at their annual fall bazaar in 1917 in the interests of wartime economy.[53] If sugar was scarce, money was plentiful, judging from the over-subscribed Victory Loan campaigns. In 1917 Cornwallites salted away $454,900 in the Victory Loan bonds and the next year's objective of $390,000 was overshot by $115,200.[54]

Women of the town found that wartime patriotism had given them new opportunities. Having moved from concentration solely on church-oriented activities to more varied fraternal and social organizations by the turn of the century, they now branched out into patriotic and service clubs that embraced women from all denominations and all levels of society. The Imperial Order Daughters of the Empire was an ideal agency for bringing women together to aid the war effort. Thus members of the first Cornwall I.O.D.E., the St. Lawrence Chapter, used the pages of the *Standard* to appeal to women and young girls in town to come to their committee rooms on Tuesdays and Fridays to secure free yarn and knit socks "for the soldiers at the front."[55] Women in East Cornwall soon followed suit. They formed a second I.O.D.E. chapter, Lady Laurier, by May of 1917, opening a "sewing room in Ruest's Hotel" for volunteer workers.[56]

The men of the 154th Battalion went overseas clad in Sutherland trews and scarlet doublets with white belts and rifle slings, marching behind their Highland Pipe Band, fitted out with Clan Ranald kilts, white shell jackets and diced glengarries with feathers. Through the prompt and decisive order of Minister of Militia Sam Hughes, who always had a soft spot for the Highlanders of the United Counties, they were given permission to bear the style and title of "154th Overseas Battalion, Highlanders" and allowed to change their pattern of clothing from that of infantry to full Highland pattern. However, as military authorities overseas decided it was wrong to send young raw recruits immediately into trench warfare, the 154th never went into battle with its new colours and clad in Highland dress. The unit split up and the men and officers drafted into other units, principally the 2nd and 21st Battalions. They did not don Highland uniform until their return from overseas when they converted to kilts in 1922 with authority to wear the Macdonell of Glengarry tartan, the only corps in the British Commonwealth to wear this tartan. At the same time the old 59th Regiment became the "Stormont, Dundas and Glengarry Highlanders" with regimental headquarters still in Cornwall. Commanding was Cornwall civil engineer W.H. Magwood, who had gone overseas with the Battalion.

Like other militia regiments that converted to wartime needs, the Stormont, Dundas and Glengarries faced a period of readjustment in the post-war period during which the unit dwindled down to Headquarters and one company at Cornwall and a single company at Alexandria. Part of the difficulty was the attitude of the returning veterans. Many preferred to get out of uniform and forget the battlefields, the slaughter, the guns and the gas. Townsmen and women appreciated this, but they also knew that veterans would need help in adjusting once more to civilian life. Others would require medical care. Still other families would face the future without the head of the household and these widows and orphans of slain soldiers would need extra help and protection. Thus, in the fall of 1917, a branch of the Great War Veterans' Association was formed in Cornwall with a five-fold purpose. First and foremost was their desire "to retain that spirit of comradeship found amongst the men in the trenches (as) it is the greatest spirit of this whole war."[58] Indeed, men returning from the second world war were just as emphatic about the almost spiritual experience the soldiers felt as trench warfare developed. It was a sense of comradeship towards each other that transcended differences they had known at home, whether of religion, ethnic background or social class. Thrown together haphazardly at the front and facing physical discomfort, danger and frequently death itself, these men from Cornwall knew that their safety and sanity often depended on the unselfishness, good humour, alertness and judgment of their comrades. Once back home, veterans spotted each other as "men who had been over there." This idea of preserving and fostering the comradeship of old soldiers was paramount in the formation of the first veterans' group. In addition, they aimed at providing places of recreation where veterans could meet together, discuss common problems, and unite their efforts to secure "fair and just treatment (from) the Government of Canada by courteously requesting the same."[59]

One of these veterans, George Williams, who remained a Legion member for over fifty years, put it in a nutshell. In a reminiscence which he broadcast over Legion Line 297 in February 1972, Williams reminded his listeners, "The main purpose (of the Legion) was then, as it is today, to assist needy veterans and their dependents, and to keep fresh the memory of our comrades who paid the supreme sacrifice."[60] Townsmen and women showed their solidarity with the returning veterans during the Labour Day celebrations on 1 September 1918 and Town Council lent its support by voting them a grant of $4,000 in 1919.[61]

When the founding of this first veterans' group was announced in the *Standard* on 11 July 1918 the writer predicted that "this Association will be one of the greatest and noblest of any in America, if not in the Empire."[62] He was right in the long run, but it took almost ten years before the first world war veterans in Cornwall really began to pull together as a group. Indeed, it was the women of the two Cornwall chapters of the Imperial Order Daughters of the Empire who took the initiative in getting a cenotaph erected in Memorial Park on Second Street. Together with public-spirited citizens and a number of veterans, they organized an impressive ceremony for the unveiling on 5 June 1925. Governor-General Baron Byng, himself a veteran, did the honours, while 104 veterans of the 154th Battalion supplied the Guard of Honour, headed by the Pipe Band of eleven Pipers and five Drummers. Among those with whom Baron Byng stopped to chat was Private Alex G. Atchison of Knox Church who had won the Military Medal.[63]

Yet even this occasion did not spark enough enthusiasm to bring the Cornwall veterans together. Remembrance Day ceremonies that November were still carried out largely through the efforts of the ladies of the I.O.D.E. A great display of Union Jacks along Pitt and Second Streets formed part of the Armistice Day celebrations along with a mammoth parade of school children and teachers to the new cenotaph at Memorial Park where each child dropped a sprig of evergreen as a memorial to those who had died in the war. What was most remarkable was the absence or at least no obvious presence of veterans or military men. Mayor Harry W. Snetsinger was there to officiate, asking everyone to bow their heads in a moment of silent prayer at eleven o'clock. Then the minister of Knox Church,

Reverend James Faulds, gave a stirring address. "The true war," he declared, "is a war against that which is ignoble and unworthy, dishonorable and injurious."[64]

This Remembrance Day ceremony at the new cenotaph was far more impressive than the previous annual observances which had been held at Central Park, where a modest cross had been erected and speeches were given from the bandstand. From now on, Cornwall's veterans began to heed the voice of the Dominion president of the Great War Veterans' Association, Sir Richard Turner, who had been urging the various small veterans' groups across the country to combine into one organization which could present the veterans' demands and views to the federal government from a united front.

Under the enthusiastic leadership of Harold Fawthrop, a member of a Baptist family which had sent four of its men overseas, the veterans met at the Cornwall High School in 1926 to form Branch 83 of the Canadian Legion. This was the veterans' organization that became the Royal Canadian Legion in 1960. Captain Frank Hunter was elected president by the 200 or so veterans who attended the initial meeting in 1926. Being so numerous, they soon found that their room at the high school was inadequate. It was again the I.O.D.E. who procured them larger quarters. Over the years they met in various places - the Bank of Nova Scotia building on Second Street, the Colquhoun block, the new Windsor Hotel, the Snetsinger Block and above Hall's hardware store, under presidents Frank Hunter, B. de Millidge, J. Victor Smyth, Harold Fawthrop, Bill Conley, Wilfred Stewart, W.H. Magwood and Fred Davidson.[65]

One of the first major events of the newly-organized Legion branch was to assist in an impressive ceremony on 1 August 1926 when the old colours of the 154th Battalion were retired. These were the colours that had been presented by the Cornwall I.O.D.E. to the wartime battalion ten years earlier just prior to the troops' embarkation for overseas. As the 154th had been officially disbanded before its return from England, its colours were now deposited in Trinity Church. Veterans of the battalion crowded into the two centre aisles of the church as their old commanding officer, Colonel A.G.F. Macdonald presented the colours to Canon W. Netten for "safekeeping, as a token of their gratitude to Almighty God by Whom alone victory is secured,...to provide a memorial to the men of all ranks who served under these Colours, and to afford an inspiration for patriotic service and sacrifice to all who may worship here."[66]

By 1931 Cornwall's veterans were sufficiently organized to acquire more permanent headquarters at the Labor Temple on north

Pitt Street. One of their major annual events in the 1930s was a field and track meet held early each August. However, it was their involvement in the meets that wiped out their financial base and disheartened members for almost a decade. Their most grandiose meet was planned for 7 August 1933, a day on which the veterans hoped to raise spirits and dispel some of the depression gloom. For this, they invested most of their capital, expecting to recoup their investment by the day's receipts. Through the efforts of Dr. J.A. Phillips, a later mayor of Cornwall, the John McMartin Memorial Gold Cup, then valued at $3,000, was put up for competition, having been donated to the Legion by the Estate in memory of Mr. and Mrs. John McMartin. This was the couple who had been so generous in their support of Cornwall's military men and cadets and for whom the reorganized Legion Branch 297 was later named.[67] Unhappily for Cornwall and for the Legion, the most disastrous fire of the town's history broke out at noon on the very day that the Legion had planned its sports event. Instead of going to the meet, crowds raced to the heart of the city to watch as strong winds chased the fire from its original spot behind Fursey's garage at 234 Pitt Street west. Believed to have been started by some young boys, the fire quickly raced along a wooden fence, sweeping into the garage on one side and into the huge Victoria skating arena on the other. Before long every business establishment along the west side of Pitt Street between Second and Third Streets was in flames, though the volunteer firemen were on the scene four minutes after the alarm sounded. Montreal and Ottawa firemen raced to Cornwall after receiving S.O.S. calls from Fire Chief George Hunter at two o'clock. By 3:30 p.m. seventeen streams of water were pouring into the flames from the Cornwall contingent that included fire-fighting equipment from the Howard Smith Paper mill, Canadian Cottons Limited, Beach Furniture, Ives Bedding and Courtauld's Limited. Eleven firemen from Montreal station No. 34 manned two pumps that effectively blocked the blaze from injuring the Royal Bank, while Ottawa firemen played another stream into the flames. It was eight o'clock before the fire was extinguished and Cornwall firemen returned to their station, exhausted. Besides Chief George Hunter and Deputy Chief Cory Moore, they included E. Kennedy, J. Warrington, W. Borthwick, J. Firn, A. Silmser, A. Parker, E. Wagoner, W.A. Milligan, A. Conliffe, H. Plumley, I. Miller, A. Wilson, F. Silmser, C. Snetsinger, W. Copeland and W. Silmser.

When the burned-out area was examined, townsmen counted thirty-one businesses along Pitt Street West, ten business places, five dwellings and the Victoria Arena on Third Street, and one store and apartment block on Pitt Street East all wiped out, amounting to a loss of $243,855, of which only $135,900 was covered by insurance. The day had been exciting, but burned-out businessmen would rather have had the attraction of the Legion's field and track meet. As for the thirty-six families left homeless, fifteen of whom had nothing left but the clothes they were wearing that lunch hour, they found quick and immediate help from the newly-formed Kinsmen Club which set up a fire relief bureau in the town hall and raised $2,000 within two weeks for the fire victims.[68]

This new service club, which proved so efficient in the emergency, had only been organized in March of 1933 by fourteen Cornwall young business and professional men; President J. Cliff Beach, Vice President D. Labarr, Secretary A.E. Hall, Treasurer O.C. Graveley, Registrar B. Cameron and Bulletin Editor G.C. Garbutt. Like the Legion itself, the Kinsmen's clubs had originated in the trenches in France where a young soldier, Harry A. Rogers, had determined to keep alive the bond of comradeship and the ideals of service that he had experienced at the front. Two years after his return to his home in Hamilton, Ontario, Rogers gathered a small group of young friends together to form the first "Kinsmen" club, the name itself evoking a sense of comradeship. Membership was limited to those under forty and their motto was "Fellowship through Service." Each club was to focus its activities upon the needs of its own particular community. On 7 August 1933, Cornwall's utmost need was to care for the homeless families, provide moral support to the many businessmen who lost their premises, and mourn with fellow townsmen over the loss of its splendid hockey and skating rink.[69]

Thus members of the new Cornwall Kinsmen Club, who since March had been waging a very successful "Give a man a job" anti-depression campaign, swung into action to aid the fire victims.[70] As for Cornwall's Legion, doubly hit by the effects of the fire which wiped out its anticipated audience at the field and track meet and by the continuing depression over the thirties which kept its treasury at a minimum, the association of veterans limped along until 1939 when its charter was returned to head office and a provisional committee was set up to reorganize the branch. With the breaking out of the second world war, Cornwall's veterans received a new charter in 1939 to become the John McMartin branch 297 of the Canadian Legion with Donald Dick as first president. When Dick enlisted for active service a second time, the branch was headed by Bill Thomas. By 1982 this offspring of the Great War Veterans'

Association had a paid-up membership of 1,500, giving Branch 297 one of the biggest Legion memberships in Ontario and making it the largest civilian organization in Cornwall.[71]

NOTES

1. *The Making of a New Cornwall*, 14.
2. *Freeholder*, 30 November 1906.
3. *Ibid*, 9 March and 9 November 1900.
4. *Old Boys' Reunion Souvenir Album*, 1906, 8.
5. Carman Miller, "A Preliminary Analysis of the Socio-Economic Composition of Canada's South African War Contingents," in *Social History*, November 1975, 219.
6. Minutes, Town Council, 15 February 1900, 242; *Freeholder*, 7 December 1900.
7. *Reporter*, 31 March 1877; *Canadian Illustrated News*, 26 January 1878.
8. *Freeholder*, 6 July 1900.
9. *Ibid*.
10. *Ibid.*, 3 August 1900; Minutes, Town Council, 1898-1902, 13 August 1900, 298.
11. William Boss, *The Stormont, Dundas and Glengarry Highlanders*, 147; for the Cadet Corps, see Alexander Caldwell and Mary Stewart, *Cornwall Collegiate and Vocational School: A Historical Sketch*, 12, their date of 1909 as the founding date of the corps is inaccurate, see Boss, 109, and *Standard-Freeholder*, 3 August 1946.
12. Minutes, Town Council, 1907-1914, 14 April 1913, 549-550.
13. *Standard-Freeholder*, 5 March 1937.
14. *Freeholder*, 19 October 1906.
15. For list, see *Old Boys' Reunion Souvenir Album*, 1906, 148-49; *Standard*, 8 June 1906.
16. *Old Boys' Reunion*, 1906, 9.
17. *Standard*, 25 May 1906.
18. Minutes, Town Council, 14 February 1912, 435; see also, H.M. Stiles, *Official History of the Cornwall Cheese and Butter Board*, 216.
19. Minutes, Town Council, 1907-14, 13 April 1908, 123; *Old Boys' Reunion*, 1906, 44 and 70; J.G. Harkness, *History of Stormont, Dundas and Glengarry*, 358.
20. *Old Boys' Reunion*, 1906, 49; Harkness, 360.
21. Minutes, Town Council, 1902-14, 31 May 1906, 517 and 1 February 1907, 11.
22. *Standard-Freeholder*, 29 June 1934; Harkness, 360.
23. Minutes, Town Council, 1907-14, 5 March 1907, 19.
24. *Ibid.*, 13 March 1907, 24-26.
25. Stiles, *Cheese Board*, 236.
26. Harkness, 360.
27. *Standard-Freeholder*, 1 September 1939; for post-war cheese factory developments, see Clive and Frances Marin, *Stormont, Dundas and Glengarry 1945-1978*, 153-56.
28. Minutes, Town Council, 1902-07, 27 October 1905, 438; *Ibid.*, 1907-14, 14 November 1910, 331; Harkness, 359.
29. *Standard-Freeholder*, 22 February and 5 May 1933; 29 June 1934; Harkness, 361.
30. *Standard-Freeholder*, 30 December 1944.
31. Minutes, Town Council, 1902-07, 14 August 1905, 415; *ibid.*, 1907-14, 2 June 1910, 291.
32. Harkness, 362.
33. Minutes, Town Council, 1902-1907, 14 July 1904, 270-71.
34. G. Meredith Smith, *The Smiths of Philipsburg*, see genealogy chart no. 1; William Wood, *The Storied Province of Quebec*, IV, 407-8; *Who's Who in Canada*, 1919-20, 1388; *ibid.*, 1925-26, 1215.

35. William Boss, *Stormont, Dundas and Glengarry Highlanders*, 112.
36. Dorothy Donihee, "In My Mother's Footsteps," 52.
37. *Freeholder*, 14 January 1915.
38. Names of those who died are engraved on the plaque in Memorial Park, Cornwall.
39. *Standard*, 17 February 1916 and 24 February 1916.
40. Boss, *Stormont, Dundas and Glengarry Highlanders*, 120-23; Harkness, 530.
41. Winifred Jerrom to Senior, 30 June 1982.
42. Mrs. I.R. Mavor, History of St. Lawrence Chapter, I.O.D.E., prepared April 1982; *Standard-Freeholder*, 29 June 1934 and 3 August 1946; Boss, *Stormont, Dundas and Glengarry Highlanders*, 123.
43. Jerrom to Senior, 30 June 1982, enclosure, "Presentation of Colours to the 154th Battalion"; Harkness, 312.
44. *Standard*, 1 June 1916.
45. *Ibid.*, 29 March 1917.
46. *Ibid.*, 8 February 1917.
47. *Ibid.*, 11 October 1917.
48. *Ibid.*, 13 December 1917.
49. *Ibid.*, 22 August 1918.
50. *Ibid.*, 12 September 1918.
51. *Standard-Freeholder*, 29 June 1934.
52. *Standard*, 26 April 1917.
53. *Ibid.*, 15 November 1917.
54. *Ibid.*, 21 November 1918.
55. *Ibid.*, 6 June 1918.
56. *Ibid.*, 10 May 1917.
57. Boss, *Stormont, Dundas and Glengarry Highlanders*, 108, 134; Jerrom to Senior, 30 June 1982, enclosure, "Presentation of Colours to the 154th Battalion."
58. *Standard*, 11 July 1918.
59. *Ibid.*
60. George Williams, "The Royal Canadian Legion in Cornwall," broadcast over Station C.J.S.S., 6 February 1972.
61. *Standard*, 4 September 1918; Minutes, Town Council, 1914-1923, 15 October 1919, 349.
62. *Standard*, 11 July 1918; *Standard-Freeholder*, 29 June 1934.
63. *Standard*, 12 November 1925; *Standard-Freeholder*, 10 October 1979; Boss, *Stormont, Dundas and Glengarry Highlanders*, 137.
64. *Standard-Freeholder*, 10 October 1979.
65. *Ibid.*, 29 June 1934.
66. Boss, *Stormont, Dundas and Glengarry Highlanders*, 139.
67. George Williams, The Royal Canadian Legion in Cornwall.
68. For details of fire see, *Standard-Freeholder*, 9 August 1933; *ibid.*, 30 December 1944; *ibid.*, 3 March 1979.
69. *Standard-Freeholder*, 13 November 1936.
70. For the Kinsmen, see *Standard-Freeholder*, 3 December 1944 and 19 February 1980; *The Story of Kinsmenship*; *Special 50th Anniversary Issue of Kin 1920-1970*.
71. *Standard-Freeholder*, 18 March 1972; *Associations, Organizations and Clubs, Cornwall Directory 1979-1980*, 150; Larry Keen, Community Programs Chairman, Royal Canadian Legion, to Senior, 14 April 1982.

Jacob Farrand Pringle, (1816-1901). Author of Cornwall's first history *Lunenburg or the Old Eastern
District*. Junior County Court Judge 1866-1878: Judge
1878-1900.
Credit: Stormont, Dundas and Glengarry Historical Society.

Regimental and King's colours of the 154th Battalion, (World War I). These colours were presented by the St. Lawrence Chapter of the I.O.D.E. Cornwall.

Credit: the United Counties of Stormont, Dundas and Glengarry, Harkness J.G. *Stormont, Dundas and Glengarry: A History 1784-1945.*

Capitol Theatre, interior 1931. Opened January 23, 1928, closed May 31, 1977, re-opened February 1978. Original seating capacity 1360, present 990.

Credit: Heritage Cornwall.

Old Cornwall Post Office.
Credit: Public Archives of Canada, neg. PA 48113.

Chapter XVI
Cornwall Organizes for Fellowship and Service

The Legion, the Imperial Order Daughters of the Empire chapters, and the new Kinsmen Club gained in importance during the early decades of the new century partly because of their special connection with war and its aftermath. A number of other fraternal, patriotic and service organizations, no less important, also emerged in the Cornwall of this period. They were part and parcel of the phenomenal growth of such societies in Canada as a whole throughout the twentieth century. In 1893 the Toronto *Globe* had listed only twenty-one clubs, societies or associations for the expanding milltown.[1] By 1918 the Cornwall *Standard* named thirty-four.[2] Then, in 1934, as the town surveyed its first 100 years as an incorporated entity, the *Standard-Freeholder* listed thirty.[3] By 1980 the directory of *Associations, Organizations and Clubs* for 1979-1980, published in both French and English, identified no less than 174. In each case, the listing was incomplete, but taken as a comparative base, they show how people in Cornwall from the late 1800s on were getting together more and more for specific fellowship and service needs, though most of the developing associations had limited memberships. Some were still being organized along religious lines such as the Roman Catholic Knights of Columbus, chartered in 1904, La Société des Enfants de Marie, founded in 1904 at the Church of the Nativity; St. Joseph's Union, active in Cornwall by 1918; the Catholic Women's League, 1921; the Holy Name Society, formed in 1924; and La Congrégation des Dames de Sainte Anne which became the largest women's parish organization at the Church of the Nativity by 1960 with a membership of 527[4] This explosion in Catholic organizations parallelled the expansion in Catholic numbers in town.

The Knights of Columbus became, for Cornwall, one of the most powerful of its service and fraternal organizations, embracing in its membership Catholic men, over eighteen, dedicated to the knightly ideals of service to their church, country and fellow men. Like the early workingman's union, the Knights of Labor, they deliberately chose a name linking their ideals to those of chivalry. Moreover, by describing themselves as Knights of Columbus, they witnessed to the world the part played by Catholics in discovering, exploring and colonizing America. Cornwall Council 755 grew from forty-five members in 1903 to its present 1982 membership of close to 1,300, making it the largest Council in Ontario, outnumbering even the Ottawa and Kingston Councils which predated it. With such a membership, the Knights of Columbus thus rival in numbers the local Legion branch, the third largest in Ontario, an indication of Cornwall's propensity to create and sustain outstandingly vibrant fraternal and service organizations.

Drawing on members from all Roman Catholic communities of Cornwall, including those of Scottish, Irish, French and Italian backgrounds, the Cornwall Knights of Columbus take pride in their adherence to the four main principles guiding the organization — charity, unity, fraternity and patriotism. As they celebrated seventy-five years of continuous service in Cornwall in 1978, their spokesman, Past Grand Knight Gus Murray, asserted, "No other Catholic society so successfully has united the Catholics of every parish...the English-speaking people, the French Canadians and the Italian minority into one modified body working without restraint or rancour for Church and Country".[5] These claims are verified by a glance at Council 755's membership from the earliest days to the present. In 1903 the first Grand Knight was Dr. P.J. Maloney. His executive read like a directory of Cornwall's leading Catholics: Alexander Langlois, deputy Grand Knight; A.T. MacDonald, recording secretary; Dr. W.B. Cavanagh, financial secretary;Dan J. Gillies, treasurer; John A. Chisholm, chancellor; Edward O'Callaghan, warden; J.E. McDonell, lecturer; J.J. Broderick, inside guard; William F. Donihee, outside guard; Rev. George Corbet, chaplain; board of trustees — C.P. Derochie, Joseph E. Chevrier, J.A. Sauriol, and J.A. McDougall.

Knights of the new Council paraded to mass at St. Columban's Church for the first time in 1903. Then, throughout succeeding generations names such as Lally, Tallon, Lavigne, Bergeron, Battista, Scully, Villeneuve and Clarkin bear witness to the continuity of family affiliation with the Order whose 1978 president, Maurice Labelle, sounded a tocsin to warn members that "we are now faced with tremendous changes in moral and societal values" and needed to adhere to the original concept of the Order as one fashioned on the "fear and love of God and fierce pride in their country."[6] The 1982 executive indicated not only the continuity of these families within the Order but also the great expansion of the Order within the French-Canadian community. For instance, Father Kevin Maloney was chaplain, Past Grand Knight A. Malcolm Macdonald was advocate and Donald V. MacDonald a trustee. Other officers were Grand Knight Claude Poirier, deputy Grand Knight Raoul Fournier, chancellor René Regnier, treasurer Réjean Bussière, recorder Gaetan Simard, financial secretary Edwin R. Joubert, lecturer Francis Lefebvre, warden Arthur Mondoux, inside guard Val Rioux, outside guard Marcel Bélanger, past Grand Knight Jack Price, programme director Louis Rioux, and trustees Maurice Labelle and Roy Johnson.

During the earlier years of their existence, the Knights of Columbus concentrated their charitable endeavours towards the relief of children and widows, especially through an insurance plan. They bought schoolbooks and clothing for needy children attending separate schools, made donations to St. Paul's Home and Nazareth Orphanage and to the Christmas Cheer Fund. In more recent years their charity, which has always extended beyond the confines of their own faith and locality, has included St. Joseph's Villa, the Multiple Sclerosis Fund and support for playgrounds in Rome. Their concern for Catholic higher education has been expressed through the provision of aid to seminarians, and scholarships, prizes and bursaries to Roman Catholic university students. Public witness of the Knights to Catholic principles has included a spectacular May Day rally in honour of the Blessed Virgin Mary during which fifteen floats depicting the Rosary were drawn through the main streets of Cornwall. Young Catholic men in Cornwall, between the ages of twelve and eighteen, absorb the principles of the Order while serving within the youth organization — Circle 640 of the Columbia Squires. This group, like the parent organization, bears testimony to the harmonious mingling of Catholics of different ethnic origin. For instance, new members initiated into the group in 1978 included Bruce Brennan, Luc Brisson, Brian and Claude Poirier, Pat Swift, Jamie Lefebvre, Curtis Lalonde and Anthony Joubert.

Catholic women in Cornwall never succeeded in associating on such a scale within a single organization. The feminine counterpart of the Knights of Columbus — L'Ordre des Filles d'Isabelle — did not have a branch in Cornwall until 1960. Though it grew in membership to 208 by 1982, and aimed "d'unir dans cette grande société fraternelle de bienveillance toutes les femmes catholiques," Les Filles d'Isabelle remained largely within the French-speaking community.[7]

At St. Columban's Church, Catholic women organized themselves into a branch of the Catholic Women's League in 1921, a year after the League's national founding. Since that date, four other parishes have founded branches — St. John Bosco in 1949. Holy Cross, founded in 1954, which became St. Peter's C.W.L. in 1979; St. Francis de Sales, 1962, and Blessed Sacrament, 1981, with a total membership in 1982 of 496. Like the Knights of Columbus, the Catholic Women's League is a fraternal and service organization whose motto "For God and Country" symbolizes its aims, while its choice of the Blessed Virgin Mary as patroness stresses its militant stance in defence of the faith. The first Cornwall branch, St. Columban's, under the presidency of Mrs. Harry Snetsinger, undertook to provide comforts for the inmates of St. Paul's old people's home, the House of Refuge, for patients at the Hotel Dieu, and, above all, to support Nazareth Orphanage. In recent years, the local branches of the Catholic Women's League have kept pace with current needs, stressing Christian family life by support of such community organizations as Birthright, which provides aid to pregnant women in distress, and Meals on Wheels, which brings hot nutritious meals to elderly people or others confined to their homes. In line with modern concerns, Cornwall women within the C.W.L. also aim to "enhance the role of women in church and society" and to promote "human rights."[9]

A number of other groups organized along denominational lines prior to the second world war. These included several women's clubs at the Methodist Church: the Young Women's Group that became the Evening Missionary Society in 1908, the young people's club known as the Epworth League, and another group called the Young Married Women's Social Club.[10] In 1926 a number of societies in Knox Church reorganized following that church's decision the previous year to join the new United Church of Canada.[11] The decision had been made by 182 members while some ninety-five members of Knox rejected the union scheme and returned to the St. John's Presbyterian fold. One of the new societies to emerge in Knox Church was the Christian Endeavour Society, formed by forty-four young men and women.[12] In the First Baptist Church a Young Women's Missionary Society was formed about 1933 to supplement the work of the older parent Women's Mission Circle that had been organized in 1880 by Jane MacArthur and Jennie Hamilton, and a Mission Band, started in 1899.[13]

The fraternal organization of the Cornwall Jewish community, B'nai Brith Lodge, was founded in 1934 by Archie Dover.[14] Aimed at promoting a high morality and standards of charity among Jews,

B'nai Brith activities included relief to soldiers overseas and entertainment of recruits at the Basic Training Centre on Marlborough Street during the Second World War, support of such international agencies as the Anti-defamation League and Hillel Foundation, and relief to victims of major disasters. The Lodge, open to all Jewish men and women over the age of twenty-one and of sound moral character, experienced a drop in membership from thirty in 1972 to twenty in 1982. Its activities have been sustained by devoted members such as Saul Schulman who served as president three times and by seven charter members who were still active by 1972.[15] Beth El Sisterhood is a second Jewish organization in Cornwall, made up in 1980 of twenty-seven women who direct their fraternal and charitable activities from the Synagogue on Amelia Street, founded in 1925. Part of their programme is to purchase equipment for the Synagogue and maintain the social hall connected with their house of worship.[16] The Cornwall Jewish Community Council is headed by David Kaye.

Other groups in the town associated along linguistic or ethnic lines. Such were Les Artisans Canadiens-Francais, established in July 1916 under the aegis of the fluently-bilingual pastor of the Church of the Nativity, Father Duncan MacDonald, who was educated at the University of Ottawa and Grand Seminary of Montreal. The aims of Les Artisans Canadiens-francais were four-fold: to perfect the French language among Francophones in Cornwall, to assist in Catholic education, to visit the sick, and to provide insurance. With Joseph E. Chevrier as president and Daniel Danis as executive representative, this new French-Canadian organization of sixty-three members parallelled the older St. Jean-Baptiste Society branch. Like the majority of fraternal and service organizations in Cornwall, Les Artisans Canadiens-francais was an all-male one whose members were part of the rising French-Canadian middle class, affluent enough to own homes or businesses that needed fire protection and whose position in life enabled them to devote time, energy and money to charitable endeavours.[17]

Women of French-Canadian origin formed a separate organization in 1925 — La Fédération des Femmes Canadiennes-Francaises under Mme Telésphore E. Lussier as president. Founded in the Hull-Ottawa region in 1914 as a response to the federal government's appeal for women's participation in the First World War efforts, Les Femmes Canadiennes-Francaises took Jeanne d'Arc as their "guide dans notre role de femmes chretiennes, gardiennes de la foi." With a French woman saint as their patron and the motto "Pour nos Foyers," early members of the Fédération in Cornwall were largely centred on the parish of the Nativity of the Blessed Virgin Mary and confined to those Catholics over eighteen who could speak French. They concerned themselves above all with the poor and needy within and without their own parish. In 1960 their works of charity were legion and acknowledged in the souvenir album prepared to honour Monsignor Joseph-Azellus Brunelle. Its editors declared, "Il nous fait plaisir de reconnaître publiquement l'oeuvre de la F.F.C.F. et de proclamer hautement leur travail et leur dévouement dans la paroisse... La F.F.C.F. à Cornwall vivra car la charité est à la base de leurs aspirations et de leur travail commun." A west End branch was established in 1929, centred on the new St. Francis-de-Sales parish, with Mrs. Alex Lafleche as president. Later, branches were also founded in the parishes of St. Felix-de-Valois and at Ste. Croix. In 1977 the various branches re-grouped into two sections the parent group remaining as "Nativité" and the others becoming Section "Fémina." To coordinate the two sections and as a liaison with the national office at Ottawa, a regional committee of five members was formed, made up of Lucille Léger, president, Gisèle Dion, vice-president, Simonne Tremblay, secretary, Marie-Reine Desrosiers, treasurer, and Pauline Fournier, past president.[18]

Over the years the Fédération grew to a total membership of 235 by 1982, including one survivor from the original charter members of 1925 — Bertha Tyo the octogenarian affectionately known as "une femme sans pareille" and whose good works include knitting over a thousand socks for prisoners of war. The Fédération became the focus for policies to promote women's participation not only in the Francophone milieu in Cornwall, but in the promotion of French culture within the community as a whole. In line with the modern emphasis on cultural preservation and expansion Les Femmes Canadiennes-Francaises welcome into their section all those who speak French, whether Roman Catholic in religion or not. Thus French-Canadian women spearheaded the move towards co-ordinated action on a cultural level to stimulate and preserve the French language and traditions in Cornwall, a move which ultimately resulted in the founding of Le Conseil de Vie Francaise de Cornwall, incorporated in June 1962.[19]

Still other Cornwallites grouped together in fraternal and service societies without denominational or ethnic limitations on their membership, usually directing their charitable efforts towards some specific category of people in need. One of the earlier clubs to include both English-speaking and French-speaking members on their executive was the Benevolent and Protective Order of Elks, organized in May 1917 with a membership of seventeen. They became well known in Cornwall by sponsoring a Christmas Fund for poor children as well as treating children to a Christmas morning movie at the Capitol Theatre.[20] Similarly, the Loyal Order of Moose, organized in 1929 with sixty-two chartered members, had a small number of French Canadians among their first members, two of whom, Percy Payette and George A. Leroux, became dictators, as their leading executive member was termed. Members of the Loyal Order of Moose had sick and death benefits for members that included the care of their orphaned children until they reached the age of sixteen. They also helped maintain a home for aged and infirm members in Florida, indicative of the trend toward mutual self help within fraternal societies prior to the great expansion in sick and welfare benefits taken over by government agencies in the post Second World War period.[21]

The first purely service club in Cornwall was the Kiwanis, formed in 1927 by thirty-seven Cornwall men who chose Peter Leclair as their president. Their first major activity in 1927 undertaken in conjunction with the Elks, was to provide a sorely-needed car for the Victorian Order of Nurses. Then, in 1928, under the presidency of Alex Caldwell, principal of Cornwall Collegiate, they began their spectacular work in aid of crippled children, first compiling a case history of all crippled children in the Cornwall area and setting up a crippled children's clinic in 1928. Their work expanded into other areas of youth work — constructing a swimming pool in Central Park at a cost of $2,000, and providing a swimming supervisor; sponsoring a summer camp for underprivileged children; distributing Christmas baskets; purchasing glasses for needy children; and sponsoring the Air Cadet Squadron in 1944. The club's membership peaked in the 1940s when it reached eight-two members who launched a burlesque hockey game and ice carnival jointly with the local Kinsmen and Lions Clubs, the proceeds of which went to buy Bren guns for the Stormont, Dundas and Glengarries then serving overseas in the Second World War. Chronicles of the Kiwanis were recorded by its first secretary, Guy Cottrell, who was, in 1972, the only surviving original member of the club, and who achieved the amazing record of perfect attendance for fifty years. By 1980 its membership had dropped to forty-five, whose chief concern was still aiding crippled children.[22]

Five Cornwall societies were organized in the early years of the century along semi-professional lines to deal with specific social needs: the Children's Aid Society, formed in March 1908; the Victorian Order of Nurses, chartered in March 1914; St. John Ambulance Society and Federated Charities of Cornwall, both founded in 1926, and the Welfare Bureau, organized in 1938.

The Children's Aid Society grew out of a meeting of fifty Corn-wallites concerned enough about the physical and moral condition of neglected or orphaned children to provide temporary shelter for them and then to locate them in free foster homes. The work of the society embraced truancy, juvenile delinquents, regulating the use made of children in the work force such as their delivering papers late at night. In the case of older children placed in homes where they were expected to work, the society received money in trust for the child from the foster parents. The Society also put its weight behind measures designed to provide a more moral community milieu for children. They urged Town Council to enforce the laws with regard to profanity on the streets, to pass a law forbidding vendors to sell cigarettes to minors, and to impose a curfew on minors.[23]

Up until 1914 the case work for children was carried out largely by Chief of Police Robert Smyth. Then, in 1914, when the Society was reorganized and the home of Mrs. George Buckland became available as a shelter for Protestant children, while Nazareth Orphanage continued as the home for Roman Catholic children, T.W. Ault, Governor of the County Jail, became agent for the Society. Receiving an allowance of $10 monthly and his expenses, Ault remained the leading figure in the operations of the society for the next twenty years until a full-time trained social worker was appointed in 1936. Ault's devotion to the children who came under his jurisdiction was acknowledged by all, though there were complaints in 1917 from the provincial government Superintendent of Neglected Children that Ault's job as Jail Governor conflicted with his work as regular agent of the Children's Aid. "We are extremely anxious to separate young children from the appearance of police and prison," the Superintendent told board members of the Children's Aid Society. The latter saw no conflict and defended Ault's dual role. "We find that the worst conditions are caused by the neglect of parents," they insisted, "and Mr. Ault's position as Jailer gives him a standing in the eyes of parents that no other Agent could have and we therefore consider it a distinct advantage."[24] Indeed, Ault's meagre wages as Agent were also a distinct advantage to the Society and, in this case, townspeople resisted the pressures of the provincial government bureaucracy to get rid of Ault. By the time an assistant was hired for him in 1936, the assistant was paid $60 a month, three times what Ault had ever received, though by this time there were 170 children in the care of the society's shelters and another twelve under its protection. As the town's population increased, so, too, did the number of children needing the Society's services. Throughout the late 1930s the numbers rose to 200; by the late 1940s they peaked to

515, cared for by a staff of nineteen workers. From then on there was a gradual decline in the number of children brought under the Society's care, 233 in homes in 1957, for instance, and 103 under the protection of the Society. The staff also experienced a slight attrition of two workers.[25]

The second major service society of a semi-professional nature to be organized in Cornwall in the early part of the century was the Victorian Order of Nurses. As early as 1897 Lady Aberdeen, wife of the governor-general, tried to encourage the founding of a local branch in Cornwall, urging Town Council to call a public meeting of ladies for that purpose.[26] It was not until 1913 that Mrs. A.F. Cameron founded the Cornwall branch and remained president for the first five years, guiding the Order when it was sustained by private subscriptions and local service organizations.

Aimed especially at providing professional and efficient care to mothers during their confinements and to their new babies, the Order began modestly with one paid nurse, Alma Thompson, who cared for some 290 patients. Her daily routine often saw her trudging through mud or snow that reached over her boottops to get to homes and schools where her services were urgently needed. Her work at schools involved her in truancy duties as well. A second nurse was hired in 1917 and a third in 1924. It is not surprising that the three nurses were overjoyed when the new service clubs, the Elks and Kiwanis, purchased them their first car in 1928. A year later a fourth nurse was engaged and these four nurses carried out ever-increasing duties over the thirties. For instance, in 1934 the four nurses made 7,284 home visits, the majority of them within the township area. Ten years later the same number of nurses made 9,580 visits, caring for the sick at home, demonstrating nursing methods to family members and aiding in the prevention of disease through educational work. Over the years from the 1940s to the 1960s the shift to hospital care for confinements and sick or injured people was evident in the change of workload for the Victorian Order of Nurses. In 1926, they attended over 200 confinements at home, their fees ranging from twenty-five cents to a dollar. In 1960 there were but two home confinements and the work of the nurses turned more and more to the care of the elderly, cancer patients, and post-surgical patients.[27]

The desperate need for home care provided by nurses and for increased medical services became more than apparent in the 1930s when Cornwall experienced severe health problems, partly due to a lack of adequate housing for those crowding into the milltown seeking jobs. Since 1911 the town's population had more than doubled from 6,598 in 1911 to 12,507 in 1935, without an accompanying increase in low rental housing. Within this expanding population, the mortality rate for infants, generally regarded as one of the more reliable indexes to the general health of a community, was nearly double that of any other section in Ontario - 100 deaths per thousand births, while the average infant mortality throughout the province was fifty-nine per thousand. Moreover, the death rate in Cornwall in the early thirties was higher than in any other community in the province.

So serious were health and housing problems in the early years of the depression, that Mayor Aaron Horovitz and Town Councillors asked the Canadian Welfare Council, Ottawa, to undertake a study of social and health conditions in Cornwall in 1935. Charlotte Whitton, Executive Director of the Council, together with two other professional social workers surveyed the town, traipsing up and down back alleys, into shacks, or garages converted into living quarters and lean-tos erected at the rear of stores, seeing for themselves how families on relief or with low incomes were living in single rooms without plumbing conveniences, their main advantage being that such accommodations cost five to eight dollars rent per month.

The investigators concluded that one of the major areas of concern was the housing shortage and subsequent high rent for what was available. Adequate accommodation for a moderate-sized family could not be had for under $20 to $25 a month; yet most breadwinners, even when employed full-time, could not manage such a rent. The survey team's remedy was to suggest to Town Council the construction of 100 to 150 homes, either financed by the municipality or privately, to rent at not more than $15 a month and that preference in the occupation of such homes be given to families whose weekly income was in the neighbourhood of $15 to $20. To make sure that the shacks vacated by families would not be taken over "by Squatters from suburban municipalities and nearby rural areas," the three women investigators urged the Town to "invoke the new by-law to condemn" such shacks as dwellings.

With regard to Cornwall's care of its neglected or orphaned children, the investigators praised the single-handed efforts of Jail Governor T.W. Ault, but were quick to urge the need of an assistant, especially to help in enforcing the truancy laws and in the juvenile delinquency area. The combined student population of the public and separate schools was roughly 3,500 in 1935, but many teenaged children withdrew from school early on work permits, thus aggravating the employment situation, as employers tended to hire the young unskilled worker for a lower wage than what would be paid to an adult man or woman. To reduce the incidence of truancy and the tendency of young people to withdraw from school prematurely, the investigating team suggested technical training facilities, a suggestion that materialized three years later when, for the first time, drafting, woodwork, machine shop, electricity and home economics were offered to high school students at Cornwall Collegiate, which henceforth became Cornwall Collegiate and Vocational School. To give adolescents a healthier climate for their leisure hours, they urged the formation of young peoples' clubs and more recreation facilities.

Efforts to coordinate private philanthropy had been made ten years earlier in 1926 when an agency, Federated Charities, was established. Its formation was largely the work of Mayor Dr. W.B. Cavanagh, a member of St. Columban's Roman Catholic Church, who had spearheaded many of the more progressive moves made by Town Council and the Board of Trade. Realizing that there was much overlapping and redundancy, not only in fund-raising for charity but also in the distribution of charity through various churches and societies, Cavanagh suggested uniting all such fund-raising and distribution through a single agency. Charlotte Whitton and her assistants, who had made a piercing survey and analysis of Cornwall's social needs, now suggested that Federated Charities become the nucleus agency around which a Family Welfare Bureau should function, dedicated to returning to a normal life those families that through ill-fortune, ill health, or immorality had been threatened. One of their strongest supporters in this move was Mary Mack, Cornwall's "Grande Dame" in every sense of the word: a woman respected for her works of charity, her verve and energy, her high tone and her sense of civic duty. Combining high intelligence with great organizational abilities and an artistic temperament, Mary Mack, a spinster daughter of United Counties Warden and Sheriff, William Mack, brought to every job or organization she touched a unique quality. Like Charlotte Whitton and her assistants, she threw herself into the welfare work of the thirties, touring every inch of the old square mile of Cornwall and chatting personally with families to learn their needs.[29]

One of the first major tasks of the new Family Welfare Bureau, established in 1938, was to create a social service exchange which would retain, in one central place, an index of all the records of families or individuals known to any of the health or social agencies of the community. Thus, welfare and social workers, whether dealing with sickness, juvenile delinquency, immorality or other aspects of family distress, would have access to a dossier of the family as a whole and know what had been done by other groups to aid the person or family in trouble. In 1944, for instance, the Welfare Bureau, which eventually became the Family Counselling Centre run so efficiently by Margaret Conliffe, gave full-time assistance to ninety-two families and part-time aid to sixty-two; made 890 home visits and carried out 758 interviews in the office.[30] Dry statistics of annual reports are but the inked numbers of what had often been the difference between hope and despair for numerous families - milk to hungry children, cod liver oil tablets to under-nourished ones, clothing from the Welfare Bureau's workshop to cover those without clothes, and above all, treating "young and old, whatever their circumstances, with dignity and respect," as Mary Mack did.[31]

Partly in response to the plea for more youth clubs, made by the team of social workers investigating Cornwall's social problems in 1935, there was an emphasis on the growth of the Scout and Guide movements in the mid-1930's. Scout troops had been in existence at St. Columban's since 1921 and at St. John's Presbyterian Church since 1926. New Scouts troops were formed at Trinity and Knox Churches in 1936, while a Guide company and Brownie Pack were organized at the Church of the Nativity in 1936 and 1939. St. Paul's United Church got its first Scout troop in 1939. Other troops were founded in the 1940s, one at the Church of the Good Shepherd in 1944 and at Nativity in 1946, the same year that a Boy Scout Association was formed in town, largely through the efforts of Lieutenant Colonel Neil Phillips, a former mayor. Other youth groups emerged: at Nativity in 1935 Jeunesse Ouvrière Catholique and Jeunesse Ouvrière Catholique Feminine; at Knox a Canadian Girls in Training group formed in 1939; and in 1937 a Boys' Band was formed by Henry Larose, its instruments bought with the help of prominent businessmen. By 1946 the band had grown to such a size that Bandmaster Fred Booth divided it into a senior and junior band. These new clubs directed towards adolescents and young people supplemented the few youth groups already established in town, including the Orange Youth Britons, formed in 1900, and the Cadet Corps at Cornwall Collegiate and Vocational School operating since 1907.[32]

The St. John Ambulance Association formed its first branch in Cornwall in 1926 under the presidency of B. de B. Millidge, holding lectures in first aid in the old Cheese Board room in the Town Hall and later transferring its activities to a room in Cornwall Collegiate and Vocational School. The first Cornwall Brigade was organized in 1941 under Superintendent F.D. Harrower and the following year a nursing division was opened under Superintendent Jean Doherty. Since 1949 George Tyo has been secretary and chief training officer, the Cornwall Branch providing superb first aid services to the town's citizens at all major festivities and walking off with the C.J. Laurin trophy for three years in a row, 1979 to 1981, awarded at the annual inspection of all Ontario Divisions. The trophy is given each year to the division contributing the highest number of public duty hours in the province. Moreover, in 1981, a Cornwall member of the St. John Ambulance Brigade, Corporal Della D'Ambrosio, won honours as the individual giving the most public duty hours in Ontario.[33]

Women's organizations did not take any great leap forward until the Second World War. To the already established organizations within various churches, and the Rebekahs, Imperial Order Daughters of the Empire, Victorian Order of Nurses, and Femmes Françaises-Canadiennes, were added the Cornwall branch of the Women's Institute in 1912, the Ladies' Orange Benevolent Association in 1920 and what became one of Cornwall's chief women's fraternal societies, the Order of the Eastern Star, a Masonic-affiliated group formed in 1930 by fifty charter members. Mrs. John Cardle was the prime mover in its initial stages when meetings were held in the Oddfellows' hall, then located in the Snetsinger block on Pitt Street. Membership was limited to women over eighteen who were related to Master Masons and who expressed a belief in a supreme being.[34]

A number of purely cultural clubs and partly industrial societies existed in pre-Second World War Cornwall. The venerable Cornwall Agricultural Society, active as early as 1845 and reorganized in 1852 under Philip Vankoughnet, did not peter out for over a hundred years. The purchase of its large Agricultural Grounds north of Ninth Street did not take place until 1940 when Town Council set aside $5,680.98 to redeem the mortgage on the property.[35] Closely allied to the Agricultural Society were the Cornwall Poultry, Dog and Pet Stock Association, formed in 1874; the extremely important Cheese Board, established in 1898 and by 1919 conducting business that out-distanced the paper and cotton mills in terms of circulating money in town; and the Pointers' Club, founded in 1913 by William Lane, Father A.J. MacMillan of Nativity Church, and Fred Quig, to establish a hunting and fishing reserve near Mount Laurier, Quebec. A Horticultural Society was formed in 1924 to foster interest in flower shows and care of public parks, and particularly to inculcate good gardening habits among children. A Game and Fish Protection Association was organized in January 1933 by avid anglers and hunters, anxious to prevent pollution in the St. Lawrence River and other fishing streams. Their first officers, Joseph Labonne, Wilfred L.G. Snetsinger, René A.

380

Danis and William Whittaker led the way in awakening the public to the dangers of water pollution. They also undertook to restock rivers and streams.[36] By 1948, the Association's spokesman, Nick Kaneb, who would become twice Cornwall's Mayor in the 1960s, urged the provincial Minister of Lands and Forests to take measures to alleviate the serious pollution problems in the Cornwall area. He also recommended the suspension of gun licenses to careless hunters.

At the cultural and entertainment levels, Cornwallites were, for most of the first part of the Twentieth century, dependent on the small public library; a thirty-piece band organized by the National Club of Cornwall in 1905 when the Citizens' Band broke up; and the Stormont, Dundas and Glengarry Historical Society, founded in 1920 to encourage research into Cornwall's past and that of the three counties. Townspeople also patronized the Cornwall Art Association, formed in 1934 largely through the efforts of Mary Mack, who had studied at the Montreal Museum of Fine Arts and in Paris; and they enjoyed the productions of the amateur dramatic groups at Trinity and St. Columban's Churches. For their entertainment, however, Cornwallites were turning increasingly to the growing number of moving picture theatres.[37]

The Art Association functioned effectively until the outbreak of the war "bringing art and music within the reach of the pupils of all the schools" and promoting special performances in town. First officers included Norman Linnett, Alexander Caldwell, Mary Mack and W.E. Hopkins. The group brought exhibitions from the National Gallery, as well as leading musicians and lecturers to Cornwall audiences, including the Hart House Quartet. The evening's concert at the old assembly hall of the Cornwall Collegiate Institute was remembered by townspeople not only for the brilliant performance by the Toronto quartet but also for Mary Mack's entrance as she moved down the main aisle of the hall, stunning in a long black velvet gown, her fair hair set simply in a single classical knot above the nape of her neck - the epitome of elegance. As one admirer said, "Miss Mack gave TONE to Cornwall."[38] Few disagreed.

Early movies in Cornwall received full and enthusiastic endorsation in 1905 when townsmen and women packed the Town Hall for three nights in a row, entranced with the silently-moving pictures. One member of the audience, James Whitham, was so impressed that he quietly abandoned his life-long trade as a cotton loom fixer to pioneer the Cornwall motion picture era. His first movie house was modest enough. Located next to the old Windsor Hotel on Water Street, the Starland could seat ninety-five on its somewhat hard kitchen-type chairs. A second movie house, the Wonderland, owned and operated by Alex MacDonald, opened within the year to rival the Starland. Whitham pushed on, transferring his movie operation to larger quarters on the site of present day Loblaw's Grocery on Second Street West. Named the Crystal Palace, the new Whitham theatre could seat 110 comfortably and charged five or ten cents, depending on the length of the entertainment provided. Accompanying the silent movies was Boggie Douglas as singing leader and pianist Hugh Kippen. A third move to larger quarters in the newly rebuilt Yates block on Pitt Street saw the Crystal Palace come into its own with a seating capacity for 340 and a full-fledged orchestra with Kippen still as pianist, Fred Airey, trombone, Earl Boscoe, drummer, and A.J. Bouley as violinist. When Whitham sold the Crystal to Nelson Charlebois and Arthur St.-Armand in 1919, he had already begun construction of his fourth movie theatre - the Palace - with a seating capacity of 820, indicative of the popularity of the new type of public entertainment as well as of the expanding population of the milltown.[39]

In company with his son-in-law, Clarence G. Markell, Whitham continued as the key figure in Cornwall's movie world, buying out his rival, the Wonderland, in 1923, while his other competitor, the Crystal Palace, went out of business in the twenties, thus leaving Whitham master of the field. He was equal to it. By 1927 he had built the Capitol Theatre on Second Street just west of Pitt Street at a cost of $250,000. With seats for 1,321, sound equipment, an eight by six screen, steam heat and an auditorium resplendent in Spanish design with baskets of carved flowers and roped bordered columns, the Capitol was the ultimate in elegance and comfort. Mayor Neil Phillips and manager Clarence Markell were on hand on opening night - January 1928 - to welcome clients and watch "The Singing Fool" with Al Jolson. From then until the 1960s when movies declined, the Capitol held its own as Cornwall's prime movie house. Its hold over Cornwallites extended into the late 1970s when they refused to allow its demolition and put up such a stalwart fight to preserve the theatre that it stands today as one of the city's protected heritage buildings.[40]

James Whitham's vision in providing Cornwall with the utmost in theatres was thus vindicated, as was his promotion of sports in town, especially lawn bowling. When the Lawn Bowling Club was formed in September of 1938, it was James Whitham who donated the land at the corner of Sixth and Sydney Streets and took charge of the beautification of the property, laying out fourteen greens, and building the clubhouse and toolshed. To honour Cornwall's movie pioneer and the generous patron of their club, members of the club perpetuated his memory by calling their club the Whitham Lawn Bowling Club.[41]

These pre-Second World War societies and clubs in Cornwall tended to divide primarily along religious and male-female lines. Only in a few organizations were men and women associated together: Federated Charities was one, B'nai Brith another, and the Stormont, Dundas and Glengarry Historical Society was mixed as were several of the youth groups in the different churches. But on the whole, fraternal and service associations continued either wholly male or female in membership. Older organizations such as the Catholic Mutual Benefit Association and the various Courts of Foresters gave way to the Knights of Columbus, while other nationalist societies such as the Sons of England, the Sons of Scotland, and Les Artisans Canadiens-Français faded away, as did a number of the more specialized clubs such as the Women's Christian Temperance Union, St. Joseph's Union, the Lord's Day Alliance and the Mechanics' Institute, indicative perhaps of the rejuvenation process necessary in most organizations that outgrow their original reason for existing or have been taken over by people whose ideas or programmes are neither identical or even amicable to those on which the societies were founded. The dying away of earlier clubs in Cornwall made way for the plethora of organized activities of every description that characterized post-Second World War Cornwall.

NOTES

1. *Globe*, Toronto, 18 November 1893.
2. *Standard*, 7 February 1918.
3. *Ibid.*, 29 June 1934.
4. For St. Joseph's Union, see *Standard*, 7 February 1918; for others, see *Paroisse de la Nativité de la B.V.M., 1887-1962, Album Souvenir, Hommages à Mgr. J.A. Brunelle, P.P., Curé de la Nativité de Cornwall, 1942-1960*; for the Knights of Columbus, see *Standard-Freeholder*, 29 June 1934; *ibid.*, 18 February 1972 and 21 November 1978; 20 March 1979; A.M. Macdonald to Senior, 7 June 1982, enclosure; for Catholic Women's League, see *Standard-Freeholder*, 29 June 1934, 3 August 1946, Mildred Cleary to Senior, July 1982, enclosures; St. Columban's Council annual report May 1981; Catholic Women's League of Canada, Alexandria, Cornwall Diocesan Council annual report, April 1982; *Catholic Women's League of Canada Constitution and Bylaws*, 1979.

5. *Standard-Freeholder*, 21 November 1978.

6. *Ibid.*

7. Zo-Anne Roy to Senior, 10 April 1982, Outline History of L'Ordre des Filles d'Isabelle, Cercle Notre Dame du Perpétuel Secours, no. 1028.

8. Mildred Cleary to Senior, July 1982, enclosure.

9. *Catholic Women's League of Canada Constitution and Bylaws*, 1979, 2; see also brochure published by Catholic Women's League.

10. Evelyn Stidwill, Early Recollections of St. Paul's United Church.

11. *Knox United Church 1846-1975*, 13.

12. *Ibid.*, 41.

13. L. Jean Cameron, First Baptist Church, 1882-1967, 6, 18-19.

14. *Standard-Freeholder*, 4 March 1972.

15. *Associations, Organizations, and Clubs, Cornwall Directory, 1979-80*, 20; *Standard-Freeholder*, 4 March 1972.

16. *Ibid.*; see also *Standard-Freeholder*, 3 August 1946.

17. *Standard-Freeholder*, 29 June 1934.

18. *Ibid.*, see also *Fédération des Femmes Canadiennes-Françaises, Statuts et Règlements*, 1975, 25; *Souvenir Album: Hommages à Mgr. J.-A. Brunelle*, 1960.

19. Gisèle Dion to Senior, 22 April 1982, enclosure Outline History of Fédération des Femmes Canadiennes-Françaises in Cornwall; for aims of Fédération, see *Statuts et Règlements*, 1975, 1-2; Jules Renaud to Senior, 25 November 1980, enclosing an account of the founding of the Franco-Centre.

20. *Standard-Freeholder*, 29 June 1934.

21. *Ibid.*

22. *Ibid.*; see also, 31 May 1944, 3 January 1945, 21 August 1946, 22 January 1957, 8 January 1972; *Associations, Organizations and Clubs, Cornwall Directory*, 1979-80, 121.

23. Research Report on Children's Aid Society, 50th Anniversary, 3, 6, 12-13.

24. *Ibid.*, 9.

25. *Ibid.*, see chart showing increase of workers; and the number of children under the Society's protection or care, 1935-1957.

26. Minutes, Town Council, 1896-98, 30 April 1897, 290-91.

27. *Standard-Freeholder*, 29 June 1934; Community Services to Families and Individuals in the Town of Cornwall, 1935: A Community Study by the Canadian Welfare Council Ottawa; Report on the Victorian Order of Nurses, Cornwall, 1945; Mrs. Earl Malcolm, History of the Victorian Order of Nurses, April 1973.

28. Details on Cornwall's health and housing problems in the 1930s come largely from A Community Study 1935 by the Canadian Welfare Council, see especially 1-8.

29. See Emily MacInnes, Tribute to Mary Mack, read before the Stormont, Dundas and Glengarry Historical Society, 17 January 1979.

30. Report on Founding and Progress of the Cornwall Family Welfare Bureau, 1944.

31. Emily MacInnes, Tribute to Mary Mack, 1979.

32. For the origin of these clubs see, *Souvenir Album: Hommages à Mgr. J.A. Brunelle*; Callan Plumodore, Boy Scouts in Canada, 10; *Standard-Freeholder*, 29 June 1934 and 15 June 1946; *Knox United Church, 1846-1975*, 41.

33. *Standard-Freeholder*, 29 June 1934; 1 February, 1947; George Tyo to Senior, 17 May 1982; Annual Report, St. John Ambulance, Cornwall Division, 1981.

34. *Standard-Freeholder*, 29 June 1934, and 22 October 1979.

35. *Cornwall Observer*, 4 September 1845; James Croil, *Dundas, or a Sketch of Canadian History*, 237; *Standard*, 13 September 1901; Minutes, Town Council, 1907-1914, 12 August 1912, 485-6, 489, see also Committee Book Town Council, 1933-1941, 29 November 1940, 366.

36. H.M. Stiles, *History of the Cornwall Cheese Board*, 18; *Standard-Freeholder*, 29 June 1934.

37. *Standard-Freeholder*, 26 March 1946, 23 August 1948; *Associations, Organizations and Clubs, Cornwall Directory*, 1979-80, 161; Emily MacInnes, Tribute to Mary Mack, 1979.

38. *Ibid.*, Standard-Freeholder, 29 June 1934.

39. *Standard-Freeholder*, 6 November 1939, 2 June 1948.

40. Eileen Merkley, *The Friendly Town That Grew*, 47-48.

41. *Standard-Freeholder*, 3 August 1946.

Miss Mary Mack, (1899-1978), Cornwall's first woman Alderman. It was said that 'Miss Mack gave TONE to Cornwall'. Picture taken for the coronation of H.M. Queen Elizabeth II, 1953.

Credit: Stormont, Dundas and Glengarry Historical Society.

Chapter XVII

Industry, Depression and Unionization

The most significant aspects of Cornwall's industrial and labour development in the first half of the twentieth century were the change-over of the Toronto Paper Company to C. Howard Smith's ownership in 1919 and its subsequent expansion by the 1960s into the city's major industry; the establishment, in 1924, of the British-owned Court-auld's viscose rayon producing plant that accounted for much of the town's population boom during the depression decade, and the unionization of both the paper and textile industries, the latter being carried out largely under communist leadership.

These were significant developments; but there were unique developments in Cornwall's industrial and unionization processes as well. It was Cornwall that led the way in industry-wide unionization of the whole Canadian textile industry and, for a brief time, was in the unique position of having one union that embraced workers from the three textile-producing companies in town - the Cornwall Textile Workers Union.[1] The town was also unique in that it enjoyed population increase and industrial expansion in the decade of the 1930s when other Canadian manufacturing towns were suffering retrenchment and unemployment because of the depression. In 1930, before the full impact of the depression had hit the country, Cornwall's industrial force of 3,673 workers, employed in forty-one industries, produced goods valued at $24,253,452.[2] Cornwall's need in 1930, then, was more for an employment agency where information could be exchanged between those offering jobs and those seeking them. Thus an "Employment Bureau" was set up for the first time in January 1930 with Fire Chief George Hunter in charge.[3]

Cornwall's status as the pre-eminent Ontario milltown of the 1880s had declined by 1923 to 23rd place, though by 1930 it had made a slight recovery, moving to 18th position in the provincial hierarchy of manufacturing centres.[4] With this decline that set in at the turn of the century, cotton workers had given up strike action, their last strike of any note being in 1901.[5] But by 1936 the *Standard-*

Freeholder boasted that employment in Cornwall's industries had reached an all-time high, with 4,779 workers bringing home annual wages of $4,144,893.[6] Frugal, hardworking and steady workers such as Stan Tilton of the papermill, for instance, could afford to buy his own home and have a cellar well stocked each year with winter foods and fuel to provide for his growing family.[7] And even without strikes for higher wages, Cornwall workers had secured an overall wage increase in 1935 of 6-1/4 percent, according to the Board of Trade's calculations.[8] Thus it may well have been the relative affluence and well-being of its workforce, rather than its poverty, that made Cornwall a more viable place for union organizers to start industry-wide unionization of textile plants in the era of the depression.

Part of this expansion occurred in Canadian Cottons where the number of workers in the three mills had increased from 1300 in the early 1930s to over 1400 by 1937, the year that Canadian Cottons experienced its first strike.[9] The town's other older established major industry, the paper mill, had increased its number of employees from 130 at the turn of the century to 348 in 1919, the year that the Toronto Paper Manufacturing Company changed hands to the Montreal-based fine paper manufacturer, C. Howard Smith. From then until the 1940s there was no spectacular rise in the number of its employees. The mill barely managed to keep up its payroll strength over the depression years, though by 1937 construction of the vanillin plant and the extension of the sulphite and soda mills started a gradual increase in its labour force.

It was in the finishing department of the paper mill that the first Cornwall strike since 1901 occurred, suddenly and almost without warning, in 1919, a portent of what became yearly occurrences in Cornwall industries from 1936 on. Between 1936 and 1972, the Department of Labour in Ottawa received no less than eighty-six reports of Cornwall strikes, three of them at the papermill and thirty-one of them at Canadian Cottons.[10] Work stoppages and wildcat strikes became so common by the 1950s that one union official, George Harrop, recalled thirty-two in one year at the Dundas mill, and Canadian Cottons officials ceased filing reports with the Department of Labour for the shorter ones. The papermill remained free of strikes once its initial effort fizzled. No other strike occurred at the plant until 1962. At the time of the 1919 strike, male workers received $2.10 to $3.45 daily; women and girls got from $1.60 to $2.10, while boys earned $1.95 daily. The company's total annual payroll in 1919 was $360,000, while the company's modest profit was $162,373.[11] These wages, company officials claimed, had doubled labour costs in the previous four years and had made the papermill workers, particularly the women, the best paid of any industry in Cornwall.[12] Nevertheless, the workers in the finishing department wanted an extra fifty cents daily. A union existed at this time, for the company's report to the Department of Labour, Ottawa, filed on 23 May 1919, reported that the workers' petition for more money had been handed to a "union clerk" on May 2 and the company's refusal to meet the wage increase was made to "their committee man." Mill manager W.J. Wallace made it clear that the company could not meet any wage increases as it had made "two substantial increases in the past year."[13] The refusal was met by a walkout of seventy-five men and women. The company's riposte was to notify the men on May 9 "to call for their pay, as we intend to proceed to fill their places, and that we consider they had gone out without just cause." By May 12 the strike was broken. Thirty-two girls resumed work and twenty-three men were re-hired at the same rate of wages and hours as before. Twenty workers were not re-hired, but whether they included union leaders or not is unknown. At any rate, the papermill came under the ownership of C. Howard Smith six months later and from then until 1962 suffered no strikes, largely because the papermill workers enjoyed better wages on the whole than their fellow workers in the textile mills, who tended to envy the papermill workers as the elite of the Cornwall workforce.[14]

The greatest expansion in the workforce occurred in the 1920s and 1930s in the textile industry, largely because of the construction of the Courtauld viscose rayon plant. This British company chose Cornwall as a location for a Canadian plant because the town could supply cheap electrical power, had a plentiful supply of water from the St. Lawrence River, and possessed a labour force well experienced in textile production.[15] From the moment in May 1924 when construction of the huge plant began on the site of the Branard Butler apple orchard east of Cornwall, workers flocked to the milltown to share in the construction and get jobs in the new plant. Sure-footed Indians from St. Regis and Caughnawaga were there to swarm over the high girders carrying heavy tools, guiding derrick-lifted beams into place and nonchalantly tossing hot rivets to welders working at a considerable distance away from them or even on a higher level.[16] Paymaster William Jones of the parent plant in Coventry, England, was there setting up his first office in the old Butler farmhouse. One of the first employees, Barry Robinson, was among the young Cornwall lads learning how to assemble equipment, filters, and pumps on the spinning machines and prepare a batch of viscose. Then, on 4 May 1925, less than a year after the first sod was turned to build the plant,

Robinson and his fellow workers excitedly fidgeted like expectant fathers, waiting to see how liquid could be turned into yarn. Robinson's job was to spin the first few ends and, at the crucial moment, as the spinning-box snatched the thread, Robinson and the whole group of Cornwall apprentices bowed their heads to catch a closer look under the machine to see when the first viscose thread produced in Cornwall would come out, the only time, as Robinson wryly recalled, "that (Cornwall) spinners have been known to bow to their machine."[17]

Paymaster William Jones found Cornwall life had its exciting moments, too. That first year the hundred employees earned about thirty-five cents an hour, paid to them in cash each week. Part of Jones' job was to fetch the money from the Bank of Montreal on Pitt Street and bring it by streetcar as far as St. Lawrence Park from where he would carry it the rest of the way on foot. However, some alert workers or police noticed that "thugs" had been watching the paymaster's movements for a number of weeks and tipped off the company's chief engineer, John R. Douglas. Big industry and big money attracted more than workers and their families: thieves and thugs wanted a share too. The company quickly switched to paying by cheque while the "thugs" switched their place of operations to a bank in Hochelaga near Montreal where two weeks later they carried out a notorious robbery.[18]

With its virtual monopoly on the production of viscose rayon in Canada and a benevolent tariff protection, Courtauld's soon drew 600 workers from the British Isles, the United States and from various areas in Canada, particularly from the province of Quebec.[19] These were part of the increasing town population of 11,126 in 1931, of whom 4,846 were French-speaking residents, 958 of them born in Quebec.[20] Thus Cornwall inhabitants of French background continued as the largest single ethnic group in town, but they were still out-numbered by 5,320 English-speaking residents, 938 of whom had been born in the British Isles. Another 304 came from the United States. The town also had, by this time, several smaller ethnic groups, the largest of which were 387 Dutch, 210 Jews, 117 Italians, and 102 Germans, as well as forty-two Asians. Among the latter were twenty-nine Chinese who formed a small congregation, connected with Knox Church. The Chinese worshipped in a vacated church at 116 Sydney Street which had earlier served the small group of Presbyterians of French-Canadian origin.[21]

This melange of Cornwallites chose the Romanian-born head of Cornwall Pants and Prince Clothing Company, Aaron Horovitz, as their mayor in 1930, the first time a Jewish mayor had ever been elected to head a Canadian municipality. In the next twenty-four years Horovitz occupied the mayoralty seat for a total of eighteen years, marking the longest time one man had held the post. He thus began a new tradition in Cornwall of long-term mayors. Dr. J.A. Phillips followed suit by serving as mayor for five years, Nick Kaneb was mayor for nine years, while the present incumbent, Gerald Parisien, has captured the seat at every municipal election since 1975.

When Cornwall first began to experience severe labour troubles in 1936, the town was, therefore, headed by a man well versed in its industrial development, being himself with his brother Louis, the owner and architect of a highly successful clothing business that was to experience labour upheavals as well.[22] But it was at Cornwall's newer viscose mill that the first strike of the 1930s erupted, taking both management and organizers of the nascent Cornwall Rayon Industrial Workers Union by surprise. In the twelve years since it began operations in Cornwall, the viscose mill had expanded rapidly. Its physical plant was no sooner up than additional wings stretched out to the east and west and its production figures soared from two million pounds of artificial silk, as the rayon yarn was called, to fourteen million pounds by 1939, despite a slow market in 1938.[23] By 1934 average weekly wages had risen to $20.32 for men while women got $12.60.[24] However, wages varied widely, some men getting as much as $50 weekly, others getting $6. Similarly, women and girls could earn as low as $6 or as high as $18. Sales and profits had risen also. In the period from 1926 to 1935 the company's sales totalled $34,891,028. Its profits over the same period were about 27 percent of its total sales: $10,556,997.[26]

This expansion at Courtauld's not only swelled its workforce from an initial 100 in 1925 to 1,753 by 1936, almost half of whom were women, it also attracted other companies to Cornwall such as the American-owned Powdrell and Alexander curtain manufacturers. They set up a branch factory in 1933 to make what would be Cornwall's most natural product: rayon and cotton curtain material. At first Powdrell and Alexander expected to employ only 150 Cornwallites and "no work was to be given to anyone who is unable to prove residence within the limits of Cornwall and the suburbs."[27] The sprawling factory went up quickly on Cumberland Street between Fourth and Fifth Streets. By 29 June 1934 it absorbed all Cornwall's unemployed, expanding its workforce to over 225 who turned out 25,000 yards of curtain daily.[28] So popular was this new type of material that the Cornwall factory could not produce enough to meet the demand even when working at full capacity every day.

A glance at the Cornwall of 1934 that was celebrating its 100th birthday as an incorporated town reveals few of the flagrant signs of economic distress that were afflicting other centres in Canada. When the Canadian racing schooner, the *Bluenose*, paid a visit to the town a year earlier enroute to the Chicago World Fair, 1,500 residents crowded to the wharf anxious to inspect the famous sailing vessel.[29] No less crowded was the Roosevelt International Bridge when it was formally opened in 1934 marking the start of the town's centennial celebrations.[30] The three-mile bridge route spanned the St. Lawrence, linking Ontario and New York just west of the Howard Smith Paper Mill, and giving vehicular traffic a quick and scenic route through Cornwall Island Indian Reservation to the United States and back. It also gave the new lacrosse factory at Cornwall Island better access to railway communication in Cornwall. Thus the small factory, begun in the early 1930s and taken over in 1945 by schoolteacher Colin Chisholm and Frank Roundpoint, a former councillor of the Mohawks on Cornwall Island, increased its production of lacrosse sticks from 2,400 in 1947 to 7,000 by 1972.[31]

While Cornwallites congratulated themselves on their 100th birthday and opened their new international bridge, they welcomed as their due the notice from Canadian Industries Limited that the company intended to build a $900,000 alkali-chlorine plant on the old Wood farm next door to the Howard Smith Paper Mill. Town fathers lost no time in agreeing to the large amount of water the plant would require and by 1935 the plant began operations. For producing a tank-car of liquid chlorine each day, the new chemical company's eighty-one employees earned thirty-five cents an hour, the rate of pay that Courtauld's had given its first employees a decade earlier.[32] Another smaller industry started in 1932, the Cornwall Brass and Iron Foundry on Sixth Street East, operated by the Leroux Brothers.[33] And when the new deluxe steamer, the *Queen Mary*, began accepting bookings for its first trans-Atlantic trip in 1936, it was a Cornwall couple whose names headed the list - Mr. and Mrs. J.H. Cline - an indication that Cornwall's older established families were not feeling the pinch.[34]

The speed with which funds were secured in May 1936 for a new ice rink to replace the old Victoria skating rink destroyed in the 1933 fire also demonstrated that ordinary Cornwallites were not unduly suffering a lack of ready money in the 1930s. Some 2,300 local residents raised $60,000 within a month to build the Cornwall Community Arena on Water Street East.[35] With seating accommodations for 1,225 and standing room for another 1,775, the Arena opened on

16 November 1936. A capacity crowd watched two local teams, the Cornwall Flyers and the Canadiens play their first game on the artificial ice rink which was lighted by thirty-two 1000-watt bulbs, each toting a huge reflector. To mark the occasion, the *Standard-Freeholder* published a souvenir supplement on 13 November 1936 reminding Cornwallites of the town's great names in hockey - Newsie Lalonde, Carson Cooper, the Denneny, Penny and Contant brothers, to name a few. Local teams such as the Canadiens, which was formed in 1926 and won the Benson Trophy of the St. Lawrence League in 1932, and the Holy Name Junior Hockey Club, coached by John Denneny and winner of the Citizen Shield of the Ottawa Hockey District in 1932 and 1933, could now practice and meet their rivals on home ice instead of having to make-do on the outdoor rink at the Cornwall Athletic Grounds or travel to Morrisburg or Iroquois for matches.[36]

The hockey players, their audiences and those who had money to spare to build the new Arena were part of Cornwall's more affluent sector. But even those "horribly in debt" in the height of the depression years, such as a couple living in the East End with their new baby - Tom and Dorothy Donihee - had their perfect moments. For the Donihees such a moment stole upon them suddenly one evening in July of 1937. It had been a "hot, humid and depressing day" for the husband and his twenty-nine-year old wife, but at last as "supper was over, the dishes done, and our dear baby tucked into sleep for the night," they slipped into their bathing suits and went for a swim in the nearby river. As dusk deepened, the sultry air cooled and the couple sat on a large rock jutting out into the water, the husband's arm protectingly around his wife. For the moment their worries over debt faded as they silently watched the great new moon creep over the horizon. "We watched it getting larger and larger, until finally it was shining across the water in a great wide ray like a path of gold coming to meet us, giving us hope and encouragement."[37]

For workers in the textile mills hope and encouragement were coming in another form - unionization. But because five of the men most active in organizing the Cornwall workers were communists or had close communist connections, the emerging unions suffered some initial hostility. The men who took the lead in organizing textile workers, first at Courtauld's in 1936, and then at Canadian Cottons in 1937, were Arthur Laverty, Frank Love, Alex Welch, Ellis Blair and Percy Laurin. The latter three were acknowledged communists; the first two were dubbed communists by management, probably justifiably so, as both had close communist connections. Laverty, Irish by birth, had had wide union experience in a number of industries in Great Britain before emigrating to Canada in 1929. Being employed at Courtauld's for five years, he was well acquainted with the town's industrial base and its growing prosperity in the midst of depression. Laverty worked steadily and quietly among fellow workers, getting some 1,100 men and women to form the Cornwall Rayon Workers Industrial Union by June 1936.[38] In the course of the strike that broke out at Courtauld's in August 1936, Laverty was dubbed a communist by company president, Henry Johnson, who had secured a dossier on Laverty's past union activities in Great Britain. Laverty, together with Love and Welch, were all eventually dropped from the strike negotiating committee at the insistence of President Henry Johnson, because they were "stated to hold communistic views."[39]

Frank Love was employed at Gallinger's Electric shop on Pitt Street, but was fired from his job, presumably for his union activities among the rayon workers at Courtauld's. He then became a full-time union organizer in Cornwall, though it is not clear who paid him, if, indeed, he was paid. The nascent Rayon Workers Union was in no position to hire an agent. Love's communist connections were more overt than those of Laverty as he had been a writer for the Progressive Arts Clubs in the early 1930s.[40] As the strike wore on and negotiations between the company and union committee hardened, neither Laverty nor Love showed any hesitation to share the limelight wih known communists from Toronto such as the *Daily Clarion* reporter, Frank Haslam, and textile union organizer, Alex Welch. All four spoke at a rally attended by some 1500 in Central Park on 30 August 1936, for instance.[41]

Alex Welch arrived post-haste from Toronto as soon as news reached that city of the wildcat walkout on 31 July of 191 Courtauld women workers, the preliminary to the more organized strike that began 11 August.[42] There was no doubt about Welch's credentials as a communist. He had been active in the communist-inspired Workers' Unity League before its demise in 1936. This was the League that unabashedly aimed at organizing "the unorganized in the mass production industries...in a militant trade union centre based on class struggle...ultimately for the overthrow of the capitalist system."[43] As Welch's new job was union organizer for the United Textile Workers of America, Cornwall was pristine grounds for his efforts.

Less obvious communists were two leading local union men, Ellis Blair, vice-president of the new Courtauld union, and Percy Laurin, who became president of the emerging union at Canadian Cottons which staged its first strike in 1937. Blair was a graduate of the Ottawa Normal School who had switched his interests from teaching to textiles. Laurin was a graduate of the Cornwall Commercial

College. Both local union leaders had gone into the textile work force though their post high school education had been in another direction. Thus there were in Cornwall that hot summer of 1936 five union organizers, all communists or with close communist connections, though rank and file union members may not have been aware of Blair and Laurin's membership in the Communist Party of Canada.[44]

The incident that brought Alex Welch promptly to Cornwall in early August 1936 was the sudden walkout of women in the reeling department of Courtauld's. They were protesting the firing of four fellow women workers over an overload dispute that centred on Mamie Lavigne, a union member who later became vice-president.[45] Much to the relief of union organizers the company backed down. Instead of firing the four women, it suspended them for a week. This action came in the wake of a meeting of 1,000 workers who demanded the re-instatement of the dismissed women.[46] Union organizers such as Frank Love regarded strike action as a last resort and "not a good resort for a new union at all."[47] Yet, once the women had started the ball rolling, union organizers pushed for concessions at a meeting with company officials on August 6. They asked for union recognition, a guaranteed forty-hour week, five to ten cents increase in the hourly rates of pay, and improved working conditions to eliminate the danger of eye injury and skin rash caused by various chemicals used in the production of viscose.[48] Management countered with a proposal for a company-type union - a Works Council. This counter-proposal was discussed by Frank Love at a second mass meeting of some 800 workers at the Royal Hotel where Alex Welch "launched a withering attack on the...Works Council." Union members then voted unanimously to affiliate with the United Textile Workers of America, a union associated with the American Federation of Labour. According to the communist *Daily Clarion* of Toronto, they gave a vote of confidence "for President Arthur Laverty", thus clearing the air as far as the union's reaction to the company's proposal for a Works Council was concerned.[49]

Then, on the night of 11 August, workers walked out a second time on the spur of the moment. This time it was men in the spinning department who, annoyed at being told not to discuss union matters while on the job, left their machines. They were soon followed by 957 men and 796 women. The next morning, while some 2,000 townsmen gathered to watch, picket lines went up around the huge plant and union members prepared to bivouac in the nearby fields to prevent movement in and out of the factory. Six policemen were on hand, called in by management, to help maintain order and prevent property damage.[50]

The strike at Courtauld's dragged on until 4 September when the company, through the efforts of a federal conciliator, agreed to a two cent increase in pay for all males, others to get as much as 40 or 45 cents extra; girls to receive from 24 to 27 cents more and were not to be required to work after six o'clock on Saturday night. Though the union dropped its demand for recognition early in the strike negotiations, the company recognized a workers' committee.[51] Working conditions were to be looked into and, by 23 October 1936, Assistant General Manager Hugh Douglas reported to the Royal Commission investigating conditions in the textile industry that "conditions leading to eye trouble are being corrected."[52] By signing an agreement with the Union, Courtauld's was probably the first company to do so in the Canadian textile industry, a step that caused "considerable comment and criticism in the industry and also in...Cornwall at the time."[53]

These triumphs for the new union, admired and envied by workers throughout the textile industry generally and particularly by those at the nearby mills of Canadian Cottons, had their price. For almost four weeks workers and merchants of Cornwall did without the usual $30,000 to $35,000 weekly Courtauld's payroll.[54] The plant itself suffered damages of some $35,086 because machines had been left running when the spinners walked out on 11 August and the viscose had hardened in the pipes, a situation that would have been disastrous to future operations had not the plant works manager, M.V. Kenyon, and other staff members worked day and night to clear the pipes before they were permanently damaged.[55] Most workers were taken back on the payroll, but a few such as president Arthur Laverty were not. In the course of the strike, mildly violent clashes occurred between workers and police on several occasions, and women showed no more reluctance to "man" picket lines than they did to initiate strike action. One of them, Dorothy Lynch, was knocked down near the mill gate by a provincial police car and suffered "slight injuries," according to the *Ottawa Evening Citizen*. Union organizer Frank Love was arrested on charges of intimidation for telling pickets not to let anyone in or out of the plant.[56] Though released on bail, Love's arrest gave an emotional charge to several mass rallies orchestrated by the union. At one in Central Park on August 29, Alex Welch addressed a crowd of 1,500, criticizing Mayor Aaron Horovitz for sending Cornwall police to the mill, which was outside town limits. During the last two weeks of the strike, a number of small scuffles occurred, one resulting in the arrest of nine men, including union vice-president Ellis Blair.[57]

Both management and union sought outside help. Company president Henry Johnson arrived late in August from England to handle company negotiations himself and he insisted that the men whom he regarded as communists be dropped from the negotiations - Laverty, Love and Welch.[58] The union had brought in Welch, Frank Haslam of the *Daily Clarion* and Felix Lazarus from Toronto, and James Potts, identified as a student at Western University, the latter three assisting at one of the mass rallies.[59] Strikers received moral and financial help from several directions, including the Canadian Commonwealth Federation and the Communist Party of Canada, the latter also arranging a private party for five girls and one man from Courtauld's who went on a speaking tour in the provincial capital on behalf of the striking union members.[60]

In fact, the intense interest which the *Daily Clarion* exhibited in the Cornwall strike, giving it almost daily reports, encouraged management and other townsmen to credit the communists with more influence in the union than they probably had. Local shopkeepers, who had revived the defunct Retail Merchants Association in July 1935, showed some sympathy with the strikers by donating prizes for a union raffle.[61] One of the merchants went so far as to eject from his premises a rival union started by Paul Rivière who claimed to have enlisted 500 Courtauld workers "tired of being out of work" and "wishing to open negotiations on a reasonable basis," an indication that a sizable number of textile workers disapproved of the strike tactics being used by Laverty's union.[62]

Finally, both sides agreed to outside arbitration. Deputy Minister of Labour for Ontario, J.F. Marsh, succeeded in getting mill management and union officials together on 19 August, but without any positive results.[63] It was not until a federal conciliator, M.S. Campbell, appeared on the scene at the urging of Stormont's Member of Parliament, Lionel Chevrier, that hard-fought negotiations ended the strike on 4 September, and Cornwall emerged with the image of a "tough union town." In Toronto, the United Textile Workers of America celebrated by issuing the first number of *The Textile Worker*, much of it devoted to the union triumph at Courtauld's in Cornwall. "Here is the first major victory of the American Federation of Labour in an unorganized industry," the editor exclaimed, "not only in Canada, but on the whole continent."[64] Victory was sweet. Within a year it included recognition of the Rayon Workers Industrial Union as bargaining agent for Courtauld's employees, with R. Harkin replacing Laverty as president. The union soon secured affiliation with the United Textile Workers of America as Federal Union 3.[65] Even if no longer president of the Courtauld union, Laverty was still at the fore in the negotiations since he was president of the National Textile Council, as well as being chief promoter of the Cornwall Textile Workers Union which embraced millhands from all three textile firms in town.

The latter union subsequently became affiliated with the newly-formed Committee for Industrial Organization. Textile company officials had watched with concern the formation of a Canadian branch of the Committee for Industrial Organization, especially as it was promoted by a group of Hamilton steelworkers, most of whom were communist.[66] Laverty took time out in the fall of 1936 to deny specifically that he intended to form an industry-wide union in Cornwall. Indeed, in 1936 his efforts were concentrated on establishing the Cornwall Trades and Labour Council and consolidating union gains in the three local textile firms.[67] Yet despite his denial in 1936, by 1937 he had formed the all-embracing Cornwall Textile Workers Union.

Unionization of Canadian Cottons and the Powdrell and Alexander curtain factory proceeded rapidly under Arthur Laverty, Percy Laurin and Ellis Blair. So, too, did the unionization of the small clothing factory owned by the town's mayor, Aaron Horovitz. When four employees were dismissed, allegedly for union activity, the whole staff of 275 walked out and stayed out until 15 September when the company agreed to a forty-four hour week, an eight-hour day with time and a half for overtime, and the discharged workers were rehired.[68]

The union situation and strike action at the three mills of Canadian Cottons were not so straightforward. Enlisting union members was not difficult, especially after the success of the Courtauld workers the previous summer. Moreover, a union already existed among the millhands of Canadian Cottons, at least since 1921 when "representatives of the Labour Union were heard by (Town) Council in reference to a minimum wage which deputation suggested should be fixed at 43-1/2 cents per hour."[69] One of the more active members of this early union was Phileas Laperle. His employment with the company began in 1902 when he took his place as an apprentice beside his father at the age of twelve, earning $3.15 every two weeks for working 120 hours.[70] In 1952 Laperle, by then a union official, claimed that "thirty years have passed since the struggle began to form a union of Cornwall Textile Workers," and that he was in the struggle at every step. A union man through and through, Laperle was also a company man through and through. He could brag that his family gave a total of 400 years' service to Canadian Cottons which learned "to treat us like human beings because we taught it how." By 1952 he was earning close to two dollars an hour for a 44-hour week, a wage hike he attributed largely to union efforts from 1937 on.[71]

Union demands for increased wages and improved working conditions began in July 1937 at a time when Canadian Cottons' 1400 workers received average weekly earnings of from $12 to $16.[72] Armand Proulx, a doffer in the Stormont mill, for instance, received 14 cents an hour plus 2-1/4 cents for each machine he doffed but, because of a slowdown in work, his pay had dropped from $13.00 to $10.50 a week. Sixteen-year-old Annette Brunet worked for four months as an apprentice without pay at the Stormont mill and then got $1.80 a day. Marcile Paquin, a cleaner at the Stormont mill, was paid $8.30 for a four-day week during which she worked nine hours a day.[73] Thus cotton workers, at the bottom of the wage scale in Cornwall textile mills, felt justified in expecting a larger slice of the company's profits, though their organizer, Arthur Laverty, put union recognition as the prime target in 1937.

In contrast with the Courtauld's month-long strike the previous summer, the Canadian Cottons strike that began 20 July 1937 was completely orchestrated by the union. Arthur Laverty handed a notice to management on 12 July, stating that the Textile Workers Union now represented 80 percent of the total workforce of 1,401 that included 319 women. Laverty listed six demands, the first being union recognition. A general pay increase of 20 percent was asked for; overtime was to be paid for all hours worked beyond a normal day; promotions to be made on a basis of seniority and efficiency; lunchrooms and smoking rooms to be provided and a lunch period granted without pay reduction; and proper ventilation to be provided in all departments needing it.[74]

Union control during the strike was evident. No violent confrontations occurred. Women were not used on picket lines nor were they on negotiating committees, as they had been in the Courtauld's strike, perhaps because their numbers at Canadian Cottons were not as great as they were at the viscose mill. Neither provincial nor local police were used, and even with provincial and federal efforts at arbitration, the strike settlement reached on 20 August was temporary, pending the recommendations of an Ontario Industry and Labor Board study of the whole textile industry.[75] Shorter walkouts continued through August, September and November of 1937, and again in February and March of 1938 before management and union reached a modus vivendi of sorts.[76] The most important feature of the settlement was that Canadian Cottons agreed to a union "closed shop" in their three Cornwall mills, the first union in the Canadian textile industry to secure such an agreement.[77] Speaking for the union, President Percy Laurin promised that "every effort is to be made...to prevent further stoppages and strikes."[78] As for the company, it insisted that the union cancel its affiliation with the National Textile Council and its officers, Arthur Laverty and Alex Welch. The latter had returned to Cornwall from the United States in 1937 to help Laverty organize the Council. With Laverty and Welch at its head, company officials regarded the Council, probably rightly so, as communist-inspired.

Company officials were not the only ones concerned about communist influence in the emerging militant unions. So, too, were labour leaders and other Cornwallites. The editor of the *Standard-Freeholder* used the front page for an anti-communist editorial on 2 December 1936. He warned townsmen to beware of communists who were trying to get candidates in municipal elections to accept their programmes. It was no idle warning. Within a year, two communist union leaders who had helped organize and secure recognition for the textile unions, Ellis Blair and Percy Laurin, secured seats on the Town Council in municipal elections.[79] However, their elections had more to do with their efficient union leadership than it did with their communist affiliation, which was not generally known at the time of their elections. Both men were re-elected in 1938 and continued active membership in their unions, Blair being named business agent for Courtauld's union, and Laurin continuing as President of Canadian Cottons union which affiliated with the United Textile Workers of America as Federal Union 2, thus receiving an earlier number than the Courtauld union which was Federal Union 3.

This second major strike victory of textile workers in Cornwall, together with the election of two prominent union men to Town Council in 1937 again produced admiration among workers throughout the industry in Canada and stimulated union activity at the Canadian Cotton Company's mills in Hamilton and Milltown, New Brunswick. Indeed, militant Cornwall workers sent Arthur Laverty to Hamilton to help cotton workers there to organize. In a flyer addressed to the "Workers of the Canadian Cotton Company" Laverty and other union organizers told them, "The Cornwall Local Union has been fighting the battle for all the Hamilton workers and the Milltown workers and gained a 5% increase last fall... The Milltown workers joined the Union, saying they would not be a drag on the Cornwall Union."[80]

At first the Cornwall unions tended to burst at the seams with self-importance and self-imposed meetings, even taking a pre-emptory tone when seeking negotiations with management to iron out minor problems over working conditions. Such a tone was assumed by Laverty in the fall of 1937 when writing to Courtauld's manager, E. Hazeley, about various matters in the engineering department. Laverty ended his letter with an abrupt "Please arrange for such a meeting early next week, preferable Tuesday."[81] Even the rank and file members began to treat the company somewhat offhandedly. Edwin Thompson, for instance, wrote a note to his boss informing him that his absence from work was due to sickness and should he be away any longer, "I will inform Mr. Laverty." This was too much for Courtauld's manager, who curtly reminded Thompson that "you are employed by Courtauld's, not by Mr. Laverty."[82]

However, as the depression deepened towards the end of the 1930s and even Courtauld's mill, which had been riding the crest of rising production and profits, began to experience a slump in sales, union-management relations became more conciliatory. In the spring of 1938, for instance, Hazeley, the manager of Courtauld's, sought the help of the union business agent, Ellis Blair, in giving "all the publicity you can" to the fact that the company was keeping one of its mills operating solely "to provide work for its employees...that it is obvious to everyone employed in no. 1 mill that the company has no need of production from that mill, owing to the large stocks that we hold."[83] This slump was short-lived. Courtauld's constructed its fourth mill in 1938 to the rear of the parent plant and adjoining the two additional mills that had been constructed in 1930 and 1934. The dividing walls in the four mills were removed, making the Courtauld's plant into one huge building, probably the biggest rayon spinning unit in the world at that time.[84] This expansion at Courtauld's in 1938 helped dispel depression fears in town.

The picture that emerges from this look at Cornwall's industrial growth, its labour force, and the strike action of the 1930s is that of a town bursting with increased population, expansion in industry, and a militant and triumphant union movement. Though tension ran high at times during the strike confrontations in 1936 and 1937, especially when violence broke out between police and men and women on the picket lines at the Courtauld plant, union leaders strove to avoid such clashes and succeeded during the subsequent strike at Canadian Cottons the following year. Moreover, the labour force moved quickly to eradicate the image that it was under radical or communist influence, even if it meant disassociating itself from the men who had done most of the hard organizing in 1936 and 1937.

Then, to gain community support and sympathy, unionists held mass rallies to explain their policies and tactics, and staged door-to-door canvasses for donations to the relief stores set up to aid striking workers. Once management found itself face to face with determined and organized unionists, prepared to sit it out for a month or more on the picket lines, it recognized the unions as bargaining agents for the mill-hands. Thus, unionists in the Cornwall textile industry led the way for the rest of Canada in organizing on an industry-wide basis and emerged as tough, moderate and responsible, just as ready to tackle rival unions, whether communist or otherwise, as they were to meet hard-nosed company management across the negotiating table.

As for the men who pioneered the industries, provided the capital needed to create and expand the plants, brought in the raw materials to be made into finished products, and who kept faith in the productive ability of the Cornwall labour force, these men watched the decade of depression with fearful eyes lest their plants succumb under the impact of the general decline in trade and employment that was overtaking the rest of the country. That Cornwall reaped the advantages of full production for most of the decade, a population boom, expansion in its industries, and unionization of its workforce during a decade of general depression speaks eloquently for those leaders of industry and of labour during that difficult decade. The remarkable point was not that there were strikes and misunderstandings, but that moderation on both sides helped resolve the difficulties before they could impose long-term hardships on the community at large or undermine the financial stability of the textile industry upon which the prosperity of the town of Cornwall depended.

NOTES

1. *Ottawa Evening Citizen*, 21 October 1936; Ralph Ellis, "Cornwall Labour and Unionization, 1936-37," term paper submitted to Department of History, McGill University, Spring 1982, 9.
2. *Standard-Freeholder*, 2 July 1932.
3. Minutes, Town Council, 15 January 1930, 425.
4. *Standard-Freeholder*, 2 July 1932.
5. Charles Lipton, *The Trade Union Movement of Canada, 1827-1959*, 108.
6. *Standard-Freeholder*, 5 February 1937.
7. Dorothy Donihee, "In My Mother's Footsteps," 25, 28-29.
8. *Standard-Freeholder*, 7 February 1936.
9. *Ibid.*, 6 August 1937; Ellis, "Cornwall Labour and Unionization," 18.
10. Strikes and Lockouts Records, 1907-1973, RG27/312, 395, 397, 405-553, 3092-3617.
11. *Standard-Freeholder*, 19 March 1979.
12. *Gazette*, Montreal, 13 May 1919; RG27/312, see No. 118, Toronto Paper Company's report of strike to Department of Labour, 23 May 1919.
13. *Globe*, Toronto, 18 May 1919.
14. *The Cornwall Mill Story*, 1970, 8, gives an account of a strike at the mill in 1920, but as details are identical to the 1919 strike, presumably this is the strike referred to.
15. *Fifty Years of Progress, Yesterday, Today and Tomorrow, Courtaulds Canada Limited, 1975*, 2.
16. See memoir of Paymaster William Jones in *Courtaulds (Canada) Limited: 30th Year in Canada*, 5.
17. *Ibid.*, 8 and 11.
18. *Ibid.*, 6.
19. *Standard-Freeholder*, 29 June 1934.
20. *Census*, 1931, ii, 743 and 424.
21. *Knox United Church 1846-1975*, 15.
22. *Standard-Freeholder*, 25 August 1937.
23. *Fifty Years of Progress*, 1975, 3; see also E. Hazeley to Ellis Blair, 7 March 1938, Greater Cornwall Textile Joint Board, Local 779 reports for 1938-1944 (MG28/1-219/80-437, box 1.)
24. *Royal Commission Report on the Textile Industry*, 1938, 279-284.
25. *Ibid.*, 300.
26. *Ottawa Morning Journal*, 31 October 1936, see Justice Turgeon's Summary of Royal Commission's investigation of the textile industry.
27. *Standard-Freeholder*, 25 February 1933.
28. *Ibid.*, 29 June 1934.
29. *Ibid.*, 2 February 1946.
30. *Ibid.*, 28 June 1958.
31. *Ibid.*, 22 February 1947; see also, *Standard-Freeholder* Business Review, 1972, 3.
32. *Ibid.*, 21 February 1934; see also, "Know Your City, Cornwall Ontario," prepared by Cornwall Collegiate and Vocational School Commercial Class XII, February 1961.
33. *Standard-Freeholder*, 1 February 1947.
34. *Ibid.*, 10 October 1934.
35. *Ibid.* 11 November 1936.

36. *Ibid.*, 13 November 1936.
37. Donihee, "In My Mother's Footsteps," 60.
38. *Standard-Freeholder*, 12 August 1936.
39. Memo by M.S. Campbell, Department of Labour Conciliator, 31 August 1936, and his final report on the Courtauld's strike, 22 September 1936, (RG27/377.)
40. Ralph Ellis, "Labour and Municipal Politics in Cornwall, 1936-1939", term paper submitted to the Department of History, McGill University, Spring, 1982, 4.
41. *Ottawa Evening Journal*, 31 August 1936.
42. *Labour Gazette*, September 1936, 774, in RG27/377.
43. For the Workers' Unity League, see *The Worker*, 28 June 1930; *Canada's Party of Socialism: The Communist Party of Canada*, 85, 37, 70-83, 100 and 112; Ian Angus, *Canadian Bolsheviks: Early Years of the Communist Party of Canada*, 281-88.
44. For identification of Blair and Laurin as communists, see *Canada's Party of Socialism: The Communist Party of Canada*, 117.
45. *Ottawa Evening Citizen*, 21 October 1936; *Labour Gazette*, September 1936, 774 in RG27/377.
46. *Daily Clarion*, Toronto, 7 August 1936.
47. Cited in Ralph Ellis, "Unionization of a Mill Town: Cornwall in 1936", term paper submitted to Department of History, McGill University, Spring 1982, 7.
48. *Standard-Freeholder*, 12 August 1936; Courtauld's report to Department of Labour, 13 August 1936 (RG27/377); see also Arthur Laverty's testimony before Royal Commission, cited in *Ottawa Evening Citizen*, 21 October 1936.
49. *Daily Clarion*, 10 August 1936.
50. For details see, Courtauld's report to Department of Labour, 13 August 1936; (RG27/377); see also, *Ottawa Evening Citizen*, 21 October 1936; Ellis, "Unionization of a Mill Town," 7.
51. *Standard-Freeholder*, 4 September 1936; *Daily Clarion*, 7 September 1936.
52. *Ottawa Morning Journal*, 23 October 1936.
53. *Standard-Freeholder* Business Survey, 1942, 22.
54. *Ottawa Evening Journal*, 4 September 1936.
55. *Ottawa Evening Citizen*, 21 October 1936.
56. *Toronto Telegram*, 21 August 1936.
57. *Ibid.*, 31 August 1936.
58. Memo and final report of Conciliator M.S. Campbell, 31 August 1936 and 22 September 1936, (RG27/377); *Ottawa Evening Journal*, 2 September 1936; and *Toronto Star*, 31 August 1936.
59. *Ottawa Evening Journal,* 31 August 1936.
60. *Daily Clarion*, 31 August 1936.
61. *Standard-Freeholder*, 17 July 1935.
62. *Ottawa Morning Journal*, 3 September 1936.
63. *Standard-Freeholder*, 19 August 1936.
64. Cited in the *Daily Clarion*, 16 October 1936.
65. *Ibid.*, 13 September 1937; see also, Shirley Dixon, president of Courtaulds, to R. Harkin, 24 May 1938 (MG28/1-219/80, 437, box 1)
66. *Canada's Party of Socialism: The Communist Party of Canada*, 102; *Ottawa Evening Citizen*, 21 October 1936.
67. *Daily Clarion*, 12 October 1936.
68. *Standard-Freeholder*, 25 August and 15 September 1937.
69. Minutes, Town Council, 11 April 1921, 468.
70. *Standard-Freeholder*, 28 August 1952.

71. *Ibid.*

72. *Royal Commission on the Textile Industry*, 1938, 286.

73. *Ottawa Morning Journal*, 23 October 1936.

74. *Standard-Freeholder*, 21 July 1937.

75. *Ibid.*, 9 and 30 August 1937.

76. *Ibid.*, 27 August, 24 November, 1937; 11 February, 28 March, 1938; see also Percy Laurin's report to Department of Labour, on the strike at Canadian Cottons, 11 February, 1938 (RG27/395).

77. *Standard-Freeholder*, 28 March and 13 May 1938.

78. *Ibid.*, 16 February 1938.

79. Minutes, Town Council, 10 January 1938, 390; Ellis continued to be elected until December 1940.

80. MG28/1-219/80-437, box 1.

81. Laverty to Hazeley, 12 November 1937. (*ibid.*)

82. Hazeley to Laverty, 13 November 1937, enclosing copy of letter to Thompson, (*ibid.*)

83. Hazeley to Ellis Blair, 7 March 1938, (*ibid.*)

84. *Standard-Freeholder*, Business Survey, 1942, 22.

Aerial view of the artificial silk, rayon, plant of Courtauld's (Canada) Ltd., Cornwall, Ontario. May 1935. Construction of the plant was started May 1924.

Credit: Public Archives of Canada. Neg. C 46217.

Mayor Aaron Horovitz, 1930-1934, 1936-1937, 1944-1945, 1949-1956. (from 'Old Home Week,' 1946 Souvenir Booklet and Program.)

Chapter XVIII

Cornwall as War Clouds Darkened

War for Cornwall meant economic prosperity and jobs for everyone. It also meant the loss of about 4,000 servicemen and women from its workforce, the grief and loneliness that accompanied war casualties and family separations, and the adjustment of much of its industry to war production.[1] The population of the square mile of town that more often than not was called a city by 1939 was nearing 14,000. English-speaking residents of Irish, Scottish and English background accounted for 6,947. Its French-speaking residents numbered 5,969. Among the 1,157 of European or Asian backgrounds, those of Dutch and Jewish origin still represented the largest of the ethnic groups - 509 Dutch and 190 Jews. Cornwallites of Italian extraction were the third ethnic group of sizable proportion - some 157 within the town limits.[2]

Another 20,000 or so inhabitants occupied the sprawling suburbs that immediately surrounded the square mile town - Smithville, Laflecheville, Garden City, Beaconfield, Riverdale and Lorneville. Being beyond the town limits, these suburbs absorbed the inflowing population, but, not being subject to zoning or building by-laws, residential and commercial developments sprang up haphazardly without adequate urban planning. Thus, while growth in the heart of the town was sluggish from 1940 until 1957, its uncontrolled suburbs ran rampant in terms of population expansion and manufacturing. It was only with the annexation of the suburbs to the city in 1957 that urban development in greater Cornwall was tackled, and the city's population jumped overnight from 17,160 to 39,764.[3]

These were part of the estimated crowd of 50,000, the largest ever assembled in Cornwall, who lined the tracks near the Canadian National Railway station on 21 May 1939 to catch a glimpse of King George VI and Queen Elizabeth as they stopped for twelve minutes in Cornwall during their tour of Canada. "Everyone was captivated by the royal pair" who waved from the observation platform of the royal train, awakening and renewing the undercurrent of loyal sentiment that swelled up as the country and its people watched war clouds darken over Europe. For Cornwallites, this visit of their King and Queen was the ninth time that members of the Royal Family had honoured the town with a visit. As far back as 1787 Prince William Henry had paid the first such visit, followed by the visit of Prince Edward, Duke of Kent, in 1792. The Prince of Wales, later Edward VII, had made Cornwall one of his stops in 1860. The Marchioness of Lorne had spent a wet day in town in 1878. Then came a visit of special importance for Cornwallites when the Duke of Cornwall and York, later King George V and his duchess, who became Queen Mary, visited the factory town in 1901. George VI had passed through the town enroute to Niagara as a naval cadet in 1913 and his older brother, the Prince of Wales, visited Cornwall in 1919.[4] In fact, the loyalist town was seldom if ever left off a royal itinerary.

It was from the whole area of this loyalist and royalist Cornwall and its growing suburbs that the call to arms was answered by over 4,000 men and women, giving Cornwall one of the highest percentages of service personnel in the country. It is not surprising that the local press boasted in 1944 that "no city in Canada has answered its call to battle more honorably".[5] Inscribed on the Roll of Honor at City Hall are the names of 3,630, representing all those whose names were forwarded voluntarily to the committee in charge of preparing the Honor Roll after the war. Thus, although the list does not contain all the names, it is likely a close approximation of the number who actually served. What the Honor Roll does show, however, is the overwhelming response to duty by both of Cornwall's major language groups. Out of the 3,630 names listed, almost half are French, an indication that members of Cornwall's French community, in proportion to the overall population, served, like their English-speaking comrades, unstintingly. Loyalist names such as Alguire, Anderson, Macdonald, Casselman, Loney, Macdonell, Barnhart, Loucks, Gallinger, Silmser and Snetsinger are interspersed with those of Bergeron, Carrière, Charlebois, Gauthier, Kirkey (Cartier), Larose, Lalonde, Landry, Lavigne, Lefebvre, Leroux, Parisien, Payette, Primeau, Rivière, Sauvé, Séguin and Tessier, to mention only a few of the hundreds of Cornwall families stemming from the founding fathers of Canada whose sons and daughters served at home and abroad from 1939 to 1945.[6]

One of the first to go overseas in December 1939 was a local boxer, Ashley Kirkey of Seventh Street. Serving in North Africa, Sicily and Italy with the Hastings and Prince Edward Regiment, Sergeant Kirkey was mentioned in dispatches, along with Sapper Hugh Daniel Cameron of Ninth Street East, for "gallant and distinguished service".[7] Before the war was over, a number of other Cornwall men would be so honoured. Two commanding officers of the Glens, Lieutenant-Colonels Roger Rowley and Donald D. Cameron, received the Distinguished Service Order and Bar. Lieutenant-Colonel Neil Gemmell received the Distinguished Service Order and the Croix de Guerre avec Etoile Vermeille.[8] For his daring action during the Ems River crossing, Captain Donald Charles Stewart was awarded the Military Cross and Captain J.R. Owen won the Medaille Militaire de Belgium. Lance-Corporal Aurele Mercier of 198 Montreal Road won the Military Medal for his action in capturing an officer and fourteen other ranks in a fortified house in Italy, Mercier "armed only with a Tommy gun".[9] Another amateur boxer and employee of Howard Smith Paper Mill, Corporal Donald James Milne, was awarded the Military Medal posthumously.[10] These were but some of the men of Cornwall whose deeds merited special citations or awards.[11]

At the start of the war Cornwall was a town whose inhabitants were, for the most part, Ontario-born and predominantly Roman Catholic. Out of a population of 14,117 in 1941, there were 8,229 Roman Catholics. United Church adherents were the next largest religious grouping with 1,943. Anglicans numbered 1,905 and Presbyterians 1,333.[12] The town's workforce totalled 4,797, most of them employed in the manufacturing industries, but there were sizable numbers elsewhere. Trade accounted for 405, town service personnel, 471, 265 in construction, 274 in transportation, 225 clerical workers, twenty-eight school teachers, ten musicians and one artist. A sign of the times was that only forty-eight described themselves as farmers.[13]

The bare bones of official statistics do not tell the whole story. Cornwall's trade, for instance, was undergoing a gradual change from small speciality shops owned by local people to larger departmental and chain stores, increasingly owned by outside financial interests. Two local businesses led the way in the conversion from small dry-goods or grocery stores into departmental stores by 1926. These were McIntyre and Campbell's drygoods store on Pitt Street, established in 1879, and Fawthrop Brothers store in the West End which branched out to include drygoods, books, china, toys, and clothing, in addition to groceries.[14] The first of the chain stores to come to Cornwall was Woolworth's, which opened on Pitt Street in 1918, employing twenty-three "lady" clerks and five men.[15] Rival five and ten-cent stores did not appear until the Federal and National stores opened on Pitt Street. One of the first of the large food chains to locate in Cornwall was Dominion Store on Pitt Street which was wiped out in the great fire of 1933. Other departmental chain stores moved into

410

the city in the mid-1940s: Metropolitan in 1946 and Zeller's in 1947, the latter closing its doors on Pitt Street in 1982.[16]

Cornwall's banking history continued on a steady course during the first half of the twentieth century, except for one jolt in 1906. This was the year of the first Old Boys' Reunion when the souvenir programme described Cornwall's three banking institutions as financial pillars of the community, none more so than the Ontario Bank with a paid-up capital of $1,500,000 and its directors "gentlemen of the highest financial standing".[17] The branch of the Ontario Bank in Cornwall, established in 1882, had been managed since 1887 by a man esteemed by all, Archibald Denny. He had kept his bank neck to neck with its major rival, the local branch of the Bank of Montreal, and ahead of the newly-established branch of the Sterling Bank. Not only was Denny founder and president of the influential Cornwall Cheese Board, he was also quartermaster of the 59th Regiment and a first-class public relations man. Every Christmas Denny courted his clients with a morocco-bound diary and desk calendar "containing all the information that a busy man likes to have at hand". Nor did he neglect the ladies. His gift to them was a combined passbook and card case designed to "call the attention of the gentle sex to the advisability of opening a savings account with the Ontario Bank".[18]

However, Cornwallites, whether of gentle or not so gentle sex, were startled one Friday in 1906 to learn from the *Standard* that the Ontario Bank's president had been arrested in Toronto for misappropriation of funds and the bank had folded. Denny was as dumbfounded as anyone else. To the hundreds who lined up on Saturday morning in front of the bank wicket, he exclaimed that there had not been the slightest inkling of any trouble beforehand. Indeed, so high was Denny's standing in the community that no one doubted him, nor had they any reason to. He prolonged banking hours on Saturday from noon to five o'clock and, while his clients were busily withdrawing their money, he was busy on the telephone making arrangements to open a branch of the Royal Bank of Canada next door. By Monday morning, 22 October, he was persuading many to transfer their money into the Royal, rather than going over to the Bank of Montreal.[19]

Thus Cornwall got its first branch of the Royal Bank of Canada in October 1906 in somewhat unusual circumstances. The branch took over the premises of the defunct Ontario Bank next door to the old Post Office on Pitt Street and remained at this address until 1967 when it moved to 212 Pitt Street. By the time that the Royal Bank branch relocated in its new building at 300 Pitt Street in March of 1980 it had grown from a one-man affair in 1906 to forty employees under manager Bill Pickard.[20] A second Cornwall branch opened at the Eastcourt Mall in April 1968, long after other bank branches had moved to the East End, indicative of the Royal's conservative approach to expansion in this area.

Other local bank branches had somewhat more conventional histories. The Bank of Commerce opened a branch in 1912 and by 1922, aware of the emergence of a separate shopping and business area servicing the eastern part of town, it established a sub-branch there, the first bank to do so. By 1925 the Sterling Bank branch, opened in 1905, was taken over by the Standard Bank of Canada and this, in turn, merged with the Canadian Bank of Commerce in 1928.[21] The Bank of Montreal, which had a branch in Cornwall as early as 1857, established itself permanently in a building located on Pitt Street East on the site of the Rossmore Hotel that burned in 1910.[22] The manager of the local branch of the Bank of Montreal saw the business potentialities of the East End and a second branch was established on Montreal Road at the corner of Marlborough Street in 1925, perhaps out-distancing the small East End sub-branch of the Bank of Commerce which closed its doors in 1936. The Bank of Montreal pushed northward after the war, opening a small branch on Pitt Street at the corner of Fourteenth Street.

The Bank of Nova Scotia moved to Cornwall in June 1928. Some indication of banking arrangements in the 1920s can be gleaned from the Bank of Nova Scotia's early records. It paid Alexander R. McLennan $1,080 a year for the premises it occupied on Second Street East in the Standard Block. Its manager, W.E. Sparham, received $3,000 annually. The accountant earned $1,000 yearly. The male clerk got $1,050, while the female clerk got $500. One other employee, described as a messenger and janitor, received $600 annually.[23] It was not until 1969 that the Bank of Nova Scotia made a cautious move towards expansion in Cornwall by opening a second branch in the new Brookdale Mall Shopping Plaza in the northwest area of the city. Thus, as Cornwall entered the war period, it was served by five banks - the Royal Bank of Canada, the Bank of Montreal, the Bank of Nova Scotia, the Canadian Bank of Commerce and, in the East End, by a second branch of the Bank of Montreal.

The town's fire and police departments were not much different in 1939 than they were at the beginning of the century. The volunteer fire brigade operated almost continuously under the capable wing of the Hunter family from 1886 until December of 1945. Only for a brief interlude from 1925 to 1933 did Charles Larose run the brigade between the demise of John G. Hunter as chief and the appointment of his son, George J. Hunter, in 1933.[24] Horses were dispensed with by 1921 when a small truck was bought to carry the hose and, by 1925, a ladder truck was acquired. A pumper was added to the equipment in 1929, but it was not until 1944 that a new La France pumper was bought. During the early war years six new men brought the strength of the brigade up to thirteen permanent members and fifteen volunteers.[25] Then, in 1945, the force became a full-time permanent force under Chief Cory Moore, its members working a sixty-hour week.[26] This was the force that faced one of Cornwall's worst downtown fires since 1933, when twelve stores were gutted and twenty-four families left homeless on Christmas Eve of 1947.[27] By 1970 the Fire Department moved into its new Station on Fourth Street that was officially opened by Mayor Nick Kaneb who headed the city's administration for most of the sixties and early seventies.

Cornwall's Fire Department increased from its 1946 complement of twenty-eight members to a force of fifty-five under Chief Hugh O'Reilly who took over the department in 1981 following the retirement of Lucien A. Carrière who had headed it since 1958.[28] Its firefighters handle as many as 644 calls a year, not all of them fires. The firemen assist in rescues of adventurous youths on the ice floes of the St. Lawrence. They provided mouth-to-mouth resuscitation for Lee Ann St. Pierre when she collapsed in a swimming pool. One of their most valuable services is training groups such as the Boy Scouts and nurses in fire safety and prevention techniques.

Police history in the twentieth century indicates that Cornwall was relatively free of serious crime. Over the years from 1900 to 1980 there was a gradual improvement in police equipment and technology, and an increase in the size of the force from seven to sixteen in 1947 and to ninety-two by 1982.[29] The jump in size of the force came about partly because of the 1957 annexation of the township area that resulted in a merger of the town and township police forces into a fifty-two man department, headed by Cornwall Police Chief, Allan G. Clarke, with the township chief, Hermidas J. Poirier, as his deputy.[30]

The police force at the turn of the century was facetiously described in the Old Boys' Reunion souvenir album of that year as the "Heaviest in Canada". Chief Robert Smyth, a pole vaulter in his youth, weighed in at 235 pounds. His two senior constables, Joseph Lalonde and George C. Crites, weighed 215 and 220 pounds respectively. These three men, together with three assistant policemen, kept the police blotter clear in 1901 except for fifty-nine Cornwallites who ended up in jail. The fifty-nine were a fair cross-section of Cornwall's society except that none were from the upper echelons. According to the jailor's report for the year, the majority were Canadian-born

Roman Catholic day labourers who were convicted mainly on charges of drunkenness or theft.[31]

The beginning of modern communications for the police began in 1907 when Chief Robert Smyth had a telephone installed in his own home. With his retirement in 1918, the Cornwall police underwent a period of instability when no less than four chiefs resigned or were fired within seven years. The appointment in 1925 of a former rookie policeman, Fred Seymour, as Chief Constable at a salary of $1600 brought a long period of stability in police leadership and control.[32] Seymour reigned supreme at police headquarters from 1925 until 1945, unperturbed by a long list of charges brought against the department and him in particular by J.H. Warrington in 1935. Although the investigation exonerated the force and its chief, Seymour was censured for carelessness in allowing a prisoner to escape, and Town Council determined to tighten up its control of the force.[33] A Board of Commissioners, made up of Mayor William A. Parisien, County Court Judge Francis T. Costello and Dr.J.A. Phillips, acting for the police magistrate, was established in July with a mandate to "take full control of the Police Force".[34] However, so much controversy surrounded the operations of the Board that it was abolished by Town Council within eight months.[35]

Town Council obviously appreciated Chief Seymour's work for by 1937 his salary was raised to $2,000, while his constables were paid $1,400. However, Council still hoped to gain more control over the force's discipline and a new post was established in 1939, that of Inspector of Police, filled by Frank H. Hunter,[36] who had been with the force since 1935. Before the year was out, Hunter enlisted in the provost branch of the Royal Canadian Air Force. A second investigation of the police force by Provincial Police Inspector W.H. Lougheed was carried out in 1943 with the result that Seymour stepped down as Chief and Frank Hunter, then a flight lieutenant in the R.C.A.F., became Chief for the next ten years.[37] A Board of Police Commissioners was again set up in 1945, composed, as before, of the mayor, the county court judge and the police magistrate.[38]

These measures were largely concerned with internal administration and the discipline of the force as it increased in size and modernized over the years, sporting a new Plymouth sedan in 1934, its officers taking courses from the St. John Ambulance Brigade, and other officers, such as Allan Clarke, being sent to take special courses at the Police School.[39] By 1955 Cornwall boasted its own Police School where Clarke, who became Chief in 1953, instructed constables in the proper use of firearms and other related subjects.[40]

414

With the erection of a new Police Headquarters on Pitt Street West in 1972, the Cornwall Police Force boasted its own indoor shooting range, private elevators for prisoners, nine police cells equipped with showers, and all the up-to-date appurtenances of a modern justice building, including a separate area for youthful offenders.[41] Another Cornwall veteran, Earl Landry, who had served in the Royal Canadian Provost Corps during the Second War and joined the Police Force in 1947, was named Chief in 1974. He pressed for a larger force to cope with the increase in police duties as the decade of the seventies wore on. By 1982 under his administration the force grew to ninety-two, including an administrative staff of eleven under Inspector Stuart McDonald, a criminal investigation branch under Detective Inspector Calvin Scott, and field operations under Inspector James Burke.[42]

In addition to the local police, Cornwall was headquarters for District II of the Ontario Provincial Police from 1948 until 1958 when some 100 office and field staff operated out of a two-storey building on Augustus Street. Serving the six counties of Stormont, Dundas, Glengarry, Prescott, Russell and Carleton, officers of the Ontario Provincial Police found that, by 1958, their Cornwall headquarters was becoming more and more cramped, lacking space for twenty-eight vehicles and increasing personnel. The decision was to remove to a more spacious location at Long Sault in 1958.[43]

These were the developments in the major municipal institutions such as fire and police protection, banking institutions and retail businesses as Cornwall approached the threshold of the war years and jumped over it. Its canal traffic had peaked in 1928 when 7,505,671 tons of freight were carried through, for the yearly tonnage of war materials from 1939 to 1945 never reached the 1928 figure.[44] But the canal's wartime importance was immediately recognized, just as it had been on the eve of the First World War. No sooner had Canada declared war on Germany than eleven officers and 250 men of the Stormont, Dundas and Glengarry Regiment took over guard duty. They were relieved by local members of the Veterans' Guard of Canada and Royal Canadian Mounted Police in October.[45] Cornwall's drydock at the eastern end of the canal, the only one between Montreal and Kingston, also took on new importance during the war as naval and merchant ships were serviced by Bingley Steel Works.

Improvements to Cornwall's streets and to the Fly Creek drainage were undertaken in the 1920s. The macadamizing of town streets at the turn of the century had not stood up to the heavier traffic of more recent years. By 1921, with Mayor J.A. Chisholm at the helm,

Town Council initiated a system of paving on a cement base with asphaltic concrete or an amiesite wearing surface. Only three miles had been constructed by 1926, but gradually the major streets were paved and granolithic sidewalks laid on both sides.[46] The first serious attempt to alleviate the Fly Creek problem was in 1924 when the Town Council under Mayor W.H. Snetsinger decided the time had come to get rid of the annual spring flooding of cellars and the unsanitary condition of the rivulet in summer. The firm of McLean and Stidwill was given a contract to lay a large trunk sewer along the Fly Creek basin to afford drainage and sewage facilities to the residents of the town through which the Fly Creek ran. The Creek continued to give its neighbours so much trouble that by 1959 efforts were renewed to divert the Creek north of Eleventh Street into a drainage ditch extending east to Gray's Creek.

Even before the war broke out and Cornwall's industry geared into high production and expansion, Cornwall's citizens were alert to the town's expansion potential and the need for proper zoning of residential and manufacturing areas. A town planning expert, Horace L. Seymour, was called in to carry out a survey which resulted in a new zoning by-law in 1940. Then, in 1943, a Town Planning Commission was formed and hired Norman D. Wilson to draw up a detailed plan for Cornwall's development. Completed in 1944, Wilson's report envisaged a seaway project that would bring "ocean port facilities within five and a half miles of the city" and forecast that the industrial expansion accompanying the power development plan would boost the city's population to 50,000 within twenty-five years.[47]

By 1940 a large percentage of Cornwall's heavy industry had been turned to wartime production. Courtauld's had a particularly heavy responsibility in the early years of the war when most of the European rayon factories fell to German arms. The firm undertook a major capital expenditure programme to modernize its viscose producing facilities and to install equipment especially designed for tire cord yarn. Mobile guns, jeeps and transport trucks overseas, as well as huge bombers, moved off on tires made from cord produced in Cornwall. The mill also made flare parachute fabric, silk for powder bags to hold the propellant charge used in heavy guns, and linings for uniforms, to mention only a few of the items produced by Courtauld's workers to aid the war effort.[48]

The other major textile plant, Canadian Cottons, made uniforms for the air force and navy, produced ticking for the army, and manufactured flannelette, eiderdowns, sheeting and nurses' clothing.

Howard Smith Paper Mill produced blueprint paper needed for scale plans for war equipment. Its machine shop was expanded to produce parts for corvettes and other war equipment while subcontract work for the Department of Munitions and Supply amounted to $8,000,000 alone in 1943.[49] Half of the wartime production at Cornwall Pants and Prince Clothing was for navy apparel. Ives Bedding Company made double-deck bunks for barracks and field ambulance beds. Sixty percent of the production at the Powdrell and Alexander Curtain factory was turned over to surgical gauze and bandage material.

Engineers and other personnel at Bingley Steel Works serviced equipment for aircraft as well as ships at the drydock. Machinists at the huge shop of Warp Tension Governors Limited, 303 Water Street, worked day and night producing tank and armoured car components. This was the Foundry and Machine Shop of the Quig Brothers who had, in 1912, taken over the foundry owned by Jacob Miller.[50] The Cornwall division of Dominion Tar and Chemical turned to full-time war production, making fibre conduits to protect underground cables and supplying materials for airport construction and casings for shells. By 1945 this plant's wartime expansion resulted in plans for a new $500,000 plant to employ 100 instead of its pre-war complement of fifty-five workers.[51]

At Cornwall's West End a wartime chemical plant was erected in 1942-43 amidst great secrecy after three farmers were notified of expropriation proceedings involving 318 acres of land to the rear of their farms on old Highway No. 2. Here the Department of Munitions and Supply began construction of a three-million dollar plant that eventually housed about fifty buildings, all fenced in and surrounded by armed guards. Spur lines from the Canadian National Railway provided ready movement of the plant's production, while another spur line connected the plant with the Cornwall Street Railway, giving its 300 workers easy transportation to and from work. Known as Stormont Chemicals, the plant produced, among other wartime products, mustard gas. The disposal of this deadly gas after the war created something of a problem for the War Assets Corporation which had the job of selling the plant as war surplus. The solution was to seal the gas in steel containers, some 2,000 tons of it, and transport it by rail to the Atlantic coast where it was taken far out to sea and dumped.[52] The plant's post-war conversion to a whey-processing operation and the manufacture of penicillin was in sharp contrast to its wartime origin.

Not only was a major part of Cornwall's industry reshaped by war's demands. Its citizens and soldiers were also caught up by wartime activities. The first and most immediate job of the officers and men of the Stormont, Dundas and Glengarry Regiment was guarding the canal.53 Mobilization of the regiment as an active service battalion took place on 18 June 1940 when two companies were recruited from the Cornwall regimental area. Others were raised in Brockville, Kingston and Peterborough. These companies became the 1st Battalion of the Regiment that served with such distinction in Europe. Other men of the regiment formed a reserve battalion whose primary role was to keep reinforcements moving steadily forward to active service units. From 1940 to 1944 some 995 men trained in the second battalion and then joined active units: 687 served in the 1st battalion, 226 went into the Royal Canadian Air Force and another seventy-six enlisted in the Royal Canadian Navy Volunteer Reserve. In addition, a total of eighty-three officers from the 2nd Battalion later joined active units.54

While soldiers presented themselves at regimental headquarters for service, townsmen and women lost no time in rolling up their sleeves and turning the town into a beehive of war-related activities. Officers' wives organized a Women's Auxiliary of the Stormont, Dundas and Glengarry Highlanders in March of 1941 with Mrs. R.F. Gray as president and Mrs. R.T.E. Hicks-Lyne, wife of the commanding officer, as honorary president.55 By the late summer of 1940 some 500 men were busy building twenty-nine wooden huts, a chapel, hospital, and a drill hall with an indoor range at the huge new Basic Training Centre on Marlborough Street. By October the lieutenant colonel who commanded the Centre all during the war, Rodolphe Larose, former commanding officer of Le Régiment de Hull, arrived to start the first group of 750 young men through their thirty days' basic training. Before the war ended Lieutenant-Colonel Larose had put 15,000 rookies through their paces, many of them enrolling for courses at Cornwall Collegiate and Vocational School, others winning sports acclaim by their hockey triumphs in the senior hockey league.56

Town Council responded to this military presence by converting the auditorium of the Town Hall into a recreation centre for service personnel - Cornwall's "Beaver Club".57 Women and girls were busy knitting and making baby layettes for the Aid to Britain campaign, while "warm clothing and substantial comforts" were sent to "our uncomplaining allies", the Russians, in the Aid to Russia campaign. Kinsmen organized the highly successful "Milk for Britain" project that helped supply British children with milk. And when it was announced in 1941 that Cornwall led the rest of Canada in its per capita purchase of War Savings Stamps, Cornwallites swelled with pride.58

Wartime housing projects got underway in 1943. Thirty-eight

houses were built in the area which had formerly been the agricultural fair grounds north of Ninth Street. New streets were eventually laid out here - Eleventh and Twelfth, Vimy, Dieppe and Dunkirk, the latter three indicative of the war theatre. Before the end of the war, another seventy-seven were built in this area, while twelve others were located on a new street, McGregor, opened up to provide a site for them.[59] Not only service personnel and veterans moved into the new housing area, but also imported workers at Cornwall's essential war industries.

Citizens responded to the Victory Loan campaigns by buying a total of $10,985,600 worth of bonds.[60] More than three million pounds of salvage was collected, much of it paper, and proceeds from the salvage campaigns, organized by Alderman William H. Gallinger, were used to purchase three Bren guns as well as to renovate the Town Hall Auditorium for the troops.[61] Cornwall's labour force also provided skilled workers for essential industries outside the town. During 1944, for example, a total of 1,377 men and women left Cornwall to work elsewhere. By that time, some of Cornwall's own men were returning from overseas and placing their names with the Selective Service Office, looking for work. Some were difficult to place as they were reluctant to return to their old jobs.[62] One man, however, had no qualms at stepping back into a job at the Howard Smith Paper Mill. He was thirty-three-year-old Captain Allen Piper of Cumberland Street who had lost both hands when a grenade exploded in his hands as he was instructing trainees in England. With indomitable spirit and the aid of medical science, Piper was fitted with artificial hands and resumed gainful employment.[63]

The need for aviation-minded youths to have an outlet to stimulate their interest in flying was realized in the early years of the war with the founding of the Air Cadet League of Canada in 1941. Within a year Cornwall had its own Air Cadet Squadron, thanks to the efforts of the Kiwanis Club and such men as dentist Dr. Mack Good, T.O. Clark, Guy Smith, Bill Surgeson, Harold Farlinger, Ed Pearson, Archie Dover, Harry Hertz, and Guy Cottrell.[64] This squadron became one of Cornwall's prides under its wartime commanding officers, T. Barrett, G. Hughes, G. Hirst, B. Comrie, and continued so after the war, attracting young men by a combined programme of air training and good citizenship.

Blood donor clinics took on a new importance during the war. The Red Cross organized periodic clinics in town, appealing to patriotic-minded people to give their blood for the "fighting men". Cornwallites came to regard this gesture as a personal and direct share in war. "If I can't go myself," they said, "perhaps my blood will save the life of someone who did." By 1944 Cornwall had passed its 10,000th donation.[65]

It was in the midst of this steady and effective support of the war effort in all areas that the residents of Cornwall were shaken out of their beds shortly after midnight on Monday, 4 September 1944. Within a space of a few minutes four distinct earthquakes rocked the town, sending over a 1000 chimneys crashing down, twisting gravestones, and causing severe damage to St. Columban's and Knox United churches. At St. Columban's rectory two big stone chimneys on either side of the roof crashed through onto the floors of the bedrooms. One of the maids, Noema Boisvenue, was saying a novena beside her bed when all of a sudden the bed shot across the room. She dashed out minutes before the big stones came tumbling through the ceiling and onto the floor where a moment before she had been praying.[66]

At the Howard Smith Paper Mill the giant smoke stack split nine feet from the top. The company's new office building was badly cracked and its chlorine plant damaged. Chemical stoneware at the Canadian Industries Limited plant was shattered and the corners of the building torn loose. More serious was the damage suffered by Ives Bedding where the east and west walls were so severely cracked that Manager Howard Gray feared both sides would have to be rebuilt. Even the Roosevelt International Bridge was injured.[67] As the shocks continued between four and five o'clock and again at seven o'clock in the morning, terrified residents fled from their homes, to join others who were kneeling in prayer along the tramway tracks on Pitt Street many clad only in their night clothes. One intrepid Cornwallite, Margaret Hollister, tried to make her way through the dense crowds of praying people to the *Standard-Freeholder* building. Though every window along Pitt Street was shattered and no repairs undertaken until the next day, she recalled, not a thing was stolen.[68]

One the most seriously injured buildings was Cornwall Collegiate and Vocational School which was so badly damaged that it was unsafe to hold classes for over a week. Central Public School had gaping holes in its walls.[69] At St. Columban's Church, the sanctuary and choir loft were severely damaged and three beautiful stained glass windows over the sanctuary were destroyed as was the pipe organ. The earthquake and the shock of the destruction to the church and rectory hastened the death of the parish's ailing pastor, Father J.M. Foley, the priest who had seen his flock through the worst days of the depression when no one was ever turned away from the rectory empty-handed. As there was no insurance covering earthquake damage,

420

the parish faced an enormous repair and renovation job that spring.

At Knox Church repairs had to be made to the entire fabric of the structure. While these were being done, its people worshipped at St. Paul's United and St. John's Presbyterian churches while the Baptists offered their Sunday School facilities to Knox children. By the spring of 1945 all the repairs had been made and paid for. Just as the Knox congregation recovered from this blow, fire broke out in the boiler room due to faulty wiring and the interior of the church was destroyed. Once more the people of Knox set about to renew their church, holding services in the basement while Atchison and Company undertook renovations.[70]

Local Member of Parliament Lionel Chevrier was on hand the next day with Mayor Aaron Horovitz to survey the havoc caused by the earthquake. The initial damage was estimated at $750,000, though officials feared it might run as high as a million dollars,[71] especially as slight tremors continued for several days, the last occurring on September 13. The centre of the quake was just forty miles to the north-east of Cornwall, an area subject to earthquakes since as far back as 1663. Other quakes had been felt in the Cornwall area in 1860, 1877, 1935, 1939 and 1940. Still another was to occur in 1946, but none was of the magnitude of the 1944 shock.[72]

In spite of war, earthquake and fire, Cornwallites went about their business quietly and often prayerfully. Perhaps it was because of these terrible visitations, endured by all townspeople, that they experienced during the war a feeling of comradeship and unity somewhat akin to that felt by their men overseas. Undaunted, they pressed for internal developments and improvements to the town. Under Mayor J.A. Phillips, Town Council sought city status in 1943 only to be coldly rebuffed by the provincial Minister of Municipal Affairs who commented that "the people of Cornwall wanted to live in a city and at the same time to...retain the status of a town for municipal purposes including assessment".[73] They had to wait another two years before they gained the glory of being a city, ready to accept the financial commitments that the status imposed. At the stroke of midnight 1 January 1945, Cornwall's 15,118 inhabitants celebrated both the New Year and their status as citizens of Ontario's newest city.[74] Eight days later an official celebration took place when Honourable George A. Drew, Premier of Ontario, was guest of honour at a banquet at the fashionable Cornwallis Hotel, marking the occasion. On hand to take the compliments was Aaron Horovitz, back in his familiar seat at "City Hall" for his third stint as Mayor, with ambitions for a new hall fit to go with Cornwall's heightened status. Before year's end, Cornwall was tagged the "Friendly City", a term that stuck until the fifties brought in a new image, that of the "Seaway City".[75]

When Mayor Horovitz brought out grandiose plans for a $250,000 City Hall to replace the 1862 Town Hall, he faced strong opposition, even though he assured citizens that the cost would be spread over a twenty-year period. Spearheading the opposition was Cornwall's first radio station, CKSF, owned by the *Standard-Freeholder* Company.[76] Located in the building on the west side of Pitt Street that had once housed the Ontario Bank, the station was opened formally on 15 February 1945 with a salute from Cornwall, England, to its sister city in Canada. Mayor Horovitz was on hand to say a few words as was Member of Parliament Lionel Chevrier. However, the new station's announcers, A.L. Bonhomme, Philip Brooks and Russell Hawkshaw threw their weight behind the protest against a new City Hall, declaring that all available building materials should be reserved for veterans' housing. Their voice of protest was joined by others such as war amputee Allan Piper, former Mayor Elzéar Emard, J.J. Tallon and Alderman Levi Miller. When the vote was put to the ratepayers on 9 July 1945 a majority of 128 voters turned thumbs down on the project and it was shelved for a couple of years until Lloyd Gallinger stepped into the mayoralty chair and succeeded in getting a favourable vote.[77] The new hall went up and Aaron Horovitz returned to power at City Hall just in time to take the bows once more as citizens joined with officials and employees of the new hall such as Basil Stone and Euclide Contant to celebrate its opening in 1949.

However, Mayor Horovitz did not get his new hall in time to celebrate the end of the war and the triumphant return of the Stormont, Dundas and Glengarry Highlanders from overseas. But this did not dampen celebrations. The home front had followed too closely the valorous conduct of their men on the field of battle in Europe. Attached to the 3rd Canadian Division, the Glens were thrown against the enemy at Bernières-sur-Mer near Caen in France, shortly after the Normandy invasion on "D" Day 6 June 1944. Their baptismal fire came in one of the bloodiest battles of the campaign in northwestern Europe as they formed part of the Allied force moving on Caen. As the Regiment moved towards Les Buissons, a small village on the outskirts of Caen, their battle cry of "Up the Glens" was heard far and wide. It was here in what the Glens soon termed "Hell's Corners" that a strong German counter-attack by shock troops of the 12th S.S. Panzer Division tried unsuccessfully to break through Canadian lines with infantry and Tiger tanks.[78]

So fierce was the engagement that even the regiment's pipers were silent so as to enable the men to hear the whine of shells and mortar in time to dive for the safety of a slit trench. By 9 July 1944 the Glens had the distinction of being the first Canadians to enter Caen. Such moments of glory were short-lived for the Glens soon faced their worst ten days' fighting in the little village of Hubert Folie, being shelled, mortared by rocket bombs and strafed by planes.[79] Then came the heavy fighting for the Falaise Gap in mid-August and a month later three days of bitter fighting to reduce Boulogne. The famous "back-door" crossing of the Scheldt Estuary by the Glens and other troops in "Buffaloes" caught the German defenders by surprise. This amphibious manoeuvre was considered by military authorities as one of the most successful of the water campaigns undertaken in Europe. Ghent was occupied by November 1944 and in March of 1945 the Glens were the second Canadian contingent to cross the Rhine, their movement hidden by the greatest smoke screen ever created, and protected by a barrage of massed artillery fire that rocked the German side of the river as though shaken by an earthquake.[80]

These were the troops honoured on the battlefield by their Scottish comrades-in-arms in February 1945 when they were presented with a set of ancient silver spoons, originally made for the Glengarry Fencibles, the Roman Catholic Regiment raised in Scotland during the Napoleonic Wars, many of whose men were among those who emigrated to Upper Canada in 1804 with their priest, Father Alexander Macdonell. The spoons had been made for the officers' mess during the time the Glengarry Fencibles were in Dublin, Ireland, helping to suppress the rebellion of 1798.[81]

It is not surprising that the people of Cornwall greeted with great joy the news of the war's end in Europe. They joined in a monster parade to the Athletic Grounds where a fireworks display, dancing and unbounded hilarity reigned on Tuesday 8 May 1945 as 10,000 people listened to speeches and engaged in "mirth-making and celebrations that outranked all previous public demonstrations held in Cornwall."[82] Then, in mid-August as rumours of peace in the Pacific floated over the airwaves and in newspapers, beverage vendors enjoyed a rush order business as queues formed up long before the regular opening time. Mayor Horovitz announced on 14 August that a two-day public holiday would mark "Victory-in-Japan" Day, for he fully anticipated that "people are going to let loose and celebrate until the small hours of the morning". Wisely, he concluded that an extra day "will give them a chance to rest up and reflect upon the seriousness of the situation. They can go to Church and thank God for the restoration of peace after so many years of mental anguish and suffering".[83] That same night the Mayor was roused at two a.m. with the news of Japan's surrender and plans went ahead for the mammoth victory celebrations that included special services of thanksgiving in all churches, a parade to Memorial Park of all of Cornwall's military personnel, organized by the Legion, and street dancing in four sections of the city.

Moving as were these celebrations, there was an even more deep-felt moment for the people of Cornwall on Saturday afternoon, 29 December 1945, when the "Counties' Own Regiment" returned home to the acclaim of thousands who lined Cornwall's streets and thronged the Canadian National Railway Station area to catch the first glimpse of the special troop train carrying the Glens. At 2:45 p.m. the skirl of the pipes was heard from Sydney Street as the 2nd Battalion, headed by Lieutenant-Colonel D.R. Dick, marched into a cleared space behind the station, bearing the colours of the 1st Battalion. Repatriated soldiers of the 1st Battalion formed to the right, while a large detachment of Legion veterans formed to the left. Promptly at 3:15 p.m. the sound of a train whistle was heard and a shout arose, "Here they are!" High-ranking officers and civilians forgot their dignity and surged forward, all anxious for that first view of "the boys". First off the train was Lieutenant-Colonel Neil Gemmell who had commanded the unit since the fighting in the Hochwald Forest area. In a few terse sentences, he summed up his men. "There wasn't a finer bunch of boys overseas...they blazed a trail of sensational victories and accomplishments in France, Belgium, Holland and Germany", declared the sandy-haired, slightly built commanding officer as he watched his men disembark at Cornwall, to be embraced and feted by loved ones whose ardour was not dampened by the chill December day.[84] The boys were home once more and that was all that mattered. Their record spoke for itself: the Glens never failed to take an objective; they never lost a yard of ground; they never lost a man - taken prisoner - in an offensive action.[85] As the 2nd Battalion greeted its comrades and handed over the Regimental Colours to be borne by the 366 men of the 1st Battalion on their last parade as a unit to the Cornwall Armoury, the people of Cornwall were as one with their returning heroes.

424

NOTES

1. *Standard-Freeholder*, 30 December 1944.
2. *Census*, 1941, ii, 92; 434-35.
3. *The Making of a New Cornwall*, 14.
4. For various accounts of Royal Visits to Cornwall, see, William Mack Alguire, *Historical Sketch of Cornwall, Greetings to Their Majesties, and Memories of former Happy Visits,* Souvenir programme, May 21, 1939, 11-19; *Gazette*, Montreal, 30 August 1792; J.F. Pringle, *Lunenburgh, or the Old Eastern District*, 140; address of Prince William Henry from Inhabitants, the town of Cornwall, 1787; James Croil, *Dundas, or a Sketch of Canadian History*, 324-25, 333; *Standard-Freeholder*, 22 May 1939 and 6 October 1979; for an expression of Cornwall royalist sentiment see Mary A. Mack to Editor, *Ottawa Journal*, 30 April 1977, re Queen's visit.
5. *Standard-Freeholder*, 30 December 1944.
6. See Honor Roll, 1939-1945, City Hall.
7. *Standard-Freeholder*, 4 January 1945.
8. *Ibid.*, 29 December 1945.
9. *Ibid.*, 30 June 1944.
10. *Ibid.*, 17 March 1945.
11. For a list of awards to officers and men of the Stormont, Dundas and Glengarry Highlanders see, William Boss, *The Stormont, Dundas and Glengarry Highlanders*, 325-26; and *Standard-Freeholder*, 29 December 1945.
12. *Census*, 1941, ii, 606.
13. *Ibid.*, vii, 244-46.
14. *Old Boys' Re-Union*, 1926.
15. *Standard*, 16 May 1918.
16. *Old Home Week 1946; Standard-Freeholder*, 19 July 1946 and 3 March 1979, see map of 1933 fire.
17. *Old Boys' Reunion, 1906*, 74.
18. *Ibid.*, 57 and 75.
19. *Standard-Freeholder*, 8 March 1980.
20. B.J. MacFarlane to Senior, 26 March 1982.
21. *Standard-Freeholder*, 29 January 1949; Alanna Little, Community Relations Officer, Canadian Imperial Bank of Canada, to Senior, 23 March 1982.
22. *Standard-Freeholder*, 3 November 1937; *Old Home Week, 1946*, 97.
23. L.G. Hodgins, Assistant Manager, Operations, Scotiabank, to Senior, 23 March 1982.
24. *Old Boys' Reunion 1906*, 68; *Standard-Freeholder*, 30 December 1944.
25. *Standard-Freeholder*, 3 August 1946.
26. *Ibid.*, 22 August 1945.
27. *Ibid.*, 26 December 1947.
28. *Ibid.*, 3 August 1946; Fire Chief Hugh O'Reilly to Elinor Senior, 25 March 1982.
29. Police Chief Earl Landry to Elinor Senior, 1 June 1982.
30. *Standard-Freeholder*, 9 February 1957.
31. *Freeholder*, 18 October 1901.
32. Minutes, Town Council, 9 March 1925, 126.
33. *Standard-Freeholder*, 24 July 1935.
34. By-law no. 19, 8 July 1935.

35. *Standard-Freeholder*, 15 January 1936.
36. Minutes, Town Council, 20 March 1939.
37. *Standard-Freeholder*, 11 September 1943.
38. *Standard-Freeholder*, 30 December 1944.
39. Minutes, Town Council, 10 February 1931 and 6 April 1934; 1 April 1938.
40. *Standard-Freeholder*, 2 January 1955.
41. *Ibid.*, 2 February 1972.
42. *Ibid.*, 19 March 1976; 3 June 1976; 30 May 1978; Police Chief Earl Landry to Senior, 1 June 1982.
43. *Standard-Freeholder*, 23 December 1947; 4 June 1958.
44. *Ibid.*, 3 August 1946.
45. *Ibid.*, 29 December 1945; Boss, 282.
46. *Old Boys' Re-Union*, 1926, 21-24, 27.
47. *Standard-Freeholder*, 3 August 1946.
48. *Ibid.*, 7 May 1945.
49. *Ibid.*
50. *Ibid.*, 30 December 1944; see also Industrial Edition, 1955, 15.
51. *Ibid.*, 30 January 1943, 29 August and 5 November 1945.
52. *Ibid.*, 5, 6 June 1942, 8 May, 3 August and 27 September 1946; see also *Old Home Week 1946*, 99.
53. *Standard-Freeholder*, 29 December 1945; Boss, 282.
54. *Ibid.*, 29 December 1945 and 3 August 1946.
55. *Ibid.*, 29 December 1945.
56. *Ibid.*, 31 December 1944, and Boss, 290.
57. Minutes, Town Council, 15 September 1942, 658.
58. *Standard-Freeholder*, 17 March 1941.
59. *Ibid.*, 19 September 1945, 24 August 1946.
60. *Ibid.*, 30 December 1944 and 3 August 1946.
61. *Ibid.*, 16 August 1945.
62. *Ibid.*, 1 March 1945.
63. *Ibid.*, 3 June 1944.
64. *Ibid.*, 25 June 1977.
65. *Ibid.*, 30 December 1944.
66. *150th Anniversary of St. Columban's Parish, 1896-1979*, 24.
67. *Standard-Freeholder*, 5 September 1944.
68. Interview with Margaret Hollister by author, 17 June 1979; see also, *Standard-Freeholder*, 8 September 1944.
69. *Standard-Freeholder*, 5 September 1974.
70. *Knox United Church, 1846-1975*, 18-19.
71. *Standard-Freeholder*, 8 September 1944.
72. For earthquakes see, *Reporter*, 10 November 1877; Croil, 160; *Standard-Freeholder*, 1 November 1935, 20 October 1939, 24 December 1940, and 14 February 1946.
73. *Standard-Freeholder*, 26 March 1943.
74. *Ibid.*, 3 and 5 January 1945.
75. *Ibid.*, 31 December 1945.
76. *Ibid.*, 29 January 1945.
77. *Ibid.*, 4, 7, 10 July 1945.

78. *Ibid.*, 29 December 1945; Boss, 186-87.
79. Boss, 201-202; *Standard-Freeholder*, 29 December 1945.
80. *Standard-Freeholder*, 29 December 1945.
81. *Ibid.*, 7 February 1945.
82. *Ibid.*, 9 May 1945.
83. *Ibid.*, 14 August 1945.
84. *Ibid.*, 31 December 1945.
85. Boss, 268.

Cornwall's Police Force, 1906, 'Heaviest in Canada'. J. Lalonde 215 lbs; Chief Smith, 235 lbs.; G.O. Crites, 220 lbs. - Total 670 lbs.
Credit: Cornwall: *Old Boys' Re-Union - 1906.*

Cornwall Collegiate Institute and Vocational School, 1940's. The school became a Collegiate Institute in 1925 and a Vocational School as well in 1937.

Credit: United Counties of *Stormont, Dundas and Glengarry: A History 1784-1945.*

Pitt Street fire at the Height of the blaze August 7, 1933.
(from a postcard printed in the 1930's).

Wartime housing development, east of Pitt Street in the Eleventh Street sector. Streets such as Vimy and Dunkirk grew out of this project.

Credit: *Standard-Freeholder*, Cornwall, October 20, 1979.

Cornwall Armouries-Headquarters S.D. & G. Highlanders. Opened in 1938. The first unit to enter Caen, to the battle cry of 'UP the Glens'. Arrived home December 29, 1945.

Credit: Ian Bowering.

Return Home to Cornwall of the S.D. & G. Highlanders from World War II, January 5, 1946. L. Col. Donald Dick, O.C., 2nd Bn. (R) handing over the colours to L. Col. Gemmill, O.C. 1st Bn.

Credit: United Counties of Stormont, Dundas and Glengarry, *Stormont, Dundas and Glengarry, A History 1784-1945.*

John Graham Harkness, (1865-1948) author,
Stormont, Dundas and Glengarry:
A History 1784-1945.
Credit: Societe Historique de Cornwall.

Edouard (Newsie) Lalonde, (1888 or 89 - 1971) 1963. The man often referred to as the top Cornwall and district athlete of the past century. 'Newsie' is holding the Mann Cup, emblematic of junior lacrosse supremacy in Canada. 'Newsie' was a member of both the Canadian Hockey and Lacrosse Halls of Fame.
Credit: *Standard-Freeholder*, Cornwall, June 24, 1967.

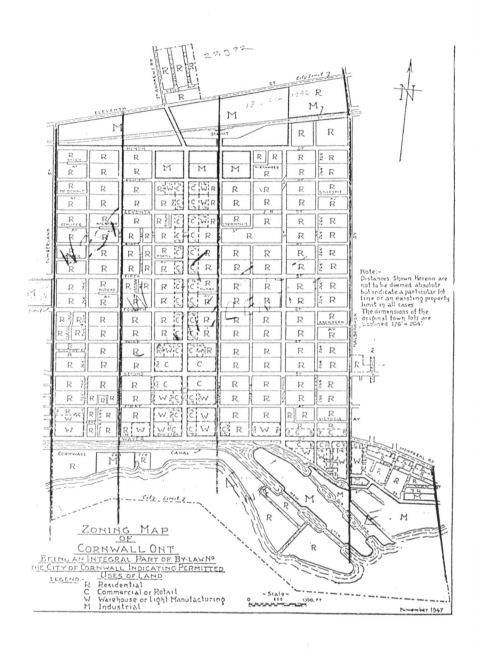

ZONING MAP
OF
CORNWALL ONT
BEING AN INTEGRAL PART OF BY-LAW Nº
THE CITY OF CORNWALL INDICATING PERMITTED
USES OF LAND
LEGEND :
R   Residential
C   Commercial or Retail
W   Warehouse or Light Manufacturing
M   Industrial

Note:-
Distances Shown Hereon are
not to be deemed absolute
but indicate a particular lot
line or an existing property
limit in all cases
The dimensions of the
original town lots are
assumed 176' x 264'.

- Scale -
0   500   1000. FT

November 1947

434

Chapter XIX

Modern Cornwall Faces Economic Doldrums

At war's end Cornwall was vibrant, confident and full of optimism, its plants expanding, veterans being absorbed into the labour force, unions maturing under cautious and capable men such as Leo Tessier, George Harrop, Eugene Charlebois, Thomas Webster and Ernest Booth. At City Hall officials were making plans for a third Old Home Week in 1946 with Canada's Governor General, Field Marshal Viscount Alexander as Veterans' Day Guest. John Graham Harkness brought out his history of Stormont, Dundas and Glengarry and Mary Mack assaulted the previously all-male conclave at City Hall to become Cornwall's first woman councillor in 1947. This buoyancy survived less than a decade. By the early 1950s foreign competition in textiles was playing havoc with Cornwall's major industry. The St. Lawrence Seaway project stemmed economic doldrums temporarily, but once the Seaway boom was over, optimism turned to gloom and the unemployed looked increasingly towards City Hall for handouts.[1]

The vibrancy of the city's economy at war's end, however, was proclaimed in such publicity brochures as the attractive Old Home Week souvenir album of 1946, the impressive booklet prepared by the Industrial Committee of Greater Cornwall in 1949-50 describing Cornwall as "the City of Opportunity", and a third thirty-two page booklet entitled "Greater Cornwall", printed in the early 1950s which detailed Cornwall's present and future potentialities.[2] In 1946 the city's promoters spoke of its thriving condition and predicted that Cornwall would become a "city of beauty and convenience" with a population of at least 50,000. By 1949 industrial spokesmen were comparing favourably the post-war "displaced persons" of Europe who were starting to swell Cornwall's workforce to those early pioneer Loyalist refugees who had founded the city in 1784. Other city businessmen hinted at the untold wealth that could come from the untapped hydro-electric power of the Long Sault Rapids.[3]

New industries thinking of making Cornwall a home base were

informed that Cornwall's tax structure allowed them a fixed assessment for a period of years, providing the ratepayers passed a by-law approving such tax favours, an indication that Cornwall's city administration had reverted to the policy used in the late nineteenth and early twentieth centuries to attract industry. The 1950 booklet listed twenty-four city industries, including four chemical firms, six textile and clothing plants, three printers, four lumber and woodworking plants, two foundries, one steel works, one paper mill and a bed factory.[4] The shift towards chemical production became more pronounced over the next twenty-five years when nine other chemical firms were established in the city.

The first new one was a small liquid fertilizer plant started in 1947 by a local man, E.J. Kaneb, whose family had emigrated to Cornwall from Massachusetts in the 1920s.[5] Kaneb's company, known as Hy-Trous, and located on Frontenac Street by 1953, was eventually bought out by Brockville Chemical Industries, a division of the giant holding company, Genstar Limited. Today both the company and its product are known as Nutrite.[6] Other chemical companies attracted to Cornwall by 1952 were Howards and Sons, located in the west end of the city, and the smaller plant of Pfizer Canada that produced citric acid. Howards made a food sweetener known as sorbital, glyceryl triascetate, and plasticizers, among other products. By 1967 it was producing phthalic andydride and in 1969 branched into the production of polyester resin. From an initial operating workforce of twenty in 1954, Howards and Sons grew to a staff of 120 by 1970, producing 50 million pounds of phthalic andydride yearly, most of which were sold in Canada. The plant was bought in 1970 by a West German-based firm, Badische Anilin Soda Fabriken (BASF) and by the late 1970s employed 152.[7] Pfizer Canada was located in Wallrich Avenue in the West End near the larger Howards and Sons plant. Drawing its main materials from Ireland, Pfizer began with a staff of eight men who came out from the original parent company of Kemball Bishop of London, England, and grew to a staff of ninety in the 1970s. In the early 1980s there was an attrition of workforce to seventy-one because of depressed economic conditions in Canada.[8]

One of the most important subsidiary chemical plants to be built in Cornwall in the post-war period was the transparent cellulose packaging firm of TCF, one of the Courtaulds group. Opening in 1953 to meet the demands of the growing number of self-service supermarkets where foods had to be protected against handling and yet visible to the buyer, TCF expanded within twenty-five years to a workforce of 340.[9] Though its products, Vynar, kept the same name, the plant switched to its parent company name in 1980, that of

British Cellophane Limited (BCL Canada).[10] Iroquois Chemicals was established in 1959 to make finishers for the Canadian furniture industry, using raw materials imported from Germany. By 1970 annual sales soared to $2,000,000 in Canada and the company opened a subsidiary company in Bissendorf, Germany, to serve European customers.[11]

Iroquois Chemicals became supplier of polyester resin for a new Cornwall firm, Fiberez of Canada. Started by David Dempster of Hydra Clene Corporation in 1958, Fiberez was sold to Wilfred Kaneb in 1959. Although its original product was fibreglass reinforced plastics, Fiberez expanded into bathtub and shower production.[12] In the sixties two chemical firms located in the city: VirChem, in 1964, a subsidiary of Virginia Chemicals of Portsmouth, Virginia, whose small Cornwall plant produces zinc hydrosulphite, a chemical used in the pulp and paper industry, and Chemcell Limited, which began operations in 1967, producing methanol from naptha feedstock for the Canadian market. By the 1970s when the federal government tariffs on imported naptha feedstocks were reduced, the small Cornwall plant went out of business.[13] Its demise was countered by the establishment of another West German-based chemical firm, Pellon Chemotextiles, which opened a plant in 1972 to produce non-woven textiles largely for the Canadian market.[14] Most of these smaller chemical plants were low-labour intensity operations, usually employing 100 or less in a combined plant-office workforce.

The trend in Cornwall's newer post-war industries, then, was towards chemical products. But in 1946 at war's end Cornwall was still primarily a mill town. Since 1891 its major industry, Canadian Cottons, had maintained a stable workforce, though its annual production and payroll underwent considerable change. In 1891 some 1,453 men, women and children produced $1,647,397 worth of goods and brought home annual wages of $446,588.[15] In 1946 the three mills employed 1500 who manufactured $6,000,000 worth of goods and earned $1,800,000 in annual wages.[16] Thus, in the fifty odd years from 1891 to 1946, Canadian Cottons had kept pace with newer technology and production methods so as to allow for a greatly expanded production level with the same sized workforce. Its last major building programme was in 1943-44 when a new four-storey building was erected adjoining the Canada Mill.[17] Then, in 1948, Canadian Cottons bought the huge Powdrell and Alexander plant and re-named it Glengarry Textiles. Thus, in the immediate post-war period, Cornwall's major textile plant showed no sign of slowing down, rather the reverse, and this in spite of sporadic labour troubles and strikes.

Union growth in Cornwall had been somewhat erratic since the 1936-37 heroic age, especially in the textile industry. Competition for the Cornwall unions between the Committee for Industrial Organization and the American Federation of Labour created tension, especially in 1941 when two Cornwall union men, J. René Laframboise and Hector Sampson, were elected president and secretary of a new body - the Textile Workers of Canada - at an organizational meeting in Ottawa under a charter granted by the Trades and Labor Congress of Canada.[18] Their activity in Cornwall on behalf of the AFL was soon countered by the rise of a new labour personality, Leo Tessier.[19] While still in his early thirties, Tessier moved rapidly up the union ladder from shop steward to committeeman and then to presidency of Courtaulds Local 3, United Textile Workers of Canada.[20] This was the wartime era of close cooperation between union and management when union officers could ask management to post lists of members delinquent in paying union dues and a union think-tank originated the idea of employees receiving a bonus for good work attendance records, thus reducing absenteeism.[21] Union men were also responsible for promoting the use of an Amalgamated Union label on clothing and educating the public to ask for the union label when making purchases.[22]

It was under Leo Tessier that the Courtaulds union became Local 779 of the Textile Workers Union of America (CIO) in March 1946,[23] thus breaking its original affiliation with the United Textile Workers of America (AFL). By 1948 it had achieved a closed union shop and checkoff. In that same year the Union boasted that its efforts had resulted in average wage increases to $1.05 an hour, more than double the basic wage rate of 1945. Company president Shirley Dixon proudly announced that the "employees of Courtaulds Limited are the highest paid workers among the textile industry throughout the Dominion."[24] This affability between union and management came at a time when Courtaulds was experiencing its largest net profit within twelve years - some $1,434,000 - and was optimistically planning to spend $10,000,000 on new equipment.[25] So affluent were some of the employees that by 1950 twenty of them got together to organize a Credit Union with David Bell as President. Before the year was out its membership grew to 619 and its management was able to declare a three percent dividend.[26]

Just as the textile industry in Cornwall was enjoying good profits and expansion at the war's end, so, too, union organization became more sophisticated. A Trades and Labour Council already existed and in 1945 its president was Malcolm Upper.[27] Then, in January

1947, a Cornwall and District Labour Council was formed with Ernest Booth as president, James Upson, vice-president, and Ernest Malyon as secretary-treasurer. Their task was to deal with the day-to-day problems affecting Cornwall unions affiliated with the Canadian Congress of Labour.[28] The founding of the Greater Cornwall Textile Joint Board on 5 April 1947 marked the creation of a new forum for expressing union policy and action. Leo Tessier headed the new body for the next three years until he became Canadian organizer for the Textile Workers Union of America and sailed for Lyons, France, in December 1950 to participate in an international labour conference on wage disparities in the textile industry between various countries.[29]

Men like Ralph McIntee, Ralph Carrara, Fernand Branchaud, and Gordon Jarrett carried on the work of the Joint Board, promoting seminars for union men on such subjects as labour law, shop steward duties, grievance procedures and contract analysis, organizing gala labour day parades and field competitions, protesting time and again against the removal of price and rent controls, insisting on the right of union representation on major drives such as the United Welfare Fund and assisting Cornwall service clubs in sponsoring Christmas theatre parties for children.[30]

It was a time, too, when the cotton mills had their own customs and comradeship. For instance, in early September 1948 the time-honoured "Bouillotte" was conducted with a programme of songs, games and a special initiation ceremony for two new loom fixers of the weave room of Dundas Mill. In a ceremony that had not varied in thirty years, R.J. Piquette, garbed in the "traditional regalia of the official initiator, acted as the tail clipper" of the two youngest members, Leo Leroux and Rheal Ouellette.[31] At another level, textile men met at the King George Hotel on 15 March 1948 to form a Cornwall and District Textile Association whose aim was to facilitate an exchange of professional knowledge, to promote sound procedures for textile processing, establish technical libraries and encourage textile research. F. Simpson and T. Hargreaves were elected president and vice-president with J.A. Dixon as secretary.[32] Thus as the new decade approached, the Cornwall textile industry was steady and confident, while its union leadership was maturing and preparing to move into the political arena.

Politicization of labour began overtly in 1943 when unionist Malcolm Upper threw his hat into the provincial election ring as a candidate for the Co-operative Commonwealth Federation (C.C.F.) party. Upper came third with 2,772 votes, a respectable showing for the party that had originated ten years earlier.[33] The C.C.F. had a branch in Cornwall in the early 1940s, if not before. A second C.C.F.

club was formed 20 July 1944 for members in the East End of town with Amedée Larin as president, Dan McIntosh and Sylvio Dalbec, vice-presidents, Arthur Roy, secretary, Malcolm Upper, treasurer, and Maurice Léger as membership chairman.[34]

This second C.C.F. Club followed on the heels of Upper's defeat in the 1943 provincial election. By 1945 the local C.C.F. party fielded candidates in both the federal and provincial elections, again running low thirds to the established Liberal and Progressive Conservative candidates. Then, in 1948, the popular union leader, Ralph McIntee, president of the Greater Cornwall Textile Joint Board, entered the provincial election as C.C.F. candidate. He secured 2,976 votes, not much more than Upper's total in 1943, but his defeat by Progressive Conservative John L. McDonald, who got 6,729 votes, put the socialist wing of labour in Cornwall on its mettle, especially as the pace of left-wing political organizing became more evident.[35] For instance, a petition, sponsored by the Cornwall Labor-Progressive Club in 1946, had secured 500 signatures. Under the chairmanship of Louis Moyville, the Club urged the return of price controls, the removal of wage freezing, and the restoration of the excess profits tax on corporations.[36]

The intrusion of Labor-Progressive politics in Cornwall sharpened the determination of C.C.F.-minded men and women to make another major thrust into federal politics in 1949. McIntee, beaten but unbowed, was appointed to head up union political action in the forthcoming election in which the C.C.F. candidate, Alex Mullin, was to cross swords with the very popular Liberal incumbent of the past fourteen years and Minister of Labour since 1945 - Lionel Chevrier.[37] Two other contestants entered the lists - former Progressive Conservative Member of Parliament for Stormont, Frank Shaver, and Lucien St. Amour of the Union of Electors. Even with Leo Tessier and Pat Conroy, secretary-treasurer of the Canadian Congress of Labour, in town to back up his campaign, Mullin came in third in the election with only 1,281 votes to Chevrier's 12,587 and Shaver's 6,661. Disgruntled, Mullin expressed his surprise "at seeing some of the men who called themselves good trade unionists" working for the old parties.[38]

Scarcely had they licked their election wounds before Cornwall labour leaders launched a devastating attack on Communist influence, not only in Cornwall unions but in Canadian labour circles generally. On 26 January 1950 the Greater Cornwall Textile Joint Board, together with Locals 779, 805 and 806, Textile Workers Union of America, CCL-CIO, printed an open letter addressed jointly to Kent Rowley, the United Textile Workers of America, TLC-AFL, the *Canadian Tribune* and the Labor Progressive Party of Canada, accusing the Communists of raiding local unions.[39] "There is not a single textile worker in Cornwall who is not aware that the Communist Party of Canada and the agents of the United Textile Workers of America A.F. of L.-T.L.C. have laboured to capture the textile industry of Cornwall for party purposes", the letter declared. Addressing Kent Rowley directly, Cornwall union leaders announced that "after nearly four years of constant disruptive propaganda on the part of the Communist movement and its fellow travellers, we accept your challenge, Mr. Rowley...to study the record."

In a surprisingly candid fashion, the writers, Thomas Duffy, president of Courtaulds Local 779, Thomas Webster, president of Canadian Cottons Local 806, and André Derouin, president of Local 805 of Glengarry Textiles, together with Archie Lebrun, president of the Greater Cornwall Textile Joint Board, boasted of the wage gains and increased benefits derived from recent contract negotiations with Canadian Cottons, describing their gains as far superior to those secured by Rowley in his negotiations on behalf of the United Textile Workers of America with Dominion Textiles of Montreal. The fur flew in all directions. Even Charles Lipton, one of the organizers for the United Textile Workers of America and future author of *"The Trade Union Movement of Canada 1827-1959"*, came in for attack. Cornwall union leaders accused him of being at the head of "20 men... in beating up two TWUA men." Going beyond union and labour matters, the Cornwall leaders attacked Rowley on the grounds that he was critical of Canadian, American, British and French foreign policy, but "no where do we find even the slightest...criticism of the Soviet Union."

They concluded their broadside with a resounding rejection of "the Communist party and all of its agents...we are convinced that the apparent conspiracy by the Communist party, its friends and fronts in the trade union movement, to raid and take over the textile workers of Cornwall and thereby dominate and disrupt the industrial life of the entire city, for party purposes, is doomed to failure." This was language all could understand, and Pat Conroy, secretary-treasurer of the Canadian Congress of Labour, made sure that affiliated unions across Canada received copies of the Cornwall letter. "The Communists' attempt to raid the established and effective textile locals of Cornwall," Conroy declared, "is of major importance to all Canadian workers." Rowley replied four days later to the "wild, false and slanderous attacks on our union...by the Cornwall Joint Board of Textile Workers of America (C.I.O.)". He declared that the authors of the open letter were seeking "to divert the attention of textile workers and of the Canadian trade union movement as a whole from the tragic situation which exists where the CIO-TWUA is in control."[40]

This fight in the union movement both in Cornwall and at the national level between the Committee for Industrial Organization and the American Federation of Labor had been brewing all during the 1940s and the charges of union raiding reached a climax with the Canadian Seamen's Union strikes in June 1946 and in June 1948 when Cornwall was the scene of bitter clashes between police and pickets and imported strike-breakers.[41] Textile union rivalry continued unabated, although in 1951 the *Standard-Freeholder* reported that the ranks of the Ontario Federation of Labour (CIO-CCL) "have been pruned almost simon-pure of Communists".[42] Indeed, the president of the Canadian Trades and Labour Congress of Canada, Percy Bengough, who was guest speaker at a labour rally at the Cornwall Collegiate and Vocational School auditorium on 15 February 1951 justified the action of the Congress "in throwing out its Communist officers on the grounds that they posed a threat to the Congress and to the country". Though he spoke to an almost empty auditorium because a Friday night hockey games had lured most of the union men to the arena, Bengough warned Cornwall labour leaders that "Communists join our organization and in many cases they do a good job so as to entrench themselves. They get control," he declared, "with the idea of ultimately destroying the organization".[43]

Cornwall labour leaders had been foremost in pruning their ranks of Communists, thereby creating an image of moderate, almost conservative union leadership as the new decade began. What they failed to realize at first was that this pruning process was the preliminary to moves at the national and international level to merge the giant rival union movements - the Committee for Industrial Organization and the American Federation of Labor. Tension between the Textile Workers' Union of America (CIO) and United Textile Workers of America (AFL) evaporated in 1956 when a merger was finally effected, resulting in the creation of the Canadian Labour Congress which was "to give workers a unified front".[44] Raiding ceased, for the luxury of bitter union infighting was only possible in times of full production and soaring sales.

Strike action at Canadian Cottons mills continued intermittently throughout the 1950s, though never for long and at no time reached the proportion of the papermill strikes of 1976 and 1980-81. Courtaulds workers walked off on a wildcat strike in July of 1956 over the "sore eye" clause in their new contract which insisted that workers must stay in the company surgery, rather than go home, when suffering sore eyes. This was the first labour trouble at Courtaulds since the initial strike of 1936.[45] Hotel workers, who had been helped in organizing their union by members of the Textile Workers of America, staged a rotating strike at Cornwall's nine hotels in the spring of 1950 after hotel owners refused recommendations handed down by a conciliation board. The strike dragged on for seventeen weeks with textile union officers and workers joining the hotel workers at the picket lines. The situation at times got out of hand when strikers tossed eggs and ornamental shrubs at customers being escorted into the hotel by police, all of whom, including the strikers, were then bombarded with clouds of pepper tossed by staff members from inside the hotel.[46] Other strikes in 1954 and 1955 by the United Brotherhood of Carpenters and Joiners were short-lived as were the two strikes of the Union of Public Employees that put City Hall out of operation for ten days in 1957 and for a period in 1959. Strikes occurred at various construction sites, especially during the heyday of the Seaway construction in the 1950s, but one instance of picketing gave unionists red faces. When Courtaulds Local 779 was having work done on the old First Baptist Church which they were converting into their Labour House, a solitary member of the Building and Construction Council, Euclide Gratton, marched back and forth in front of the building, protesting that the work was being done by a non-union contractor. Embarrassed viscose workers quickly explained that the use of a non-union contractor had been an oversight.[47]

Throughout the sixties trade unionists continued to nominate workingclass men as candidates for the renamed socialist party, the New Democratic Party - William Kilger in 1963, and John Trew, a former president of Courtaulds Local 779, in 1965, but the labour vote never became tied to any one party in Cornwall.[48] When a New Democratic Party candidate, thirty-one-year old school teacher George Samis, succeeded in getting 9,934 votes in a by-election to the Ontario Legislature in 1974, he did so without any special support from labour. The subsequent success of this part-French native of Montreal in retaining the Cornwall seat that had been held throughout the sixties by Conservative Fern Guindon and throughout the fifties by Liberals, was as much due to Samis's personal record and his espousal of Franco-Ontarian interests as it was to any increasing labour support for his candidacy.[49]

Union activity in Cornwall's second major industry, the Howard Smith Paper mill, parallelled that of the textile industry. The paper industry rode the crest of full post-war production, its work force increasing from 1,000 employees in the early 1950s to 1,500 by the end of the decade.[50] Developments such as the use of lignin extract from soda pulp waste liquor for making arborite, the installation of the giant No. 1 paper machine that John Entwistle of Cornwall had constructed, and the opening of the chlorine dioxide and pulp bleaching plant in 1957 all indicated the sound operating basis of the company that attracted the attention of Toronto financiers like E.P. Taylor.

Union members reaped part of the benefits of this growing plant. Organized in 1937 by Elbert Gallinger and Harry Kirby with the aid of textile union leaders, Locals 212 and 338 were headed in 1949 by John McGillivrary and Thomas Harris.[51] These leaders were quick to urge their members to be moderate in wage demands, declaring that "wages and benefits built up during the war years to the point that we are now satisfied that our efforts should be directed to maintaining this position, rather than contributing to further inflationary trends through increased wage demands".[52] This theme was repeated two years later when Harris was host, along with the new president of Local 212, Leonard Hart, at a dinner at the King George Hotel. Here J.P. Burke, president of the International Brotherhood of Pulp, Sulphite and Paper Mill Workers gave figures and facts to show that, in the fourteen years since 1937 when the paper mill unions were first organized, the basic wage rate had increased from thirty-six cents an hour to $1.14 in 1951, making an 180% percent increase in wages during a time when the cost of living had increased by 88 percent. This meant that negotiated wage gains had far outstripped the cost of living and had thus substantially raised living standards for the employees. What was more, Burke added, "We have established a good record and haven't put the company out of business".[53]

A few months later, the president of the company, E. Howard Smith, the son of the founder, attended a dinner at the Cornwallis Hotel honouring 240 long-service employees. A graduate in mechanical engineering of McGill University, E. Howard Smith had spent a number of years as plant manager at the Cornwall mill in the 1920s and knew personally some of those being feted. His address held a note of warning. The time has come, he said, "to stop expanding and consolidate" because the paper making industry was moving into a highly competitive period with a buyer's market.[54] Nevertheless the Howard Smith Paper Mill workers were given a shorter forty-four hour week in the fall of 1952, still retaining the same pay as though they worked a forty-eight hour week.[55]

By 1957 as employees of Howard Smith welcomed a new wage agreement that brought their base labour rate to $1.60 an hour and made plans to open their own Credit Union, changes occurred at the corporate level of the company that reverberated down to the lowest level of operations.[56] This was the shift of control from the family-based Howard Smith interests of Montreal to the Toronto-based E.P. Taylor interests. The shift of control occurred shortly after the death of Chairman of the Board, Harold Crabtree, in the spring of 1956. Over the summer the large Crabtree holdings were sold to E.P. Taylor, then in control of Argus Corporation which, in turn, controlled Dominion Tar and Chemical Company.[57] By 1957 Dominion Tar and Chemical had 53.3 percent interest in the Cornwall Mill, having acquired 16 percent of the shares in the summer of 1956 and, by an additional exchange of three and one-half shares Dominion Tar and Chemical for one share of Howard Smith, the Company, whose Board of Directors was headed by E.P. Taylor, acquired an additional 354,588 Howard Smith shares.[58]

When news reached head office in Montreal that Dominion Tar and Chemical now owned the controlling interest in the Cornwall plant, the president, E. Howard Smith, already ill with stomach ulcers, retired, rather than continue as chairman of the Board, an appointment offered to him by the new owners. In a sense, the wheel had turned full cycle. C. Howard Smith had bought out the Crabtree interests in 1916.[59] In 1956 the Crabtree family sold their Howard Smith shares to the Taylor interest, thus not only shifting the company's financial base back to Toronto, its original base, but, in turn, providing the Cornwall plant with a broader financial base from which to expand.

This expansion included No. 6 paper machine that went on stream in 1960, a giant designed to produce 40,000 tons of paper a year. Six years later No. 7 paper machine was christened with great pomp and ceremony. Closed circuit television allowed a unique hookup between Cornwall and Toronto for the occasion. From a Toronto hotel ballroom, Premier John Robarts, surrounded by W.N. Hall, president of what by now was Domtar Limited, Stormont M.P.P. Fern Guindon, and J.H. Robertson, vice-president of Domtar, watched the screen as Mayor Elzéar Emard in Cornwall approached "Super Seven" with a bottle of champagne. At a signal from Mr. Robarts, the mayor swung the bottle which refused to break. Undaunted, the Mayor grasped a second bottle which he dashed against the machine with gusto, showering himself and nearby officials with bubbly champagne and shattered glass. Thus did Super Seven officially go on stream. These additions over the sixties changed the small plant of 1882 into a Cornwall colossus worth $66,000,000, whose employees brought home $13,000,000 in wages in 1967.[60]

The story of the Cornwall papermill, then, was one of continued expansion. The textile story was somewhat different. It was in the early 1950's that danger signals became apparent. Union men such as Ralph McIntee spoke of "a pall of gloom spreading over industry because of foreign competition and dropping employment". In 1952 representatives of Canadian Cottons' Local 806, Textile Workers' Union of America, met with four federal cabinet ministers, including their local Member of Parliament, Lionel Chevrier, to demand federal action to relieve textile unemployment. The next year, McIntee was spokesman for union officials in deploring the Fair Trade Pact between Canada and Japan. The Pact, he said, was "a severe blow to the textile industry (which) is already suffering from low-priced imports". City Hall was behind both management and labour in their efforts to halt "the dumping of American, English and other textiles on our markets". In 1953 Mayor Aaron Horovitz offered to head a civic delegation to federal cabinet ministers to protest the Japan-Canada Fair Trade Pact. According to McIntee, "Cornwall has been losing $2,000,000 in wages each year because of the dumping", and he urged Canadian textile manufacturers to become more daring in their style, colours and over-all quality in order to compete with foreign textiles.[61]

Some gestures at modernization of plant equipment had been made by Canadian Cottons as the pace of foreign competition quickened. Time and quality control efficiency experts were brought in, usually from American-based companies, who time-clocked individual millhands during their work performance and compared them to American standards of productivity, frequently concluding that Canadian productivity levels were inferior. Tension over time and quality control studies, sagging sales, markets flooded with foreign textiles, the slow pace of modernization of the three Cornwall mills, and frequent wildcat strikes all combined to crush Cornwall's oldest industry.

Canadian Cottons paid quarterly dividends for the last time in 1953 and that same year announced the shutdown of the Stormont Mill, the first of the Cornwall mills to be liquidated.[62] Its closure threw 385 employees out of work. The City's bleak unemployment picture was emphasized by the *Standard-Freeholder* on 5 February 1954 when it disclosed that the number of jobless during January had reached 3,610, the highest since the National Selective Service office opened in Cornwall in 1941. Unemployment benefits paid out in January alone totalled $200,000. This figure for a single month seemed astronomical when compared with the entire yearly payment in 1951 of $440,181.[63] Nor was this the whole story. Canadian Cottons' neighbouring textile firm, Courtaulds, was also experiencing hard times. It had weathered the 1952 spring crisis when 1,015 employees had been laid off, but with the introduction of a new type of high tenacity rayon filament, stronger than ordinary viscose, Courtaulds hoped to secure a new market.[64] By April of 1952 the company was rehiring again. However in July of 1954 Courtaulds began to experience market difficulties again and laid off 500 from the filament plant for six weeks.[65] When to this was added the news that the venerable Ives Bedding plant would close its doors after fifty years of operations and throw its sixty-five skilled workmen on the job market as well, Cornwall's economic picture was far from satisfactory.[66]

Adding to the economic uncertainty in the spring of 1954 was the shakeup at the top level of Canadian Cottons Limited when both President J. Irving Roy and Vice-president MacMillan Boyd resigned amidst news that the company had suffered a loss of $900,000 during the first half year, a loss attributed to the encroachment on company sales by low-priced imports, especially from the United States.[67]

Stepping into the presidency of Canadian Cottons at this crucial time was L.C. Bonnycastle of Toronto, the man who was to remain at the helm as the old cotton firm limped along, through strike after strike, especially in 1957, when there were seventeen illegal walkouts and work stoppages.[68] Union and company officials often worked together to try to stem the tide of disruptions, many of them short-lived and often associated with workload disputes involving female employees.[69] On 11 May 1957 Canadian Cottons placed a full-page advertisement in the *Standard-Freeholder* describing the illegal walkout of its employees and grimly drawing attention to a possible closure of its operations in Cornwall. Nevertheless, in June and October both male and female employees were annoyed over pay cutbacks under what was called the "red circle" quota clause in their work contract. Then on 17 October seven men in the converting plant walked out protesting a cut of twenty-five cents per hour because they had not attained levels of production set up in engineering surveys and in effect throughout the textile industry. Other workers refused to cross picket lines set up by the seven men, and thus the whole plant of 1300 workers was shut down. The union executive disclaimed responsibility for the walkout and said so in a letter to the company.

Mayor Lloyd George "Archie" Lavigne tried to get company and union officials together to "cut short a situation which can do nothing but bring harm to the City", but the meeting stalemated. While women shared picketing duties with men and union members set up a tent on Mattice Farm to serve coffee and sandwiches to pickets, the company issued announcements all day long saying that the gates of the mills were open for workers to return to work. Top union officials from New York and Toronto converged on the Cornwallis Hotel on 4 November in an effort to sort out the difficulties with Jack B. Paddon, vice-president of Canadian Cottons. Then on 6 November the company issued a strong statement declaring that "it is impossible to conduct a successful operation under such conditions. Assurances must be forthcoming from a strong and reliable union executive that these illegal strikes will cease for all time".[70]

Members of Local 806 Textile Workers' Union of America, representing the Canadian Cottons' workers, held a series of emergency meetings at Nativity parish hall on 8 and 10 November under their president, Ralph McIntee, and by 11 November they agreed to resume work with the proviso that the contentious "red letter" clause be discussed in continuing negotiations with the company.[71] At another level, Cornwall's ailing cotton industry was championed in the House of Commons by Stormont's Member of Parliament, Albert Lavigne, who protested vigorously against the government sending a buying mission abroad "instead of emphasizing the sale of Canadian goods".[72]

An uneasy truce existed between Canadian Cottons Company officials and their workers throughout 1958. Management pointed to foreign competition as the major source of the company's difficulties, though domestic rivals, especially Quebec textile firms, were also competing for the Canadian market. Manager V.H. Bruneau minced no words when he spoke to the Cornwall Rotary Club in April 1959. "The textile industry of Canada hasn't anything to cheer about," he mournfully pointed out. "The real trouble began when Japan, China and India decided to expand their textile trade," Bruneau stated. "With low labor costs, and long hours, it soon became apparent that these countries could manufacture similar products to those made right here in Cornwall and land them in Canada in some cases for little more than the cost of our raw materials". He urged that the "Canadian textile industry receive the protection it requires...that imports are necessary, but not to the extent that they destroy sound industry".[73]

Foreign competition and the unstable labour situation were part of the reasons for the demise of Cornwall's oldest textile company. Still, the announcement on 7 December 1959 of the company's closure came as a shock. Layoffs for the 1300 employees began on 12 December. A large part of the company's equipment was sold to

Dominion Textiles of Montreal.[74] Other equipment went as far afield as Venezuela where seven Cornwall men, including union business agent, Frank Querat, journeyed in order to help install the Cornwall machinery in the Texfin Company plant and to teach textile skills to Venezuelan workers.[75] The old Stormont mill, vacant since its closure in 1954, was destroyed in a spectacular Halloween night fire in 1961, believed to have been the work of pranksters.

President L.C. Bonnycastle and company director B.H. Rieger were the two men of the defunct company who remained through the various company changeovers, first from Canadian Cottons to Canman Industries Limited in 1960 which acquired all the common shares of Canadian Cottons at $27 each. They were also among the directors of the holding company, Canadian Corporate Management Company, which took over Canman Industries in 1965 and were still directors in 1981.[76] When the full story of Canadian Cottons' final financial dealings are unravelled, a third factor in the company's demise may emerge. Apart from the foreign sales competition and the unsteady labour situation, the men at the corporate level may have decided to liquidate the Cornwall operations in order to gain access to the accumulated surplus of the company, together with the proceeds of the sale of its assets, for use elsewhere. Supplementary letters patent had been applied for and acquired by Canadian Cottons in October 1959, giving the company power to carry on business in industries other than textiles.[77]

As a good-will gesture, Canadian Cottons vice-president Jack Paddon, led a group of Cornwall businessmen back to the very spot in the United States from which some of the city's Loyalist founders had fled two hundred years earlier. This was to Manchester, New Hampshire, which, like other manufacturing centres in the New England states, had fallen on hard times, its mills closing and capital moving south to areas where organized unions were less powerful. Here in Jeremiah French's old home town, Cornwall businessmen viewed a defunct textile mill which had been taken over by a citizens' committee who had succeeded in attracting new businesses to the site. The moral for Cornwall businessmen was to go and do likewise, and they did. Spurred by the city's industrial commissioner, Edgar May, they formed a company called the Cornwall Industrial Development Limited (CIDL) in September 1959 and, with J.R. Whitehead as president, bought the East End property of Canadian Cottons for $675,000.[78] The Glengarry Cottons property was sold separately for $200,000 to National Grocers. Gradually small businesses began to rent space in the empty cotton mills and the Ontario government rented space for a trade school, but no longer did lights from Cornwall's huge textile factories cast a bright light for miles up and down the St. Lawrence River.

The plight of the textile trade in Cornwall was of major concern to Transport Minister Lionel Chevrier who envisaged the development of the St.Lawrence Seaway and power project not only as a panacea for the economic ills of his home town, but as a boon for the country as a whole. No sooner had the textile union delegation from Cornwall assailed him and four of his cabinet colleagues in Ottawa in 1952 than Chevrier returned to Cornwall in May, hailed as "Mr. Seaway". Here he spoke confidently at the official opening of the Seaway model exhibition at the Armouries.[79] Like Chevrier, Mayor Aaron Horovitz saw the giant project as the source of "a bright future for Cornwall". Retailers and hotelmen would benefit from the arrival of thousands of construction workers and contractors, while cheap hydro-electric power would attract diversified industries.[80] If New York State dragged its feet in agreeing to the project, Chevrier talked about Canada going it alone with the canal system on the Canadian side.[81]

As the spring of 1954 lengthened into summer with no definite word on an agreement, rumours began to fly that the United States would join the Seaway project only if the "international" section of canals were built on the American side of the river.[82] Little by little Cornwallites received news that compromises and accommodations were being hammered out at the negotiating table between Canadian and American authorities. Chevrier fought tooth and nail to keep the locks and channel on the Cornwall side and nearly succeeded.[83] However, by 10 August 1954 when the start of construction was ushered in by an official ceremony involving New York State Governor Thomas Dewey, Prime Minister Louis St. Laurent, Ontario Premier Leslie M. Frost, and Robert Saunders, Chairman of Ontario Hydro, Cornwallites sensed that their fears were real and that the locks and channel would both go to the American side. Thus, as the dignitaries gathered at Maple Grove, just west of Cornwall on the site of the old Loyalist homestead of the French family, and prepared to turn the first sod for the Seaway construction, a group of Cornwallites formed a Citizens' Joint Action Committee to prepare a petition. In no uncertain terms, they demanded an all-Canadian Seaway, convinced that the future development of the city depended vitally on such an arrangement.[84]

During the early years of construction, Chevrier managed to get $30,000,000 worth of dredging operations and land excavations done on the Cornwall side in anticipation of a future deep-sea Canadian channel.[85] News releases throughout 1955 continued to hint that an "All-Canadian Seaway"[86] could be a possibility in ten years time if traffic became heavy enough. But these decisions, like the later closure of the old Cornwall Canal and the loss of 150 local jobs through the transfer of canal shop operations to St. Lambert, were beyond Chevrier's control.[87] As president of the St. Lawrence Seaway Authority, Chevrier did his best to protect Cornwall interests, but he lost out to more powerful American and Canadian interests.[88] His frustration and disappointment became increasingly evident and by 1957 he resigned from the project that had been his dream, while the new federal Member for Stormont, Progressive Conservative Grant Campbell, seldom let him forget that the Eisenhower Locks should have been on the Canadian side.[89]

Within five years from the time that the first Seaway sod was turned, the area and people to the west of Cornwall were more than uprooted. Eight small communities, involving 6,500 people and 500 homes, were shunted to make way for the project that cost Canada $329,025,700. Some 12,300 labourers and Hydro workers drained the Long Sault Rapids, built the Moses-Saunders power dam and a huge generating station, created the 35-mile long Lake St.Lawrence and constructed the Seaway Bridge connecting Cornwall with Massena, New York.[90] For these five years Cornwall citizens happily welcomed the thousands of workers and millions of Seaway dollars. And it is not surprising that when construction ended, there was a sense of let-down. Yet, neither Massena, New York, nor St. Lambert, Quebec, which got the coveted locks and the deep-sea channels, turned into great oceanports. Moreover, the Seaway operated at a loss up until 1980 when toll increases were introduced in the expectation that the Seaway operations would come out of the red for the first time.[91] Thus, in the long term, Cornwall may still be the chief beneficiary of the Seaway project, compared to Massena and St. Lambert, in that it has the power project to back up potential industry.

Cornwall received some immediate compensation for its disappointment in not getting the international locks and channel. An eight-storey Seaway Authority building was constructed in the heart of the city at the corner of Pitt and Second Streets. By 1958 it towered above its neighbours on the spot that the old Gothic Post Office had graced for almost half a century. The impact of the Seaway construction was felt in other directions than increased trade for the city's merchants. Housing became scarce and rents soared, forcing many mothers to join fathers as breadwinners and rent-payers. Social welfare agencies found that these "tight money" conditions in the homes where both parents were out working and neglected children frequently dropped out of school made for strained family relations and greatly increased caseloads.[92]

One of the direct results of the Seaway project was the erection in 1958 of the city's new filtration and water purification plant. Erected on the western outskirts of the city at a cost of $1,730,000, the filtration plant was considered the most modern one in all North America at the time of its opening.[93]

The city had received a mandatory order from the Ontario Department of Health in 1951 to provide better water protection for its citizens, but it was not until the pressure of incoming Seaway workers put a strain on the city's water system that construction began in 1956 on an overhead tank at Marlborough and Ninth Streets. It was also this pressure of population that speeded up the city's plans to annex most of the township in 1957, thus bringing its assessment up to $55,000,000 and increasing its responsibilities with regard to schools, roads, police and fire protection to the additional 30 square miles that Cornwall now covered.[94]

All this construction, expansion and development of municipal facilities and institutions gave the city and its citizens a sense of forward motion, even after the Seaway project ended and many of the migrant workers began to drift away. There was still the official opening of the Seaway in 1959 to give a sense of accomplishment to what had been a project of herculean dimensions. Queen Elizabeth and Prince Philip arrived on the Royal yacht *Britannia* to share with President Dwight Eisenhower the initial honours of opening the Seaway in Montreal. Then, while Cornwallites waited patiently in the thickest fog ever to hit Eastern Ontario, the *Britannia* nosed its way through the envied St. Lambert Locks to head towards Cornwall. However, the fog delayed the Royal yacht so that many of the elaborate plans drawn up by Dr. J.A. Phillips and his Cornwall royal tour committee had to be shelved. When the *Britannia* finally berthed at Snell Lock, Massena, the Royal couple reached Cornwall where 5,000 school children, senior citizens, invalids and other Cornwallites roared their welcome at the Athletic Grounds, captivated by the personal charm and warmth of their monarch and Prince Philip.[95]

Yet an under-current of ill-will had become evident. The night before the Queen's arrival, vandals ransacked Horovitz Park which had been decorated for the occasion. A Union Jack was torn down and thrown across a fountain. Park tables and benches were upturned, and white paint was splashed over the decorative gates unveiled the previous year in honour of Mayor Aaron Horovitz who had died in

1957.[96] The tightly-knit prosperous city of the war years had given way to a more impersonal one. The Friendly City had evolved into the Seaway City.

NOTES

1. See, for instance, *Standard-Freeholder*, 26 November 1970.
2. *Old Home Week*, 1947, 7-9.
3. *Ibid., City of Opportunity*, 1950, 4-5.
4. *City of Opportunity*, 1950, 10, 13-15.
5. *Standard-Freeholder*, 3 December 1960.
6. Bruce McDonell, Plant Superintendent, to Elinor Senior, 7 January 1982.
7. Monique St. Onge, Public Relations, BASF, to Senior, 11 March 1982; *Scott's Industrial Directory of Ontario Manufacturers*, 1979, 2-9; *Chemistry in Canada*, June 1970, 27.
8. *Scott's Industrial Directory of Ontario Manufacturers*, 1979, 2-9; *Chemistry in Canada*, June 1970, 27; G. Sullivan, Plant Manager to Senior, 31 May 1982.
9. "TCF'S Twenty-Fifth Anniversary", in *Standard Freeholder*, 17 June 1978, 8A.
10. *Fifty Years of Progress: Courtaulds (Canada) Limited*, 1975, 3 and 11.
11. *Iroquois Chemicals*, 1; *Chemistry in Canada*, June 1970, 28; D.L. Segur, President, Iroquois Chemicals, to Senior, 28 May 1982.
12. Dave Hall, Manager, Fiberez of Canada, to Senior, 7 January 1982.
13. *Chemistry in Canada*, June 1970, 26.
14. A. Stark, President, Pellon Chemotextiles, to Senior, 19 January 1982.
15. *Census*, 1891, iii, 120 and 377.
16. J.G. Harkness, *History of Stormont, Dundas and Glengarry*, 236.
17. *Standard-Freeholder*, 17 October 1944.
18. *Ibid.*, 17 March 1941.
19. For details on Tessier's career, see obituary in *Standard-Freeholder*, 16 April 1968.
20. Leo Tessier to Drummond Giles, 25 April 1944 (MG28/1-219/80-437, box 1).
21. Tessier to Giles, 12 June and 3 November 1944 (*ibid.*)
22. *Standard-Freeholder*, 15 November 1956.
23. *Ibid.*, 8 March 1946.
24. *Ibid.*, 13 July 1948.
25. *Ibid.*, 11 June 1948.
26. *Ibid.*, 16 February 1951.
27. *Ibid.*, 23 January 1945.
28. *Ibid.*, 3 January 1947.
29. *Ibid.*, 17 January 1949 and 3 November 1950.
30. For these union activities see *Standard-Freeholder*, 17 January, 9 March and 5 November 1949; 22 December 1950, 13 February, 3 March and 20 April 1951; 6 and 21 November 1956.

31. *Standard-Freeholder*, 14 September 1948.
32. *Ibid.*, 16 March 1948.
33. R. Lewis, *History of Electoral Districts*, 359.
34. *Standard-Freeholder*, 20 July 1944.
35. Lewis, *History of Electoral Districts*, 359.
36. *Standard-Freeholder*, 23 September 1946.
37. *Ibid.*, 17 January 1949.
38. *Ibid.*, 6 and 28 June 1949.
39. A copy of this Open Letter, dated 26 January 1950, is filed in the newspaper file of the Greater Cornwall Textile Joint Board collection in the Public Archives, Ottawa.
40. *Standard-Freeholder*, 30 January 1950.
41. *Ibid.*, 31 May and 3 June 1946; 11 and 12 June 1948.
42. *Ibid.*, 5 February 1951.
43. *Ibid.*, 3 March 1951.
44. *Ibid.*, 1 February 1951; 27 May 1952; 16 May 1956.
45. *Ibid.*, 3 July 1956.
46. *Ibid.*, 17 May 1950.
47. *Ibid.*, 14 April 1961.
48. *Ibid.*, 21 January 1952; 20 March 1963 and 18 September 1965; R. Lewis, *History of Electoral Districts*, 360.
49. See N.D.P. information brochure on George Samis, April 1981; George Samis to Senior, 8 March 1982.
50. *Standard-Freeholder*, 8 May 1957.
51. For early organization, see *Standard-Freeholder*, 7 February 1953; Senior interview with P.D. Connolly, Manager, Labour Relations, Domtar Fine Papers, 18 March 1983.
52. *Standard-Freeholder*, 11 May 1949.
53. See extracts of J.P. Burke's speech in *Standard-Freeholder*, 1 February 1952.
54. *Standard-Freeholder*, 28 April 1952.
55. *Ibid.*, 1 October 1952.
56. For Credit Union, see *The Cornwall Mill Story*, 1970, 22; for wage agreement see *Standard-Freeholder*, 8 May 1957.
57. See *Financial Post Survey of Industrials*, 1957, 143; *The Cornwall Mill Story*, 1970, 20; G. Howard Smith to Senior, 26 August, 27 September, 8 November 1982; Senior interview with Mrs. Emily Evans Kellander, secretary to E. Howard Smith from 1928 to 1957, 6 March 1983.
58. See *Financial Post Survey of Industrials*, 1957, 339.
59. William Wood, *Storied Province of Quebec*, iv, 407-408.
60. *The Cornwall Mill Story*, 1970, 23 and 28.
61. For the various comments on economic conditions, see *Standard-Freeholder*, 12 and 22 March, 1952; 28 and 31 October and 6 November 1953.
62. *Financial Post Survey of Industrials*, 1959, 120; *Standard-Freeholder*, 12 December 1953.
63. *Standard-Freeholder*, 28 February 1952.
64. *Ibid.*, 9, 26 January and 28 February 1952.
65. *Ibid.*, 8 July 1954.
66. *Ibid.*, 31 March 1954.
67. *Ibid.*, 25 January 1954.
68. *Ibid.*, 6 November 1957.
69. *Ibid.*, 19 March and 9 May 1957.

70. For details of the 1957 strikes, see *Standard-Freeholder*, 27 June, 25, 29, 31 October, 4, 7 November 1957.

71. According to an advertisement published by Canadian Cottons, the Red Circle Rates were wage rates being paid to about seventy workers, which were badly out of line with those being earned by the rest of the millhands. The Company claimed that the reduction of these Red Letter Rates had been agreed to by the Union during contract negotiations. See, "An Open Letter to Employees of Canadian Cottons Limited", in *Standard-Freeholder*, 28 October 1957; see also, *Standard-Freeholder*, 11 and 17 November 1957.

72. *Standard-Freeholder*, 11 December 1957.

73. *Ibid.*, 21 April 1959.

74. *Ibid.*, 7 December 1959.

75. *Ibid.*, 12 November 1960.

76. *Financial Post Survey of Predecessor and Defunct Companies*, 1981, 31; *Financial Post Survey of Industrials*, 1982, 94-95.

77. *Financial Post Survey of Industrials*, 1960.

78. *Standard-Freeholder*, 5 February 1960.

79. *Ibid.*, 29 May 1952.

80. *Financial Post*, 15 August 1953.

81. *Standard-Freeholder*, 10 July 1953.

82. *Ibid.*, 26 June 1954.

83. In a personal interview on 17 December 1981 with the writer, Eric Reford, President of Reford Steamship Company, Montreal, a staunch Progressive Conservative, confirmed that Chevrier fought valiantly throughout the negotiations to protect Cornwall's interests.

84. Standard-Freeholder, 11 August 1954.

85. Bud Henson, St. Lawrence Seaway Authority, Cornwall, interview with James MacDonald, 14 July 1980.

86. *Standard-Freeholder*, 28 June 1955.

87. *Ibid.*, 6 and 15 November 1969.

88. See St. Lawrence Seaway Authority Fact Sheet 1203, 3-5.

89. Jenny Colucci to editor, *Standard-Freeholder*, 8 February 1980.

90. For details, see *Star Weekly*, Toronto, 27 June 1959, 8; see also, *Standard-Freeholder*, 26 June 1954.

91. Sultan Jessa's interview with Ernest Piossi, vice-president, Eastern Region of the St. Lawrence Seaway Authority, Montreal, in *Standard-Freeholder*, 26 June 1979.

92. *Standard-Freeholder*, 28 June 1958.

93. *Ibid.*, 25 January, 1958; City By-law 386, 10 October 1955.

94. *Standard-Freeholder*, 28 June 1958.

95. Minutes City Council, 16 January 1959, 5; *Standard-Freeholder*, 26 June 1979.

96. *Standard-Freeholder*, 24 June 1959.

R.H. Saunders Generating Station, Ontario Hydro. Construction on this project started on August 10, 1954 was completed in 1958. The construction of the Seaway uprooted eight communities, 6,500 people and 300 homes at a cost of $329,025,700. 12,300 labourers were employed to make the 33-mile-long Lake St. Lawrence.

Chapter XX

Twentieth Century Schools and Churches

Church and school development in the twentieth century reflects primarily the expansion in the Roman Catholic population and the difficulties of financing separate high schools. This expansion was obvious in the West End in the early 1920s when Monsignor George Corbet of St. Columban's Church established a small chapel in the suburb of Beaconfield.[1] Corbet succeeded also in procuring the services of seven Presentation Brothers from Ireland for the Centre Ward Boys' School. Working closely with Corbet, the Presentation Brothers fulfilled the long-time aspirations of Cornwall's Roman Catholic community by opening a boys' high school, Gonzaga, at the corner of York and Third Streets, in 1925.

The Presentation Brothers continued to teach in the parish schools of St. Columban's until 1959 when new Ontario Department of Education regulations required them to undertake additional studies at the Ontario Normal College. Judging this to be an unnecessary expense for the brothers who were already well qualified and experienced teachers, the Order withdrew them from Cornwall for services in Ireland and Quebec.[2] Part of Monsignor Corbet's plan in opening the boys' high school was to foster a vocation for the priesthood among devout young Catholics. He was largely successful in this, as many graduates from Gonzaga went on to study for the priesthood. However, the rapid expansion of the elementary school population - over 2,500 in 1934 - put such pressure on the two St. Columban's parish schools that by 1936 Gonzaga was forced to become an elementary school to accommodate the overflow from the old Centre Ward School.[3]

It was this population pressure that resulted in two new Roman Catholic parishes being established in 1936. The small chapel in Beaconfield could no longer cope with the numbers in the West End and thus the parish of St. Francis-de-Sales was established for Catholics west of Cumberland Street. Expansion to the east of the town was relieved by the formation of the parish of St. Felix-de-Valois with a western boundary fixed at Guy Street. The two new parishes took steps not only to erect churches but also to establish schools, the one in the west parish opening in the basement of the new church on Second Street West in 1939. The new eastern parish established its first school for 450 pupils at the corner of Belmont and Easton Streets the same year.[4]

Then, as Cornwall's population continued to increase because of war-time industrial expansion, Roman Catholic schools expanded east, west and north even before additional parishes had been established. A second school associated with St. Francis-de-Sales parish opened in the area north of the Canadian National Railways tracks. This was the area known as "Garden City" where squatters had established themselves in the depression era and built rough dwellings. The owner of much of the land, Dan Cameron, sub-divided his property into building lots which he sold cheaply to many of the day labourers living there. Because Cameron allowed the new owners and the squatters to use part of his land to plant gardens, it became known as "Garden City". It was in this area of poor housing, devoid of proper sewerage facilities, roads or sidewalks, that parishioners from St. Francis-de-Sales began plans for a school, especially as pupils found it hard to undertake the long walk of over a mile to attend the parish school on Second Street West.

Truancy in the area was rampant and it was hoped that the opening of Notre Dame School in 1942 at the corner of Notre Dame and Twelfth Streets would alleviate this problem. The seriousness of the situation was underlined by the report of the truancy officer a few months after Notre Dame opened. He pointed out that out of 100 pupils enrolled, only forty were attending, a situation he attributed to the apathy of parents and the habit of children in this area to treat school attendance cavalierly.[5] Indeed, up until the post-war years, probably the majority of pupils coming out of elementary schools still went straight into the workforce where jobs were available, rather than continue into high school.

The opening of the first Roman Catholic School in Garden City accented the need for a separate parish there. The pioneer priest sent into the area was one well fitted by temperament and training for the task. Alcime Poirier at thirty-six had had a career as a cheese-maker in Alexandria before emigrating to the United States as a day worker. Deeply stirred by a call to the priesthood, he returned to studies, first in Quebec and then at the Diocesan Seminary in Ottawa. Just as the need was urgent in Garden City, Father Poirier was ordained in 1943, ready to take over the new parish in 1944. It was given the name of St. John Bosco in honour of the Italian saint of the nineteenth century who had founded the Order of Salesians, the priests of St. Francis-de-Sales, whose primary mission was to recruit abandoned or poor children and train them as farmers or industrial workers.[6]

The boundaries of St. John Bosco extended in the east to Marlborough Street, in the west to Brookdale Avenue, southward to a line between Sixth and Seventh Streets, and stretched northwards to Eamer's Corners. The new parish reflected the realities of Cornwall's growth in that its boundaries reached well into the township area. When the first service was held in the basement church at the corner of York and Ninth Streets on 2 December 1944, there were 673 families on the parish roll with a total membership of 3,135 souls.[7] It took another ten years before the Church of St. John Bosco rose above its foundation and fostered the founding of four other parishes: Ste. Theresa of Lisieux in 1955, Saints Martyrs Canadiens and Christ the King at Eamer's Corners in 1964 and Blessed Sacrament in 1965.

Concomitant with this expansion in parishes was the increase in schools. Indeed, once again, in some cases, the schools paved the way for the establishment of parishes. Just as the founding of Notre Dame School preceded the establishment of the parish of St. John Bosco, so, too, did the founding of St. Theresa's School in 1952 precede the formation of the parish of St. Theresa of Lisieux in 1955. Other schools growing up within the parish were the St. John Bosco School opened in 1945 and located in the church basement until its own building was erected on Eighth Street between Augustus and York Streets in 1947; St. Joseph's School, 1945, east of McConnell Avenue near Track Road; Sacred Heart School, opened in 1946 at the corner of Aubin and Fifteenth Streets, originally as an all-French school, but converting into an all-English one by 1957; St. Mary's School at Eamer's Corners, 1952, operating as a bilingual school until 1957 when it became an all-English school; St. Paul's School, established in 1954, at the corner of Marlborough and Ninth Streets; and St. Gabriel's School, built in 1957 on Reneal Street, an all-French School which absorbed French-language students from the other parish schools of St. John Bosco Parish. Finally, in 1960, the original Roman Catholic school of this northern parish, Notre Dame, closed its doors and became the site of the amalgamated Roman Catholic School Board of Stormont, Dundas and Glengarry Counties. A new Notre Dame Senior School was built in 1959-60 on Fifteenth Street West. The great expansion in schools, then, took place in the northern area towards which so much of Cornwall's expanding population was gravitating.

In the east, parish schools at Nativity and St. Felix-de-Valois both felt the pressure of numbers, too. Nativity parish had, in 1922, under its pastor, Father Duncan MacDonald, made plans for a new convent and a brick school. The latter was to take the place of the small frame building at the corner of Edward Street and Montreal Road known as L'Ecole de Bois, that now consisted of four classrooms into which as many as 160 to 170 pupils crowded each day. When the new Nativity school opened in 1924, its enrolment swelled to 673 boys and girls. Thus it was necessary to continue using L'Ecole de Bois for the primary grades while the new school served the older students. By 1927 Nativity schools were so crowded that for the first time the rotary system, disliked by students, parents and teachers alike, was temporarily set up. It was into this situation that the new bilingual separate school inspector, S.J. Gratton, stepped in 1928. He pressed for the building of another school, St. Louis de Gonzague, which, with its twelve classrooms, became the boys' school for Nativity parish while the old Nativity School became the girls' school and the rotary system was dropped. By this time Nativity parish had swollen to over 1,300 families.

Along with this expansion of schools in the parish of the Nativity, there was also expansion eastward in the parish of St.-Felix-de-Valois. A second parish school was erected in 1944, St. Albert the Great, whose enrolment levelled off at about 200 pupils. Both parish schools as well as those of Nativity were not only separate Roman Catholic schools, labelled bilingual, they were in reality French-language schools. Similarly, the new schools of St.-Francis-de-Sales in the West End of Cornwall and one of the St. John Bosco Schools were, or soon became, largely French-language institutions as well.[8]

The financial strain of coping with so many new school buildings and the increase in the number of teachers' salaries caused a crisis for the separate school board in the early 1940s. Even with the advantage of having so many of its teachers from religious orders and consequently prepared to take much lower salaries than lay teachers, separate school boards could not keep up with the expense of the expansion process. In some instances, Roman Catholics chose the lower public school tax structure rather than continue to support the separate system by paying higher taxes.[9] The situation became so serious that the school board was close to bankruptcy and some suggested abandoning completely the Catholic schools. At a special meeting in May 1948, convoked by Bishop Rosario Brodeur, it was decided to save the schools at all costs. A policy of retrenchment was instituted. Kindergarten classes were suppressed. The number of students in each class was increased to forty-five, and religious teachers were asked to teach more at reduced salaries. Then, too, new provincial legislation eased the plight of the separate school system. Larger provincial grants were made to Roman Catholic schools, and the crisis passed.

Instead of defeatism, Cornwall's Roman Catholics took a new lease on their educational life by pushing forward with the building of schools in the east and west flanks of the city. With the founding of a new parish, Holy Cross, to serve families living nearer their work at the Courtauld's plant in the East End, a school was built on Anthony Street in 1949 even before the parish church was erected. So great was the student pressure in this area that Holy Cross soon became the largest Roman Catholic elementary school in the greater Cornwall area. By 1970 its enrolment numbered over 600 pupils housed in a twenty-two classroom school. Still another French-language school opened in the East End in 1955, Immaculate Conception, located on McConnell Avenue. Roman Catholic school expansion crested in the early 1960s with the building of St. Peter's School on Second Street East in 1963. Built to service the predominantly English-speaking families moving into the new low-rental housing project known as Glenview Heights, St. Peter's School was enlarged in 1965 to cope with an enrolment of some 260 pupils. In the West End, parents in the Riverdale area of St.-Francis-de-Sales parish applied for a separate school in 1955. When this suburb was annexed to the city in 1957, a new school was built, known as St. Anne's. Mirroring the general population of this area, St. Anne's School population of some 200 was almost equally divided between English and French-speaking pupils and represented one of the truly bilingual schools in the city.

This growth of bilingual or all French-language elementary schools reflected the steady influence of L'Association Canadienne Française d'Education d'Ontario, an agency formed in 1910 which had as its patrons Les Saints Martyrs Canadiens and as a motto, "Garde le Dépôt." Members of ACFEO, such as Joseph E. Chevrier and Daniel Danis, strove to advance Cornwall's French Canadian sector by a "vigilant protection of all (its) interests...rights and privileges".[10] The increase in bilingual schools also represented the influence of the new French organization, Société des Artisans Canadiens Français, of which the founding officers in 1916 were Joseph Chevrier, president, and Daniel Danis, executive officer. Father Duncan MacDonald of Nativity Church was chaplain.[11] By 1934 the Artisans Canadiens Français had over 200 members dedicated, among other things, to "perfecting the French language." The older St. Jean Baptiste Society of Cornwall also lent its weight to promoting bilingual or all-French schools, especially in the pre-war period. Finally, the influence of such bilingual school inspectors as S.J. Gratton and Dr. Laurier Carrière helped spur the trend towards bilingualism in the separate school system.

In addition to expansion within the elementary school system, Roman Catholics also pressed forward with immediate plans to open schools at the senior level. The Clerics of St. Viateur, who had established classical colleges at Rigaud, Joliette and the Gaspé in the province of Quebec, opened the Collège Classique de Cornwall in the fall of 1949. In this way, Cornwall reasserted its ancient status as a seat of higher learning in the province, for the new college not only prepared students for junior and senior matriculation but soon affiliated with the University of Ottawa and was able to offer degrees in philosophy and arts. Using a remodelled double house on Lawrence Avenue, the Collège Classique de Cornwall, with four teaching brothers, welcomed their first thirty-five male students. Directing the college was a former Royal Canadian Air Force chaplain, Father J.J. Downs, who had taught for twenty-seven years at the brothers' Collège Classique at Rigaud.[12] By 1955 the College had outgrown its somewhat primitive first site. With Member of Parliament Lionel Chevrier as president of the Association of the Friends of Cornwall Classical College, the Clerics of St. Viateur were able to purchase property to the east of the city limits on Windmill Point.[13] Here in a beautiful location on the bank of the St. Lawrence, the Collège Classique de Cornwall increased its enrolment to 230 students, staffed by fifteen priests.[14]

The opening of the Collège Classique meant that, for the first time, boys of French background could go to high school in an all French school, rather than move from French elementary schools into the unfamiliar English-language atmosphere of Cornwall Collegiate and Vocational School where many of them dropped out by Grade Nine, disheartened by the difficulties in meeting the English literature and grammar standards maintained by the students who had gone through the English system from early childhood. English Catholic students in Cornwall faced difficulties, too, in moving from separate elementary schools into Cornwall's public high school. For English Catholic male students, this problem had been alleviated temporarily by the founding of Gonzaga High School, but with the reversion of Gonzaga to an elementary school, all Roman Catholic students had to complete their high school education at Cornwall Collegiate and Vocational School. This procedure often meant severe educational re-adjustments for many students who found that their preparation for high school was somewhat dis-similar to that acquired by those who had followed the public school system.

Girls of French background acquired a privately-supported high school in the early 1950s when l'Académie St.-Michel opened its doors in the former old people's home known as Glen-Stor-Dun beyond the eastern boundaries of the city.[15] Operated by the Sisters of the Sacred Heart, the girls' academy started in September 1952 with eighty pupils and fourteen teachers. Like the Collège Classique de Cornwall, l'Académie St.-Michel soon had to be enlarged by ten additional classrooms to cope with increasing enrolment. This enrolment reflected the buoyant atmosphere of the Cornwall of the immediate post-war years and the 1950s period of the Seaway construction. The retrenchment and recession of the 1960s, which saw Cornwall designated a depressed area by the provincial government, played havoc with its privately supported institutions of higher learning. By 1968 the Clerics of St. Viateur were forced to close the doors of their college, and they sold their property to the government-financed St. Lawrence College of Applied Arts and Technology. L'Académie St.-Michel collapsed financially a year later. A similar fate befell Holy Cross Academy for girls. With the demise of these three vibrant institutions in Cornwall, there arose within the French community more strident demands for a publicly-financed all French high school. The more articulate took their cue from the French Language Advisory Committee formed on a province-wide basis in 1969 with the major objective of securing public French-language secondary schools.

While these developments were occurring within the separate system of Cornwall in the period prior to World War II and after, protestant churches and public schools underwent renovations and extensions to existing buildings to cope with enlarged congregations and school enrolments, though these never came near the population explosion experienced within the Roman Catholic community. This is readily evident by a comparison of Cornwall elementary school figures as follows:[16]

	Public Schools	Separate Schools
1948	932	2375
1958	2876	6144
1968	2894	6819
1978	1819	4783

Before the war all protestant children in Cornwall and its suburbs attended either Central Public School or the East Front or West Front

Township schools. Central Public School remained the sole elementary school in the town proper for almost a century. Built in 1884 at the corner of Second and Amelia Streets, Central School was enlarged in 1921 and 1931 to allow its student population to expand to a capacity of 1,000. Its imposing and well-kept schoolgrounds drew favorable comments from visitors to the city, many of whom drove past the school that faced the old No. 2 Highway connecting Montreal and Toronto prior to the completion of the Macdonald-Cartier trans-Canada highway north of the city in 1967.[17] Students at Central Public School showed their mettle during the war years when they purchased $18,611 worth of war savings stamps which was used towards the purchase of a training plane for the Royal Canadian Air Force. The plane was named the "County of Stormont" in honour of the public school children of the county who had made the purchase possible.[18]

East Front School, familiarly known as the "Red School House", was built in 1934 and was enlarged to four storeys in 1945 to house 125 pupils.[19] The West Front School had been in existence since before the turn of the century, as had Gladstone Public School on Baldwin Avenue in the East End.[20] The former closed its doors for the last time in the early 1960s. Gladstone Public School had disappeared from Baldwin Avenue long before, but another school of that name was erected at 825 McConnell Avenue in the post-war school boom.

Cornwall Collegiate and Vocational School was the pride of the town's protestant population. Growing gradually from an enrolment of 240 pupils and a staff of nine teachers in 1918 to a greatly enlarged building in 1946 with a total day and night student body of 1,100, the high school enjoyed a long stable administration from 1918 to 1939 under Principal Alexander Caldwell.[21] An Irish Presbyterian who joined the C.C.V.S. staff in 1912, Caldwell was an ardent Latin specialist and a gifted teacher who combined classical scholarship with the more practical task of teaching commercial subjects, even continuing to serve in the commercial department after he stepped down as principal. With Caldwell as head of C.C.V.S. for the longest administrative term in the school's history and another member of St. John's Presbyterian Church, Frederick MacMillan, as principal of the other major public school in town — Central — for thirty years from 1927 to 1957, leadership in the public school system in Cornwall for most of the first half of the twentieth century was securely and safely under the wing of two members of St. John's Presbyterian Church. MacMillan's successor as chief officer at Central Public

School for the next eighteen years until his retirement in 1975 was Arthur Youngs, a dedicated member of St. Paul's United Church, who chronicled the history of that congregation just as MacMillan and other members did for St. John's Church. With Christian men of this calibre at the helm in the Cornwall public school system, parents had few fears that secular humanism would run rampant in their schools.

During the war years the vocational department of Cornwall Collegiate and Vocational School played a vital role in providing the army and the city's industrial plants with skilled technicians. More than 3,000 men passed through the school taking courses in welding and radio mechanics on a three-shift basis, twenty-four hours a day. The commercial department gave crash courses as well to train men and women for the expanding corps of civil servants needed in war time.[22] At one time more than 500 military personnel from the giant Basic Army Training Camp on Marlborough Street attended night classes at C.C.V.S., stretching the staff's working capabilities to their limits. And, as many of the regular high school students went directly from their classrooms into the armed forces, there were days of sorrow when staff and students received news that boys who had been in school but a short time ago would not be returning from overseas. At war's end there were ninety-one names on the new memorial plaque erected by the Students Council.[23]

Classroom shortage was so acute in 1945 — some teachers had as many as fifty to sixty students per class — that C.C.V.S. was forced to stagger the timetable to accommodate its student population.[24] Similar overcrowding was experienced at Central Public School where it was feared that they would have to open up the third floor which had been unused and condemned as a fire hazard since 1931.[25] Demands for additional elementary public schools and extensions to C.C.V.S. thus took on a new urgency, as did requests for the establishment of a vocational and technical centre in Cornwall, put forward by the Cornwall District Rehabilitation Committee under the chairmanship of Neil Philips.[26] Particular emphasis was laid on the plight of returning veterans who needed up-grading in their skills to procure peace-time employment.[27]

Student pressure on Cornwall Collegiate and Vocational School was eased in 1950 with the opening of a bilingual high school — St. Lawrence — on the northeast corner of McConnell and Second Streets. Built to accommodate 500 students in the largely French-speaking East End, the new high school boasted several unique features. It was not only Cornwall's first bilingual public high school;

it was the first such high school in the entire province. Thus Cornwall made educational history once more. Moreover, St. Lawrence High was the only provincial high school with an agricultural department. In addition, it could award four different diplomas in commerce. When St. Lawrence High School opened its doors for the first time in September of 1950, Principal Remi Lalonde and his staff of nineteen teachers, twelve of them of French background and most of them educated at the bilingual University of Ottawa, welcomed 375 students who poured into the thirteen new classrooms.[28]

Not only was the new high school to help alleviate the shortage of space at the senior high school level, it was also to unravel the paradox existing in Cornwall whereby a segment of the French-Canadian community complained loudly and bitterly that they were being irrevocably assimilated into the English-language sector, while segments of the English community complained just as loudly, though not so bitterly, that the town was "divided by a very definite division line running the length of McConnell Street." According to these social analysts, "on the east the French population lived and on the west those of Anglo-Saxon stock. No one transgressed this cultural wall and there was little communication or positive action between the two ethnic groups."[29] Anyone who dropped around at the Canadian Legion on a Friday night for a glass of beer or spent a day at St. Francis-de-Sales School in the West End of the city knew that assimilation was not total nor cultural barriers impenetrable.

A glance at Canadian census figures for 1951 and 1961 indicates that, with annexation of the suburbs to the city in 1957, Cornwall's French sector numerically outdistanced its English-language sector, and bilingualism, rather than decreasing, took a jump forward. For instance, in 1951 there were 7,073 Cornwallites of French background, 4,602 of whom gave French as their mother tongue. Ten years later, out of 23,452 French inhabitants, 18,496 gave their mother tongue as French. With regard to bilingualism, 5,689 claimed competency in both French and English in 1951; in 1961 the number was 18,996. These statistics indicate that Cornwall's French population was far from facing extinction, either culturally or linguistically. Yet the fear and perhaps the danger of cultural extinction lingered. Indeed, anyone born on the North American continent knew that a mother tongue could be lost within a single generation. Thus, it was thought that a bilingual high school, located in the East End, and drawing young people from both language groups to a cultural and educational milieu would create a friendly bridge over cultural walls and, even if it did not halt assimilation, at least the process would be in both directions. Yet, for some members of the French-Canadian community, St. Lawrence High School was but "un premier pas" towards an ultimate objective, that of attaining an all French-language high school.[30]

By 1960 St. Lawrence High School's enrolment had shot up to 1,209 and its programme expanded to include a full technical course, designed to entice students to continue their studies after they reached sixteen. How successful the high school was in establishing its identity as a Roman Catholic bilingual high school in the first decade of its existence is indicated by the fact that Nativity Parish devoted a whole page of its souvenir album of 1960 to the school. The album was prepared in honour of the beloved Pastor of the parish, Monsignor Joseph-Azellus Brunelle, who had suffered a coronary thrombosis and announced his retirement with a simple statement, "Le Curé est pour la paroisse et non pas la paroisse pour le curé".[31] It was Monsignor Brunelle who had counselled L'Association canadienne-francaise d'Education de l'Ontario in much of its efforts to preserve French culture,[32] and the writers of the *Souvenir Album* acknowledged that the founding of St. Lawrence High School "dans les limites de sa paroisse" gave him great satisfaction.[33] Initially, then, St. Lawrence High School had been acclaimed by both French and English in Cornwall.

However, by the early 1960s criticisms were being levelled at the bilingual high school. The most frequent was that it was "still an English-language school serving a predominantly French student body".[34] Many of its students came from English-language elementary schools, often Roman Catholic ones, and it was difficult for the fluently-bilingual staff to maintain French instruction in the later grades, because English students could not always understand and the teachers would switch to English. Indeed, by 1965, apart from French language classes, only history and geography were taught in French.[35]

Whatever its shortcomings as a bilingual high school, St. Lawrence High certainly eased the pressure on Cornwall Collegiate and Vocational School. Yet the latter still had to press for expansion and renovations in anticipation of the post-war baby boom enrolment expected to hit the high school level in the late 1950s. The long-sought-for approval for the construction of an $1,160,000 addition to C.C.V.S. came from City Council in 1955. This projected a 37-room extension for 920 students and the demolition of part of the old school building.[36] For C.C.V.S. it meant an anticipated expansion in student enrolment from its 1955 figure of 853 day students to a possible 1,350 enrolment. Indeed, the projected peak enrolment was under-estimated. By 1964, C.C.V.S.'s enrolment crested at 1,724 and gradually levelled off to an average 1,450 for the remainder of the 1960s. For most of the 1970s, the student population hovered between 1,334 and 1,492. By 1982 it had settled at 1,275.[37]

Just as high school enrolment peaked and declined in the 1960s, so, too, did pressure on the elementary public school system. The city got its second public school in 1949 with the building of Memorial Park on Third and Bedford Streets, its name appropriately chosen by School Trustee C.C. Beech to honour the city's war heroes.[38] Indeed, one of them, C.E. Petepiece, who served overseas as an officer in the Canadian army, became its first principal and remained so until his retirement in 1976. The city's newest one-story public school was ready for the fall term of 1950, sporting red doors with lime, green and mauve pastel-coloured interior walls. Roughly T-shaped with four entrances, Memorial Park was the ultimate in classroom modernity. Its enrolment peaked in 1964 with over 300 students. By 1982 it had levelled off at 180.[39]

Demands for a third public school began almost as soon as Memorial Park School opened its doors. Money to buy a school site became available in 1950, but the wherewithal to erect the school did not materialize until June 1954, when the School Board was authorized to borrow $160,000 to build Sydney Street Public School between Seventh and Eighth Streets. With rooms built to accommodate at the most thirty-five students each, the six classroom school opened in January 1955 with 213 pupils.[40]

At the same time two other public schools were opened: Viscount Alexander Public School at 1401 Dover Road in the extreme West End and Vincent Massey Public School at 1520 Cumberland Street North. Enrolment at the former declined from a peak figure in 1969 of 325 to 245 in 1982. Vincent Massey's enrolment in 1982 was 214.[41] The new Gladstone Public School on McConnell Street rounded out the expansion in the public school system in the 1950s.

The era of the 1960s saw the erection of one further public school, Sir John Johnson, situated on Mohawk Drive, its name proclaiming allegiance to the man who founded the city almost two hundred years earlier. Sir John Johnson School catered not only to children living in trailer camps on the northwestern fringe of the city but also was part of the new system of busing by which pupils from the inner city were picked up early in the morning and driven to the new school where they remained the whole day, eating their lunch at the school. Teachers and students of Sir John Johnson pulled a tour de force in public relations one day in June 1961 shortly after the official opening of the school when they invited Sir John Johnson of London, England, to come to Cornwall to unveil the plaque perpetuating the name of his illustrious ancestor.[42]

School expansion in the 1960s was largely at the secondary level with the erection of the huge windowless General Vanier Secondary School at the corner of Cumberland and Fifteenth Streets at a cost of $4,744,975.[43] Designed by local architect William R. Mack, General Vanier Secondary School was ready for its first students in September of 1967. By 1979 it had 1,487 students, with a projected decline in enrolment to 976 by 1983.[44] The separate school system erected two junior high schools in 1967, Bishop MacDonell for English-speaking students and Senior Jean XXIII for French-language students.

With the closing of three French-language senior educational institutions - Collège Classique de Cornwall, Académie St-Michel and Holy Cross - in the late 1960s, students from these schools crowded into the bilingual St. Lawrence High School. The school had been experiencing a steady upward climb in its enrolment throughout the 1960s in any event, but by 1968 enrolment had reached 1,737. Two years later there were 2,116 students, giving St. Lawrence High School the largest student population in the city. This pressure of enrolment, together with the introduction of provincial legislation in 1968 permitting the establishment of public French-language high schools, stimulated the demands by French parents and clergy for a publicly-financed high school where most of the teaching would be in the French language. Among those who approached the Cornwall School Board in 1968 to ask that St. Lawrence High School be declared a French language institution were Jeannine Séguin, Clément Charette, Robert Brault, Bernard Bertrand, Rhéal Martel, Jules Renaud and Fathers Bernard Guindon and P.E. Claude.[45] The School Board accepted the principle of a separate French language school, but delayed action pending the amalgamation of the regional school boards.

By 1970, the School Board agreed to a shift system for two years, partly to ease the crowded school situation and partly to initiate what became, in effect, a French language school within the St. Lawrence High School system. A morning shift, from eight to one o'clock, was attended by about 1,350 students who were taught in English. The afternoon shift from one to six o'clock was attended by 750 students who were taught in French.[46] The French shift dropped the English half of its name and a separate administration was set up under Jeannine Séguin as principal and Jules Renaud as vice-principal.[47]

These moves caused bitterness, not only among teachers and students, but also in the wider Roman Catholic community of Cornwall, for the conflict within St. Lawrence High School was primarily among Roman Catholics. Board Trustees, teachers and students were, for the most part, Catholics. Indeed, members of the first Board of Trustees of St. Lawrence High School in 1950 were not only Catholics, they were all French as well. And the tension ran as high within the French community of Cornwall as it did in the English sector. The slogan, "Nous la voulons, nous l'aurons", (what we want, we shall have), was more frequently and stridently heard by the spring of 1973, but not all students and parents at St. Lawrence High were shouting it.[48] The president of the Parents Association, Eugène Legault, for instance, bitterly declared that it was "le groupe de francophones, sous l'influence de certains professeurs, qui auraient commencé à vouloir se séparer de l'autre groupe".[49] English-language students who had chosen to attend the East End high school in order to learn French and to mix with French students felt spurned by the wish of those French-language students who wanted the school for themselves.

Tension reached a climax on 14 March 1973 when a section of the students in the French language shift formed a committee of eight, headed by nineteen-year-old Roger Dubé, and initiated an 18-day student strike. The strike committee set up headquarters in the parish hall of Nativity Church where an assembly of parents, media and clergy pledged their support. The provincial government sent Professor Thomas Symons who mediated a settlement whereby the school building would be turned over to the French-language shift and a new high school would be built on Second Street East between Anthony and Danis Streets to house the bilingual St. Lawrence-St. Laurent High School.

By the fall of 1974 a new building was ready for the old St. Lawrence-St. Laurent High School when Principal René Brisson welcomed 932 students. Its enrolment climbed to 1,067 by 1976 and then levelled off at 751 in 1981. The all French-language high school was re-named La Citadelle, a name inspired by the writings of the French Roman Catholic writer, Antoine Saint-Exupéry. Described by vice-principal Jules Renaud as "une école dynamique et...ouverte à toute la communaute française", La Citadelle's enrolment increased from 758 in its first year to 1,070 in 1976 and by 1981 had declined to 1,004.[50] For a large segment of the French-Canadian community, it represented the fulfilment of long-sought linguistic aspirations. These had been gradually encouraged by the growth of institutions such as the magnificent Nativity Guard, organized in 1952 by Monsignor J.-A. Brunelle, and dedicated to increasing Catholic faith and Christian morals.[51] These parish right-hand men to the priest took as their motto "A Genoux devant Dieu - Debout devant les Hommes". By

1958 they had a full complement of 100 members, clad in elegant uniforms of navy jacket with yellow trim, light blue trousers with a yellow stripe down the outside, and a peak cap in navy and light blue.[52] On the occasion of their 25th anniversary in 1977, Nativity Guards, under their president, Arnold Fobert, played host to the 32nd reunion of the Gardes Paroissiales from all over the neighbouring province of Quebec, Cornwall being the only Ontario city having such an organization.[53] With their close fraternal ties to members of parish guards in Quebec, Nativity Guards kept a nice balance between their defence of the faith, their protection of linguistic aspirations and concern for the whole community of Cornwall.

Another institution that brought the French sector of Cornwall closer to their roots in the province of Quebec was the Caisse Populaire. This was a form of banking system associated with the parish. Under Monsignor J.-A. Brunelle's guidance, a branch was established at Nativity parish in 1953 and moved into the new hall in 1954. It was eventually renamed La Caisse Populaire de l'est de Cornwall. A second Caisse Populaire was established at St. John Bosco parish in 1953, becoming eventually La Caisse Populaire Nord de Cornwall.[54] These institutions, together with various other organizations such as Le Conseil de Vie Française de Cornwall, founded in 1961, under-pinned the growing militancy of Cornwall's Francophone community. Le Conseil de Vie subsequently undertook the running of the very successful and popular "La Semaine Française" each June in Cornwall. It also organized a Franco-centre on Montreal Road as a rallying point for all French-language activities in Cornwall, determined to "protect Francophone customs and traditions along with its religious character and to promote them as much as possible". With its motto, "Alone we can do little, together we can do anything", the Franco-centre attracted to its doors many of the organizations that formerly met in parish halls such as Guides and Scouts, Knights of Columbus, no. 7229, of Sainte-Croix parish, and le Club Richelieu, founded in 1948 by Fred Lefebvre as a service club specially devoted to children.[55] It was also instrumental in founding La Societe historique de Cornwall in the mid-1970s, dedicated to preserving documents relating to Francophone activities in the Cornwall area. At its head are Father C.E. Claude, Jules Renaud and Fernande DeSerres-Fobert.

The somewhat unsteady growth of a Francophone press and radio in Cornwall also spurred the aspirations of the French-Canadian community. The first French-language newspaper, *L'Avenir de Cornwall*, was founded in 1932 by Charles Michaud. The weekly five-cents a copy newspaper ceased publication in 1934 and it was not until 1950 that a second French newspaper appeared, *L'Etoile de Cornwall*. Founded by Jacques Garneau and printed at first by *Le Droit* of Ottawa, the new Cornwall Francophone newspaper was taken over by Mme. Laurier Carrière and Elphège Guindon. Father C.E. Claude of Le Collège Classique de Cornwall ran *L'Etoile de Cornwall* from 1955 to 1959 when it became a bilingual journal. In the wake of the student strike at St. Lawrence High School, a monthly magazine called *Francor* made its appearance under the initiative of Father Claude. This publication ceased in 1977. A number of Francophones then persuaded *Le Carillon de Hawkesbury* to publish *Le Journal de Cornwall*, its first issue appearing on the streets of Cornwall on 26 August 1977. With Roger Duplantie as director and André Paquette as editor, the new French weekly gained a circulation of 3,000 by 1982. By contrast, the French owners and editors of *Cornwall Weekly News*, Robert A. Brunet and Raymond Blaquière, built up their English-language newspaper from a small weekly "ad market" with a circulation in 1972 of 1,500 copies to a weekly newspaper in 1982 with a circulation of 18,000.

French-language radio broadcasting began in 1948 over CKSF when Roland Forget provided a daily hour of French programming. In 1958 Station CJSS-TV opened with a bilingual permit, giving all day broadcasts in French on Saturday until 1960. French radio station CFML was opened in 1959 under Mme Madeleine Laframboise. Then, in 1971, Bernard Bertrand secured a license for a bilingual cablevision station.

These developments in the French sector of Cornwall's schools, churches, and media in the post-war period were the most spectacular in terms of numbers of people involved and widespread prominence. The strike at St. Lawrence High School received sympathetic coverage across Canada, especially from newspapers such as the Toronto *Globe and Mail* and the Ottawa *Le Droit*. The Montreal *Gazette* gave front page coverage plus a second page to Cornwall's Francophone achievements, crediting Yolande Charron, animator of L'Association canadienne-française de l'Ontario, with much of their success, especially with regard to new recommendations by the Davis government in June 1982. With such new powers, Mme Charron believed that school administrators could now insist on the use of the French language both in and out of the classrooms at such schools as La Citadelle.[56]

Less spectacular were developments within the protestant churches in the post-war decades. St. Paul's United Church succumbed reluctantly to the jaws of the giant demolition machines in 1978, not long after one of its parishioners, Arthur Youngs, wrote a brief history of the church, ending his account with a poignant thrust, "It is OUR CHURCH,...situated on the north-east angle of a planned Downtown Redevelopment Area....Will it, of necessity, become a VICTIM of replacement, being considered an OBSTACLE to PROGRESS?"[57] The congregation's decision to sell the church to developers of a mid-town shopping complex came after much soul searching and pressure. Its last pastor, Reverend Gary Stokes, in a final moving sermon, challenged the congregation to emulate the people of Israel who, when they had to leave Egypt, took with them an ark containing the two stone tablets on which the Ten Commandments were engraved. The move for the people of St. Paul's United Church was not so distant, but it was just as heavy-hearted as they watched their church being destroyed. They made their way to Knox United Church where the people of that congregation had extended an invitation to them as early as January of 1978 "to come to Knox to worship, in case of need."[58] Knox United Church was in sound financial, spiritual and fraternal order with Robbert Pentinga in the pulpit and Robert Olding as chairman of the Congregational Board and its church membership numbered 903.[59] The two congregations continued to worship together in the church which then became Knox-St. Paul's United.

Members of the Salvation Army also found themselves rooted out of the First Street West Citadel that had been their spiritual home since 1904. Urban renewal plans for the Civic Complex in Lamoureux Park called for the removal of the Salvation Army Barracks once the historic Cornwall Canal had been filled in. Thus the Salvation Army vacated its old barracks in 1962 for a new Citadel at Fifth and York Streets. With the renaming of St. Lawrence High School in 1975, this gave Cornwall two citadels on its flanks, one guarding against cultural assimilation, the other on guard against moral contamination.[60]

The town's Anglicans increased in numbers from 1,164 at the turn of the century to 3,693 in 1961, but experienced a slight decline in numbers to 3,455 by 1971. Trinity Memorial maintained a fairly steady growth in numbers. When the church was consecrated in 1884 there were 180 families on the parish roll. In 1981 the roll contained the names of 1,599 individuals, approximately 400 families, whose yearly offerings amounted to $163,431, probably the largest of all church offerings in Cornwall.[61] Its sister church, the Church of the Good Shepherd, in the East End, had a fairly steady growth in members from 134 in 1925 to 339 in 1949. Then church membership fell off to 168 by 1969. Declining numbers at the Church of the Good Shepherd and at the St. John the Evangelist Church in nearby Lancaster prompted the two Anglican parishes to combine in 1976 as the Parish of St. Lawrence East, both churches being served by one rector.[62] An indication that the fruits of the "permissive society" of the 1960s had reached Cornwall was evident in the setting up in the parish hall of the Church of the Good Shepherd a group called "Our House", dedicated to helping young people addicted to drugs.[63]

The larger Anglican parish of Trinity Memorial in the post-war period had outgrown the small hall that had been built through the generosity of Canon J.S. Mountain in 1884 and enlarged in 1908. A three-year building campaign was started in 1951 to erect a new hall with an auditorium big enough to seat 750 for concerts and 500 people for banquets. The proposed hall was also to have sufficient Sunday School rooms, a modern kitchen, washrooms, and committee rooms. It was ready for dedication the next year. By 1979, the "new" hall had become not only the pivot for activities of Trinity Memorial people but also the centre for numerous town activities such as the Red Cross Blood Donor Clinics and the meeting place of many service organizations whose members generously contributed to additional renovations undertaken that year under its energetic rector, Reverend J. Bain Peever.[64]

Perhaps the most far-reaching development within the local Anglican churches in the 1960s was the re-direction of missionary work by the church's central governing body. Emphasis was henceforth to be placed on financial support of local ministries and projects in foreign mission fields, rather than sending missionaries from Canada. Thus foreign missions were to be weaned, just as the Cornwall mission church was in the nineteenth century, from dependence on outside missionary priests, but not necessarily from dependence on outside money. This new policy meant that the Anglican Church's most powerful women's organization, the Women's Auxiliary, would have to revamp its major commitment — that of funding missionaries to foreign countries and to Canada's far north. In 1928, for instance, the Women's Auxiliary in Canada supported thirty-four missionaries in overseas fields and paid the salaries of seventeen missionaries and seventy-six mission helpers in home fields.[65] The first inkling of this change in missionary policy came to the Women's Auxiliary at their annual meeting in 1964 when the Primate, Archbishop Howard Clark, "warned us that no organization must exist for its own sake but rather for the sake of Christ's Church". Elaborating further, the Primate said, "Individuals must continually be on guard that they do not belong to the structure long after the purpose for the structure has ceased to exist".[66]

Anglican churchwomen in Cornwall and other places took the hint and dissolved the Women's Auxiliary, for a time returning to the overall loosely-structured parish organization of the nineteenth century in which purely "women's" groups were somewhat frowned upon. At a meeting on 31 January 1966, the women of Trinity Memorial received advice from various representatives of ex-women's groups at Knox and St. Paul's churches. These churches had already undergone similar re-structuring of their various societies, and their representatives gave Trinity women the benefit of their experiences in weathering the re-organization. Delegates from as far afield as Montreal and Waterloo also tendered suggestions and encouragement for the change. After pondering the various suggestions, Trinity women chose a new organization which took the name of "Anglican Church Women". The soul-searching that went into the formation of the new structure was not without its bleak moments. One life-long devoted member of Trinity's Women's Auxiliary admitted that "the amalgamation of the various societies caused pain to some persons who withdrew and did not return to active participation".[67]

The town's Presbyterians had experienced uneven growth over the past 100 years, almost doubling in numbers from 648 in 1861 to 1,125 in 1901, but losing out in 1925 when Knox Presbyterian Church joined the United Church of Canada. Presbyterian numbers then increased steadily from 1,099 in 1931 to a peak in 1961 of 2,807. The post-war population decline began to affect their numbers and by 1971 there were 2,430. Membership at St. John's Presbyterian Church reflected this demographic picture. In 1905 there were 283 families; in 1924, 458. In 1964 the number soared to 900 and by 1981 there were 470 families and individuals connected with the church, in all 828 individual members whose yearly offerings were in the neighbourhood of $145,000.[68] Reverend Doctor W. L. MacLellan guided the St. John's flock from 1955 to 1974, when he was succeeded by Reverend Fred Rennie.

A restructuring of the whole church organization, not just women's groups, was attempted within Presbyterian ranks in the early 1970s when Cornwall Presbyterians adopted the general suggestions outlined in the Lamp Report sent to them by General Assembly. These called for setting up four committees — worship and nurture, policy and planning, mission and outreach, finance and maintenance. Representatives from various organizations at St. John's were to be included on these committees to "ensure a fair cross-section of the congregation from which well-balanced conclusions could be reached". However, the feeling soon grew that there was too much overlapping and the umbrella committees at St. John's disappeared, leaving the more traditional church structure intact.[69]

Two new Baptist congregations were established in the post-war years, taking their place beside the parent First Baptist Church. The latter had outgrown its small church at 130 Sydney Street and members made plans for an impressive new church at the corner of York and Third Streets, the cornerstone being laid in November 1960 by the wife of Prime Minister John Diefenbaker.[70] The establishment of Calvary Baptist Church on Brookdale Avenue in 1952 and of Fellowship Baptist Church, organized in 1973 with a church erected on Helen Street off McConnell Avenue North in 1980, indicated the extent of growth of Baptist members in Cornwall. While they had declined to only forty-nine in 1911, their numbers by 1931 had risen to 234 and by 1961 they numbered 627. Church figures for First Baptist Church show a corresponding pattern. In 1920 there were 150 church members. In 1960 there were 300 and their numbers peaked in 1969 at 330.[71]

The Cornwall Pentecostal Church at 507 Pitt Street began as a basement church in 1949 after brethren had worshipped in various locations since coming to Cornwall in 1923. By 1954 the church was erected above its foundations and the fellowship grew to include 130 families under the pastoral care of Reverends George Bussey and Stephen Bussey who also held services at Brookdale Shopping Plaza.[72] Another post-war protestant church was erected in Cornwall - St. Matthew's Lutheran Church, built at 1509 Second Street West. This congregation grew out of the substantial number of Lutherans who emigrated from Scandinavia and Germany in the 1950s. While the number of Lutherans had declined to only thirteen in 1941, by 1961 they numbered 183. At first they held simple worship services in private homes. After 1961 Lutheran services were conducted in the Viscount Alexander Public School in Riverdale until a church was built in 1965. In conjunction with the Reformed Church at Eamers Corners, St. Matthew's Lutheran Church undertook to sponsor one of the exiled Vietnamese families which came to Cornwall. In 1980 the congregation of about 100 secured a permanent rector, Reverend Ed Bastian.[73]

Other religious groups such as the Mormons, Jehovah Witnesses, Church of Christ and Seventh Day Adventists appeared in post-war Cornwall, probably attracting some of those who showed up in the 1971 census which, for the first time, indicated a substantial number of Cornwallites - some 565 - who openly acknowledged that they had "no religious affiliation" whatever. The Mormons increased from eleven in 1951 to ninety-five in 1971. The Seventh Day Adventists hold services at 1509 Second Street West, while the Jehovah Witnesses, who doubled in numbers from 100 in 1961 to 205 in 1971, meet to worship at 305 Thirteenth Street West. Those connected with the Church of Christ meet in their church on Tollgate Road East.

The new Roman Catholic churches to the north, east and west accounted, in part, for the decline in numbers in the older Roman Catholic parishes. For instance, Nativity Church had a total of 4,950 parishioners in 1950; 8,121 in 1970, and 3,402 in 1981.[74] Its first off-shoot, St.-Felix-de-Valois, celebrated its 25th anniversary in 1963, giving thanks to its pastors, Curé Irenée Gauthier and Vicaire Arthur Forest, both Clerics of St. Viateur. By 1982 St.-Felix-de-Valois Church, under Father Denis Laurier, a Cleric of St.-Viateur, served 640 families and 280 single persons.[75]

Further east, an offshoot of St. Felix-de-Valois emerged in 1954 - Holy Cross Parish - which originally was a bilingual one. Like its school which became the largest elementary one in the city, Holy Cross Church rapidly grew in numbers to 750 families by 1962.[76] By 1978 the parish divided when English Masses were discontinued. Services for English-speaking parishioners were temporarily held at the cafeteria of the new St. Lawrence High School until St. Peter's Church was erected still further east.[77] By 1981 Sainte-Croix, as it was henceforth known, served 786 French Roman Catholic families. A list of the parish activities indicates the scope of parish life. There were 850 of its parish children in separate schools or universities; seventy parishioners were involved in the charismatic movement; 218 members were Knights of Columbus; thirty were choral members; 121 were in the Age d'Or; forty were active in the cursillo movement; ninety were Dames de Ste-Anne; forty-eight were Daughters of Isabella; eighty-two boys and girls were in the Scout-Guide move-ment; one member was in the Pro-Life movement; 122 couples were in Marriage Encounter Groups and fifty boys served as altar boys.[78] Sainte-Croix's vigorous Catholic Women's League owed much of its impetus to Dorothy Donihee who, as provincial president in 1954, organized the parish branch. This C.W.L. branch was in the vanguard of parish social and moral issues - assisting the Hungarian Relief Fund in 1957, donating funds to a missionary priest in Chile for his Crusade of Rosaries, holding catechism classes for pupils in public schools, fighting against abortion legislation in 1974, and studying pornographic material on news stands in 1977, to mention a few.[79]

Just as vigorous were the new Catholic parishes to the north. Paroisse Saints Martyrs-Canadiens was established in 1963 to serve the north-east area of the city bounded by Boundary Road where the number of largely French-speaking parish families increased from 300 in 1963 to 340 in 1982.[80] Paroisse Christ-Roi was established in 1964 with Father Roger Desrosiers as the founding priest. This parish, whose church was built in 1968, grew to 385 families by 1982.[81]

Had John Collins and William Dummer Powell of Loyalist days been sent to the Cornwall of the 1970s, they would have been astonished at the proliferation of churches and schools in the village they had condemned for its lack of such institutions. In 1982 there were twelve protestant places of worship, one synagogue, and eleven Roman Catholic churches. Thirty-six schools dotted the landscape: eleven public elementary schools, twenty-one separate Roman Catholic ones of which fourteen were French-language schools, and four senior high schools, two English-language, one bilingual and one French-language. Nor was this the total educational picture.

By the late 1960s Cornwall had taken its place once more as a seat of higher learning when Collège Classique de Cornwall began giving post-secondary courses through its affiliation with the University of Ottawa. Its buildings at Windmill Point and its association with the University of Ottawa were taken over by St. Lawrence College in 1968 when courses in business, technology and child education were offered to some initial 150 students. By 1969 the Cornwall Adult Retraining Centre, in existence since 1961, was transferred to the new college and, in 1973, St. Lawrence College took over the Cornwall Regional School of Nursing, operating since 1966.[82] The enlarged college became the St. Lawrence College of Applied Arts and Technology.

A second post-high school training centre came to Cornwall in 1978 when the Department of Transport decided to move the Transport Canada Training Institute from Ottawa to the Loyalist city on the bank of the St. Lawrence. A unique building, using for the first time a total energy system that recovered heat generated by equipment, lighting and the sun, was erected on Montreal Road in East Cornwall, capable of housing 625 students. Marine navigators, pilots, air controllers and all personnel connected with transport technology take courses pertinent to their fields at the new Transport Institute that houses, in addition to seventy-five classrooms, some forty-five laboratories and thirty computer training areas.[83]

As Cornwall branched out into more modern areas of specialized training, one of its most honoured and ancient institutions of higher learning collapsed in 1963. The Cornwall Commercial College that first opened its doors in 1896 and produced over the next half century many of Canada's best trained secretaries survived only a year after the death of its founder, George Smith, who remained principal throughout the College's entire existence.[84]

Whatever tensions still permeated the Loyalist settlement as it approached its 200th birthday, they were not the result of a lack of schools and churches. If anything, there were too many such institutions by the late 1970s, and school boards and church bodies were contemplating closures.[85] Tensions arose not only over linguistic policies and practices within the schools and churches, but also because of modern tendencies within church and school bureaucracies such as the liturgical changes in both Roman Catholic and Protestant services, amalgamation of parish societies into new organizations with different goals than those of the more traditional ones such as missionary groups and women's auxiliaries, and the gradual inclusion of programmes such as sex education in schools and parish educational work.[86]

Cornwallites were still quarrelsome, quick to take offense at anticipated encroachments on what they regarded as their rights, and ready at a moment's notice to form committees to protest real or imaginary grievances. They were also just as ready to forget such grievances, temporarily at any rate, and crowd into St. Felix-de-Valois parish hall any night from Monday to Friday to enjoy an evening of bingo.[87] Here aging matrons of Anglo-Saxon heritage soon caught on to French numbers while their French counterparts rubbed shoulders with them in the congenial atmosphere of the 1960s and 1970s when bingo was at its height, beckoning one and all, French and English, young and old, men and women, to a night's outing at one of the numerous games being staged at various church halls around the city, the proceeds of which often went towards building new churches or parish halls. Such social gatherings would not have puzzled Collins and Powell at all. Pioneer settlers of the town had also found ways to amuse themselves on the long winter nights.

NOTES

1. *Stormont-Dundas-Glengarry Old Boys' Re-Union, 1926*, 15; Rudolph Villeneuve, *Catholic Education in Cornwall, Ontario, Yesterday, Today and Tomorrow*, 22.

2. Villeneuve, 8; *150th Anniversary of St. Columban's Parish, 1829-1979*, 39.

3. *Standard-Freeholder*, 29 June 1934.

4. *Ibid.*, 17 November 1939; Villeneuve, 22.

5. Villeneuve, 27-28.

6. *Paroisse St.-Jean-Bosco, Cornwall, 1944-1969*, 2.

7. For details on Catholic schools, see Villeneuve, 16, 18, 25-29, 32.

8. For bilingual identification, see Villeneuve, 45; for all French identification see statement in Jules Renaud, Chairman of the Stormont, Dundas and Glengarry Separate School Board, *Standard-Freeholder*, 26 March 1979.

9. Villeneuve, 18.

10. Diocesan Archives, Cornwall, see file on ACFEO.

11. *Standard-Freeholder*, 29 June 1934.

12. *Ibid.*, 13 February 1950.

13. *Ibid.*, 29 January 1955.

14. *Ibid.*, 22 June 1979.

15. *Paroisse St.-Jean-Bosco, Cornwall, 1944-1969*, 31.

16. Adapted from figures in Clive and Frances Marin, *Stormont, Dundas and Glengarry, 1945-1978*, 586 and 592.

17. For details, see Marin, 127-28; *Old Home Week, 1946*, 43; Principal David Hickey to Elinor Senior, 13 January 1982; Arthur Youngs, Central Public School, in *Cornwall Weekly News*, 21 September 1977.

18. *Standard-Freeholder*, 29 June 1944.

19. *Ibid.*, 29 August, 13 September 1945, 16 May 1946.

20. Villeneuve, 3; see also Dorothy Donihee, "In My Mother's Footsteps", 33-37.

21. Alexander Caldwell and Mary Stewart, *Cornwall Collegiate and Vocational School; An Historical Sketch*, 10; *Old Home Week, 1946*. 45; *Standard-Freeholder*, 28 September 1946.

22. *Standard-Freeholder*, 1 June 1945.

23. *Ibid.*, 30 May 1947; Caldwell and Stewart, 12.

24. *Standard-Freeholder*, 8 September 1945.

25. *Ibid.*, 2 October 1945.

26. *Ibid.*, 6 April 1945.

27. *Ibid.*, 2 November 1945 and 14 December 1945.

28. *Souvenir* of the official opening of Ecole Secondaire St-Laurent/St.Lawrence High School, June 1951.

29. Former St. Lawrence High School student John Gault's article in *Maclean's Magazine*, January 1974.

30. Jules Renaud, "L'Ecole Secondaire La Citadelle de Cornwall", 1.

31. Monsignor J.-A. Brunelle's letter to his parishioners cited in *Album Souvenir: Hommages à Mgr. J.-A. Brunelle, P.P., Curé de la Nativité de Cornwall, 1942-1960*, 59.

32. *Ibid.*, 64.

33. *Ibid.*, 41.

34. Jules Renaud, "Ecole Secondaire La Citadelle de Cornwall", 1.

35. *Ibid.*

36. *Standard-Freeholder*, 11 January 1955.

37. G.E. Armstrong to Senior, 26 April 1982; see also enrolment figures compiled by G.E. Armstrong.

38. *Standard-Freeholder*, 9 February and 5 May 1949.

39. David McCleary to Senior, 4 March 1982.

40. *Standard-Freeholder*, 5 and 12 January 1955.

41. Principal C.A. Andrews to Senior, 19 January 1982; Principal T.D. Magee to Senior, 25 May 1982.

42. *Standard-Freeholder*, 22 June 1961.

43. *Ibid.*, 27 December 1966.

44. *Ibid.*, 26 March 1979.

45. Jules Renaud, "Ecole Secondaire La Citadelle de Cornwall", 1-2.

46. *Globe and Mail*, Toronto, 24 March 1973.

47. Jules Renaud, "Ecole Secondaire La Citadelle de Cornwall", 3-4.

48. *Ibid.*, 4.

49. *Le Droit*, Ottawa, 22 March 1973.

50. Jules Renaud, "Ecole Secondaire La Citadelle de Cornwall", 5.

51. *Souvenir Album: Hommages à Mgr. Brunelle*, 43.

52. *Standard-Freeholder*, 28 June 1958.

53. Message of Ed Lumley, M.P. for Stormont-Dundas, to Nativity Guards, *25th Anniversaire, Garde Nativité 1952-1977*, Cornwall, 9.

54. *Souvenir Album: Hommages à Mgr. Brunelle*, 48; Paroisse St.-Jean-Bosco, Cornwall, 1944-1969, 19; Jules Renaud to Senior, 14 February 1983.

55. For Franco-centre see account by Jules Renaud; for Le Club Richelieu, see *Standard-Freeholder*, 17 February 1949, 3 January 1972; see also *Album Souvenir: Hommages à Mgr. Brunelle*, 65.

56. *Gazette*, Montreal, 5 June 1982.

57. Arthur Youngs, "St. Paul's United Church", 9 February 1978.

58. *Knox United Church, Annual Report, 1978*, 7.

59. *Ibid.*, 23.

60. *Standard-Freeholder*, 15 March 1973.

61. *Souvenir Booklet: Trinity Parish Church Building Campaign, 8 April 1951*; see also, Statistical Returns, Trinity Memorial Church, 1 January to 31 December 1981.

62. Reverend G.H. Worden to Senior, 3 May 1982.

63. *Ibid.*

64. *Trinity Memorial Church Hall 1952, Renovation 1979*, 2.

65. Winifred Jerrom, "Our Story: W.A. and A.C.W."

66. *Ibid.*

67. *Ibid.*

68. Reverend Fred H. Rennie to Senior, 11 May 1982.

69. Fred MacMillan et al, "History of St. John's Church, Cornwall, 1787-1975", 41-42.

70. L. Jean Cameron, First Baptist Church, 1882-1967, 11-12.

71. Myrla Scott to Senior, 27 August 1982.

72. Reverend S. Bussey to Senior, July 1982; *Standard-Freeholder*, 10 August 1979, see advertisement on church page.

73. T. Matlachowski to Senior, 15 April 1982.
74. Fernande DeSerres-Fobert, Historique de la Paroisse de la Nativité depuis sa fondation, see statistical charts in appendix.
75. Father Denis Laurier to Senior, July 1982.
76. *Le Journal de Cornwall*, 28 September 1979, 21.
77. *Ibid.*, 18.
78. Status animorum of the parish for 1981.
79. *Le Journal de Cornwall*, 28 September 1979, 16-17.
80. Father Jacques Houle to Senior, July 1982.
81. Denise Giroux to Senior, 30 April 1982.
82. *Standard-Freeholder*, 21 December 1962; 20 December 1966.
83. *Ibid.*, 29 November 1973.
84. *Ibid.*, 25 January 1947; Marin, 350-51.
85. See, for instance, *Standard-Freeholder*, 26 March and 16 May 1979.
86. For sex education at the parish level see, for example, *Trinity Memorial Church Hall 1952, Renovation 1979*, 2.
87. For bingo notices see *Paroisse de la Nativité de la B.V.M. Cornwall, 1887-1962: 75th Anniversaire*, 23; and *25 Ans D'Histoire pour la Paroisse Sainte-Croix* in *Le Journal de Cornwall*, 28 September 1979.

Nativity Church, 1970's (Eglise de la Nativité de la B.V.M.).

Credit: Societe Historique de Cornwall.

St. Felix de Valois, 1983.
Credit: Societe Historique de Cornwall.

St. Columban's, 1983.
Credit: St. Columbans Parish.

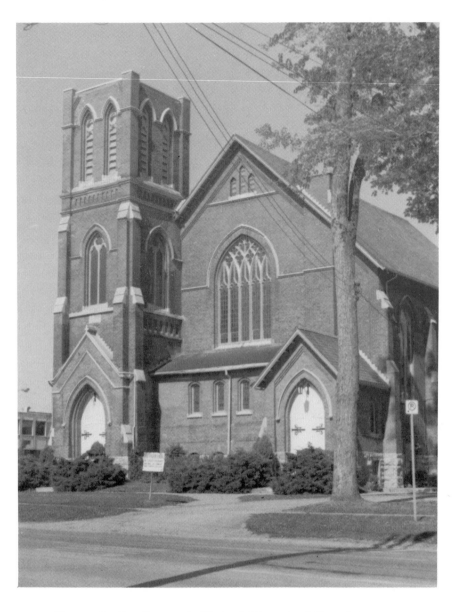

Knox - St. Paul's 1970's (United Church of Canada).
Credit: Heritage Cornwall.

Chapter XXI

Cornwall's New Image

Cornwall's self-image in the early 1960s was anything but positive. Tagged by the federal government as a "depressed" area needing tax incentives to attract new industries after the end of the Seaway construction and the closing of Canadian Cottons, the city saw a new generation of some 5,100 young people arrive on a jobless market.[1] For a time Cornwall had the unenvied record of having the highest percentage of unemployed of any city in Ontario.[2] These job-seekers lined up at the unemployment bureau and began to frequent the welfare agencies, unwillingly but gradually assuming a "handout" mentality.[3]

Such a mentality was far different from that prevailing in town for the past two hundred years. Yet it bore a marked resemblance to the attitude of the Loyalist founders of the town who had had to depend on the bounty of the British government for almost a decade while they awaited the outcome of the American revolutionary war and then began the process of re-settling on pioneer lands such as Cornwall. During this time the Loyalists had become such experts in the art of applying for handouts, that the government had to take a firm, unpopular but salutary step in cutting off all subsidies, thus forcing the Loyalists to pull up their bootstraps and become self-sufficient. Many were reduced to lower standards of living than they had been accustomed to, but eventually they established a viable and, for some generations, a thriving economy in Cornwall.

Part of this thriving economy had been the cotton textile mills. When they closed in 1959, there was a tendency both in Cornwall and at the federal level to link the demise of the cotton mills with the loosening of trade regulations that allowed foreign textiles easier access to the Canadian market. Thus, in the immediate wake of the textile debacle in Cornwall, federal leaders, accused of being partly to blame, were inclined to favour incentives or subsidies for industries planning to locate in Cornwall. Other sectors in Cornwall itself tended to look increasingly towards City Hall to solve economic difficulties. One aspect of this expectation was that City Hall could and should undertake long-term economic planning by buying up potential industrial sites and providing them with sewage and water facilities so as to attract new labour-intensive industry.

City Hall did provide impetus towards economic recovery though it took almost a generation before fully-serviced industrial parkland was available at $5,000 an acre, the cheapest in Eastern Ontario.[4] But providing such facilities and industrial sites is not done overnight. City Hall set up a Cornwall Planning Board as early as 1951, composed of eight members appointed by Council, with the Mayor as an ex-officio member.[5] Citizens of the calibre of Dr. J.A. Phillips, Wilfred Kaneb, S. Smolkin, L.P. Gosselin, Dorothy Donihee, E.J. Legault, Ernest Booth, Raymond Lefebvre, George Charlebois and M. Jean Cameron devoted time and talent to considering ways and means to make Cornwall a more agreeable place to live in, both as a place of work and as a home town.[6]

With annexation in 1957, the city's administration expanded to include professionals such as a chief administrative officer, an industrial commissioner and a city planning expert. Thus, side by side with the elected Councillors, there grew up an enlarged bureaucracy which began to assume some of the duties previously handled by Council committee heads. The extension of the city's boundaries beyond the original one mile square also meant a re-shaping of wards for electoral purposes. Over the nineteenth century there had been a slight change from two wards to three: East, Centre and West. Then, when city status was attained in 1945 a fourth ward was created by dividing Centre Ward in two. In 1957 came the final division into six more or less oblong wards reaching from Highway 401 down to the river banks.

Businessmen headed the municipal hierarchy for most of the years from the early depression to the present. Aaron Horovitz returned three times as mayor throughout the thirties, forties and fifties for a total of eighteen years as chief magistrate. Hotelman Nick Kaneb ruled the roost all through the sixties, except for two years when the popular obstetrician, Dr. Elzéar Emard, was mayor. Then another businessman, a thirty-three-year old native of Windsor, Ontario, Ed Lumley, was persuaded to tackle the job in 1972 at a time when the city's economy had again taken a turn for the worse.[7] Lumley had settled in Cornwall in 1964 as a partner in a soft-drink vending company, fast attracting attention as a responsible family man, full of energy and optimism. When Lumley moved from municipal office to even tougher tasks at the federal level as Member of Parliament for Stormont and Minister of Trade, his place as mayor was filled by another businessman, fifty-six-year old Gerald Parisien. Cornwall-born Parisien had been an independent merchant for twenty-five years following four years' service overseas with the Royal Canadian Artillery. As President of the Cornwall Retail Merchants' Association, Parisien was urged to enter municipal politics in 1959 as candidate for Ward 4, the central section of the city. He has been at City Hall ever since. Even during the five years from 1970 to 1975 when he was not serving on Council, Parisien was news editor and political analyst for Radio Station CJSS and thus covered City Council.[8]

When Nick Kaneb became Mayor in 1961 he faced the challenge of raising public morale for Cornwall's citizens were shattered by the turnabout situation of finding their city a "depressed" area. Kaneb was well aware of its problems. Coming to Cornwall from Massachusetts as a child of four, he had been brought up and educated in Cornwall, going on to Clarkson College and McGill University for post-secondary education. His administrative talents were early recognized. Besides heading the Cornwall Board of Trade, the Lions Club and the Cornwall Curling Club, he became chairman of the Eastern Ontario Development Organization and president of the Ontario Hotel Association.[9]

With such a background and a six-year apprenticeship as alderman, Kaneb captured the mayor's chair just as the bottom fell out of the job market. Among other things, the forty-five-year old mayor is credited with attracting fourteen new industries to town that directly or indirectly provided 2,000 jobs and thus erased Cornwall's image as a "depressed" area by 1965.[10] Under Kaneb, major harbour developments were undertaken and the first tourism promotion council established, as well as the adult retraining centre.[11] Kaneb was on hand, too, for the opening of the $306,000 civic recreation centre on the east side of the Athletic Grounds in 1961.[12] The centre was named the Bob Turner Memorial Centre in honour of the city's first full-time recreation director, who had died suddenly in 1962.[13]

Along with the rest of Canada, Cornwall perked up for the 1967 Centennial celebrations marking the country's 100th birthday. An Old Home Week from June 30 to July 9 was organized during which Queen Elizabeth and Prince Philip made a twenty-minute cavalcade tour through town, greeting Stormont Member of Parliament Lucien Lamoureux, Mayor and Mrs. Kaneb, and others before boarding the Royal yacht, *Britannia*, which was berthed in Cornwall Harbour.[14] This time there was no fog to throw the programme out of kilter, as there had been in 1959. The city's special centennial project was the Simon Fraser Centennial Library whose greatly expanded facilities superseded the old Cornwall Library. Born amid centennial celebrations in Cornwall, too, was the Centennial Choir, which went on to win numerous honours at music festivals in Ottawa and Toronto and then in 1977 won top honours as the best amateur choral group in Ontario. Founded by R. Brian McCartney, head of the Music Department of Cornwall Collegiate and Vocational School and General Vanier Secondary School, the choir drew its original members from the A Capella Girls' Choir of CCVS and the Edgar Shaw Hansen Singers. In 1976 the choir performed at the international Eisteddfod at Llangollen in North Wales.

It was during Kaneb's mayoralty that Courtaulds Limited pulled ahead briefly as Cornwall's key industry, expanding into tufted carpets, polystyrene insulating board and the production of nylon yarn, though it closed out its fibreglass boat division in 1961.[15] Dwindling sales forced Courtaulds to discontinue rayon yarn production in June 1969, a hard decision for President N.I. Battista, a Cornwall man, educated in city schools. The closure meant the end of jobs for 650 employees.[16] Courtaulds then relocated its Montreal-based Versatile Knitting Division in Cornwall in 1973, but the market for stretch-knit fabrics folded, and by 1976 this division ceased production. Other products proved just as short-lived. The ten-year-old nylon process was phased out in 1974 and in 1980 Caravelle Carpets closed, leaving the Courtaulds operations greatly curtailed. From a workforce in the 1940s and 1950s of over 2,000, the plant had dwindled down to 899 in 1979.[17] Employees at Courtaulds watched management's efforts to diversify production, satisfied that the company was doing its best to keep the Cornwall plant operating despite the business recession. Labour relations remained stable since the late thirties and strikes were unheard of.

Cornwall's emerging industrial giant, the Howard Smith Paper Mill (Domtar) that had changed hands in 1957 and by 1966 had installed two new huge paper machines, began to experience labour problems in the 1960s. A short strike erupted in May 1962, the first at the plant since 1919.[18] Strikes occurred again in June 1967 and January 1968, the latter precipitated by the arrival of efficiency experts, brought in from Chicago to study plant operations. Workers in the shipping, mailing and finishing departments walked off the job, complaining that they were not receiving fair work schedules and loads.[19] As the efficiency experts left the plant they were booed by strikers who shook their car and warned them not to come back. Like the one-day strike in 1967, this wildcat strike was quickly settled. A conciliator from the Department of Labour was called in after Mayor Nick Kaneb orchestrated a conference between union and company officials.[20]

Far more serious was the 188-day strike in 1975-76 when Domtar net earnings dropped from $35,000,000 in 1975 to $10,600,000 in 1976.[21] Workers walked off the job in mid-September 1975 and remained off until late in March 1976, adamant in their job security demands to retain in the work contract the seniority clause "last man in, first man out".[22] As the town's largest single employer, anything affecting Domtar affected the whole city. Time and again Mayor Gerald Parisien intervened to bring union and company officials to the negotiating table. Two of his own aldermen, Matthew Holden and Aimé Leblanc, were among the strikers.[23] Federal Minister of Labour John Munro met with members of the Canadian Papermakers' Union in late November, assuring them that the paper company must not refuse negotiations on the grounds of the federal wage and price control programme.[24] Behind the scenes in Ottawa, Stormont-Dundas's M.P., Ed Lumley, worked urgently and effectively to bring company and union officials to the negotiating table. At another level, the Member of the Provincial Parliament, George Samis, and the editor of the *Standard-Freeholder* urged the Ontario Minister of Labour to attempt a settlement.[25]

For the 1,300 on picket lines in Cornwall it was a cold and dreary Christmas season in 1975. Not only was the Domtar workforce out; so, too, were employees of Dominion Tape and MCA Records (Compo).[26] The Domtar offer in January 1976 of a 14 percent wage increase in the first year, 8-1/2 percent in the second and 8 percent in the third year, without a cost of living allowance, was rejected by strikers, but by February workers reduced their wage demands.[27] On 23 March news of a strike settlement was received by all Cornwallites with thankfulness. The controversial seniority clause remained unsettled, but a cost of living allowance was retained in the new contract which was retroactive to 1 April 1975, giving the workers on the average an extra $600.

The employees of the MCA Record Company, a subsidiary of Decca and the Music Corporation of America, were out on strike even longer than Domtar workers - over 194 days. The workers, whose spokeswoman was Denise Martineau, treasurer of Local 539 of the International Union of Electrical, Radio and Machine Workers, were militant. Headlines such as "Welfare Looks Good to Cornwall Workers" and "Company Can Pack Up and Leave" were ominously prophetic.[28] When workers rejected a company offer of a 45 percent wage increase, Vice-president Richard Bibby announced in February 1976 that the firm would close its Cornwall operations "because of insoluble labour problems".[29] The plant had opened in 1963 and received an Ontario Development Grant in 1969, its workforce expanding at times to as many as 400. In announcing the closure, Bibby said that his product could be produced cheaper elsewhere.[30] He raised the question of Canadian productivity in relation to that of American, saying that a recent settlement in a United States record plant was lower than the final offer he had made to his Cornwall employees.[31]

This question of lower Canadian productivity compared to American standards had also been raised during the Domtar strike when Manager William Welsh suggested that Domtar was having difficulty in competing with American paper companies because Americans made "fine paper better, faster, and cheaper than in Canadian mills like Cornwall".[32] Union leaders such as Wilfred Oliver, national negotiator for the Canadian Paperworkers' Union, discounted such claims as "Hogwash" and feared that they were "destroying the morale of workers".[33] Bitterness lingered after the lengthy and costly strike. The Montreal *Gazette* added its own barb some months after the settlement by suggesting that the company allowed the strike to drag on because it had large inventory on hand and sales demand was down.[34]

An uncertain market after the strike settlement added to economic anxieties and forced Domtar to lay off temporarily 1,000 workers in November 1976, thus vindicating the workers' fears about job security.[35] Still, the viability of the Cornwall papermill was evident to employees such as the Loyalist descendant Fred Empey. Empey took to the columns of the *Standard-Freeholder* in January of 1977 to proclaim that both pride and loyalty were strong among Domtar's employees.[36] By 1979 the governments of Ontario and Canada signed a $15,750,000 agreement with Domtar to modernize its pulp and paper making facilities at Cornwall and at two other mills. In addition, Domtar announced a five-year $112 million dollar capital investment programme, in which the Cornwall mill, the company's largest, would be one of the prime benefactors.[37]

In less than a year millhands were out on strike once more. Seven long months dragged on from late October 1980 until 26 May 1981 before contract negotiations were settled and the paper machines began to roll once more. For the people of Cornwall the end of the longest strike in the city's history brought a release from pent-up tension and hopes that Domtar sales staff could coax back old customers and find new ones. For no matter how much city planners and federal and regional industrial experts might aspire to the ideal economy of diversified industry, Cornwall's major bread basket is a huge pile of wood chips. As these blow across Second Street in an overhead eighteen-inch pipe at the speed of ninety miles an hour to feed the giant digesters and paper machines so that Domtar workers keep up an annual output of 235,000 tons of fine paper every year, Cornwallites put up with the occasional odour that fills the air. Old-timers look askance at pamphlets put out by the company's environmental specialists who promise that such air and water pollution will be controlled. "When we don't smell the papermill, then we know we're in trouble", the oldsters insist, with a wry wink. Millhands agree. In 1982 some 1,482 carried home $48,000,000 in annual wages from the paper mill, indifferent to the occasional smell caused by upsets in mill machinery. City Hall will welcome the eventual elimination of paper mill odours in town, but it welcomes even more the growing revenue from the mills, some $1,500,000 in taxes in 1982.[38]

It was against this background of economic recession and labour unrest that Kaneb's administration established a civic task force to study the city's economy and unemployment problem. In its initial report in the fall of 1970, the task force urged that Cornwall be designated "a slow-growth area", a recommendation that neither the federal Minister of Economic Development, Jean Marchand, nor the editor of the Standard-Freeholder found acceptable. At a dinner at the Cornwallis Hotel in November 1970, Marchand laid it on the line to Cornwall business and municipal leaders, saying it was time for Cornwall to do something for itself. He promised that federal incentives to industry would be available for Cornwall if those incentives were to be a decisive factor in any company's decision to locate there.[39] The editor of the Standard-Freeholder derided the suggestion that Cornwall be declared a slow-growth area. "This is hand-out thinking of the worst sort, the kind of thinking which has sapped Cornwall's strength since the closing of the Cornwall Canal and the opening of the Seaway", he thundered.[40]

The civic task force's more positive recommendation was to expand the budget and staff of the industrial commissioner, W. Laurier Courville, who had taken on the onerous job in 1969. By freeing Courville from non-industrial promotion duties, the civic task force expected that the industrial commissioner could put forth all his efforts in pursuing new industries for the city. A direct result of the civic task force's report and the visit of the federal Minister of Economic Development was a study, not of Cornwall's economic problems, but of Cornwall's industrial opportunities, a step away from the negative thinking of the sixties.

Undertaken at the behest of the Department of Regional and Economic Expansion, the study was done by management consultants of Price Waterhouse Associates, operating out of Ottawa. A team of eight men arrived in town in January 1971 to interview more than 100 business, community and government leaders. By August their report reached Mayor Kaneb's desk. Most people, institutions and even cities cannot bear too close a scrutiny without a few imperfections being noticed. Cornwall was no exception. The first general criticism by the management consultants was that Cornwall was not aggressive enough in getting "its fair share of new industries", in comparison to similar Ontario communities. Although they emphasized that the successful growth of the city was the responsibility of all the people, not just the civic government, the Price Waterhouse consultants made it clear that the city's industrial commissioner must take the lead as "marketing" agent not only of industrial sites but of the community as a whole. This meant that Cornwall must attract potential industry by an image of a progressive community with alert, capable and socially-responsible community leaders, the very qualities which corporate industry was expected to show once it locates in any urban community.[41]

Coming in an election year, the $75,000 report probably led to the downfall of Kaneb's administration. The *Standard-Freeholder* remarked that the "city's record has been anything but impressive... even with the generous federal and provincial incentives...available in the Cornwall district", and suggested that "the planning and super-salesmanship needed to bring new jobs to Cornwall has been lacking."[42] Six years earlier the same media had praised Kaneb for the number of new industries he had attracted to Cornwall.[43]

The new broom that was to sweep away Cornwall's defeatist attitude and ghost-town image was the man for whom the word "defeat" did not exist. Ed Lumley swept into office as mayor in 1972, convinced that "Cornwall can and will blossom forth as one of Ontario's most progressive cities. We must never look back, but ahead with all the enthusiasm and energy at our disposal."[44] Unpretentious and hard-working, Lumley recognized unemployment as Cornwall's number one problem. "Over twice the national average and three times the provincial average," he admitted frankly.[45] He pointed to the lack of new industries - 100 requests in eighteen months but no firm commitments. As for taxes, he acknowledged that Cornwall's were already one of the highest in the country and increasing, just to keep up with current expenses. His six-point plan of action to remedy the ills and set priorities echoed many of the recommendations of the Price Waterhouse Report. After an immediate review and analysis of the city's industrial development policies and practices, he wanted top selling personnel on all potential industrial projects with a special impetus on the expansion of local industry and a re-evaluation of the tourist industry. The new mayor also pledged himself to create a "new spirit of teamwork on City Council" which, in turn, would generate a spirit of enthusiasm throughout the city.[46]

Seldom has a city accepted more fully the professional advice it sought. Throughout the three years that Lumley headed the city's administration, most of the major recommendations of the Price Waterhouse Report were put into force. Council was reorganized and the city's industrial development programme revamped immediately.[47] In his appraisal of the first three months of his administration, Lumley spoke of the cooperation and enthusiasm of all sectors in the city, particularly that of the local and national press which "have replaced the tarnished image of the past with one of (Cornwall's) progress", so much so that prospective industries had noticed the change. The Federal representative, the Honourable Lucien Lamoureux, Speaker of the House of Commons, and provincial representative Fern Guindon, both provided wholehearted support with the result that "persons on unemployment and welfare are on the decline".[48]

The Cornwall Royals were part of Cornwall's improved image. Just as the new mayor was jubilantly announcing an upward swing generally, Cornwall's junior hockey team won the Quebec Junior Hockey League championship and went on to bring home the Canadian championship that fall when they defeated the Peterborough Petes and the Edmonton Oil Kings in Ottawa for the Memorial Cup.[49] This national hockey triumph stirred Cornwall as few other events have since the old Cornwall Flyers had battled their way to victory over the Ottawa City League, the Ottawa District League, the Ontario League and finally the Eastern Canada Championships to reach the Allan Cup finals in 1937-38.[50] If their hockey team, which began the season near the bottom in 1972, could put Cornwall on the winning map across Canada, so could the city. The *Standard-Freeholder's* A. Cunningham epitomized the changed outlook in a cartoon captioned "The Last Shall be first! The Good Book lets us know - Orv Tessier and His Royals Really Proved it So!!!"[51]

Industrial Commissioner Laurier Courville struck an optimistic note, too, in his report to the citizens by way of the *Standard-Freeholder's* 1972 annual industrial edition. Courville pointed out that the unemployment figure peaked at 18.5 percent in 1971 at a time when 1,500 local students were flooding the labour market looking for summer work, a timely reminder that computerized and fluctuating statistics, as useful as they are, can sometimes be the source of undue concern. On the bright side, Courville reported that St. Lawrence

College had the best employment record in Canada in 1971. All its graduates had found work. Even Prime Minister Pierre Elliot Trudeau waxed whimsical in his 1972 message to the people of Cornwall, quoting the first lines of Dickens's *Tale of Two Cities*: "It was the best of times, it was the worst of times...it was the spring of hope, it was the winter of despair".[52]

By March 1973 Mayor Lumley's annual report to the people of Cornwall radiated confidence and hope. Unemployment had dropped to 15 percent and at one time during the year had been down to 10 percent. There had been a 37 percent increase in construction and by the end of 1973 it was expected that the new industrial park would be fully serviced and thus more attractive to industry. The city's decision to hire a full time city planning expert and actively promote tourism were part of Lumley's overall plan to revitalize the city.[53] He praised the efforts of Member of Parliament, Honourable Lucien Lamoureux, in securing federal grants through the Department of Regional Economic Expansion. These grants went towards expansion in such plants as Howards and Son, Morbern, which manufactured polyurethane-coated fabrics, Prince Clothes, and Sovereign Seat Covers. DREE grants also contributed towards luring several new firms to Cornwall: Pellon, Cornwall Appliances, Versatile Knitting and Levi Strauss. Pellon and Levi Strauss proved enduring, while the two other DREE-supported ventures collapsed.[54]

Just as important was the hint in Lamoureux's annual report to Cornwallites that the Act establishing the Department of Regional and Economic Expansion allowed, in addition to federal industrial incentives such as Cornwall already received, "infra-structure" assistance, a new phrase that was soon on every tongue in Cornwall and with good reason. Lamoureux described precisely how the people of Cornwall could go about getting such infra-structure grants. If the city was designated a "special area" by both federal and provincial governments, then it could apply for even more generous grants to help with the planned Civic Complex - a venture partly spurred by the Royals' triumph, and such other projects as the plan to reclaim the canal lands that eventually became one of Cornwall's beautiful riverside parks named in honour of the man who did so much to procure the wherewithal to turn the waterfront into "Lamoureux" Park. Lamoureux urged that citizens' groups work closely with elected representatives at the three levels of government - municipal, provincial and federal. "This is the challenge which has to be met," he said, "if the Cornwall area is to have any chance to solve its employment and other economic problems in the immediate future."[55]

Before the year was out, Mayor Lumley had learned all about infra-structures. *Standard-Freeholder* headlines on 26 February 1974 announced, "Cornwall Strikes it Rich". Federal and provincial infra-structure grants totalling $14,169,000 were to pour into the city over the next three years to build the Civic Complex, service the canal lands, turn Water Street into a four-lane highway, complete sewer and road services to the city's industrial plaza and develop into a recreational area the 500 acres of former Loyalist land in the West End, known as Hydro lands, and re-named to honour Member of Provincial Parliament Fern Guindon. Cornwall was the first Canadian city to benefit from the infra-structure programme, costs of which were to be shared equally by the Ontario and Canadian governments. Nor was this all the good news. Coupled with the announcement of the infra-structure grants was the hint that an industrial incentive of $3,400,000 was to be spent to provide services for a new industry to be built in the West End, described by Lamoureux as "one of the largest and most desirable industries for this whole area." Although policy dictated that the name of the prospective firm would not be made public until all negotiations were settled, Cornwallites knew within a few weeks that it was Combustion Engineering that would locate in Cornwall's West End and provide eventually employment for a possible 1,000 workers.[56] When to all this was added the announcement the previous fall that the new $50,000,000 Transport Canada Training Institute would be located in Cornwall, bringing 350 teaching and administrative staff to the city as well as employing 100 to 150 local staff, Cornwall's cup of good fortune was running over.[57]

The city continued in a state of euphoria throughout the year. Mayor Ed Lumley could not believe that the infra-structure dream had come true. "Had someone told me two or even one year ago that we'd get $14 million, I would have told him he was crazy".[58] The long hours put in by the mayor and his administrators, including particularly Alderman Douglas Webster, City Engineer Charles Adams and City Treasurer Robert Hamilton, in preparing the brief, had paid off. Indeed, Don Jamieson, the federal minister responsible for the Department of Regional and Economic Expansion, described the brief as a masterpiece and one that other municipalities should use as a model.[59] Along with the prospect of federal and provincial funding for Cornwall's downtown face-lifting operations and industrial expansion came the pleasing news that the city's unemployment rate had dropped to 6 percent, the lowest in years.[60]

So impressed were federal Liberal leaders at Mayor Lumley's handling of the infra-structure negotiations and his leadership in raising morale in Cornwall's business and industrial circles that they urged him to run as Liberal candidate for the Stormont riding when its incumbent of the past twelve years, the Honourable Lucien Lamoureux, resigned to accept the post as Canadian Ambassador to Belgium and Luxembourg. Thus Cornwall municipal politics again proved a stepping off stage for entry into the larger stage of federal politics. For the energetic mayor of Cornwall it meant a dual job for a short time as he continued to occupy the mayoralty seat after winning the Stormont seat. He then went on to capture the Stormont seat in each subsequent election, moving up rapidly as Chairman of the House of Commons Steering Committee on Regional Development, then as secretary to the minister of Regional Economic Expansion and to the Minister of Finance, and was appointed Minister of State for Trade on 3 March 1980.[61] Thus Cornwall and Stormont's liaison with the corridors of power in Ottawa remained intact and, at the federal political level, the area maintained its age-old reputation: as Stormont goes, so goes the nation.

While Lumley was on hand at the federal level to keep an eye on Cornwall's interests, his place at City Hall was filled by Gerald Parisien whose long apprenticeship as alderman throughout the sixties gave him a thorough grounding in municipal politics. Not only had he served as chairman of the Industrial, Public Works and Labour Relations committees, he also served on the Finance, Parks and Recreation, and Traffic committees as well. The administration he took over was composed of a Council of twelve, elected every three years, and a bureaucracy that increased from thirty-four in 1972 to thirty-eight in 1982. The larger city organization beyond City Hall includes 470 employees. These, together with City Hall staff, take home a total annual pay of $13,236,750.[62]

Of the twelve aldermen in 1983, four are involved in teaching - Dick Aubry, Guy Leger, Brian Lynch and Earl Myers; two are women - Terri Lalonde, manager of the Seaway Valley Tourist Council, and Jan Samis, wife of Member of Provincial Parliament George Samis; five, including the mayor, are or have been associated with business or industry - Francis Guindon, Angelo Lebano, Aimé Leblanc, Ray Lalonde, and Gerald Samson; and one is a lawyer - William Wise. These aldermen meet the second and fourth Monday of each month in the Council Chambers to debate current policies, enact municipal laws and administer the annual revenue of close to $43,000,000.[63] The city's seventeen separate departments are under the general supervision of Chief Administrator Charles F. Adams. Departmental heads in 1983 are Frank McDonald, Commissioner of Finance; G. Walsh, Commissioner of Development; Richard Allaire,

City Clerk; Laurier Courville, Assistant to the Chief Administrator; Michael Otis, Director of Planning; W.L. Moskowitz, Director of Economic Development; William A. Knight, Director of Engineering Services; Hugh O'Reilly, Fire Chief; S. Seguin, Director of Public Works; Si Miller, Director of Parks and Recreation; Miss F. Flanigan, Director, Social Services; R.N. Douglas, Director of Personnel; F. Lyonnais, Comptroller; Ed Landry, Chief of Police; Gordon S. Robertson, Transit Manager; and William Upper, Manager, Civic Complex. Had Cornwall's first municipal body, the 1834 Board of Police, been able to look into the future to foresee the enormous expansion from four elected representatives and a city bureaucracy of about fourteen to a Council of twelve and a city organization of 508 employees by 1983, they would scarcely have credited what they saw.

In the eight years since Parisien has headed the city's administration, there has been unprecedented commercial growth in the downtown area. Pitt Street Mall, the pet project of businessman George Assaly, opened in September 1978, diverting traffic to the east and west so that shoppers and strollers could enjoy the treed and fountained downtown mall.[64] Two years later Cornwall Square shopping centre opened on the east side of Pitt with forty-nine different shops spaciously occupying the huge shopping complex.[65] Designed to keep in Cornwall much of the estimated $25,000,000 being spent annually in shopping centres in Montreal and Ottawa, Cornwall Square is part of Cornwall's new progressive image.[66] Oldtimers regretted the loss of St. Paul's Church and other familiar landmarks to the east of Pitt Street, but industrial developers and urban promoters saw the re-vitalized downtown area as one of their ace cards in attracting industry.

Along with this downtown commercial expansion, two other shopping malls had already been established - Brookdale Mall Shopping Plaza in the West End, which underwent a $5,000,000 expansion programme in 1979, and the Eastcourt Mall.[67] Yet, recession stalked the path of commerce in the early 1980s. Mayor Parisien, who became president of the Association of Municipalities of Ontario, encouraged worried businessmen to "hang on". Cornwall was the "shopping mecca" for Eastern Ontario...."When the recession ceases, we'll be OK", insisted the mayor whose administration has been marked by such sound fiscal policies that the city's credit listing earned the coveted AA rating.[68]

The slump in retail sales in 1982 was coupled with the closure of two textile firms that had located in the new industrial plaza just seven years earlier - Riverside Yarns and Cornwall Spinners.[69] Cornwall

Spinners was a carpet factory erected over 1974-75 by Mussa H. Amlani and his sons after their parent plant had been nationalized by the Bangladesh government.[70] Riverside Yarns was a Canadian-owned company whose Cornwall plant made texturized synthetic yarn mainly for the Dupont plant at Coteau-du-Lac. In spite of difficult market conditions, both firms enjoyed a moderate expansion until 1980. Their closures in 1982 threw about 600 Cornwallites out of work.[71]

Cornwall labour leaders joined with textile manufacturers' representatives, retailers and other union leaders in an unprecedented show of solidarity to urge the federal government to impose import quotas on textiles. Courtaulds general manager, William Cowling, had urged this in 1978 when he stated unequivocally, "the free trade policies of the federal government have been responsible for a steady decline of the textile industry in Canada."[72] Roy Collins, manager of the Greater Cornwall Textile Joint Board, reiterated this stand in 1982: "Foreign imports are ripping (the textile) industry to shreds". Cornwall's federal Member of Parliament, Ed Lumley, was with Industry Minister Herb Gray when the textile delegation pleaded their case, Collins emphasizing that "no one can compete with a country (Taiwan) with an hourly wage of 60 cents...our hourly wage is already lower than most industry in Canada. Our workers are not grossly overpaid...they just want to live like other Canadians".[73] Neither Lumley nor Gray could give much hope for changed trade policies because of Canada's participation in the General Agreement on Trade and Tariffs (GATT), but they promised the textile united front they would see what could be done.

Several smaller firms established in the 1960s and 1970s survived the recession. These include a West German-based firm, Karl Gutmann Incorporated, that manufactures furniture for computer and related equipment and employs about fifty-five people; C-Tech, a locally-owned electronics plant producing sonar scanning equipment and employing 100; Julius Resnick Canada Company which makes handbags; and Eastern Pottery, a Canadian-owned company that produces toilet bowls, tanks and sinks.[74] However, attempts to revive Cornwall's textile industry proved futile, and with the closure of Caravelle Carpets, Cornwall Spinners and Riverside Yarns and the retrenchment in the Courtaulds operations, Cornwall's image as a textile town declined and it took on the image of a factory town of diversified industry with the Domtar paper mill dominating local production.

500

NOTES

1. *Ottawa Journal*, 6 June 1965.
2. *Standard-Freeholder*, 24 June 1967.
3. *Ibid.*, 26 November 1970.
4. *Ibid.*, 19 March 1977.
5. By-law 1090, 13 January 1961.
6. Minutes, City Council Committee Book, 1961, 27 December 1961, 494; Cornwall Planning Board Minutes, 5 February 1951, 14 January 1957.
7. *Canadian Parliamentary Guide*, 1981, 289; Senior interview with Mrs. Ed Lumley, 11 March 1983.
8. Mayor G. Parisien to Senior, 10 March 1982.
9. *Standard-Freeholder*, 3 December 1960.
10. *Ibid.*, 9 January 1965.
11. *Ibid.*, 18 March 1972.
12. *Ibid.*, 2 January 1962.
13. Parks and Recreation Committee, Council Minutes, 25 February 1960, 172.
14. *Standard-Freeholder*, 24 June 1967.
15. *Ibid.*
16. *Ibid.*, 28 June 1979.
17. *Scott's Industrial Directory, Ontario Manufacturers*, 1979, 2-91; J.G. Harkness, *A History of Stormont, Dundas and Glengarry*, 363.
18. Strikes and Lockouts, RG27/552/no. 89.
19. *Ibid.*, RG27/3591/no. 67-277 and 3595/no. 68-023.
20. *Standard-Freeholder*, 26 and 30 January 1968.
21. *Ibid.*, 19 March 1977.
22. *Ibid.*, 2 February 1976.
23. *Ibid.*, 27 June 1976.
24. *Ibid.*, 28 November 1975.
25. *Ibid.*, 5 December 1975 and 20 February 1976.
26. *Ibid.*, 24 December 1975.
27. *Ibid.*, 5 January and 6 February 1976.
28. *Ibid.*, 21 October and 15 November 1975.
29. *Ibid.*, 12 February 1976.
30. *Ibid.*, 27 November 1975.
31. *Ibid.*, 12 February 1976.
32. *Ibid.*, 28 December 1976.
33. *Ibid.*
34. *Ibid.*; *Gazette*, Montreal, 30 June 1976.
35. *Ottawa Citizen*, 19 November 1976.
36. *Standard-Freeholder*, 7 January 1977.
37. *Ibid.*, 20 December 1979.
38. For statistics on Domtar payroll and taxes, see Sheila Kyte, secretary to Domtar Resident Plant Manager, W.V. Emory, to Senior, 4 June 1982.

39. *Standard-Freeholder*, 26 November 1970.
40. *Ibid.*
41. Price Waterhouse Report, 1971, 103-105.
42. *Standard-Freeholder*, 1 October 1971.
43. *Ibid.*, 9 January 1965.
44. *Ibid.*, 18 March 1972.
45. See political pamphlet entitled "Vote Lumley" 1971.
46. *Ibid.*
47. *Standard-Freeholder*, Industrial Review, 18 March 1972.
48. See Mayor Ed Lumley's Report, *Standard-Freeholder*, 18 March 1972.
49. *Standard-Freeholder*, 18 March and 29 September 1972.
50. *Ibid.*, 24 June 1967.
51. *Ibid.*, 18 March 1972.
52. *Ibid.*
53. *Ibid.*, 17 March 1973.
54. *Ibid.*
55. *Ibid.*
56. *Ibid.*, 21 December 1974; by 1982 the plant employed about 240, Blair Munro, Time Study Analyst, Combustion Engineering, to Senior, 13 June 1982.
57. See Lumley Pamphlet, 1975, 3; *Standard-Freeholder*, 22 March 1974 and 29 November 1975.
58. *Standard-Freeholder*, 26 February 1974.
59. *Ibid.*, 31 December 1974.
60. See interview with Industrial Commissioner Laurier Courville and Alderman Douglas Webster, in *Standard-Freeholder*, 31 December 1974.
61. *Canadian Parliamentary Guide*, 1981, 561 and 289; Householder Newsletter, Ed Lumley, M.P., December 1974, 1-2; Senior interview with Mrs. Ed Lumley, 8 March 1983.
62. City Clerk R. Allaire to Senior, 30 December 1982.
63. Financial Statement, Corporation of the City of Cornwall, 1981, 1.
64. *Standard-Freeholder*, 30 September 1978.
65. *Ibid.*, 31 March 1980.
66. *George Samis, Queen's Park Report*, 1978, 3.
67. *Standard-Freeholder*, 22 November 1979.
68. *Ibid.*, 25 November 1982; Parisien to Senior, 10 March 1982.
69. *Standard-Freeholder*, 19 March 1976.
70. *Ibid.*, 31 March 1980.
71. *Ibid.*, 15 July 1982; Gordon A. Fox, Personnel Manager, Riverside Yarns Ltd., to Senior, 27 May 1982.
72. *Standard-Freeholder*, 28 March 1978.
73. *Ibid.*, 15 July 1982.
74. For a list of the major manufacturing firms in Cornwall in 1972, see *Standard-Freeholder*, 18 March 1972; Vice-president Wolfgang Salzer, Karl Gutmann Inc., to Senior, 5 January 1982.

Aerial view of Domtar Fine Papers and the Seaway International Bridge, 1981. The north span of the bridge was opened to traffic on July 3, 1962. It is 1,624.8 metres long (5,330 feet), the roadway is 8.2 metres wide (27 feet) and offers a 36.6 metre clearance (120 feet).
Credit: Domtar Fine Papers, Montreal.

United Counties Museum in the 'Wood House'. This house was built by William Wood from limestone intended for a blockhouse, around 1840. Wood's descendants lived in the house until 1953. It opened as a museum operated by the Stormont, Dundas and Glengarry Historical Society, September 1957.

Cornwall Civic Complex, opened October 1976, cost $8,000,000. The facility includes the Ed. Lumley Arena with a maximum seating capacity of 5,500 and a convention centre that hosts on the average 15 events a year.   Credit: Cornwall Civic Complex.

Cornwall Royals Winners of the Memorial Cup, 1972, 1980 and 1981.

Cornwall Royals, 1982-83.

First row, left to right: Joe Mantione, Eric Calder, Paul Emard, President; Roy Russell, Jocelyn Guevremont, Coach; Doug Gilmore, Dennis Schrapp.

Second row, left to right: Mario Boisvert, Assistant Trainer; Rob Norman, Roy Millari, Mike Tomlak, Jim Kyte, Dave Shellington; Kevin Skilliter, Steve Ouderkirk, Head Trainer.

Third row, left to right: Steve Driscoll, Doug Archie, Dave Sikorski; Pierre Baril, Brent Loney, Scott Birnie, Ian

Mr. George Samis, M.P.P. for Cornwall and
Cornwall Township, since 1974.

The Honourable Ed. Lumley, Minister for Trade
and Commerce, M.P., P.C. Member of Parliament for Stormont, Dundas since 1974, Mayor
for the City of Cornwall December 1971 to
December 1974.

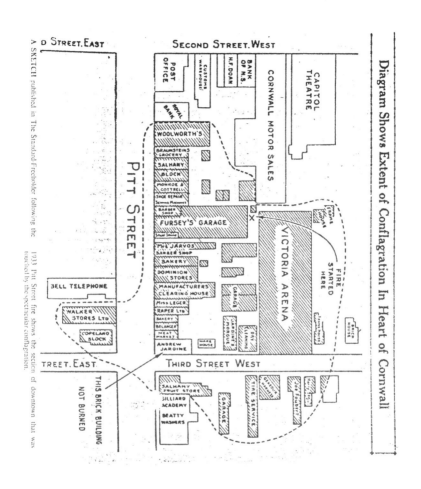

Cornwall Fire of 1933.

Cornwall City Council, 1983-85

Mayor G.J. Parisien

Alderman R. Aubry

Alderman F. Guindon

Alderman R. Lalonde

Alderman T. Lalonde

Alderman A. Lebano

Alderman A. Leblanc

510

Alderman G. Leger   Alderman B. Lynch   Alderman E. Myers

Alderman J. Pescod   Alderman J. Samis   Alderman Wm. Wise

511

Chapter XXII

The Glue That Keeps Cornwall Together

While the municipality of Cornwall basked in the enjoyment of sound financial policies and the town's industrial sector rolled with the punches as Canadian and world market conditions wavered over the years from the early 1950s to the present, Cornwallites, whether employed or unemployed, were seldom idle. Time and talents were directed into existing fraternal, service and cultural associations and often new ones were created to deal with specific modern needs. The war and post-war period witnessed a trend in voluntary organizations towards health-related areas, physical or mental. Taking the lead in this new direction was the local branch of the Canadian Red Cross Society, formed a short time after the outbreak of World War II at a crowded meeting in the auditorium of the Cornwall Collegiate and Vocational School. An indication of the importance of the new Red Cross branch was its rostrum of officers. Member of Parliament Lionel Chevier accepted the post of honorary president while the manager of the Howard Smith Paper Mill, Brydone de Millidge, took the office of president. He was assisted by no less than four vice-presidents: Mrs. Donald Ross-Ross, former Mayor W.A. Parisien, Mary Mack and Mrs. J.A. Chevrier.[1]

Mrs. Ross-Ross took charge of the war work that included bandage and dressing preparations, knitting and the first blood clinics in 1943 at Corbet Hall on Fourth Street. After the war the work of the Red Cross expanded to include tuberculosis clinics at which school children were X-rayed; setting up a "loan cupboard" from which hospital beds, wheelchairs and crutches could be borrowed; a Homemaker service, first organized in 1947 and originally designed to fill the place of the mother in the home when she was incapacitated; and swimming and safety water courses. In the 1980s the branch continues to carry out these services as well as an emergency service for victims of fires and other disasters.[2]

The spirit of service and the varied backgrounds of the Red Cross membership were typical of most of the city's service organizations.

The president in 1981, for example, was an immigrant to the city from Tanzania, Sultan Jessa, who has worked his way up at the *Standard-Freeholder* to become one of the newspaper's top staff writers. Working closely with him is former alderman Larry Keen, Doe Dube, Marjorie McCoy and one of the charter members, Mrs. Donald Ross-Ross. Dr. Indu Gamghir is chairman of the major disaster planning committee. It was this type of dedicated service and teamwork that Mayor Gerald Parisien commended when he spoke at the annual meeting of the Red Cross in 1981. "You are the glue, along with other like organizations", he said, "that keeps a community together".

It was out of the war experience that the Red Cross local branch developed. So, too, did a number of other Cornwall associations including the group, inspired by an idea of Rupert Moncrieff, who began the collection of dimes to be used towards the purchase of Hurricane fighters. Moncrieff's idea was taken up by people in other Canadian cities and by 1942 some 57,000 dimes had been forwarded to the Finance Minister in Ottawa.[4] Cornwall's Navy League branch was formed in 1944 under the aegis of Lt.-Col. Neil Phillips and Mrs. Archie Dover.[5] The Ladies Auxiliary of the Legion was founded in 1945, and like the Legion itself, proved to be one of the best glues for binding society together. Although it is an all-female organization, the Ladies Auxiliary takes its mentalité from the wartime experience of close cooperation and liaison between men and women. Members proudly proclaim that their "goal is to work with and assist the Royal Canadian Legion". Among their most valued services are visits to veterans at St. Joseph Villa, the Glen-Stor-Dun Lodge and St. Lawrence Estate. In 1980 the Auxiliary's membership numbered 190, whose executive was headed by Mrs. Rita Marsolais, Mrs. Winnaford Campeau and Mrs. Eva Watson.[6]

The local branch of the Stormont, Dundas and Glengarry Highlanders 1st Battalion Association was founded in February 1947 when Major R.P. Milligan invited all local Glens to an organizational meeting. Major J.A.M. Pete MacNeil was named president and Lt. Robert Dixson secretary by those attending who included, besides Major Milligan, Lt. Charles McGuire, Cpl. Allan Cameron, Pte. William Lalonde, Pte. Joe Sommerville, Sgt. Colin Bates, Lt. Mack Cameron, Cpl. Howard Bailey, Sgt. Douglas Cameron and Major Clarence Petepiece. The object of the new association was to keep alive the comradeship that had existed during the war and to pass along the traditions of the regiment to those who followed. The first of the popular annual reunions of the Glens was held in the Cornwall Armoury in 1948. Present-day reunions attract back to battalion headquarters as many as 250 former Glens. The 1st battalion Association also spearheads plans for return visits to the European battlefields on special anniversaries. Thus thirty years after allied troops crashed on the beaches of Normandy on D-Day, 6 June 1944, Cornwallite Lt.-Col. Don Stewart led a delegation of veterans back to the same ground. Another means of keeping ties is the publication of Sitrep (Situation Report), first edited in 1970 by Major Reg Dixon.[7]

Three other war-related societies were formed shortly after war's end. Ex-navy men got together to form the Cornwall Navy Club in 1948.[8] Then in 1949 a local chapter of the Silver Cross Women was formed with Florence Pridden as first president and Ida Alguire as secretary. After thirty years of service in looking after the interests and welfare of widows and mothers of men who had made the supreme sacrifice, the Silver Cross Women, which began with a membership of fifty-two, closed out their association in 1979. Seven members met for a final Christmas supper at which special guest Mayor Gerald Parisien accepted their colours. The last president was Ida Alguire and secretary was Florence Pridden, a mute testimony to the dedication of the women who sought and gave comfort when comfort was needed.[9]

Air service personnel established a veterans organization in 1950 with the chartering of Cornwall and District Wing 424, Royal Canadian Air Force Association. Prominent in the formation were H.G. Williams, Chief of Police, Frank H. Hunter, George Fox, Dalton McAlear and Grant McMillan. Like other such associations, Wing 424 takes part in many charitable and community programmes, but is especially devoted to "developing physical, mental and moral wellbeing in our nation's youth, particularly Air Cadets". This is evident in their keen support of the Kiwanis-sponsored Air Cadet Squadron no. 325. In 1982 the 121 regular and seventy-eight associate members of Wing 424 were presided over by Francis Guindon and Robert Franklin. One of the Wing's most spectacular contributions was to share in the 1974 project of bringing to Cornwall the Silver Star T-33 training jet that stands on a pedestal outside the Royal Canadian Air Force Association headquarters on Water Street.[10]

Sea Cadets were organized in Cornwall in 1953 under the auspices of the Navy League local branch and a Ladies Auxiliary of the Navy League was formed the same year to help support the new Royal Canadian Sea Cadet Corps Stormont.[11] Two cadets of this corps captured the top Canadian Sea Cadet award - Chief Petty Officer Peter Meyer won it in 1976 and Chief Petty Officer Dan Bissonnette in 1979.[12] The kilted cadet corps of Cornwall Collegiate and Vocational

School that had been organized in 1907 declined in the late 1960s. So, too, did the Royal Canadian Army Cadet Corps 2403, organized at St. Lawrence High School in 1951. Forty-five young men reorganized the latter corps in 1970 and now Corps 2403 trains at the Cornwall Armoury.[13]

These, then, were the offspring of war and armed forces organizations that continued after the war in Cornwall. The 1940s saw a number of other clubs and organizations emerge. Three were to become prominent service clubs in the city: the Lions, organized in 1940, and the Richelieu Club, founded in 1948, both inspired by hotelman Fred Lefebvre, and the Optimists Club, chartered in 1948 under Norman C. Ross as president. All three are directed mainly towards helping young people. In addition to operating St. Lawrence Park, which in the 1940s had a swimming pool, sports field and other outdoor facilities, the Lions Club raised $402,000 towards the war effort and other club projects. It was the Lions Club, too, which donated $3,500 to the Sea Cadets to buy two training boats. One of the club's major projects in the late 1970s was the purchase of a $50,000 surgical microscope for the Hotel Dieu Hospital.[14]

Determined to look on the sunny side of life at all times, local Optimists began with a dinner-dance at the Cornwallis Hotel and from then on the fifty-five charter members, in spite of several unsuccessful fund-raising projects, went on to prove their spurs as "Friends of Youth", sponsoring Venturers, Scouts and Cubs, promoting the Optimist Pipe Band which has won numerous awards and was several times selected to lead the St. Patrick's Day parade in Montreal, and above all, underwriting the cost of equipment and uniforms for as many as 400 boys in minor football in Cornwall. The Optimists enticed their wives to form a parallel club, Opti-Mrs. Club, organized in 1950.[15]

The North End Social Club, founded in 1948, is also geared towards helping young people. Its activities include sponsoring majorettes, lacrosse, softball and minor hockey. Directed towards more professional areas were several other clubs founded in the 1940s. These included the Junior Chamber of Commerce, the Jaycees, 1945[16], the Cornwall Community Council, 1946; the local branch of the Engineering Institute, formed in 1946 with Donald Ross-Ross as provisional chairman;[17] the Home and School Association, organized in 1947 around a group of parents and teachers of Cornwall Public School with John A. Stewart as acting president and Mrs. Abe Miller as vice-president;[18] the Firefighters' Association, local 849, founded in 1946, and undertaking both charitable and educational work including fire prevention in schools, distributing gifts at hospitals at

Christmas and sharing in the Jerry Lewis Muscular Distrophy campaigns; and the Cornwall Musicians' Guild, Local 800, chartered in 1951 with Moses Augi as president. This Guild had grown to a membership of 300 by 1982 with Michael Heenan, Kenneth McLaren, H. Bradley Lewis and Lucien (Duke) Decoste at its head, ready and anxious to protect the interests of their members and to see that they are paid "properly and promptly for their services".[19]

A group of young people "fed up with black leather jacket gangs, motor-cycles and souped-up hot rods" met at Alexander Park in October 1958 to organize a club for teen-agers. Calling themselves "Gay Jeans", a name which in the 1950s was still used in its traditional meaning, the group was headed by Donald Stone, Joyce Sullivan, Ann Barlow, Sharon Pearce, Betty McCrae, Jacqueline Deguire and Kenneth Bergeron, with Rudy Payment, a member of the Bob Turner Memorial Arena staff as recreational advisor.[20]

Several women's groups took root in the post-war days. In 1946 Mrs. Donald Ross-Ross, Mrs. J.H. Summerskill, Mrs. Lionel Chevrier, Mrs. Robert Kershaw and Mrs. Aaron Horovitz organized the Women's Canadian Club of Cornwall to foster an interest in public affairs of the country by presenting prominent speakers such as John Fisher and the Honourable Lionel Chevrier.[21] The Federation of Business and Professional Women local branch was established in 1954 with Mrs. Rosamonde Laberge as president and Miss Ada Adams as vice-president.[22] The following year Miss L. Jean Cameron sparked the founding of the Cornwall branch of the Canadian Federation of University Women. Their aims were to stimulate intellectual activity, preserve historic buildings, promote social life among university women, and cooperation in public services such as education, particularly by means of a scholarship programme. By 1980 the Club had seventy members, of whom fifty-seven were among the charter members, representing twenty-six different universities and ninety-three degrees.[23] Les Femmes d'aujourd'hui was founded in the fall of 1974 by Paule Pelletier to serve as a social gathering club of all French-speaking women in Cornwall. Open to any woman "able to converse fluently in French", the club was given its name by Madeleine Germain.[24]

Cornwall's Rotary Club was the last of the city's major men's service clubs to be organized. Founded in 1950 under the sponsorship of the Massena, New York, Rotary Club, the local club was first headed by Al Gardner, resident manager of the Provincial Paper Mills Company. With a membership based on business and professional men at the senior management level, the Rotary Club's first money-making event was a circus in the Water Street Arena in 1951. Much of the club's philanthropy is directed towards assisting the blind. On their twenty-fifth anniversary in 1975 they donated a car to the local Canadian Institute for the Blind, which had been founded in 1949 and which, in 1979, offered its services to 108 blind people in the city and 237 in the total Cornwall district.[25] Other Rotarian projects included sponsoring tennis tournaments in the city, supporting the Rotary student exchange programme in which Canadian students are sent to a foreign country for a year's study and foreign students are brought to study at a Canadian university. Part of the $225,000 raised by local Rotarians and contributed to the community over the years since 1950 was used to buy an electromyography unit donated to Hotel Dieu Hospital in 1980, marking the 75th anniversary of the founding of Rotary International.[26]

The trend towards health-related organizations took a spurt forward in the 1970s, though there had been several such associations organized earlier such as the local branch of the Canadian Cancer Society, formed in 1953 with Lt.-Col. A.M. Irvine as president and Mrs. W.C. Sullivan and Magistrate P.C. Bergeron as vice-presidents.[27] By 1981 the local Cancer Society branch's annual dinner meeting was attended by fifty-one members under president William Costello. One of the guest speakers was Benson Stidwill, president of the Cornwall Ostomy Association, formed in the 1970s. The Arthritis Society branch was first organized in 1967, but became inactive until 1973 when Ralph Flath became president of the re-organized group of forty members. A clinic for arthritis sufferers was set up in 1975 with Mrs. Della Hilldrup as nurse and the following year Mrs. Hilldrup was awarded the Volunteer of the Year Award.[28]

Fifteen men and women met one night in November 1951 to set up a Fresh Air Camp Committee to provide annual summer camps for children who would not otherwise be able to attend camp. Among those spearheading the new association was Fred Stevens who announced that it was the local Kiwanis Club, which had begun operating fresh air camps nine years earlier, that was behind the present group in their efforts.[29] Another group of thirty-two parents organized a Council for the Exceptional Child in 1964, their aim to offer help to the exceptional child and the child's parents. The first workshop established by the Cornwall District Association for the Mentally Retarded was in the old Show Mart which opened in 1965 with Klass De Vries as director. Known as Arc (Adult Retraining Centre), the Centre was a place where workers repaired lawnchairs, and made articles such as addressograph plates, ceramics, posters and other articles for sale. At first thirty-five people over eighteen years of age were employed at ARC Industries, but in 1977 larger quarters for the workshop had to be found when the number of people engaged in the workshop had increased to sixty.[30] In 1975, a society called "Open Hands" was formed with the object of providing a home for physically and mentally handicapped children. Headed by Heidi Berger and Nick Battista in 1979, Open Hands had six counsellors to provide help to such children.

Senior citizens also joined the togetherness trend of the 1950s by meeting at Trinity Church Hall, some 60 men and women, to form a Senior Citizens' Club under the auspices of the Kinettes.[31] Members worked hard on various fund-raising projects which eventually provided enough money to open a Senior Citizens Centre right in the heart of Cornwall on the Pitt Street Mall in the 1970s. The need for senior citizens' housing units made itself felt in the community of the 1970s when two of Cornwall's tallest buildings went up to service its senior citizens - one at Sixth and Adolphus Streets, a second at First and Augustus Streets. A third housing unit for senior citizens was erected on Montreal Road near Navitity Church.[32] A home for old people had been established when Glen-Stor-Dun Lodge opened in what was once the old House of Refuge and Industry. When this building became inadequate, a new Glen-Stor-Dun Lodge for the aged was opened in 1952 east of Cornwall.

Superannuated teachers of Cornwall and the three counties formed a Retired Teachers Association in 1973 with Campbell Fraser, Mrs. Roland Schaeffer, L. Jean Cameron, and Mrs. H.R. Smith at its head. By the late 1970s the Association had 258 members who kept abreast of pension and other related matters as well as organized trips and conferences. Some of the most successful trips to Ottawa, Kingsmere, Quebec City, the Stratford Festival and New York City have been largely due to the efforts of Trip Convenor Laura Sabourin, named "Personnalité de l'Année", by the Cornwall Chambre de Commerce during the year of the woman.[33]

For boys of ten to eighteen years who were experiencing difficulties at home or in society generally, a juvenile detention home, Laurencrest, was established in 1968 in the north end of Cornwall. As many as twenty-eight boys lived at the home at various times, attending local schools and receiving specialized help in adjusting to society.[34] Directed by John McKee in the early 1970s, the home was largely the work of Family Court Judge Percy Bergeron, who retired in 1972 after thirty-seven years on the bench and who was honoured by being made a Knight of St. Gregory by Pope John XXIII.

Other adolescent boys were helped by the Big Brothers of Cornwall, a group organized in 1972 and headed by Father Kevin Maloney,

Alderman Brian Lynch and Donald Belanger in the late 1970s. Bringing the various children's and youth's services in the Cornwall District under an umbrella agency was the job of the Children's Services Council. This agency was established in 1977 at the behest of the provincial government.[35]

Two societies were formed in Cornwall in response to the abortion issue that became prominent in the late 1960s and 1970s when federal legislation softened existing abortion laws. A branch of Pro-Life was formed in 1975, dedicated to promoting a respect for human life from the time of conception until natural death. Active in this society, which grew to 400 members by the late 1970s, were Micheline Ouellette, Suzanne Beaulieu and Frank Burke.[36] A second organization, Birthright, was established in 1977. It offers help to pregnant women in distress who wish to bear their children. Heading this organization in the late 1970s were Marilyn Bergeron, Juanita Courville, Nancy MacGregor, Jean Maynard and Claudette Steer, who, together with thirty other members, organized an emergency telephone service and a drop-in centre. A second Women's Centre with a crisis telephone service was opened in 1975 with twenty-seven executive members and volunteers ready to assist any woman in trouble. Heading this Centre in the late 1970s were Judy Auger, Roberta Velley and Yolande Charron.[37]

Cornwall's Children's Aid Society maintained a policy of forbidding abortions for wards of the society unless two medical doctors declared that the mother's life was gravely endangered by the pregnancy. When the Society was pressed in 1983 by a fifteen-year-old ward who wished to abort her child, Director Tom O'Brien upheld the Society's policy in not authorizing the abortion.[38] Twenty years earlier the head of the Children's Aid Society would not have had to face such a decision. In 1965 Cornwall's two hospitals had no recorded abortions. In 1970, the year after federal legislation allowed hospitals to set up therapeutic abortion committees, there were six abortions at the Cornwall General Hospital. By 1975 the number had increased to thirty-three abortions and by 1980 there were seventy-nine. Over the years from 1965 to 1975 there was a doubling of live births at the Cornwall General Hospital: 228 in 1965, 421 in 1970 and 484 in 1975.[39] Thereafter the Cornwall General Hospital amalgamated its obstetrical department with the new Hotel Dieu Hospital which opened on McConnell Avenue in 1955. From then on deliveries were performed at the Hotel Dieu Hospital and abortions at the Cornwall General Hospital. In 1977 there were 1,061 babies born at the Hotel Dieu Hospital and in 1978 there were 1,035.[40]

The old Hotel Dieu Hospital on Water Street in the West End of the city was renamed Macdonell Memorial Hospital, in memory of Sister Janet Macdonell, one of the sisters of the Religious Hospitallers of St. Joseph, who founded the hospital.[41] Today Macdonell Memorial Hospital's 122 beds are used by chronically-ill and rehabilitation patients. A fourth Cornwall Hospital was located on the eastern outskirts of the city, St. Lawrence Sanitorium, which opened in 1937 for 100 patients with lung diseases. By 1946 it had proved its worth. The death rate from tuberculosis in the Cornwall district had sharply declined, and by the 1970s the hospital closed its doors.[42]

Cultural associations blossomed in the post-war era, especially in music, live drama and historically-oriented societies. The Cornwall Community Concert Association was organized in the 1944-45 season with Drummond Giles, manager of Courtaulds, as first president, and Alexander Caldwell as vice-president. In its first two years, it succeeded in providing first-class musical entertainment for nearly 1,000 members.[43] The Cornwall Music Conservatory opened in 1947, largely due to the efforts of R. Stewart Hall, an associate of the Toronto Conservatory of Music, Carson Martin and Margaret Peachey. Located at first on the original site of the old Bishop Strachan grammar school, the Conservatory trains students for violin, voice, piano and instrumental music and prepares them for the Toronto Conservatory of Music examinations.[44]

Jeunesses Musicales of Canada made its debut in Cornwall in 1961. Its main goal was to promote classical music for young people and provide an opportunity for young artists to perform. By 1980 its membership of seventy-five was headed by Mrs. Pat Rudden, Mrs. William Harris and Jean-Claude Gélinas.[45] One of the best promoters of classical music in Cornwall was the annual Music Festival sponsored since 1955 by the Kinsmen. It was out of this musical milieu that Cornwall pianist, Louise-Andrée Baril, a pupil of Rosemonde Laberge, achieved international acclaim when she performed at Carnegie Hall, New York, in 1973. Besides the Centennial Choir organized in 1967, choral ensembles included the Cornwall Ecumenical Choir, founded by Lynne Francis in 1973 with the express purpose of bringing major oratorical works to the Cornwall public.

The sixty-member choir's first performance of Handel's Messiah attracted such numbers that Knox United Church and both its halls were filled and people had to be turned away from the doors. Since that time, the choir has sung numerous works by Handel, Haydn, Bach, Mozart, Mendelssohn, Vivaldi, Benjamin Britten and Vaughan Williams. Its present executive includes Margaret Bradbury, Ethel

Harrison and Jean Weber.[46] Le Cercle Ste. Cécile was a group of young people of Nativity Church who organized in the early 1950s for tennis and, under Mgr. J.-A. Brunelle, their aims broadened to include drama. Then under the direction of Joseph Riel, they became well-known as a choral group.[47] By 1979 Cornwall boasted its own Symphony Orchestra conducted by Cornwallite Brent McLaren. Its inaugural concert was given 30 May 1979 at St. Jean Bosco Church.[48]

Dramatics were not entirely neglected in the post-war period. Alice Richmond organized a drama group in 1951 and during the 1960s St. Columban's Drama Club produced such musicals as The Sound of Music, The King and I, and Brigadoon. Cornwall Little Theatre was started in 1960 with the object of presenting live theatre to Cornwall audiences. In 1965 the more ambitious Glen Productions was organized, drawing many of its member from the older Operatic Society which had concentrated largely on performances of Gilbert and Sullivan's light opera. In 1965 the more ambitious Glen Productions was organized under the direction of Ron Sullivan, Andy Trasuk, Rick Forrester and Luc Groulx. They produced such musicals as South Pacific and Hello Dolly. The Glen also sponsored theatre, cabarets, the Glen Concert Series and Glen Singers. In 1975 City Council formed the Cornwall Arts Development Committee to further the arts.

In the 1970s a number of purely Francophone musical and theatrical associations were founded. These included Association des Jeunes Musiciens Francophones de Cornwall, 1979, emphasizing the teaching of music in French; Les Concertistes, 1975, promoting concerts by and for young Francophones; Ecole de Ballet de Cornwall, 1975, giving Francophone students ballet instruction in French; and L'Ensemble Musique et Harmonie, founded in 1972 by Michele Cadotte to promote French choral works and to teach music for the Mass. French theatre was promoted by Roland Chevrier who wrote and produced several plays, using the company Les Copains de l'Art. In 1977 Le Théâtre Chez-Nous was founded by Lise Davidson whose company presents mainly French comedies.[49]

In the heyday of dance bands, Pearson's Central Ballroom on Sydney Street, the Labor Temple on York Street, and the more fashionable Cornwallis Hotel and Oasis Pavillion resounded to Burton Heward's Rhythm Knights and Charles James' Orchestra, among others. Heward's first band included Dan Robertson, Mac Norris, Levi Leroux, Jack Gibson, Hamilton Kirkey, Charles Stewart, with Heward on the drums. Later additions to the band were Hal Lee, Harvey Boileau, Charles Heward, Dick Loucks, Len DeCarle, Lionel Bouley, Eric Hudd, Gerry Burgess, and vocalists Shirley McAteer and Ed Lalonde. Charles James' Orchestra was composed of Paul Comeau, Larry and Joseph Desrosier, Fern Moquin, Oliver Duhaime, and Rheal Groulx.[50]

Cornwall got its own commercial television station in 1959 when Stanley Shenkman set up station CJSS-TV with well-equipped studios. The French-language radio station CFML (CFIX) which went on the air the same year under the direction of Madeleine Laframboise was sold in 1977 to Veerendra D. Adhiya, a lawyer who came to Canada from India in 1966 but he was not successful in his application to operate a French-language radio station in Cornwall.[51]

As for historically-oriented associations there is, in addition to the Stormont, Dundas and Glengarry Historical Society, La Société Historique Canadienne-Française de Cornwall, founded in 1975 to promote interest in the history of the Francophones of Cornwall. The older Historical Society had spearheaded, over the years since 1920, interest in Cornwall's past and in preserving its historical buildings and artifacts. The Society was largely responsible for the conversion of the old Wood home on Second Street into the United Counties Museum which opened its doors in 1956.[52] More recently the Society spurred the move to restore Inverarden, the home built to the east of the city in 1816 by fur-trader John McDonald of Garth. Under the direction of personnel from Parks Canada, this charming regency cottage was restored and renovated to become one of Cornwall's main tourist attractions under Curator Ian Bowering.[53] In the mid-1970s the Historical Society also took the lead in promoting the project of having a history of Cornwall written as part of the city's Bi-Centennial celebrations in 1984.[54] Thus, when the Bi-Centennial Committee was set up under Alderman Angelo Lebano, and now headed by Robert Pearson, one of its priorities was to hire a historian for the job.

A number of Parks Canada personnel working out of Cornwall such as Dr. Robert J. Burns and Dennis Carter-Edwards, together with other Cornwallites, formed the Local Architectural Conservation Advisory Committee, two members of which, Dr. Norbert Ferré and Nick Lambooy, were appointed by the city. The aim of LACAC, now Heritage Cornwall, is to identify historical sites and buildings worthy of conservation and to "focus attention on the physical heritage of the city as it nears its bicentennial".[55] One of the ways LACAC does this is by publishing *Heritage Cornwall*, a booklet of pictures and stories on Cornwall's historic architecture.

Cornwall has been fortunate in the quality and number of its historian-writers. Judge Jacob Farrand Pringle and lawyer John Graham Harkness have both produced lasting histories of the United Counties in which Cornwall is the centrepiece, just as the more recent well-written and thoroughly-researched work by Clive and Francis Marin will take its place as a classic county history.[56] Other Cornwallites such as Dorothy Donihee and Eileen Merkley chose to write memoirs.[57] Still others such as Bill Gallant and Father Rudolph Villeneuve concentrated on such areas as the Royals hockey team and Catholic education in Cornwall.[58] The only Cornwallite to win the Governor-General's award for non-fiction was Roger Caron, author of *Go-Boy*, in which the author describes his life of crime as a youth and his subsequent terms in jail. In 1977 a number of Cornwall writers got together to form a local branch of the Canadian Authors' Association.

Perhaps the most important source of Cornwall's history is the *Standard-Freeholder*. Cornwall's local newspaper and its predecessors have done the job of unfolding the city's history day by day since 1 April 1941 and prior to that once, twice, or three times weekly. Staff writers such as Alex Mullin, Russ Dewar and Sultan Jessa not only have provided first-class reporting, but often their writing has touched deeply into the hearts of Cornwallites. This has been particularly true of their feature stories on Cornwall personalities such as sportsmen John Denneny and Newsie Lalone and artist Bob Eadie. Other feature articles on Cornwall's past such as those written by Bernard Chevrier on John Sandfield Macdonald have helped to instill in Cornwallites an interest and love of their heritage. From the early 1940s when the local newspaper became a daily prepared by a staff of thirty-four until today, the *Standard-Freeholder* has built up a circulation of over 17,000, produced since 6 December 1976 in off-set by a staff of about fifty and delivered by some 300 carriers. The Fleming family of Owen Sound were the owners of the *Standard-Freeholder* from the early 1930s until 1959 at which time it was bought by the Thomson Newspaper chain.

Two of Cornwall's most vibrant organizations, the Legion and the Kinsmen, continue to provide the city with fellowship and service of a high quality. Among the Kinsmen's more recent projects have been turning the YM-YWCA into a bilingual Day-Care Centre; replacing the VON car; and, by a donation of $70,000, helping to finance the new wing of the Simon Fraser Library. This wing houses the F.B. MacMillan Room for children which was opened in May 1979. In many of their projects, the Kinsmen have been helped by their wives who organized a Kinette Club in 1942.[59]

The steady growth of the John McMartin Memorial Branch No. 297 of the Royal Canadian Legion by the extension of membership to sons and daughters of veterans has meant that the Cornwall branch has continued to be one of the largest in the province. In recognition of their services on the home front during the war, Legion members were given a substantial grant by the city. They used this to buy Judge R.B. Carman's home which had been more recently occupied by Member of Parliament for Stormont in 1926, Arnold Smith. Legion members built a new wing in 1958 to house the Sir Winston Churchill Auditorium. And it is at Legion headquarters that Cornwall's unofficial forum exists, familiarly dubbed "Senators' Corner". Here all issues at City Hall, Queen's Park and Parliament Hill are thrashed out with gusto, merriment and great thoroughness, none more so than the 1983 municipal budget with its snippet of information about an $8,000 bill for coffee at City Hall. So intense was the discussion at Senators' Corner over that item that most City Hall Legion members hovered on the brink of going on the coffee wagon for the rest of their lives.

In addition to their self-imposed duties as guardians of public policy, members of Legion Branch No. 297 undertook several major post-war projects. These included their 1967 Centennial project to relocate the cenotaph and build a memorial fountain in Legion Memorial Park; to sponsor the Golden Tulip programme in 1976 and award fifty bursaries of $150 each to students in Cornwall secondary schools as part of the Legion's golden anniversary celebrations; and the presentation of a $25,000 organ to the new Cornwall Civic Complex in 1978. The Cornwall branch was honoured in 1981 when one of its past presidents, Larry Keen, was acclaimed Ontario Command Provincial President for a three-year term.[60]

One of Cornwall's newest and fastest growing organizations, whose membership embraces the three counties, is the St. Lawrence Branch of the United Empire Loyalists' Association. Organized at Morrisburg on 16 October 1977, the new Loyalist branch attracted fifty-three to its initial meeting which was presided over by Ian McMartin and Keith Casselman. A month later at a second meeting held at Viscount Alexander School in Cornwall, R. Melvin Scott was elected president with Mrs. Donald Hare and Stanley McNairn, vice-presidents, and Lynne O'Brien area genealogist.[61] St. Lawrence Branch had a predecessor. In 1934 the Loyalists' Society of Stormont was headed by W. Mack Alguire, with John H. Cline and William H. Gallinger as vice-presidents. During the celebrations marking the centennial of the city, this forerunner of the St. Lawrence Branch inserted in the *Standard-Freeholder* a tribute entitled "Hail to the United Empire Loyalists AD 1784-1934".[62]

These Loyalist descendants of the original pioneer settlers of Cornwall, together with thousands of other Cornwallites, were among the boisterous, joyous crowd that filled cars, trucks and buses to speed to Dorval Airport, Montreal, on Monday, 12 May 1980, to greet their conquering heroes, the Cornwall Royals Hockey team which had just won the Memorial Cup in playoffs out west against the Peterborough team. As the cavalcade neared Cornwall, pockets of cars, parked along the highway between Lancaster and Cornwall, honked their horns and fans waved banners. The Cornwall fire department engine waited on the overpass, its lights flashing a welcome in the dark. Through crowded streets of cheering, waving citizens, the bus carrying the Royals slowly wove its way to the Cornwall Civic Complex where the team had been the No. 1 tenants of the Ed Lumley arena ever since the Complex opened. Not since the Stormont, Dundas and Glengarry Highlanders returned from overseas had Cornwall witnessed such a homecoming.[63] This second national championship, captured by the Cornwall hockey team, put the city on the map once more as the 1980s began. The Royals repeated their victory in 1981, giving the hockey city a winning streak that led to anticipated victories in other directions.

The 1981 census showed that Cornwall's population had stabilized after a slight decline in the early 1970s. In 1971 there were 47,220 people in Cornwall. By 1976 their number had dropped to 46,121, but by 1981 the population had risen slightly to 46,144.[64] By comparison, Cornwall's neighbouring Loyalist-based municipalities of Kingston and Brockville suffered slight population declines throughout the seventies. Kingston's urban population in 1976 was 56,032. In 1981 it was 52,616. Brockville had 19,903 people in 1976 and 19,896 in 1981.[65] Thus Cornwall, in terms of population, had far outstripped Brockville and was catching up to Kingston by the 1980s.

The youth section of Cornwall's population numbered 11,140 in 1981. This meant that almost one quarter of the city's citizens were under the age of nineteen. For those city authorities who looked back longingly to the baby-boom days of the early 1960s when Cornwall's teen-agers and younger children numbered 19,322 out of a total population of 43,639, the 1981 figure sent fears of an ageing population shivering down their spines.

The trend that sharpened Francophone aspirations and spearheaded their efforts to emphasize French culture and education in Cornwall was the decline in French as a mother language among Cornwallites. This trend is apparent in the following table culled from available Statistics Canada census figures:

Mother Tongue	1951	1961	(post	1971	1981
English	11,939	23,919	annexation)	27,630	28,630
French	358	18,496		18,165	15,960

Languages spoken

English only	10,763	21,078	-	-
French only	423	3,476	-	-
French & English	5,689	18,996	-	-

Ethnic origin

British	8,301	15,765	20,135	-
French	7,073	23,452	23,320	-

With such a French-language pattern emerging in the post-war period, a section of the city's Francophone community became more strident in their demands for all-French schools, including those at the kindergarten level and for all-French day-care centres, financed by the municipality. The stridency reached its peak in 1977 when one of the stormiest meetings of the Stormont, Dundas and Glengarry Separate School Board was held. During a four-hour long meeting, a group of French parents persisted in their demand to restrict French-language schools to pupils fluent in French "to ensure the survival of French schools and French culture".[66] A softer tone prevailed by 1979 when Chairman of the Separate School Board, Jules Renaud, spoke of the Board's basic Catholic philosophy of education within a pluralistic society. This philosophy recognized, he declared, "an openness to diverse cultures, as well as the privileged position occupied by the language and culture of the two founding nations of Canada which give our country characteristics clearly different from those of our powerful southern neighbour".[67]

The plurality of Cornwall society was demonstrated anew in 1979 with the arrival of a group of twenty-three Vietnamese refugees, one of whom spoke English fluently and one of whom spoke French fluently.[68] These newest immigrants quickly merged into the congenial milieu of the Seaway City, at first undertaking custom sewing in their temporary living quarters at motels and later in their more permanent homes.[68] As far as labour spokesmen were concerned, those who made Cornwall their home were entitled to whatever jobs were available. Garfield Poitras, president of the 5000-member Cornwall and District Labor Council, emphasized this in March 1979. The Council's priority, he said, "will be fight to keep local people working on local jobs which benefit the whole community.[70] This was the conciliatory attitude generally that began to spread in the early 1980s as Cornwall approached its 200th birthday, giving the city a renewed claim to being the "Friendly Bilingual City" that had existed in the late 1960s.[71]

However, the Cornwall of the 1980s bears little resemblance to the gloom and doom Cornwall of the 1950s and 1960s. Proof enough

526

of that were the shenanigans that shook up the city as St. Patrick's Day neared in 1983. Citizens were startled on Monday 14 March to learn from their radios and television that a meteorite-like object had crashed on the lawn of City Hall and lay there hissing and smoking. Police blocked off all the streets surrounding City Hall and fire engines clanged to the rescue to examine the mysterious object, while puzzled and worried workers and drivers backed away and tried to manoeuvre to work by side-streets. Other citizens kept their ears peeled to the radio to learn what was going on. By nightfall the *Standard-Freeholder* had the story. The Lord Mayor of Cork in Ireland and his Councillors had invited Cornwall to be their "twinning city" during Cornwall's bi-centennial year's celebrations in 1984 and, as a goodwill gesture, they had "hurled...the Cornwall-Canadian Blarney Rock" across the Atlantic to land on the lawn of City Hall.

No sooner had the excitement over the arrival of the Blarney Rock subsided than Pitt Street Mall was suddenly and unexpectedly invaded - not by a solitary Irish colleen who had on previous St. Patrick's Days paraded up and down to remind Cornwallites of the great day - but by such a crowd of shamrock - bedecked and "Erin Go Bragh" leprechauns, Clansmen, fiddlers and kilted singers that restaurants and shops were emptied in a moment. At the head of the invading force was a workman pushing a works department wheelbarrow on which sat a huge box covered with green foil and floating with green ribbons. Beside him swaggered a solitary piper, his Scottish tartar bagpipe covered with bright green velvet. Next came Acting Mayor Brian Lynch with bits of green trailing from his tweed hat. With him walked Cornwall's tall, burly lawyer, Patrick Rudden, sporting a vivid green bowtie, green streamers flying in the wind, and, perched on the top of his touselled steel-grey hair, was the brightest green miniature bowler hat, securely held in place by a narrow elastic band. Dancing and leaping about the acting mayor and his companion was Cornwall's official leprechaun.

A broad Kelly green carpet had been laid along the Mall some time earlier and two tables set thereon. Here the wheelbarrow was trundled and the huge package lifted up on one table. Irish melodies poured from the nearby bandstand where a fiddler, accordionist, guitarist and singers of the Clansmen added to the festivities. As the package was unwrapped, the crowd surged forward to hear Acting Mayor Lynch explain that here was an ersatz Blarney Rock, but a Blarney Rock nevertheless, and Patrick Rudden had been named its offical keeper. A more delightfully confused story has rarely been unfolded. It seems that some hitches had occurred in the hurling of the Rock and it was still on its way across the Atlantic. That did not daunt City Hall. Cornwall's city fathers came up with a Blarney Rock of their own, hastily quarried, a leprechaun confided, from a back concession Loyalist farm. There it sat, waiting to provide a prized "chip off the old rock" to the first 500 Cornwallites to line up at the second table to sign a waiting guest book that was to be sent to the people of Cork as a token of appreciation and fellowship.[72]

If Cornwall's Irish came into their own on St. Patrick's Day, 1983, other Cornwallites of diverse backgrounds took the centre of the stage on July 1st when the city's first Multi-Cultural Festival was held at the Civic Complex by the Chamber of Commerce. For over thirteen hours ten ethnic groups displayed their musical, dancing and vocal artistry before more than 2,000 spectators. While enjoying the traditional dancing and music of Chinese, East Indian, Saudi Arabian, North American Indian, Polish, Scottish, Dutch and Italian Cornwallites, guests sampled food and drink native to the nationalities represented. This is the glue, as Mayor Gerald Parisien declared, that binds the people of Cornwall together.

NOTES

1. *Standard-Freeholder*, 16 October 1939.

2. *Ibid.*, 9 October 1947; 19 and 26 November 1979.

3. Canadian Red Cross Society, Cornwall Branch, Annual Report, 1981, 2.

4. *Standard-Freeholder*, 26 February 1942.

5. *Ibid.*, 3 November 1944.

6. *Associations, Organizations and Clubs, Cornwall Directory*, 1979-80, 152.

7. For details on the 1st Battalion Association, see *Standard-Freeholder*, 25 May 1974; Major Reg Dixon to Senior, 20 May 1982; John Angus McDonald, secretary, 1st Battalion, to Senior, 20 August 1982.

8. *Standard-Freeholder*, 30 June 1948; *Old Home Week*, 1946, 81.

9. *Standard-Freeholder*, 10 December 1979; see Committee Book, City Council, 25 April 1963, 693, re plot of land on Tollgate Road offered to Silver Cross Women as a memorial park.

10. Belva Webster, secretary Wing 424 to Senior, 29 July 1982; *Cornwall Weekly News*, 1 June 1977; *Standard-Freeholder*, 13 March 1950; 23 September, 1974, and 14 May 1977.

11. *Standard-Freeholder*, 31 January 1953 and 30 May 1978.

12. *Ibid.*, 12 September 1979.
13. *Ibid.*, 30 November 1979.
14. *Ibid.*, 24 January 1945, 13 October and 22 November 1948; 5 February 1972 and 28 November 1979.
15. *Ibid.*, 26 March 1979.
16. *Ibid.*, 3 August 1946.
17. *Ibid.*, 11 September 1946.
18. *Ibid.*, 8 October 1947.
19. *Ibid.*, 26 September 1950; Secretary-treasurer H. Bradley Lewis to Senior, 17 March 1982.
20. *Standard-Freeholder*, 30 October 1958.
21. *Ibid.*, 3 August 1946, 2 November 1945, 18 September 1961.
22. *Ibid.*, 24 January 1955.
23. L. Jean Cameron and M. Louisa MacArthur, Canadian Federation of University Women, Cornwall Club, Twenty-fifth Anniversary, 27 May 1980.
24. *Standard-Freeholder*, 30 May 1978.
25. *Associations, Organizations and Clubs, Cornwall Directory*, 1979-1980, 29.
26. *Standard-Freeholder*, 16 February 1980.
27. *Ibid.*, 31 January 1953; Mrs. Cathie Thain, unit secretary, Cornwall and District, Canadian Cancer Society, to Senior, 18 March 1982.
28. Belva Webster, History of the Arthritis Society, 1967-1977.
29. *Standard-Freeholder*, 30 November 1951.
30. *Ibid.*, 19 March 1977.
31. *Ibid.*, 20 February 1953.
32. *Ibid.*, 22 March 1974 and 21 March 1975.
33. History of Stormont, Dundas and Glengarry Superannuated Teachers of Ontario, District 25, September 1982, prepared by L. Jean Cameron, Angus McKenzie, Mrs. Olive Higgins and Laura Sabourin.
34. *Standard-Freeholder*, 18 March 1972, 17 March 1973, 22 March 1974.
35. Mrs. Rachelle Lecours, executive coordinator, to Senior, 20 May 1982.
36. *Associations, Organizations and Clubs, Cornwall Directory*, 1979-1980, 142.
37. *Ibid.*, 19 and 188; Marilyn Bergeron to Senior, 30 June 1982.
38. *Gazette*, Montreal, 15 January 1983.
39. Live birth-abortion statistics, supplied by Cornwall General Hospital to Senior, 7 December 1982.
40. Margaret G. Ferguson, Staff Development, Cornwall General Hospital, to Senior, 7 December 1982; *Standard-Freeholder*, 26 March 1979.
41. *Hotel Dieu Jubilee*, 30.
42. *St. Lawrence Sanitorium*, 1937-38; *Standard-Freeholder*, 26 October 1945, 27 and 30 September 1972, 24 February 1973; *Old Home Week*, 1946, 41.
43. *Standard-Freeholder*, 3 Aug. 1946.
44. *Standard-Freeholder*, 25 Oct. 1947, and 1 Sept. 1950.
45. *Associations, Organizations and Clubs, Cornwall Directory*, 1979-1980, 114.
46. Margaret Bradbury to Senior, 24 June 1982.
47. *Album Souvenir, Hommages à Mgr. J.-A. Brunelle*, 1942-1960, 39.
48. *Standard-Freeholder*, 31 May 1979.
49. *Répertoire 1979-1980 des associations, organizations et clubs de Cornwall.*
50. *Standard-Freeholder*, 2 Aug. 1975 and 14 Dec. 1979.
51. *Globe and Mail*, Toronto, 21 Nov. 1981; Veerendra D. Adhiya to Senior, 11 Mar. 1982.
52. *Standard-Freeholder*, 24 June 1967.

53. *Ibid.*, 12 May 1980.

54. Stanley McNairn, President, Stormont, Dundas and Glengarry Historical Society, and L. Jean Cameron, Secretary, to Clerk, United Counties, 15 Nov. 1976.

55. *Heritage Cornwall*, LACAC, i, see forward by Dr. R.J. Burns.

56. Clive and Francis Marin, *Stormont, Dundas and Glengarry 1945-1978* (Belleville, 1982).

57. Dorothy Donihee, In My Mother's Footsteps, unpublished memoirs; Eileen Merkley, *The Friendly Town that Grew: A Reminiscence of Cornwall, Ontario* (Cornwall, 1978).

58. Bill Gallant, *The Frozen Stage: History of the Cornwall Royals* (Ottawa, 1981); Rudolph Villeneuve, *Catholic Education in Cornwall, Ontario, Yesterday, Today and Tomorrow* (Cornwall, 1971).

59. *Standard-Freeholder*, 3 Aug. 1946; 21 Mar. 1975; 25 May 1979.

60. Larry Keen, Community Programmes Chairman, Branch No. 297, to Senior, 14 April 1982.

61. Florence G. English to Senior, 26 July 1982.

62. *Standard-Freeholder*, 29 June 1934.

63. *Ibid.*, 13 May 1980.

64. *Census*, 1971, i, part 3, Bulletin 1.3-3, 3-4; *Statistics Canada Census*, 1981, iii, 101.

65. *Statistics Canada, Census*, 1981, iii, 97.

66. *Standard-Freeholder*, 31 Dec. 1977.

67. *Ibid.*, 26 Mar. 1979.

68. *Ibid.*, 30 May 1979.

69. *Ibid.*, 31 Mar. 1980.

70. *Ibid.*, 26 Mar. 1979.

71. *Ibid.*, 24 June 1967.

72. See announcement by Business People of Cornwall City Centre given to each recipient of a "Chip off the Old Block", St. Patrick's Day, 17 March 1983. *Standard-Freeholder*, 18 Mar. 1983.

Select Bibliography

Unpublished sources

Cornwall
City of Cornwall Archives:
Town Council Committee Book 1933-1941.
Financial Statements.
Honor Roll 1939-1945.
Parks and Recreation Committee Council Minutes 1960.
Planning Board Minutes.
Police Commissioners, Board of 1945-59.
Town and City By-laws.
Cornwall Chamber of Commerce:
Minutes of Board of Trade 30 April 1890 to 24 November 1916.
Correspondence of Board of Trade 1890-1942.
Cash Book 1890-1956.
Cornwall Airport Brief submitted to Cornwall City Council 1977.
Diocesan Archives of Alexandria at Cornwall:
L'Association Canadienne Française d'Education d'Ontario collection.
Father Charles Murray, "Reminiscences", 1886.
Société Saint-Jean-Baptiste Papers, Cornwall.
Eglise de la Nativité de la Bienheureuse Vierge Marie.
Registres des Baptîmes, Mariages et Sépultures de la Congrégation Canadienne
Française de l'Eglise de la Nativité de la Sainte Vierge.

Simon Fraser Centennial Library:
Cornwall Town Council Minute Books 1868-1944.
Cornwall Football Club Minute Book 1899.
Cora MacMillan, "The Mohawk Indians of Cornwall Island", paper prepared for the
    Cornwall Centre Women's Institute, November 1968.
Norman A. McNairn, "A personal approach to history: Outline of John McNairn,
    U.E."
Regulations governing Police Force of the Town of Cornwall, 1911.
Callan J. Plumadore, "History of the Boy Scout Movement in Cornwall, 1975".
Price Waterhouse Associates, "A review of the Industrial Opportunity Study for the
    Cornwall Area", prepared for the Department of Regional Economic Expansion,
    Ottawa, 1971.
Trinity Church Register of burials 1813-1846; Subscribers List 1805 and floor plan of
    the Strachan Church.
Victorian Order of Nurses, Report on, 1945, Cornwall; and "Victorian Order of
    Nurses: 75 Years in Canada, 60 Years in Cornwall", prepared by Mrs. Carl
    Malcolm, 1973.

531

City plans deposited at the Simon Fraser Centennial Library:
"The Making of a New Cornwall 1963-1983: An Urban Renewal Study", prepared for the City Council by E.G. Faludi and Associates, Toronto, 1962.
"Cornwall Central Business District Renewal Scheme, Phase One", by E.G. Faludi and Associates, Cornwall 1968.
"Cornwall Downtown Redevelopment Plan", prepared by A.M. Ismaily, Cornwall, 1977.
"City of Cornwall Zoning By-law, no. 751, 1969", by Paul Landry and Garry Wood, "Central Area Planning: City of Cornwall", 1977.
"City of Cornwall Industrial Commission", 1956 and 1967.
"Report of the Post-War Planning and Rehabilitation Committee", 1945.
Norman D. Wilson, "Elements of a City Plan", Cornwall, 1944.
Senior Collection deposited at the Simon Fraser Centennial Library: Letters and documents from individuals, firms, institutions and organizations to author contained in boxes of research notes, including:
Canadian Red Cross Society, Cornwall, Branch Annual Report, 1981.
Catholic Women's League of Canada, Alexandria, Cornwall Diocesan Annual Report, April, 1982.
Children's Aid Society, Outline of History from records and Minute Books 1908-1958, on the 50th Anniversary of the Society.
"La Citadelle, Cornwall: une école secondaire de langue française: nous la voulons, nous l'aurons", a collection of documents and newspaper clippings on La Citadelle.
"Community Services to Families and Individuals in the Town of Cornwall, Ontario, 1935: A Community Study made at the request of His Worship, the Mayor of Cornwall", prepared by the Canadian Welfare Council, Ottawa, under Bessie Touzel, Muriel Tucker and Charlotte Whitton.
Fernande DeSerres-Fobert, "Historique de la Paroisse de la Nativité depuis sa fondation", 1982.
Gisèle Dion, "Outline history of the Fédération des Femmes Canadiennes-Françaises in Cornwall", 1982.
Ralph Ellis, "Unionization of a Mill Town: Cornwall in 1936", unpublished term paper presented to the History Department, McGill University, spring 1982.
Ralph Ellis, "Cornwall Labour and Unionization 1936-37", unpublished term paper presented to the History Department, McGill University, spring 1982.
Ralph Ellis, "Labour and Municipal Politics in Cornwall, 1936-39", unpublished term paper presented to the History Department, McGill University, spring 1982.
Ralph Ellis, "The Economic, Social and Demographic Impact of the Cornwall Canal: 1834-1843", unpublished term paper presented to the History Department, McGill University, spring 1982.
"Founding and Progress of Cornwall Family Welfare Bureau, Report on", 1944.
Rosemary Joy, "Genealogical Notes on the Matthias Snetsinger Family".
Fred MacMillan, Dr. Simon Fraser and Philip Robertson, "History of St. John's Church, Cornwall, 1787-1975".
Winifred Mavor, "History of St. Lawrence Chapter, I.O.D.E.", April 1982.
Winifred Mavor, "History of the Cornwall Golf and Country Club", 1982.
Harry Moffatt, "Early History of Curling in the Cornwall Area", 1980.
Jules Renaud, "Account of the Founding of the Franco-Centre", 1980.
Jules Renaud, "L'Ecole Secondaire: La Citadelle de Cornwall".

Zo-Anne Roy, "Outline History of L'Ordre des Filles d'Isabelle, Cercle Notre Dame du Perpétuel Secours no. 1028".

Hannah Lawrence Schieffelin, letter 4 Dec. 1780, in *New York Genealogical and Biographical Records*, 1941, vol. 72.

Hereward Senior, "The Loyalists in Quebec: A Study in Diversity", paper presented to the Canadian Historical Association at the Learned Societies Conference, Halifax, 3 June 1981.

"St. John Ambulance Annual Report," Cornwall, 1981.

"St. Lawrence-Seaway Authority Fact Sheet, 1203".

Evelyn Stidwill, "Early Recollections of St. Paul's United Church", Cornwall, 1966.

Trinity Memorial Church, "Statistical Returns", 1 Jan. to 31 Dec. 1981.

Arthur Youngs, "Freemasonry in Cornwall and Area first recorded in the late 1700s", 1980.

Stormont, Dundas and Glengarry Historical Society Collection deposited in the Simon Fraser Centennial Library. Among the items used from this collection were:

Mrs. Garnet Alguire, "How the Seaway and Power Project Affected this Community", paper read to the Cornwall Centre Women's Institute, August 1960.

Mack W.R. Alguire, "History of the Mail Service", printed in *Standard-Freeholder*, 15 Feb. 1955.

L. Jean Cameron, Angus McKenzie, Olive Higgins and Laura Sabourin, "The Story of S.D.G. Superannuated Teachers of Ontario, District 25", September 1982.

L. Jean Cameron and M. Louisa MacArthur, "Canadian Federation of University Women, Cornwall Club, Twenty-Fifth Anniversary", 27 May 1980.

Dorothy Donihee, "In My Mother's Footsteps", Cornwall 1979.

Know Your City, Cornwall, Ontario, paper prepared by Commercial Class XII, Cornwall Collegiate and Vocational School, February 1961.

Emily MacInnes, "Tribute to Mary Agnes Mack", paper presented to the Stormont, Dundas and Glengarry Historical Society, 17 January 1979.

Lyall Manson and Mary Mack, "Waterfront Inventory", paper presented to the S.D.G. Historical Society, January 1972.

Prince William Henry, Address to, by the Citizens of Cornwall, 1787.

J. Allan Walters, "Royal Towns, the St. Lawrence River and the Bay of Quinte Townships", paper presented to the S.D.G. Historical Society, 19 January 1977.

C. Hume Wilkins, "Stormont, Dundas and Glengarry", paper presented to the S.D.G. Historical Society, 17 January 1972.

Arthur Youngs, "St. Paul's United Church", February 1978, YM-YWCA brochure, Cornwall, c. 1959.

St. Columban's Church:
Births, Marriages and Deaths Registers 1834-38 and 1886-1931.

Trinity Church:
Canon Jacob J.S. Mountain, Will of, Cornwall, 25 June 1902.
Register of Births, Deaths and Marriages, 1835.

United Counties Museum:
Frank B. Risteen, "Some Highlights in the Life of Cornwall's founder: Sir John Johnson", paper presented to the Stormont, Dundas and Glengarry Historical Society, 17 March 1976.

Privately held:
> Barnhart Genealogy, prepared by Dr. Barnhart and held by Mr. and Mrs. Benson Stidwill, Cornwall.
> Members Register, Oriental Lodge of Oddfellows, Cornwall, no. 163, 1884-1981, and Officers Roll Book, Oriental Lodge, no. 163, 31 Dec. 1913 to 30 June 1969, held by G. Revill, Cornwall.

Montreal

Archdiocese de Montréal Archives:
> Bishop J.J. Lartigue Letters.
> Kingston Diocese Letters, 1836-1842, file 255.

McCord Museum:
> Miscellaneous Masonic Papers, 12291.

McGill University:
> John McDonald of Garth Autobiographical Notes 1791-1816 CH3.S39.
> Statement by some Inhabitants of Cornwall that changes in the road made by John McDonald are not detrimental to the general public, 17 June 1817, CH222. S200.

Privately held:
> Orange Warrant for Hugh McCallum, Loyal Orange Lodge no. 880, Cornwall, 14 March 1870, held by Mrs. Leslie Roberts, Montreal; facsimile is in Senior Collection in Simon Fraser Centennial Library, Cornwall.

Ottawa

Diocesan Archives (Anglican):
> Trinity Church Papers 59.

Public Archives:
> Assessment Returns, Cornwall, 1829-1843, RG5/B26/6.
> British Military Records, RG8/C series.
> Buchanan Papers, MG24/D16/107.
> Civil Secretary's Correspondence, RG5/CI/210-212, 223, 225.
> Colborne Papers, MG24/A40.
> Dorchester Papers, MG23/GII/6.
> Governors, Lieutenant-Governors and Administrators' Correspondence, Upper and Lower Canada, 1763 to 1841, MG11/Q series.
> Ogle R. Gowan, Memoirs of the Rebellions 1837-38, in Ferguson Papers, MG27/IE/v.
> Greater Cornwall Textile Joint Board Collection, MG28/1-219.
> Haldimand Papers, MG21.
> Sir John Johnson, correspondence, warrants, accounts and related records of, MG19/F2.
> King's Royal Regiment of New York, Orderly book of 1st Battalion kept by Captain Samuel Anderson, May 1779 - August 1780, and Memorandum Book kept by Adjutant John Valentine, Account Book and Roll, 1782-1784, MG23/B23.
> Labour, Department of, Strikes and Lockout Records, 1907-1973, RG27.
> Land Board Records, RG1/L1-4.
> John Sandfield Macdonald Papers and Letters, MG24/B30.
> Bishop Alexander Macdonell Letters, 1836-1839, MG24/J13.
> Ralph E. McIntee Papers, MG30/A87.
> Militia Records, 1774-1814, RG4/B29.
> Militia Records, RG9/IC6.

Peter O'Brian Papers, MG24/G71.
James Pringle Papers, MG24/I29.
Jacob Farrand Pringle Papers, MG24/G44.
Simcoe Papers, 1793-1795, MG24/K2.
State Papers, Upper Canada, 1791-1841, RG1/E3.
Civil and Provincial Secretaries' Correspondence, Lower Canada, "S" series, RG4/A1.
Upper Canada Sundries, RG5/A1.
War Office, 28.
Wily Memoirs, MG29/E1.

TORONTO
Provincial Archives
Nancy Cameron letter, 12 May 1785, MU 2098.
Canniff Papers, MU492.
Crown Land Papers, Stormont County Surveys, RG1/A7.
Eastern District Quarter Sessions 1826-1835, MG9/D8.
General Quarter Sessions of the Peace for the Eastern District, Minutes of, RG22/7.
Strachan Papers.
University of Toronto:
James R. Miller, "Town of Cornwall 1784-1867", unpublished M.A. thesis, 1967.
T. Phillips, "History of Cornwall", unpublished M.A. thesis.
Upper Canada Village:
Paul Fortier, "Accommodation for Militiamen in the Eastern and Johnstown Districts of Upper Canada during the War of 1812", 1977.
James Smart, "St. Lawrence Project: Events in Military History 1760 to 1814".
University of Western Ontario:
Ruth Bleasdale, "Irish Labourers on the Cornwall, Welland and Williamsburg Canals in the 1840s", unpublished M.A. thesis, September, 1975.

Published sources
Books, articles and pamphlets
Aren Akweks, *History of the St. Regis Atkesasne Mohawks.* Malone, New York, 1948.
_____ *Album Souvenir: Hommages à Mgr. J.-A. Brunelle, P.P., Curé de la Nativité, Cornwall, 1942-60.*
William Mack Alguire, *Historical Sketch of Cornwall. Greetings to Their Majesties, and Memories of Former Happy Visits, Souvenir Programme. 21 May 1939.*
J.B. Allaire, *Dictionnaire biographique du clergé Canadien-Français.* Montreal 1908-1934.
Brother Alfred, *Catholic Pioneers in Upper Canada.* Toronto, 1947.
Jeffery Amherst, *The Journal of,* ed. by J. Clarence Webster. Toronto, 1931.
Ian Angus, *Canadian Bolsheviks: Early Years of the Communist Party of Canada.* Montreal, 1981.
_____ *Second report of the Bureau of Archives for the Province of Ontario,* part I and II, 1904, Toronto, 1905.
_____ *Third report of the Bureau of Archives for the Province of Ontario,* 1905, Toronto, 1906.

_____ Sixteenth report of the Department of Archives for the Province of Ontario, 1920. Toronto, 1921.
_____ Report of the Public Archives of Canada. Ottawa, 1884-1889.
_____ Report of the Public Archives of Canada. Ottawa, 1890.
Frederick H. Armstrong, Handbook of Upper Canadian Chronology and Territorial Legislation. London, 1967.
_____ Associations, Organizations and Clubs, Cornwall Directory, 1979-1980.
H. Belden, Illustrated Historical Atlas of the Counties of Stormont, Dundas and Glengarry, Ont., compiled, drawn and published from personal Examinations and Surveys. Toronto, 1879.
Darby Bergin, The Cornwall Canal: Its Location and construction, breaks and present condition, a speech delivered in the House of Commons. Ottawa, 1889.
A.N. Bethune, Memoir of the Right Reverend John Strachan. Toronto, 1870.
Ruth Bleasdale, "Class Conflict on the Canals of Upper Canada in the 1840s", in Labour/Le Travailleur, spring 1981, 9-39.
Richard H. Bonnycastle, The Canadas in 1841. 2 vols. London, 1842.
William Boss, Stormont, Dundas and Glengarry Highlanders, 1783-1951. Ottawa, 1952.
Alfred Leroy Burt, The Old Province of Quebec. Toronto, 1968.
Alexander Caldwell and Mary Stewart, Cornwall Collegiate and Vocational School. Cornwall, 1956.
Brian Cameron, A Brief History of Knox United Church, Cornwall, 1846-1975. Cornwall, 1975.
L. Jean Cameron, First Baptist Church, Cornwall, 1882-1967, Eighty-fifth Anniversary, June 15, 1882 — June 15, 1967. Cornwall, 1967.
Francis W. Campbell, Fenian Raids of 1866 and 1870. Montreal, 1904.
Patrick Campbell, Travels in the interior inhabited parts of North America in the years 1791 and 1792. Edinburgh, 1937.
Robert Campbell, A History of the Scotch Presbyterian Church, St. Gabriel Street. Montreal, 1887.
_____, Canada Directory, 1851.
_____, Canada's Party of Socialism: History of the Communist Party of Canada, 1921-1976. Toronto, 1982.
_____, Canadian Parliamentary Guide. Ottawa, 1981.
_____, Canadian Parliamentary Guide. Ottawa, 1975.
William Canniff, Settlement of Upper Canada. Toronto, 1869, reprinted Belleville, 1971.
J.M.S. Careless, Brown of the Globe: 1818-1850, The Voice of Upper Canada, i. Toronto, 1959.
Charlotte Bruce Carey, "Sketch of the Bruce Family" in Annual Transactions, United Empire Loyalists' Association. iii. Toronto, 1900. 50-52.
Philip Carrington, The Anglican Church of Canada. Toronto, 1963.
J. Smyth Carter, The Story of Dundas, being a history of the County from 1784 to 1904. Iroquois, 1905.
_____, Catholic Women's League of Canada, Constitution and By-laws. 1979.
_____, Census, Returns for the Town of Cornwall and the Townships of Cornwall and Roxborough, prepared by Alexander McDonell, Assessor, 1829. Ed. by Robert Burns and Daphne Howells, 1978.
_____, Census, Canada, 1851-1981.
_____, Chemistry in Canada. June 1970. 26-28.
Lionel Chevrier, The St. Lawrence Seaway 1954-1957. Toronto, 1959.

Willis Chipman, "The Life and Times of Major Samuel Holland, Surveyor-General 1764-1801", in *Ontario Historical Society Papers and Records*. xxi. Toronto, 1924, 11-90.

George Corbet, *A Retrospect: First Catholic Diocese in Upper Canada and the Evolution of the Catholic Separate School System*. Cornwall, 1921.

_____, *Greater Cornwall: the Friendly City*. Board of Trade booklet. Cornwall c. 1951.

_____, *Cornwall, Ontario: City of Opportunity*. Prepared by the Industrial Committee of Greater Cornwall. Cornwall, 1950.

_____, *The Cornwall Canal, also Correspondence on the subject of the recent Break in the Cornwall Canal*. Ottawa, 1889.

_____, *Directory of Cornwall Curling Club*. 1981-82.

_____, *Cornwall General Hospital Bylaws*. Cornwall, 1898.

_____, *Cornwall City Directory 1933-34*.

_____, *Welcome to Cornwall: the Friendly Seaway City*. c. 1967.

_____, *The Cornwall Mill 1881-1981: A Century of Achievement*. Cornwall, 1981.

_____, *The Cornwall Mill Story*. Cornwall, 1970.

_____, *The Cornwall Tribute, a piece of plate presented to the Honourable and Venerable John Strachan, D.D., Archdeacon of York, by forty-two of his former students, educated by him at Cornwall*. Cornwall, July 1833.

Joseph Cosette, "Father Pierre Rene Floquet", in *Dictionary of Canadian Biography*, iv, 270-271.

N. Omer Coté, *Political Appointments, Parliaments and Judicial Bench in the Dominion of Canada, 1867-1895*. Ottawa, 1896.

N. Omer Coté, *Supplement to Political Appointments, Parliaments and the Judicial Bench in the Dominion of Canada 1896-1903*. Ottawa, 1903.

J.O. Coté, *Political Appointments and Elections in the Province of Canada from 1841 to 1865*. Ottawa, 1866.

_____, *Courtaulds (Canada) Limited, Yesterday...today and tomorrow, 50th anniversary 1925-1975*. Cornwall, 1975.

_____, *Courtaulds: a Brief History*. London, 1975.

_____, "Courtaulds (Canada) Limited: 30th Year in Canada" in special issue of *The Rayon Reel*, October 1955.

_____, *Covenant Chapter, no. 113, G.R.C. Royal Arch Masons, 1894-1944: Fiftieth Anniversary*. Cornwall, 1944.

Gerald M. Craig, *Upper Canada: the Formative Years 1784-1841*. Toronto, 1963.

Gerald M. Craig, "John Strachan", in *Dictionary of Canadian Biography*, ix. 751-766.

Donald Creighton, *The Empire of the St. Lawrence*. Toronto, 1956.

James Croil, *Dundas: or a sketch of Canadian History, and more particularly of the County of Dundas, one of the Earliest Settled Counties in Upper Canada*. Montreal 1861.

E.A. Cruikshank, *Record of the Service of the Canadian Regiments in the War of 1812*. Cornwall, 1915.

E.A. Cruikshank, "A Memoir of Lt.-Col. John Macdonell, of Glengarry House", in *Ontario Historical Society Papers and Records*, 1925. xxii. 20-59.

E.A. Cruikshank, "A Journey from Montreal to Kingston in 1791", in *Ontario Historical Society Papers and Records*. xxi. Toronto, 1924.

E.A. Cruikshank, *The Settlement of the United Empire Loyalists on the Upper St. Lawrence and the Bay of Quinte in 1784*. Toronto, 1966.

Joseph Denieffe, *A Personal Narrative of the Irish Revolutionary Brotherhood*. New York, 1906, reprinted Shannon, 1969.

J.A. Derome, *La Canada écclesiastique: almanach annuaire du clergé Canadien*. Montreal 1914.

Thomas Doige, *Montreal Directory: An Alphabetical list of merchants, traders and householders residing in Montreal*. Montreal, 1819.

_____, *Agreement between Domtar Fine Papers, Cornwall, and Office and Professional Employees International Union Local 418*. 1981-1984.

_____, *Some Questions and Answers about Domtar's Cornwall Mill and the Environment*.

_____, *Domtar Fine Papers, Cornwall, Ont., Labour Agreement 1981-1984 for members of Canadian Papermakers Union, C.L.C., Locals 212 and 338*.

A.G. Doughty and D.A. McArthur, *Documents relating to the Constitutional History of Canada, 1791-1818*.

William Dunlop, *Recollections of the War of 1812*.

Matilda Edgar, *Ten years of Upper Canada in Peace and War, 1805-1815, being the Ridout Letters with Annotations*. Toronto, 1890.

_____, *Financial Post Survey of Predecessor and Defunct Companies*. 1981.

_____, *Financial Post Survey of Industrials*, 1957, 1959, 1960 and 1982.

Edith Firth, *The Town of York 1815-1834*. Toronto, 1966.

_____, *Fly Creek Drainage Study, Final Report*. The Raisin Region Conservation Authority. Ottawa, 1977.

L.J. Flynn, *Built on a Rock: The Story of the Roman Catholic Church in Kingston, 1826-1976*. Kingston, 1976.

F.J. French, "Jeremiah French: U.E. Loyalist", in *Ontario Historical Society Papers and Records*. xxi. 1924. 181-182.

Mary Beacock Fryer, *King's Men: Soldier-Founders of Ontario*. Toronto, 1981.

Bill Gallant, *The Frozen Stage: History of the Cornwall Royals*. Ottawa, 1981.

_____, *25th Anniversaire, Garde Nativité*. 1952-1977.

John Gault, "Losing on the Plains of Cornwall", in *Maclean's Magazine*, vol. 87, no. 1. January 1974.

Heather Gilbert, *Awakening Continent: The Life of Lord Mount Stephen*. i. Aberdeen, 1965.

Jean L. Gogo, *A History of the Cornwall General Hospital*.

Robert Gourlay, *Statistical Account of Upper Canada, compiled with a view for a Grand System of Emigration*. i. London, 1822 and 1866.

John S. Grant, "Reminiscences", in *Standard-Freeholder*, 28 September 1946.

Rhodes Grant, "Settlement of the Counties traced by an Area Resident; a Descendant of Angus Grant who was with Sir John Johnson on the Trek" in *Standard-Freeholder*, 5 July 1976.

Ernest Green, "Notes on the Empey (Impey) Family of Stormont", in *Ontario Historical Society Papers and Records*, xxvii. 1931. 392-399.

Michèle Guay, "Jean (John) François-Marie-Joseph Macdonell", in *Dictionary of Canadian Biography*. ix. 485-86.

Edwin C. Guillet, *Early Life in Upper Canada*. Toronto, 1933.

Joseph Hadfield, *An Englishman in America, 1785, being the Diary of Joseph Hadfield, edited and annotated by Douglas' S. Robertson*. Toronto, 1933.

John H. Hanson, *The Lost Prince*. New York, 1854.

John Graham Harkness, *A History of Stormont, Dundas and Glengarry, 1784-1945*. Ottawa, 1946.

Robert A. Harrison, *The New Municipal Manual for Upper Canada containing votes of decided cases and a full analytical index.* Toronto, 1859.

J.L.H. Henderson, *John Strachan.* Toronto, 1969.

George Heriot, *Travels through the Canadas.* London, 1807.

_____, *Histoire de Cornwall - Experience '78: Un projet études canadiennes.* Cornwall, 1978.

J. Mackay Hitsman, *Incredible War of 1812: A Military History.* Toronto, 1965.

Bruce W. Hodgins, *John Sandfield MacDonald.* Toronto, 1971.

Bruce W. Hodgins, "Philip VanKoughnet" in *Dictionary of Canadian Biography,* x, 693-94.

Elizabeth Hoople, *The Hooples of Hoople's Creek,* Toronto, 1967.

_____, *Hotel Dieu Jubilee 1897-1922.* Cornwall.

Franklin B. Hough, *A History of St. Lawrence and Franklin Counties, New York, from the earliest period to the present time.* Albany, 1853.

Franklin B. Hough, translator and editor, *Memoir upon the late war in North America between the French and English 1755-1760, followed by observations upon the theatre of the Actual War and by new Details concerning the manners and customs of the Indians; with topographical maps.* 2 vols. Roxbury, Mass., 1866.

_____, *25 Years of Progress: Being an Account by word and picture of the Accomplishments of the first quarter century of Howard Smith Paper Mills Limited and Affiliated Companies.* June 1937.

George S. Jarvis, "Reminiscences", in *Canadian Illustrated News,* 26 January 1878.

Robert Jefferson, *Faith of our Fathers: the Story of the Ottawa Diocese.* Ottawa, 1957.

Winifred Jerrom, "Our Story, the W.A. and the A.C.W.", in *Angelion,* Cornwall, spring, 1980.

Sir John Johnson, *The North American Johnsons: A short Story of Triumph and Tragedy.* London, 1963.

J.K. Johnson, "Donald Aeneas Macdonell", in *Dictionary of Canadian Biography,* x. 469-470.

J.K. Johnson, "George Stephen Jarvis", in *Dictionary of Canadian Biography,* x. 379-380.

J.K. Johnson, "Col. James Fitzgibbon and the Suppression of Irish Riots in Upper Canada", in *Ontario History,* lvii. 1966. 139-155.

J.K. Johnson, *The Canadian Directory of Parliament 1867-1967.* Ottawa, 1968.

_____, *Journal, Appendix to, Legislative Assembly, 1843,* no. 2. iii.

Gregory S. Kealey and Bryan D. Palmer, "The Bonds of Unity: the Knights of Labor in Ontario, 1880-1900", in *Histoire Sociale/Social History,* xiv. no. 28, November 1981, 369-411.

Gregory S. Kealey, ed. *Canada Investigates Industrialism: The Royal Commission on the relations of Labor and Capital, 1889.* Toronto, 1973.

William Kingsford, *History of Canada.* vii, Toronto, 1898.

William Kingsford, *The Canadian Canals: their History and Cost.* Toronto, 1865.

_____, *The Story of Kinsmenship: Special 50th Anniversary issue of Kin 1920-1970.*

_____, *History of District Six: the Association of Kinsmen.* Brockville, 1966.

_____, *Kinscope: The Kinsmen Club of Cornwall,* vol. 48, no. 12, April 1982.

_____, "Knights of Columbus Council 755, 75th Anniversary 1903-1978, Cornwall", in *Standard-Freeholder,* 21 November 1978.

John Knox, *An Historical Journal of the Campaigns in North America for the years 1757, 1758, 1759 and 1760.* 3 vols. Toronto, 1914.

Otto Langmark and Kent Baker, *The Official Plan of the City of Cornwall 1968.*

Roderick Lewis, *Centennial Edition of a History of the Electoral Districts, Legislatures and Ministries of the Province of Ontario 1867-1968.* Toronto, 1968.

Sydenham B. Lindsay, "The Romance of Louis XVII", in *Gazette,* Montreal, 16 June 1922.

Charles Lipton, *The Trade Union Movement of Canada, 1827-1959.* Toronto, 1973.

_____, *Liste des Terrains concedés par la couronne dans la Province de Québec de 1763 au 31 Décembre 1890.* Montreal, 1891.

G. Murray Logan, *Scottish Highlanders and the American Revolution.* Halifax, 1976.

_____, *Lovell's Ontario Directory.* 1871.

_____, *Vote Lumley.* Cornwall, 1971.

Edward Lumley, *Householder Newsletter.* Ottawa, December 1974.

James R. McCartney, "Sectarian Strife in Dundas County: A Lutheran-Episcopalian Land Endowment Controversy", in *Ontario History,* liv, June 1962, 69-86.

Herbert S. McDonald, "Memoir of Col. Joel Stone: a U.E.L. and the Founder of Gananoque", in *Ontario Historical Society Papers and Records,* xviii, 1920, 59-90.

John A. MacDonald, *Troublous Times in Canada: A History of the Fenian Raids of 1866 and 1870.* Toronto, 1910.

John Alexander Macdonell, *Sketches, illustrating the early settlement and history in Glengarry, in Canada, relating principally to the revolutionary war of 1775-1783, the war of 1812-14, and the rebellion of 1837-38, and the services of the King's Royal Regiment of New York, the 84th Royal Highland Emigrant Regiment, the Royal Canadian Volunteer Regiment of Foot, the Glengarry fencible or British Highland Regiment, the Glengarry Light Infantry regiment, and the Glengarry militia.* Montreal, 1893.

John MacLennan, "Early Settlement of Glengarry" in *Transactions of the Celtic Society of Montreal.* Montreal 1884-1887.

Mary Mack, "History of Bishop Strachan Memorial Trinity Church" in *Souvenir of the Dedication of the Restored and Modernized Memorial Pipe Organ.* 1968.

George Mainer, "Solomon Yeomans Chesley", in *Dictionary of Canadian Biography,* x, 163-164.

Clive and Frances Marin, *Stormont, Dundas and Glengarry 1945-1978.* Belleville, 1982.

Eileen Merkley, *The Friendly Town that Grew.* Cornwall, 1978.

Nick and Helma Mika, *United Empire Loyalists: Pioneers of Upper Canada.* Belleville, 1976.

A.J.B. Milborne, *Freemasonry in the Province of Quebec 1759-1959.* Knowlton, 1960.

Carman Miller, "A Preliminary Analysis of the Socio-Economic Composition of Canada's South African War Contingents", in *Histoire Sociale/Social History,* November 1975, 219-237.

_____, *Mitchell's Canada Gazetteer and Business Directory, 1864-65.*

Henry Morgan, *Canadian Men and Women of the Time: A Handbook of Canadian Biography.* Toronto, 1898.

A.C. Morice, "A Canadian Pioneer: Spanish John", in *Canadian Historical Review,* x, 1929, 212-235.

_____, *Paroisse de la Nativité de la B.V.M. 1887-1962: 75th Anniversaire.* Cornwall, 1962.

_____, *New Democratic Party informtion brochure on George Samis.* April, 1981.

_____, *Notre Histoire racontée par Nicole Hamelin, Linda Lamothe et Marc-Andre Bernier*. Cornwall, 1981.

Anne Nyland, "History of the Cornwall Public Library", 1982.

John Cosens Ogden, *A Tour Through Upper and Lower Canada by a Citizen of the United States*. Litchfield, 1799.

_____, *Old Boys' Reunion at Cornwall, Ontario, August 11-15, 1906; Souvenir of Stormont, Dundas and Glengarry*.

_____, *Old Boys' Re-Union at Cornwall, Ontario, July 31st August 7th, 1926: Official Souvenir Booklet*.

_____, *Old Home Week, City of Cornwall and the United Counties of Stormont, Dundas and Glengarry, August 3 to 10, 1946: Souvenir Booklet and Program*.

_____, *Parliamentary Register*, 7 March 1823.

Dorothy J. Phelps, *John Strachan Comes to Cornwall, 1803-1812*. Cornwall, 1976.

Dorothy J. Phelps, *Trinity, Bishop Strachan, Memorial Church, 1869-1978: As I See It*. Cornwall, 1978.

Pierre Pouchot, *Memoirs sur la Dernière Guerre de l'Amérique septentrionale, entre La France et l'Angleterre par M. Pouchot, Chevalier de l'Ordre Royal et Militaire de St. Louis, ancien capitaine au Régiment de Béarn, Commandant des forts de Niagara et de Levis, en Canada*. Yverdon, 1781.

Richard Preston, *Kingston before the War of 1812: A Collection of Documents*. Toronto, 1959.

Jacob Farrand Pringle, *Lunenburgh, or the Old Eastern District*. Cornwall, 1890; reprinted Belleville, 1980.

_____, *Recueil de Jeux, presented by La fédération des Femmes, Section Femina*, prepared by Paule Geoffrion, Michel Mayer, and Cyrille Aubin. Cornwall, 1981.

J.E. Rea, *Bishop Alexander Macdonell and the Politics of Upper Canada*. Toronto, 1974.

T.A. Reed, "John Strachan's Journey from Montreal to Kingston in December 1799", in *Ontario History*, xlii, 1950, no. 4, 213-217.

_____, *Répertoire 1979-1980, des associations, organizations et clubs de Cornwall*.

_____, *Report on the State of the Militia*. Ottawa, 1857, 1865, 1866, 1870.

William D. Reid, *Death Notices of Ontario*. Lambertville, New Jersey, 1980.

William D. Reid, *The Loyalists in Ontario: the Sons and Daughters of the American Loyalists of Upper Canada*. Lambertville, New Jersey, 1973.

Frank B. Risteen, *The Founding of Cornwall*. Toronto, 1968.

Frank B. Risteen, "How Cornwall was Founded", in *Standard-Freeholder*, 9 December 1965.

John Ross Robertson, *The Diary of Mrs. John Graves Simcoe, wife of the First Lieutenant Governor of the Province of Upper Canada, 1792-1796*. Toronto, 1911.

John Ross Robertson, *History of Freemasonry in Canada*, 2 vols. Toronto, 1899.

Duc de la Rochefoucauld-Liancourt, *Travels through the United States of North America, the Country of the Iroquois, and Upper Canada in the years 1795, 1796, and 1797*. ed. by William R. Riddell. Toronto, 1916.

Thomas Rolph, *A brief account together with observations made during a visit in the West Indies, and a tour through the United States in parts of the year 1832-33, together with a Statistical Account of Upper Canada*. Dundas, Upper Canada, 1836.

Donald Ross-Ross, A.L. Farnsworth, and G.B. Stidwill, *History of Engineering in the Cornwall Area: a paper marking the 75th anniversary of the Engineering Institute of Canada*, submitted by the Cornwall Branch, E.I.C., reproduced through the courtesy of Howard Smith Division, Domtar Pulp and Paper Limited. Cornwall, 1962.

S. Rowe, "The Anderson Record from 1699 to 1896", in *Ontario Historical Society Papers and Records*, vi, 1905, 109-135.

_____, *Royal Commission on the Textile Industry*. Ottawa, 1938.

Milton Rubincam, *The Old United Empire Loyalists List: Centennial of the Settlement of Upper Canada by the United Empire Loyalists 1784-1884*. Toronto 1885; reprinted Baltimore, 1969.

_____, "Salvation Army: 85th Anniversary in Cornwall", in *Standard-Freeholder*, 15 March 1973.

George Samis, *Queen's Park Report,*. 17 October 1974.

Charles R. Sanderson, ed. *The Arthur Papers*. iii. Toronto, 1957.

_____, *150th Anniversary St. Columban's Parish, 1829-1979*. Cornwall, 1979.

_____, *An Historical Sketch of St. Columban's Parish, Cornwall, Commemorative of the opening of the new Church, June 1896*. Cornwall, 1896.

_____, "25 Ans d'Histoire pour la Paroisse Sainte-Croix," in *Le Journal de Cornwall*, 28 September 1979.

_____, *25th Anniversaire de la Paroisse Saint-Félix-de-Valois*, Cornwall, 26 et 27 Mai, 1962.

_____, *25th Anniversaire de la Paroisse de St. Jean-Bosco, 1944-1969*.

_____, *St. Lawrence High School/Ecole Secondaire Saint-Laurent Official Opening*. June 1951 and 22 November 1974.

_____, *Campus: St. Lawrence College Saint-Laurent*, iii, no. 1, March 1975.

_____, *Campus: St. Lawrence College Saint-Laurent*, "We're Ten Years Old", 1967-1977.

Myrla Scott, *History of the First Baptist Church, Cornwall, 1882-1982*. Cornwall, 1982.

_____, *Scott's Industrial Directory of Ontario Manufacturers*. 1978, 1979.

Robert L. Séguin, *Le mouvement insurrectionnel dans la Presqu'île de Vaudreuil 1837-38*. Montreal, 1955.

Robert Sellar, *History of the County of Huntingdon*. Huntingdon, 1888.

Elinor Senior, *British Regulars in Montreal: An Imperial Garrison, 1832-1854*. Montreal, 1981.

Elinor Senior, *Roots of the Canadian Army in the Montreal District 1846-1870*. Montreal 1981.

Elinor Senior, "The Glengarry Highlanders and the Suppression of the Rebellions in Lower Canada 1837-38", in *Journal of the Society for Army Historical Research*, lvi, no. 227, London, 1978, 143-159.

Elinor Senior, "Loyalist Regiments after the American Revolution", in *Canadian Genealogist*, ii, no. 1, 1980, 31-46.

Hereward Senior, *The Fenians and Canada*. Toronto, 1978.

Hereward Senior, "John Hillyard Cameron: Canadian Scot and Orange Grand Master", in *Scottish Tradition*, ix/x, Guelph, 1981-82, 116-135.

Hereward Senior, *Orangeism: The Canadian Phase*. Toronto, 1972.

_____, *Services français à Cornwall*, prepared by Michele Morin, Andre Dion and Pascale Charest. Cornwall, 1981.

Adam Shortt and A.G. Doughty, *Documents relating to the Constitutional History of Canada 1759-1791*, Ottawa, 1918.

542

Adam Shortt and A.G. Doughty, *Canada and its Provinces*. xvii. Toronto, 1914.

Wilbur H. Siebert, "The Loyalists and the Six Nation Indians in the Niagara Peninsula", in *Transactions of the Royal Society of Canada*, section ii, 1915, 79-100.

John Graves Simcoe, *Correspondence*, ed. by E.A. Cruikshank. 5 vols. Toronto, 1923-1931.

Alison Smith, "John Strachan and Early Upper Canada, 1799-1814", in *Ontario History*, lii, 1960, 158-173.

G. Meredith Smith, *The Smiths of Philipsburg and St. Johns, Quebec, 1768-1975*. Montreal, 1976.

Robert Smith, "Reminiscences of Cornwall 1885-1932", An address presented to the Stormont, Dundas and Glengarry Historical Society, 15 January 1932.

W.H. Smith, *Canada, Past, Present and Future*, 2 vols. 1852, reprinted, Belleville, 1974.

W.H. Smith, *Canadian Gazetteer, comprising statistical and general information respecting all parts of the Upper Province or Canada West, with a map of the Upper Province*. Toronto, 1846.

_____, *Société Saint-Jean Baptiste, Programme Souvenir*, 26 Juin 1932.

Hugh Joseph Somers, *Life and Times of the Honourable and Right Reverend Alexander Macdonell, D.D., First Bishop of Upper Canada, 1762-1840*. Washington, 1931.

G.W. Spragge, "The Cornwall Grammar School under John Strachan 1803-1812", in *Ontario Historical Society Papers and Records*, xxxiv, 1942, 61-84.

C.P. Stacey, "Michael Murphy: A Fenian Interlude", in the *Canadian Historical Review*, xv. no. 2, June, 1934, 133-154.

George C. Stanley, *Canada's Soldiers, 1604-1954: the Military History of an Unmilitary People*. Toronto, 1954.

_____, *State Papers, Upper Canada*, 1891, i.

_____, *State Papers of Vermont, Sequestration, Confiscation and Sale of Estates*, ed. by Mary Greene Nye, vi. 1941.

Charles James Stewart, *Report of a Missionary Journey made by...through Upper Canada in 1820*, ed. by J.J. Talman. London, 1942.

G.B. Stidwill, *The Mountains and Trinity Church*. Cornwall, 1965.

H.M. Stiles, *Official History of the Cornwall Cheese and Butter Board*. Cornwall, 1919.

William L. Stone, *Life of Joseph Brant - Thayendanegea, including the border wars of the American Revolution and sketches of the Indian campaigns*. 2 vols. Albany, 1865.

_____, *Stormont, Dundas and Glengarry Highlanders: A Brief History, 1784-1945, presented to members of the First Battalion upon their return from overseas*. Cornwall, 1945.

H.C. Stuart, *The Church of England in Canada, 1759-1793, from the Conquest to the establishment of the See of Quebec*. Montreal, 1893.

J.J. Talman, *Report of a Missionary Journey made by the Honourable and Reverend Charles James Stewart through Upper Canada in 1820*. London, 1942.

Cyprien Tanguay, *Répertoire général du clergé canadien*. 2 vols. Montreal, 1893.

Howard Temperley, "Frontierism, Capital and the American Loyalists in Canada", in *American Studies*, 13, I, Cambridge University, 1979, 5-27.

_____, "TCF's twenty-fifth anniversary," in *Standard-Freeholder*, 17 June 1978.

_____, *Souvenir booklet: Trinity Parish Building Campaign*. Cornwall, 1951.

_____, *Trinity Memorial Church Stewardship Programme*, 1979.

_____, *Trinity Memorial Church, Re-dedication by the Right Reverend Bishop W.J. Robinson*, October 1977.

_____, *Trinity Memorial Hall, 1952, renovation, 1979.*

_____, *University of Toronto, School of Social Works: Round Table on the Impact on the human-well being of a rapidly evolving industrialization.* Cornwall c. 1957.

Rudolph Villeneuve, *Catholic Education in Cornwall, Ontario, Yesterday, Today and Tomorrow.* Cornwall, 1971.

Rudolph Villeneuve, *The Signs of the Times: A Diocese in Transition, Diocese of Alexandria.* Cornwall, 1969.

Rudolph Villeneuve, *Youth Today and What They Want, a sociological Survey of the Youth of Cornwall,* 1968.

Robert Vogel and Terry Copp, *Maple Leaf Route: Caen.* Alma, Ontario, 1983.

F.A. Walker, *Catholic Education and Politics in Upper Canada.* Toronto, 1955.

James T. Watt, "Anti-Catholicism in Ontario Politics 1894", in *Ontario History,* lix, no. 2, June 1967, 57-67.

Issac Weld, *Travels through the States of North America and the Provinces of Upper and Lower Canada during the years 1795, 1796 and 1797.* London, 1799.

C. Hume Wilkins, "Stormont, Dundas and Glengarry", paper presented to the Stormont, Dundas and Glengarry Historical Society, 17 January 1972.

George Williams, "The Royal Canadian Legion in Cornwall", an address broadcast over Radio Station CJSS, 6 February 1972.

Alan Wilson, "John Colborne", in *Dictionary of Canadian Biography,* ix, 137-144.

William Wood, *The Storied Province of Quebec,* iii, iv. Toronto, 1931-32.

_____, *York Almanac,* 1803.

A.H. Young, "The Mission of Cornwall, 1784-1812", in *Ontario Historical Society Papers and Records,* xxv, 1929, 481-497.

Arthur Youngs, "Central Public School", in *Cornwall Weekly News,* 21 September 1977.

Maps, Plans and Views

Map of the Province of New York, prepared for William Tryon, Captain-General and Governor, by Guy Johnson, 1771.

An Exact Chart of the River St. Lawrence from Fort Frontenac to the Isle of Anticosti, by Thomas Jeffreys, 25 May 1771.

Map of the Inhabited Parts of Canada from French Surveys; with the Frontiers of New York and New England from the large Survey by Claude-Joseph Sauthier, prepared by William Faden, 25 February 1777.

Map of the Province of New York in North America, prepared by order of Major-General William Tryon, 1 January 1779.

James Peachey, View of Johnstown, 16 July 1784 (PAC: C1512).

Patrick McNiff Map, 1 November 1786 (PAC: H2/400).

Plan of Part of His Majesty's Province of Quebec, from Montreal Westward, 16 March 1790, copied by J.H. Brigly, December 1908 (PAC: H1/400).

Plan of the Township of Cornwall, by William Chewett, 1792 (PAC: V3/440).

A Short Topographical Description of His Majesty's Province of Upper Canada in North America to which is annexed a Provincial Gazetteer, drawn up by David William Smyth, Surveyor-General of Upper Canada, at the desire of Major-General Simcoe, 1st October, 1799, published by W. Faden, Geographer to His Majesty, London, 1799.

Township of Cornwall, drawn by William Browne, 1823 (PAC: F/430).

Map of...Town of Cornwall, 1862, by H.F. Walling, published by D.P. Putnam, Prescott, 1862 (PAC: V1/420).

Map of Cornwall in The New Topographical Atlas of the Province of Ontario, published by Miles and Company, Toronto, 1879, p. 81.

Plan of the Town of Cornwall, East Cornwall, Lorneville and the Glebe Lot, in H. Belden, *Illustrated Historical Atlas of Stormont, Dundas and Glengarry*, Toronto, 1879, p. 52.

Map of Cornwall, drawn by Charles E. Goad, 1895, revised 1916 and 1947.

St. Lawrence Waterway: Prescott to Montreal, Plan Showing Project for Improvement, Plan No. 1450, Ottawa, 1932.

Map of Cornwall, c. 1930. (PAC: F440).

Map of the City of Cornwall and Suburbs, drawn for S.A. Renouf Advertising Company, Toronto, and distributed by W.A. Parisien Estate, Cornwall, c. 1945.

Elements of a City Plan for Cornwall, Wilson and Bunnell, Consulting Engineers, 1944.

Zoning Map of Cornwall, Ontario, 1947.

Map of Cornwall: Locate in Cornwall, the Logical Spot for Rail, Road, and River Transportation, 1950.

Map of Cornwall, prepared under R.C. Adams, 1957.

Plan of the City of Cornwall, prepared under C.F. Adams and drawn by A.J. Laplante, 1969.

Cornwall and the Port of Massena, aerial photographs taken by the Department of Energy, Mines and Resources, Ottawa, 1975, and published by the United States Geological Survey, Virginia, 1977.

Plan of the City of Cornwall, prepared under G.A. Walsh, and drawn by A.J. Laplante, n.d.

NEWSPAPERS

Cornwall	Approximate dates of publication
Advertiser	1863-1866
L'Avenir de Cornwall	1932-1934
Chronicle	1845
Constitutional	1850-1863
Economist	1860-1863
L'Etoile de Cornwall	1950-1959
Freeholder and Eastern District Gazette	1846-1932
Gazette and Eastern Counties Chronicle	1867-1875
Le Journal de Cornwall	1977 - present
News	1882-1885
Observer	1831-1849
Reporter and Eastern Counties Gazette	1876-1885
Standard	1886-1932
Standard-Freeholder	1932 - 1941

Daily Standard-Freeholder	1941 to present
Weeky News	1972 to present
Glengarry	Dates useful for references to Cornwall
News	May 1896
Kingston	
Gazette	13 September 1811
Chronicle and Gazette	27 September 1834
Frelighsburg, Quebec	
Missiskoui Standard	21 November 1837
Montreal	
Canadian Illustrated News	26 January 1878
Gazette	3 May, 12 July, 30 August 1792,
	16 April 1878, 15 January 1983
Herald	14 December 1822
La Minerve	4 June 1866
Le Pays	12 April 1866
Morning Courier	1 March 1836
Transcript	2 December 1837
Vindicator	17 and 21 October 1834
Ottawa	
Citizen	19 November 1976
Le Droit	30 November 1937
Evening Citizen	21 October 1936
Evening Journal	31 August 1936
Journal	6 June 1965, 30 April 1977
Morning Journal	3 September, 23 and 31 October
	1936
Quebec City	
Gazette de Québec	1 January and 7 September 1786,
	28 February 1788
Mercury	5 June 1866
Morning Chronicle	1 March 1836
Toronto	
Daily Clarion	August to October 1936
Financial Post	15 August 1953
Globe	17 October 1870, 18 May 1919
Globe and Mail	24 March 1973, 21 November
	1981
Leader	3 and 7 September 1866
Saturday Globe	18 November 1893
Star Weekly	27 June 1959
Upper Canada Gazette (York)	23 July 1818
Weekly Register (York)	18 July 1822
The Worker	28 June 1930

Selective Index

Gallinger, Clarence 333
Gallinger, Elbert 444
Gallinger, (Lt.) George Henry 354
Gallinger, (Lt.) John 99
Gallinger, Lloyd 422
Gallinger, (Pt.) R.J. 354
Gallinger, (Pt.) S.P. 354
Gallinger, William H. 419, 524
Gallows Hill 117, 129
Gamghir, (Dr.) Indu 513
Garneau, Jacques 472
Gananoque 75
Gardner, Al 516
Gault, Andrew Frederick 226-227
Gault, Archibald 320, 332
Gault, Ralph 333
Gault, Robert Leslie 226-227
Gauthier, Curé Irenée 477
Gauthier, J.T.A. 307
Gélinas, Jean-Claude 520
General Stores 202
George VI, King 408
Gemmel, (Lt.-Col.) Neil 410, 424, 432
General Synod 326
Gallent, Bill 523
Germain, Madeleine 516
Gibbons, William 321, 323, 327
Gibson, Jack 521
Gibson, John 193
Giles, Drummond 520
Gill, J. 322
Gilley, James 184
Gillies, Dan J. 322, 369
Glen Productions 521
Glen-Stor-Dun Lodge 517
Goldstein, Samuel L. 321
Good, (Dr.) Mack 419
Goodall, (Dr.) John 185
Gore, (Col.) Charles 142
Gordon, Robert 195
Gosselin, L.P. 488
Gourdan, (Father) Anthony 19
Gourlay, Robert 115
Graham, John 239
Graham, John W. 259
Grant, George A. 321
Grant, Lionel 320
Grant, Robert 125
Gratton, Euclide 443
Gratton, S.J. 460, 462
Graveley, C.A. 322
Graveley, Edward A. 318, 321
Gray, (Capt.) Andrew 103
Gray, Herb 500
Gray, Howard 420
Gray, (Maj.) James 33-36, 39, 41, 52, 53, 55, 57, 67, 73, 79, 99

Gray, Matthew 74
Gray, (Mrs.) R.F. 418
Gray, (Solicitor-General) Robert Isaac
    Dey 67, 99, 152
Gray, (Maj.) S. Morgan 349
Greenwood, Samuel 334, 348
Grocers and General Stores 202
Groulx, Rheal 521
Guindon, (Father) Bernard 469
Guindon, Elphège 472
Guindon, Fern, 443, 445, 495, 497
Guindon, Francis 498, 514

Hadfield, Joseph 51
Haines (Haynes), (Sgt.) Michael 59
Haldimand, (Maj.-Gen.) 15, 16, 18
Haldimand, (Gov.) Frederick 19-24,
    33, 37, 41-43
Hall, James 323
Hall, R. Stewart 520
Hall, W.N. 445
Hamilton, (Capt.) C.D. 354
Hamilton, (Dr.) Charles J. 316, 318,
    319, 321
Hamilton, Jennie 297, 326, 371
Hamilton, R.J. 7
Hamilton, Robert 497
Hampton, (Maj.-Gen.) Wade 106, 107
Hare, (Mrs.) Donald 524
Hargreaves, T. 439
Harkin, R. 397
Harkness, J.G. 336
Harkness, John Graham 433, 435, 522
Harrington, M.F. 322
Harris, Thomas 444
Harris, (Mrs.) William 520
Harrison, Ethel 520-521'
Harrison, Henry Joseph 318
Harrop, George 388, 435
Harrower, F.D. 379
Hart, Christine 12
Hart, Leonard 444
Harvey, John 224, 228
Haslam, Frank 394, 397
Hastie, (Rev.) James 240
Hawkshaw, Russell 422
Hay, John 196
Hazeley, E. 401
Heenan, Michael 516
Heritage Cornwall, booklet 522
Hermiston, (Mrs.) H. 327
Hermiston, Stuart H. 354
Hertz, Harry 419
Hessel, A. 322
Hessel, William 183

566

The paper that makes up this book was donated courtesy
DOMTAR FINE PAPERS.